ISBN 978-0-484-62107-6
PIBN 10260920

For support please visit www.forgottenbooks.com

1966
FEDERAL HANDBOOK
FOR
SMALL BUSINESS

A SURVEY OF SMALL BUSINESS PROGRAMS IN THE FEDERAL GOVERNMENT AGENCIES

JANUARY 31, 1966

PRINTED FOR THE USE OF THE

SENATE SELECT COMMITTEE ON SMALL BUSINESS

AND THE

HOUSE SELECT COMMITTEE ON SMALL BUSINESS

U.S. GOVERNMENT PRINTING OFFICE

54-543

WASHINGTON : 1966

For sale by the Superintendent of Documents, U.S. Government Printing Office
Washington, D.C., 20402 - Price 65 cents

II

FOREWORD

This is the second edition of the Federal Handbook for Small Business. The first edition was published in 1962 and was enthusiastically received by the American small business community.

Its purpose is to provide in one comprehensive volume information on all the Federal programs of interest to small business.

Each agency of the Federal Government having a program beneficial to small business firms has participated in the preparation of the data contained herein. The publication of this Handbook is sponsored jointly by the Senate Small Business Committee and the House Small Business Committee.

JOHN SPARKMAN,
Chairman, Senate Small Business Committee.
JOE L. EVINS,
Chairman, House Small Business Committee.
JANUARY 31, 1966

Table of Contents

DEPARTMENT OF THE TREASURY

Internal Revenue Service

DEPARTMENT OF JUSTICE

FEDERAL TRADE COMMISSION

VETERANS ADMINISTRATION

ATOMIC ENERGY COMMISSION

TENNESSEE VALLEY AUTHORITY

EXPORT-IMPORT BANK

Small Business Administration

GENERAL

Although various Government departments and agencies provide services to small business, the Small Business Administration (SBA) is the one agency that was created by Congress solely to advise and assist the Nation's small businesses. This action recognized that while the more than 4.5 million small businesses play a distinct and vital role in the national economy, they generally operate at a distinct disadvantage as compared with large business. Larger firms can more readily finance growth and research, find it easier to deal with the Government—the Nation's largest customer—and have less difficulty overcoming management and related problems.

The SBA serves small business in six ways:

1. By lending money to small businessmen, directly or indirectly.

2. By helping small business get a fair share of Government contracts and surplus Government property.

3. By providing information and assistance regarding management, and by sponsoring research into the management problems of small firms.

4. By developing and presenting helpful material in the foreign trade field.

5. By providing production and products assistance.

6. By providing informative publications on subjects of interest to small business.

The SBA assists all types of small business—manufacturing, wholesaling, retailing, service, and other firms—and has established different size standards for different types of business. Congress defined a small business as one that is independently owned and operated and not dominant in its field, and instructed SBA to establish more detailed standards.

The SBA complied by spelling out specific standards which govern eligibility of firms for business loans, for financial aid through SBA-licensed small business investment companies and SBA loans to State and local development companies, and for help in obtaining Government contracts, and property being sold by the Government. Under SBA's definition, about 95 percent of all business is classified as small business.

BUSINESS LOANS

An essential part of the service SBA offers small businessmen is counseling by financial experts. Sometimes a specialist can show a businessman that it would be inadvisable or unnecessary for him to borrow money.

If borrowing does appear to be the answer to a firm's problems, the SBA may participate with a bank in a loan, or may make a "direct" (100 percent) loan, for the following purposes:

• Purchase of machinery, equipment, facilities, supplies, materials.

• Working capital.

• Business construction, conversion or expansion.

While most business loans are small—some are even under $1,000—the SBA, under its statute, may lend a small business as much as $350,000 as the Agency's share of a participation or a direct loan.

Before SBA may make a direct loan, it must make certain that the firm applying for the loan cannot secure adequate financing at a reasonable rate from a bank or other private source.

When a small businessman can secure some, but not all, of the money he needs from a private source, SBA may participate in the loan for as much as 90 percent of the loan. However, SBA may not provide its share of the loan immediately if the private lender is willing to lend its own funds, with a portion guaranteed by SBA.

Generally, a loan may be for as long as 10 years with interest on SBA's share set at a maximum of $5\frac{1}{2}$ percent. When a bank or private lender participates with the SBA in a loan it may, and frequently does, set a rate higher than $5\frac{1}{2}$ percent on its share of the loan, providing the rate is legal and reasonable. (If the private institution will set a rate lower than $5\frac{1}{2}$ percent, SBA will also lower its rate, but not below 5 percent.)

Where SBA's participation involves a guaranty, the private lender, who initially advances all the loan funds, may set the interest rate on the entire loan.

SPECIAL PARTICIPATION PLANS

To provide increased assistance to small firms and to encourage greater bank participation in

1

loans, SBA has devised several special participation loan plans. Although the interest rate remains the same, the loans vary somewhat from the regular participation loans as follows:

Small Loan Program. The Small Loan Program is designed specifically to meet the needs of very small businesses, including new enterprises, many of which have in the past been unable to obtain loans because of lack of adequate collateral. Under this program great stress is put on the character of the applicant, his past record for handling obligations, and his future business prospects. Loan may be made in amounts not to exceed $15,000 for direct SBA loans, or bank participation loans where the SBA portion does not exceed $15,000, up to 6 years.

Simplified Bank Participation Plan. This is a streamlined plan in which the small businessman deals entirely with the bank and follows the bank's instructions in preparing and submitting credit information. Because the SBA depends largely on the bank's judgment of the soundness of the proposed loan, quick action can be taken on applications.

Under this plan, SBA's share may be up to $350,000 or 75 percent of the total loan, whichever is smaller. Maximum maturity is usually 10 years.

Early Maturities Participation Plan. The SBA recognizes fully the value of local financing of small businesses. At the same time it is aware that banks often are accustomed to lending money only for short periods of time. The SBA therefore devised the "Early Maturities Participation Plan" under which a bank may participate for as little as 2 years and SBA will continue its share of the credit for as much as an additional 8 years. The SBA's share of the loan may be up to $350,000.

Another plan combines some of the "early maturities" and "simplified participation" advantages.

POOL LOANS

The SBA makes loans to corporations formed by "pools" or groups of small businesses to: (1) obtain raw materials, equipment, inventory or supplies for use by group members, (2) obtain the benefits of research and development for the members of the group, or (3) establish facilities for these purposes.

The maximum amount that SBA can advance alone or as its share is $250,000, multiplied by the number of small businesses which are members of the pool.

The interest rate on pool loans is 5 percent and loans may be made for as long as 20 years.

AREAS OF UNEMPLOYMENT

As a means of stimulating business activity and thereby increasing job opportunities in areas of substantial unemployment, SBA makes loans at 4 percent interest to small firms in these areas. This rate applies to a direct SBA loan and to the Agency's share of an immediate participation loan. The 4-percent rate is applicable in areas which had

been designated as redevelopment areas by the Area Redevelopment Administration or designated by the Department of Labor as having substantial unemployment.

ELIGIBILITY REQUIREMENTS

To be considered for an SBA loan, a small business must meet certain general credit requirements. For example, as required by the Small Business Act, a loan must be "of such sound value or so secured as reasonably to assure repayment." An applicant must be of good character, and must have enough capital in the business so that, with SBA assistance, it will be possible for him to operate on a sound financial basis.

As a public agency responsible for taxpayers' money, SBA has unique additional responsibilities as a lender. For example, it will not make loans to an individual who derives any part of his gross income from gambling activities. Nor will it make loans for speculation in any kind of real or personal property.

The size requirements for firms and their affiliates for business loans generally are as follows:

● Manufacturing: Small if 250 or fewer employees, large if more than 1,000 employees, and either small or large, depending on industry, if between the 250 and 1,000 limits. Special size standards are established for various manufacturing industries.

● Retail: Annual sales of $1 million or less.

● Wholesale: Annual sales of $5 million or less.

● Service trades: Annual receipts of $1 million or less.

● Trucking: Annual receipts of $3 million or less.

● Construction: Average annual receipts of $5 million or less for preceding 3 fiscal years.

Special size standards have been worked out as the result of studies of certain businesses.

Food canning, for example, is small if the firm has 500 or fewer employees excluding agricultural employees.

Other examples: A retail grocer that handles fresh meats is a small business if his annual sales are $2 million or less; a retail automobile dealer is small if his limit is $3 milion or less; a retail aircraft dealer is small if his annual sales are $3 million or less; a department store is considered small if its annual sales do not exceed $3 million.

In general, a business that provides services is small if its annual receipts are $1 million or less. However, there are exceptions, for example: Hotels, motels, and power laundries, are considered small business if they do no more than $2 million worth of business annually; trailer courts or parks for transients, $100,000 or less; hospitals, 100 beds or less, excluding cribs and bassinets; motion picture production and picture services, $5 million.

Shopping centers are considered small if their assets do not exceed $5 million; net worth, $2½ million; average net income, after Federal income taxes, for applicants preceding 2 fiscal years, $250,-000; and it does not lease more than 25 percent of the gross leasable area to large businesses.

A warehousing business is considered small if its annual receipts do not exceed $3 million. A business engaged in air transportation is small if its employees do not exceed 1,000 persons. A grain storage business is considered small if it does not have in excess of 1 million bushels capacity and annual receipts of $1 million.

Inasmuch as the standards are general and subject to change, the small business owner should consult the nearest SBA field office for current standards.

INDIRECT FINANCING

The SBA has two other basic but indirect ways of providing small business with necessary finances. These are (1) through the Agency's Small Business Investment Company program, and (2) through its program of loans to State and local development companies.

SMALL BUSINESS INVESTMENT COMPANIES

Under the Small Business Investment Act, SBA licenses, regulates, and helps to provide financing of privately and publicly owned small business investment companies, commonly termed SBIC's.

These investment companies have the function of providing equity capital and long-term loans to small businesses, and may furnish advisory and consulting services as well.

An SBIC may begin operations with as little as $300,000 paid-in capital and surplus, which the SBA may match by the purchase of the SBIC's subordinated debentures. Under exceptional circumstances, as, for instance, in an area where no SBIC's are now located or where the operating expenses of the SBIC are to be subsidized, the beginning capital requirement may be as low as $150,000. To help with the growth of the SBIC, SBA may purchase additional subordinated debentures from the SBIC, up to a total of $700,000 on a matching basis with the private capital in the company.

After an SBIC has invested or lent a substantial part of its money to small businesses, it may borrow operating funds from SBA. These loans may total as much as 50 percent of the company's paid-in capital and surplus, but may not exceed $4 million. Subordinated debentures sold to SBA are considered part of the SBIC's capital and surplus for this purpose. Thus $700,000 in private capital makes an SBIC eligible for $700,000 in subordinated debenture funds, plus another $700,000 in operating loans from SBA, for a total of $2,100,000 available for investment in small concerns.

The interest rate on subordinated debentures is

5 percent per annum. For operating loans, it ranges from 5¼ percent if a bank or other financial institution participates with SBA in the loan to the SBIC, to 5½ percent if SBA makes a direct loan from its own funds.

SBIC's are encouraged to borrow operating loans from private sources. The maximum permitted ratio of debt to an SBIC's capital and surplus is four to one.

Liberal tax provisions have helped SBIC's to flourish and to provide money for small businesses as well as to attract investors. An SBIC has a 100 percent exemption on taxes for dividends it receives from investments in small businesses, and may deduct from ordinary income losses sustained through sales of convertible debentures or stock obtained through conversion, or by exercising warrants. Also, in some circumstances an SBIC may qualify for "pass-through" treatment, so that the individual investor can treat profits received from SBIC operations as capital gains, taxed at the maximum rate of 25 percent. On the other hand, losses sustained by the investor in the sale of his SBIC stock may be deducted from ordinary income.

Financing agreements by an SBIC must provide for financing for at least a 5-year period and loans may be for as long as 20 years. Loans of less than 5 years' maturity may be made when they are necessary or desirable to protect previous SBIC investments, or, to a limited extent, as part of a sound financing package for the small concern.

An SBIC may furnish financial assistance to a single small enterprise in an amount not exceeding 20 percent of the investment company's capital and surplus.

If a small firm needs more funds than one SBIC can provide, several SBIC's may participate in meeting the firm's requirements. However, no financing for more than $500,000 may be made by more than 5 SBIC's without SBA approval.

A small business investment company may finance a small business by any of the following methods, including various combinations:

1. By purchasing debentures which are convertible into stock of the small firms.
2. By purchasing capital stock in the small business, with or without warrants to purchase additional stock.
3. By purchasing debt securities, with or without warrants to purchase stock.
4. By any other acceptable instrument of equity financing.
5. Through long-term loans to the business.

A list of SBIC's may be obtained from any SBA office.

Eligibility Requirements. For purposes of SBIC financing, a company qualifies as small if (a) it meets the business loan size standards indicated previously or (b) it does not have assets exceeding $5 million, does not have a net worth exceeding $2.5 million, and its average net income, after

Federal income taxes, for the preceding 2 years did not exceed $250,000.

LOCAL DEVELOPMENT COMPANIES

An additional SBA method of helping small business with its long-term financing problems is through the local development company which assists in the financing of small business concerns in their area.

A local development company is incorporated under the laws of the State of operation for the purpose of furthering the economic development of the community and its environs, with authority to promote and assist the growth and development of small business concerns in a specific area within the State covered by its operation. It may be organized as a profit or nonprofit corporation and shall be principally composed of and controlled by local persons residing or doing business in the area of operation. The local development company may borrow up to $350,000 for a period of 25 years to assist any identifiable small business concern. The proceeds of the loans may be used for the acquisition of land, construction, expansion or modernization of buildings and the purchase of machinery and equipment. The local development company may be required to furnish no less than 20 percent of the project cost and SBA will loan up to 80 percent. SBA's interest rates are 5½ percent but they will be reduced to 5 percent if a bank will participate at a similar lower rate. If the area is an area of substantial unemployment, the interest rate will be 4 percent.

STATE DEVELOPMENT COMPANIES

A State development company is an enterprise incorporated under and pursuant to special legislative act to operate on a statewide basis with authority to promote and assist the growth and development of small business concerns within the State. It is organized and controlled by individuals and corporations (usually lending institutions) residing or doing business in the State. The prime purpose of the State development company shall be to assist the economic development and rehabilitation of the State and any monetary profits to the shareholders of members must be merely incidental to its primary purpose. SBA may lend to this type of development company as much as the company's total outstanding borrowings from all other sources. Maturities may be for as long as 20 years with interest rate at 5 percent except that SBA will charge only 4 percent when the development company uses the funds for long-term loans in areas of substantial unemployment.

ADDITIONAL INFORMATION ON LOANS AND LOAN SOURCES

The SBA programs described briefly above are set out in more detail in various publications available without charge from any SBA field office or from the SBA, Washington 25, D.C.

In addition, the Small Business Administration has published a pamphlet, "Loan Sources in the Federal Government," which is available upon request. Revised and expanded in August 1963, it lists loan sources believed to be of major interest to the small business owners under the following six classifications:

1. *Commercial, Industrial, and Financial Loans.* In addition to the Small Business Administration, this section lists the Treasury Department, Federal Reserve System, Federal Home Loan Banks, Maritime Administration, and the Economic Development Administration of the Department of Commerce.

2. *Agricultural Loans.* This section includes Farm Credit Administration, Rural Electrification Administration, Farmers Home Administration, and Commodity Credit Corporation.

3. *Housing and Community Development Loans.* Included are Community Facilities Administration, Public Housing Administration, Urban Renewal Administration, and Federal Housing Administration.

4. *Veterans Loans* made by the Veterans Administration.

5. *Natural Resources Loans* made by the Department of the Interior include loans by the Bureau of Reclamation, Bureau of Commercial Fisheries, and Bureau of Indian Affairs.

6. *International Loans* are made by the Export-Import Bank of Washington and the Agency for International Development.

For further information check the loan entries in the Index of this publication.

ECONOMIC OPPORTUNITY LOANS

In connection with the Anti-Poverty Program, SBA is responsible for implementation of title IV of the Economic Opportunity Act of 1964. Under this program, comprehensive assistance is available to low-income persons or those who will hire them, who cannot secure credit from any other source. Emphasis is on expansion of business and job opportunities.

Community-organized-and-operated Small Business Development Centers (SBDC's) are the prime means by which the program is executed. The Board of Directors of the SBDC is drawn from a broad base of business, banking, and other local leaders. It includes representatives of the people who are to be helped. Wherever possible, the SBDC operates in conjunction with an overall Community Action Program. The SBDC prescreens loan applications, helps arrange for management training, identifies unmet demands which can be met by small concerns, and promotes the interests of local small business community and economic development generally.

The final credit decision remains in the hands of SBA. Economic Opportunity Loans may be made for up to $25,000 at a maximum maturity of 15 years. The interest rate on SBA's share of the loan is ordinarily 5½ percent except in localities classified by the Area Redevelopment Administration as areas of substantial and persistent unemployment, where the rate is 4 percent. Credit standards for Economic Opportunity Loans are more liberal than in other SBA lending programs. Prime emphasis is placed on the character of the applicant and the projected performance of the firm. No loan applications will be denied solely because of insufficient collateral. The applicant must, however, furnish reasonable assurance that the loan will be repaid.

Equal in importance to financial assistance to small firms under the program is the management assistance available. Where necessary, a loan applicant may be required—in some cases as a precondition of the loan—to undertake management training to upgrade his skills and improve his business. Management training may take a variety of forms. One-to-one counseling may be offered by SBA specialists, the volunteer Service Corps of Retired Executive (SCORE), or local groups like the SBDC itself. Other regular SBA Management Assistance programs—workshops, courses, and the like—are also available.

DISASTER LOANS

The Small Business Administration has a disaster loan program available to small businessmen and others. One type of loan covers physical damage; others cover economic injury. The maximum maturity of all types is 20 years and SBA may advance the entire amount or may join in a loan with a bank or other private lending institution. There is no statutory limitation on the dollar amount of disaster loans.

PHYSICAL DAMAGE LOANS

Individuals, businesses, and nonprofit organizations, including churches, are eligible for loans in storm, flood, and other major disaster areas to help repair or rebuild homes and profit and nonprofit institutions, and to help replace lost or damaged furnishings or business machinery, equipment, and inventory. Loans are conditioned on tangible property losses in areas designated disaster areas by SBA.

The loan limit is determined by the actual tangible loss.

The interest rate on SBA's share of this type of disaster loan and on the private lender's share for home construction or repair is 3 percent per annum. On other than home loans, the private lender may establish its own rate on its share of the loan, providing it is within reasonable limits.

In disaster areas, rehabilitation assistance is often given jointly by the American Red Cross and SBA, with part of the applicant's loss being covered by a grant from the Red Cross and part by a loan from SBA.

ECONOMIC INJURY LOANS

Major or Natural Disaster. When the President of the United States or the Secretary of Agriculture declares a major disaster area because of a major or natural disaster, a small business suffering a substantial economic injury directly attributable to the disaster is eligible for a loan to provide ordinary working capital, replenish normal inventories, and pay financial obligations (except bank loans) which the borrower would have been able to meet had it not been for the resulting loss of revenue.

The amount of a loan is determined by the working capital needs of the applicant, taking into account possible economies which would be appropriate during a period of reduced business.

The borrower is charged 3 percent for SBA's share of the loan while a participating financial institution may fix its own rate on its share, within reasonable limits.

Diseased Products Loans. The SBA also makes loans to small business firms suffering substantial economic injury as the result of inability to process or market a product for human consumption because of disease or toxicity through natural or undetermined causes. Such loans are made to help small firms to reestablish their businesses, at the 3 percent interest rate, up to 20 years.

Displaced Small Businesses. The SBA also makes low-interest disaster loans to eligible small businesses physically displaced by Federally-aided urban renewal, highway, and other construction programs. The loans provide financial assistance in relocating applicants in a suitable and reasonable location, comparable to that which they previously occupied, including limited upgrading and necessary modernization.

The interest rate on SBA's share of this type of loan is established annually on a statutory formula based on the average annual interest rate on all interest-bearing obligations of the United States. The rate through June 30, 1966, is 3⅞ percent.

Nonprofit, charitable, eleemosynary, homes, apartment houses, and other investment properties, and religious institutions, as well as small businesses established after the Federal project was approved, are not eligible for this type of loan.

GOVERNMENT BUYING AND SELLING

Each year the U.S. Government does billions of dollars worth of business with private companies, both in buying needed goods and services and in disposing of surplus Government property. The SBA is charged with assisting small businessmen to secure a fair share of that business.

It has been a natural tendency, over the years, for Government representatives to buy from or sell to large organizations that have national reputations and that can deal in large amounts. For example, it is simpler to agree to a single contract with a well-known big business than to negotiate smaller sales or purchase contracts with several small businesses.

Also, while it is comparatively easy for large companies to keep informed on Government activities and to deal directly with the Government, it has traditionally been difficult for small businessmen—without Washington representatives and Government contacts—to learn what the Government is in the market to buy, and what it has to sell.

The Small Business Administration tries in various ways to minimize the disadvantages the small businessman faces when dealing with the Government.

GOVERNMENT PURCHASE CONTRACTS AND SUB-CONTRACTING

The U.S. Government is the world's largest buyer and SBA provides assistance to small firms so they can secure a fair share of the Government's prime contracts and subcontracts.

Specialists in SBA field offices advise small businessmen which Government agencies are prospective customers. The small businessmen are told how to have their names placed on bidders lists and how to obtain drawings and specifications for specific contracts.

In addition to answering specific questions, SBA publishes "The U.S. Government Purchasing, Specifications and Sales Directory," which lists principal goods and services bought by each Government agency. The directory is sold by the Government Printing Office; see the "For Sale" section, page 11. Another booklet, "Selling to U.S. Government," explains how to sell to the Government and how to find subcontract opportunities. It is available from SBA field offices.

Small Business Set-Asides. Government procurement officials at military and civilian purchasing offices review proposed contracts to determine which ones can be set-aside for competitive bidding by small business. Before a purchase may be set aside, there must be a reasonable expectation that a sufficient number of small firms will bid so the Government is assured of receiving a satisfactory price.

Potential Sources Program. SBA representatives review proposed Government purchase contracts for which there has been inadequate small business competition. If the representatives believe small firms are capable of performing the contracts, they have SBA offices find small companies that want to bid on them through the facilities inventory and recommend that contracting officials solicit the firms for bids.

Subcontract Program. The SBA develops subcontract opportunities for small businesses by encouraging prime contractors to increase their subcontracting to small concerns. In addition, SBA informs small firms of these opportunities and assists them in properly presenting their capabilities to contractors.

The most important part of the program is arranging cooperative subcontracting programs for small business with prime contractors and large subcontractors.

In its efforts to secure a larger percentage of subcontracts for small business, SBA continually works with the largest contract-awarding agencies, the Department of Defense and the General Services Administration.

The SBA obtains from these and other appropriate procurement agencies information and records concerning subcontracting by the procuring agency's prime contractors. In addition, when requested to do so, Government prime contractors must consult with SBA through the appropriate purchasing agency to provide subcontract opportunities for small business. Regulations direct contractors to keep records of their subcontracting work.

The SBA is empowered to suggest small concerns as subcontractors when it appears that they might not otherwise be solicited.

Although it varies somewhat with each contractor, the cooperative subcontracting programs for small business generally cover the following points: (1) placing a fair proportion of the prime contractor's total purchase of materials, supplies and services with small businesses; (2) extending invitations to bid to small firms whenever there are known small business sources through the facilities inventory; (3) permitting SBA to review requirements and recommend small concerns to participate; (4) furnishing adequate specifications, drawings, or purchase descriptions so that small firms can prepare bids intelligently; (5) specifying reasonable delivery schedules, allowing sufficient time for preparing bids, and when economically feasible, purchasing in quantities which can be furnished by small business; (6) providing SBA with sufficient information for evaluation of the results.

Inventory of Small Plant Facilities. The Small Business Act empowers SBA to make a complete inventory of all productive facilities of small business concerns. In carrying out this activity, the Agency maintains a centralized facilities register of small business productive facilities. This inventory is used principally in assisting the registered companies in their efforts to obtain prime and subcontracts, in locating new sources for Government purchasing offices, in locating scarce or specialized machine tools and equipment when calls are received for them, also, concerns with research and development capabilities, and small business firms in the forestry and forest products industry for use in connection with the timber sales set-aside program. Small firms may register by completing a questionnaire available at any SBA office.

Prime Contract Referral. Small firms interested in selling to the Government should have their names placed on contracting agencies bidder lists so they will receive notices of Government purchases directly from the contracting office. However, until a small business is placed on the bidders lists, the SBA, if requested, will notify the firms of current bidding opportunities which are suited to their facilities.

Contract Financing. The simplest form of contract financing under a fixed price contract is that of partial payments. Partial payments are made for material delivered, received, and accepted; thus as a contractor makes partial delivery of completed items, he receives payment to finance continuing production costs.

Progress Payments. Progress payments may be made under a fixed-price contract that involves a long tooling up period, a long production run before any deliveries can be made, or a product which cannot be delivered in units. Progress payments do not require delivery and payments may be made on the basis of a certain amount of work done or a percentage of costs incurred. Small business firms may request progress payments whether or not the invitation for bid (IFB) provides for them, without jeopardizing their bid.

Eligibility Requirements. A small business concern for the purpose of Government procurement is a concern, including its affiliates, which is independently owned and operated, is not dominant in the field of operation in which it is bidding on

54-548°—66——2

Government contracts and can further qualify under the criteria set forth below.

GOVERNMENT PROCUREMENT

The following definitions are applicable to concerns bidding on a Government procurement contract:

(a) *Manufacturing*: Concerns are considered as small if number of employees do not exceed 500 persons and large if its number of employees exceeds 1,000 persons. Within this range, the size standards vary from industry to industry. In the petroleum industry a concern is considered small if its employees do not exceed 1,000 persons and its crude oil capacity does not exceed 30,000 barrels per day.

(b) *Construction*: A concern is considered small if its average annual receipts do not exceed $7½ million for the preceding 3 fiscal years.

(c) *Nonmanufacturer*: Small if the number of employees does not exceed 500 persons and must furnish products manufactured in the United States by small business manufacturers.

(d) *Services*: A concern is classified as small if its annual recipts do not exceed $1 million for the preceding 3 fiscal years; engineering services or naval architectural services—$5 million; motion picture production or motion picture services—$5 million.

(e) *Transportation*: A concern is classified as small if its number of employees does not exceed 500 persons, except air transportation—not exceeding 1,000 employees, and trucking and/or warehousing—annual receipts do not exceed $3 million.

(f) *Research, development, and testing*: A concern is classified as small if its number of employees does not exceed 500 persons.

GOVERNMENT SUBCONTRACTING

A concern bidding on government subcontracts is considered as small under the following conditions:

(a) Subcontracts of $2,500 and less (all industries) number of employees do not exceed 500 persons.

(b) Subcontracts exceeding $2,500, except nonmanufacturing—qualifies as a small business concern if it meets the size standards as indicated in (a) through (f) above; nonmanufacturers—number of employees does not exceed 500 persons.

SALES OF GOVERNMENT PROPERTY

In the submission of a bid or proposal for the purchase of Government-owned property, a concern must meet the following size standards to be considered as a small business concern:

(a) *General—manufacturers:* Number of employees does not exceed 500 persons; *nonmanufacturers:* average annual sales or receipts for bidder's preceding 3 fiscal years do not exceed $5 million; and *stockpile purchasers:* (primarily engaged in purchase of materials not domestically produced) average annual sales or receipts for bidder's preceding 3 fiscal years do not exceed $25 million.

(b) *Timber:* Number of employees do not exceed 500 persons and primarily engaged in the logging or forest products industry.

Certificates of Competency. A certificate of competency—frequently called a "COC"—is a statement that a small business, or a "small business pool," is technically and financially capable of carrying out a specific Government contract.

On occasion, when a small business submits the lowest competitive bid, the Government contracting officer questions the ability of the management, the physical facilities, and other factors relating to capacity or financial resources which would affect the firm's ability to perform a contract of that size, and produce the quality required in the time allotted.

After rejecting the lowest bidder for such reasons, the contracting officer advises SBA. The Agency, in turn, contacts the small firm to find out if it wishes to apply for a certificate of competency.

If the firm applies, SBA specialists make an on-site study of the company's resources, management, performance record, and financial status. The company's plans to secure financing, personnel and equipment to perform the contract are reviewed. At times the company may submit an application for an SBA loan along with its request for a certificate of competency, and SBA would take this into consideration.

Then, if SBA is convinced that the company possesses or has access to the necessary credit or productive capacity to perform the contract successfully, the Agency issues a certificate of competency that is binding on the contracting officer.

The COC is valid only for the specific contract involved. A firm fully capable of handling one contract, does not necessarily have the qualifications to handle another. Each case is treated individually.

When a company is awarded a contract as the result of a COC, SBA requires the company to report regularly on the performance of the contract. If the firm encounters difficulties, SBA assists by providing help in obtaining needed financing, by providing engineering advice and assistance, and by locating scarce materials and equipment.

BUYING FROM THE GOVERNMENT

Each year the U.S. Government sells, leases, and otherwise disposes of considerable amounts of real and personal property and natural resources. It is the responsibility of the Small Business Administration to advise and assist small businesses in obtaining a fair proportion of the total sales.

Property of almost every kind and variety, from machine tools to minerals, may be found in the Federal Government's stockpile and inventory.

These items are made available for purchase by businessmen when they are declared surplus.

General Services Administration supervises the disposition of civilian agency goods and the Department of Defense handles the disposal of surplus developed by the military. GSA handles the sale of real property for all Government agencies. Sale of natural resources, such as timber and surface minerals, are conducted by the Federal agencies responsible for the Nation's public resources program.

Regional SBA offices are apprised of available Government surplus items through sales brochures and bid invitations. When small businesses register with these regional offices and make their needs and interests known, they are informed of the location and sales dates of suitable production and construction equipment, and natural resources such as timber.

By SBA agreements with the Forest Service of the Agriculture Department, the Bureau of Land Management of the Interior Department, and the Department of Defense, small logging and milling concerns are afforded the opportunity to bid on those sales of Federally owned timber.

MANAGEMENT INFORMATION

In addition to providing information in connection with its loan program and selling to—and buying from—the Government, the SBA also provides information and assistance to small businessmen to help them do a better job of starting or managing a small business.

The SBA efforts to supply this type of information and assistance are accomplished through individual counseling, management courses and conferences, workshops, and publications.

RETIRED EXECUTIVES ASSIST SMALL BUSINESS OWNERS

A Service Corps of Retired Executives (SCORE) was established by SBA on a national basis in October 1964. This is an effort to utilize the skills and knowledge of retired business executives who are willing to work with small business owners needing their advice and assistance.

The essence of SCORE is a "Businessman-to-Businessman Advisory Relationship." SCORE's objective is to make the small owner/operator a better manager by helping him reach a balanced approach to his business.

SCORE volunteers will, with the guidance of SBA personnel, counsel SBA borrowers, recipients of certificates of competency and other businessmen seeking advice and guidance. They will also be used as instructors or discussion leaders in SBA's management courses, conferences and workshops.

MANAGEMENT COURSES AND CONFERENCES

The successful operation of a small business calls for considerable knowledge of management skills and techniques, and SBA has arranged with leading educational institutions throughout the Nation, trade and professional associations and local business and civic groups, to present a program of helpful administrative management courses.

Designed to broaden and strengthen management abilities, the courses are generally taught by experienced educators and successful businessmen, and cover business planning, organizing, staffing, directing, and controlling. Another form of assistance is through 1-day management conferences arranged on some subject of current interest, such as the tax laws. Small business owners and managers may secure current information about courses and conferences in their area from their SBA field office.

IMP HELPS BUSINESS HELP ITSELF

SBA's Intraindustry Management Program (IMP) is designed to make use of the natural relationships which exist between large and small businesses and between trade associations and their members. Large manufacturers, wholesalers and trade associations are being encouraged to share their management knowledge with their suppliers, distributors, dealers, and members by offering programs of management guidance and assistance for the small firm owner-manager. SBA has developed packaged materials which are used as guidelines for the development of new and improvement of existing management training programs.

SBA WORKSHOPS ASSIST PROSPECTIVE BUSINESSMEN

To help prevent the high proportion of casualties among new businesses and recognizing that many difficulties experienced by small business owner-managers are due to inadequate preparation and analysis prior to opening a business, SBA conducts 1-day workshops.

The workshops, which have been conducted by agency specialists, are designed to deal with fundamentals of good management which can be applied to new businesses of all kinds. They emphasize the need for both technical and managerial experience, for understanding what is required in the fields of financing, law, and management, and where to go for assistance. Discussions are held on subjects such as personal qualifications for successful business management; initial capital requirements and sources of financing; locating a business; buying a going concern; types of business organizations; business regulations; tax and insurance; and management requirements of a small business.

MANAGEMENT PUBLICATIONS

The SBA publishes a wide range of management and technical publications of value to established or prospective operators of small businesses.

They include a series of free publications obtainable from SBA offices and a series of publications which are sold for a small charge by the Superintendent of Documents, Washington 25, D.C. Lists of both are available from SBA offices.

Free Series. The five series whose individual titles are distributed without charge by SBA's field and Washington offices are as follows: (1) "Management Aids for Small Manufacturers," designed to supply information on sound business administration; typical title—"Steps in Incorporating a Business"; (2) "Small Marketers Aids," prepared for owners of small retail, wholesale, and service enterprises; typical title—"Are You Kidding Yourself About Profits"; (3) "Technical Aids for Small Manufacturers," covers significant developments in such fields as materials, processes, equipment, and maintenance; typical title—"Is Worker Fatigue Costing You Dollars?"; (4) "Small Business Bibliographies" reference sources for owners and managers; typical title—"Selling by Mail Order"; (5) "Management Research Grant Program"; typical title—"Small Business and Pattern Bargaining."

For-Sale Series. The four series whose individual titles are sold at nominal prices by the Superintendent of Documents are as follows: (1) "Aids Annuals," updated versions of the Management, Technical, and Small Marketers Aids no longer available individually; (2) "Small Business Management Series," discussions-in-depth of management subjects, usually prepared on a contract basis by recognized authorities on important management subjects; (3) "Starting and Managing Series," basic, general book on starting a business, followed by books on starting and managing service stations, credit and collection services, etc.; (4) "Small Business Research Series," results of academic studies of small business problems including procedures and techniques; typical title—"The First Two Years: Problems of Small Firm Growth and Survival."

SBA AS SMALL BUSINESS SPOKESMAN

SBA champions the cause of small business before other Government agencies. It tries to assure that these other agencies consider the welfare and interests of small business firms in their policies, programs, regulations, and actions.

Whether SBA will actually intercede with another agency on behalf of small business will depend on its determination that the proposed action will directly result in a sufficiently adverse economic disadvantage to the small business community compared to large business and that the action will not result in a substantial conflict of economic interest within the small business community itself.

SMALL BUSINESS DEFENSE PRODUCTION ADJUSTMENT PROGRAM

The present trend toward shifts in Government defense spending necessitates measures to insure that these shifts do not unduly affect the small business community. Small Concerns are more severely affected by the shifts than larger companies, and they require guidance and help.

The problem of adjustment to changing defense requirements necessitates positive steps by the small business concerns to obtain and to retain a fair proportion of Government contracts and subcontracts in accordance with declared congressional policy. These steps, embodied in Small Business Production Adjustment Program are designed to accomplish the following:

1. *Upgrading* of small business capabilities, i.e., building up existing small business industrial competence in order to enable small business concerns to undertake production of defense items for which they were hitherto lacking in capabilities.

2. *Diversification*: Where upgrading is neither impossible nor insufficient to occupy the full productive capabilities of a small business concern, assistance will be rendered in order to enable the small company to manufacture new products, in addition to those presently made.

In order to carry out this diversification, a New Product Development Program will provide technical, marketing, and financial assistance to small concerns.

3. *Conversion*: Where the above measures do not appear useful, small firms will be rendered varied assistance to enable them to convert their facilities to new products (military or civilian) altogether.

4. *Extension of Procurement Assistance*: Recognizing that there will be a steadily decreasing Government subcontract workload, the Procurement Assistance Program will be extended so as to encourage large commercial product manufacturers to undertake a voluntary small business subcontracting program, similar to the one now mandatorily in effect under Public Law 87–305.

PUBLICATIONS

FREE FROM SBA

The SBA publishes a wide variety of helpful publications that are available free from any SBA office:

SBA—What It Is—What It Does. Summarizes SBA assistance to small businesses, describes Agency organization, and lists field office locations.

SBA Fact Sheet No. 4–SBA Services to Small Businesses. One-page synopsis of services available from SBA.

SBA Business Loans. Explains SBA loan policies and programs, eligibility requirements and loan application procedures.

Limited Loan Participation Plan. Describes a loan plan of special interest to small retail, wholesale, service and other businesses with sound management, good earnings and credit records, but limited tangible collateral.

Bank–SBA Participation Loan Plans. A guide for banks with an explanation of the types of SBA-bank participation loans, loan procedures and requirements, and the advantages these loans give to small firms, banks, and communities.

Here's How America's Banks Can Strengthen Their Communities and the Nation. A leaflet for banks explaining SBA's Simplified Bank Loan Participation Plan.

SBA Fact Sheet No. 1—Simplified Bank Loan Participation Plan. One-page synopsis of this special loan plan, how it works, and advantages it offers banks.

How An SBA Loan Can Help Your Business. A leaflet containing facts on how SBA loans help small manufacturing, retail, service, and wholesale firms.

SBA Loans to Privately Owned Health Facilities. A leaflet explaining SBA financial assistance available to privately owned hospitals, convalescent and nursing homes, and medical and dental laboratories.

Key Features of SBA Lending Programs. A chart describing the various SBA business and disaster loan programs—who is eligible, amounts available, interest rates, maturities, and collateral requirements for each type loan.

SBIC Financing for Small Business. Explanation of how SBIC's provide money for growth to small business concerns.

ABC of Selling to U.S. Government. Information on Government buying methods, locating purchasing agencies and learning what they buy, and how to have an opportunity to bid on Government contracts and orders.

SBA Disaster Loans for Businesses and Homes. Describes SBA assistance available to victims of natural disasters such as storms and floods, and to small business suffering economic injury from drought or excessive rainfall.

SBA Fact Sheet No. 3—SBA Loans for Displaced Small Businesses. One-page synopsis of how SBA helps small firms displaced by Federally-aided urban renewal, highway and other construction projects.

Loans to State and Local Development Companies. Explains SBA loans available to State and Local Development Companies that use the loans to help qualified small businesses or to establish new businesses.

Does Small Business in Your Community Need Capital? A leaflet explaining how SBA loans help local development companies assist small businesses with plant construction, expansion, modernization, or conversion.

Long-Term Capital for Small Business. A leaflet explaining how small businesses can obtain long-term capital through SBA loans to State development companies.

SBA Services for Community Economic Development. How SBA helps low-income rural communities and substantial unemployment areas increase employment, strengthen and diversify business and assist small firms hurt by economic dislocations.

Small Business—A Keystone of Rural Area Development. A leaflet describing how Federal and State Governments are cooperating to achieve balanced farm, industry and community development in underdeveloped rural areas.

Small Business Pooling for Defense Production, Research and Development. The purpose, formation, approval, and operation of "pools" or groups of small businesses desiring to undertake defense production or research and development.

List of Small Firms Interested in Performing Research and Development. Classification of firms according to fields in which they have indicated they are interested in performing contract research for the Government or private enterprise. Also contains data on firms facilities, and scientific staffs.

SBA Services for the Forest Products Industries. Explanation of SBA programs of interest to small loggers, sawmills, planing mills, plywood and veneer plants, wood products manufacturers and distributors and lumber yards.

How SBA Helps Small Construction Firms. An outline of how SBA can assist small construction contractors.

The Facts . . . Construction Set-Asides for Small Business. A leaflet explaining the joint efforts of SBA and other Government agencies in giving small firms a better opportunity to obtain Government construction contracts through competitive bidding.

FOR SALE

In addition the *U.S. Government Purchasing, Specifications and Sales Directory* was sold for 60¢ (new edition expected to be priced higher) by the Government Printing Office in Washington, D.C. This publication lists Government purchasing and sales offices, what they buy or sell, and the specifications for goods or services bought or sold.

EMPLOYEE-EMPLOYER RELATIONSHIPS

SBA's management and technical publications include studies relating to various phases of employee-employer relationships.

Examples in the personnel management field include "Is Your Labor Turnover Cost Too High?" "Incentive Techniques for Small Businesses," "Saving Manpower in Industry," "Reducing Accident Costs in Small Plants," "Reducing Accident Costs Through Safe Working Conditions," "Using Deferred Compensation in Small Business," "Employee Relations for Small Retailers," "Managing Women Employees in Small Business." All of these are available free from SBA offices.

Others available for a small cost from the Superintendent of Documents, Washington 25, D.C., are "Employee Suggestion System for Small Plants," 15¢; "Sales Training for the Smaller Manufacturer," 20¢; "Health Maintenance for Greater Efficiency," 25¢; "Personnel Management Guide for Small Business," 25¢.

SBA FIELD OFFICES

NORTHEASTERN AREA

Boston, Mass. 02210, Sheraton Building, 470 Atlantic Avenue
Augusta, Maine 04330, 20 Willow Street
Concord, N.H. 03301, 18 School Street
Hartford, Conn. 06103, Federal Office Building, 450 Main Street
Montpelier, Vt. 05601, Federal Building, Post Office and Courthouse, 2d Floor, 87 State Street
Providence, R.I. 02903, 611 Smith Building, 57 Eddy Street

NEW YORK AREA

New York, N.Y. 10004, 42 Broadway
Santurce, Puerto Rico 00908, San Alberto Condominio Building, 1200 Ponce de Leon Avenue, Post Office Box 9442
St. Thomas, U.S. Virgin Islands 00802*, Post Office Box 806
Syracuse, N.Y. 13202, Chimes Building, Room 711, 500 South Salina Street
Buffalo, N.Y. 14203*, Federal Building, Room 9, 121 Ellicott Street

MIDDLE ATLANTIC AREA

Philadelphia, Pa. 19107, Jefferson Building, 1015 Chestnut Street
Baltimore, Md. 21202, 521 Calvert Building, Fayette and St. Paul Streets
Clarksburg, W. Va. 26301, Old Post Office Building, 227 West Pike Street
Charleston, W. Va. 25301*, 3000 U.S. Courthouse and Federal Building, 500 Quarrier Street, Room 3000
Cleveland, Ohio 44113, Standard Building, 1370 Ontario Street
Toledo, Ohio 43602*, Federal Office Building, 234 Summit Street
Columbus, Ohio 43215, Beacon Building, 50 West Gay Street
Cincinnati, Ohio 45202*, 4515 Federal Building
Newark, N.J. 07102, 10 Commerce Court
Pittsburgh, Pa. 15222, Federal Building, 1000 Liberty Avenue
Richmond, Va. 23226, Post Office Box 8565, 1904 Byrd Avenue
Washington, D.C. 20417, 1321 H. Street NW. (Mezzanine)

*Branch office.

SOUTHEASTERN AREA

Atlanta, Ga. 30303, 52 Fairlie Street NW.

Birmingham, Ala. 35205, South 20th Building, 908 South 20th Street

Charlotte, N.C. 28202, American Building, 201 South Tryon Street

Columbia, S.C. 29201, 1801 Assembly Street

Jackson, Miss. 39201, 322 U.S. Post Office and Courthouse Building, Capital and West Streets

Jacksonville, Fla. 32202, 47 West Forsyth

Louisville, Ky. 40202, 1900 Commonwealth Building, Fourth and Broadway

Miami, Fla. 33130, 912 Federal Office Building, 51 SW. First Avenue

Nashville, Tenn. 37219, Security Federal Savings & Loan Building, 500 Union Street

Knoxville, Tenn. 37902*, 233 West Cumberland Building, 301 West Cumberland Avenue

MIDWESTERN AREA

Chicago, Ill. 60604, Federal Office Building, Room 437, 219 South Dearborn Street

Des Moines, Iowa 50309, 850 Insurance Exchange Building, Fifth and Grand Avenue

*Branch office.

MIDWESTERN AREA—con.

Detroit, Mich. 48226, 1200 Book Building, 1249 Washington Boulevard

Marquette, Mich. 49855*, 502 West Kaye Avenue

Indianapolis, Ind. 46204, Century Building, 36 South Pennsylvania Street

Kansas City, Mo. 64106, 911 Walnut Street

Madison, Wis. 53703, Commercial State Bank Building, 114 North Carroll Street

Milwaukee, Wis. 53203*, Straus Building, 238 West Wisconsin Avenue

Minneapolis, Minn. 55402, Lewis Building, 603 2d Avenue South

St. Louis, Mo. 63102, Federal Building, 208 North Broadway

SOUTHWESTERN AREA

Dallas, Tex. 75201, Mayflower Building, 411 North Akard Street

Albuquerque, N. Mex. 87101, 102 U.S. Courthouse, Fifth and Gold Streets, SW.

Houston, Tex. 77002, 802 Federal Office Building, 201 Fannin Street

Little Rock, Ark. 72201, 377 Post Office and Courthouse Building, 600 West Capital Avenue

SOUTHWESTERN AREA—con.

Lubbock, Tex. 79401, 204 Federal Office Building, 1616 19th Street

Marshall, Tex. 75671, Marshall National Bank, Post Office Box 1315, 101 East Austin Street

New Orleans, La. 70130, 845 Federal Office Building, 610 South Street

Oklahoma City, Okla. 73102, 807 U.S. Post Office Building, Third and Robinson

San Antonio, Tex. 78204, 410 South Main Avenue

ROCKY MOUNTAIN AREA

Denver, Colo. 80202, Federal Office Building, 1961 Stout Street

Casper, Wyo. 82601, Western Building, 300 North Center

Fargo, N. Dak. 58102, 300 American Life Building, 207 North Fifth Street

Helena, Mont. 59601, Post Office Box 1690, 205 Power Block, Corner Main and 6th Avenue

Omaha, Nebr. 68102, 7425 Federal Building, 215 North 17th Street

Salt Lake City, Utah 84111, 2237 Federal Building, 125 South State Street

Sioux Falls, S. Dak. 57102, 402 National Bank of South Dakota Building, 8th and Main Avenue

ROCKY MT. AREA—con.

Wichita, Kans. 67202, 301 Board of Trade Building, 120 South Market Street

PACIFIC COASTAL AREA

San Francisco, Calif. 94102, Federal Building, 450 Golden Gate Avenue, Box 36044

Anchorage, Alaska 99501, 632 Sixth Avenue, Suite 450, Post Office Box 999

Boise, Idaho 83702, Room 408, Idaho Building, 216 North Eighth Street

Honolulu, Hawaii 96813, 1149 Bethel Street, Room 402

Agana, Guam 96910*, Ada Plaza Center Building, Post Office Box 927

Los Angeles, Calif. 90013, 312 West Fifth Street

Las Vegas, Nev. 89104*, 1721 East Charleston Street

Phoenix, Ariz. 85004, Central Towers Building, 2727 North Central Avenue

Portland, Oreg. 97205, 330 Pittock Block, 921 SW. Washington Street

San Diego, Calif. 92101, 110 West C Street

Seattle, Wash. 98104, 1206 Smith Tower, 506 Second Avenue

Spokane, Wash. 99201, American Legion Building, Room 300, North 108 Washington Street

General Services Administration

The General Services Administration is responsible for a wide variety of Government-wide functions pertaining to procurement, supply, storage, distribution, and maintenance of real and personal property and nonpersonal services; utilization and disposal of real and personal surplus property; transportation, traffic, and public utilities management and services; and records and paperwork management. These responsibilities are carried out by assigning, regulating, or performing such functions for executive agencies in accordance with the dictates of economy, efficiency, or improved service, or when otherwise in the best interests of the Government. GSA is responsible for managing assets valued at over $11 billion.

Different segments of the agency's overall responsibility are delegated by the Administrator to each of the six Services of GSA, as shown on the organizational chart on page 21.

The primary functions of interest to the small businessman include:

1. Prescribing Government-wide procurement policies through the issuance of Federal Procurement Regulations applicable to all executive agencies.

2. Procurement and contracting for requirements which are common to two or more Federal agencies. These requirements include a wide variety of categories, such as office supplies, office furniture and equipment; hardware and hand tools; plumbing, heating and electrical supplies; lighting fixtures and lamps; nonmilitary vehicles and motor vehicle parts and accessories; refrigerators, air conditioners and water coolers; firefighting equipment, paper and paper products; paints, waxes, adhesives, and brushes; janitorial supplies; floor coverings and household and quarters furniture, etc.

(The procedures for contacting GSA are for information on the sale of such items described under the subsequent heading of GSA Business Service Centers.)

3. Contracts for design and construction of Government buildings throughout the country, and supplies and materials necessary for their repair, remodeling, and maintenance.

4. Contracts for the appraisal, leasing, and disposal of real property.

5. Contracts for the disposal of Government-owned surplus personal property.

6. Contracts for procurement and disposal of strategic and critical stockpile materials.

7. Contracts for special services, such as window washing, stenographic reporting, furniture repair and refinishing, sound recording and reproducing, repair of tires, tubes, office machines, etc.

A detailed description of the above functions is contained under subsequent headings for each of the GSA Services.

GSA BUSINESS SERVICE CENTERS

In dealing with GSA, the businessman has the distinct advantage of convenient contact points, strategically located in major cities throughout the United States, which provide factual information, counseling, and assistance on Government business opportunities (see map on page 23 for locations).

These centers are daily engaged in providing small businessmen with the following services:

• Information concerning procurement of Government goods and services.

• Counseling on how to do business with the Government—the facts on what steps to take, what forms to use, and whom to contact.

• Detailed information and guidance on such subjects as:

> Locations of contracting offices;
>
> How to get on Bidders' Mailing Lists;
>
> How and where to obtain Government specifications;
>
> How to establish Government-consumer demand and promote sales;
>
> How to introduce new products to Government supply systems;
>
> How to keep informed on current bidding opportunities.

• Assistance by trained personnel, whose primary function and interest is to make available their time and ability to fit the needs of the individual businessman requesting their help.

• Providing reference copies of Government regulations, catalogs, bid invitations, and other materials of interest, and supplying copies of mailing list applications, specifications, and related forms and publications.

In addition, these centers continuously seek to stimulate and maintain the small businessman's interest and capability in doing business with GSA and other Government agencies by:

13

● Publication of bidding opportunities in trade and other news media—in addition to the Department of Commerce "Commerce Business Daily."

● Distribution of publications which are helpful to small business concerns interested in obtaining contracts, including such recent booklets as:

Doing Business with the Federal Government
Sale of Government Personal Property
Disposal of Surplus Real Property
Public Building Design and Construction
Leasing Space to the Government
A Guide to Specifications and Standards of the Federal Government

● Followup contacts with individual small firms previously counseled to identify their successes, failures, problem areas, etc., to determine what further action should be taken to increase their opportunities and capacity to compete effectively for Government contracts, and to encourage future participation in Government procurement and sales opportunities.

● Participation in local business opportunity meetings sponsored by State and local business, or governmental groups.

● Maximum utilization of trade journals, the local press, chambers of commerce, trade associations, State development corporations, mayors' and governors' advisory groups, local business and civic organizations, small business councils, etc.

FEDERAL PROCUREMENT REGULATIONS SYSTEM

In order to better understand the policies of the Federal Government with regard to small business participation in Government procurement, the businessman should be familiar with the Federal Procurement Regulations System.

The Federal Procurement Regulations System consists of two major elements: (a) the Federal Procurement Regulations, which contain basic procurement policies and procedures applicable to all Government agencies, and (b) implementing and supplementing regulations of individual procurement agencies. Both the Federal Procurement Regulations and the agency implementing and supplementing regulations are published in Title 41 of the Code of Federal Regulations. Such codification and publication make it easier for all business concerns, and especially small business, to readily attain and understand the Government's "contracting ground rules" and to participate in Government procurement. These regulations cover procurement from commercial sources by all executive agencies, and generally provide uniform policies and procedures for worldwide application.

Examples of policies and procedures which are significant to the small businessman are:

● Small business concerns shall be afforded an equitable opportunity to compete for prime contracts and subcontracts.

● Bidders' mailing lists shall include all established and potential small business suppliers who have made acceptable application for inclusion, or who appear from other information (including recommendations by the Small Business Administration representative) to be qualified for inclusion therein.

● Procurement of property and services shall be divided into reasonably small lots (not less than economic production runs) in order to permit bidding on quantities less than the total requirements.

● Applicable specifications, plans, and drawings either shall be furnished with invitations for bids and requests for proposals or, when not so furnished, information as to locations where they may be obtained or examined shall be furnished.

● Any individual procurements or class of procurements, or any appropriate part thereof, shall be set aside for the exclusive participation of small business concerns on the basis of an appropriate (1) joint determination by a Small Business Administration representative and the contracting officer, or (2) a unilateral determination by the contracting officer.

● In the event of equal low bids, preference shall be given to small business concerns in each priority category established for award.

● Proposed procurements and contract awards shall be published in the Department of Commerce. "Commerce Business Daily."

● The maximum amount of time practicable shall be allowed for preparation and submission of bids and proposals.

● Delivery schedules shall be established on a realistic basis which will encourage small business participation to the extent consistent with the actual requirements of the Government.

● Each contractor having a prime contract which exceeds $500,000 and which, in the opinion of the contracting officer, involves substantial subcontracting opportunities shall be required to establish a small business subcontracting program.

PUBLIC BUILDINGS SERVICE

CONTRACTS FOR DESIGN

Almost all new construction and larger alteration projects for which GSA has responsibility are designed by architect-engineer firms or individual architects and individual engineers. Architect-engineers are selected from those who inform GSA of their interest in designing Federal buildings. The architect for the particular project usually contracts for site topographical surveys and soil tests. Professional engineering services are included in the design contract for new construction and major extensions. Separate contracts may be made for professional engineering services where the requirements are basically of an engineering nature.

During fiscal year 1964, GSA awarded 534 design contracts to small business concerns which resulted in designs with a total improvement cost of approximately $413 million.

CONSTRUCTION CONTRACTS

Construction contracts are awarded to the lowest responsible bidder on the basis of competitive bids received after public advertising. When bids are solicited for new construction projects, a notice is placed in a newspaper in the city in which the work is to be performed. Notices also appear in various trade journals, contract notices and report publications, and technical publications serving the construction industry, and the Department of Commerce publication, "Commerce Business Daily."

Preinvitation notices are mailed to firms and individuals who have indicated an interest in bidding on the larger new construction and alteration projects. Notices are also sent to postmasters and building custodians, chambers of commerce, and bid rooms in the area in which construction work is to be performed.

GSA construction and alteration projects estimated to cost $500,000 and under, with few exceptions, are set aside for exclusive bidding by small businesses.

In fiscal year 1964, GSA negotiated locally approximately 11,000 projects which cost under $2,000 at a total cost of almost $7 million. In addition, formally advertised contracts for almost 2,000 projects were awarded at a total cost of over $166 million. All but a few of the very largest of these projects were awarded to small business.

LEASING OF SPACE

General purpose space needed for office, storage, or special use, is leased by GSA in urban centers throughout the United States and in Puerto Rico. GSA does not lease any property in foreign countries, nor does it lease new construction, privately built, for Postal purposes.

Outside of urban centers, the Departments of Agriculture, Commerce, and Defense lease general purpose space under authority granted by GSA.

Leases are obtained by soliciting offers for negotiation or by advertising for sealed bids. In either case, GSA encourages the broadest possible participation among owners and managers of acceptable commercial space. Owners and managers interested in offering commercial space to GSA may contact the regional office having jurisdiction over the area in which the space is located. See GSA regional map, page 23.

BUILDING MAINTENANCE AND REPAIR PROCUREMENTS

In the maintenance and operation of buildings and space, GSA purchases a wide variety of equipment, supplies, materials, and services. Purchases from other than Government sources of supply are usually contracted for by authorized buildings management officials from local businessmen throughout the United States.

DEFENSE MATERIALS SERVICE

PROCUREMENT

GSA procures materials for the national stockpile in accordance with purchase directives issued by the Office of Emergency Planning. Most stockpile objectives have been met, and current procurement of materials for the stockpile by GSA is limited to one item—jewel bearings. In addition, some materials in the stockpile are being upgraded to higher use forms.

Stockpile programs which have assisted small business include rotation to prevent deterioration of materials such as cordage fibers where many of the companies involved are small units. In addition, most of the contracts for supplies and for handling, testing, maintenance, and other services are made with small business concerns.

DISPOSAL

Programs to dispose of excess materials in the national stockpile, Defense Production Act, and other inventories also are designed to encourage small business participation. These excess materials inventories primarily are the result of a change in stockpile policy some years ago by the Office of Emergency Planning, to provide for a 3-year emergency rather than the previous 5-year basis, but also may result from changes in supply-requirements estimates, development of substitute materials, and other factors.

Disposal plans are developed by GSA as authorized by OEP, and must avoid serious disruption of the usual markets of producers, processors, and consumers and adverse effects on the international interests of the United States. In developing disposal plans, GSA consults the Departments of the Interior, Commerce, State, Agriculture, Defense, Labor, and other governmental agencies concerned.

Disposals are made over a sufficient period of time so that sales in any one year are limited to a prudent and reasonable percentage of total annual consumption.

All sales to industry are on a competitive basis, with GSA retaining the right to reject any or all bids considered unacceptable. In planning sales of each material, GSA selects the specific method which will maximize competition and the consequent return to the Government. Care is exercised to insure that sales are made at prices which would not be disruptive of markets.

While most materials are offered on a sealed-bid basis, the public auction method has been used in a number of cases, such as feathers and down and silk waste. Sales of rubber and some other materials are negotiated by phone, just as the commodity exchanges operate, on the basis of prevailing market prices, which fluctuate during the course of any given day, and are subject to allowances for quality and condition.

In order to maximize participation by small business concerns, some portions of the disposal of excess materials have been restricted to, or set aside for, small business bidders, as in the solicitations for the sale of cadmium, aluminum, and nickel. To obtain maximum competition and bidding from all segments of the trade including small business, all materials offered for sale are described in detail and divided into appropriate size lots.

Sales of excess materials totaled $167.1 million in fiscal year 1964. Rubber, tin, and aluminum accounted for almost 80 percent of the total, and various lots of some 25 other excess metals, minerals, ores, and agricultural commodities made up the rest.

GSA gives advance notice to the trade of proposed procurements and sales under these programs. Procurement upgrading, rotation and sales of materials are handled by the Defense Materials Service, Central Office, in Washington, D.C., and procurement of supplies and services is mainly arranged by the GSA regional offices.

TRANSPORTATION AND COMMUNICATIONS SERVICE

The Federal Procurement Regulations require the inclusion in all contracts, in amounts exceeding $5,000, a clause covering the Utilization of Small Business Concerns. Further, the clause with regard to Utilization of Small Business Concerns is contained in Standard Form 32 (June 1964 edition) under item 21 thereof. Consequently, in any transportation contract awarded through formal advertising or through negotiation, the clause pertaining to the Utilization of Small Business Concerns becomes a part of the contract.

With respect to movements of public property under Government bills of lading (contracts), it is the policy of TCS to place with small car-

riers a fair proportion of the total traffic movement by each mode of transportation.

Each Regional TCS Director collaborates with his respective GSA Business Service Center in the advertisement of invitations to bid for transportation services and utilizes their services in the public opening of sealed bids. Detailed information regarding these services may be obtained by contacting the nearest Business Service Center (see map, p. 23).

AUTOMOBILE REPAIR CONTRACTS, RENTALS

At present there are 90 motor pools in operation by GSA, which total is expected to exceed 100. At each interagency motor pool location, GSA enters into automobile repair contracts. Repair contracts are also entered into in other cities within the region where there is a high concentration of federally owned vehicles.

In addition, the GSA interagency motor pools contract for short-term rental of U-drive vehicles. These contracts provide for commercially rented vehicles at each motor pool location and each major trading or population center in each of the 10 regions.

UTILIZATION AND DISPOSAL SERVICE

Programs of the Utilization and Disposal Service of concern to the small businessman primarily involve the sale of real and personal property, and the repair and rehabilitation program.

SALES OF PERSONAL PROPERTY

The General Services Administration and the Department of Defense are the principal Government outlets for the sale of personal property. Sales include thousands of different technical and common-use type items ranging from shoes to airplanes—and in quality, from unused to scrap.

Kinds of Property Sold. Personal property offered for sale by the Government is property that is no longer needed by any agency of the Federal Government to discharge its responsibilities or not required for nonfederal use by the States for education, public health, civil defense, or public airport purposes.

A wide variety of personal property is being sold periodically. Included are automotive and other vehicles, aircraft, hardware, plumbing and heating equipment, paper products, office supplies and equipment, drugs and medical items, wearing apparel, textiles, industrial equipment, and many others.

The property which is offered for sale may be unused or used. It may be in good condition; may require minor or extensive repair or rehabilitation; or may be offered for sale as scrap.

Where Government Property Is Sold. The military installations of the Army, Navy, Air Force, and Marine Corps hold the greatest portion of the Federal Government's inventory of personal property, and thus they generate the largest quantities of property which become available for sale. Such property is sold by the military services through Defense Surplus Sales Offices that have been assigned specific geographic areas of responsibility in the United States.

The General Services Administration conducts sales of personal property for many civil agencies of the Government. These sales usually include a wide variety of consumer-type items. Such sales may be conducted where the property is located or from a consolidated sales point.

How To Obtain Sales Information. As property becomes available for public sale, catalogs or other types of announcements are distributed to those on the mailing list who have expressed an interest in bidding on the types of property being offered within designated geographical areas.

Each of the ten GSA Regional Offices maintains a mailing list for its sales of property located in the geographical area which it serves. For general information about sales conducted by GSA, a businessman may have his name placed on the mailing list by writing to the GSA Business Service Center which serves the geographical area in which he is interested in participating in personal property sales. The addresses of these offices are listed on page 22.

The Department of Defense maintains a centralized mailing list for sales conducted by the Defense Surplus Sales Offices. For inquiries concerning such property and to have his name placed on the mailing list, a businessman should write to the Defense Surplus Bidders Control Office, The Federal Center, Battle Creek, Mich., 49016.

Mailing lists are broken down by types of commodities and also by geographical areas of buyer interest. Therefore, requests for inclusion on the mailing lists should provide:

1. Full name of individual or business concern.
2. Complete address.
3. Commodities or types of property desired (i.e., passenger automobiles, construction equipment, machine tools, etc.).
4. Geographical area in which it is desired to inspect and bid on property.

The catalogs received will describe the property, indicate its specific location, include dates and time for inspection, and give other detailed information regarding the sale.

In addition to sales catalogs which are mailed to potential buyers appearing on mailing lists, notice to the public of sales may also be provided in one or more of the following ways:

1. Through newspapers, radio or television announcements.
2. In trade journals and periodicals.
3. Through notices placed in public buildings, such as post offices, town halls, administrative offices at county seats, and others.
4. Through announcement in the Department of Commerce publication "Commerce Business Daily." This daily publication contains a listing of the larger current sales of personal property. It may be obtained at a subscription rate of $15 a year ($57 for airmail delivery) by writing to the U.S. Department of Commerce, Administrative Service Office, Room 1300, New Post Office Building, 433 West Van Buren Street, Chicago, Ill., 60607.

How Property Is Sold. Personal property is normally sold on a competitive basis to the highest responsible bidder.

Sales are open to the general public and property is offered in quantities calculated to encourage participation by business concerns of all sizes, as well as individuals.

The principal competitive sales methods used in Government selling are:

Sealed Bid in which "Invitations for Bid" containing all sales terms and conditions, description of the property, and understandable instructions are mailed to potential buyers. Notice to the public is given through one or more of the several ways mentioned above. Bidders enter on the "Invitation for Bid" form the prices they are willing to offer, sign, and return it to the Government office specified along with the required deposit. These bids are opened publicly on the announced date, awards are made, and successful bidders are notified.

Public Auction in which the traditional commercial auctioning methods are followed. Catalogs which include instructions are provided potential buyers, and public notice is given in the usual manner. Professionally qualified auctioneers are used.

Spot Bid in which the buyer writes out his bid and places it in a bid box. Successful bidders are then determined and awards made for each item or lot. The buyer then arranges for prompt removal of the property. Here, again, information regarding the property and instructions for placing bids are supplied to those on mailing lists and the usual public notice is provided. In many cases a provision is made which enables prospective purchasers who find it impossible to attend the sale in person to submit mailed bids.

General Conditions of Sale. Close attention should be given to the instructions provided in sales brochures and announcements concerning scheduled sales.

Bidders are customarily required to submit a deposit with their bids, generally amounting to 20 percent of the total bid. For successful bidders the sales brochure will describe the steps necessary to complete payment and remove the property. For unsuccessful bidders, deposits will be refunded promptly.

All bidders are urged to inspect the items on which they plan to bid since the property is offered on an "as-is, where-is" basis.

SALES OF REAL PROPERTY

Real property offered for sale by the Government is known as surplus; that is, it is property no longer needed by any agency of the Federal Government to perform its functions.

The General Services Administration is the principal Government agency responsible for the sale of surplus real property to the public. Sales for fiscal year 1964 were approximately $340 million, based on acquisition cost to the Government.

What Real Property Does the Government Sell?
The types of real property available for sale range from unimproved rural and urban land to improved commercial and industrial facilities. This surplus property consists of residences, residential lots, factories, office buildings, warehouses, and nearly every type of property sold on the commercial market.

How Is Sales Information Obtained? Scheduled sales of real pro erty are widely publicized through paid advertising and announcements and are listed daily in the publication, "Commerce Business Daily." (See pp. 17, 24–25 for information on where to obtain copies.)

Mailing lists are maintained in each GSA regional office of persons or firms who have indicated an interest either in a particular property or a type of property which might become available for sale within the region. Each GSA regional office also has a complete list of real property available for sale throughout the United States, the Commonwealth of Puerto Rico, and the Virgin Islands.

To obtain information or to have his name placed on a mailing list for specified real or personal property or for particular types of property which might become available for sale, the businessman should write to or visit the Business Service Center at the General Services Administration office nearest him (see map, p. 23) or to the Utilization and Disposal Service, General Services Administration, Washington, D.C., 20405.

A pamphlet, "Disposal of Surplus Real Property," describing the real property sales program and how property may be obtained is available, without charge, from any office of the General Services Administration.

How Is Surplus Real Property Sold? Surplus real property is normally sold on a competitive basis to the highest acceptable bidder, either by sealed bid or public auction. Sales are open to the general public and property is parceled for sale in a manner which makes it attractive to the widest available market, including individuals and small business concerns whenever possible.

PROPERTY REHABILITATION PROGRAM

The Property Rehabilitation Division of UDS is responsible for the rehabilitation (repair and refinishing) of items of personal property such as office furniture, household and quarters furniture, hospital and institutional furniture, office machines, i.e., typewriters, adding machines, major

household appliances, i.e., kitchen ranges, refrigerators, washers, dryers, etc., and mattresses and other items as may be included in the future.

For this purpose, the program depends primarily on small business concerns for the actual repair and refinishing of the items described.

Contracts are obtained through competitive bidding procedures released by individual regional offices located in major cities of the United States (see map, p. 23). These contracts involve, for the individual business concern, a sales volume that ranges from several thousand dollars to more than a hundred thousand dollars a year, depending upon the volume of business present in a given area and the size of the establishment.

The general trend is toward expansion of the number of contracts to be utilized and the volume of work involved. The type of rehabilitation performed is comparable to that practiced commercially and usually includes furnishing transportation of items to and from customer agencies within an acceptable transportation range.

FEDERAL SUPPLY SERVICE

The Federal Supply Service contracts for or purchases more than a billion dollars worth of material or services each year, to supply the needs of executive agencies. This purchasing is carried out by buying divisions located in each of GSA's 10 regional offices and by a Procurement Operations Division in GSA's Central Office in Washington, D.C., with a branch office in New York City.

An extremely wide variety of goods and services is purchased by these buying activities but only a relatively small portion of the total purchases are for items used by GSA itself. The Service's primary responsibility is to keep other agencies supplied with the materials and services they need to carry out their respective program operations. Vast quantities of general products and items, other than strictly military material, are procured and supplied to military activities.

These supply support programs are accomplished through the following types of procurement and supply activities.

GSA SUPPLY DEPOT PROGRAM

GSA supply depots are located in each of the regional offices shown on the map on page 23, and stock thousands of items of general commodities repetitively required by Federal agencies.

The items carried in Stores Stock are those which are consumed or needed in the day-to-day operations of Federal agencies, and which can be most advantageously furnished through storage and issue.

Replenishment of stores stock items is accomplished through definite quantity purchases, or through the establishment of term contracts against which replenishment orders are issued as

stocks are depleted. As in the case of the Federal Supply Schedule Contracts Program mentioned below, contracting is handled on either a central or regional basis depending upon the character of the commodity involved. When term contracts are awarded centrally particular attention is given to the issuance of invitations on a zone basis in order to provide maximum opportunities for small businesses to compete. When consolidated definite quantity contracting is found to be the most advantageous method of procurement, large lots are carefully scrutinized and adjusted with the objective of making maximum reasonable use of the production and distribution capacities of small business concerns.

A majority of the items shown in the Stores Stock Catalog are replenished either through local purchase action on a definite quantity basis by the regional offices, or by the issuance of delivery orders against regional or national term contracts. Regional term contracts are particularly advantageous to small business concerns since they cover a continuing requirement which can reasonably be estimated in advance. A large proportion of the local purchasing which is not included in regional term contracts is handled through small purchase procedures prescribed in the Federal Procurement Regulations which are specifically designed to simplify procurements from small business concerns.

Prospective suppliers may review the items carried in the GSA Stores Stock Catalog by referring to copies of the catalog which are available for inspection at any of the regional Business Service Centers, or copies may be purchased through the Superintendent of Documents, Government Printing Office, Washington, D.C., 20402.

FEDERAL SUPPLY SCHEDULE CONTRACTS

In terms of dollar value and range of items covered, the Federal Supply Schedule Program is the largest program carried out by the Federal Supply Service. The Federal Supply Schedules are an organized listing of contracts against which Federal agencies may place delivery orders as needs develop. These schedules are published by GSA and made available to all agencies having an anticipated need. They cover a definite range of items which are available for direct delivery from the supplier to the requisitioning or using agency at prices, and under contracting conditions, which have been established in advance. They do not obligate the Government to purchase any definite quantity. Each is a required source for some specified group of Federal agencies, or for Federal agencies located in a specified area. Schedule contracts are available as an alternate source of supply for Federal agencies which are not required by regulation to use them on a mandatory basis.

Federal Supply Schedule contracts are handled on either a central or regional basis depending upon the character of the commodity involved. Schedule contracts awarded centrally are zoned to provide maximum opportunities for small businesses to compete.

Under this program "indefinite quantity" or "term" contracts are awarded for items which are in common and recurring use by the various Federal agencies. Information concerning the range of commodities involved in this program can be obtained from a review of the Federal Supply Schedule Checklist and Guide, published quarterly, which contains a general index of the commodities and a list of the schedules currently in effect. More detailed information concerning the contracting policies for specific items may be secured from regional GSA Business Service Centers.

CONSOLIDATED PURCHASE PROGRAM

Certain Federal agencies' requirements, such as motor vehicles, household and quarters furniture and coal, constitute a large and easily predictable volume that can be consolidated into periodic procurement cycles. The total quantities needed are incorporated into definite quantity invitations for bids for direct delivery to the ordering agency. This program is also conducted on both a national and regional basis, depending on the character of the commodity involved. Whenever feasible, portions of these procurements are set aside for small business concerns.

SPECIAL PURCHASE PROGRAMS

In addition to the regular programs discussed above, the Federal Supply Service on a continuing basis undertakes special purchase programs which normally involve only the requirements of a single agency. For example, purchases of a wide variety of supplies are made on behalf of the Agency for International Development for shipment overseas. In addition to a special program carried out by AID to publicize the procurements, the Federal Supply Service has adjusted its techniques to encourage small business participation. For example, the purchasing is decentralized and handled through simplified open market procedures whenever possible. Export arrangements have been established so that the small business supplier desiring to participate does not have to be an export merchant and in many cases may offer his domestic item as packaged for domestic use with GSA handling all matters of export packing and shipping.

SIMPLIFIED PROCEDURES AID SMALL BUSINESS

Contract forms, methods, and procedures have been simplified to make it easier for small business concerns to participate in FSS programs. An up-to-date list of commodities normally purchased is available and streamlined methods of placing new suppliers' names on mailing lists have been developed. Certain types of contracts are personally delivered to small business contractors at which time terms and conditions are reviewed to help them avoid pitfalls and difficulties which might otherwise occur. In addition, quality control inspectors assist small business firms in meeting contract requirements and in solving production, delivery, and quality control problems.

The Federal Supply Service is interested in keeping the Federal Supply System up-to-date through the introduction of new and improved items. For this purpose counseling services are provided at each GSA's Business Service Centers and special procedures are used to assure prompt and receptive processing of supplier applications to introduce new and improved items into the Federal Supply System.

INSPECTION OF PURCHASED COMMODITIES

Government procurement regulations require that materials and services purchased be inspected prior to acceptance and payment by the Government. This inspection may be performed at source (supplier's plant) or at destination (consignee location).

The supplier, prior to submitting a bid, should thoroughly review the contractual requirements. Special attention should be given to any referenced technical specifications in order to insure that the supplier thoroughly understands what will be required, and evaluates his capability of meeting these requirements before submitting a bid.

Effort is made to prevent costly errors in contracting for Government supplies by having a preproduction meeting between a cognizant Government inspector and the supplier. At such a meeting a thorough review should be made of the governing specifications.

It has been the experience of Government inspection activities that most rejections of contractor's materials are due to an incorrect interpretation of the technical specifications by the contractor. It is a requirement in contracts that suppliers establish proper quality controls over production of the required product, and submit to the Government inspection representative for acceptance only materials that have been inspected, tested, and found to comply with contract specification requirements.

RELATIONSHIP OF FEDERAL SPECIFICATIONS AND STANDARDS TO SMALL BUSINESS

Small business concerns are often unfamiliar with the purpose and use of the various types of specifications and standards in use in the Federal Government. The following explanation is intended to provide a better understanding of this important phase of Federal Government supply operations.

Wherever feasible, the Federal Government makes its procurements on a competitive basis. Federal specifications and standards provide the basis for achieving this objective. Specifications provide clear and accurate descriptions of the product or service being procured, and specify the minimum requirements for quality and construction of materials and equipment necessary for an acceptable product. Standards reduce to a minimum the number of qualities, sizes, colors, varieties, and types of materials and commodities being procured.

Federal specifications and standards are designed for the protection of the Government, in that it must secure the best product at the lowest competitive price to meet the service needs of the Federal agencies. Participation by large and small suppliers on an equal basis in supplying Government requirements broaden sources of supply and assures greater supplier participation.

In order to assure that small business gets its fair share of Government procurements, Federal specifications are thoroughly coordinated with all segments of industry, small as well as large, located in representative geographical areas of the country. By this means, the small producer plays a part in the development of the specifications and his interests are reflected. In addition, Federal specifications are coordinated with technical societies and associations, trade associations, and with using Federal agencies.

Evaluation of New Items. Firms interested in having new products included in the Federal Supply System may fill out the appropriate application at any GSA regional office. If evaluation indicates procurement of the item would be in the best interest of the Government, the item will be included in the Federal Supply System.

Availability of Federal Specifications, Standards, and Handbooks. An index of all current specifications, standards, and handbooks is issued as of January 1, each year with cumulative monthly supplements being issued during the year. Copies of the Index and Supplements may be purchased on a subscription basis from the Superintendent of Documents, U.S. Government Printing Office, Washington, D.C., 20402. The current domestic subscription cost is $1.50 and checks or money orders should be made payable to "Superintendent of Documents."

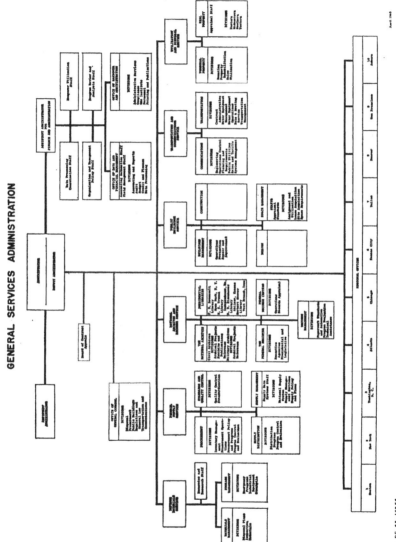

GENERAL SERVICES ADMINISTRATION

Copies of current Federal Specifications and Standards needed by business concerns for Government bidding and contracting purposes are available without charge from any of the GSA Business Service Centers (see map, p. 23). Complete libraries, and copies wanted by individuals or organizations not involved in Government bidding and contracting, may be purchased through the GSA Business Service Center in Washington, D.C., at the prices shown in the index or supplement thereto. Orders should be accompanied by check, postal money order, cash, or Government Printing Office coupons in the proper amounts for the particular documents and quantities needed. Checks and money orders should be made payable to the "General Services Administration." Government Printing Office deposit account numbers will be honored. Government bidders who are not certain exactly what specifications are needed should make inquiry directly to the particular Government agency contracting office which is requesting bids.

GSA REGIONAL OFFICES AND BUSINESS SERVICE CENTERS

Frank J. O'Connor
Regional Director of
  Business Affairs
General Services
  Administration
U.S. Post Office and
  Courthouse
Boston, Mass. 02109
Tel: 223-2868

John F. Clark
Regional Director of
  Business Affairs
General Services
  Administration
30 Church Street
New York, N.Y. 10007
Tel: 264-1234

William F. Donlin, Jr.
Regional Director of
  Business Affairs
General Services
  Administration
7th and D Streets SW.
Washington, D.C. 20407
Tel: WOrth 3-4147

William W. Barron
Regional Director of
  Business Affairs
General Services
  Administration
1776 Peachtree Street NW.
Atlanta, Ga. 30309
Tel: 526-5661

John F. Daley
Regional Director of
  Business Affairs
General Services
  Administration
219 South Dearborn Street
Chicago, Ill. 60604
Tel: 828-5383

Thomas W. Lacy
Regional Director of
  Business Affairs
General Services
  Administration
1500 East Bannister Road
Kansas City, Mo. 64131
Tel: EMerson 1-7200

Randolph M. Jackson
Regional Director of
  Business Affairs
General Services
  Administration
1114 Commerce Street
Dallas, Tex. 75202
Tel: RIverside 9-3355

Price J. George
Regional Director of
  Business Affairs
General Services
  Administration
Denver Federal Center,
  Building 41
Denver, Colo. 80225
Tel: 233-6689

Robert J. Ireland
Regional Director of
  Business Affairs
General Services
  Administration
49 Fourth Street
San Francisco, Calif.
  94103
Tel: 556-2114

Mrs. Margaret Bayless,
  Manager
Business Service Center
General Services
  Administration
417 South Hill Street
Los Angeles, Calif. 90013
Tel: 688-3210

John J. Murphy
Regional Director of
  Business Affairs
General Services
  Administration
Federal Office Building
909 First Avenue
Seattle, Wash. 98104
Tel: 583-5558

BIBLIOGRAPHY OF GSA PUBLICATIONS

The following publications are available, without charge, from field offices of GSA, Small Business Administration and Department of Commerce:

Doing Business With the Federal Government
A Guide to Specifications and Standards of the Federal Government

The following guides are available, without charge, from GSA Business Service Centers:

Sales Promotion in Selling to the Federal Government
Leasing Space to the Government
Public Building Design and Construction
Government Business Opportunities
Federal Supply Schedule—Checklist and Guide
Disposal of Surplus Real Property
Sale of Government Personal Property

The following publications may be purchased from the Superintendent of Documents, Government Printing Office, Washington, D.C., 20402:

Federal Procurement Regulations, $7.50
Index of Federal Specifications, Standards and Handbooks, $1.50
Common Shipping Faults and Their Remedies, 25¢
Help Prevent Loss and Damage, 30¢
How To Prepare and Process U.S. Government Bills of Lading, 35¢
Stores Stock Catalog, $2.25

GSA REGIONAL OFFICES AND BUSINESS SERVICE CENTERS

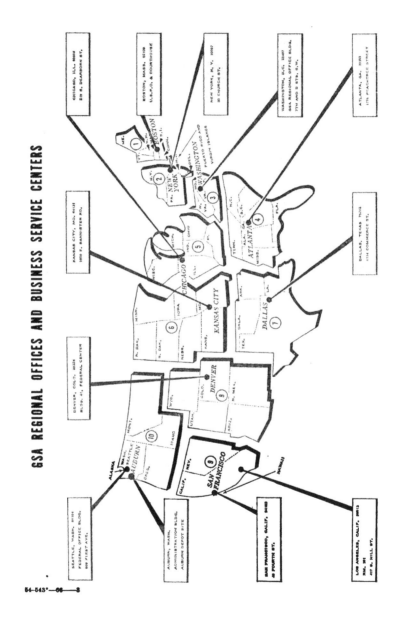

CHICAGO, ILL. 60604
219 S. DEARBORN ST.

BOSTON, MASS. 02109
U.S.P.O. & COURTHOUSE

NEW YORK, N. Y. 10007
26 CHURCH ST.

WASHINGTON, D.C. 22407
GSA REGIONAL OFFICE BLDG.
7TH AND D STS., S.W.

ATLANTA, GA. 30303
1776 PEACHTREE STREET

KANSAS CITY, MO. 64131
1500 E. BANNISTER RD.

DALLAS, TEXAS 75202
1114 COMMERCE STREET

DENVER, COLO. 80225
BLDG. 41, FEDERAL CENTER

SEATTLE, WASH. 98104
FEDERAL OFFICE BLDG.
909 FIRST AVE.

AUBURN, WASH.
ADMINISTRATION BLDG.
AUBURN DEPOT SITE

SAN FRANCISCO, CALIF. 94102
49 FOURTH ST.

LOS ANGELES, CALIF. 90012
RM. 391
457 S. HILL ST.

Department of Defense

SELLING TO THE MILITARY

INTRODUCTION

To sell to the Department of Defense, business firms must identify those offices which buy the supplies or services the firm has to offer, or has a capability to offer.

Business firms must compete for Defense work and meet terms of contracts awarded, just as is the case in selling to commercial firms.

The Department of Defense wants to do business with all competent firms in order to get competition among those who offer products or services that are required. Purchasing activities particularly want small business firms and firms in labor-surplus areas to offer their products to supply Defense needs.

Business firms, too, must help themselves by learning how the Department of Defense conducts its business, and by seeking out those military purchasing offices which buy supplies and services the firm can supply.

Remember . . . basic principles followed in selling within the commercial business field equally apply in selling to the Department of Defense.

● Learn your customer's needs, his buying policies and practices, and where buying is done.

● Follow leads to search out selling opportunities in all segments of Defense organization.

This pamphlet is intended to provide business firms, which have little or no experience in selling their products or services to the Department of Defense, with basic steps and initial contacts for locating sales opportunities.

PART I

MAKING YOUR CAPABILITIES KNOWN

● Complete "Bidder's Mailing List Application" (p. 27), along with "Bidder's Mailing List Application Supplement" (p. 29). Additional copies of these forms are available at all Defense procurement offices.

● Send completed forms to each Defense procurement office that has buying responsibility for products or services you can furnish.

● Principal purchasing offices of Department of Defense and the types of commodities and services they buy are listed under part II.

Many procurement offices will supply a checksheet of the commodities and services they buy so you can specifically identify those which your firm can produce. Care should be exercised in completing the forms and in describing supplies or services you have to offer. If possible, the number of the Government specification your supplies meet or can be made to meet should be indicated.

Specifications for items used by the military are generally available at procurement offices which have responsibility for buying the item. Specifications can also be secured from the *Naval*

Supply Depot (ATTN: Code DCI), 5801 Tabor Avenue, Philadelphia, Pa., 19120 (Telephone: RAndolph 8–1212, ext. 528 or 530). The particular specifications desired should be identified by number and title in your request.

Each procurement office that has your firm on its "bidders' lists" will forward "Invitations for Bids" (IFB's) or "Requests for Proposals" (RFP's) as requirements develop for supplies or services you have offered. When your firm receives IFB's or RFP's, a bid or proposal should be offered or the purchasing office should be informed that the firm is unable to bid but desires to remain on the active bidder's list. Otherwise, the firm may be dropped from the bidders' list.

Opportunities should be sought continuously to be included on the bidders' lists of the various Defense procurement offices which have buying responsibility for supplies and services your firm has to offer.

COMMERCE BUSINESS DAILY

The "COMMERCE BUSINESS DAILY" is a valuable source of information to businessmen in identifying products and services which individual procurement offices currently plan to buy. This Federal publication lists:

24

• Current Defense Department proposed procurements estimated to exceed $10,000 and civilian agency procurement expected to exceed $5,000;
• Recent contract awards—which provide "leads" to subcontracting opportunities;
• Surplus sales information; and other information helpful to businessmen who seek to participate in Federal procurement activities.

The "Commerce Business Daily" is published Monday through Friday and may be purchased on annual subscription for $15 by regular mail or $42 for an airmail edition. Checks or money orders should be made payable to the "U.S. Department of Commerce" and mailed to:

U.S. Department of Commerce
Administrative Services Office
Room 1300, New Post Office Building
433 West Van Buren Street
Chicago, Ill., 60607

The "Daily" is also available for inspection at each of the 60 field offices of the Small Business Administration, the 34 field offices of the Department of Commerce and at approximately 700 cooperating offices, including many local chambers of commerce.

SUBCONTRACTING

One of the greatest opportunities small business firms have for participating in Department of Defense business, other than contracting directly with a Defense Agency, is by subcontracting with firms that have Department of Defense contracts. Opportunities in the subcontracting field are often overlooked by small business firms.

Department of Defense contracts in the amount of $500,000 or more, having substantial subcontracting possibilities, require that the contractor maintain a Defense Small Business Subcontracting and Labor Surplus Area Program. Such contractors are required to designate a Small Business Liaison Officer who administers the company subcontracting program. These programs are designed to assist small business firms and to afford them opportunities to participate in Defense work as subcontactors. The Commerce Business Daily is useful in identifying firms which offer subcontracting opportunities.

LOCAL PURCHASES

Certain needs of each military camp, post, base, station, or installation are met by a purchasing office at the installation. Such purchases are generally for small quantities of items or specific services needed by the installation initiating the purchase. For the most part such purchases are made from sources near the purchasing installation. Business firms should investigate the requirements of military installations within their geographical area.

MILITARY EXCHANGE SERVICES

Each military exchange located at installations in the United States purchases or contracts for its own needs. The exchange officer, or his representative, should be contacted at each military installation where business firms desire to offer their products or services. This may be accomplished by writing or telephoning the exchange officer at each military installation.

MILITARY COMMISSARY STORES

Items sold through military commissary stores are purchased by either (1) Defense Personnel Support Center, 2800 South 20th St., Philadelphia, Pa., 19101, or (2) individual military commissary stores at installations where stores are located. Information on how to participate in supplying needs for commissary stores may be obtained by writing or telephoning the Defense Subsistence Supply Center or the Commissary Store Officer at the nearest military installation.

SOURCES OF INFORMATION ON DEFENSE PROCUREMENT

There are many offices within the Department of Defense, and in other Government agencies, that provide guidance and information to assist business firms and individuals who seek opportunities to participate in supplying Department of Defense requirements. There are one or more military procurement offices in virtually every major city in the United States. These offices are equipped to provide information and guidance to individuals and business firms on how they can compete for Defense work. Small Business Specialists on the staff of these major military procurement offices are anxious to assist small business firms in obtaining information on (1) military procurement; (2) being placed on appropriate bidders' lists; and (3) identifying subcontract opportunities.

Other Government agency field offices, including those of the Small Business Administration, General Services Administration, and the Department of Commerce are also equipped to assist business firms in locating opportunities to participate in military procurement. Further, many local chamber of commerce offices have facilities to provide similar guidance.

FEDERAL PROCUREMENT INFORMATION OFFICES IN WASHINGTON, D.C.

These offices do not let contracts or make purchases but are available for the purpose of providing information and guidance on Federal procurement activities.

Defense Procurement Information Office, Office of the Assistant Secretary of Defense (Installation and Logistics), Washington, D.C. Room 3D777, Pentagon, Tel: OXford 7-1481.

Army Small Business Adviser, Office of the Assistant Secretary (Installations and Logistics), Department of the Army, Washington, D.C. Room 2E591, Pentagon, Tel: OXford 7-8113.

Navy Small Business Adviser, Office of Naval Material, Department of the Navy, Washington, D.C. Room 2203A, 18th and Constitution Avenue. Main Navy Building, Tel: OXford 6-7612.

Air Force Small Business Adviser, Office of the Deputy Chief of Staff (Systems and Logistics), Directorate of Procurement Policy, Department of the Air Force, Washington, D.C. Room 4C279, Pentagon, Tel: OXford 7-4126.

Defense Supply Agency Small Business Adviser, Directorate of Procurement and Production, Defense Supply Agency, Cameron Station, Alexandria, Va. Room 119A, Building 4, Cameron Station, Tel: OXford 8-1471.

Director of Business Services, General Services Administration, Region No. 3, 7th and D Streets SW., Washington, D.C. Room 7604, Tel: WOodley 3-4147.

Small Business Advisory Service Center, Small Business Administration, 811 Vermont Avenue NW., Washington, D.C. Main Lobby, Tel: DUdley 2-3848.

Business Service Center, Department of Commerce, 14th and Constitution Avenue NW., Washington, D.C. Main lobby, Tel: WOodley 7-5201.

STANDARD FORM 129—AUGUST 1952 PRESCRIBED BY GENERAL SERVICES ADMINISTRATION SEC. 1-8-202 129-102	BIDDER'S MAILING LIST APPLICATION	INITIAL APPLICATION
		REVISION

All answers should be typed or printed. See reverse for information and instructions.

TO:	DATE OF THIS APPLICATION

1. NAME OF APPLICANT	2. ADDRESS TO WHICH BIDDING FORMS ARE TO BE MAILED

3. ADDRESS OF MAIN BUSINESS OFFICE	4. HOW LONG IN PRESENT BUSINESS

5. TYPE OF ORGANIZATION (Check one)
☐ INDIVIDUAL ☐ PARTNERSHIP ☐ CORPORATION

6. IF INCORPORATED, INDICATE IN WHICH STATE

7. NAMES OF OFFICERS, MEMBERS OR OWNERS OF CONCERN, PARTNERSHIP, ETC.

(A) PRESIDENT	(B) VICE PRESIDENT
(C) SECRETARY	(D) TREASURER

(E) OWNERS OR PARTNERS

8. AFFILIATED CONCERNS (Name, location, and in detail, controlling interest in each)

9. PERSONS OR CONCERNS AUTHORIZED TO SIGN BIDS AND CONTRACTS IN YOUR NAME (If agent, so specify)

NAME	OFFICIAL CAPACITY

10. PERSONS TO CONTACT ON MATTERS CONCERNING BIDS AND CONTRACTS (If agent, so specify)

NAME	OFFICIAL CAPACITY	TELEPHONE NO.

11. INDICATE CLASSES OF EQUIPMENT, SUPPLIES, MATERIAL, AND/OR SERVICES ON WHICH YOU DESIRE TO BID (Use attached list, if any)

12. CATEGORY (See definitions on the reverse of this form and check below the category which applies to the applicant)

☐ (A) MANUFACTURER OR PRODUCER ☐ (C) REGULAR DEALER (Type 2)
☐ (B) REGULAR DEALER (Type 1) ☐ (D) SERVICE ESTABLISHMENT

13. NUMBER OF PERSONS NOW EMPLOYED	14. FLOOR SPACE (Square feet)		15. NET WORTH	
	MANUFACTURING	WAREHOUSE	DATE	AMOUNT

16. THIS SPACE FOR USE BY THE GOVERNMENT	17. I certify that the information supplied herein (including all pages attached) is correct and that neither the applicant nor any person (or concern) in any connection with the applicant as a principal or officer, so far as is known, is now debarred or otherwise declared ineligible by any agency of the Federal Government from bidding for furnishing materials, supplies or services to the Government or any agency thereof.
	SIGNATURE OF PERSON AUTHORIZED TO SIGN THIS APPLICATION
	18. NAME AND TITLE OF PERSON SIGNING (Please type or print)

INFORMATION AND INSTRUCTIONS

Persons or concerns wishing to be added to a particular agency's bidder's mailing list for supplies or services shall file this properly completed and certified Bidder's Mailing List Application, together with such other lists as may be attached to the application form, with each procurement office of the Federal agency with which they desire to do business. *The application shall be submitted and signed by the principal as distinguished from an agent, however constituted.*

After placement on the bidder's mailing list of an agency, a supplier's failure to respond (*submission of bid, or notice in writing that you are unable to bid on that particular transaction but wish to remain on the active bidder's mailing list for that particular item*) to Invitations for Bids will be understood by the agency to indicate lack of interest and concurrence in the removal of the supplier's name from the purchasing activity's bidder's mailing list for the items concerned.

CATEGORY DEFINITIONS
(See Item No. 12)

A. **MANUFACTURER OR PRODUCER** means a person (or concern) owning, operating, or maintaining a factory or establishment that produces, on the premises, the materials, supplies, articles, or equipment of the general character of those listed in item No. 11.

B. **REGULAR DEALER** (*Type 1*) means a person (or concern) who owns, operates, or maintains a store, warehouse, or other establishment in which the materials, supplies, articles, or equipment of the general character listed in item No. 11 are bought, kept in stock, and sold to the public in the usual course of business.

C. **REGULAR DEALER** (*Type 2*) in the case of supplies of particular kinds (*at present, petroleum, lumber and timber products, coal, machine tools, raw cotton, green coffee, or hay, grain, feed, and straw*) "REGULAR DEALER" means a person (or concern) satisfying the requirements of article 101 (b) of the regulations, as amended from time to time, prescribed by the Secretary of Labor under the Walsh-Healey Public Contracts Act (41 U. S. Code 35–45).

D. **SERVICE ESTABLISHMENT** means a concern (*or person*) which owns, operates, or maintains any type of business which is principally engaged in the furnishing of nonpersonal services, such as (*but not limited to*) repairing, cleaning, redecorating, or rental of personal property, including the furnishing of necessary repair parts or other supplies as part of the services performed.

BIDDER'S MAILING LIST APPLICATION SUPPLEMENT

Form Approved
Budget Bureau No. 22-R091.6

IF ADDITIONAL SPACE IS REQUIRED, ATTACH SEPARATE SHEET AND REFER TO ITEM NUMBER

1 NUMBER OF EMPLOYEES	OPERATIONS AT	ENGINEERING	PRODUCTION	OTHERS	TOTAL
	MAXIMUM LEVEL				
	MINIMUM *(During last 2 yrs.)*				
	PRESENT LEVEL				

2. CONTRACTS HELD WITH ARMED SERVICES DURING PAST 3 YEARS *(List separately)*

CONTRACT NUMBER	DESCRIPTION OF ITEMS	DOLLAR VALUE

3. TYPES OF EQUIPMENT, COMPONENTS, MATERIAL OR SERVICES NOW BEING MANUFACTURED, PERFORMED, OR DEVELOPED *(Commercial and Military)*

4. FLOOR SPACE *(Sq. ft.)*

ENGINEERING	LABORATORY	TOTAL FLOOR SPACE *(Including warehouse and manufacturing space)*

5. BRIEF DESCRIPTION OF BUILDINGS *(Type of construction and use)*

6. MACHINERY AND EQUIPMENT [1]

7. TESTING AND/OR LABORATORY FACILITIES [1]

8. ADDRESSES *(Including counties)* OF FACTORIES, FOUNDRIES, MINES, OR YARDS, IF ANY *(Specify)*

9. SECURITY CLEARANCE *(If applicable, check highest clearance authorized by clearing agency)*

FOR KEY PERSONNEL			FOR PLANT ONLY	
TOP SECRET				
SECRET	CONFIDENTIAL		SECRET	CONFIDENTIAL

LIST DEPARTMENTS WHICH HAVE GRANTED SECURITY CLEARANCE AND DATES GRANTED

10. INCLOSURES *(Check)* ☐ FINANCIAL STATEMENTS, INCLUDING OPERATING STATEMENTS ☐ DESCRIPTIVE LITERATURE
☐ ADDITIONAL INFORMATION ATTACHED ☐ BROCHURE ☐ CATALOG ☐ PHOTOGRAPHS

11. I CERTIFY THAT THE INFORMATION SUPPLIED HEREIN *(Including any attachments)* IS CORRECT

DATE	NAME AND ADDRESS OF APPLICANT	SIGNATURE

[1] Give brief, representative outline of type and condition of machinery, equipment (6), and facilities (7) available; if not owned by firm, give status in detail.

DD FORM 558-1
1 AUG 55

EDITION OF 1 JAN 54 IS OBSOLETE.

PART II

DEPARTMENT OF THE ARMY MAJOR BUYING OFFICES

The Department of the Army's missions for Research and Development, and Procurement and Production, are the responsibility of the Assistant Secretary of the Army (Research and Development) and the Assistant Secretary of the Army (Installations and Logistics) respectively. Both of these offices are policy offices. No actual contracting is accomplished by either of these offices, nor do they maintain bidders lists.

The U.S. Army Materiel Command has responsibility for the major part of the research and development and materiel procurement functions formerly assigned to the Army technical services. However, there are certain missions and functions assigned to other elements of the Army, which are as follows:

The U.S. Army Corps of Engineers is responsible for contracting for military construction, maintenance, and repair of buildings, structures and utilities, and civil works such as river and harbor improvement, flood control, hydroelectric power, public utility services and related projects.

The Army Medical Service provides supplies and services for the support of Army Medical Centers and General Hospitals under the command jurisdiction of The Surgeon General. The Army Medical Service does not procure standard items of medical material. Such items are purchased by the Defense Medical Supply Center, a procuring activity of the Defense Supply Agency. Procurement responsibilities remaining at the Army Medical Service consist of the following:

1. Contracts for supplies and services in direct support of missions at major hospitals and medical centers. Mission support items for the Army Medical Service consist of medical, dental, laboratory and hospital equipment and supplies; X-ray and photographic equipment and supplies; hospital furnishings; kitchen equipment, drugs and chemicals; occupational and physical therapy supplies; equipment, supplies, and services required for plant maintenance.

2. Contracts for research and development in areas of basic and applied medical and scientific research applicable to medical treatment supplies and equipment.

3. Contracts for medical and hospitalization services under the provisions of the Medical Care Act (Public Law 85-861).

The Continental Armies: Purchases in this area (generally identified as "local purchases") consist of the many items needed in the daily operations of posts, camps, and stations of the Department of the Army. Most of these items are obtained from local business sources or from stocks of other Government agencies. Items purchased are generally commercial type rather than military; are not complex or are less complex than items procured by major procurement offices. Post, camp, and station procurement also includes minor construction, repairs, and utilities, painting, and other supplies and services incidental to the "housekeeping" activity of the installation concerned.

Headquarters, U.S. Army Materiel Command
Washington, D.C.
Telephone: Code 202, OXford 7-4447 or 7-5978

The U.S. Army Materiel Command, with headquarters in Washington, D.C., has materiel procurement functions formerly assigned to the Army technical services. Except for those items procured and furnished the Army under Department of Defense single-department procurement programs or by the Defense Supply Agency, or authorized for procurement from the General Services Administration, the U.S. Army Materiel Command supervises all Army procurement which is accomplished at the Separate Activities and Detachments listed on page 31 or the "Commands" listed on pages 32 to 34.

SEPARATE ACTIVITIES

U.S. Army Harry Diamond Laboratories
Washington, D.C. 20438
Area Code: 202 244-7700

U.S. Army Natick Laboratories
Natick, Mass. 01762
Area Code: 617 653-1000

U.S. Army Pictorial Center
35-11 35th Avenue
Long Island City, N.Y. 11106
Area Code: 212 AStoria 4-3100

*Watertown Arsenal
Watertown, Mass. 02172
Area Code: 617 926-1900

PROCUREMENT DETACHMENTS

U.S. Army Chicago Procurement Detachment
623 South Wabash Avenue
Chicago, Ill. 60605
Area Code: 312 WEbster 9-6000

U.S. Army Cincinnati Procurement Detachment
Federal Office Building
550 Main Street
Cincinnati, Ohio 45202
Area Code: 513 381-2200

U.S. Army New York Procurement Detachment
207 West 24th Street
New York, N.Y. 10011
Area Code: 212 ORegon 7-3030

U.S. Army Southwest Procurement Agency
55 South Grand Avenue
Pasadena, Calif. 91109
Area Code: 213 SYcamore 6-0471

U.S. Army Northwest Procurement Agency
1515 Clay Street
Oakland, Calif. 94604
Area Code: 415 834-4121

*Closing.

Major subordinate commands of the U.S. Army Materiel Command responsible for procurement and the types of materiel they procure are:

Headquarters, U.S. Army Mobility Command
Building 230, Detroit Arsenal, Warren, Mich.
Telephone: 756-1000 Area Code 313

Mission: Exercises integrated commodity management of tactical wheeled and general-purpose vehicles and aeronautical, air delivery, surface transportation, mapping, geodesy, electric power generation, construction and services, barrier, bridging, stream crossing, petroleum handling, and general support equipment and supplies, including design and development; product, production, and maintenance engineering; procurement, production, industrial readiness planning; and cataloging.

U.S. Army Mobility Equipment Center
4300 Goodfellow Boulevard
St. Louis, Mo. 63120
Area Code: 314 EVergreen 2-8200

U.S. Army Engineer Research & Development Laboratories
Fort Belvoir, Va. 22060
Area Code: 703 781-8200

U.S. Army Aviation Materiel Command
12th and Spruce Streets
St. Louis, Mo. 63166
Area Code: 314 MAin 2-2688

U.S. Army Transportation Research Command
Fort Eustis, Va. 23604
Area Code: 703 878-3306

U.S. Army Tank-Automotive Center
Detroit Arsenal
Warren, Mich. 48090
Area Code: 313 756-1000

Headquarters, U.S. Army Missile Command
Redstone Arsenal, Ala. 35809
Telephone 876-5441 or 876-3567 Area Code 205

The U.S. Army Missile Command is responsible for integrated commodity management of free rockets, guided missiles, ballistic missiles, target missiles, air defense missile fire coordination equipment, related special purpose and multisystem test equipment, missile launching and ground support equipment, missile fire control equipment, and other associated equipment including (1) design and development, (2) product, production, and maintenance engineering, (3) procurement, production, and industrial mobilization planning, (4) cataloging and standardization, (5) wholesale inventory management and supply control, (6) new equipment training, design of pertinent training devices, and technical assistance to users. The Missile Command is responsible for conducting or managing basic and applied research with respect to assigned materiel development.

Major Commodity Areas

Free rockets, guided missiles, ballistic missiles, target missiles, multisystem test equipment, and associated equipment.

Buying offices:

Directorate of Procurement and Production	Purchasing and Contracting Division
U.S. Army Missile Command	U.S. Army Missile Support Command
Redstone Arsenal, Ala.	Redstone Arsenal, Ala.

Headquarters, U.S. Army Weapons Command

Rock Island Arsenal, Rock Island, III.   61202

Telephone: 794-5336   Area Code 309

The U.S. Army Weapons Command is a major subordinate Command of the U.S. Army Materiel Command and contracts for weapons system, including artillery weapons, infantry weapons, secondary armament for vehicles, crew-served weapons, and aircraft weapons systems; combat vehicles including tanks, armored personnel carriers, self-propelled artillery and missile launchers, tank bulldozers, flamethrowers, armament adaption kits and associated equipment. Also, research, design and development; product production, and maintenance engineering; procurement, production and industrial mobilization planning; cataloging and standardization; wholesale inventory management and supply control; such stock control, storage, distribution, surveillance, and depot maintenance as may be assigned; new equipment training, design of pertinent training devices, and technical assistance to users.

Major Commodity Areas

Weapons and combat vehicles:

Rock Island Arsenal Rock Island, Ill. 61202 Area Code: 309 794-5336	Contracts for replenishment spare parts for artillery, artillery mounts, recoil mechanisms, carriages, limbers, and loaders; handcarts; arms racks; target materiel (except aerial drones); training devices and associated equipment for the foregoing items; common tools; tool sets; shop equipment; and raw materials, and hardware items used in arsenal manufacturing operations.
Springfield Armory Springfield, Mass. 01101 Area Code: 413 REpublic 9-6011	Contracts for replenishment spare parts for individual weapons, machineguns, grenade launchers, secondary armament for combat and tactical vehicles, aircraft armament subsystems (gun type), spotting weapons mounts and pods; clips; links; linkers; delinkers; training devices, and associated equipment for the foregoing items; and raw materials and hardware items used in arsenal manufacturing operations.
Watervliet Arsenal Watervliet, N.Y. 12189 Area Code: 518 ARsenal 3-4610	Contracts for mortars; recoilless rifles; cannon assemblies and components; training devices, associated equipment, and replenishment spare parts for the foregoing items; and raw materials and hardware items used in arsenal manufacturing operations.

Headquarters, U.S. Army Munitions Command

Dover, N.J.   07801

Telephone: 328-4040 or 328-3011   Area Code 201

The U.S. Army Munitions Command is responsible for integrated commodity management of nuclear and non-nuclear munitions. This responsibility includes research, design, and development; product, production, and maintenance engineering: procurement and production; procurement, production, and industrial mobilization planning; related activities.

Major Commodity Areas

Nuclear and non-nuclear ammunition, rocket and missile warhead sections, and demolition items; chemical, biological and radiological materiel; propellants and explosives; flamethrowers and agents and incendiaries; fire control; mines, non-nuclear bombs, grenades and pyrotechnics; meteorological and propellant actuated devices.

Installations

U.S. Army Edgewood Arsenal
Edgewood Arsenal, Md. 21010
Area Code: 301: 676–1000

U.S. Army Biological Laboratories
Fort Detrick, Frederick, Md.
Area Code: 301 MOnument 3–4111

Frankford Arsenal
Bridge and Tacony Street
Philadelphia, Pa. 19137
Area Code: 215 535–2900

Joliet Arsenal
Joliet, Ill. 60436
Area Code: 815 423–5511 (Elwood, Ill.)

Picatinny Arsenal
Dover, N.J. 07801
Area Code: 201 328–4106, 328–4104

U.S. Army Ammunition Procurement and Supply Agency
Joliet, Ill. 60436
Area Code: 815 423–5511 (Elwood, Ill.)

U.S. Army Pine Bluff Arsenal
Arsenal, Ark. 71603
Area Code: 501 JEfferson 4–4600

U.S. Army Rocky Mountain Arsenal
Denver, Colo.
Area Code: 303 ATlas 8–0711

Headquarters, U.S. Army Electronics Command

Fort Monmouth, N.J. 07703
Telephone 535–1997 Area Code 201

The mission of the U.S. Army Electronics Command includes the research and development and the procurement and production of electronic materials for the Army.

Major Commodity Areas

Communications, Electronic Warfare, Combat Surveillance, Night Vision, Automatic Data Processing, Radar, and Meteorological Materiel.

Installations

U.S. Army Electronics Command
Fort Monmouth Procurement Division
Directorate, Procurement and Production
Fort Monmouth, N.J. 07703
Area Code: 201 535–1729

U.S. Army Electronics Command
Fort Meade Procurement Division
Directorate, Procurement and Production
9800 Savage Road
Fort George G. Meade, Md. 20755
Area Code: 301 PArkway 5–4400

U.S. Army Electronics Command
Philadelphia Procurement Division
Directorate, Procurement and Production
225 South 18th Street
Philadelphia, Pa. 19103
Area Code: 215 KI 6–3200

U.S. Army Electronics Command
Washington Procurement Division
Directorate, Procurement and Production
814 North St. Asaph Street
Alexandria, Va. 22314
Area Code: 202 OXford 5–5369

Headquarters, U.S. Army Test and Evaluation Command

Aberdeen Proving Ground, Md. 21005
Telephone: 272–4000 Area Code 301

The mission of the U.S. Army Test and Evaluation Command is to command those assigned research activities, proving grounds, installations, boards, and facilities required to test equipment, weapons, and materiel systems; to plan and conduct tests of materiel intended for use by the U.S.

Army or developed by the Army for use by other departments of the Government and to assure efficient and economic use of test facilities.

Installations

Aberdeen Proving Ground
Maryland 21005
Area Code: 301 272-4000

U.S. Army Electronic Proving Ground
Fort Huachuca, Ariz.
Area Code: 602 458-3311

Dugway Proving Ground
Dugway Procurement Division
Salt Lake City, Utah
Area Code: 801 524-2097

Jefferson Proving Ground
Madison, Ind.
Area Code: 812 273-1428

White Sands Missile Range
New Mexico 88002
Area Code: 915 678-1401

Yuma Proving Ground
Yuma, Ariz. 85364
Area Code: 602 788-8321

Headquarters, U.S. Army Supply and Maintenance Command
Washington, D.C. 20315
Telephone: OXford 7–5978 Area Code 202

The mission of the U.S. Army Supply and Maintenance Command is the supervision of supply, transportation, and maintenance functions at approximately 150 field installations and activities formerly administered by the headquarters of the 7 technical services.

Depots

Atlanta Army Depot
Forest Park, Ga. 30050
Area Code: 404 366-5460

New Cumberland Army Depot
New Cumberland, Pa. 17070
Area Code: 717 234-4961

Sharpe Army Depot
Lathrop, Calif. 95330
Area Code: 209 466-6071

Anniston Army Depot
Anniston, Ala. 36202
Area Code: 205 237-6611

Blue Grass Army Depot (see Lexington Army Depot)
Richmond, Ky. 40475
Area Code: 606 623-2210

Letterkenny Army Depot
Chambersburg, Pa. 17201
Area Code: 717 264-5111

Navajo Army Depot
Flagstaff, Ariz. 86003
Area Code: 602 774-7161

Pueblo Army Depot
Pueblo, Colo. 81001
Area Code: 303 947-3341

Red River Army Depot
Texarkana, Tex. 75502
Area Code: 214 792-7122

Savanna Army Depot
Savanna, Ill. 61074
Area Code: 273 273-2211

Seneca Army Depot
Romulus, N.Y. 14541
Area Code: 15 585-4481 (Geneva, N.Y.)

Sierra Army Depot
Herlong, Calif. 96113
Area Code: 916 827-2111

Tooele Army Depot
Tooele, Utah 84074
Area Code: 801 882-2550

Umatilla Army Depot
Hermiston, Oreg. 97838
Area Code: 503 567-6421

Fort Wingate Army Depot
Gallup, N. Mex. 87301
Area Code: 505 863-6891

Lexington Army Depot
Lexington, Ky. 40507
Area Code: 606 299-1221

Sacramento Army Depot
Sacramento, Calif. 95801
Area Code: 916 456-7841

Tobyhanna Army Depot
Tobyhanna, Pa. 18466
Area Code: 717 894-8301

Charleston Army Depot
North Charleston, S.C. 29406
Area Code: 803 SHerwood 7-5241

Granite City Army
Granite City, Ill.
Area Code: 618 GLenview 2-7300

Corps of Engineers

The Corps of Engineers contracts with civilian contractors for construction, maintenance, and repair of buildings, structures, and utilities for the Department of the Army. The Corps of Engineers also is responsible for civil works such as river and harbor improvement, flood contol, hydroelectric power, and related projects. Inquiries concerning military construction or civil works should be sent to the following offices:

Office	Mail and/or office address
Office of Chief of Engineers	Building T-7, Washington, D.C.
USA Engineer Waterways, Experiment Station.	Post Office Box 631, Vicksburg, Miss., Halls Ferry R.D., Vicksburg, Miss.
USA Engineer Division, Lower Mississippi Valley.	Post Office Box 80, Vicksburg, Miss., Mississippi River Commission Building, Vicksburg.
USA Engineer District, Memphis	Post Office Box 97, Memphis 1, Tenn., West Memphis, Ark.
USA Engineer District, New Orleans	Foot of Prytania Street, New Orleans 9, La.
USA Engineer District, St. Louis	420 Locust Street, St. Louis 2, Mo.
USA Engineer District, Vicksburg	Post Office Box 60, Vicksburg, Miss., U.S. Post Office and Courthouse Building, Vicksburg.
USA Engineer Division, Missouri River	Post Office Box 1216, Omaha, Nebr., 215 North 17th Street.
USA Engineer District, Kansas City	1800 Federal Office Building, 911 Walnut Street, Kansas City 6, Mo.
USA Engineer District, Omaha	215 North 17th Street, Omaha 2, Nebr.
USA Engineer Division, New England	424 Trapello Road, Waltham, Mass.
USA Engineer Division, North Atlantic	1216 Federal Office Building, 90 Church Street, New York 7.
USA Engineer District, Baltimore	Post Office Box 1715, Baltimore 3, Md., 24th and Maryland Avenues, Baltimore 18, Md.
USA Engineer District, New York	111 East 16th Street, New York 3, N.Y.
USA Engineer District, Norfolk	Post Office Box 119, Norfolk, Va., foot of Front Street, Norfolk, Va.
USA Engineer District, Philadelphia	Post Office Box 8629, Philadelphia, Second and Chestnut Streets, Philadelphia, Pa.
USA Engineer Division, North Central	536 South Clark Street, Chicago, Ill.
USA Engineer District, Buffalo	Engineer Park, foot of Bridge Street, Buffalo, 7, N.Y.
USA Engineer District, Chicago	536 South Clark Street, Chicago, Ill.
USA Engineer District, Detroit	Post Office Box 1027, Detroit 31, Mich., 150 Michigan Avenue, Detroit 26.
USA Engineer District, Rock Island	Clock Tower Building, Rock Island, Ill.
USA Engineer District, St. Paul	1217 U.S. Post Office and Customhouse, 180 East Kellogg Boulevard, St. Paul, Minn.
USA Engineer Division, North Pacific	210 Customhouse, Portland 9, Oreg.
USA Engineer District, Alaska	Box 7002, Anchorage, Alaska.
USA Engineer District, Portland	628 Pittock Block SW., 10th Avenue and Washington Street, Portland 5, Oreg.
USA Engineer District, Seattle	1519 South Alaskan Way, Seattle, Wash.
USA Engineer District, Walla Walla	Building 602, City-County Airport, Walla Walla, Wash.
USA Engineer Division, Ohio River	Post Office Box 1159, Cincinnati, Ohio, Cincinnati Gas and Electric Annex, 315-335 Main Street, Cincinnati, Ohio.
USA Engineer District, Huntington	Post Office Box 2127, Huntington 19, W. Va., 502 Eighth Street, Huntington, W. Va.
USA Engineer District, Louisville	Post Office Box 59, Louisville, Ky., 830 West Broadway, Louisville, Ky.
USA Engineer District, Nashville	Post Office Box 1070, Nashville, Tenn., 306 Federal Office Building, Seventh Avenue and Broadway, Nashville, Tenn.
USA Engineer District, Pittsburgh	564 Forbes Avenue, Manor Building, Pittsburgh, Pa.
USA Engineer Division, South Atlantic	Post Office Box 1889, Atlanta, Ga., 30 Pryor Street, Atlanta, Ga.
USA Engineer District, Charleston	Post Office Box 905, Charleston, S.C., Municipal Marina, Charleston, S.C.
USA Engineer District, Jacksonville	Post Office Box 4970, Jacksonville, Fla., 575 Riverside Avenue, Jacksonville, Fla.

Office	Mail and/or office address
USA Engineer District, Cape Canaveral	Post Office Box 1042, Merritt Island, Fla.
USA Engineer District, Mobile	Post Office Box 1169, Mobile, Ala., 2301 Airport Boulevard, Mobile 7, Ala.
USA Engineer District, Savannah	Post Office Box 889 Savannah, Ga., 200 East St. Julian Street, Savannah.
USA Engineer District, Wilmington	Post Office Box 1890, Wilmington, N.C., 308 Customhouse, Wilmington.
USA Engineer Division, South Pacific	U.S. Appraisers Building, 630 Sansome Street, San Francisco, Calif.
USA Engineer District, Sacramento	Post Office Box 1739, Sacramento, Calif., 650 Capital Avenue, Sacramento 8, Calif.
USA Engineer District, San Francisco	180 New Montgomery Street, San Francisco.
USA Engineer Division, Southwestern	Santa Fe Building, 1114 Commerce Street, Dallas 2, Tex.
USA Engineer District, Albuquerque	Post Office Box 1538, Albuquerque, N. Mex., 517 Gold Avenue, Albuquerque, N. Mex.
USA Engineer District, Fort Worth	Post Office Box 1600, Fort Worth, Tex., 100 West Vickery, Fort Worth.
USA Engineer District, Galveston	Post Office Box 1229, Galveston, Tex., 606 Santa Fe Building, Galveston.
USA Engineer District, Little Rock	Post Office Box 867, Little Rock, Ark., 700 West Capital, Little Rock, Ark.
USA Engineer District, Los Angeles	Post Office Box 17277, Foy Station, 751 South Figueroa Street, Los Angeles 17, Calif.
USA Engineer District, Tulsa	Post Office Box 61, Tulsa, Okla., 616 South Boston Avenue, Tulsa, Okla.
Army Map Service	6500 Brooks Lane NW., Washington, D.C.

Army Medical Service

The Army Medical Service provides health services for the Army and, as assigned, for the Navy and Air Force; develops and supervises policies and plans, provides and conducts programs, establishes standard, technical procedures, organization and doctrine, and conducts medical research and development relating to the health of the Army and develops, provides and services medical materiel required by the Army, and as assigned, for the Navy and Air Force and for foreign aid programs; and prescribes the curricula of the Army Medical Service schools and separate courses of instruction which are composed predominantly of medical professional material.

Office of the Surgeon General, Washington, D.C.

U.S. Army Medical R. & D. Command, Office of The Surgeon General (A)
18th Street and Constitution Avenue NW.   20315

Makes contracts for research in medical sciences, devices, processes, and techniques.

Walter Reed Medical Center, Washington, D.C.
RAndolph 3-1000

Valley Forge Army Hospital, Phoenixville, Pa.
WEllington 3-5863

Letterman Army Hospital, Presidio of San Francisco, Calif.
JOrdan 1-2211

Madigan Army Hospital, Tacoma, Wash.
JUniper 8-3611

Fitzsimons Army Hospital, Denver, Colo.
EMpire 6-5311

Brooke Army Medical Center, Fort Sam Houston, Tex.
CApital 2-8411

William Beaumont Army Hospital, El Paso, Tex.
LOgan 5-4611

Local procurement of:
Nonstandard medical supplies and equipment.
Research equipment.
Animals for research.
Limited quantities of drugs and biologicals.

Headquarters, U.S. Continental Army Command
Fort Monroe, Va. Tel: 737-3221
(Local Procurement at Posts, Camps, and Stations)

Posts, camps and installations under the Continental Army Command are authorized to buy from local sources of supply such as:

Automotive: Spare parts for vehicles; automotive tools; reconditioning of motors; target frames; miscellaneous hardware.

Housekeeping: Supplies such as food, petroleum products, miscellaneous office supplies and equipment, small kitchen utensils and appliances and services, such as laundry, drycleaning and alterations, office machine rentals and repairs, burials, commissary store equipment.

Chemicals: Phosphates, ammonia, denatured alcohol—parts for decontamination units, gas mask parts.

Electrical: Communications equipment, such as telephone and telegraph equipment, including such subcomponents, as adapters, amplifiers, controls dials, generators, wet- and dry-type batteries, intercommunication equipment such as sound recording and reproduction equipment (reproducing tape, turntables, microphones) and television equipment.

Construction: Minor construction (repairs and rehabilitation), custodial services, air-conditioning packing and crating of household goods, miscellaneous hardware, such as handtools, nails, screws, and electrical fixtures; miscellaneous plumbing and heating items, building construction items such as paint, lumber, cement blocks, bricks, glass; agricultural items, such as grass seed, weed killer, tree sprays, insect and rodent control and chemicals. Major subordinate commands of the U.S. Continental Army Command, responsible for procurement and the locations of the posts, camps and stations under their command are:

Headquarters, 1st U.S. Army
Fort George G. Meade, Md.

Boston Army Base
666 Summer Street
Boston, Mass.

Fort Devens
Ayer, Mass.

U.S. Army Training Center
Fort Dix
Wrightstown, N.J.

Camp Drum
Watertown, N.Y.

Fort Hamilton
Brooklyn, N.Y.

Fort Jay
Governors Island
New York, N.Y.
First U.S. Army Recruiting District
Governors Island
New York, N.Y.

U.S. Army Support Center
Niagara Falls, N.Y.

Fort Slocum
New Rochelle, N.Y.

Fort Totten
Bayside, Long Island, N.Y.

Fort Wadsworth
Staten Island, N.Y.

U.S. Army Armor Center
Fort Knox, Ky.

Fort George G. Meade
Md.

Fort Miles
Lewes, Del.

Fort Monroe
Hampton, Va.

Carlisle Barracks
Carlisle, Pa.

Headquarters, XXI U.S. Army Corps
Indiantown Gap Military
    Reservation
Annville, Pa.

U.S. Army Engineer Center
    and Fort Belvoir
Fort Belvoir, Va.

U.S. Army Transportation
Center and Fort Eustis
Fort Eustis, Va.

XX U.S. Army Corps
Fort Hayes
Columbus 18, Ohio

U.S. Army Quartermaster Corps
and Fort Lee
Fort Lee, Va.

U.S. Army Intelligence Center
and Fort Holabird
Baltimore 19, Md.

Headquarters, 3d U.S. Army
Fort McPherson, Ga.

Fort Benning
Columbus, Ga.

Fort McClellan
Anniston, Ala.

Fort Stewart
Hinesville, Ga.

Fort McPherson
Atlanta, Ga.

Fort Gordon
Augusta, Ga.

XII U.S. Army Corps
Atlanta, Ga.

Fort Jackson
Columbia, S.C.

IV U.S. Army Corps
Birmingham, Ala.

Fort Bragg
Fayetteville, N.C.

Fort Rucker
Ozark, Ala.

Fort Campbell
Fort Campbell, Ky.

Headquarters, 4th U.S. Army
Fort Sam Houston, Tex.

Fort Polk
Leesville, La.

Fort Chaffee
Fort Smith, Ark.

Fort Sam Houston
East Grayson Street and North New
  Braunfels Avenue
San Antonio, Tex.

Fort Hood
Killeen, Tex.

Fort Wolters
Mineral Wells, Tex.

Fort Sill
Lawton, Okla.

Headquarters, VIII U.S. Army Corps
708 Colorado Street
Austin, Tex.

Fort Bliss
El Paso, Tex.

Headquarters, 5th U.S. Army
1660 East Hyde Park Boulevard, Chicago, Ill.

Fort Riley
Junction City, Kans.

Fort Benjamin Harrison
Indianapolis 16, Ind.

Fort Sheridan
Highwood, Ill.

Fort Carson
Colorado Springs, Colo.

Fort Wayne
6301 West Jefferson Avenue
Detroit, Mich.

Camp McCoy
Sparta, Wis.

U.S. Army Support Center
St. Louis, Mo.

Headquarters, XIV U.S. Army Corps
1006 West Lake Street
Minneapolis, Minn.

U.S. Army Support Detachment
Chicago, Ill.

Fort Custer
Battle Creek, Mich.

Camp Atterbury
Edinburg, Ind.

Fort Leavenworth
Leavenworth, Kans.

Fort Leonard Wood
Waynesville, Mo.

Headquarters, XVI U.S.
 Army Corps
Omaha, Nebr.

Fort Lawton
Seattle, Wash.

Fort Douglas
Salt Lake City, Utah

Presidio of San Francisco
San Francisco, Calif.

Fort Lewis
Tacoma, Wash.

Fort Lesley J. McNair
4th and P Streets SW.
Washington, D.C.

Fort Myer
Arlington, Va.

Headquarters, VI U.S. Army Corps
Battle Creek Federal Center
Battle Creek, Mich.

Headquarters, 6th U.S. Army
Presidio of San Francisco, Calif.

Fort Irwin
Barstow, Calif.

Fort MacArthur
San Pedro, Calif.

Fort Ord
Monterey, Calif.

Headquarters, Military District of Washington
U.S. Army, Washington, D.C.

Cameron Station
5010 Duke Street
Alexandria, Va.

DEPARTMENT OF THE NAVY MAJOR PURCHASING OFFICES

Bureaus and Offices

Chief, Bureau of Naval Weapons
Department of the Navy
Washington, D.C. 20360
Tel: 202 OXford 6-7470

Guided missiles, airframes, aircraft engines, propellers, instruments, armament and fire-control systems, ground handling equipment for aircraft and missiles, electronic equipment, antisubmarine equipment, parachutes, flight clothing, navigation equipment, high-energy fuels, photographic equipment and services, meteorological equipment, aircraft training equipment, catapults, naval guns, torpedoes, and research and development needs for these items.

Chief, Bureau of Ships
Department of the Navy
Washington, D.C. 20360
Tel: 202 OXford 6-3362

Ships and ship repair, minesweeping gear, shipboard and deck machinery, propellers and shafting, internal combustion and gas turbine engines, refrigeration and air-conditioning equipments, motors and motor-generator sets, interior communication systems, and electronic equipment including radar, radio, radiac, etc., navigation systems, sonar, and small boats including research and development needs for these items.

Chief, Bureau of Yards and Docks
Department of the Navy
Washington, D.C.
Tel: 202 OXford 6-3281

Cranes, powerplants, piledrivers, dredges, major boiler plants and electrical generators, and permanent facilities (including acquisition and disposal of real estate). This Bureau is responsible for the Navy's construction projects, as well as station maintenance and repair, including public utilities services. Contracts for such projects, however, are let through the Directors, District and Area Public Works Offices. (See subsection on Navy Construction, pp. 48 and 49.)

Commandant of the Marine Corps
(Code CSG)
Headquarters, U.S. Marine Corps
Washington, D.C.
Tel: 202 OXford 4-1919

Electronics equipment, construction equipment, specialized vehicles and equipment peculiar to the Marine Corps such as landing vehicles, trailer-mounted compressors, welders, generators, floodlight sets, etc., repair parts for specialized Marine Corps equipment.

Chief of Naval Research
Department of the Navy
Washington, D.C.
Tel: 202 OXford 6-6650

Responsible for basic and applied research, including fundamental studies, in such fields as electronics, chemistry, and physics, and serves to coordinate the research programs of the technical bureaus.

Chief, Bureau of Naval Personnel
Department of the Navy
Washington, D.C.
Tel: 202 OXford 4-2835

Responsible for procurement of training services from educational institutions and of training publications.

Chief, Bureau of Supplies and
Accounts,
Department of the Navy
Washington, D.C.
Tel: 202 OXford 6-4680

Does not do any actual procurement or let contracts, but exercises technical control over the field purchasing activities—including all of those listed except the technical bureaus, the Marine Corps, the Military Sea Transportation Service, Office of Naval Research, Administrative Office, and Navy Training Devices Center.

Administrative Office
Department of the Navy
Washington, D.C.
Tel: 202 OXford 6-7666

Services and material for the internal operation of the Navy Bureaus and Offices. Office services, office equipment rental, computer services and rental, printing, binding, and editing services.

Navy Purchasing Offices

Navy Purchasing Office
Washington Navy Yard
Building 200
Washington, D.C. 20690
Tel: 202 OXford 8-2957/8-2958

Machine tools (metal and wood working, portable and stationary), industrial equipment for shops, including boilers, ovens, electric motors, transformers, and generators, forgings, metallurgical testing, welding, warehousing, pumps, test stands. Musical instruments, electrical measuring or indicating instruments, steel plates and shapes, air-conditioning and refrigeration equipment (industrial and domestic). Missile containers, missile components, electric and electronic components, antennas, radar components, mine components. Research, development, test and analytical services and material as requested by naval activities in the Washington, D.C., area.

Officer in Charge
Navy Purchasing Office
Third Ave. and 29th St.
Brooklyn, N.Y. 11232
Tel: 212 STerling 8-5000

Research, development, test and analytical material and services. Ships machinery and hardware. Engineering and technical services. Also general procurement for activities in the New York area (e.g., ships' store items, nonstandard equipment and supplies, training devices, etc.).

Officer in Charge
Navy Purchasing Office
929 South Broadway
Los Angeles, Calif. 90015
Tel: 213 688-2721

Responsible for purchasing requirements of all Naval activities in the 11th Naval District in excess of their local purchase authority (normally $2,500). Majority of purchases are items of a technical nature, including research and development requirements, and supplies and services for support of R. & D. Naval activities in Southern California.

Inventory Control Points

Commanding Officer
Navy Aviation Supply Office
700 Robbins Ave.
Philadelphia, Pa. 19111
Tel: 215 RAndolph 8-1212

Weapons; aircraft gunnery fire-control components; airframe structural components; aircraft components and accessories; aircraft launching, landing, and ground handling equipment; small craft; marine hardware and hull items, buoys; tire rebuilding and tire and tube repair materials; gas turbines and jet engines, aircraft, and components; engine accessories; mechanical power transmission equipment; bearings; metalworking machinery; wrapping and packaging machinery; special industry machinery; materials handling equipment, non-self-propelled; rope, cable, chain and fittings; firefighting, rescue and safety equipment; pumps and compressors; furnace, steamplant, and drying equipment and nuclear reactors; plumbing fixtures and accessories; pipe, tubing, hose and fittings; valves, nonpowered; maintenance and repair shop equipment; handtools, hardware and abrasives; prefabricated and portable buildings; lumber, millwork, plywood, and veneer; wallboard, building paper and thermal insulation materials; communication equipment; electrical and electronic equipment components; electric wire, and power and distribution equipment; lighting fixtures and lamps; miscellaneous alarm and signal systems; instruments and laboratory equipment; photographic supplies; chemicals and chemical products; armament training devices; furniture; household and commercial furnishings and appliances; food preparation and serving equipment; office supplies; books, maps, and other publications; floor polishers and vacuum cleaners; paint and artists' brushes; containers, packaging and packing supplies; textiles, leather and furs; clothing and individual equipment; beverages, nonalcoholic; fuels, lubricants, oils and waxes, nonmetallic fabricated materials; metal bars, sheets and shapes; chemical reproductions; printing and related services; technical publications.

Commanding Officer
Navy Ships Parts Control Center
Mechanicsburg, Pa. 17055
Tel: 717 766-8511

Electrical and mechanical assemblies; power distribution equipment; transformers; alarms and signal systems; communication equipment; electrical fittings and fixtures; precision machine work; firefighting and safety equipment; drafting equipment; ferrous blooms and billets; ammunition and rockets and related products and components; rocket launchers, missiles and component parts; bombs, weapons and weapon parts; chemical products, cutting tools for machine tools and other machine tool accessories; gages and thermometers, minesweeping gear and repair parts; marine hardware and hull items; navigation equipment; gaskets, packing materials and assemblies; pipes and tubes; survival at sea equipment; vales; friction and nonfriction bearings; heaters; shipboard furniture; hose and hose assemblies; non ferrous ingots and pigs; optical components; motors; batteries; bandsaw blades; welding, flame-cutting and metallizing equipment and supplies.

Commanding Officer
Navy Electronic Supply Office
Great Lakes, Ill. 60088
Tel: 312 336-3500

Antennas and antenna accessories; amplifiers; attenuators; batteries; bearings; cable; cable assemblies; cabinets and test benches; capacitors; cavities; circuit breakers; coils; conduit and conduit fittings; connectors; contacts; brushes and electrodes; converters; crystals, filters; fuses and fuse holders; generators; hardware; handsets; indicators; insulation; insulators; jackboxes; keyers; lamps and lighting fixtures; loudspeakers; meters and measuring equipment; microphones and accessories; mixers; modulators; modules and printed circuit assemblies; motors; networks; oscillators; instrument panels; receivers; recorders and components; pressure regulators; relays, contactors and solenoids; resistors; semiconductor devices; tube shields and insert; sockets; sound recording equipment; stuffing tubes; switches; terminal boards; terminals and lugs; transformers; transmitters; tubes, tuners; waveguides and accessories; wire.

Navy Supply Centers and Depots

Commanding Officer
U.S. Naval Supply Center
Naval Base
Norfolk, Va. 23511
Tel: 703 444-3051

General procurement for Naval activities and ships in the Fifth Naval District and Atlantic Ocean Areas (e.g., operating supplies; maintenance and repair components and equipment; laboratory and test equipment; communications equipment; some research, development, test and evaluation).

Commanding Officer
U.S. Naval Supply Center
Oakland, Calif. 94614
Tel: 415 TWinoaks 3-4224

General procurement for Naval activities in the Twelfth Naval District and Pacific Ocean Area overseas ships and bases (e.g., miscellaneous ship and marine equipment; engine accessories; communication equipment; electrical and electronic equipment and components; pipe, tubing, hose, and fittings; cable, chain, and fittings; various services including funeral, printing, laundry, and equipment repair; general supply-type items; ship stores' resale items, etc.).

Commanding Officer
U.S. Naval Supply Depot
ATTN: Purchase Department
Great Lakes, Ill. 60088
Tel: 312 DElta 6-3500

General procurement for Naval activities in the Michigan, Indiana, Illinois, Wisconsin, Minnesota, Iowa, Missouri, North Dakota, South Dakota, Nebraska, Kansas, Colorado, and Wyoming area (e.g., chemicals and chemical products; laboratory equipment; toiletries; books, maps, and other publications; general supply-type items, etc.).

Commanding Officer
U.S. Naval Supply Center
Charleston, S.C. 29408
Tel: 803 SHerwood 7-4171

General procurement for certain Naval activities in the North Carolina, South Carolina, Georgia, Florida, Alabama, Tennessee, and Mississippi area (e.g., chemicals and chemical products; electrical motors; electrical control equipment; miscellaneous furniture and fixtures; general supply-type items, etc.).

Commanding Officer
U.S. Naval Supply Depot
Newport, R.I. 02840
Tel: 401 841-2686

General procurement for certain Naval activities in the Maine, New Hampshire, Vermont, Massachusetts, Rhode Island area (e.g., electronic and electrical components; chemicals and chemical products; automotive supplies; galley equipment and supplies; general supply-type items, etc.).

Commanding Officer
U.S. Naval Supply Depot
Seattle, Wash. 98119
Tel: 206 ATwater 3–5200

General procurement for Naval activities in the Washington, Oregon, Idaho, Montana area and Alaska (e.g., artists' supplies, chemicals and chemical products; blueprinting services; corrosion preventive compounds; divers' equipment; electrical hardware; laboratory equipment and supplies; general supply-type items, etc.).

Commanding Officer
U.S. Naval Supply Center
Pearl Harbor, Hawaii
Tel: 808–4711, Ext. 54161
(Mail Address: Box 300, Navy No. 128, FPO, San Francisco, Calif. 96614)

General procurement for Naval activities in the Hawaiian Islands and other Pacific Ocean area activities and operating forces as may be required.

Commanding Officer
U.S. Naval Supply Depot
Guam, Mariana Islands
Tel: 33–4111
(Mail Address: Navy No. 926, FPO, San Francisco, Calif. 96635)

General procurement for ashore and afloat activities in the Mariana Islands area (e.g., bakery and dairy products, fresh shell eggs; automotive and heavy equipment repair parts; tires and tubes; building and construction materials; hardware; electrical, plumbing and safety equipment; prescription glasses; diving gear; office machines and supplies; air-conditioning units and parts; various gases; electronic parts; paint; periodicals, printing; rubber stamps; lubricants; plywood; photographic supplies; EAM cards and forms; washing machines; refrigerators; tape recorders. Services include repair of office machines; outboard motors; tire recapping; renovation of recreational areas; packing and crating of household goods; termiteproofing of military quarters; laundry and drycleaning and stevedoring.

Navy Shipyards and Repair Facilities

Commander
Boston Naval Shipyard
Boston, Mass. 02129
Tel: 617 242–1400

General procurement for certain Naval activities in the New England area (e.g., electrical wire and cable; welding wire and electrodes; chemicals; hardware; refrigeration and air-conditioning equipment; electronic test equipment; power-distribution equipment; measuring instruments; non-icing windows; sound-detecting equipment; abrasives; aluminum ladders; food preparation and serving equipment).

Commander
Puget Sound Naval Shipyard
Bremerton, Wash. 98314
Tel: 206 478–7355

General procurement for Naval activities in Northwest United States, including major shipboard components including pumps, davits, hoisting equipment, metal sheets, and switchgear. Also shipboard repair components including special valves, piping, and electrical items; normal shipyard requirements for production shops and maintenance items; special electronic components including oscillographs, pressure transducers, programmers, rate gyrotest turntables, and power supplies.

Commander
Charleston Naval Shipyard
Naval Base
Charles, S.C. 29408
Tel: 803 SHerwood 7–4171

General procurement for operation and maintenance of Charleston Naval Shipyard (e.g., chemicals, electrical and electronic equipment, hardware, gangways, blasting sand, liquid oxygen, deck coverings, lead ballast weights, submarine equipment and supplies).

Commander
Philadelphia Naval Shipyard
Naval Base
Philadelphia, Pa. 19112
Tel: 215 HOward 5–1010

General procurement for certain Naval activities in the Pennsylvania, South New Jersey, Delaware, and Ohio area (e.g., shipboard doors, latches and scuttles, shipboard airvent covers and manhole covers, gangways, hydraulic cylinders, boat davits, slipring assemblies, blasting sand, liquid oxygen, lithographic forms).

Commander
Portsmouth Naval Shipyard
Portsmouth, N.H. 03804
Tel: 207 439–1000

Procurement of materials required in the development, construction, repair and alteration of submarines, including hull steel, special corrosion resisting steel, pipe and tubing, valves and fittings of all types, castings, pumps and motors, antenna masts, propellers, controllers and panels, alarm and signal systems, metal furniture, air compressors, gages, test equipments, power transmission equipments, etc. Contracting for services include design engineering printing of instruction booklets, piping fabrications, office machine repair and maintenance, laundry services, transportation of household goods, etc. General procurement of plant operation and maintenance items for Naval activities in the northern New England area.

Commanding Officer
U.S. Naval Submarine Base
New London, Conn. 06342
Tel: 203 449-3011

Submarine equipment and supplies, alarm and signal systems, compressed gases, dairy and bakery provisions for various activities and vessels in the New London area; repair parts for miscellaneous equipment; disposal of radioactive waste material; safety equipment; electrical hardware; laboratory supplies; automotive repair parts; sandblasting supplies; miscellaneous equipment for maintenance and repair shops; stone and gravel.

Commanding Officer
U.S. Naval Station
Key West, Fla. 33040
Tel: 305 296-3511

Communication equipment, electrical equipment, engine accessories and components, ship and marine equipment, laundry supplies, sundries.

Commanding Officer and Director
U.S. Navy Underwater Sound Lab.
Fort Trumbull
Port London, Conn. 06321
Tel: 204 443-8361

Instrumentation for research and development.

Navy Aviation Activities

Commanding Officer
Naval Air Engineering Center
Philadelphia, Pa. 19112
Tel: 215 HOward 5-1000 or 5-1020

Research, development, test and analytical services and materials for aircraft launching, recovery and landing-aid systems (carrier and land-base); spare parts for catapult and arresting gear; machine tools and metalworking machinery. Electronic environmental and laboratory testing equipment to support research, development, test and evaluation of aerospace pilot protective survival equipment; aeronautical accessories, powerplants, structure and materials; technical representative services for aviation systems and equipment; and technical documentation and engineering services for naval weapons.

Commanding Officer
U.S. Naval Air Development Center
Johnsville, Pa. 18974
Tel: 215 OSborne 5-7000

Procurements for research and development in the fields of antisubmarine warfare, aeronautic electronics, aeronautical instruments, aeronautical photography, aviation medicine, and attendant equipment and support services.

Commanding Officer
Naval Avionics Facility
21st St. and Arlington Ave.
Indianapolis, Ind. 46218
Tel: 317 FLeetwood 7-8311 or 7-8129

Procurement of materials and services required for development, preproduction manufacturing, repair and overhaul of airborne fire-control hardware and test equipment.

Commanding Officer
Naval Air Station
Jacksonville, Fla. 32212
Tel: 305 389-7711

Aircraft components and accessories; ship and marine equipment; vehicular equipment components; tires and tubes; engines, turbines and components; engine accessories; mechanical power transmission equipment; bearings; woodworking machinery and equipment; service and trade equipment; special industry machinery; rope, cable, chain, and fittings; refrigeration and air-conditioning equipment; firefighting, rescue and safety equipment; pumps and compressors; plumbing, heating, and sanitation equipment; water-purification and sewage-treatment equipment; pipe, tubing, hose, and fittings; valves, maintenance, and repair shop equipment; handtools; measuring tools, hardware and abrasives; lumber, millwork, plywood, and veneer; construction and building materials; communication equipment; electrical and electronic equipment components; electric wire and power and distribution equipment; lighting fixtures and lamps; alarm and signal systems; medical, dental, and veterinary equipment and supplies; instruments and laboratory equipment; photographic equipment; chemicals and chemical products; furniture; household and commercial furnishings and appliances; food preparation and serving equipment; office machines and data-processing equipment; office supplies; cleaning equipment and supplies; brushes, paints, sealers, and adhesives; containers, packaging, and packing supplies; textiles, leather and furs; subsistence; fuels, lubricants, oils, and waxes, and miscellaneous items.

Commanding Officer
U.S. Naval Air Station
Memphis, Tenn. 38115
Tel: 901 872-1711

Engine accessories, firefighting and safety equipment, chemical and chemical products, metalworking machinery.

Commanding Officer
U.S. Naval Air Station
Patuxent River, Md. 20670
Tel: 301 VO 3-8111

Communication equipment, compressed gases, firefighting equipment and supplies, chemical products, barometers, electrical supplies and components.

Commanding Officer
U.S. Naval Air Station
Pensacola, Fla. 32508
Tel: 305 GLendale 5-3211

General procurement for certain Naval activities in the Florida, Alabama, Mississippi, and Louisiana areas (e.g., hardware, plumbing, and electric wire and power and distribution equipment; firefighting, rescue, and safety equipment; electrical and electronic equipment components; aeronautical material; tools and attachments for metalworking and woodworking machinery; chemicals and chemical products; miscellaneous maintenance and repair-shop specialized equipment; lubrication and fuel dispensing equipment; paint; etc.).

Commanding General
Marine Corps Air Station
Cherry Point, N.C. 28533
Tel: 919 447-2111

Weapons; guided missiles, launchers and handling and servicing equipment; airframe structural components; aircraft components and accessories; aircraft ground servicing equipment; small craft; marine hardware and hull items; railroad track materials; bicycles; vehicular equipment components; engine accessories; mechanical-power transmission equipment; bearings; tools and attachments for woodworking machinery; metalworking machinery; service and trade equipment; special industry machinery; service and trade equipment; gardening implements and tools; materials handling equipment; rope, cable, chain, and fittings; refrigeration and air-conditioning equipment; maintenance and repair-shop equipment; handtools; measuring tools; office machines and data-processing equipment; office supplies and devices; firefighting, rescue and safety equipment; pumps and compressors; furnace, steamplant and drying equipment, and nuclear reactors; plumbing, heating, and sanitation equipment; water purification and sewage treatment equipment; pipe, tubing, hose, and fittings; valves; hardware and abrasives; prefabricated structures and scaffolding; lumber, millwork, plywood, and veneer; construction and building materials; medical, dental, and veterinary equipment and supplies; photographic equipment; chemicals and chemical products; food preparation and serving equipment; books, maps, and other publications; containers; packaging and packing supplies; tires and tubes; excavating and highway maintenance; communications equipment; electrical and electronic-equipment components; electric wire, and power-distribution equipment; lighting fixtures and lamps; alarm and signal systems; instruments and laboratory equipment; training aids and devices; furniture; household and commercial furnishings and appliances; musical instruments, phonographs, and home-type radios; cleaning equipment and supplies; brushes, paints, sealers, and adhesives; textiles, leathers, and furs; clothing and individual equipment; agricultural supplies; dairy foods and eggs; fuels, lubricants, oils, and waxes; nonmetallic fabricated materials; metal bars, sheets, and shapes; signs, advertising displays and identification plates; smokers' articles and matches.

Commanding Officer
U.S. Naval Air Station
Corpus Christi, Tex. 78419
Tel: 512 TErminal 5-8211

General procurement for certain Naval activities in the Louisiana, Arkansas, Oklahoma, Texas, and New Mexico area (e.g., firefighting, rescue, and safety equipment; electrical and electronic equipment components; aircraft engine fuel-system components; aircraft engine electrical system components; miscellaneous aircraft engine accessories, and all commercial-type items used by the Navy).

Navy Ordnance Activities

Commanding Officer
Naval Ammunition Depot
Crane, Ind. 47522
Tel: 812 854-2511

Pyrotechnics, some conventional ammunition and components parts and explosives; electrical and electronic equipment and supplies; instruments and laboratory equipment; special metallic and nonmetallic fabricated materials.

Commanding Officer
U.S. Naval Ordnance Plant
Forest Park, Ill. 60130
Tel: 312 FO 6-2700

Electrical and electronic components; test equipment; castings and forgings (ferrous and nonferrous), raw materials (ferrous and nonferrous), miscellaneous machine tools; bearings, laboratory equipment and supplies; electric motors, torpedo components; torpedo and automotive batteries.

Commanding Officer
U.S. Naval Ordnance Plant
Louisville, Ky. 40214
Tel: 502 361-2641

Wood and steel containers; production jigs and fixtures; ferrous and nonferrous castings and forgings; parachute packs; bomb fins; guided missile warheads; boosters and sustainers; mine parts; solonoid and control valves; and manufactured ordnance parts.

Commanding Officer
U.S. Naval Ordnance Plant
Macon, Ga. 31201
Tel: 912 788-6700

Metals and plastics (powders, bars, stampings, extrusions, and ammunition component parts), chemicals (polyvinyl chloride, strontium nitrate, barium nitrate, silicon, etc.), explosives (priming mixtures, delay compositions, high explosives, and propellants), paper and wood packaging (boxes and nestings).

Commanding Officer
U.S. Naval Ammunition Depot
McAlester, Okla. 74501
Tel: 918 GArden 3-6330

Conventional ammunition and component parts and explosives; electrical and electronic equipment and supplies; instruments and laboratory equipment; special metallic and nonmetallic fabricated materials.

Commanding Officer
U.S. Naval Propellant Plant
Indian Head, Md. 20640
Tel: 301 743-2111

Inorganic chemicals; precision tools; engine accessories; defusers; explosive devices such as ignitors, initiator assemblies and squibs; metalworking machinery; intercommunication equipment; electrical equipment; liquid- and gas-flow measuring instruments; laundry services.

Commander
U.S. Naval Weapons Laboratory
Dahlgren, Va. 22448
Tel: 703 NOrth 3-2511

Experimental research and development services; missile warheads and explosive components; engine accessories; woodworking machinery and equipment; metalworking machinery.

Commanding Officer
U.S. Naval Ordnance Laboratory
Silver Spring, Md. 20910
Tel: 301 434-7100

Research and development in naval ordnance items, particularly in the area of underwater devices and fusing. Various mechanical and electronic items, as well as test equipment to support the research and development effort. A wide variety of small purchase items generally procured in the local trade area.

Commanding Officer
U.S. Naval Ordnance Test Station
China Lake, Calif. 93557
Tel: (via Ridgecrest, Calif.)
FR 7-7411

Research and development and testing equipment in connection with missiles, rockets, etc.

Commanding Officer
U.S. Naval Torpedo Station
Keyport, Wash. 98345
Tel: 206 478-8434

Electrical and electronic equipment and supplies, testing instruments, metals, plastics, torpedo components, chemicals, hardware, machine-shop equipment and miscellaneous maintenance supplies.

Commanding Officer and Director
U.S. Navy Mine Defense Laboratory
Panama City, Fla. 32402
Tel: 305 234-2281

Underwater sound equipment; sound-recording and reproducing equipment; electrical-control equipment; radio and television equipment; instruments and laboratory equipment; lubricating and fuel-dispensing equipment.

Other Navy Activities

Commanding Officer and Director
U.S. Naval Training Device Center
Port Washington, N.Y.

Responsible for the procurement of training aids and devices for personnel of the Army, Navy, Marine Corps, and other DOD activities. Includes procurement of hardware and research and development effort necessary for training devices designed to simulate actual conditions in areas such as shiphandling, communications, gunnery, fire-control, operational flight training, weapons systems trainers, human engineering. Engineering services for various devices.

Director
U.S. Naval Research Laboratory
Washington, D.C. 20390
Tel: 202 JOhnson 3-6600

Environmental chambers; nuclear instrumentation; systems such as optical, infrared, radar, sonar, radioastronomy, reactor, radiation stabilizer, telemetry, memory, environmental, vacuum, and cryogenics with associated instrumentation and components; equipments for crystal processing; data processing; materials testing and navigation; antennas; lasers, masers; research and cryogenic magnets; instrumentation for satellites and oceanographic research; machine tools; metallurgical instruments; laboratory instruments; equipment and supplies; communication equipment; electronic components; chemicals, insulating materials; special and routine metals; and maintenance services.

Commander
U.S. Naval Oceanographic Office
Washington, D.C. 20390
Tel: 301 REdwood 6-2700

Experimental research and development services for Oceanographic Shipboard Survey Systems; data processing; various types of test equipment, sound-recording and reproduction equipment; instrument and laboratory equipment; photographic, lithographic and all types of printing equipment.

Superintendent
U.S. Naval Academy
Annapolis, Md. 21402
Tel: 301 268-7711

Pennants and flags; boat repairs (small craft); aluminum and wood boat masts; study desks; drafting supplies; diploma cases; janitor supplies; motion-picture machines; optical supplies and services; sails for small craft; sailcloth (duck or cotton, dacron, nylon); radio materials.

Commanding Officer and Director
David W. Taylor Model Basin
Washington, D.C. 20007
Tel: 301 EMpire 5-2000

Sound-recording and reproducting equipment; electrical control equipment; cameras; instruments and laboratory equipment; electronic components; radio hardware; underwater television equipment; fasteners; machine and hand tools; optical equipment; metals; insulating materials; photographic supplies; and janitorial supplies.

Marine Corps Activities

Commanding General
Marine Corps Supply Activity
1100 South Broad St.
Philadelphia, Pa. 19146
Tel: KIngsley 6-2000

Repair parts for tactical equipment and vehicles; electronic components; engineering components and spare parts; athletic equipment.

Commanding General
Marine Corps Supply Center
Albany, Ga. 31704
Tel: 912 435-3451, Ext. 511 or 512

Automotive spare parts and accessories; electronic components and spare parts; miscellaneous electrical and plumbing supplies; safety equipment; abrasives; spare parts for materials-handling equipment; packing and packaging equipment and supplies; food for resale.

Commanding General
Marine Corps Supply Center
Barstow, Calif. 92312
Tel: 831-1445, Ext. 224 or 821

Automotive spare parts and accessories; electronic components and spare parts; miscellaneous electrical and plumbing supplies; safety equipment; abrasives; spare parts for materials-handling equipment; packing and packaging equipment and supplies; food for resale.

Commanding General
Marine Corps Base
Camp Lejeune, N.C. 28542
Tel: 231-3540, Ext. 75570

Repair parts for maintenance of buildings, grounds and equipments; plumbing, heating and sanitation equipment; pipe, tubing, and fittings; valves; hardware and abrasives; construction and building materials; books and publications; recreational and athletic; food for resale.

Commanding General
Marine Corps Base
Camp Pendleton, Calif. 92056
Tel: 714 722-4111, Ext. 2922 or 2924

Repair parts for maintenance of buildings, grounds and equipment; plumbing, heating and sanitation equipment; pipe, tubing, and fittings; valves; hardware and abrasives; construction and building materials; books and publications; recreational and athletic equipment; food for resale.

Commandant Marine Corps Schools Quantico, Va. 22134 Tel: 703 875–9706, Ext. 2–0721	Hardware, plumbing, electrical, building and groundkeeping supplies in support of Marine Corps Educational Center including office and training supplies, training aids and technical books; specialized equipment and supplies for test and evaluation; special rifle team equipment and related supplies in support of the Marine Corps Marksmanship Training Unit; schools, supplies, and equipment for five dependents' schools; commercial vehicle parts; laundry supplies and equipment; items for Marine Corps museums and common grocery-type items for the Sales Commissary.
Commanding General Marine Corps Recruit Depot Parris Island, S.C. 29905 Tel: JA 4–2111, Ext. 4692	Plumbing and heating fixtures and accessories; fire-fighting and safety equipment and components; books, publications, and periodicals; condiments; vehicular and construction equipment; repair parts (commercial); general housekeeping supplies; alteration services for military clothing; stevedoring and local drayage services; periodic service inspection on various types of office machines.
Commanding General Marine Corps Recruit Depot San Diego, Calif. Tel: 831–1540	Plumbing and heating fixtures and accessories; firefighting and safety equipment and components; books, publications, and periodicals; condiments; vehicular and construction equipment; repair parts (commercial); general housekeeping supplies; alteration services for military clothing, stevedoring and local drayage services; periodic service inspection on various types of office machines.
Commanding General Marine Corps Base Twentynine Palms, Calif. Tel: 831–1850, Ext. 813	Repair parts for maintenance of buildings, grounds, and equipment; plumbing, heating and sanitation equipment; pipe, tubing, and fittings; valves; hardware and abrasives; construction and building materials; books and publications; recreational and athletic equipment; food for resale.

Navy Construction

Contracts for construction projects and major station maintenance and repair are awarded by the following area offices:

District Public Works Officer
1st Naval District
495 Summer St.
Boston, Mass. 02210
  Tel: LIberty 2–5100
(Maine, New Hampshire, Vermont, Massachusetts, and
  Rhode Island including Block Island.)

District Public Works Officer
3d Naval District
90 Church St.
New York, N.Y. 10007
  Tel: REctor 2–9100
(Connecticut, New York, also the northern part of
  New Jersey, including the counties of Monmouth,
  Middlesex, Somerset, Hunterdon, and all counties
  north thereof.)

District Public Work Officer
4th Naval District
Building No. 1, Naval Base
Philadelphia, Pa. 19112
  Tel: 755–3955
(Pennsylvania, Ohio and Delaware, also the southern
  part of New Jersey, including the counties of Mercer,
  Burlington, Ocean, and all counties south thereof.)

Area Public Works Office, Chesapeake
U.S. Naval Station, Washington Navy Yard Annex
Washington, D.C. 20390
  Tel: 202 OXford 8–3300
(District of Columbia, the counties of Anne Arundel,
  Prince Georges, Montgomery, St. Marys, Calvert, and
  Charles in Maryland and the counties of Arlington,
  Fairfax, Stafford, King George, Prince William, and
  Westmore and the city of Alexandria in Virginia.)

Director, Atlantic Division
Bureau of Yards and Docks
Naval Base
Norfolk, Va. 23511
  Tel: MAdison 2–8211
(Atlantic Area—Maryland, West Virginia, Virginia,
  Kentucky, and eastern part of North Carolina, including counties of Gates, Chowan, Washington,
  Beaufort, Craven, Jones, Onslow, and all counties
  east thereof, except counties indicated in APOW,
  Ches.)

Director, Southeast Division
Bureau of Yards and Docks
U.S. Naval Base
Charleston, S.C. 29408
Tel: SHerwood 7-4171
(North Carolina, less those counties listed in the Atlantic Division, South Carolina, Georgia, Florida, Alabama, Mississippi, and Tennessee.)

Director Public Works Office
8th Naval District
Building No. 16, Naval Station
New Orleans, La. 70140
Tel: FOrest 6-2311
(Louisiana, Arkansas, Oklahoma, Texas, and New Mexico.)

District Public Works Officer
9th Naval District
Building No. 1A
Great Lakes, Ill. 60088
Tel: 336-3500
(Michigan, Indiana, Illinois, Wisconsin, Minnesota, Iowa, Missouri, North Dakota, South Dakota, Nebraska, Kansas, Colorado, and Wyoming.)

Area Public Works Officer, Caribbean
Navy No. 116, Fleet Post Office
New York, N.Y. 09592
Tel: San Juan 72-20080
(Puerto Rico, Virgin Islands, Trinidad, and Panama Canal Zone.)

Director, Southwest Division
Bureau of Yards and Docks
1220 Pacific Highway
San Diego, Calif. 92132
Tel: BElmont 2-3871
(Arizona, Clark County in Nevada; southern part of California including the counties of Santa Barbara, Kern, and San Bernardino, and all counties south thereof.)

District Public Works Officer
12th Naval District
San Bruno, Calif. 94067
Tel: JUno 3-1640
(Utah, Nevada, less Clark County; northern part of California, including the counties of San Luis Obispo, Kings, Tulare, Inyo and all counties north thereof.)

Director, Northwest Division
Bureau of Yards and Docks
Seattle, Wash. 98119
Tel: ATwater 3-5200
(Washington; Oregon; Idaho; Montana; also:
Officer in Charge
Bureau of Yards and Docks
Contracts in 17th Naval District.)

District Public Works Officer
14th Naval District
Navy No. 128, Fleet Post Office
San Francisco, Calif. 90614
Tel: Pearl Harbor 4711
(Hawaiian Islands and islands to the westward and southward including the Midway Islands, Jure, Wake, Johnston, and Palmyra Islands, Kingham Reef and Kwajalein Atoll (Marshall Islands).)

DEPARTMENT OF THE AIR FORCE MAJOR PURCHASING OFFICES

San Antonio Air Materiel Area
Kelly Air Force Base
San Antonio, Tex. 78241
Tel: 923–5411, Ext. 64192

Nuclear bombs; nuclear projectiles; nuclear warheads and warhead sections; nuclear demolition charges; nuclear rockets; conversion kits, nuclear ordnance; fuzing and firing devices, nuclear ordnance; nuclear components; high explosive charges, propellants and detonators, nuclear ordnance; specialized test and handling equipment, nuclear ordnance; miscellaneous nuclear ordnance; airframe structural components; parachutes and aerial pickup, delivery and tiedown equipment; miscellaneous aircraft accessories and components; aircraft arresting barrier and barricade equipment; aircraft launching equipment; aircraft ground servicing equipment; airfield specialized trucks and trailers; gasoline reciprocating engines, except aircraft and components; gasoline reciprocating engines, aircraft and components for engines assigned to San Antonio AMA; diesel engines and components; steam turbines and components; gas turbines and jet engines, aircraft and components for turbines and jet engines assigned to San Antonio AMA; miscellaneous engines and components; engine fuel system components, nonaircraft; engine fuel system components, aircraft; engine electrical control components, nonaircraft; engine electrical system components, aircraft; engine cooling system components, nonaircraft; engine air and oil filters, strainers and cleaners, nonaircraft; miscellaneous engine accessories, nonaircraft; torque converters and speed changers; gears, pulleys, sprockets and transmission chain; belting, drive belts, fan belts and accessories; miscellaneous power transmission equipment; gas generating equipment; self-contained refrigeration units and accessories; refrigeration and air conditioning plants and components; fans and air circulators, nonindustrial; nuclear reactors; motor vehicle maintenance and repair shop, specialized equipment; aircraft maintenance and repair shop, specialized equipment; lubrication and fuel dispensing equipment; miscellaneous maintenance and repair shop, specialized equipment; motors, electrical; electrical control equipment; generators and generator sets, electrical airborne; transformers, distribution and power station; converters, electrical; rectifying equipment, electrical; batteries, primary; batteries, secondary; miscellaneous electrical power and distribution equipment; indoor and outdoor electrical lighting fixtures; electrical vehicular lights and fixtures (aeronautical) airborne; electric portable and handlighting equipment; electric lamps; ballasts, lampholders and starters; nonelectrical lighting fixtures; traffic and transit signal systems; shipboard alarm and signal systems; aircraft alarm and signal systems; miscellaneous alarm and signal systems; electrical and electronic properties measuring and testing instruments; chemical analysis instruments; physical properties testing instruments; laboratory equipment and supplies; time measuring instruments; optical instruments; geophysical and astronomical instruments; hazard detecting instruments, and apparatus; scales and balances; drafting, survey, mapping instruments; liquid and gas flow, liquid level and mechanical motion measuring instruments; pressure, temperature and humidity measuring and controlling instruments; combination and miscellaneous instruments; chemicals; dyes; gases, compressed and liquefied; pest control agents and disinfectants; miscellaneous chemical specialties; storage and shipping containers applicable to aircraft jet engines; storage and shipping containers applicable to aircraft reciprocating engines assigned to San Antonio AMA; boxes and containers, recruiting and advertising; gas cylinders; tents and tarpaulins; specialized flight clothing and accessories; liquid propellants, fuels and oxidizers.

Warner Robins Air Materiel Area Robins Air Force Base Warner Robins, Ga. 31094 Tel: 926-5871	Guns through 30 millimeter, support items, launchers, rockets, and pyrotechnics; miscellaneous weapons; aircraft gunnery fire control components/replacement parts; aircraft bombing fire control components/replacement parts; guided missile components (MGM-13B, CGM-13C), guided missile remote control systems (MGM-13B, CGM-13C); launchers, guided missile (MGM-13B, CGM-13C); guided missile handling and servicing equipment (MGM-13B, CGM-13C); airframe structural components; miscellaneous aircraft items; special services aircraft structural components; aircraft propellers; trucks and truck tractors; trailers; tractors, wheeled; metal working machinery; road clearing and cleaning equipment; firefighting equipment; decontaminating and impregnating equipment; safety and rescue equipment; driers, dehydrators, and anhydrators; air purification equipment; guided missile maintenance, repair, and checkout specialized; equipment (MGM-13B, CGM-13C); radio and television communication equipment, airborne; radio navigation equipment, airborne; radio navigation equipment, airborne-special services; intercommunication and public address systems, airborne; radar equipment, airborne; miscellaneous communication equipment, airborne; sets, kits, outfits of measuring tools; food preparation and serving equipment (special purpose).
Mobile Air Materiel Area Brookley Air Force Base Mobile, Ala. 36615 Tel: 438-6011, Ext. 7271	Compressors and vacuum pumps; power and hand pumps; heat exchangers and steam condensers; industrial furnaces, kilns, lehrs and ovens; industrial fan and blower equipment; plumbing fixtures and accessories; space heating equipment and domestic water heaters; pipe and tube; hose and tubing, flexible; fittings and specialties: hose, pipe and tube; valves, powered; valves, nonpowered; hand tools (special purpose); hardware and abrasives; prefabricated and portable buildings; bridges, fixed and floating; storage tanks; scaffolding equipment and concrete forms; prefabricated tower structures; miscellaneous prefabricated structures; ammunition and explosives (except items assigned to Army Ordnance) guided missile components (Titan II); guided missile remote control systems (Titan II); launchers, guided missile (Titan II); guided missile handling and service equipment (Titan II); tires and tubes, pneumatic, aircraft; ammunition maintenance and repair shop specialized equipment; guided missile maintenance, repair and checkout specialized equipment; resistors; capacitors; filters and networks; circuit breakers; switches; connectors, electrical; lugs, terminals, and terminal strips; relays, contactors, and solenoids; coils and transformers; piezoelectric crystals; electron tubes, transistors, and rectifying crystals; miscellaneous electrical and electronic components; cameras, motion picture; cameras, still picture; photographic projection equipment; photographic developing and finishing equipment; photographic equipment and accessories; photographic sets, kits, and outfits; training aids; armament training devices; operational training devices; communication training devices; ammunition boxes, packages, and special containers.
Oklahoma City Air Materiel Area Tinker Air Force Base Oklahoma City, Okla. 73145 Tel: 732-7321, Ext. 2601	Guided missile; aircraft fixed wing; aircraft hydraulic vacuum and deicing system components; aircraft air conditioning, heating, and pressurizing equipment; gas turbine and jet engines; and components, nonaircraft; engine cooling system components, aircraft; engine air and oil filters, strainers, and cleaners, aircraft; turbosuperchargers; miscellaneous engine accessories, aircraft; telephone and telegraph equipment, ground; teletype and facsimile equipment, ground; radio and television communication equipment, ground; radio navigation equipment, ground; intercommunication and public address systems, ground; sound recording and reproducing equipment, ground; underwater sound equipment; visible and invisible light communication equipment; miscellaneous communication equipment, nonairborne; navigational instruments; flight instruments; automatic pilot mechanisms and airborne gyro components; engine instruments; meteorological instruments and apparatus, ground; engine containers.

Sacramento Air Materiel Area McClellan Air Force Base Sacramento, Calif. 95652 Tel: 922-1511, Ext. 26219	Guided missile components (Atlas, Titan I, and Thor); guided missile remote control systems (Atlas, Titan I, and Thor); launchers, guided missile (Atlas, Titan I, and Thor); guided missile handling and service equipment (Atlas, Titan I, and Thor); tanks, auxiliary fuel, and components (external) and airframe structural components; space vehicle remote control systems; space vehicle handling and servicing equipment; rocket engines and component spares (Atlas, Titan I, and Thor); guided missile maintenance, repair, and checkout specialized equipment (Atlas, Titan I, and Thor); radar equipment (ground); resistors; capacitors; filters and networks; circuit breakers; switches; connector, electrical; lugs, terminal, and terminal strips; relays, contactors, and solenoids; coils and transformers; piezoelectric crystals; electron tubes, transistors, and rectifying crystals; headsets, handsets, microphones, and speakers; electrical insulators and insulating materials; electrical hardware and supplies; electrical contact brushes and electrodes; antennas, waveguides, and related equipment; synchros and resolvers; cable, cord, and wire assemblies, communication equipment; miscellaneous electrical and electronic components; generator and generator sets, electrical; wire and cable, electrical.
Wright-Patterson AF Base 2750th Air Base Wing Dayton, Ohio 45433 AC 513 257-1110	Contract technical services; specialized procurement.
2802 Inertial Guidance and Calibration Group Newark Air Force Station Newark, Ohio 43055 AC 513 344-9481	Specialized test equipment.
Hq. Military Airlift Command Scott Air Force Base Belleville, Ill. 62226 AC 618 256-2123	Airlift.
Military Airlift Command 1350 Motion Picture Squadron Wright-Patterson Air Force Base Dayton, Ohio 45433 AC 513 255-5728	Motion picture production; script; foreign translations; commercial prints.
Aeronautical Systems Division Wright-Patterson Air Force Base Ohio 45433 Tel: 257-1110, Ext. 55322	Complete development and acquisition program for aeronautical systems and their components and related Government-furnished aerospace equipment (GFAE) including but not limited to aircraft engines, aircraft wheels and brakes, airborne communication systems, aircraft bombing and navigation systems, aircraft instruments; Department of Defense central procurement responsibility for ground and aerial cameras, photographic processing equipment. Responsible for AFSC planning for limited war.
Research and Technology Division Systems Engineering Group Wright-Patterson Air Force Base Ohio 45433 Tel: 253-7111	Exploratory and advanced development programs in air breathing, electric, and advanced propulsion, fuels, and lubricants, flight vehicle power, site support, electronic components, optronics and photo material, inertial components, vehicle electromagnetic environment, aerospace vehicle applications such as reconnaissance, navigation and guidance, electronic warfare, materials, sciences, metals and ceramics, nonmetallic materials, manufacturing technology, and materials application, flight vehicle dynamics, performance, control, launching, alighting, and structures, crew station, environmental control, and escape, aerodynamic and decelerators. Basic and applied research in bioastronautics, in human engineering, training, environmental stress criteria and life support. Basic research in selected areas of physical and mathematical science.
Ballistic Systems Division Norton Air Force Base San Bernardino, Calif. 92400 Tel: 382-8553	Development and acquisition of all BSD ballistic missile systems, activation of designated missile sites, related studies to determine feasibility of future systems and advanced ballistics weaponry state-of-the-art.

Space Systems Division
Air Force Unit Post Office
Los Angeles, Calif. 90045
Tel: 643-2855

To plan program and manage qualitatively superior space systems and related equipment; acquisition of space systems and equipment and manages the research, development engineering and test, on orbit tracking, telemetry control, recovery, installation and check out of assigned space systems. (SSD)

Electronic Systems Division
L. G. Hanscom Field
Bedford, Mass. 01731
Tel: 274-6100, Ext. 2244

Complete acquisition program for electronic electromagnetic information and communications systems and equipment.

Aerospace Medical Division
Brooks Air Force Base
San Antonio, Tex. 78235
Tel: 532-8811, Ext. 6227

Life sciences, human factors, aerospace medicine, biosciences, biomedicine, behavioral sciences, space medicine, biotechnology, human engineering, human resources, aviation medicine, and space biology.

Air Force Flight Test Center
Edwards Air Force Base
Muroc, Calif. 93523
Tel: 258-2111, Ext. 6227

Complete test and evaluation of new and research aircraft, parachute and deceleration devices. Research and development of rocket propulsion systems, rocket engines and new propellant formulations (liquid and solid) with associated fuel flow and capative test support equipment. Flight test instrumentation, simulation, tracking and data acquisition and reduction equipment.

Air Force Special Weapons Center
Kirtland Air Force Base
Albuquerque, N. Mex. 87117
Tel: 247-1711, Ext. 2017

Testing and engineering in the field of nuclear weapons and associated equipment. Specific engineering interests include: telemetry; instrumentation; weapons/aircraft flight characteristics; high-speed camera techniques. Provides air support to the Atomic Energy Commission in the conduct of live nuclear tests in the Zone of Interior and in preparation for the Air Force support role in oversea testing.

Air Force Eastern Test Range
Patrick Air Force Base
Cocoa, Fla. 32925
Tel: 485-7545, Ext. 6151

Test range instrumentation involving radar, trajectory computers and recorders, tracking and target analysis, wire communications, radio communications, programing timing and firing systems, telemetry receiving; data storage, data separation and presentation, optics and telemetry data reduction.

Air Force Western Test Range
Vandenberg Air Force Base
Lompoc, Calif. 93437
AC-805 866-3818

Specializes in polar orbit launches of satellites and supports the operational training launches of the Strategic Air Command missiles. (WTR)

Rome Air Development Center
Griffiss Air Force Base
Rome, N.Y. 13442
Tel: 330-4020

Surveillance, electronic intelligence, communications, computer and data-processing techniques, textual data-processing, intelligence, extraction from aerial reconnaissance, data presentation, high-power electromagnetic generators, receivers, transmission line components, microelectronics applications, reliability and maintainability, survivability, propagation, vulnerability reduction, electronic countermeasures and electromagnetic weapons.

Air Force Missile Development
Center
Holoman Air Force Base
Alamogordo, N. Mex. 88330
Tel: 473-6511, Ext. 3861

AFMDC: Conduct of category II testing of aircraft reconnaissance systems operation of the central inertial guidance test facility, support of flight and static test of ballistic missile nose cones, and reentry systems. Operation of ballistic missile reentry system data center. Operation of AFSC high-speed test track. Horizontal rocket engine testing up to 500,000 pounds thrust. R. & D. and human factors and execution of Air Force responsibilities at the White Sands Missile Range.

Air Proving Ground Center
Eglin Air Force Base
Valparaiso, Fla. 32542
Tel: 881-6668, Ext. 2843

Research, development, test, and evaluation of guns and other aircraft weapons, ammunition, rockets, bombs, and fire-control components and systems.

Arnold Engineering Development
Center
Arnold Air Force Station, Tenn.
37389
Tel: 455-2611, Ext. 509

Aerodynamics, research and development of powerplants related to operation and tests of air breathing propulsion systems, i.e., turbojet, ramjet, and turboprop. Problems associated with high-temperature materials and the unique mechanical, electrical, and thermodynamic problems all related to the construction of large and complex engine-test facilities and wind tunnels involving heavy construction of complicated machinery and associated ducting.

Base Procurement

This consists of supplies and services, including minor construction, required for the daily operation of Air Force bases, worldwide. In the United States, those bases are under various commands: Tactical Air Command, Military Air Transport Service, Air Defense Command, Air Training Command, Strategic Air Command, Alaskan Air Command, etc. At each command headquarters there is an Executive for Small Business. Each individual base also has a designated small business specialist. These bases are listed below:

Alabama

Montgomery:
Maxwell Air Force Base (AF)
Base Procurement Office
Mrs. Ruth R. Hunter
Area Code: 205 265-5021, Ext. 7201

Selma:
Craig Air Force Base (AF)
3615 Pilot Training Wing
Capt. Chester A. Holland
Area Code: 205 TR 4-7431, Ext. 53206

Alaska

Anchorage:
Elmendorf Air Force Base
Lt. Eldon R. Gunderson
APO Seattle 98733
Tel: 373-4230

Fairbanks:
Eielson Air Force Base
Mr. Donald M. Smith
APO Seattle 98742
Tel: 754-2209

Arizona

Chandler:
Williams Air Force Base (AF)
3525 Pilot Training Wing
Mr. Matthew A. Jannuzzi
Area Code: 602 YU 8-2611, Ext. 667

Phoenix:
Luke Air Force Base (AF)
Base Procurement Office
Mr. John J. Anderson
Area Code: 602 WE 5-9311, Ext. 2629

Tucson:
Davis Monthan Air Force Base (AF)
Base Procurement Office
Mr. Eugene L. Sierras
Area Code: 602 793-3131

Arkansas

Blytheville:
Blytheville Air Force Base (AF)
Base Procurement Office
Mr. Francis M. Nordeen
Area Code: 501 PO 3-3931, Ext. 246

Jacksonville:
Little Rock Air Force Base (AF)
825 Combat Support Group
Mr. James M. Hull
Area Code: 501 YU 5-3301

California

Camarillo:
Oxnard Air Force Base (AF)
414 Combat Support Squadron
Mrs. Zella A. Haug
Area Code: 805 486-1631, Ext. 3216

Fairfield:
Headquarters Western Transport Air Force (AF)
Procurement Division
Travis Air Force Base
Capt. Arvid G. Shaw
Area Code: 707 438-2516

Travis Air Force Base (AF)
1501 Air Base Group
Mr. Donald R. Bertholdi
Area Code: 707 438-2811

Ignacio:
Hamilton Air Force Base (AF)
28 Air Division
Lt. Stephen D. Thomas
Area Code: 415 884-7711, Ext. 3324

Lompoc:
Vandenberg Air Force Base (AF)
Base Procurement Office
Mr. William C. Key
Area Code: 805 866-5001

Los Angeles:
Lookout Mountain Air Force Station
1352 Photo Group
Mrs. Florence A. Thorn
Area Code: 213 654-4100, Ext. 44

Marysville:
Beale Air Force Base (AF)
456 Combat Support Group
Mr. Louis A. Fields
Area Code: 916 634-2041

Merced:
Castle Air Force Base (AF)
Base Procurement Office
Mr. William R. Mann
Area Code: 209 RA 3-1611, Ext. 2802

Riverside:
March Air Force Base (AF)
22 Combat Support Group
Mr. Ralph G. Christiansen
Area Code: 714 Moreno Long Dist. Oper. 20, Ext. 2046

California—Continued

Sacramento:
Mather Air Force Base (AF)
3535 Navigator Training Wing
Mr. John Solberg
Area Code: 916   EM 3-3161, Ext. 2740

Victorville:
George Air Force Base (AF)
Base Procurement Office
Mr. Paul Waas
Area Code: 714   CH 6-8611, Ext. 2337

Colorado

Colorado Springs:
USAF Academy Procurement Office
Mr. Lester A. Shoemaker
Area Code: 303   472-2332

Ent Air Force Base
4600 Air Base Wing
Mr. Robert S. Nevroth
Area Code: 303   635-8911, Ext. 6641

Denver:
Lowry Air Force Base (AF)
Lowry Technical Training Center
Mr. Joe P. Piccola
Area Code: 303   DU 8-5411, Ext. 44471

Connecticut

Windsor Locks:
Bradley Field
905 Troop Carrier Group (AF)
Mrs. Ernestyne E. Clark
Area Code: 203   NA 8-3377, Ext. 58

Delaware

Dover:
Dover Air Force Base (AF)
1607 Air Base Group
Capt. Wm. F. McGovern
Area Code: 302   734-8211, Ext. 617

Florida

Homestead:
Homestead Air Force Base (AF)
19 Combat Support Group
Mr. Jack Ford
Area Code: 305   ED 6-7327

Orlando:
Hq. Air Photographic and Charting Service (AF)
Procurement Division
Orlando Air Force Base
Mrs. Edith C. Light
Area Code: 305   841-5611, Ext. 2002

McCoy Air Force Base (AF)
306 Combat Support Group
Mr. Lloyd F. Kruckemyer
Area Code: 305   855-3210, Ext. 438

Florida—Continued

Pamana City:
Tyndall Air Force Base (AF)
73 Air Division
Mr. Ray P. Gatliff
Area Code: 305   286-2111, Ext. 25261

Tampa:
MacDill Air Force Base (AF)
Base Procurement Office
Maj. John Colianna
Area Code: 813   836-1411, Ext. 3232

Georgia

Albany:
Turner Air Force Base (AF)
484 Combat Support Group
Mr. Edwin J. Mulholland
Area Code: 912   432-3000

Marietta:
Dobbins Air Force Base (AF)
918 Troop Carrier Group
Irene V. Rogers—Mr. Joseph Nix
Area Code: 404   428-4461, Ext. 705

Savannah:
Hunter Air Force Base (AF)
63 Troop Carrier Wing
Lt. Eddie G. Freret
Area Code: 912   234-4461, Ext. 28141

Valdosta:
Moody Air Force Base (AF)
3550 Pilot Training Wing
Lt. Robert A. Law
Area Code: 912   ED 3-4211, Ext. 453

Hawaii

Honolulu:
Hickam Air Force Base (AF)
Pacific Air Force Base Command
Maj. Lloyd E. Bell

Idaho

Mountain Home:
Mountain Home Air Force Base (AF)
9 Strategic Aerospace Wing
Mr. Herbert J. Pennings
Area Code: 208   828-2479

Illinois

Belleville:
Scott Air Force Base (AF)
1405 Air Base Group
Mr. Leonard R. Pranger
Area Code: 618   256-3036

Illinois—Continued

Chicago:
O'Hare International Airport
928 Troop Carrier Group
Mrs. Ethel C. Tonkin
Area Code: 312   296–4411, Ext. 583

Rantoul:
Chanute Air Force Base (AF)
Technical Training Center
Mr. Thomas G. Stark
Area Code: 217   TW2–3111, Ext. 4112

Indiana

Columbus:
Bakalar Air Force Base
930 Troop Carrier Group
Mr. Robert M. Bardin
Area Code: 812   373–2501, Ext. 351

Peru:
305 Combat Support Group
Bunker Hill Air Force Base (AF)
Mr. Howard E. Smith
Area Code: 317   MU 9–2211, Ext. 2131

Iowa

Sioux City:
Sioux City Municipal Airport (AF)
4644 Support Squadron
Mr. Jeffrey Dargis
Area Code: 712   252–4141, Ext. 308

Kansas

Salina:
Schilling Air Force Base (AF)
Base Procurement Office
Mr. Clifford L. Nyberg
Area Code: 913   AV 5–3285

Topeka:
Forbes Air Force Base (AF)
815 Combat Support Group
Mr. A. H. Stratton
Area Code: 913   UN 2–1234, Ext. 5431

Wichita:
McConnell Air Force Base (AF)
Base Procurement Office
Capt. Marvin G. Spallina
Area Code: 316   685–1151

Louisiana

Alexandria:
England Air Force Base (AF)
Base Procurement Office
Mr. Wm. H. Dunn
Area Code: 318   443–4561, Ext. 553

Shreveport:
Barksdale Air Force Base (AF)
2 Combat Support Group
Mr. James L. Ingram
Area Code: 318   425–3117

Maine

Bangor:
Dow Air Force Base
Base Procurement Office
Mr. Lloyd G. Sargent
Area Code: 207   989–2300, Ext. 2121

Limestone:
Loring Air Force Base (AF)
42 Combat Support Group
Lt. Phillip J. Carney
Area Code: 207   FA 8–7311, Ext. 2284

Massachusetts

Chicopee Falls:
Westover Air Force Base (AF)
814 Combat Support Group
Mr. Edward J. Kennedy
Area Code: 413   557–3507

Falmouth:
Otis Air Force Base (AF)
551 Combat Support Group
Mr. Robert L. Marelli
Area Code: 617   968–4461

Michigan

Kinross:
Kincheloe Air Force Base (AF)
507 Combat Support Group
Mr. Gilbert F. Peterman
Area Code: 906   495–5611, Ext. 2380

Marquette:
K. I. Sawyer Air Force Base (AF)
Base Procurement Office
Mr. Morris E. Woodridge
Area Code: 906   346–6511, Ext. 2300

Mt. Clemens:
Selfridge Air Force Base (AF)
1st Combat Support Group
Helen M. Bourdage
Area Code: 313   463–0511, Ext. 24206

Oscoda:
Wurtsmith Air Force Base (AF)
Base Procurement Office
Mr. Roy L. Lemons
Area Code: 517   SE 9–3611, Ext. 2132

Minnesota

Duluth:
Duluth Municipal Airport (AF)
343 Fighter Group
Maj. Joseph Gambucci
Area Code: 218   727–8211, Ext. 240

St. Paul:
Minneapolis-St. Paul International Airport (AF)
934 Troop Carrier Group
Mrs. Julia S. Kulmala
Area Code: 612   PA 1–2915, Ext. 270

Mississippi

Biloxi:
Keesler Air Force Base (AF)
Technical Training Center
Mr. Barnard R. Chevalier
Area Code: 601   ID 2-1561, Ext. 38081

Columbus:
Columbus Air Force Base (AF)
454 Combat Support Group
Mr. Fred B. Gilliland
Area Code: 601   434-7517

Missouri

Richards-Gebaur Air Force Base (AF)
328 Combat Support Group
Mr. Leonard W. Shriver
Area Code: 816   331-1200, Ext. 526

Knob Noster:
Whiteman Air Force Base
351 Combat Support Group
Mr. Orville D. Meyer
Area Code: 816   LO 3-5511, Ext. 267

Montana

Glasgow:
Glasgow Air Force Base (AF)
Base Procurement Office
Mr. Louis W. Blanchette
Area Code: 509   CH 7-2161, Ext. 4419

Great Falls:
Malmstrom Air Force Base (AF)
341 Combat Support Group
Mr. Angus W. Clunie
Area Code: 406   731-3743

Nebraska

Lincoln:
Lincoln Air Force Base (AF)
818 Combat Support Group
Mr. Glen R. Carrigan
Area Code: 402   GR 7-6011, Ext. 2128

Omaha:
Offutt Air Force Base (AR)
3902 Air Base Wing
Mr. William W. Vaughan
Area Code: 402   294-4351

Nevada

Las Vegas:
Nellis Air Force Base (AF)
Base Procurement Office
Mr. Vance O. Taylor
Area Code: 702   DU 2-1800, Ext. 22151

Nevada—Continued

Reno:
Stead Air Force Base (AF)
3635 Flying Training Wing
Mr. Forrest F. Glenn
Area Code: 802   FI 9-0711, Ext. 285

New Hampshire

Manchester:
Grenier Field, Manchester Municipal Airport (AF)
902 Troop Carrier Group
Mr. Arthur J. Clare
Area Code: 603   NA 4-4031, Ext. 362

Portsmouth:
Pease Air Force Base
817 Combat Support Group
Mr. Paul E. Weller
Area Code: 603   GE 6-0100, Ext. 336

New Jersey

Wrightstown:
Headquarters Eastern Transport Air Force
Procurement Division
McGuire Air Force Base
Sgt. Stanley R. Gerst
Area Code: 609   724-2100, Ext. 2024

McGuire Air Force Base (AF)
1611 Air Base Group
Capt. Wm. D. Bell
Area Code: 609   724-2100, Ext. 3120

New Mexico

Clovis:
Cannon Air Force Base (AF)
Base Procurement Office
Mr. Dominic A. Schreiber
Area Code: 505   SU 4-3311, Ext. 293

Roswell:
Walker Air Force Base (AF)
6 Strategic Aerospace Wing
Mr. H. L. Gremillion
Area Code: 505   348-8383

New York

Long Island:
West Hampton Beach (AF)
Suffolk County Air Force Base
52 Combat Support Group
CWO Howell L. Broxton
Area Code: 516   289-1900, Ext. 472

Newburgh:
Stewart Air Force Base (AF)
4603 Air Base Group
Mr. Joseph T. Curry
Area Code: 914   562-1300, Ext. 550

New York—Continued

Niagara Falls:
Niagara Municipal Airport (AF)
4621 Air Base Group
Mr. Roderic R. Madore
Area Code: 716 297-4100, Ext. 294

Plattsburgh:
Plattsburgh Air Force Base (AF)
Base Procurement Office
Mr. Paul R. Pierson
Area Code: 518 565-5218

North Carolina

Fayetteville:
Pope Air Force Base
Base Procurement Office
Mr. Roger L. Hawley
Area Code: 919 396-4111, Ext. 51155

Goldsboro:
Seymour-Johnson Air Force Base (AF)
Base Procurement Office
Mr. Battle R. Tunstall
Area Code: 919 RE 5-1121, Ext. 275

North Dakota

Grand Forks:
Grand Forks Air Force Base (AF)
Base Procurement Office
Lt. A. D. Berquist
Area Code: 701 594-6571

Minot:
Minot Air Force Base (AF)
862 Combat Support Group
Mr. William W. Pirkle
Area Code: 701 TE 7-1161, Ext. 5054

Ohio

Columbus:
Lockbourne Air Force Base (AF)
801 Combat Support Group
Mr. R. H. Brown
Area Code: 614 491-8211, Ext. 7341

Dayton:
Wright-Patterson Air Force Base (AF)
Base Procurement Office
Mr. Henry T. Brown
Area Code: 513 257-1110, Ext. 72324

Vienna:
Youngstown Municipal Airport (AF)
910 Troop Carrier Group
Mrs. Mary Jean Michael
Area Code: 216 FR 4-1551, Ext. 212

Ohio—Continued

Wilmington:
Clinton County Air Force Base (AF)
906 Troop Carrier Group
Mr. George R. Goodman
Area Code: 513 FU 2-3811, Ext. 3188

Oklahoma

Altus:
Altus Air Force Base (AF)
Base Procurement Office
Mr. Ernest L. Sadler
Area Code: 405 HU 2-8100, Ext. 7320

Burns Flat:
Clinton Sherman Air Force Base (AF)
Base Procurement Office
Mr. Glen D. Peck
Area Code: 405 LO 2-3121, Ext. 342

Enid:
Vance Air Force Base (AF)
Base Procurement Office
Mr. A. H. McMullen
Area Code: 405 AD 7-2121, Ext. 210

Oregon

Klamath Falls:
Kingsley Field (AF)
408 Combat Support Squadron
Virginia A. Brower
Area Code: 503 882-4411, Ext. 420

Portland:
Portland International Airport (AF)
337 Combat Support Squadron
Helen T. Barber
Area Code: 503 288-5611, Ext. 354

Pennsylvania

Corapolis:
Greater Pittsburgh Airport (AF)
911 Troop Carrier Group
Miss Laverna R. Cerceo
Area Code: 412 FE 1-2609, Ext. 253

Willow Grove:
Willow Grove Air Reserve Facility (AF)
912 Troop Carrier Group
Mr. George L. Zwolak
Area Code: 215 OS 2-4300, Ext. 386

South Carolina

North Charleston:
Charleston Air Force Base (AF)
1608 Air Transport Wing
Mr. Robert C. McCollister
Area Code: 803 747-4111, Ext. 2063

South Carolina—Continued

Myrtle Beach:
  Myrtle Beach Air Force Base (AF)
  Base Procurement Office
  Mrs. Marie J. Repec
  Area Code: 803   HI 8-3131, Ext. 444

Sumter:
  Shaw Air Force Base (AF)
  Base Procurement Office
  Capt. Virgil V. Carlsen
  Area Code: 803   775-1111

South Dakota

Rapid City:
  Ellsworth Air Force Base (AF)
  821 Combat Support Group
  Mr. Donald S. Galbraith
  Area Code: 605   399-2721

Tennessee

Smyrna:
  Sewart Air Force Base (AF)
  Base Procurement Office
  Capt. Lonnie J. Rowin
  Area Code: 615   675-6211

Texas

Abilene:
  Dyess Air Force Base (AF)
  Base Procurement Office
  Mr. Roy J. Bishop
  Area Code: 915   OW 6-2581

Amarillo:
  Amarillo Air Force Base
  Amarillo Technical Training Center
  Mrs. Mildred F. Walker
  Area Code: 806   DI 9-1511, Ext. 8133

Austin:
  Bergstrom Air Force Base (AF)
  Base Procurement Office
  Miss Vivian A. Anderson
  Area Code: 512   EV 5-4100, Ext. 420

Big Spring:
  Webb Air Force Base
  Base Procurement Office
  Mr. Floyd A. Henderson
  Area Code: 915   AM 4-2511, Ext. 606

El Paso:
  Biggs Air Force Base (AF)
  95 Combat Support Group
  Mr. Thomas J. Smith
  Area Code: 915   LO 6-6711, Ext. 24201

Fort Worth:
  Carswell Air Force Base
  824 Combat Support Group
  Miss Dorothy G. Carroll
  Area Code: 817   PE 8-3511, Ext. 253

Texas—Continued

Houston:
  Ellington Air Force Base (AF)
  2578 Air Base Squadron
  Mrs. Mary Y. Kerr
  Area Code: 713   HU 7-1400, Ext. 667

Laredo:
  Laredo Air Force Base (AF)
  Base Procurement Office
  Mr. Forest Morris
  Area Code: 512   RA 3-9121, Ext. 681

Lubbock:
  Reese Air Force Base
  3500 Pilot Training Wing
  Maj. Joseph V. Sullivan
  Area Code: 806   885-4511, Ext. 314

San Antonio:
  Lackland Air Force Base (AF)
  Lackland Military Training Center
  Lt. G. H. Madeley
  Area Code: 512   OR 4-3411, Ext. 3328

Sherman:
  Perrin Air Force Base
  4780 Air Defense Wing
  Mr. S. J. Hallett
  Area Code: 817   787-2971, Ext. 8295

Waco:
  James Connally Air Force Base (AF)
  3565 Navigator Training Wing
  Mrs. Ethel S. Morrow
  Area Code: 817   SW 9-3611, Ext. 563

Wichita Falls:
  Sheppard Air Force Base (AF)
  Technical Training Center
  Mrs. Artie Sauer
  Area Code: 817   881-2511, Ext. 2005

Virginia

Hampton:
  Langley Air Force Base (AF)
  Base Procurement Office
  Maj. Kenneth A. Clark
  Area Code 703   764-3246

Washington

Everett:
  Paine Field (AF)
  57 Combat Support Squadron
  Mr. Robert F. Collins
  Area Code 206   353-1161, Ext. 258

Moses Lake:
  Larson Air Force Base (AF)
  4629 Strategic Aerospace Wing
  Mr. Thomas F. Mortensen
  Area Code 509   769-7081

Washington—Continued
Spokane:
   Fairchild Air Force Base (AF)
   92 Combat Support Group
   Mr. Walter J. Anderson
   Area Code 509   CH 7-2161

Tacoma:
   McChord Air Force Base (AF)
   25 Air Division
   Mr. Charles L. Wilk
   Area Code 206   588-2121, Ext. 2531

Wisconsin

Madison:
   Hqs. 327 Fighter Group (AF)
   Truax Field
   Mr. G. H. Hagen
   Area Code: 608   249-5311, Ext. 153

Wisconsin—Continued
Madison—Continued
   Truax Field (AF)
   30 Air Division
   Mr. Theodore R. Carey
   Area Code: 608   249-5311, Ext. 663

Milwaukee:
   General Billy Mitchell Field (AF)
   933 Troop Carrier Group
   Mrs. Alice E. Ward
   Area Code: 414   HU 1-6400, Ext. 251

Wyoming

Cheyenne:
   Francis E. Warren Air Force Base (AF)
   809 Combat Support Group
   Mr. L. B. Nelson
   Area Code: 307   775-2947

DEFENSE SUPPLY AGENCY
Cameron Station, Alexandria, Va., 22314

The mission of the Defense Supply Agency (DSA) is to provide common supplies and services to the Military Departments, other elements of the Defense Department, and to Federal civil agencies, as assigned by the Secretary of Defense.

The Agency is the supplier to the Military Departments and other customers of such necessities as food, clothing and textiles, medical, chemical, general, industrial, construction, fuel, and electronics supplies. It manages an inventory of idle industrial plant equipment and maintains central records of all plant equipment owned by the Defense Department. It procures and distributes food and sanitation supplies and medical kits for the Civil Defense fallout shelter program.

In the service field, DSA administers the Federal Supply Catalog for the Defense Establishment, Federal civil agencies, and other users and supervises Defense-wide programs for materiel utilization, technical documentation services, coordinated procurement, and surplus property disposal.

In 1964 the Secretary of Defense directed that contract administration services also should come under management of DSA. This consolidation of some 200 Army, Navy, Air Force, and DSA field contract offices is engaged in such functions as quality assurance, production expediting, industrial security, and payment of contractors.

Interested bidders and suppliers should deal directly with appropriate Supply Centers and Depots.

Defense Personnel Support Centers

Commander
Defense Personnel Support Center
2800 South 20th Street
Philadelphia, Pa. 19101
Area Code: 215   HOward 5-2000,
   Ext. 023, 638
AUTOVON: 231-1460

Hospital and surgical clothing and textiles; household furnishings; textile fabrics; yarn and thread; notions and apparel findings; padding and stuffing materials; leather; shoe findings and soling materials; tents and tarpaulins; flags and pennants; underwear and outerwear; footwear; hosiery; badges and insignia; luggage; and, specialized flight clothing.

Drugs, medicines, biologicals, official reagents; surgical dressings materials; medical, surgical, dental, and opticians instruments, equipment, and supplies, X-ray equipment and supplies; hospital furniture, equipment, utensils, and supplies; and, medical sets, kits, and outfits.

Subsistence of all types, perishable and nonperishable for distribution in the United States and overseas. The range and variety of such purchases cover all types and kinds of meat and meat products, fresh fruits and vegetables, dehydrated items, seafood or water foods, cereals, dairy products, poultry, and other related food items. Canned, packaged fresh, frozen items are purchased in car-lot and less-than-car-lot quantities. Large quantities are purchased after nationwide competition, while less-than-car-lot quanties are procured locally by the individual regional headquarters.

Commander
Defense Construction Supply Center
3990 E. Broad St.
Columbus, Ohio 43215
Area Code: 614 236-3541
AUTOVON: 231-3720

Diesel engines and components; gardening implements and tools; construction, mining, excavating, and highway maintenance equipment; conveyors, winches, hoists, cranes, and derricks; firefighting equipment; pumps and compressors; plumbing, heating, and sanitation equipment; water purification and sewage treatment equipment; pipe, tubing, hose, and fittings; valves; prefabricated structures and scaffolding; lumber, millwork, plywood, and veneer; other construction and building materials; and, supplies, repair parts, and miscellaneous items applicable to automotive and construction equipment, warehouse trucks, and trailers.

Sub-Offices (Specializing in Lumber)

Atlanta Regional Procurement Sub-Office
Defense Construction Supply Center
Defense Supply Agency
Post Office Box 1889
Atlanta, Ga. 30301
Area Code: 404 526-6644

Portland Regional Procurement Sub-Office
Defense Construction Supply Center
Defense Supply Agency
783 Pittock Block
Portland, Oreg. 97205
Area Code: 503 227-7681

Commander
Defense Electronics Supply Center
1507 Wilmington Pike
Dayton, Ohio 45401
Area Code: 513 252-6551, Ext. 26218
AUTOVON: 551-1530

Resistors; capacitors; filters; networks; relays; contactors; solenoids; coils; transformers; piezoelectric crystals; electron tubes; transistors; rectifying crystals; headsets; handsets; microphones; speakers; antennas; waveguides and related equipment; synchros; resolvers and miscellaneous electronic components; fuses; lighting arresters; circuit breakers; and, switches.

Commander
Defense Fuel Supply Center
Cameron Station
Alexandria, Va., 22314
Area Code: 202 OXford 8-8401

Chemicals and specialties including cleaners, solvents, and fluids having a petroleum base; gasoline and jet fuel; fuel oils; packaged petroleum products; cutting, lubricating, and hydraulic oils and greases; miscellaneous waxes, oils, and fats; pest control agents and disinfectants; petroleum base liquid propellants and fuels; natural and synthetic minerals; and solid fuels.

Commander
Defense General Supply Center
Bellwood, Petersburg Pike
Richmond, Va. 23212
Area Code: 703 275-3617
AUTOVON: 555-3370

Service and trade equipment; furniture; food preparation and serving equipment; office supplies; musical instruments; recreational and athletic equipment; cleaning equipment and supplies; toiletries; materials handling equipment; self-contained refrigeration units and accessories; fans and air circulators; photographic supplies; floor coverings; miscellaneous household and commercial furnishings and appliances; bags and sacks; drums and cans; boxes, cartons, and crates; bottles and jars; packaging and packing bulk materials; paper and paperboard; rubber fabricated materials; plastic fabricated materials; glass fabricated materials; refractories and fire surfacing materials; electrical hardware, lighting equipment, and supplies; cable, cord, and wire assemblies; lugs, terminals, and terminal strips; electrical insulators and insulating materials; electrical contact brushes and electrodes; chemicals; compressed gases; dyes; pest control agents and disinfectants.

Commander
Defense Industrial Supply Center
700 Robbins Avenue
Philadelphia, Pa. 19111
Area Code: 215   RAndolph 8-1212,
    Ext. 7049
AUTOVON: 231-3840

Hardware and abrasives; metal bars, rods, sheets, and shapes; bearings; chain and wire rope and fittings; electrical wire and cable; fiber rope, cable, and twine; blocks, tackle, slings, and rigging; rivets, nails, screws, and bolts; metal screening; packing and gasket materials; and, knobs and pointers.

Subsistence Regional Headquarters

Chicago Subsistence Regional Hdqrs, DPSC
536 South Clark Street
Chicago, Ill. 60605
Area Code: 312   828-5009

Columbia Subsistence Regional Hdqrs, DPSC
1813 Main Street   •
Columbia, S.C. 29201
Area Code: 803   254-1606

Fort Worth Subsistence Regional Hdqrs, DPSC
Felix at Hemphill Streets
Fort Worth, Tex. 76115
Area Code: 817   WA 4-2261

Kansas City Subsistence Regional Hdqrs, DPSC
623 Hardesty Avenue
Kansas City, Mo. 64124
Area Code: 816   221-7000

Los Angeles Subsistence Regional Hdqrs, DPSC
929 South Broadway
Los Angeles, Calif. 90015
Area Code: 213   688-3555

New Orleans Subsistence Regional Hdqrs, DPSC
4400 Dauphine Street
New Orleans, La. 70140
Area Code: 504   947-5571

New York Subsistence Regional Hdqrs, DPSC
Third Avenue and 29th Street
Brooklyn, N.Y. 11232
Area Code: 212   ST 8-5000

Oakland Subsistence Regional Hdqrs, DPSC
2155 Webster Street
Alameda, Calif. 94505
Area Code: 415   523-4252

Richmond Subsistence Regional Hdqrs, DPSC
% Defense General Supply Center
Bellwood, Petersburg Pike
Richmond, Va. 23219
Area Code: 703   275-3851 Autovon: 555-3311

Seattle Subsistence Regional Hdqrs, DPSC
Pier 91
Seattle Wash. 98119
Area Code: 206   AT 3-5200

Defense Supply Agency Depots

Procurement of local support supplies and services is effected at the following DSA-operated activities:

Defense Depot Memphis
Memphis, Tenn. 38115
Area Code: 901   458-4411
AUTOVON: 631-1490

Defense Depot Ogden
Ogden, Utah 84401
Area Code: 801   399-3474
AUTOVON: 553-1460

Defense Depot Tracy
Tracy, California 95376
Area Code: 209   835-1180
AUTOVON: 831-1490

Special Assistants for Small Business—Defense Contract Administration Services

Headquarters, DCAS:
    Mr. George C. Tolton
    Mr. John V. Weesner
    Headquarters, Defense Supply Agency
    Cameron Station
    Alexandria, Va. 22314
    Area Code: 202   OX 8-9605

DCASR, Atlanta:
    Mr. Adee F. Thompson
    3100 Maple Drive NE.
    Atlanta, Ga. 30305
    Area Code: 404   261-7310, Ext. 295

DCASD, Orlando:
    Mr. DeFarest A. Long, Jr.
    Orlando Air Force Base
    Building 2516
    Orlando, Fla. 32813
    Area Code: 305   841-5611, Ext. 2077

DCASR, Boston:
    Mr. Edward Fitzgerald
    Mr. John McManus
    666 Summer Street
    Boston, Mass. 02210
    Area Code: 617   542-6000, Ext. 876

DCASD, Rochester:
Mr. Robert A. McMillan
317 Child Street
Rochester, N.Y. 14611
Area Code: 716 328-7670

DCASR, Chicago:
Mr. Victor J. Ripp
Mr. John C. Mras
O'Hare International Airport
Post Office Box 8758
Chicago, Ill. 60666
Area Code: 312 296-4411, Ext. 2388

DCASD, Indianapolis:
Mr. Robert Raney
Finance Center, U.S. Army
Building 1
Fort Benjamin Harrison, Ind. 46249
Area Code: 317 LI 6-9211

DCASD, Milwaukee:
Mr. Dean Stevenson
744 North Fourth Street
Milwaukee, Wis. 53202
Area Code: 414 BR 2-4003

DCASR, Cleveland:
Mr. Harold A. Johns
Mr. Robert W. Livingston
1367 East Sixth Street
Cleveland, Ohio 44114
Area Code: 216 861-4960, Ext. 463 or 464

DCASD, Cincinnati:
Mr. Gene Luke
Federal Office Building
550 Main Street
Cincinnati, Ohio 45202
Area Code: 513 684-2200, Ext. 3914

DCASD, Dayton:
Mr. Paul E. Birkhold
Bldg. 70, Area C
Wright-Patterson AFB
Dayton, Ohio 45433
Area Code: 513 253-711, Ext. 70240

DCASR, Dallas:
Mr. George R. Phillips
Mr. George Koury, Jr.
500 South Ervay Street
Dallas, Tex. 75201
Area Code: 214 RI 9-3207

DCASR, Detroit:
Mr. Donald B. Leahy
Mr. Norman Rautio
1580 E. Grand Boulevard
Detroit, Mich. 48211
Area Code: 313 923-0100, Ext. 307/516

DCASD, Grand Rapids, Mich.:
(To be serviced by DCASR, Detroit)

DCASR, Los Angeles:
Mr. Edgar L. Harris, Jr.
11099 So. LaCienega
Los Angeles, Calif. 90045
Area Code: 213 643-1000

DCASD Phoenix:
Mr. Charles P. Fink
3800 North Central Avenue
Phoenix, Ariz. 85012
Area Code: 206 261-4391

DCASR, New York:
Mr. Theodore M. Everett
770 Broadway
New York, N.Y. 10003
Area Code: 212 OR 7-3030, Ext. 494 or 498

DCASD Garden City:
Mr. Wilbur V. Gould, Jr.
605 Stewart Avenue
Garden City, Long Island, N.Y. 11533
Area Code: 516 PI 1-8000

DCASD Newark:
Mr. Vincent J. Farrell
240 Route 22
Springfield, N.J. 07081
Area Code: 201 379-7950

DCASR, Philadelphia:
Mr. Albert B. Feldman
Mr. John F. Malley
Mr. John A. Walter
2800 South 20th Street
Philadelphia, Pa. 19101
Area Code: 215 271-3371 or 271-3372

DCASD Pittsburgh:
Mr. George Kuhn
1610 South Federal Building
1000 Liberty Avenue
Pittsburgh, Pa. 15222
Area Code: 412 644-5072

DCASR, St. Louis:
Mr. Harold W. Nutt
Mr. Kenneth E. Kichline
4300 Goodfellow Boulevard
St. Louis, Mo. 63120
Area Code: 314 EV 2-8200, Ext. 525 or 748

DCASD Twin Cities:
Mr. Roma T. Schumacher
2305 Ford Parkway
St. Paul, Minn. 55116
Area Code: 612 690-1721, Ext. 214

DCASO Denver:
  Mr. Ralph E. Wilson
  3800 York Street
  Denver, Colo. 80205
  Area Code: 303 825–1161

DCASR, San Francisco:
  Mr. William R. Graham
  866 Malcolm Road
  Burlingame, Calif. 94010
  Area Code: 415 692–0300

DCASD Seattle:
  Mr. Arthur W. Perry
  Building 5D
  U.S. Naval Air Station
  Seattle, Wash. 98115
  Area Code: 206 523–0550

SURPLUS PERSONAL PROPERTY

INTRODUCTION

This pamphlet is prepared to assist individuals, business concerns, and other organizations of all sizes and classifications, desiring to participate in the sale of surplus and foreign excess property of the Department of Defense and U.S. Coast Guard, excluding real property, and to answer questions which logically arise concerning such property, and how it may be purchased.

Department of Defense property originates at Defense Supply Agency, Army, Navy, Air Force, and Marine Corps installations. The Defense Supply Agency has been assigned primary responsibility for the Department of Defense sales program. For the purpose of this publication the terms "surplus" and "foreign excess" are synonymous except that surplus refers to property located in the United States, Puerto Rico, and the Virgin Islands and foreign excess refers to property in all other areas.

This pamphlet applies to the sale of Department of Defense property of general commercial use either in its original form or as scrap. It does not apply to real estate, contractor inventory (property in the possession of contractors performing military contracts), or to material of primarily military application. Normally, property classified as arms, ammunition, and implements of war is not sold in its original form to the general public; it is either demilitarized or reduced to scrap to preclude the possibility of reconditioning it for further use or sale and to safeguard security information.

The General Services Administration has overall responsibility for the disposal of real estate, including both land and buildings. Information on the disposal of surplus real property for public or private use may be obtained from the General Services Administration, Washington 25, D.C.

Information on the disposal of contractor inventory by the military services may be obtained from one or more of the following offices of the Army, Navy or Air Force:

Commanding General
Army Materiel Command
Attention: AMCPP-PS
Washington, D.C. 20315

Chief of Naval Material
Field Contract Administration Division
Code MAT 255
Washington, D.C. 20360

Contract Management Division (SCKAP)
Directorate of Contract Management
Headquarters, Air Forces Systems Command
Andrews Air Force Base
Washington, D.C. 20331

Prospective buyers are encouraged to use available facilities described herein for information and assistance.

WHY THERE IS MILITARY SURPLUS

The Department of Defense retains only usable property for which there is a current or foreseeable requirement. Property is declared surplus when it (1) becomes excess to military requirements because of changes in defense needs or unsuitable because of wear and tear or obsolescence, and (2) cannot be used by any other Federal Government activity.

The property is thereafter made available for donation to certain designated recipients authorized by law to obtain such property. Information on how to acquire Federal surplus personal property for health, educational, and civil defense purposes and Federal surplus real property for health and educational purposes under the donation program administered by the Department of Health, Education, and Welfare may be obtained from the U.S. Department of Health, Education, and Welfare, Office of Field Administration, Surplus Property Utilization Division, Washington, D.C., 20201 or the General Services Administration, Washington, D.C., 20405.

Only that property which survives rigid utilization and donation screening is offered for sale to the general public.

TYPES OF SURPLUS AVAILABLE

Surplus property sold by the Department of Defense is grouped into 496 classes to correspond with commercial and private buying interests. Ten of these classes are for scrap (property having value for its basic material content) and waste (garbage, trash, and other refuse generated in the normal course of operations). The remaining classes are for usable property (property suitable for use either as complete items or for recovery of usable parts). All classes are described on pages 73–80.

CONDITION OF PROPERTY

Surplus property is usually sold without any warranty as to condition or fitness for any purpose. However every effort is made to adequately describe its condition by the use of such descriptive terms as "unused," "used-reconditioned," "used-usable without repair," "used-repair required," "used-suitable for recovery of parts," "scrap," or "waste."

METHODS OF SELLING SURPLUS

Sales are conducted whenever there is sufficient surplus property to interest prospective buyers and to warrant the cost of disposal. Sales are open to the general public and property is offered in such reasonable quantities as to encourage participation by business concerns of all sizes, as well as individuals. As a rule, the property is sold by one of the following methods:

Sealed Bid Sale. Normally, this method is used to sell large quantities of individual items of surplus property having a commercial or technical application which are of interest to divergent buyer groups on a local, regional, or national market area basis. Scrap and waste materials are usually sold by this method.

Prospective bidders are notified by Standard Forms 114, "Sale of Government Property, Invitation, Bid and Acceptance," normally referred to as "Invitations for Bid" or "IFB's." These forms list and describe the property and specify the place and conditions of sale, location of property, inspection and sale dates, and the person to contact for further information. Invitations for bid are mailed well in advance of the date of sale (bid opening date) to allow sufficient time for inspection of the property. The prospective buyers enter the prices they will pay for the property on the "Invitation for Bid," sign and return it to the specified selling activity along with the required deposit. These bids are then publicly opened on the specified date of sale. Subsequently, awards are made and the bidders are notified.

Auction Sale. This method is used when a substantial quantity or variety of property having wide commercial application is being offered for sale. Catalogs listing and describing the property and specifying the conditions of sale, location of property, and inspection and sales dates are distributed well in advance of the sale to prospective buyers. In auction sales, "mailed in" bids are not acceptable; bidders must be present to participate. Qualified auctioneers assist in lotting, advertising, and conducting the auction.

Spot Bid Sale. Normally, this method is used when there is a variety of commercial type property for which there is substantial interest and demand in a local or regional market area. The prospective buyers inspect the property and submit bids on forms provided by the selling activity. In spot bid sales, "mailed in" bids are acceptable and awards are made item by item as the sale progresses.

Negotiated Sale. While the majority of surplus personal property is sold by publicly advertising for bids, negotiated sales are authorized in certain limited circumstances, as, for example, where acceptable bids have not been received after public advertising or where the particular disposition is necessary because of public exigency, public health, safety or national security. All negotiated sales of property located in the continental United States with proceeds in excess of $1,000 must be submitted to the appropriate committees of Congress before the contract is made. Negotiated sales may also be used where the disposal will be to States, territories, possessions, political subdivisions thereof, or tax-supported agencies therein

where the estimated fair market value of the property and other satisfactory terms of disposal are obtained by negotiation. States or municipalities who are interested in acquiring specific items of surplus by this method should get in touch with the nearest Defense Surplus Sales Office for assistance. The specific items you desire should be accurately described in detail as much as possible in order that you may be afforded prompt service. States and municipalities can also participate in the competitive bid method of sale (sealed bid, spot bid, and auction) with the general public. However, once surplus property has been cataloged for a competitive bid sale and offered to the public, it is no longer available for negotiated sales.

Retail Sale. Retail sales are conducted at certain military installations that generate property having appeal to the general public. This method of sale offers small quantities of individual items of property at fixed prices based on the current market value. Persons interested should contact the Defense Surplus Sales Office which serves the geographical area in which they are located to find out the nearest military installation that conducts retail sales.

DEFENSE SURPLUS SALES OFFICES

Surplus property of the Department of Defense located in the United States is sold through Defense Surplus Sales Offices located throughout the continental United States. Each Defense Surplus Sales Office (DSSO) is assigned a given number of military installations within a geographical area and is responsible for conducting the sale of surplus personal property held by these installations. This includes preparation of invitations for bid combining related types of property, bid openings, making awards, and concluding all contractual arrangements. The addresses of the DSSO's and their assigned military installations are listed on pages 67–70.

SPECIALIZED DEFENSE SURPLUS SALES OFFICES

The Defense Surplus Sales Office, Tucson, Ariz., conducts sales of all Army, Navy, Air Force, Marine Corps, Defense Supply Agency and U.S. Coast Guard aircraft on a national basis. The Defense Surplus Sales Office, Brooklyn, N.Y., conducts the sale of naval vessels stricken from the Naval Vessel Register on a worldwide basis and all barges, regardless of size, and powerdriven or self-propelled vessels exceeding 40 feet in length within the continental United States. Other vessels are sold by the Sales Offices presently serving the military installations having custody of such vessels. The Defense Surplus Sales Office, Philadelphia, Pa. and the Defense Surplus Sales Office, Pueblo Army Depot, Pueblo, Colo., conduct sales of precious metals such as silver, amalgam, platinum, palladium, and rhodium, including platinum tipped spark plugs. In addition these four Defense Surplus Sales Offices sell other classes of surplus property for the military installations assigned to them. See pages 67-70 for addresses.

PRINCIPAL CONDITIONS OF SALE

Inspection. The condition of surplus property is described as accurately as possible in the invitation for bid or catalog. However, you are urged to inspect property carefully before bidding to satisfy yourself concerning its condition. Department of Defense surplus property is not sold by sample.

Deposits and Payment of Balances. The invitation for bid will specify the amount of deposit (normally 20 percent of bid), if required, and the time by which the balance must be paid. Be sure that your deposit, when required, is adequate to cover your total bid. Deposits and payments may be made in cash, or if authorized by the Invitation For Bid in any form of credit instrument payable to the Treasurer of the United States, including personal checks.

Bid Deposit Bonds. Bid deposit bonds may be used in lieu of a bid deposit, providing the invitation for bid permits their use. Most invitations do permit the use of the bonds but they are not permitted in certain types of sales involving unusual contractual arrangements. Bid deposit bonds afford a convenience to the buyer who intends to bid frequently for the purchase of surplus or foreign excess property. They eliminate the need for handling substantial amounts of money and attendant risks. The types of bid deposit bonds available are: (1) Deposit Bond—Individual Invitation. Sale of Government Personal Property (Standard Form 150) and (2) Deposit Bond—Annual Sale of Government Personal Property (Standard Form 151). These forms, along with instructions for their use, may be obtained from the nearest Defense Surplus Sales Office or from the Defense Surplus Bidders Control Office, The Federal Center, Battle Creek, Mich., 49016.

Deposit Bond—Individual Invitation (SF 150) is required each time a bid is submitted. This type of deposit bond must be executed by an approved surety company listed in Treasury Department Circular 570, "Companies Holding Certificates of Authority as Acceptable Sureties on Federal Bonds and as Acceptable Re-insuring Companies," or by individual sureties each time a bid is submitted. The Deposit Bond—Individual Invitation is then forwarded with the bid to the sales office conducting the sale for approval and acceptance in lieu of the required bid deposit up to the amount specified in the bond.

The Deposit Bond—Annual (SF 151) may be used instead of the bid deposit required by the invitation for bid for any and all bids submitted throughout a fiscal year (from July 1 of the current year through June 30 of the following year). This bond must also be executed by an approved surety company listed in Treasury Department

Circular 570 or by individual sureties. When completed, an original and one executed copy of the bond must be mailed to the Defense Surplus Bidders Control Office, The Federal Center, Battle Creek, Mich., 49016, for approval. Applicants will be notified when the bond has been approved and be given the serial number assigned. All sales offices will be notified of the approved Annual Bid Bond and serial number. Thereafter, in submitting bids, the serial number of the bond may be shown in the space provided for giving the form of the bid deposit. This will be accepted as adequate security provided the penal sum of the bond is sufficient to cover the deposit requirements of the total bid submitted.

Awards. Awards normally are made to the highest responsible and responsive bidder. Awards are not made when the bids received do not represent a fair price to the Government and are not commensurate with the market value of the property offered. In such cases, the property may be reoffered at a later date.

Removal of Property. Property may not be removed from Government premises until full payment is made. Arrangements must be made by the successful bidder to remove the property from Government premises within the time limit prescribed in the invitation for bid.

Withdrawal Policy. The Government reserves the right to withdraw any surplus property from sale when it is determined to be in the best interests of the Government.

SALE OF FOREIGN EXCESS AND EXPORT OF DOMESTIC SURPLUS

The sale of "foreign excess" (defined in the introduction) is conducted under procedures similar to those used for domestic surplus. The sale of foreign excess and the export of domestic surplus into foreign countries must, by law, conform to the foreign policy of the United States. Addresses of overseas sales offices are listed on pages 70-72.

DEFENSE SURPLUS SALES OFFICES AND ASSIGNED MILITARY INSTALLATIONS, CONTINENTAL UNITED STATES

Defense Surplus Sales Office

U.S. Naval Supply Depot, Post Office Box 660, Newport, R.I., 02844. (Sells property located in Maine, New Hampshire, Massachusetts, Rhode Island and Connecticut).

Military Installation	Location
Naval Air Station	Brunswick, Maine
Dow Air Force Base	Bangor, Maine
Loring Air Force Base	Limestone, Maine
Portsmouth Naval Shipyard	Portsmouth, N.H.
Pease Air Force Base	Portsmouth, N.H.
Boston Army Base	Boston, Mass.
Fort Devens	Ayer, Mass.
Springfield Armory	Springfield, Mass.
Watertown Arsenal	Watertown, Mass.

Military Installation	Location
Boston Naval Shipyard	Boston, Mass.
L. G. Hanscom Field	Bedford, Mass.
Otis Air Force Base	Falmouth, Mass.
Westover Air Force Base	Chicopee Falls, Mass.
Boston Procurement District	Boston, Mass.
U.S. Naval Air Station	Quonset Point. R.I.
U.S. Naval Construction Battalion Center	Davisville, R.I.
U.S. Naval Supply Depot	Newport, R.I.
U.S. Naval Submarine Base	New London, Groton, Conn.

Federal Building, 830 Third Avenue, Brooklyn, N.Y. 11232. (Sells property located in New York.)

Military Installation	Location
New York Naval Shipyard	Brooklyn, N.Y.
Fort Tilden	Long Island, N.Y.
Suffolk County Air Force Base	Long Island, N.Y.
Schenectady Army Depot	Schenectady, N.Y.
Seneca Army Depot	Romulus, N.Y.
Watervliet Arsenal	Watervliet, N.Y.
U.S. Army Support Center	Niagara Falls, N.Y.
Camp Drum	Watertown, N.Y.
Griffiss Air Force Base	Rome, N.Y.
Plattsburgh Air Force Base	Plattsburgh, N.Y.
Stewart Air Force Base	Newburgh, N.Y.
U.S. Military Academy	West Point, N.Y.

Philadelphia Naval Shipyard, Building 652, Philadelphia, Pa., 19112. (Sells property located in Pennsylvania, New Jersey, and Delaware.)

Military Installation	Location
Philadelphia Naval Shipyard	Philadelphia, Pa.
U.S. Naval Supply Depot	Philadelphia, Pa.
Frankford Arsenal	Philadelphia, Pa.
Tobyhanna Army Depot	Tobyhanna, Pa.
U.S. Naval Supply Center	Bayonne, N.J.
U.S. Naval Air Station	Lakehurst, N.J.
U.S. Naval Ammo Depot	Earle, N.J.
Fort Dix	Fort Dix, N.J.
Fort Monmouth	Red Bank, N.J.
Picatinny Arsenal	Dover, N.J.
McGuire Air Force Base	Wrightstown, N.J.
Dover Air Force Base	Dover, Del.

Fort Holabird, Baltimore, Md., 21219. (Sells property located in Pennsylvania, District of Columbia, Maryland, and Virginia.)

Military Installation	Location
Marietta Air Force Station	Marietta, Pa.
Letterkenny Army Depot	Chambersburg, Pa.
New Cumberland Army Depot	New Cumberland, Pa.
Defense Depot, Mechanicsburg	Mechanicsburg, Pa.
Harry S. Diamond Laboratory	Washington, D.C.
U.S. Naval Station	Washington, D.C.
Aberdeen Proving Ground	Aberdeen, Md.
Andrews Air Force Base	Brandywine, Md.
Edgewood Arsenal	Edgewood, Md.
U.S. Coast Guard	Baltimore, Md.
Fort George G. Meade	Odenton, Md.
U.S. Naval Academy	Annapolis, Md.
U.S. Naval Air Station	Patuxent River, Md.
U.S. Naval Propellant Plant	Indian Head, Md.
U.S. Naval Training Center	Bainbridge, Md.
Fort Belvoir	Fort Belvoir, Va.
U.S. Marine Corps School	Quantico, Va.

Military Installation	Location
U.S. Marine Corps Air Station	Quantico, Va.
Fort Myer	Arlington, Va.
U.S. Naval Weapons Laboratory	Dahlgren, Va.

U.S. Naval Supply Center, Building SDA-224, South Annex, Norfolk, Va., 23511. (Sells property located in Virginia and North Carolina.)

Military Installation	Location
U.S. Naval Supply Center	Norfolk, Va.
Norfolk Naval Shipyard	Portsmouth, Va.
U.S. Naval Air Station	Norfolk, Va.
U.S. Naval Amphibious Base, Little Creek	Norfolk, Va.
U.S. Naval Weapons Station	Yorktown, Va.
Fort Eustis	Fort Eustis, Va.
Fort Lee	Fort Lee, Va.
Hampton Roads Army Terminal	Norfolk, Va.
Richmond Defense, General Supply Center	Richmond, Va.
Langley Air Force Base	Hampton, Va.
Fort Bragg	Fort Bragg, N.C.
Pope Air Force Base	Fayetteville, N.C.
Seymour Johnson Air Force Base	Goldsboro, N.C.
Camp Lejeune	Camp Lejeune, N.C.
U.S. Marine Corps Air Station	Cherry Point, N.C.

U.S. Naval Air Station, Post Office Box 1261, Yukon Branch, Jacksonville, Fla., 32230. (Sells property located in Alabama and Florida.)

Military Installation	Location
Brookley Air Force Base	Mobile, Ala.
Eglin Air Force Base	Valparaiso, Fla.
Tyndall Air Force Base	Panama City, Fla.
U.S. Naval Air Station	Pensacola, Fla.
U.S. Navy Mine Defense Laboratory	Panama City, Fla.
U.S. Naval Air Station	Jacksonville, Fla.
U.S. Naval Air Station	Cecil Field, Fla.
7th Coast Guard District	Miami, Fla.
U.S. Naval Station	Key West, Fla.
Patrick Air Force Base	Cocoa Beach, Fla.
Orlando Air Force Base	Orlando, Fla.
MacDill Air Force Base	Tampa, Fla.
Homestead Air Force Base	Homestead, Fla.
U.S. Army Aviation Center, Fort Rucker	Ozark, Ala.
Moody Air Force Base	Valdosta, Ga.
Turner Air Force Base	Albany, Ga.
U.S. Naval Air Station	Glynco, Ga.
Marine Corps Supply Center	Albany, Ga.

Atlanta Army Depot, Post Office Box 644, Forest Park, Ga., 30050. (Sells property located in Tennessee, Alabama, Georgia, and South Carolina.)

Military Installation	Location
Sewart Air Force Base	Nashville, Tenn.
Anniston Army Depot	Anniston, Ala.
Redstone Arsenal	Huntsville, Ala.
Maxwell Air Force Base	Montgomery, Ala.
Fort Benning	Columbus, Ga.
Fort Stewart	Hinesville, Ga.
U.S. Naval Ordnance Plant	Macon, Ga.
Hunter Air Force Base	Savannah, Ga.
Robins Air Force Base	Warner Robins, Ga.
Atlanta Army Depot	Forest Park, Ga.
U.S. Naval Air Station, Atlanta	Marietta, Ga.
Dobbins Air Force Base	Marietta, Ga.

Military Installation	Location
Fort Gordon	Augusta, Ga.
Charleston Army Depot	Charleston, S.C.
Naval Supply Center	Charleston, S.C.
Charleston Air Force Base	Charleston, S.C.
Marine Corps Recruit Depot	Parris Island, S.C.
Fort Jackson	Columbia, S.C.
Myrtle Beach Air Force Base	Myrtle Beach, S.C.
Shaw Air Force Base	Sumter, S.C.

Defense Construction, Supply Center, Columbus, Ohio, 43215. (Sells property located in Michigan, Indiana, Ohio, and Kentucky.)

Military installation	Location
Detroit Arsenal	Warren, Mich.
Detroit Procurement District	Detroit, Mich.
Fort Wayne	Detroit, Mich.
U.S. Naval Air Station	Grosse Ile, Mich.
Selfridge Air Force Base	Mount Clemens, Mich.
Wurtsmith Air Force Base	Oscoda, Mich.
Fort Benjamin Harrison	Indianapolis, Ind.
Jefferson Proving Ground	Madison, Ind.
U.S. Naval Ammunition Depot	Crane, Ind.
U.S. Naval Avionics Facility	Indianapolis, Ind.
Bunker Hill Air Force Base	Peru, Ind.
Cleveland Procurement District	Cleveland, Ohio
Defense Construction Supply Center	Columbus, Ohio
Erie Army Depot	Port Clinton, Ohio
Ninth Coast Guard District	Cleveland, Ohio
Lordstown Military Reservation	Warren, Ohio
Defense Electronics Supply Center	Dayton, Ohio
Lockbourne Air Force Base	Columbus, Ohio
Wright-Patterson Air Force Base	Dayton, Ohio
Cincinnati Procurement District	Cincinnati, Ohio
Blue Grass Army Depot	Richmond, Ky.
Fort Campbell	Ft. Campbell, Ky.
Fort Knox	Fort Knox, Ky.
Lexington Army Depot	Lexington, Ky.
U.S. Naval Ordnance Plant	Louisville, Ky.

Rock Island Arsenal, Rock Island, Ill., 61202. (Sells property located in Michigan, Illinois, Wisconsin, and Minnesota.)

Military installation	Location
K. I. Sawyer AFB	Gwinn, Mich.
Kincheloe AFB	Kinross, Mich.
Rock Island Arsenal	Rock Island, Ill.
Savanna Ordnance Depot	Savanna, Ill.
Fort Sheridan	Fort Sheridan, Ill.
Joliet Arsenal	Joliet, Ill.
U.S. Naval Supply Depot	Great Lakes, Ill.
Coast Guard Supply Depot	Great Lakes, Ill.
U.S. Naval Ordnance Plant	Forest Park, Ill.
Chanute AFB	Rantoul, Ill.
Camp McCoy	Sparta, Wis.
Milwaukee Coast Guard Base	Milwaukee, Wis.
Truax Field	Madison, Wis.
U.S. Naval Air Station Twin Cities	Minneapolis, Minn.
Duluth International Airport	Duluth, Minn.

Defense Depot Memphis, Memphis, Tenn., 38115. (Sells property located in Tennessee, Mississippi, Louisiana, Arkansas, Missouri, and Illinois.)

Military Installation	Location
Defense Depot Memphis	Memphis, Tenn.
U.S. Naval Air Station	Memphis, Tenn.
Columbus AFB	Columbus, Miss.

Military Installation	Location
Greenville AFB	Greenville, Miss.
Keesler AFB	Biloxi, Miss.
U.S. Naval Construction Battalion Center	Gulfport, Miss.
8th U.S. Coast Guard District	New Orleans, La.
Barksdale AFB	Shreveport, La.
England AFB	Alexandria, La.
U.S. Army Transp. Terminal Command	New Orleans, La.
Fort Polk	Leesville, La.
U.S. Naval Auxiliary Air Station	New Iberia, La.
Hq. Support Activity	New Orleans, Algiers, La.
Blytheville AFB	Blytheville, Ark.
Little Rock AFB	Jacksonville, Ark.
Fort Chaffee	Ft. Smith, Ark.
Pine Bluff Arsenal	Arsenal, Ark.
St. Louis Procurement Dist., U.S. Army	St. Louis, Mo.
2d U.S. Coast Guard District	St. Louis, Mo.
USAF Aeronautical Chart and Information Center	St. Louis, Mo.
Fort Leonard Wood	Waynesville, Mo.
Scott AFB	Belleville, Ill.
Granite City Army Depot	Granite City, Ill.

Post Office Box 5739, Oklahoma City, Okla., 73110. (Sells property located in Missouri, Oklahoma, Kansas, and Nebraska.)

Military Installation	Location
Lake City Army Ammunition Depot	Independence, Mo.
Richards-Gebaur AFB	Grandview, Mo.
Whiteman AFB	Knob Noster, Mo.
Tinker AFB	Oklahoma City, Okla.
Clinton-Sherman	Foss, Okla.
Altus AFB	Altus, Okla.
Fort Sill	Lawton, Okla.
U.S. Navy Ammunition Depot	McAlester, Okla.
Atchison Army Storage Facility	Atchison, Kan.
Ft. Leavenworth	Leavenworth, Kan.
Ft. Riley	Junction, Kan.
U.S. Naval Air Station	Olathe, Kan.
Forbes AFB	Topeka, Kan.
McConnell AFB	Wichita, Kan.
Schilling AFB	Salina, Kan.
U.S. Naval Ammunition Depot	Hastings, Neb.
Lincoln AFB	Lincoln, Neb.
Offutt AFB	Omaha, Neb.

Fort Worth Army Depot, Post Office Box 6988, Fort Worth, Tex. 76115. (Sells property located in Texas.)

Military Installation	Location
Reese AFB	Lubbock, Tex.
Amarillo AFB	Amarillo, Tex.
Red River Army Depot	Texarkana, Tex.
Sheppard AFB	Wichita Falls, Tex.
Perrin AFB	Sherman, Tex.
Kelly AFB	San Antonio, Tex.
Randolph AFB,	San Antonio, Tex.
Ft. Sam Houston	San Antonio, Tex.
Texas Group Atlantic Reserve Fleet	Orange, Tex.
U.S. Naval Air Station	Corpus Christi, Tex.
Ellington AFB	Houston, Tex.
Bergstrom AFB	Austin, Tex.
Laredo AFB	Laredo, Tex.
Laughlin AFB	Del Rio, Tex.

Military Installation	Location
Ft. Worth Army Depot	Ft. Worth, Tex.
Carswell AFB	Ft. Worth, Tex.
U.S. Naval Auxiliary Air Station	Kingsville, Tex.
U.S. Naval Air Station	Dallas, Tex.
Fort Hood	Killeen, Tex.
Fort Wolters	Mineral Wells, Tex.
Dyess AFB	Abilene, Tex.
Goodfellow AFB	San Angelo, Tex.
James Connally AFB	Waco, Tex.
Webb AFB	Big Spring, Tex.

Pueblo Army Depot, Building 126, Pueblo, Colo., 81004. (Sells property located in North Dakota, South Dakota, Wyoming, Nebraska, Colorado, and New Mexico.)

Military Installation	Location
Grank Forks AFB	Grand Forks, N.D.
Minot AFB	Minot, N.D.
Ellsworth AFB	Rapid City, S.D.
Black Hills Army Depot	Igloo, S.D.
Francis E. Warren AFB	Cheyenne, Wyo.
Sioux Army Depot	Sidney, Neb.
Fitzsimons Army Hospital	Denver, Colo.
Fort Carson	Colorado Springs, Colo.
Lowry AFB	Denver, Colo.
Pueblo Army Depot	Pueblo, Colo.
Rocky Mountain Arsenal	Denver, Colo.
Ft. Wingate Army Depot	Gallup, N. Mex.
Cannon AFB	Clovis, N. Mex.
Kirtland AFB	Albuquerque, N. Mex.

Post Office Box 58, Defense Depot Ogden Station, Ogden, Utah, 84401. (Sells property located in Montana, Idaho, and Utah.)

Military Installation	Location
Glasgow Air Force Base	Glasgow, Mont.
Malmstrom Air Force Base	Great Falls, Mont.
Mountain Home Air Force Base	Mountain Home, Idaho
Hill Air Force Base	Ogden, Utah
Tooele Army Depot	Tooele, Utah
Defense Depot Ogden	Ogden, Utah

Davis-Monthan Air Force Base, Tucson, Ariz., 85708. (Sells property located in Arizona, New Mexico, and Texas.)

Military installation	Location
Davis-Monthan Air Force Base	Tucson, Ariz.
Fort Huachuca	Sierra Vista, Ariz.
Luke Air Force Base	Glendale, Ariz.
U.S. Naval Air Facility	Litchfield Park, Ariz.
Navajo Army Depot	Flagstaff, Ariz.
Williams Air Force Base	Chandler, Ariz.
Holloman Air Force Base	Alamagordo, N. Mex.
Walker Air Force Base	Roswell, N. Mex.
Biggs Air Force Base	El Paso, Tex.
Fort Bliss	El Paso, Tex.

U.S. Naval Supply Center, 937 North Harbor Drive, San Diego, Calif., 92132. (Sells property located in California and Nevada.)

Military installation	Location
U.S. Naval Ordnance Test Station	China Lake, Calif.
U.S. Naval Supply	Long Beach, Calif.
U.S. Naval Air Station North Island	San Diego, Calif.
U.S. Naval Air Station	Point Mugu, Calif.

Military Installation	Location
U.S. Marine Corps Air Station El Toro	Santa Ana, Calif.
U.S. Naval Construction Battalion Center	Port Hueneme, Calif.
U.S. Naval Air Station	San Diego, Calif.
U.S. Naval Supply	San Diego, Calif.
U.S. Naval Weapons Station	Seal Beach, Calif.
Marine Corps Supply center	Barstow, Calif.
Fort Irwin	Barstow, Calif.
Fort MacArthur	San Pedro, Calif.
Camp Pendleton	Oceanside, Calif.
Marine Corps Base	Twenty-Nine Palms, Calif.
Edwards Air Force Base	Edwards, Calif.
George Air Force Base	Victorville, Calif.
March Air Force Base	Riverside, Calif.
Norton Air Force Base	San Bernardino, Calif.
Vandenberg Air Force Base	Lompoc, Calif.
Nellis Air Force Base	Las Vegas, Nev.

U.S. Naval Supply Center, Building 502, Oakland, Calif., 94614. (Sells property located in California and Nevada.)

Military installation	Location
U.S. Naval Air Station	Alameda, Calif.
U.S. Naval Weapons Station	Concord, Calif.
U.S. Naval Air Station	Moffett Field, Calif.
U.S. Naval Supply Center	Oakland, Calif.
Mare Island Naval Shipyard	Vallejo, Calif.
San Francisco Naval Shipyard	San Francisco, Calif.
Beale Air Force Base	Marysville, Calif.
Castle Air Force Base	Merced, Calif.
Hamilton Air Force Base	Ignacio, Calif.
Travis Air Force Base	Fairfield, Calif.
McClellan Air Force Base	Sacramento, Calif.
Fort Ord	Monterey, Calif.
Sacramento Army Depot	Sacramento, Calif.
Sharpe Army Depot	Lathrop, Calif.
Sierra Army Depot	Herlong, Calif.
U.S. Naval Ammunition Depot	Hawthorne, Nev.
Stead Air Force Base	Reno, Nev.

Post Office Box 4050, Seattle, Wash., 98119. (Sells property located in Washington and Oregon.)

Military installation	Location
Fairchild Air Force Base	Spokane, Wash.
U.S. Naval Torpedo Station	Keyport, Wash.
Larson Air Force Base	Moses Lake, Wash.
McChord Air Force Base	Tacoma, Wash.
Fort Lewis	Tacoma, Wash.
13th Coast Guard Dist.	Seattle, Wash.
Paine Field	Everett, Wash.
Puget Sound Naval Shipyard	Bremerton, Wash.
U.S. Naval Supply Depot	Seattle, Wash.
U.S. Naval Air Station, Whidbey Island	Oak Harbor, Wash.
Portland International Airport	Portland, Ore.
Umatilla Army Depot	Hermiston, Ore.

MAILING ADDRESSES OF SELLING ACTIVITIES LOCATED OUTSIDE OF CONTINENTAL UNITED STATES

Alaska:
Redistribution and Marketing Activity
Elmendorf Air Force Base
Anchorage, Alaska
Commanding Officer
U.S. Naval Station
Navy No. 127
c/o Postmaster
Seattle, Wash., 98790

Azores:
Redistribution and Marketing Activity
Lajes Field, Terceira, Azores

Canada:
Crown Assets Disposal Corporation (CADC)
219 Argyle Avenue
Ottawa 2, Ontario, Canada

Commanding Officer
U.S. Naval Station
Navy No. 103, Fleet Post Office
New York, N.Y., 09597

Caribbean Area:
Redistribution and Marketing Activity
Kindley Air Force Base
St. George, Bermuda

Commanding Officer
U.S. Naval Station
Navy No. 138, Fleet Post Office
New York, N.Y., 09587

Property Disposal Office
Antilles Command, USARSO
Fort Buchanan, P.R.

Redistribution and Marketing Activity
Ramey Air Force Base
Aguadilla, Puerto Rico

Commanding Officer
U.S. Naval Station
Navy No. 116 Fleet Post Office
New York, N.Y., 09592

Armed Forces Disposal Center
Fort Amador, Canal Zone

Commanding Officer
U.S. Naval Station
Navy No. 188, Fleet Post Office
New York, N.Y., 09585

Commanding Officer
U.S. Naval Supply Depot
Navy No. 115, Fleet Post Office
New York, N.Y., 09593

Crete:
Redistribution and Marketing Activity
Iraklion Air Station, Iraklion, Crete

England:
USAFE/UK Redistribution & Marketing Center
RAF Station, Molesworth, England

Europe and Middle East:
U.S. Army Property Disposal Detachment, Frankfurt [1]
52 Elbestrasse, Frankfurt/Main, Germany
(or APO 757, New York, N.Y.)

France:
USAFE/France Redistribution & Marketing Center
Toul-Rosieres AB, France

Germany:
USAFE/Germany Redistribution & Marketing Center
Mainz-Kastel, Germany

Greenland:
Royal Greenland Trade Department (RGTD)
Standgade, Copenhagen, Denmark

Greece:
USAF 7206 Support Group
Redistribution and Marketing Activity
Athenai Airport, Athens, Greece

Guam, Mariana Islands:
Commanding Officer
U.S. Naval Supply Depot
Navy No. 926, Fleet Post Office
San Francisco, Calif., 96635

Hawaii:
Commanding Officer
U.S. Naval Supply Center
Navy No. 128, Fleet Post Office
San Francisco, Calif., 96614

Iceland:
Air Forces Iceland
Keflavik Airport, Iceland

Italy:
Redistribution & Marketing Center
Aviano AB, Aviano, Italy
Redistribution and Marketing Activity
Brindisi AS, Brindisi, Italy

Commanding Officer
U.S. Naval Support Activity
Navy No. 510, Fleet Post Office
New York, N.Y., 09578

Japan:
Director of Property Disposal
U.S. Army Depot, Japan
Post Office Box 3
Kamimizo Post Office
Sagamihara-shi
Kanagawa-ken, Japan
(or APO 343, San Francisco, Calif.)

Commanding Officer
U.S. Naval Supply Depot
Navy No. 3923, Fleet Post Office
San Francisco, Calif., 96647

Korea:
U.S. Army Property Disposal Agency, Korea
Seoul, Korea
APO 301, San Francisco, Calif.

Libya:
Redistribution & Marketing
Wheelus AB, Tripoli, Libya

Morocco:
Commanding Officer
U.S. Naval Air Facility
Navy No. 214, Fleet Post Office
New York, N.Y., 09583

Okinawa:
Property Disposal Branch
U.S. Army Supply Services Command
Ft. Buckner, Ryukyu Islands
APO 48, San Francisco, Calif.

Pakistan:
Redistribution and Marketing Activity
Peshawar Air Station, Pakistan

Philippine Islands:
Commanding Officer
U.S. Naval Supply Depot
Navy No. 3002, Fleet Post Office
San Francisco, Calif., 96642

Commanding Officer
U.S. Naval Station
Navy No. 961, Fleet Post Office
San Francisco, Calif., 96639

Spain:
Redistribution and Marketing Activity
Torrejon Air Base
Torrejon De Ardoz, Spain

---

[1] This activity maintains a central bidders list for the designated geographical area.

Spain—Continued
Redistribution and Marketing Activity
Moron Air Base, Moron, Spain

Commanding Officer
U.S. Naval Station
Navy No. 537, Fleet Post Office
New York, N.Y., 09576

Redistribution and Marketing Activity
Zaragoza Air Base, Zaragoza, Spain

Taiwan (Formosa):
Redistribution and Marketing Activity
Taiwan Air Station, Taiwan

Turkey:
Redistribution and Marketing Activity
Headquarters TUSLOG
Ankara, Turkey

Viet Nam:
Property Disposal Office
Logistics Director
Army Section, HQ,MAAG
(APO 143, San Francisco, Calif.)

SURPLUS PROPERTY BIDDERS LIST

The Department of Defense has a single contact point for any person interested in purchasing surplus property from military installations within the continental United States. This contact point, called the Defense Surplus Bidders Control Office, maintains a single "bidders list" for all military departments. The Department of Defense surplus property bidders list is arranged to show each person's buying interests, both geographically and with respect to classes of surplus property.

To have your name included in the list, send the Department of Defense Surplus Property Bidders Application (Parts I and II) at the back of this pamphlet to the Defense Surplus Bidders Control Office, The Federal Center, Battle Creek, Mich., 49016.

To complete Part I of the Department of Defense Surplus Property Bidders Application you should:

1. Fill in the blanks provided for your name, address, city, state and ZIP CODE. The ZIP CODE for your delivery area may be obtained by asking your Letter Carrier or local Post Office.

2. Answer the five inquiries by placing a check mark in the proper blocks.

To complete Part II of the Department of Defense Surplus Property Bidders' Application you should:

1. Refer to the "Classes of Surplus Personal Property Sold By The Department of Defense" described on pages 73 through 80 and select the numbers assigned to the classes of surplus property you are interested in purchasing. For your convenience an index to the classes of surplus personal property sold will be found on page 73.

2. Then, on Part II of the application, write in the numbers of the classes of surplus property (use numbers shown on pages 73 through 80) in

which you are interested in purchasing and the geographical areas (use code numbers shown on page 80) in which you wish to inspect and bid on surplus property. If you desire to purchase any items in Classes 1905A through 1990 (Ships, Small Craft, Pontoons and Floating Docks), please note that there are four geographical areas provided, namely, East of the Mississippi River (including Gulf Ports), West of the Mississippi River, Overseas Only and Worldwide. Note: Since costs of transportation and inspection are borne by the purchaser, care should be taken to restrict the geographical area(s) accordingly.

Remove the completed Department of Defense Surplus Property Bidders Application, Parts I and II, and mail to:

Defense Surplus Bidders Control Office
The Federal Center
Battle Creek, Mich. 49016

Whenever the property in which you have expressed an interest is placed on sale in the geographical areas you designated, you will be sent an invitation for bid. Invitations for bid provide detailed information regarding the terms and conditions of sale, location of the property, its description, condition, quantity, dates it may be inspected, time and date of bid opening, payment and removal of property, and other details.

A list of successful bidders which shows the prices that were acceptable to the Government on the various items awarded is prepared after each sale and is sent to each bidder who submitted a bid in response to the Invitation for Bid. The list is prepared by and is available at the Defense Surplus Sales Office which conducted the sale.

In the interest of economy the Defense Surplus Bidders Control Office continually reviews the record of sales participation of bidders listed on the Department of Defense Surplus Property Bidders List for the purpose of removing the names of those individuals and firms who have not demonstrated an interest in the property offered for sale in catalogs distributed to them. Distribution of sales catalogs represent a significant cost to the Government and must be controlled in this manner.

In addition to invitations for bid which are mailed to potential buyers appearing on the bidders list, notices of sale are posted in public buildings and the mediums of radio, television, trade organizations, newspapers, and periodicals are used to advertise sales.

For information and inclusion on the bidders list for property located in Alaska, Hawaii, and other areas outside the continental United States, contact the appropriate sales office listed on pages 70–72.

CLASSES OF SURPLUS PERSONAL PROPERTY SOLD BY THE DEPARTMENT OF DEFENSE

Index

SCRAP AND WASTE

Class No.

8305A — Textiles including Synthetic Fabric (e.g., canvas, parachutes, etc.).

9450A — Paper (e.g., newsprint, manila cards, etc.).

9450B — Rubber (e.g., tires and tubes all types etc.).

9450C — Miscellaneous (e.g., leather, plastic, fiberglass etc.).

9450D — Exposed Film and Spent Hypo Solution.

9450E — Waste Oil, Jet Fuels, Paints, Chemicals, Waxes and Lubricants.

9450F — Food Waste (e.g., garbage, grease, fat, bones, contaminated foods, etc.).

9670A — Ferrous Metals, Light and Heavy (e.g., cans for detinning purposes, cast iron, wrought iron and steel, black and galvanized, alloy-free turnings, alloy-free production scrap, stripped and unstripped engine blocks, steel shelving, production cuttings, shapes and forms and all industrial shapes and forms). Excludes magnetic and nonmagnetic stainless steels.

9670B — High Temperature Alloys (e.g., nickel-copper, nickel-silicon, nickel-chromium, nickel-chromium-iron, nickel-chromium-cobalt, nickel-molybdenum). Includes magnetic and nonmagnetic stainless steels.

9680A — Nonferrous Metals: Aluminum, Magnesium, Lead, Zinc, Copper, Brass, etc. Includes various types of military aircraft sold for recovery of basic metal content, parts and components (e.g., B-25, B-26, F-80, F-86, F-89, F-100, etc.).

USABLE ITEMS

Weapons

1005 — Guns (small arms) (e.g., hand operated bolt action rifles, 22, 30 caliber, sporting and riot type shot guns and component parts and accessories; bayonets, bayonet-knives, etc.).

Fire Control Equipment

1210 [1] — Fire Control Directors.

1220 [1] — Fire Control Computing Sights and Devices.

1230 [1] — Fire Control Systems, Complete.

1240 [1] — Optical Sighting and Ranging Equipment (e.g., range and height finders, telescopic sights, optical instruments integrated with fire control equipment).

1250 [1] — Fire Control Stabilizing Mechanisms.

1260 [1] — Fire Control Designating and Indicating Equipment.

1265 — Fire Control Transmitting and Receiving Equipment, except Airborne.

1270 [1] — Aircraft Gunnery Fire Control Components.

1280 [1] — Aircraft Bombing Fire Control Components.

1285 [1] — Fire Control Radar Equipment, except Airborne.

1287 [1] — Fire Control Sonar Equipment.

1290 [1] — Miscellaneous Fire Control Equipment.

[1] Certain items in this property category number are required to be demilitarized. Specific information will be given in the invitation for bid when issued.

Ammunition and Explosives

Class No.
1305   Ammunition (commercial types in serviceable condition readily available on the commercial market) (e.g., hardware or sporting goods stores, etc.).
1375 [2]   Explosives (e.g., blasting and demolition materials, smokeless powder, etc.).

Guided Missile Equipment

1450 [1]   Guided Missile Handling and Servicing Equipment (e.g., specially designed trucks and trailers, slings, hoists, jacks, etc.).

Aircraft; and Airframe Structural Components

The Defense Surplus Sales Office, Tucson, Ariz., conducts sales of all Army, Navy, Air Force, Marine Corps, Defense Supply Agency and U.S. Coast Guard aircraft on a national basis. The only types of aircraft that are authorized for sale are commercial type, cargo, and passenger carrying in each of the following property categories numbers 1510A, 1510B, 1510C, and 1520. Military type aircraft must be demilitarized and sold for recovery of basic metal content, parts and components (see property category number 9680A).

1510A   Single Engine Aircraft.
1510B   Twin Engine Aircraft.
1510C   Multi-Engine Aircraft.
1520   Aircraft, Rotary Wing (e.g., helicopters).
1560A   Airframe Structural Components, etc., peculiar to Single Engine Aircraft.
1560B   Airframe Structural Components, etc., peculiar to Multi-Engine Aircraft.
1560C   Airframe Structural Components, etc., peculiar to Helicopters.

Aircraft Components and Accessories

1610   Aircraft Propellers and Component Parts.
1620   Aircraft Landing Gear Components.
1630   Aircraft Wheel and Brake Systems.
1640   Aircraft Auxiliary Fuel Tanks.
1650   Aircraft Hydraulic, Vacuum, and De-icing System Components.
1660   Aircraft Air Conditioning, Heating, and Pressurizing Equipment.
1670 [1]   Parachutes and Aerial Pick Up, Delivery, and Cargo Tie Down Equipment.
1680   Miscellaneous Aircraft Accessories and Components.

Aircraft Launching, Landing, and Ground Handling Equipment

1710   Aircraft Arresting, Barrier, and Barricade Equipment (e.g., shipboard and land based types).
1720 [1]   Aircraft Launching Equipment (e.g., catapults, etc.).
1730   Aircraft Ground Servicing Equipment (e.g., energizers, engine preheaters, mooring assemblies, beaching equipment, passenger loading ramps, maintenance platforms, slings, hoists, airfield specialized lift trucks and trailers, etc.).
1740   Airfield Specialized Trucks and Trailers.

Space Vehicle Equipment

1850 [1]   Space Vehicle Handling and Servicing Equipment (e.g., specially designed trucks and trailers, slings, hoists, jacks, etc.).

---

[1] Certain items in this property category number are required to be demilitarized. Specific information will be given in the invitation for bid when issued.
[2] The purchaser must certify on certain items in this property category that he is a user of, or manufacturer, or processor of, or dealer in the materials and is capable of complying with all applicable Federal, State, and local laws. Specific information will be given in the invitation for bid when issued.

Ships, Small Craft, Pontoons, and Floating Docks

The Defense Surplus Sales Office, Brooklyn, N.Y., conducts the sale of naval vessels stricken from the Naval Vessel Register on a worldwide basis and all barges, regardless of size, and power-driven or self-propelled vessels exceeding 40 feet in length within the continental United States. Other vessels are sold by the Sales Office presently serving the military installations having custody of such vessels.

Class No.
1905A   Aircraft Carriers (for scrapping only).
1905B   Battleships, Cruisers, Destroyers (for scrapping only).
1905C   Landing Ships (e.g., LST, LSM, LSMR, LSSL, etc.).
1950D   Minehunters, Minesweepers, Minelayers.
1905E   Submarines (for scrapping only).
1910   Transport Vessels, Passenger and Troop.
1915   Cargo and Tanker Vessels.
1920   Fishing Vessels.
1925A   Ferry.
1925B   Harbor Utility Craft.
1925C   Repair Ships.
1925D   Tugs (e.g., TTB, YTL, ATA, etc.).
1930A   Fuel Barge, Gasoline Barge, Water Barge.
1930B   Lighters (open and covered).
1935   Barges and Lighters, Special Purpose (e.g., derrick, piledriver, torpedo testing barges, barge-mounted cranes, etc.).
1940A   P.T. Boats.
1940B   Patrol Craft (e.g., PC, PCS, SC, YP, PCE, etc.).
1940C   Seaplane Tenders.
1940D   Small Craft under 40 feet in length powered and non-powered (e.g., lifeboats, rowboats, whaleboats, motor launches, etc.).
1945   Pontoons and Floating Docks (e.g., pontoon ramps, etc.).
1950   Floating Dry Docks.
1955   Dredges.
1990   Miscellaneous (all other vessels and service craft not included in property category numbers 1905A through 1955).

Ship and Marine Equipment

2010   Ship and Boat Propulsion Components (excludes engines and turbines).
2020   Rigging and Rigging Gear.
2030   Deck Machinery.
2040   Marine Hardware and Hull Items (e.g., anchors, hatches, rudders, oars, etc.).
2050   Buoys.
2060   Commercial Fishing Equipment (excludes fishing vessels).
2090   Miscellaneous Ship and Marine Equipment (e.g., sails, marine furniture, ladders, etc.).

Railway Equipment

2210   Locomotives.
2220   Rail Cars (e.g., trailed cars, self-propelled cars, etc.).
2230   Right-Of-Way Construction and Maintenance Equipment, Railroad (e.g., locomotive cranes, snowplows, tamping machines, etc.).
2240   Locomotive and Rail Car Accessories and Components.
2250   Track Materials, Railroad (e.g., rails, frogs, fish plates, etc.).

Motor Vehicles, Trailers, and Cycles

2310A   Passenger Motor Vehicles (e.g., sedans, station wagons, etc.).
2310B   Ambulances and Hearses.
2310C   Buses.

Class No.

2320A Trucks and Truck Tractors (e.g., panel, delivery, and pickup trucks, etc.).
2320B Amphibain Vehicles.
2320C Jeeps.
2330 Trailers (e.g., semitrailers, house trailers, semitrailer dollies, etc.).
2340 Motorcycles, Motor Scooters and Bicycles.
2350 [1] Tanks and Self-Propelled Weapons.

Tractors

2410 Tractors, Full Track, Low Speed (e.g., caterpillar and crawler, etc.).
2420 Tractors, Whelled (e.g., agricultural and industrial wheeled tractors, etc.).
2430 Tractors, Track Laying, High Speed.

Vehicular Equipment Components

2510 Vehicular Cab, Body, and Frame Structural Components (e.g., automobile, trucks and trailer bodies, frames, etc.).
2520 Vehicular Power Transmission Components (e.g., transmissions, clutches, drive shafts, differentials, power takeoffs, hydraulic motors, universal joints, etc.).
2530 Vehicular Brake, Steering, Axle, Wheel, and Track Components (e.g., wheel and brake assemblies, track assemblies steering assemblies, etc.).
2540 Vehicular Furniture and Accessories (e.g., heaters, defrosters, winterization kits, seat assemblies, mirrors, curtains, etc.).
2590 Miscellaneous Vehicular Components (e.g., a-frames, bulldozer blades, crane booms, etc.).

Tires and Tubes

2610 Tires and Tubes, Pneumatic, except Aircraft.
2620 Tires and Tubes, Pneumatic, Aircraft.
2630 Tires, Solid and Cushion (includes rubber track laying treads).
2640 Tire Rebuilding and Tire and Tube Repair Materials (excludes vulcanizing machinery and equipment).

Engines, Turbines and Components

2805 Gasoline Reciprocating Engines, except Aircraft; and components.
2810A Gasoline Reciprocating Engines (Single and In-Line Engines), Aircraft; and Components (e.g., R–1340, Allison, Lycoming, Drone engines, etc.).
2810B Gasoline Reciprocating Engines (Multi-Engines), Aircraft; and Components (e.g., R–2800, R–3350).
2815 Diesel Engines and Components.
2820 Steam Engines, Reciprocating and Components.
2825 Steam Turbines and Components.
2830 Water Turbines and Water Wheels; and Components.
2835 Gas Turbines and Jet Engines, except Aircraft; and Components (e.g., air-borne auxiliary and ground gas turbine power units for aircraft engine starting, etc.).
2840 [1] Gas Turbine and Jet Engines, Aircraft and Components (e.g., turbo-prop and turbo-jet engines, etc.).
2845 [1] Rocket Engines and Components.
2895 Miscellaneous Engines and Components (e.g., wind and compressed air engines).

[1] Certain items in this property category number are required to be demilitarized. Specific information will be given in the invitation for bid when issued.

Engine Accessories

Class No.

2910 Engine Fuel System Components, Nonaircraft (e.g., fuel tanks, lines, filters and pumps, carburetors, etc.).
2915 Engine Fuel System Components, Aircraft (e.g., fuel pumps, filters, controls, valves, etc.; excludes aircraft fuel tanks).
2920 Engine Electrical System Components, Nonaircraft (e.g., generators, spark plugs, coils, distributors, voltage regulators, ignition harness, starters, magnetos).
2925 Engine Electrical System Components, Aircraft.
2930 Engine Cooling System Components, Nonaircraft.
2935 Engine Cooling System Components, Aircraft.
2940 Engine Air and Oil Filters, Strainers, and Cleaners, Nonaircraft.
2945 Engine Air and Oil Filters, Strainers, and Cleaners, Aircraft.
2950 Turbosuperchargers.
2990 Miscellaneous Engine Accessories, Nonaircraft (excludes electrical starters).
2995 Miscellaneous Engine Accessories, Aircraft.

Mechanical Power Transmission Equipment

3010 Torque Converters and Speed Changers.
3020 Gears, Pulleys, Sprockets, and Transmission chain.
3030 Belting, Drive Belts, Fan Belts, and Accessories.
3040 Miscellaneous Power Transmission Equipment.

Bearings

3110 Bearings, Antifriction, Unmounted.
3120 Bearings, Plain, Unmounted.
3130 Bearings, Mounted.

Woodworking Machinery and Equipment

3210 Sawmill and Planing Mill Machinery.
3220 Woodworking Machines (excludes hand held power driven tools).
3230 Tools and Attachments for Woodworking Machinery.

Metalworking Machinery

3411 Boring Machines.
3412 Broaching Machines.
3413 Drilling Machines.
3414 Gear Cutting and Finishing Machines.
3415 Grinding Machines.
3416 Lathes (excludes speed lathes).
3417 Milling Machines.
3418 Planers.
3419 Miscellaneous Machine Tools (e.g., shapers, speed lathes, etc.).
3422 Rolling Mills and Drawing Machines.
3424 Metal Heat Treating Equipment.
3426 Metal Finishing Equipment.
3428 Foundry Equipment and Supplies (excludes crucible furnaces, cupola furnaces and foundry hand tools).
3431 Electric Arc Welding Equipment (excludes welding supplies and associated equipment).
3432 Electric Resistance Welding Equipment.
3433 Gas Welding, Heat Cutting and Metalizing Equipment.
3436 Welding Positioners and Manipulators.
3438 Miscellaneous Welding Equipment.
3439 Miscellaneous Welding, Soldering, and Brazing Supplies and Accessories.
3441 Bending and Forming Machines.
3442 Hydraulic and Pneumatic Presses, Power Driven.
3443 Mechanical Presses, Power Driven (includes forging presses).

Class No.
3444 Manual Presses.
3445 Punching and Shearing Machines.
3446 Forging Machinery and Hammers (excludes forging presses).
3447 Wire and Metal Ribbon Forming Machines.
3448 Riveting Machines (excludes power driven hand riveting machines).
3449 Miscellaneous Secondary Metal Forming and Cutting Machines.
3450 Machine Tools, Portable.
3455 Cutting Tools For Machine Tools (excludes flame cutting tools).
3456 Cutting and Forming Tools For Secondary Metalworking Machinery.
3460 Machine Tool Accessories.
3465 Production Jigs, Fixtures, and Templates.
3470 Machine Shop Sets, Kits, and Outfits.

Service and Trade Equipment

3510 Laundry and Dry Cleaning Equipment.
3520 Shoe Repairing Equipment.
3530 Industrial Sewing Machines and Mobile Textile Repair Shops (excludes shoe sewing machines).
3540 Wrapping and Packaging Machinery.
3550 Vending and Coin Operated Machines.
3590 Miscellaneous Service and Trade Equipment (includes barber chairs, kits, hair clippers and shears, etc.).

Special Industry Machinery

3605 Food Products Machinery and Equipment (excludes kitchen and galley equipment).
3610 Printing, Duplicating, and Bookbinding Equipment.
3615 Pulp and Paper Industries Machinery.
3620 Rubber Working Machinery.
3625 Textile Industries Machinery.
3630 Clay and Concrete Products Industries Machinery.
3635 Glass Industries Machinery.
3640 Tobacco Manufacturing Machinery.
3645 Leather Tanning and Leather Working Industries Machinery.
3650 Chemical and Pharmaceutical Products Manufacturing Machinery.
3655 Gas Generating Equipment (excludes meteorological equipment).
3695 Miscellaneous Special Industry Machinery (includes specialized logging equipment, petroleum refinery machinery, shoemaking machinery, optical goods manufacturing machinery, etc.).

Agricultural Machinery and Equipment

3710 Soil Preparation Equipment (includes planting equipment and cultivating equipment).
3720 Harvesting Equipment.
3730 Dairy, Poultry, and Livestock Equipment.
3740 Pest, Disease, and Frost Control Equipment.
3750 Gardening Implements and Tools.
3760 Animal Drawn Vehicles and Farm Trailers.
3770 Saddlery, Harness, Whips, and Related Animal Furnishings.

Construction, Mining, Excavating, and Highway Maintenance Equipment

3805 Earth Moving and Excavating Equipment.
3810 Cranes and Crane-Shovels (excludes barge-mounted cranes).
3815 Crane and Crane-Shovel Attachments.
3820 Mining, Rock Drilling, Earth Boring, and Related Equipment.
3825 Road Clearing and Cleaning Equipment.

Class No.
3830 Truck and Tractor Attachments (includes equipment for mounting on trucks and tractors, such as bulldozers, augers, blades, snowplows, sweepers, etc.).
3835 Petroleum Production and Distribution Equipment (includes wellheads, pumping equipment and gas distribution equipment).
3895 Miscellaneous Construction Equipment (e.g., asphalt heaters and kettles, concrete mixers, pile drivers, cable laying, lashing, spinning, and reeling equipment, etc.).

Materials Handling Equipment

3910 Conveyors.
3920 Material Handling Equipment, Non-self-Propelled (includes dolly trucks, pushcarts, handcarts, wheelbarrows, hand trucks, and material handling trailers).
3930 Warehouse Trucks and Tractors, Self-Propelled (includes fork lift trucks, straddle trucks, cab, body, and frame structural components and springs, etc.).
3940 Blocks, Tackle, Rigging, and Slings.
3950 Winches, Hoists, Cranes, and Derricks.
3960 Elevators and Escalators.
3990 Miscellaneous Materials Handling Equipment (includes skids and pallets).

Rope, Cable, Chain, and Fittings

4010 Chain and Wire Rope.
4020 Fiber Rope, Cordage, and Twin.
4030 Fittings for Rope, Cable, and Chain.

Refrigeration and Air Conditioning Equipment

4110 Self-Contained Refrigeration Units and Accessories.
4120 Self-Contained Air Conditioning Units and Accessories.
4130 Refrigeration and Air Conditioning Plants and Components.
4140 Fans and Air Circulators, Nonindustrial.

Fire Fighting, Rescue, and Safety Equipment

4210 Fire Fighting Equipment.
4220 Marine Lifesaving and Diving Equipment (excludes lifesaving boats).
4230 Decontaminating and Impregnating Equipment.
4240 Safety and Rescue Equipment.

Pumps and Compressors

4310 Compressors and Vacuum Pumps.
4320 Power and Hand Pumps.
4330 Centrifugals, Separators, and Pressure and Vacuum Filters.

Furnace, Steam Plant, and Drying Equipment

4410 Industrial Boilers.
4420 Heat Exchangers and Steam Condensers.
4430 Industrial Furnaces, Kilns, Lehrs, and Ovens (excludes food industry ovens, metal heat treating and laboratory type furnaces).
4440 Driers, Dehydrators, and Anhydrators.
4450 Industrial Fan and Blower Equipment.
4460 Air Purification Equipment (includes electronic precipitators and dust collectors).

Plumbing, Heating, and Sanitation Equipment

4510 Plumbing Fixtures and Accessories.
4520 Space Heating Equipment and Domestic Water Heaters.
4530 Fuel Burning Equipment Units.
4540 Miscellaneous Plumbing, Heating, and Sanitation Equipment (includes incinerators, destructors, septic tanks and garbage disposal units).

Water Purification and Sewage Treatment Equipment

Class No.

4610 [2] Water Purification Equipment (includes filtration equipment and lifesaving water stills).
4620 [2] Water Distillation Equipment, Marine and Industrial.
4630 Sewage Treatment Equipment.

Pipe, Tubing, Hose, and Fittings

4710 Pipe and Tube (includes metal pipe and tube, rigid pipe and tube of plastic, synthetic rubber, or other nonmetallic material for other than underground, electrical, or laboratory use).
4720 Hose and Tubing, Flexible (includes metallic and nonmetallic flexible hose and tubing, hydraulic, air, chemical, fuel and oil hose assemblies).
4730 Fittings and Specialties: Hose, Pipe, and Tube (includes plumbing fittings and specialties, lubrication fittings, pipe joints, including expansion joints, etc.).

Valves

4810 Valves, Powered.
4820 Valves, Nonpowered.

Maintenance and Repair Shop Equipment

4910 Motor Vehicle Maintenance and Repair Shop Specialized Equipment (excludes hand tools).
4920 Aircraft Maintenance and Repair Shop Specialized Equipment.
4925 Ammunition Maintenance and Repair Shop Specialized Equipment.
4930 Lubrication and Fuel Dispensing Equipment.
4931 Fire Control Maintenance and Repair Shop Specialized Equipment.
4933 Weapons Maintenance and Repair Shop Specialized Equipment.
4935 [1] Guided Missile Maintenance, Repair, and Check-out Specialized Equipment (includes checkout equipment and test equipment specially designed for use with guided missiles and guided remote control systems).
4940 Miscellaneous Maintenance and Repair Shop Specialized Equipment (includes paint spraying equipment).
4960 [1] Space Vehicle Maintenance, Repair, and Check-out Specialized Equipment (includes checkout and test equipment specially designed for use with space vehicles, including remote control systems).

Hand Tools

5110 Hand Tools, Edged, Nonpowered.
5120 Hand Tools, Nonedged, Nonpowered.
5130 Hand Tools, Power Driven.
5133 Drill Bits, Counterbores, and Countersinks: Hand and Machine.
5136 Taps, Dies and Collets: Hand and Machine (excludes punching, stamping, and marking dies).
5140 Tool and Hardware Boxes.
5180 Sets, Kits, and Outfits of Hand Tools.

Measuring Tools

5210 Measuring Tools, Craftsmen's.
5220 Inspection Gages and Precision Layout Tools.
5280 Sets, Kits, and Outfits and Measuring Tools.

[1] Certain items in this property category number are required to be demilitarized. Specific information will be given in the invitation for bid when issued.
[2] The purchaser must certify on certain stills and distilling apparatus in this property category that he will comply with the provisions of the Internal Revenue Code and with regulations issued thereunder. Specific information will be given in the invitation for bid when issued.

Hardware and Abrasives

Class No.

5305 Screws.
5306 Bolts.
5307 Studs.
5310 Nuts and Washers.
5315 Nails, Keys, and Pins.
5320 Rivets.
5325 Fastening Devices.
5330 Packing and Gasket Materials.
5335 Metal Screening.
5340 Miscellaneous Hardware.
5345 Disks and Stones, Abrasive.
5350 Abrasive Materials.
5355 Knobs and Pointers.

Prefabricated Structures and Scaffolding

5410 Prefabricated and Portable Buildings.
5420 Bridges, Fixed and Floating (excludes pontoons and floating docks).
5430 Storage Tanks.
5440 Scaffolding Equipment and Concrete Forms.
5445 Prefabricated Tower Structures.
5450 Miscellaneous Prefabricated Structures (includes bleachers, grandstands, etc.).

Lumber, Millwork, Plywood, and Veneer

5510 Lumber and Related Basic Wood Materials.
5520 Millwork (e.g., door frames, doors, window frames, and window sashes).
5530 Plywood and Veneer.

Construction and Building Materials

5610 Mineral Construction Materials, Bulk.
5620 Building Glass, Tile, Brick, and Block.
5630 Pipe and Conduit, Nonmetallic.
5640 Wallboard, Building Paper, and Thermal Insulation Materials.
5650 Roofing and Siding Materials.
5660 Fencing, Fences, and Gates.
5670 Architectural and Related Metal Products (includes door frames, fixed fire escapes, gratings, staircases, window sash, etc.).
5680 Miscellaneous Construction Materials (includes metal lath, airplane landing mats, traction mats, etc.).

Communication Equipment

5805 Telephone and Telegraph Equipment.
5815 Teletype and Facsimile Equipment.
5820 Radio and Television Communication Equipment, except Airborne (excludes home type radio and television equipment).
5821 Radio and Television Communication Equipment, Airborne.
5825 Radio Navigation Equipment, except Airborne.
5826 Radio Navigation Equipment, Airborne.
5830 Intercommunication and Public Address Systems, except Airborne.
5831 Intercommunication and Public Address Systems, Airborne.
5835 Sound Recording and Reproducing Equipment (excludes phonographs, home type, and dictating machines).
5840 [1] Radar Equipment, except Airborne.
5841 [1] Radar Equipment, Airborne.
5845 [1] Underwater Sound Equipment (includes only communication types of infrared equipment).
5895 Miscellaneous Communication Equipment.

Electrical and Electronic Equipment Components

5905 Resistors.
5910 Capacitors.
5915 Filters and Networks.

Class No.
5920   Fuses and Lightning Arresters.
5925   Circuit Breakers.
5930   Switches.
5935   Connectors, Electrical.
5940   Lugs, Terminals, and Terminal Strips.
5945   Relays, Contactors, and Solenoids.
5950   Coils and Transformers.
5955 [1] Piezoelectric Crystals (includes processed unmounted crystals, etc.).
5960   Electron Tubes, Transistors, and Rectifying Crystals.
5965   Headsets, Handsets, Microphones and Speakers.
5970   Electrical Insulators and Insulating Materials.
5975   Electrical Hardware and Supplies.
5977   Electrical Contact Brushes and Electrodes.
5985   Antennas, Waveguides, and Related Equipment.
5990   Synchros and Resolvers (includes autosyn motors, selsyn generators, synchro receivers, torque amplifiers, etc.).
5995   Cable Cord, and Wire Assemblies: Communication Equipment.
5999   Miscellaneous Electrical and Electronic Components (includes light switches, microwave chokes, permanent magnets, etc.).

Electric Wire, and Power and Distribution Equipment

6105   Motors, Electrical.
6110   Electrical Control Equipment.
6115   Generators and Generator Sets, Electrical.
6120   Transformers: Distribution and Power Station.
6125   Converters, Electrical.
6130   Rectifying Equipment, Electrical.
6135   Batteries, Primary.
6140   Batteries, Secondary.
6145   Wire and Cable, Electrical.
6150   Miscellaneous Electric Power and Distribution Equipment.

Lighting Fixtures and Lamps

6210   Indoor and Outdoor Electric Lighting Fixtures.
6220   Electric Vehicular Lights and Fixtures.
6230   Electric Portable and Hand Lighting Equipment.
6240   Electric Lamps.
6250   Ballasts, Lampholders, and Starters.
6260   Nonelectric Lighting Fixtures.

Alarm and Signal Systems

6310   Traffic and Transit Signal Systems.
6320   Shipboard Alarm and Signal Systems (e.g., motor order indicators, ship's draft indicators, ship's speed indicators, total revolution indicators, etc.).
6330   Railroad Signal and Warning Devices.
6340   Aircraft Alarm and Signal Systems (e.g., aircraft crew warning signals, audible landing gear alarms, oil pressure warning signals, etc.).
6350   Miscellaneous Alarm and Signal Systems (e.g., alarm bells, buzzers, fire alarm switchboards, foghorns, siren alarms, under voltage alarms, etc.).

Medical, Dental, and Veterinary Equipment and Supplies

6505 [4] Drugs, Biologicals, and Official Reagents.
6510   Surgical Dressing Materials.
6515   Medical and Surgical Instruments, Equipment, and Supplies.
6520   Dental Instruments, Equipment, and Supplies.

[1] Certain items in this property category number are required to be demilitarised. Specific information will be given in the invitation for bid when issued.
[4] Certain items in this property category number are sold only to registered manufacturers of narcotic drugs.

Class No.
6525   X-Ray Equipment and Supplies: Medical, Dental, Veterinary.
6530   Hospital Furniture, Equipment, Utensils, and Supplies.
6532   Hospital and Surgical Clothing and Textile Special Purpose Items (e.g., clinic coats, surgical operating coats and trousers, etc.).
6540   Opticians' Instruments, Equipment, and Supplies.
6545   Medical Sets, Kits, and Outfits.

Instruments and Laboratory Equipment

6605   Navigational Instruments (e.g., azimuths, gyro compasses, drift meters, navigational computers, aircraft octants, plotting boards, aircraft sextants, marine sextants, etc.).
6610   Flight Instruments (e.g., airspeed indicators, bank and turn indicators, venturi tubes, etc.).
6615   Automatic Pilot Mechanisms and Airborne Gyro Components.
6620   Engine Instruments (includes all engine instruments, including aircraft, marine, and vehicular; fuel pressure gages, manifold pressure gages, oil pressure gages, fuel mixture indicators, engine oil and fuel warning devices).
6625   Electrical and Electronic Properties Measuring and Testing Instruments (includes all basic types of test instruments designed for communication and electronic equipment, such as ammeters, voltmeters, ohmmeters, multimeters, and similar instruments, etc.).
6630   Chemical Analysis Instruments (e.g., gas analyzers, hydrometers, etc.).
6635   Physical Properties Testing Equipment (e.g., balancing machines, hardness testers, industrial X-Ray machines, magnaflux testing equipment, torque bearing testers, etc.).
6640   Laboratory Equipment and Supplies.
6645   Time Measuring Instruments.
6650   Optical Instruments (e.g., binoculars, microscopes, telescopes, etc.).
6655   Geophysical and Astronomical Instruments (e.g., geodetic, oceanographic, and seismographic instruments, etc.).
6660   Meteorological Instruments and Apparatus (e.g., wind direction and speed detectors, radiosonde sets, meteorological balloons, etc.).
6665   Hazard-Detecting Instruments and Apparatus (e.g., mine detectors, gas detecting equipment, radiac equipment, water testing sets, etc.).
6670   Scales and Balances (e.g., household, industrial, postal and laboratory scales and balances, etc.).
6675   Drafting, Surveying, and Mapping Instruments.
6680   Liquid and Gas Flow, Liquid Level, and Mechanical Motion Measuring Instruments (e.g., electrical counters, engine tachometers, gas and liquid flowmeters, speedometers, etc.).
6685   Pressure, Temperature, and Humidity Measuring and Controlling Instruments (e.g., altimeters, barometers, gages, etc.).
6695   Combination and Miscellaneous Instruments (e.g., recording lie detectors, light-time recorders, meter registers, etc.).

Photographic Equipment

6710   Cameras, Motion Picture.
6720   Cameras, Still Picture.
6730   Photographic Projection Equipment.
6740   Photographic Developing and Finishing Equipment.
6750   Photographic Supplies.
6760   Photographic Equipment and Accessories.
6770   Film, Processed.
6780   Photographic Sets, Kits, and Outfits.

Chemicals and Chemical Products

Class No.

6810 Chemicals (includes nonmedicinal chemical elements and compounds, such as naphtha solvents, acetone, etc.).
6820 Dyes.
6830 Gases: Compressed and Liquefied (e.g., technical nitrogen, oxygen, etc.).
6840 Pest Control Agents and Disinfectants (includes insect repellents, fungicides, insecticides, rodenticides, week killers, etc.).
6850 Miscellaneous Chemical Specialties (e.g., antifogging compound, antifreeze, deicing fluid, etc.).

Training Aids and Devices

6910 Training Aids (e.g., cutaway models, map reading instruction kits, scale models, vehicle training aids, etc.).
6920 [1] Armament Training Devices (e.g., target panels, rifle targets, silhouette targets, etc.).
6930 [1] Operational Training Devices (e.g., link trainers, flight simulators, etc.).
6940 [1] Communication Training Devices (e.g., telephone training aids, electronic circuit trainers, etc.).

Furniture

7105 Household Furniture.
7110 Office Furniture.
7125 Cabinets, Lockers, Bins, and Shelving.
7195 Miscellaneous Furniture and Fixtures (e.g., library furniture, cashiers' stands, theater furniture, etc.).

Household and Commercial Furnishings and Appliances

7210 Household Furnishings (e.g., bed blankets, mattresses, and pillows, etc.).
7220 Floor Coverings.
7230 Draperies, Awnings, and Shades.
7240 Household and Commercial Utility Containers.
7290 Miscellaneous Household and Commercial Furnishings and Appliances.

Food Preparation and Serving Equipment

7310 Food Cooking, Baking, and Warming Equipment.
7320 Kitchen Equipment and Appliances.
7330 Kitchen Hand Tools and Utensils.
7340 Cutlery and Flatware.
7350 Tableware.
7360 Sets, Kits, and Outfits: Food Preparation and Serving.

Office Machines and Data Processing Equipment

7410 Punched Card System Machines (e.g., key punch sorting and tabulating machines, etc.).
7420 Accounting and Calculating Machines.
7430 Typewriters and Office Type Composing Machines.
7440 Automatic Data Processing Systems: Industrial, Scientific, and Office Types (e.g., electronic data counters, digital computers, magnetic tape, etc.).
7450 Office Type Sound Recording and Reproducing Machines (e.g., dictating machines, sound recorders, sound recording tape, transcribing machines, etc.).
7460 Visible Record Equipment (e.g., visible index cabinet files and rotary files, etc.).
7490 Miscellaneous Office Machines (e.g., cash registers, check signing and writing machines, label printing machines, etc.).

[1] Certain items in this property category number are required to be demilitarised. Specific information will be given in the invitation for bid when issued.

Office Supplies and Devices

Class No.

7510 Office Supplies.
7520 Office Devices and Accessories.
7530 Stationery and Record Forms (excludes standard forms approved for Government wide use).

Books, Maps, and Other Publications

7610 Books and Pamphlets.
7640 Maps, Atlases, Charts, and Globes.

Musical Instruments, Phonographs, and Home-Type Radios

7710 Musical Instruments.
7720 Musical Instrument Parts and Accessories.
7730 Phonographs, Radios, and Television Sets: Home Type.
7740 Phonograph Records.

Recreational and Athletic Equipment

7810 Athletic and Sporting Equipment (e.g., basketballs, footballs, boxing gloves, etc.).
7830 Recreational and Gymnastic Equipment.

Cleaning Equipment and Supplies

7910 Floor Polishers and Vacuum Cleaners.
7920 Brooms, Brushes, Mops, and Sponges.
7930 Cleaning and Polishing Compounds and Preparations.

Brushes, Paints, Sealers, and Adhesives

8010 Paints, Dopes, Varnishes, and Related Products.
8020 Paint and Artists' Brushes.
8030 Preservative and Sealing Compounds.
8040 Adhesives.

Containers, Packaging, and Packing Supplies

8105 Bags and Sacks.
8110 Drums and Cans.
8115 Boxes, Cartons, and Crates.
8120 Gas Cylinders (e.g., compressed gas and acetylene cylinders, liquid gas tanks, etc.).
8125 Bottles and Jars.
8130 Reels and Spools.
8135 Packaging and Packing Bulk Materials (e.g., baling wire, waterproof barriers, corrugated and wrapping paper, etc.).
8140 Ammunition Boxes, Packages, and Special Containers (e.g., steel ammunition boxes, etc.).

Textiles, Leather, and Furs

8305B Textile Fabrics (e.g., airplane cloth, burlap, canvas, cotton cloth, elastic webbing, etc.).
8310 Yarn and Thread.
8315 Notions and Apparel Findings.
8320 Padding and Stuffing Materials.
8325 Fur Materials.
8330 Leather.
8335 Shoe Findings and Soling Materials.
8340 Tents and Tarpaulins.
8345 Flags and Pennants.

Clothing and Individual Equipment

8405 Outerwear, Men's (e.g., breeches, rain coats, field jackets, knit caps, overalls, parkas, ponchos, etc.).
8410 Outerwear, Women's (e.g., blouses, rain coats, dresses, etc.).
8415 Clothing, Special Purpose (includes safety, protective, and athletic clothing, etc.).
8420 Underwear and Nightwear, Men's.
8425 Underwear and Nightwear, Women's.
8430 Footwear, Men's.
8435 Footwear, Women's.
8440 Hosiery, Handwear, and Clothing Accessories: Men's.

Class No.	
8445	Hosiery, Handwear, and Clothing Accessories: Women's.
8450	Children's and Infants' Apparel and Accessories.
8460	Luggage.
8465	Individual Equipment (e.g., ammunition belts, intrenching tool carriers, sleeping and duffel bags, flying goggles, sun glasses, etc.).
8475 [1]	Specialized Flight Clothing and Accessories.

Agricultural Supplies

8710	Forage and Feed.
8720	Fertilizers.
8730	Seeds and Nursery Stock.

Live Animals

8820	Live Animals (e.g., horses, mules, and working dogs).

Fuels, Lubricants, Oils, and Waxes

9110	Fuels, Solid.
9120	Fuel Gases.
9130	Liquid Propellants and Fuels, Petroleum Base.
9135	Liquid Propellant Fuels and Oxidizers, Chemical Base.
9140	Fuel Oils.
9150	Oils and Greases: Cutting, Lubricating, and Hydraulic.
9160	Miscellaneous Waxes, Oils, and Fats.

Nonmetallic Fabricated Materials

9310	Paper and Paperboard.
9320	Rubber Fabricated Materials.
9330	Plastics Fabricated Materials.
9340	Glass Fabricated Materials.
9350	Refractories and Fire Surfacing Materials.
9390	Miscellaneous Fabricated Nonmetallic Materials (e.g., asbestos fabricated materials, cork and fibre sheets, etc.).

Nonmetallic Crude Materials

9420	Fibers: Vegetable, Animal, and Synthetic (e.g., nylon and rayon fibers, silk, wool, etc.).
9430	Miscellaneous Crude Animal Products, Inedible (e.g., unprocessed feathers and downs, etc.).
9440	Miscellaneous Crude Agricultural and Forestry Products.

Metal Bars, Sheets, and Shapes

9505	Wire, Nonelectrical, Iron and Steel.
9510	Bars and Rods, Iron and Steel.
9515	Plate, Sheet, and Strip: Iron and Steel.
9520	Structural Shapes, Iron and Steel.
9525	Wire, Nonelectrical, Nonferrous Base Metal.
9530	Bars and Rods, Nonferrous Base Metal.
9535	Plate, Sheet, Strip, and Foil: Nonferrous Base Metal.
9540	Structural Shapes, Nonferrous Base Metal.
9545 [2]	Plate, Sheet, Strip, Foil, and Wire: Precious Metal.

Ores, Minerals, and Their Primary Products

9610	Ores (including basic radioactive materials).
9620	Minerals, Natural and Synthetic.
9630	Additive Metal Materials and Master Alloys.

[1] Certain items in this property category number are required to be demilitarized. Specific information will be given in the invitation for bid when issued.
[2] The Defense Surplus Sales Office, Philadelphia, Pa., and the Defense Surplus Sales Office, Pueblo Army Depot, Pueblo, Colo., conduct sales of precious metals such as silver, amalgam, platinum, palladium, and rhodium, including platinum-tipped spark plugs.

Class No.	
9640	Iron and Steel Primary and Semifinished Products.
9650	Nonferrous Base Metal Refinery and Intermediate Forms.
9660 [2]	Precious Metals, all types (e.g., silver, amalgam platinum, palladium, and rhodium, etc., including platinum tipped spark plugs).

Miscellaneous

9905	Signs, Advertising Displays, and Identification Plates.
9925	Ecclesiastical Equipment, Furnishings, and Supplies.
9930	Memorials: Cemeterial and Mortuary Equipment and Supplies.
9999	Miscellaneous Items (includes only those items which cannot conceivably be classified in any existing property category).

GEOGRAPHICAL AREAS AND ASSIGNED CODES

Alabama	01	Nebraska	28
Arizona	03	Nevada	29
Arkansas	04	New Hampshire	30
California (N) *	05	New Jersey	31
California (S) *	52	New Mexico	32
Colorado	06	New York	33
Connecticut	07	North Carolina	34
Delaware	08	North Dakota	35
District of Columbia	09	Ohio	36
Florida	10	Oklahoma	37
Georgia	11	Oregon	38
Idaho	13	Pennsylvania	39
Illinois	14	Rhode Island	40
Indiana	15	South Carolina	41
Iowa	16	South Dakota	42
Kansas	17	Tennessee	43
Kentucky	18	Texas (N) *	44
Louisiana	19	Texas (S) *	53
Maine	20	Utah	45
Maryland	21	Vermont	46
Massachusetts	22	Virginia	47
Michigan	23	Washington	48
Minnesota	24	West Virginia	49
Mississippi	25	Wisconsin	50
Missouri	26	Wyoming	51
Montana	27	(81–84) **	

*Provision has been made for those bidders desiring to buy surplus property specifically in northern or southern California or northern or southern Texas. California (N) represents that portion of the State above the 36° parallel and California (S) represents that portion below the 36° parallel; Texas (N) represents that portion of the State above the 31° parallel and Texas (S) represents that portion below the 31° parallel. For the purpose of this instruction, an east-west line from the towns of Shoshone to Lucia, Calif., serves as the 36° parallel. An east-west line from the towns of Wiergate to Van Horn, Tex., serves as the 31° parallel. However, bidders who desire to purchase surplus property in the entire States of California or Texas should so indicate by using both code numbers for the northern and southern areas provided for each of these States.

**If you desire to bid on any items in Classes 1905A through 1990 (Ships, Small Craft, Pontoons and Floating Docks), there are four geographical areas provided, namely:

East of the Mississippi River (including Gulf Ports)	81
West of the Mississippi River	82
Overseas Only	83
Worldwide	84

See instructions for using code numbers on page 72.

DEFENSE LOGISTICS SERVICES CENTER
DEPARTMENT OF DEFENSE
SURPLUS PROPERTY BIDDERS APPLICATION

PART I

NAME (Firm or Individual)

_____

(Last)   (First)   (Middle)

ADDRESS _____

_____

CITY_____ STATE_____ ZIP CODE_____

DLSC CONTROL NO._____
                        (Leave Blank)

ADP'S CODE(S)_____

Please answer the inquiries below by placing a check mark in the proper blocks:

1. I am interested in bidding on the following types of sales:
   ☐ Sealed Bid   ☐ Auction
   ☐ Spot Bid   ☐ All Sales

2. I intend to submit bids in surplus sales on the following basis:
   ☐ Regularly   ☐ Occasionally   ☐ One Time

3. I intend to purchase surplus property:
   ☐ For Use   ☐ For Direct Resale
   ☐ For Indirect Resale (for material content or parts to fabricate an item, etc.)

4. Surplus property purchased will be for:
   ☐ Domestic Use   ☐ Foreign Use

5. Type of Buyer:
   ☐ Commercial   ☐ Unit (or Ultimate Con-
   ☐ Institutional   sumer)
   ☐ Industrial   ☐ Professional
   ☐ Governmental

        *   *   *   *
Failure to furnish complete information could delay or preclude placement of your name on the Department of Defense Surplus Property Bidders List.
        *   *   *   *

NOTE: See instructions for completion on page 72.

Explanatory Notes for Basis of Bidding

Regularly—To fall within this classification a bidder bids regularly and would normally bid in *not less* than 20 surplus sales within a year.

Occasionally—To fall within this classification a bidder bids infrequently and would normally bid in *not more* than 19 surplus sales within a year.

One Time—To fall within this classification a bidder bids only to the extent necessary in surplus sales to purchase a specific item(s) and would normally not anticipate a continuing bidding interest thereafter.

Definitions of Types of Buyers

Commercial Buyer—is one who buys in connection with operations in the field of trade and commerce. Examples—retailers, wholesalers, agents, dealers, brokers, etc.

Industrial Buyer—is one who buys in connection with the production or fabrication of goods or services. Examples—mines, farms, fisheries, factories, laundries, hotels, restaurants, banks, etc.

Unit Buyer (or Ultimate Consumer)—is one who buys for family or individual use.

Professional Buyer—is one who buys in connection with the maintenance of a professional service. Examples—doctors, lawyers, accountants, engineers, consultants, etc.

Institutional Buyer—is one who buys in connection with the administration of an institution. Examples—hospitals, schools, etc.

Governmental Buyer—is one who buys in connection with the administration of a government. Examples—towns and cities, counties, states, nations, etc.

DEFENSE LOGISTICS SERVICES CENTER
DEPARTMENT OF DEFENSE
SURPLUS PROPERTY BIDDERS APPLICATION

PART II

I am interested in bidding on the following classes of surplus in the geographical areas indicated.

CLASSES OF SURPLUS (Use Class Numbers Shown)	GEOGRAPHICAL AREAS (Use Code Numbers Shown)

National Aeronautics and Space Administration

INTRODUCTION

The National Aeronautics and Space Administration was established by Act of Congress in 1958 for the following purposes:

1. To conduct research for the solution of problems of flight within and outside the earth's atmosphere, and develop, construct, test, and operate aeronautical and space vehicles.

2. To conduct activities required for the exploration of space with manned and unmanned vehicles.

3. To arrange for the most effective utilization of the scientific and engineering resources of the United States and for the cooperation by the United States with other nations engaged in aeronautical and space activities for peaceful purposes.

4. To provide for the widest practicable and appropriate dissemination of information concerning NASA's activities and their results.

ORGANIZATION

NASA has 10 research centers and 4 additional field offices, and its Headquarters is in Washington, D.C. Among those centers is the Jet Propulsion Laboratory at Pasadena, Calif., which is operated by the California Institute of Technology under a contract with NASA.

A brochure, "Selling to NASA," can be secured from the Small Business Specialist at any one of the procurement offices listed. The brochure briefly describes the various activities of NASA, its procurement organization, the various Field Centers and installations, and some of the programs and projects assigned to the Field Centers. It also contains a brief description of some of the other activities and programs at Headquarters which would be of interest to business concerns such as the availability of scientific and technical publications through the Office of Technical Services and the program to support research originating through unsolicited proposals.

NASA PROCUREMENT REGULATION

NASA's procurement policies and procedures are issued by the Office of Procurement at Headquarters. The NASA Procurement Regulation (NPC–400) contains the procedures for NASA contracting officers and contractors. A copy may be purchased from: The Superintendent of Documents, Government Printing Office, Washington, D.C., 20402.

WHAT NASA BUYS

Each of the research centers purchases laboratory equipment, tools, supplies, and services for use at that center. Also, some contracts are made for construction and maintenance of facilities. However, much of the major construction is contracted by the Corps of Engineers or the Bureau of Yards and Docks.

The largest dollar portion of NASA's contracting is for research and the development of new items such as space vehicles, satellites, electronic components, and tracking equipment. There are very few contracts placed for items in production quantities.

WHERE NASA BUYS

A limited amount of contracting is done at NASA Headquarters. The Headquarters Contracting Division contracts for certain requirements initiated by Headquarters offices and the Supply Branch, Administration Services Division, Office of Administration purchases office supplies and services, furniture and equipment, printing, reproduction, graphic arts services, and Headquarters support items in limited quantities. The main research and development contracts are made at the research centers and field installations. Each center makes the contracts in support of the projects that are assigned to it.

The centers and field offices are as follows:

Ames Research Center
Moffet Field, Calif. Tel: 961–1111

Electronics Research Center
575 Technology Square
Cambridge, Mass. 02139. Tel: 491–1500

Flight Research Center
Box 273
Edwards, Calif. 93523. Tel: CLifford 8–2111

Goddard Space Flight Center
Greenbelt, Md. 20771. Tel: 474–9000

John F. Kennedy Space Center
Cocoa Beach, Fla. 32931. Tel: 783-8008

Jet Propulsion Laboratory
California Institute of Technology
4800 Oak Grove Drive
Pasadena, Calif. 91103. Tel: 354-4321

Langley Research Center
Hampton, Va. 23365. Tel: 722-7961

Lewis Research Center
Cleveland, Ohio. 44135. Tel: 433-4000

Manned Spacecraft Center
Houston, Tex. 77001. Tel: WAlnut 8-2811

Marshall Space Flight Center
Huntsville, Ala. 35812. Tel: 877-1000

Space Nuclear Propulsion Offices:
21000 Brookpark Road
Cleveland, Ohio 44135. Tel: 433-4000

Nuclear Rocket Development Station
Post Office Box 1
Las Vegas, Nev. 89023. Tel: 734-3011

Wallops Station
Wallops Island, Va. 23337. Tel: VA 4-3411

Western Operations Office
150 Pico Boulevard
Santa Monica, Calif. 90406. Tel: 451-7411

Each procurement office maintains its own source list and solicitation of bids or proposals for its procurement requirements are made from the list. In addition, the requirements which are estimated to cost $10,000 or more are published in the Department of Commerce Business Daily.

Those business firms interested in competing for NASA procurement awards should register with each field center or installation by completing the Standard Form 129 and such special commodity or field of interest list which the specific center may issue to cover its own particular needs.

Many of the major programs at NASA are of a nature which require a contractor to have substantial technical and physical resources. This does not, however, preclude smaller companies from participating in the program. In addition to prime contracting, there is a substantial amount of subcontracting opportunities. Subcontractors are selected by the prime contractors and deal directly with them rather than with NASA. NASA publishes, in the Commerce Business Daily, those large requirements which offer subcontracting opportunities. The notice published at the time of the initial solicitation contains a description of the requirement, the names and addresses of those concerns being invited to compete and instructions that those interested in subcontract work in the program contact the invitees directly. This enables the potential subcontractor to contact the prime contract competitors in the early stages of the procurement process. Notices of awards are also published in the Commerce Business Daily to assist those firms interested in subcontract work.

SUBJECTS OF SPECIAL INTEREST

UNSOLICITED RESEARCH PROPOSALS

Any company which has a research idea original in nature and concept, having application to aerospace technology, may submit it to NASA as an unsolicited proposal. This will be evaluated and, if accepted, negotiations will be conducted for a contract. Such proposals should be sent to the Office of Grants and Research Contracts, National Aeronautics and Space Administration, Washington, D.C., 20546.

PATENTS

The National Aeronautics and Space Act of 1958 includes provisions for the disclosure of inventions and the handling of patent applications which differ in some details from the procedure used by other Government departments and agencies. NASA has issued regulations implementing the statutory provisions. To obtain full details of current policies, a request may be made to the Office of the General Counsel, National Aeronautics and Space Administration, Washington, D.C., 20546.

QUALITY CONTROL

NASA requires every practical means of assuring the quality of the items, including subcontract items, purchased for its space program. Copies of the specifications issued for this purpose may be obtained from NASA installations inviting proposals, or from NASA Headquarters, Code KR, Washington, D.C., 20546.

SMALL BUSINESS PROGRAM

NASA has an active small business program. Many procurements are set aside for the sole participation of small business concerns. Each NASA installation, as well as Headquarters, has a small business specialist available to counsel and assist small business companies.

TECHNOLOGY UTILIZATION

Also of interest to small business are the activities of the NASA Office of Technology Utilization.

This office publishes information on innovations and other new technology resulting from NASA's activities in industrially-oriented formats. These consist of a range of documents from one page innovation reports to book length surveys of areas of technology such as Valve Technology, Inorganic Coatings and Micro-electronics.

Information on these publications is sent to addressees on the mailing list of the NASA Technology Utilization Division, Washington, D.C., 20546. They are also for sale by the Government Printing Office and the Department of Commerce Clearinghouse for Scientific and Technical Information.

In early 1962 NASA initiated an experimental regional dissemination center program in order to assist and encourage the widest possible dissemination and utilization of the publications of the Technology Utilization Division and all other NASA generated research results. At that time a pilot program was begun with Midwest Research Institute in Kansas City, Mo. Since that time and based on this early experience NASA has initiated seven other experimental programs at:

	Starting date
Indiana University (Bloomington)	January 1962.
Wayne State University (Detroit)	January 1964.
University of Maryland	April 1964.
University of Pittsburgh	May 1964.
North Carolina Science & Technological Research Center	June 1964.
Southeastern State College, Durant, Okla	February 1964.
University of New Mexico (Albuquerque)	May 1965.

Using all the information gathering and processing tools available within NASA, the centers are able to provide current awareness service, retrospective searching of all material, supplementary information services, and provide the documents or microfilm with the speed and relevance that can best be achieved on a local basis.

While the program is still young, the four computer-equipped centers (Indiana, Wayne State, Pittsburgh, and North Carolina) are enrolling member companies so as to provide industrial financial support for the centers. To date they have enrolled approximately 90 companies which pay from $1,500 to $5,000 annually depending on the size of the company and the extent to which they intend to use the center.

Department of Commerce

provides ready access to the reports and publications of the Department and direct assistance to business on its domestic and foreign business programs.

Among services available at a Field Office are: Assistance on every phase of entering or expanding an export business; counseling on domestic marketing potentials and current business trends; leads on specific opportunities for selling goods and services both domestic and overseas; guidance in keeping up with new technology; sale of all U.S. Government publications useful to business; and help in obtaining information on Government policies and regulations affecting domestic or international business.

GENERAL

The Department of Commerce, under its statutory mandate, is directed "to foster, promote, and develop the foreign and domestic commerce of the United States." Its business activities are planned and directed to the interests of all business—small, medium, and large. The services and functions of the Department are of concern to small businesses, and are planned and executed with their interests in mind.

This Department's procurement procedures are conducted pursuant to the Federal Procurement Regulations as issued by the General Services Administration. The Department has designated an official who serves as liaison officer with the Small Business Administration in implementing procurement policies with reference to small business concerns.

OFFICE OF FIELD SERVICES

An essential part of trade development and service to small business is rendered on a local basis by the Office of Field Services. Operating through 42 field offices located in commercial and industrial centers in the United States, this organization

LIST OF FIELD OFFICES

Albuquerque, N. Mex. 87101
U.S. Courthouse
William E. Dwyer
Director
Area Code: 505 247-0311
Anchorage, Alaska 99501
306 Loussac-Sogn Building
Clyde S. Courtnage, Director
Area Code: 907 272-6331
Atlanta, Ga. 30303
4th Floor, Home Savings Building
75 Forsyth Street NW.
Daniel M. Paul, Director
Area Code: 404 526-6000
305 U.S. Customhouse
Gay and Lombard Streets
Carroll F. Hopkins, Director
Area Code: 301 Plaza 2-8460
Birmingham, Ala. 35205
Suite 200-201
908 South 20th Street
Gayle C. Shelton, Jr., Director
Area Code: 205 325-3327
Boston, Mass. 02110
Room 230, 80 Federal Street
Paul G. Carney, Director
Area Code: 617 CA 3-2312
Buffalo, N.Y. 14203
504 Federal Building
117 Ellicott Street
Robert F. Magee, Director
Area Code: 716 842-3208

Charleston, S. C. 29403
Federal Building, Suite 631
334 Meeting Street
Paul Quattlebaum, Jr., Director
Area Code: 803 747-4171
Charleston, W. Va. 25301
3002 New Federal Office Building
500 Quarrier Street
J. Raymond DePaulo, Director
Area Code: 304 343-6196
Cheyenne, Wyo. 82001
6022 Federal Building
2120 Capitol Avenue
Joseph D. Davis, Director
Area Code: 307 634-5920
Chicago, Ill. 60604
1486 New Federal Building
219 South Dearborn Street
Anthony J. Buchar, Director
Area Code: 312 828-4400
Cincinnati, Ohio 45202
8028 Federal Office Building
550 Main Street
Robert M. Luckey, Director
Area Code: 513 684-2944
Cleveland, Ohio 44101
4th Floor, Federal Reserve Bank Building
East 6th Street and Superior Avenue
Charles B. Stebbins, Director
Area Code: 216 241-7900

Baltimore, Md. 21202

85

Dallas, Tex. 75202
Room 1200, 1114 Commerce Street
Harry C. Meyers, Director
Area Code: 214
RIverside 9-3287

Denver, Colo. 80202
16407 Federal Building
20th and Stout Streets
Charles E. Brokaw, Director
Area Code: 303
297-3246

Des Moines, Iowa 50309
1216 Paramount Building
509 Grand Avenue
Raymond E. Eveland, Director
Area Code: 515
284-4222

Detroit, Mich. 48226
445 Federal Building
Frank A. Alter, Director
Area Code: 313
226-6088

Greensboro, N.C. 27402
412 U.S. Post Office Building
Joel B. New, Director
Area Code: 919
275-9111

Hartford, Conn. 06103
18 Asylum Street
James E. Kelley, Director
Area Code: 203
244-3530

Honolulu, Hawaii 96813
202 International Savings Building
1022 Bethel Street
H. Tucker Gratz, Director
Tel: 588977

Houston, Tex. 77002
5102 Federal Building
515 Rusk Avenue
Edward Fecteau, Director
Area Code: 713
228-0611

Jacksonville, Fla. 32202
512 Greenleaf Building
208 Laura Street
William Bruce Curry, Director
Area Code: 904 354-7111

Kansas City, Mo. 64106
Room 2011, 911 Walnut Street
Nathan L. Stein, Director
Area Code: 816
FR 4-3141

Los Angeles, Calif. 90015
Room 450, Western Pacific Building
1031 South Broadway
Stanley K. Crook, Director
Area Code: 213
688-2833

Memphis, Tenn. 38103
345 Federal Office Building
167 North Main Street
John M. Fowler, Director
Area Code: 901
534-3214

Miami, Fla. 33130
928 Federal Office Building
51 Southwest First Avenue
Marion A. Leonard, Director
Area Code: 305
350-5267

Milwaukee, Wis. 53203
Straus Building
238 West Wisconsin Avenue
David F. Howe, Director
Area Code: 414
BR 2-8600

Minneapolis, Minn. 55401
306 Federal Building
110 South Fourth Street
Ernest G. Booth, Director
Area Code: 612
334-2133

New Orleans, La. 70130
909 Federal Office Building, South
610 South Street
Edwin A. Leland, Jr., Director
Area Code: 504
527-6546

New York, N.Y. 10001
61st Floor, Empire State Building
350 Fifth Avenue
Arthur C. Rutzen, Director
Area Code: 212
LOngacre 3-3377

Philadelphia, Pa. 19107
Jefferson Building
1015 Chestnut Street
David Jamieson, Director
Area Code: 215
597-2850

Phoenix, Ariz. 85025
New Federal Building
230 North First Avenue
Donald W. Fry, Director
Area Code: 602
261-3285

Pittsburgh, Pa. 15222
2201 Federal Building
1000 Liberty Avenue
John Donley, Director
Area Code: 412 644-2850

Portland, Oreg. 97204
217 Old U.S. Courthouse
520 Southwest Morrison Street
James W. Goodsell, Director
Area Code: 503
226-3361

Reno, Nev. 89502
2028 Federal Building
300 Booth Street
Jack M. Howell, Director
Area Code: 702
784-5203

Richmond, Va. 23240
2105 Federal Building
400 North 8th Street
William S. Parker, Director
Area Code: 703
649-3611

St. Louis, Mo. 63103
2511 Federal Building
1520 Market Street
Alfred L. Rascher, Jr., Director
Area Code: 314
MA 2-4243

Salt Lake City, Utah 84111
3235 Federal Building
125 South State Street
Stephen P. Smoot, Director
Area Code: 801
524-5116

San Francisco, Calif. 94102
Federal Building, Box 36013
450 Golden Gate Avenue
Philip M. Creighton, Director
Area Code: 415
556-5864

Santurce, P.R. 00907
Room 628, 605 Condado Avenue
James W. Shoaf, Director
Tel: 723-4640

Savannah, Ga. 31402
235 U.S. Courthouse and Post Office Building
125-29 Bull Street
James W. McIntyre, Director
Area Code: 912
232-4321

Seattle, Wash. 98104
809 Federal Office Building
909 First Avenue
William H. Flood, Director
Area Code: 206
583-5615

BUSINESS AND DEFENSE SERVICES ADMINISTRATION

BDSA is concerned with the advancement of business and with improvement in profits, productivity and employment. Its services are available to business of all sizes, and many of them are especially helpful to small business. The Small Business Administration calls on BDSA to aid in counseling small business firms.

BDSA industry and commodity specialists deal with more than 424 industries, concentrating on such areas as production, marketing, technological changes and the outlook for each in the United States and abroad. They provide business and industry with analyses and data which few businessmen could effectively gather for themselves and which are essential to sound business planning and growth.

The 26 industry divisions of BDSA are equipped to assist the businessman, large or small, with problems of foreign or domestic trade. Assistance may be obtained by mail or by a personal visit to the Department or any of the 42 Commerce Department regional field offices.

The BDSA industry divisions are grouped in the following offices:

Office of Chemicals and Consumer Products
Office of Construction and Materials Industries
Office of Industrial Equipment
Office of Marketing and Services
Offices of Metals and Minerals
Office of Scientific and Technical Equipment
Office of Textiles

BDSA major publications include the annual U.S. Industrial Outlook, which analyzes past trends in industry, reviews major problems and projects levels of output, and eight industry periodicals.

GOVERNMENT-BUSINESS RELATIONS

BDSA represents the Secretary of Commerce in a continuous interchange of ideas between business and Government so that each is fully informed of the policies, views, objectives, programs and problems of the other as they affect national economic growth.

The agency analyzes and assesses the impact of imports on U.S. industry in the development of U.S. commercial policy, and provides advice on international business opportunities, tariff questions, commodity problems, and market prospects abroad.

BDSA also administers the Defense Materials System of priorities to expedite military, atomic, and space programs. It reviews stockpile requirements and studies the effects of stockpile aquisitions and disposal on industry.

TRADE ASSOCIATIONS LIAISON

The Department has encouraged the growth of trade associations, professional societies and chambers of commerce for the past 52 years. The BDSA Trade Associations Liaison Staff is the Department center for information on trade associations and other nonprofit groups. It also can direct a member of any of these organizations to the industry division specializing in his business.

CLEARINGHOUSE FOR TECHNICAL SERVICES

The Clearinghouse for Federal Scientific and Technical Information (formerly the Office of Technical Services) supplies the industrial and technical communities with unclassified information about Government-generated science and technology in defense, space, atomic energy, and other national programs. It makes readily available at low cost, research reports which may aid in the development of a new product, solve a processing problem, or increase productivity through technical improvement. It also furnishes information on research in progress and provides referral to specialized technical information centers for data on specific engineering problems.

In February 1964, the White House announced that the Federal Council for Science and Technology had recommended that the U.S. Department of Commerce expand its "Clearinghouse" function, building upon the existing information services of the Office of Technical Services. Subsequently, the Clearinghouse for Federal Scientific and Technical Information was established. It is located in Springfield, Va.

The fiscal year 1966 program for the Clearinghouse anticipates the availability and dissemination of 64,000 documents covering new scientific and industrial research developments. Some

39,000 of these reports are from U.S. sources and 25,000 from foreign sources.

BUREAU OF INTERNATIONAL COMMERCE

The Bureau of International Commerce (BIC) of the U.S. Department of Commerce is concerned with export promotion and with assisting U.S. business in all its operations toward that objective. In providing this help, BIC makes no distinction between small and big business but, in practice, all BIC services to promote sales of American products abroad are especially useful to smaller U.S. firms.

With its many publications—starting with the weekly magazine, International Commerce—to provide detailed information on specific markets abroad and how to sell to them, and with its variety of low-cost marketing aids, BIC offers a complete "how to do it" package of particular use to smaller companies which cannot afford complete export promotion departments of their own.

BIC's overseas promotion programs, including trade centers, trade missions, and trade fairs, give all American firms opportunities to introduce their products abroad at a small cost. Consequently, these programs are especially popular with smaller companies.

BIC's commercial intelligence program is a marketing information service providing reports on overseas trade outlets—agents, distributors, licensees, buyers, and suppliers. They include:

Trade lists—names and addresses of selected groups of foreign firms, grouped by commodity, industry, or type of product. U.S. companies can locate agents by corresponding with firms on these lists.

World Trade Directory reports—comprehensive digests describing the operation of individual firms including experience, sales competence, financial resources, and names of their trade connections.

Agency Index Service—a register of foreign agents of U.S. firms to be found in each Foreign Service post of the United States including names of local firms in each area which handle U.S. products.

Other commercial intelligence services include market report circulation, assistance in adjusting trade complaints, and identifying and assisting U.S. businessmen who travel abroad.

BIC publications provide timely coverage of foreign market developments and techniques of overseas selling. Publications include "Overseas Business Reports," comprehensive studies of specific country markets, and how-to-get-started handbooks such as "What You Should Know About Exporting." In addition the Small Business Administration, which cooperates with BIC especially in assisting smaller firms to plan and carry out export expansion activities, provides a useful handbook, "Export Marketing for Smaller Firms."

NATIONAL EXPORT EXPANSION COUNCIL

The National Export Expansion Council (NEEC) and the 42 Regional Export Expansion Councils (REEC) encourage and assist small business in the export field. This is done by means of conferences, workshops, and individual counseling to seminars, give instruction in export operations. In cooperation with the Commerce Department Field Offices, these educational activities are often cosponsored by universities and business organizations.

The Commerce Department and the Small Business Administration are engaged in a joint program to encourage small business participation in export trade. In support of the program, SBA will expand its series of cosponsored business opportunity conferences to cover exporting subjects, and will include these same subjects in its management courses.

TRADE CENTERS

U.S. Trade Centers—permanent overseas merchandise marts for American products—are in Frankfurt, London, Bangkok, Milan, Tokyo, and Stockholm. Through Bureau of International Commerce sponsored shows, a U.S. firm can test a selected market where the demand for U.S. goods is combined with dollar resources. The first Center opened in London on June 26, 1961.

A Trade Center show is undertaken only after market research indicates profitable sales in the area for a specific product line. Each show is preceded by a promotional campaign to attract the largest possible number of buyers, agents, and distributors.

These displays are designed to assist small firms in entering new markets overseas. Of 3,532 exhibitors in Trade Center shows from June 1961 through June 1965, 1,907 were small firms. Manufacturers interested in more details may contact the Bureau of International Commerce, U.S. Department of Commerce, Washington, D.C.

TRADE MISSIONS

Trade Missions are sent to promising markets overseas. Each Mission consists of five or six volunteer businessmen accompanied by two Department of Commerce trade specialists. These missions carry specific trade and investment proposals to international markets. The Trade Mission program was established in November, 1954. Through November 1965, 165 trade missions, including 29 industry-organized, Government-approved missions were sent abroad. They carried 18,000 business proposals from U.S. industry to oversea businessmen and returned with 26,000 new trade and investment opportunities.

Any U.S. firm may submit Business Proposals for any or all U.S. Trade Missions.

TRADE FAIRS

U.S. commercial exhibitions are staged overseas at major international trade fairs to sell American goods in the world's leading markets. This commercial program was inaugurated by the Bureau of International Commerce in 1963.

The cost of participating in U.S. Commercial Exhibitions is nominal and includes exhibit space and a share of the cost of the market surveys and the advertising campaign which precedes the exhibition.

Many companies that have participated in the BIC trade fairs program never before had exported their products. These companies made their first oversea sales at U.S. Exhibitions.

The Commerce Department also conducts exhibitions behind the Iron Curtain and in the developing nations on behalf of the U.S. Information Agency to tell the story of American free enterprise and to introduce U.S. products into areas that can be expected to become markets in the future.

OFFICE OF BUSINESS ECONOMICS

This Office creates measures of the functioning of the economy, such as gross national product (GNP) and the balance of international payments, and engages in economic research and analysis. Using its material on the amount of personal income received in each State, OBE produces regional studies down to the county level. Its monthly publication Survey of Current Business makes available a broad range of economic intelligence, including the latest data on production, prices, and shipments in a variety of industries. A biennial Business Statistics volume supplements the magazine, furnishing historical and explanatory material. OBE publications are made available to small business throughout the Department's field offices.

ECONOMIC DEVELOPMENT ADMINISTRATION

Through EDA, the Federal Government, in cooperation with the States and local communities, helps business enterprises get started and existing firms expand in areas of high unemployment or low family income.

Loans are made for the purchase of land, buildings, machinery, and equipment. The amount of the loan is limited to 65 percent of the total cost. There are no top or bottom limits to the size of an EDA industrial or commercial loan.

EDA also can guarantee up to 90 percent of related working capital loans made by private lending institutions.

EDA also makes loans and grants to depressed communities for public works which will promote industrial development, and can provide technical assistance to help solve economic problems.

Goal of the EDA program is to enable depressed communities to stabilize and diversify their economies and create new job opportunities.

This is done by promoting successful and sustained industrial and commercial growth. The resulting projects help make a community capable of supporting additional people and thus able to make the most of its natural and human resources.

Financial assistance under the EDA program is available to high unemployment urban areas, rural areas with low family income, certain Indian reservations and Indian-owned land areas, and those areas which have lost, or are about to lose, their major source of employment.

Economic development districts, containing two or more redevelopment areas, also are authorized so that projects of broader geographical significance may be planned and carried out.

The Secretary also can approve multi-State economic development regions, and encourages the States involved to form regional planning commissions to promote economic development.

UNITED STATES TRAVEL SERVICE

Established in June 1961, the USTS serves the travel industry by encouraging tourism to the U.S.A. Operating through 11 oversea posts located in strategic areas, USTS disseminates, through advertising media and personal contact, promotional materials for the stimulation of additional tourism to the U.S.A. It directly serves the travel industry by working with other Federal agencies for the reduction of unnecessary barriers to travel and by working with State and local community groups in the development of "host facilities." USTS program calls for the development of a travel statistics program for general use throughout the industry.

ENVIRONMENTAL SCIENCE SERVICES ADMINISTRATION—WEATHER BUREAU

WEATHER WISE IN BUSINESS

In recent years businessmen have been discovering new ways to use weather information to their advantage: To improve efficiency, to increase profits, and to reduce losses imposed by weather changes or hazards.

Many of man's economic endeavors are exposed directly to the weather and its changes. Agriculture, outdoor construction, river dependent industries and transportation are major examples, while innumerable small businessmen operate under conditions where goods or services are affected directly by climate and weather.

Considerable money and ingenuity is devoted to the problems of "Engineering around the Weather." We have houses, automobiles, offices, and even baseball fields which protect us from rain, snow, and wind and which are heated or cooled for our peak comfort and efficiency. Refrigeration, air conditioning, insulating, and waterproofing are all examples of thriving new industries which have emerged as a result of man's attempts to control his weather.

Weather determines the clothes we wear, the kinds of houses we build, the food we eat, the kinds of recreation we enjoy. It also affects business indirectly in such factors as labor, sources of supply, and consumer attitudes.

With these economic considerations in mind the alert businessman is going to keep his weather eye peeled to seek the best information he can get from the professional sources available to him. Most of the public weather services of the U.S. Weather Bureau can be applied to the needs of business, but some industries are finding it profitable to seek specialized operational guidance from qualified private meteorologists. These private weathermen serve in either a staff or consulting capacity to correlate weather conditions to a single industry's planning or operational procedures.

No attempt will be made here to provide fixed rules or policies which will fit any situation. Specific answers can come only from analysis of particular problems in individual businesses. This article is intended only to furnish guidelines on the types and the uses of meteorological information available.

The weatherman today is in a better position than ever before to help the businessman take advantage of the weather—to use it as a valuable ally and lessen its threat as an enemy. Many of the tremendous scientific and technological developments of recent years have been adapted to meteorological uses and have helped advance the accuracy of weather forecasting.

Observations and Daily Forecasts. Today the Weather Bureau receives reports from a network of over 700 hourly reporting stations forming a grid network across the nation. In addition, thousands of daily observations of temperature and precipitation are made by contract observers and cooperative observers.

These accurate, on-the-spot observations are incorporated with a vast input of other meteorological data, including upper air soundings, to derive the 24- to 48-hour forecast which is issued every day, usually every 6 hours. These daily short-range predictions are broadcast over radio and TV and used by the local newspaper and on the telephone weather dialing system.

Keeping abreast of the daily forecasts is most important. Conditions can change abruptly, and the weatherman includes these changes in the earliest possible report. For greatest validity the weather-conscious businessman should check the updated sources of radio or telephone reports for new information. In many cities a teletypewriter machine connected to the Public Service Weather circuit can be installed for a nominal fee in your office for immediate reference. In this case you must lease a teletypewriter machine from the local telephone company and furnish the necessary paper.

The Federal Aviation Agency also broadcasts twice-hourly weather reports in cooperation with the Weather Bureau over a special radio frequency at local airport stations. These reports cannot be received on regular AM–FM receivers, but special equipment can be purchased to monitor them on the 200 to 415 kilocycle band, or between 108 and 118 megacycle short wave band. Information on the proper frequency for a particular locality can be obtained from the FAA who operate the equipment.

Five-Day Extended Forecasts. The second type of general forecast is the 5-day extended forecast issued by the Weather Bureau every Monday, Wednesday, and Friday morning. These are less specific and detailed than the 24-hour forecasts. Predictions are made in terms of variations above and below normal conditions, primarily for temperatures and precipitation.

They offer an extended look at the weather to permit long-range planning and to allow provisions for unexpected fluctuations in production, sales and service demands. It must be recognized that they have lower validity than the short-range forecast and provide an entirely different range of usefulness. The 5-day extended forecasts are also disseminated by all media including the Public Service Weather teletypewriter circuit.

Thirty-Day Outlook. The third general type of forecast is the long-range 30-day outlook. This overview of the weather is published on or about the 15th and 30th of the month by the Weather Bureau's Extended Forecast Division in Washington, D.C. They offer supplementary resumés of the previous 30-day period, climatological charts, and maps.

The 30-day outlook is not a specific forecast, but an outlook of expected trends over a prolonged period for the larger geographical segments of the country. Like the 5-day forecast it indicates expected fluctuations above or below normal for the time of the year and the section of the country and does not deal with conditions that might exist in a given spot at a given time. Many newspapers and magazines throughout the country publish both the maps and text of the 30-day outlook, or "Average Monthly Weather Outlook," as it is officially titled. Copies may be purchased on a subscription basis from the Superintendent of Documents, Government Printing Office, Washington, D.C.

Special Forecasts. In addition to the general forecasts issued by the Weather Bureau, special forecasts are issued as needed, such as severe weather forecasts, hurricane and tornado advisories and warnings, flood forecasts, and extreme low or freezing temperature forecasts.

Storm warnings and severe weather advisories can yield untold savings if properly heeded. If you are in a coastal area which could be swept by a hurricane, in a low-lying area that could be subject to flooding, or in a zone of high tornado frequency, you should be constantly alert to the potential dangers. Be in a position to get all the up-to-the-minute storm warnings and advisories. For any one location their occurrence can be considered rare, but a history of past hurricane and flood damage is available to point out locations which are particularly susceptible.

Climatological Records. Weather data in the categories of both day-to-day conditions and cumulative conditions over long periods of time are called climatology and are important aids for the weatherwise businessman. The Environmental Data Service—a major component of the Environmental Science Services Administration—has the responsibility for operating the National Weather Records Center, the world's largest centralized climatological archive, located at Asheville, N.C. This is the central repository for all weather data obtained by Government agencies, and every effort has been made to insure that some copy of every meteorological record collected in the United States and its possessions is stored there.

The National Weather Records Center checks and prepares observations for publications and provides, at cost, copies of original records, hand and machine tabulations, chart and map analyses, relationship studies, etc.,[1] to the general public, industry, agriculture, and to other Government agencies. These records form the basis for research into seasonal, annual, and perennial weather cycles and changes, and the statistical analyses of them has formed the basis for many of today's forecasting techniques.

Using Weather Information. The use of weather information by industry and business must be fitted to both the needs of the businessman and the realistic capabilities of the weatherman. Figure 1 is presented to show the general relationship between time scales, meteorological tools, and the typical related problems.

For the best use of weather information to obtain greater profits or greater savings a systematic approach is advisable. The following steps will be useful in establishing a procedure:

Define the problem.

Delineate types of action which can be taken for economic gain.

---

[1] For more extensive listing see Key to Meteorological Records, Documentation No. 4.11. Selective Guide to Published Climatic Data Sources Prepared by U.S. Weather Bureau, 1963.

Select the type of information needed.
Establish a routine procedure for getting the information.
Use the information in a systematic way.

TIME SCALES & TOOLS FOR WEATHER-RELATED DECISIONS

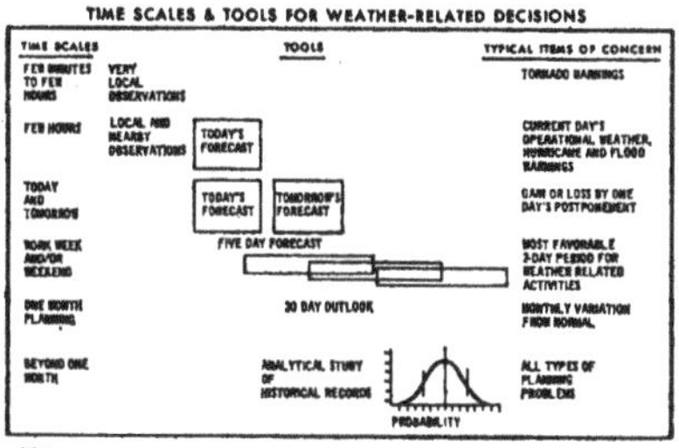

FIG. 1

If the operational decision is a renewable one needing attention at the same time each morning, and affecting only that one day's operation, use current observations plus the early morning forecast of that day's expected weather.

If an activity requires less than one full day of outdoor exposure and can be postponed, use both today's and tomorrow's forecast to make the best choice.

If the timing of a 2-day workload such as hay harvesting is the problem, use a forecast which gives general long range anomalies. Do not expect the same precision in timing that characterizes today's forecast.

Climatological records of past weather furnish a gold mine of information applicable to many types of long range planning problems. Even procedures designed to give guidance in short range decisions can be tested on historical records.

The relationship between weather and the marketing of either goods or services may not always be clear cut, but a review of past business records may provide a clue to its importance. The following hypothetical questions offer some idea of the broad range of this relationship:

How much does your own and/or your customers' fuel consumption increase as the temperatures go down?

What percentage of the car parking spaces were filled in the shopping center parking lot on 10 snowy days as compared with 10 clear, dry days?

What weather conditions do we need to divert sales clerk personnel to in-store rearrangement of displays?

Was the 100 percent sales increase of a particular insecticide in a 10 day period tied to a particular weather sequence?

Approximately how many extra thousand room air-conditioners were sold last month in city X due to the extra heat on 5 very hot days?

Are the dollars spent on snow removal more closely related to the hours of snow-fall duration or snow-fall amounts?

If the need is for a specific past record which is already published the local library may already have such information or a copy can be obtained by purchase from the National Weather Records Center, Asheville, N.C.

If the need is for a duplicate copy of data which are in the archives but not already published they are available from the National Weather Records Center for the cost of duplication.

If the need is for past information at specific locations other than the points where observations were actually made, consideration should be given to using the services of a professional meteorological consultant who is capable of estimating the most probable data for that specific location.

Analytical studies involving large numbers of man-hours or machine time in their execution each present their own peculiar set of circumstances. In some instances industrial firms may use the talents of their nonmeteorological personnel to deal with weather related problems. In most cases it is advisable to seek professional assistance either on a staff or consulting basis. The professional would be expected to know what meteorological data are needed and where and how it can most economically be processed.

Figure 2 illustrates the concept of economic use of professional assistance whenever weather-related problems reach high dollar concern.

RECOMMENDED ACTION

FIG. 2

Industrial Meteorological Services. Non-Government meteorologists fit into one of two categories: (a) Private consultants [2]—either individuals or groups of meteorologists who work on a consulting basis for one or more clients, (b) industrial meteorologists—individuals working as regular employees for business and industrial firms, insurance firms, utilities, etc. Individuals in both of

[2] "What Is a Consulting Meteorologist?" American Meteorological Society.

these groups are considered here to be in the field of industrial meteorology.[8]

Industrial meteorology is the application of meteorological knowledge to specific industrial problems in order to yield a direct economic advantage. Private weather services seldom claim their forecasts are more accurate than those of the U.S. Weather Bureau. Their staffs are small, and they can't duplicate the Government's extensive network of reporting stations. In fact, most of the firms base their forecasts largely on information on temperature, winds, rainfall, and barometric pressure received over the Weather Bureau's leased wire system. The Weather Bureau furnishes its data free, though the firms must pay for the private wire link to the Bureau.

The private services, many of which concentrate on serving customers in a limited area, can watch for weather conditions of particular importance to a client. Besides sending out periodic forecasts, they tailor their information to the needs of the individual client. The fees paid for this service are directly comparable to those in other consulting professions.

The old saw, "It's an ill wind that blows no good" has a unique relevancy to the case of the modern businessman. More and more they are realizing the value of planning and operating in partnership with the weather. Some will choose to pay private meteorologists to help chart their course, others will determine their own procedures. But by an intelligent use of today's weather techniques they all stand to gain from the modern business-weather relationship.

OFFICE OF STATE TECHNICAL SERVICES

Small business benefits in many ways from the State Technical Services program—through technical information services, technical referral services, and extensive workshops and seminars in advanced technology suitable for local industry. Each State has been requested to designate an agency or institution to develop a 5-year plan for the economic and industrial growth of the State. The designated agency also develops, coordinates, and administers the annual technical services program. The services available are provided through qualified institutions such as colleges or universities. For the names of the designated agencies, write to the Office of State Technical Services, Department of Commerce, Washington, D.C., 20230.

PATENT OFFICE

The Patent Office examines patent and trademark applications to determine the patentability of an invention or the registrability of a trade-

mark. Successful applicants receive benefits under the patent and trademark statutes. The rights to a patent or trademark may be purchased from the patentee or registrant by any person or firm.

A patent may be granted to any person who invents or discovers any new or useful process, machine, manufacture, or composition of matter, or any new and useful improvement thereof. A patent gives the inventor the right to exclude others from making, using, or selling his invention throughout the United States for a period of 17 years.

At the end of the 17-year period the patent becomes a part of the public domain at which time any one may manufacture, produce, and sell the patented invention.

Of particular interest to businessmen is the Official Gazette, a weekly publication of the Patent Office, containing the more than 1,200 patented disclosures in all fields of scientific endeavor. The Gazette provides a means of communication between inventors and manufacturers who are interested in their products.

On file in the public search room at the Patent Office are the more than 3,200,000 U.S. patents and 7 million foreign patents which can aid businessmen in their search for new products and solutions to problems in the descriptions of patented inventions that are in force and expired ones.

A trademark includes any word, name, symbol or device, or any combination thereof, adopted and used by a manufacturer or merchant to identify his goods and distinguish them from those manufactured or sold by others. In order to be eligible for registration, a mark must be in use in commerce which may lawfully be regulated by Congress. A trademark registration remains in force for 20 years, and may be renewed.

Information about patents and trademarks can be obtained from any field office of the Department of Commerce or by writing to the Commissioner of Patents, Washington, D.C., 20231.

BUREAU OF THE CENSUS

The Bureau of the Census gathers and publishes statistics of many kinds that may be useful to the businessman: Statistics about numbers of people, by age, race, sex, occupation, income, and other characteristics; about consumer buying intentions; about homes and new houses; about business and industry, imports and exports; statistics for areas ranging from city blocks, and census tracts (small areas roughly equivalent to neighborhoods), up to cities, metropolitan areas, counties, States, and the Nation.

When the businessman wants facts about his area that have a bearing on his market and his prospects, he can get answers from Census Bureau data as to how many customers, how many employed, how many in each income group, how many own homes and how many rent, how many have moved into or out of the areas recently, and how many competitors in his own line of business there are in his area.

Many businessmen depend on business publications, trade associations, or chambers of commerce to select and interpret Census Bureau statistics. The businessman who wants to study the facts for himself may obtain copies of reports at nominal cost. (See list of selected Bureau of the Census publications.)

NATIONAL BUREAU OF STANDARDS

The national measurement system maintained and developed by NBS is of major importance to the small businessman. By using NBS calibration services and standard materials, he can insure his ability to meet high accuracy requirements specified in defense and space contracts, and thus obtain his share of subcontracts. The same measurement ability enables him to make products or replacement parts compatible with the products of other manufacturers.

Where the small businessman deals in goods and services which are dispensed by weight and measure, his State Weights and Measures Department, with the technical support of the NBS Office of Weights and Measures, is his safeguard against inaccuracy. The small businessman whose specialty is invention receives important support from the NBS Office of Invention and Innovation. Engineering standards, standards of practice, commercial standards, international standards, for which NBS provides a technical basis, all promote a more uniform national and international marketplace, and thus expand the small businessman's sales opportunities.

One of the Bureau's most valuable aids to the small businessman is its dissemination of technical information. NBS develops information in specific fields—metallurgy, polymers, building materials and techniques, data processing, etc.; NBS collects and distributes reports on all unclassified Government research through its Clearinghouse for Federal Scientific and Technical Information; and the NBS Office of Technical Resources packages this information by subject and makes it available to the small businessman through State Economic Development Agencies.

SELECTED PUBLICATIONS

(Available from U.S. Department of Commerce Field Offices)

OFFICE OF FIELD SERVICES

Commerce Business Daily. A daily list of U.S. Government procurement invitations, subcontracting leads, contract awards, sales of surplus property, and foreign business opportunities.

BUREAU OF INTERNATIONAL COMMERCE

BIC Checklist, published semiannually, lists all publications of the Bureau of International Commerce. Free.

Publications noted in the checklist are available from the Commerce Department's Publication Sales and Distribution Branch of the Office of Administrative Services, Washington, D.C., 20230, or from any of the Department of Commerce Field Offices.

International Commerce is the principal periodical published in the international affairs area of the U.S. Department of Commerce. A weekly news magazine, it offers authoritative and concise international marketing information and reports demonstrating and explaining potential advantages to American businessmen in profitable international sales of U.S. products.

Commerce Business Daily offers a daily synopsis of U.S. Government proposed procurement, subcontracting leads, contract awards, sales of surplus property, and foreign business opportunities.

Overseas Business Reports replaced the 3-part World Trade Information Service in reporting basic and authoritative information needed by exporters, importers, investors, manufacturers, researchers and all who are concerned with international trade and economic conditions throughout the world.

Export Expansion Council News. Once per month this newsletter reports activities of Export Expansion Councils in 42 cities throughout the U.S.A.

The Market Series handbooks are designed to provide a current evaluation of the nature and scope of a country's market, describing the present import pattern, distribution facilities, and trade practices, as well as an analysis of the market for selected commodities.

Trade Mission Reports. Opportunities for U.S. trade with countries that are visited by U.S. trade missions.

Trade Lists. These are available to help U.S. firms find customers, agents, distributors, licensees, and sources of supply abroad. Each list gives names and addresses of firms handling a specific commodity in one foreign country. Each list also contains a summary of basic trade and industry data, including a brief analysis of foreign trade in the commodity covered, government regulations affecting trade, and other useful information.

What You Should Know About Exporting. A how-to-get-started handbook designed as a basic reference for the American businessman interested in opening profitable new overseas markets for his products. 1965. 38 pp.

World Trade Directory Reports. Carry basic commercial and financial information on specific foreign firms and individuals. Data furnished on a given firm usually cover the type of organization, method of operation, lines handled, size of firm, sales territory, names of owners and officers, capital, sales volume, general reputation in trade and financial circles, and names of any U.S. firms represented by the foreign firm and serving as its supplier. They are prepared by the U.S. Foreign Service, and represent a consensus of reliable sources of information. $1 er report. If information on a particular firm is not on file in Washington, it will be requested from the Foreign Service. To minimize delay, businessmen may authorize telegraphic request and reply, for which the Department of State will bill them direct. Available from the Bureau of International Commerce, Commercial Intelligence Division, U.S. Department of Commerce, Washington, D.C., 20230, or from any of the Department's field offices.

OFFICE OF BUSINESS ECONOMICS

Survey of Current Business. A monthly publication. Provides analytical and explanatory material regarding the Nation's economic activity.

BUSINESS AND DEFENSE SERVICES ADMINISTRATION

Nonperiodical Publications

BDSA Publications. A checklist of publications that includes data on monthly and quarterly industry reports as well as all other BDSA publications. July 1965. Free.

The U.S. Industrial Outlook. (Annual study of trends and prospects for selected major industries.)

Aids to Modernization: A Bibliography (1964). 9 pp.

Aids to Modernization: How To Succeed by Really Trying (1964). 38 pp.

Aluminum Fact Book (1963). 90 pp.

Chemical Statistical Directory No. 3 (1964). 195 pp.

Confectionery Sales and Distribution, 1964 (1965). 20 pp.

Construction Machinery and Equipment, 1962 (1964). 16 pp.

Current Status and Commercial Prospects for Radiation Preservation of Food (1965). 174 pp.

Foreign Market Surveys—Selected Foreign Countries (1965).

Gas Characteristics and Factors of Gas Distribution in Western Europe (1965). 10 pp.

Market Information on Electronic Products—Selected Foreign Countries (1964).

Market Information on Business Machines in Argentina (1965). 5 pp.

Market Information on Material Handling Equipment and Automated Warehousing Systems in Sweden (1965). 5 pp.

Market Information on Motion Pictures in Greece (1964). 3 pp.

Market Information on Photographic Products in Japan (1965). 3 pp.

Market for U.S. Scientific, Industrial and Technical Instruments and Equipment in France (1965).

Market for U.S.-type Residential Heating Equipment in France (1964). 4 pp.

Markets for Men's and Boys' Clothing in Western Europe (1964). 63 pp.

Measuring Metropolitan Markets: A Guide to the Use of U.S. Government Data (1963). 48 pp.

Outlook for American Gas Appliances and Equipment in the Netherlands (1964). 11 pp.

Outlook for U.S.-Type Residential Heating Equipment in Italy (1964). 4 pp.

Principal Sources of Statistical Data on Textiles and Apparel (1964). 19 pp.

Salad Dressing, Mayonnaise & Related Products (industry survey) 1964 (1965). 14 pp.

Selling in Italy (1965). 12 pp.

The Cotton Textile Cycle: Its Nature and Trend (1963). 42 pp.

The Japanese Electronic Industries (1964). 8 pp.

The Japanese Motion Picture Industry (1965). 3 pp.

The Japanese Watch and Clock Industry (1965). 8 pp.

The Market for Automatic Vending Machines in Austria (1963). 40 pp.

The Market for Automatic Vending Machines in the United Kingdom (1963). 36 pp.

The Market for Books in India (1964). 6 pp.

The Market for Costume Jewelry in West Germany (1963). 28 pp.

The Market for Selected Photographic Products in the United Kingdom and France (1964). 27 pp.

The Market for Semiconductor Devices in West Germany and Italy (1964). 24 pp.

The Market for U.S. Electrical Components in Western Germany and Berlin (1964). 45 pp.

The Market for U.S. Scientific, Industrial and Technical Instruments and Equipment in France (1965).

The Motion Picture Industry of the Federal Republic of Germany (1965). 4 pp.

The Turkish Motion Picture Industry (1965). 3 pp.

The United States Foreign Trade in Photographic Goods, 1963 (1964). 33 pp.

United States Lumber Imports, 1964 (1965). 6 pp.

United States Lumber Exports, 1964 (1965). 11 pp.

Water Service Pipe Requirements by Water Utilities, 1950–80 (1964). 4 pp.

Water and Sewerage Works Pressure Pipe Requirements, 1940—1975 (1964). 8 pp.

World Motor Vehicle Production and Registration, 1963–64 (1965). 6 pp.

World Survey of Abrasive Products, 1957–62 (1963). 30 pp.

World Survey of Civil Aviation—Continental Europe and Ireland (1965). 57 pp.
World Survey of Civil Aviation—United Kingdom (1965). 16 pp.
World Trade in Machine Tools, 1959–60 (1963). 16 pp.

Periodical Publications

Chemicals Industry Report. Quarterly. $1 yr. ($1.25 foreign). C41.35.
Containers and Packaging Industry Report. Quarterly. 75¢ yr. ($1 foreign). C41.33.
Construction Review. Monthly. $3 yr. ($4 foreign). C41.30/3.
Copper Industry Report. Quarterly. 75¢ yr. ($1 foreign). C41.33.
Marketing Information Guide. Monthly. $2 yr. ($2.75 foreign). (Includes annual cumulative index.) Annotations of selected current marketing materials. C41.11.
Printing and Publishing Industry Report. Monthly. $1 yr. ($1.25 foreign). C41.18.
Pulp, Paper, and Board Industry Report. Quarterly. 75¢ yr. ($1 foreign). Single copy 20¢. C41.32.

CLEARINGHOUSE FOR FEDERAL SCIENTIFIC AND TECHNICAL INFORMATION (FORMERLY OFFICE OF TECHNICAL SERVICES)

U.S. Government Research and Development Reports.
Selective Bibliographies.
Technical Translations.
Government-wide Index to Federal Research and Development.
"Packaged" Government Research and Development Information for Industry.

BUREAU OF THE CENSUS

Population Census, 1960. Figures on the growth and movement of the population and its social and economic characteristics.
Housing Census, 1960. Data on the supply and condition of housing and its facilities and equipment.
Agriculture Census, 1964. Figures on value of farm land and buildings; value of farm products sold, by source; characteristics of farm operators; crops; and livestock and poultry and their products.
Business Census, 1963. Statistics on establishments, sales, payroll, and personnel, by kind of business, for retail trade, wholesale trade, and selected services.
Manufactures Census, 1963. Data on establishments, employment, payroll, value added by manufacture, and value of shipments.
Mineral Industries Census, 1963. Figures on establishments, employment, payroll, value added in mining, and value of shipments.

Transportation Census, 1963. Figures on passenger transportation, including home-to-work travel and travel patterns for a panel of households; on the characteristics and use of private and commercial trucks, by State and geographic division; on commodity transportation by shipper groups, production areas, and commodity groups; and on for-hire buses and trucks.
Commercial Fisheries Census, 1963. Data that will show number of fisheries, employment, payroll, and receipts from fishing activities, by major type of catch, for States and regions.
Governments Census, 1962. Figures that measure costs of local governmental services and sources of revenue.

Current series of reports of the Bureau of the Census also provide statistics to assist small business in studying economic and social trends and in developing its growth potential:
Current Population Reports (monthly, annual, or biennial).
Current Housing Reports (quarterly and annual).
U.S. Foreign Trade Reports (monthly and annual).
County Business Patterns (latest, 1964; annual effective with that issue).
Current Industrial Reports (monthly, quarterly, semiannual, or annual).
Current Reports on State and Local Governments (annual).
Current Construction Reports (monthly and annual).
Current Reports on Business (weekly, monthly, and annual).
Business Cycle Developments (monthly).

NATIONAL BUREAU OF STANDARDS [4]

Technical News Bulletin. Research reported in digest form, Monthly, $1.50 yr.
Journal of Research. Full research papers. Published in four sections: A. Physics and Chemistry, issued six times per year, $4.00 yr.; B. Mathematics and Mathematical Physics, quarterly, $2.25 yr.; C. Engineering and Instrumentation, quarterly, $2.25 yr.; D. Radio Science, monthly, $9.00 yr.

Publications of the NBS Clearinghouse for Federal Scientific and Technical Information:
U.S. Government Research Reports. Department of Defense and other agencies except AEC and NASA, semimonthly, $15.00 yr.
Nuclear Science Abstracts. Atomic Energy Commission reports and nuclear science literature worldwide, semimonthly, $30.00 yr.
Scientific and Technical Aerospace Reports. National Aeronautics and Space Administration and other agency research reports in aerospace fields, semimonthly, $25.00 yr.

---

[4] All publications available from Superintendent of Documents, U.S. Government Printing Office, Washington, D.C., 20402.

Technical Translations. Translations of significant Slavic and Oriental research available from the Clearinghouse and other sources, semimonthly, $12.00 yr.

U.S. TRAVEL SERVICE

Semi-Annual Report of the Secretary of Commerce on the United States Travel Service. Reports numbered first through eighth.

U.S. Entry and Exit Requirements for Foreign Visitors.

Activities of the United States Travel Service.

Marketing the United States as a Tourist Destination.

Suggestions for Persons Desiring to Enter the Travel Agency Business.

Pleasure and Business Visitors to the U.S. by Port of Entry and Mode of Travel. Tables cover the last 6 months of 1963, the first 6 months of 1964, calendar year 1964, and the first 6 months of 1965.

Overseas Visitor Survey, Honolulu International Airport, November 1962.

Overseas Visitor Survey, Miami International Airport, July 1963.

Idlewild International Airport Survey of Visitors to the United States, June 13–19, 1962.

Summary of Attitude Research of Potential Travelers to the USA from Selected Countries, October 4, 1963.

Market Research on Attitudes on Potential Travellers to the U.S.A., June 1962.

The Future of Tourism in the Pacific and Far East, June 1961.

The Market in Great Britain for Travel to the United States, October 1965.

Temporary Visitors to the United States by Country or Region of Last Permanent Residence. Reports issued monthly and annually.

PATENT OFFICE

Patents and Inventions, an information aid for inventors.

General Information Concerning Patents.

Answers to Questions Frequently Asked About Patents.

Questions and Answers About Trademarks.

General Information Concerning Trademarks.

Patents: Spur to American Progress.

Roster of Attorneys and Agents Registered to Practice Before the U.S. Patent Office.

Department of Labor

GENERAL

Some of the services of the Department of Labor of particular interest to small business are discussed below. Further information is obtainable by mail or by visit or telephone to Labor Department offices. A list of all regional offices is furnished at the end of the narrative section.

BUREAU OF APPRENTICESHIP AND TRAINING

Small businesses comprise the great bulk of industrial enterprises which use the services of the Bureau, which is in the Labor Department's Manpower Administration, in developing and improving their apprenticeship and training activities. For example, programs in the construction, tool and die, and printing and publishing industries account for a very large proportion of all firms served by the Bureau.

These are programs predominantly involving small concerns which employ from one to five apprentices or trainees. Such businesses are not large enough to employ full-time services of a personnel and training staff. While the Bureau services many large industrial programs in a number of different ways, it is the small to medium-sized, owner-directed business which forms the core of the Bureau's apprenticeship and training activity.

To achieve widest results, the Bureau works with the trade associations in these industries and, where appropriate, with the unions active in such industries to bring about communitywide and nationwide agreements on recommended training standards.

SERVICES

Specifically, some of the services available to small businesses through the Bureau of Apprenticeship and Training are the following:

1. Advising and aiding in the establishment of an apprenticeship and training program to fit local needs.

2. Assisting in devising ways to improve present training practices and to solve personnel problems arising from lack of training plans.

3. Developing and servicing on-the-job-training programs, with provisions for reimbursement of employer training costs under the Manpower Development and Training Act.

4. Aiding local industry in getting together as a group to set up programs and solve common apprenticeship and training problems.

5. Advising on assistance available through local vocational schools, or otherwise, in providing needed instruction in subjects related to a particular trade or industry; similarly advising with respect to aptitude and interest testing facilities of the public employment service available to aid in improving the trainee selection.

6. Obtaining the aid of the local vocational school in providing special courses for presently employed workers, other than apprentices or new trainees, to improve their competence and extend their employment opportunities.

7. Helping analyze training needs likely to arise from the makeup of the industry's present work force with respect to age, retirement prospects, expansion possibilities, and other factors.

8. Making available to these small business enterprises the results of statistical and technical studies of trends in the employment and training of apprentices, and the methods used by successful program operators to achieve satisfactory results.

PUBLICATIONS

Listed below are some of the publications issued by the Bureau:

1. *National Apprenticeship Program.*

2. *Trade and Industry Nos. 1 through 7*, covering sample apprenticeship schedules in electronics and electrical industry, personal service occupations, metal working trades, automotive work, and the construction industry.

3. *National Apprenticeship Standards*, such as: Painting and decorating, carpentry, photoengravers, and truck mechanics.

4. *Employer's Guide to On-the-Job Training*, covering the aid provisions of the Manpower Development and Training Act.

5. *Apprenticeship and Economic Change*, a study of apprenticeship in the U.S. and how economic factors affect this training.

BUREAU OF EMPLOYMENT SECURITY

The State Employment Services are affiliated with the U.S. Employment Service, a part of the Bureau of Employment Security of the Manpower Administration in the Department of Labor. They provide businessmen with many services which are helpful in meeting personnel needs and in solving manpower problems.

The Employment Service is of particular help to small and medium-sized businesses which do not maintain complete personnel departments and which therefore may not be equipped internally to resolve all employment management problems as they arise.

SERVICES

With experience based on years of cooperative research with industry on personnel matters, the Employment Service helps small business to:

1. Determine the basic requirements of particular jobs and locate workers who have the necessary qualifications.

State Employment Services recruit workers in all occupations—professional, clerical, service, skilled, semiskilled, and unskilled categories. They are organized to meet the small businessman's particular specifications for current and future manpower requirements.

2. Select workers best qualified to meet job requirements through improved interviewing and testing techniques.

Working with several of the larger universities and nationally recognized industrial psychologists, the Employment Service has developed a comprehensive testing program. These tests cover trade tests to measure occupational skills already acquired, and aptitude tests to measure potentiality for learning new ones.

3. Analyze the cause, and assist in the reduction of excessive personnel turnover.

Underutilization of skills, lack of opportunity for promotion, working conditions, wages, and supervision are among the factors which contribute to absenteeism and high turnover. The Employment Service, through its tools and techniques, can make suggestions that will assist the small business in analyzing the causes of high turnover and absenteeism. Such analysis helps the small business to determine what can be done to maintain a vigorous, stable work force.

4. Plan personnel expansions and obtain needed workers. The Employment Service is also equipped to give the small business practical help in manpower planning through job analysis and occupational classification. Local Employment Service offices can be of assistance regarding the application of these tools and methods in the solution of small business manpower problems.

5. Locate applicants with required skills in other communities if they are not available locally.

If workers with the required skills are not available locally, they can be recruited through a nationwide clearance placement system. Through the process of clearance, a small business employer with an opening for a certain type of worker, and an applicant who is qualified for that job—each in a different city—are often brought together.

6. Have as a worker resource persons who have received occupational training which was established under Federal legislation, such as the Manpower Development and Training Act, because qualified workers were not available.

The Employment Service identifies occupational training courses in progress so that employers may make job offers to trainees; or initiates occupational training or refers applicants for training on an individual basis to other training courses, if it is not feasible to establish a separate course; or arranges with the Bureau of Apprenticeship and Training for development of on-the-job training programs for interested employers.

7. Use Employment Service area labor information to plan for plant expansion, new plant locations, training programs, and market analysis for sales departments.

Data on employment and unemployment trends, demand for and availability of workers by occupations, area labor outlook, wages, labor turnover, and related factors are available at the Employment Service. Such information, compiled on an area, industry, or occupational basis may be of help to the small business in planning recruiting activities, training programs, and expansion or location of new plants or establishments.

Companies in areas classified by the Bureau of Employment Security as having above average unemployment are given preferential consideration in the award of such contracts and in areas with persistently high unemployment they may be eligible for 4 percent loans. If small business firms are interested in bidding on Federal procurement contracts or in obtaining low cost Small Business Administration loans, Employment Service local offices, on request, will provide information on area classification.

In addition to these varied types of assistance, the Employment Service offices can assist the small business in determining appropriate personnel records and in relating veterans' service training to civilian occupations.

OFFICE OF LABOR-MANAGEMENT AND WELFARE-PENSION REPORTS

This Office administers all Department of Labor functions under the Labor-Management Reporting and Disclosure Act and the Welfare and Pension Plans Disclosure Act. Both laws, which provide for public disclosure, have reporting requirements applying to employers.

Disclosure files for reports filed under the Labor-Management Reporting and Disclosure Act are located in LMWP's 24 area offices. Disclosure files for reports submitted under the Welfare and Pension Plans Disclosure Act are in Washington, D.C.

All area offices and 12 resident offices provide technical assistance and compliance services and have available reporting forms which are required under the Act.

LABOR-MANAGEMENT REPORTING AND DISCLOSURE ACT

This statute requires reports from labor organizations as well as labor organization officers and employees, and from employers and labor relations consultants to help insure ethical financial practices in labor-management relations.

Form LM-10 must be filed by those employers who have been involved in certain financial transactions with labor organizations, union officers or employees, and labor relations consultants or who have made expenditures where the object relates to employee's or union's activities. (See Section 203 of the Act.) Not all employees are required to report, but those who made reportable payments in the enumerated activities should submit reports within 90 days after the close of the employer's fiscal year. In addition to Form LM-10, Technical Assistance Aid No. 4 explains in detail the reporting requirements.

LABOR RELATIONS CONSULTANTS

Labor relations consultants must report any agreement or arrangement they may have with employes to persuade employees how to exercise their rights to bargain or to obtain information about employees' union activities. Form LM-20 must be filed by the consultant within 30 days after entering into the reportable agreement or arrangement. Form LM-21 is to be filed within 90 days after the end of the consultant's fiscal year and report the amount of money received and disbursed during the year in connection with labor relations advice and services.

WELFARE AND PENSION PLANS DISCLOSURE ACT

Reporting requirements of this Act apply to employers and employer associations, among others, which administer private welfare and private pension plans. These plans, financed through the purchase of insurance or otherwise, may cover medical, surgical or hospital care or benefits, or benefits in the event of sickness, accident, disability, death, or unemployment.

Administrators of employee benefit plans subject to the Act must disclose plan provisions and financial operations by means of a description of the plan and annual reports, as well as secure fidelity bonding of persons who handle funds or other property.

Form D-1 covering plan descriptions, to be filed within 90 days after the plan is established, must be completed by administrators of plans with 26 or more participants.

Form D-2 covering annual financial reports, to be filed within 150 days after the end of the plan year, must be completed by administrators of plans with 100 or more participants. The abbreviated Form D-3 covering annual reports, also filed 150 days after the end of the plan year, is for plans with fewer than 100 participants. (The plan administrator files D-2 or D-3, not both.)

In addition to the reporting forms, the following pamphlets are available dealing with general questions concerning employee benefit plans: "Questions and Answers on the Welfare & Pension Plans Disclosure Act," "Fidelity Bonding Under the Welfare and Pension Plans Disclosure Act," and "Rights of Pension Plan Participants."

BUREAU OF LABOR STANDARDS

In carrying out its basic function of promoting sound labor standards for advancing the well-being of workers and for increasing efficiency in production, the Bureau of Labor Standards' services in the field of occupational safety are available to State Labor Departments, management, labor, civic organizations, and others and through them to small business.

SERVICES

Major phases of the Bureau's work in promoting occupational safety include:

1. Conducting safety training for State safety personnel, unions, longshore and harbor workers, and Federal employees.

2. Assisting State Labor Departments to conduct special safety programs in high accident rate industries.

3. Assisting States, unions, and other interested groups in the technical aspects of developing safety codes.

4. Developing and publishing technical information relating to accident prevention.

5. Providing technical consultation to States, employers, unions, and the general public on various aspects of safety.

6. Establishing and enforcing safety and health standards in the longshoring and ship repairing industries under Public Law 85-742.

7. Servicing the President's Conference on Occupational Safety.

8. Developing standards for safe employment of youth, including farm-employed minors.

PUBLICATIONS

Some recent safety publications of the Bureau of Labor Standards are:

Occupational Safety Aides:
Conducting a Job Hazard Analysis—LS 163.
Elements of a Safety Program—LS 164.
Good Housekeeping—LS 166.
Inspecting for Safety—LS 170.
Office Safety—LS 171.
Safe Lifting—LS 175.
Safeguarding Machinery—LS 176.
Safety Committee Activities—LS 177.
Safety Training Techniques—LS 180.
Supervisory Responsibility for Safety—LS 181.
Trips, Slips and Falls—LS 183.

Mechanical and Physical Hazards Series

Bulletins:
216—Control of Electrical Shock Hazards. (Rev. 1962.) 15 pp.
219—Mechanical Handling of Materials. 1960. 29 pp.
231—Personal Protective Equipment. 1961. 26 pp.
232—Fire Protection for the Safety Man. 1961. 25 pp.
239—Mechanics for the Safety Man. 1962. 21 pp.
240—Rigging Cargo Gear. 1962. 23 pp.
246—Maintenance and Safety. 1962. 15 pp.
256—Static Electricity. 1963. 20 pp.

Environmental and Chemical Hazards Series

Bulletins:
207—Controlling Noise Hazards. 1959. 8 pp.
222—Chemistry for the Safety Man. (Rev. 1965.) 26 pp.
226—Respiratory Protective Equipment. 1961. 34 pp.
241—Chlorine Handling in Stevedoring Operations. 1962. 9 pp.
259—The Use and Handling of Compressed Gases. 1963. 30 pp.
265—The Inorganic Acids. 1964. 27 pp.

Organization and Administration Series

Bulletins:
211—Control of the Physical Environment. 1960. 13 pp.
223—The Consultative Approach to Safety. 1960. 9 pp.
247—Fundamentals of Accident Prevention. 1962. 14 pp.
255—Using Injury Statistics. 1963. 18 pp.
67—Safety Subjects.

197—Principles and Techniques of Mechanical Guarding.
198—Occupational Health Hazards.
263—Proceedings, President's Conference on Occupational Safety (1956, 1958, 1960, 1962 and 1964).

Regulations under Public Law 85–742:
Safety and Health Regulations for Longshoring.
Safety and Health Regulations for Ship Repairing.
Safety and Health Regulations for Shipbreaking.
Safety and Health Regulations for Ship Building.
Cargo Gear Certification; Regulations Governing Accreditation of Persons to Carry out and the Procedures to be followed in Cargo Gear Certification.

Safety Code Comparison Charts: A comparison of State Safety Codes, in selected subjects, and those of nationally recognized standards setting organizations.

1. Demolition (Building Construction)—June 1960.
2. Ladders (Building Construction)—July 1960.
3. Sanitation—September 1960.
4. Mechanical Power-Transmission Apparatus—September 1960.
5. Floor and Wall Openings—November 1960.
6. Scaffolds—October 1961.
7. Welding and Cutting—January 1962.
8. Use, Care and Protection of Abrasive Wheels—January 1962.
9. Rubber Mills and Calenders—January 1962.
10. Woodworking Machinery—February 1962.
11. Cranes, Derricks, and Hoists—June 1962.
12. Textile Safety—August 1962.
13. Power Presses—October 1962.
14. Laundry Machinery and Operations—February 1963.
15. Powered Industrial Trucks—April 1963.
16. Window Cleaning—July 1963.
17. Excavation—November 1963.
18. Fixed Ladders—December 1963.
19. Metal Ladders—February 1964.
20. Wood Ladders—August 1964.

BUREAU OF LABOR STATISTICS

The Bureau of Labor Statistics publishes a large amount of information which is used by small business. In addition, data are assembled in response to individual requests, often in connection with consultation in one of the Bureau's regional offices.

Using some types of data, the businessman can compare the record of his own plant or store with that in his industry as a whole or in his locality. Other statistics are regularly used by companies planning a branch in another area. The long experience of BLS regional officers in applying available information to the problems presented has proved invaluable in both types of situation.

PUBLICATIONS

Published material may cover many individual cities or regions, or the States, or it may be available only for the United States as a whole. Some series are available for individual manufacturing and mining industries (men's workshirts or hand tools, e.g.) ; others extend also to various types of retail establishments, construction activities, utilities, services, etc. Some statistics appear monthly, others at irregular intervals. In addition to Bureau of Labor Statistics publications, the regional offices have at hand much detailed information published by other agencies within the region, or in some cases unpublished, but available for use.

Types of industry and area data published by the BLS and constantly used by businessmen include:

Turnover rates: Lay-offs, quits, hires, per thousand employees.

Average hours of production workers.

Average earnings of production workers.

Trends of individual prices, wholesale and retail, over a period of years.

Percent of income spent for different types of commodities and services by consumers of different ages, incomes, occupations, etc.

The cost of a moderate-level budget for a family of four, or for an elderly couple, in various cities.

Work injuries in specific industries.

Work stoppages in each industry.

Wage rates of individual occupations in various areas; union scales in certain industries.

Supplementary benefits such as vacations, pensions, etc. in various industries and labor areas.

Provisions of current labor-management contracts.

Current wage developments.

Ten-year projections of number in population and labor force.

Employment trends by industry, by area, in past years.

BLS regional directors often address groups of businessmen on subjects related to labor and economic developments in the region. Addresses of the BLS and its regional offices, together with a selected list of BLS publications, follow:

Monthly Labor Review: monthly journal; articles and statistics. Annual subscription rate $7.50. Single issues 75 cents.

Employment and Earnings: monthly. Annual subscription rate $4.00. Single issues 50 cents.

Employment and Earnings Statistics for the United States, 1909–64: $3.50 per copy.

Current Wage Developments: monthly; data on specific wage settlements. Free upon request.

Directory of National and International Labor Unions in the United States, 1963: biennial. Fifty cents per copy.

Analysis of Work Stoppages, 1964: annual. Thirty-five cents per copy.

Wholesale Prices and Price Indexes: monthly. Free upon request.

Consumer Price Index: monthly. Free upon request.

Occupational Outlook Quarterly: February, May, September, December. Annual subscription rate $1.25. Single issues 35 cents.

For additional items, and for prices, see Bureau of Labor Statistics Catalog of Publications, issued semiannually; or consult the Bureau of Labor Statistics, U.S. Department of Labor, at any of the following addresses:

Washington, D.C., 20212; 18 Oliver Street, Boston, Mass., 02110; 341 Ninth Avenue, New York, N.Y., 10001; 1371 Peachtree Street NE., Atlanta, Ga., 30309; 219 South Dearborn Street, Chicago Ill., 60604; 450 Golden Gate Avenue, Box 36017, San Francisco, Calif., 94102; 1365 Ontario Street, Cleveland, Ohio, 44114.

SERVICES

Following is an example of use of the type of information cited: A manufacturer requested data bearing on possible location of a small branch plant in a given region. The BLS regional office was able to obtain and supply information as to:

Levels of earnings in the area, wage rates by occupation, and current labor costs; cost of building materials; the relative trend in recent years in local consumer prices, and the cost of supporting a family there; labor-management relations, history of work stoppages, habitual labor turnover rates in the industry in the State; employment trends in the industry in the State in recent years; other area information requested, including local population and neighborhood factors that would affect the local demand for the product; some scattered information on the local availability of skilled and other workers, and of young persons having enough education to make training possible.

OFFICE OF VETERANS' REEMPLOYMENT RIGHTS

The Office provides direct assistance in connection with the reemployment rights of ex-servicemen, reservists and members of the National

Guard, and promotes employer compliance and understanding with the reemployment requirements of the Universal Military Training and Service Act.

The employer is obligated to reemploy the ex-serviceman in the position he would have had if he had remained on the job instead of entering military service. Seniority rights of the veteran are protected by certain automatic progression provisions where those rights would have been available to him had he not gone into service. The employer carries out his obligation by making available to the ex-serviceman a working position which takes into account the time spent in the service.

Representatives of the Office of Veterans Reemployment Rights are available in 19 major cities and are listed in telephone directories under the U.S. Labor Department heading. Employers in any area may secure information or assistance in interpreting the law by writing to the U.S. Labor Department, Washington, D.C., 20210.

OFFICE OF MANPOWER, AUTOMATION, AND TRAINING

The Office of Manpower, Automation and Training (OMAT) of the Manpower Administration is responsible for planning, research, and evaluation of U.S. Department of Labor activities under the comprehensive manpower program. This includes planning and evaluation of the Department's manpower training activities and planning, developing, and conducting a comprehensive manpower research effort.

The broad manpower program authorized under the Manpower Development and Training Act (MDTA) is designed to: (1) Meet critical needs of workers in shortage occupations—including professional, scientific, and apprenticeable categories; (2) Help the labor force adjust to technological developments, foreign competition, relocation of industry, shifts in demands for workers, other changes in the structure of the economy; (3) Improve job opportunities for unemployed workers.

Employers benefit from training programs that give the work force skills in line with the rapidly changing labor requirements of American industry. In addition, individual employers and employer groups may participate directly in approved MDTA on-the-job training programs under agreements with the Secretary of Labor.

Employers and industries in designated redevelopment areas are helped to meet existing manpower needs through approved local worker training programs. Previously authorized under the Area Redevelopment Act, training programs in redevelopment areas are now covered by the newly amended MDTA.

Experimental and demonstration projects study the complex training problems of particularly dis-advantaged and "hard-core" unemployed and provide occupational training and remedial services—including basic literacy and educational training where appropriate—specifically tailored to the needs of the trainees.

Manpower and automation research conducted by or contracted by OMAT cover the causes, requirements, and impact of automation; shortages in critical occupations and other factors which affect the manpower picture; and new techniques and factors affecting manpower training programs. Results of such research studies are published by OMAT.

Information on training activities and programs is available from the local office of the State Employment Service or the U.S. Department of Labor, Manpower Administration, Washington, D.C., 20210. Publications on manpower topics and information on the research program are available from the U.S. Department of Labor, Manpower Administration, Office of Manpower, Automation and Training, Washington, D.C., 20210.

WAGE AND HOUR AND PUBLIC CONTRACTS DIVISIONS

The Divisions administer the Fair Labor Standards Act, which establishes standards of minimum wage, overtime, equal pay, and child labor for employees engaged in certain kinds of interstate activity, and the Walsh-Healey Public Contracts Act, which provides minimum wage, overtime, child labor, and safety and health standards for employees engaged in work on Government supply contracts in excess of $10,000.

The field staff of the Divisions is decentralized to more than 400 field offices and field stations in important commercial and industrial centers throughout the country and in 11 regional offices in Atlanta, Boston, New York, Birmingham, Cleveland, Chicago, Kansas City, Dallas, Nashville, San Francisco, and Chambersburg, Pa. This method of administration assists employers, especially small businesses, because the services of the Divisions are brought close to the employer, eliminating the need for long trips or expensive telephone calls in order to obtain information and guidance; and the Divisions' representatives are well informed on the industry characteristics and problems in the area and thus are able to discuss the requirements and application of the Acts in terms that are meaningful to local employers.

PUBLICATIONS

Copies of interpretative bulletins, regulations, orders, and rulings which constitute official statements are made available at no cost to employers. In addition, the Divisions have developed nontechnical publications on virtually all of these matters which furnish simple explanations of the laws and the more widely applicable regulations and procedures in terms that are readily understood by the small businessman and the general public. Simple language pamphlets on how the Fair Labor Standards Act and the Public Contracts Act apply to specific industries have also been developed for use by employers.

Among the publications available are:

The Handy Reference Guide to the Fair Labor Standards Act.

The Fair Labor Standards Act, as Amended.

Interpretative Bulletin, Part 779 (The Fair Labor Standards Act as Applied to Retailers of Goods and Services).

Interpretative Bulletin, Part 780 (Exemptions Applicable to Agriculture, Processing of Agricultural Commodities, and related subjects).

A Quick Look at Hours Worked (pamphlet).

Retail and Service Enterprises and Establishments (pamphlet).

Information on the Equal Pay Act of 1963 (pamphlet).

How the Fair Labor Standards Act Operates in "Our Town" (pamphlet).

SERVICES

The Divisions encourage employer groups to request participation by staff members at meetings to discuss various aspects of the laws and the Divisions' activities. The Divisions' investigators not only check for compliance with the Acts but also discuss fully with employers every aspect of the laws' application to their business and inform employers about the assistance that can be obtained from local offices concerning future problems or questions.

Every effort is made to help employers achieve voluntary compliance, and avoid inadvertent violations which could, if left uncorrected, result in substantial back wage liabilities.

Higher minimum wages resulting from the Fair Labor Standards Act provide employees at the lower end of the income scale with greater purchasing power. Increases in wages to this group of workers are immediately reflected in greater demands for consumer goods and services. The Fair Labor Standard Act also helps reduce unfair competition among employers which may stem from wages or hours. In the same manner the Walsh-Healey Public Contracts Act eliminates unfair competition in these areas among bidders for Government work. These labor standards assure employers who comply that they will not operate at a competitive disadvantage in comparison with other employers.

REGIONAL OFFICES OF THE U.S. DEPARTMENT OF LABOR

1371 Peachtree Street NE., Room 110
Atlanta, Ga. 30309

18 Oliver Street
Boston, Mass. 02110

Wolf Avenue and Commerce Street
Chambersburg, Pa. 17201

New Federal Office Building
219 South Dearborn Street
Chicago, Ill. 60604

740 Engineers Building
1365 Ontario Street
Cleveland, Ohio 44114

1114 Commerce Street, Room 207
Dallas, Tex. 75202

832 Equitable Building
730—17th Street
Denver, Colo. 80202

2212 Federal Office Building
911 Walnut Street
Kansas City, Mo. 64106

U.S. Courthouse Building, Room 726
801 Broad Street
Nashville, Tenn. 37203

900 Parcel Post Building
341 Ninth Avenue
New York, N.Y. 10001

10064 Federal Building
450 Golden Gate Avenue
Post Office Box 36017
San Francisco, Calif. 94102

2008 Smith Tower Building
506 Second Avenue
Seattle, Wash. 98104

New York Department Store Building
Street
Fortaleza Corner San Jose
Post Office Box 4631
San Juan, P.R. 00908

Department of the Interior

GENERAL

The Department of the Interior's primary responsibility is in the conservation for wise use of major aspects of the Nation's basic resources, concerning which it has been collecting and interpreting facts for over a century. Its relationship to industry and business—small or large—is essentially one of making available this storehouse of information, and this the Department seeks to do with its many reports and publications, constantly updated to reflect the changing economic and social scene.

The Department administers the use and disposal of public lands and a number of funds for loans and grants supporting private enterprise, exploration and research. It also offers assistance in the industrial and commercial development of Indian lands and the Territories.

Under appropriate subheadings, these many programs of assistance to small business—informational, technical, and financial—are described below, and addresses are given for many of the Department's more than 2,000 field offices.

Representing the entire Department in the field, and available for general information and assistance, are the nine Regional Coordinators of the Office of the Secretary, whose addresses are:

Northeast Region:
Regional Coordinator
U.S. Department of the Interior
Blake Building, 59 Temple Place
Boston, Mass. 02111. Tel: 617 CA 3–2073

Missouri Basin Region:
Regional Coordinator
U.S. Department of the Interior
Federal Office Building, Room 5311
316 North 26th Street
Post Office Box 2530
Billings, Mont. 59103. Tel: 406 245–6373

Alaska Region:
Regional Coordinator
U.S. Department of the Interior
Post Office Box 711
Juneau, Alaska 90801. Tel: 907 JU 6–3870

Southwest Region:
Regional Coordinator
U.S. Department of the Interior
Federal Building, Post Office Box 1467
Muskogee, Okla. 74402. Tel: 918 683–3429

Pacific Southwest Region:
Regional Coordinator
U.S. Department of the Interior
125 South State Street
Salt Lake City, Utah 84111. Tel: 801 524–5625 or 524–5626

104

Pacific Northwest Region:
Regional Coordinator
U.S. Department of the Interior
Federal Building, Room 107
1002 Northeast Holladay Street, Post Office Box 3621
Portland, Oreg. 97208. Tel: 503 234–8250

Southeast Region:
Acting Regional Coordinator
U.S. Department of the Interior
c/o Southeastern Power Administration
Elberton, Ga. 30635. Tel: 404 283–3263

North Central Region:
Regional Coordinator
Ohio River Appalachia Area
Department of the Interior
Federal Office Building, Room 7034
550 Main Street
Cincinnati, Ohio 45202. Tel: 513 381–2197

Regional Coordinator
Upper Mississippi Western Great Lakes Area
Department of the Interior
Lincoln Building, Room 113
303 Price Place
Madison, Wis. 53705. Tel: 608 238–5390

PROCUREMENT ASSISTANCE TO SMALL BUSINESS

Substantially, all procurement by the Department of the Interior is accomplished through field installations located at or near the site of the work being performed. In conducting its purchase and contracting program, each transaction is reviewed to determine its susceptibility to the Small Business "set-aside" program, and, wherever possible, Invitations for Bids reserve portions of the transaction for negotiation with small business concerns.

The following field offices of the Department of the Interior have been designated by the Secretary as participants in the program, and maintain continuous liaison with the appropriate field offices of the Small Business Administration:

Aberdeen, S. Dak.; Bureau of Indian Affairs
Albuquerque, N. Mex.; Bureau of Indian Affairs
Amarillo, Tex.; Bureau of Mines
Anchorage, Alaska; Alaska Railroad
Atlanta, Ga.; Bureau of Sport Fisheries and Wildlife
Billings, Mont.; Bureau of Indian Affairs
Boise, Idaho; Bureau of Reclamation
Denver, Colo.; Geological Survey
Denver, Colo.; Bureau of Reclamation
Denver, Colo.; Bureau of Land Management
Ephrata, Wash.; Bureau of Reclamation
Gallup, N. Mex.; Bureau of Indian Affairs
Menlo Park, Calif.; Geological Survey
Minneapolis, Minn.; Bureau of Sport Fisheries and Wildlife

Muskogee, Okla.; Bureau of Indian Affairs
Omaha, Nebr.; National Park Service
Philadelphia, Pa.; National Park Service
Phoenix, Ariz.; Bureau of Indian Affairs
Pittsburgh, Pa.; Bureau of Mines
Portland, Oreg.; Bureau of Land Management
Portland, Oreg.; Bonneville Power Administration
Portland, Oreg.; Bureau of Indian Affairs
Portland, Oreg.; Bureau of Sport Fisheries and Wild-
life
Richmond, Va.; National Park Service
Roanoke, Va.; National Park Service
Sacramento, Calif.; Bureau of Reclamation
Salt Lake City, Utah; Bureau of Reclamation
San Francisco, Calif.; National Park Service
Santa Fe, N. Mex.; National Park Service
Seattle, Wash.; Bureau of Commercial Fisheries
Tulsa, Okla.; Southwestern Power Administration
Washington, D.C.; Bureau of Land Management
Washington, D.C.; Geological Survey
Washington, D.C.; Bureau of Indian Affairs
Washington, D.C., National Park Service

GEOLOGICAL SURVEY

TOPOGRAPHIC MAPS AND INVESTIGATIONS

Available to small business are the published
results of geologic, mineral and water resources
investigations and topographic maps of the Nation,
its territories and possessions.

RESEARCH ACTIVITIES

The work of the Geological Survey includes
fact-finding and research activities concerning the
earth and its resources. Of direct application to
certain problems of Small Business are the results
of the Survey's investigations of geology, mineral
and water resources and the preparation of topographic maps. The results of the investigations
are published in Survey bulletins, professional
papers, water-supply papers, circulars, and topographic and geologic maps and hydrologic atlases.
The results of many investigations are published
by cooperating Federal and State agencies and in
technical and scientific journals.

INFORMATION AND INQUIRIES

As a service to Small Business and the general
public, the Survey maintains information and inquiries offices, and libraries as follows:

Map Information Office. A center for data on
maps and mapping is maintained for the public
in Room 1028, General Services Administration
Building, Washington, D.C. Here, topographic
maps are available for purchase and questions are
answered concerning sources and status of mapping, geodetic control data and aerial photographs.

Libraries. A reference library of approximately
300,000 volumes on geology and related subjects
is open to all interested persons in Room 1033,
General Services Administration Building, Washington, D.C. Somewhat smaller libraries are also
maintained at Denver Federal Center, Denver 2,
Colo., and Pacific Coast Field Center, U.S. Geological Survey, Menlo Park, Calif.

Photographic Library. More than 100,000 Survey photographs, indexed by geologic subject and
geographical location, are available for purchase
at cost from Geological Survey, Denver Federal
Center, Denver 2, Colo.

Public Inquiries Offices. Public Inquiries Of-
fices are located at 15426 Federal Building, Denver,
Colo.; 8102 Federal Building, 125 South Street,
Salt Lake City, Utah; 108 Skyline Building,
Anchorage, Alaska; 602 Thomas Building, Dallas,
Tex.; 7638 Federal Building, 300 North Los
Angeles Street, Los Angeles,[1] and 504 Custom
House, San Francisco, Calif.; and South 157
Howard Street, Spokane, Wash. Each has a
library of Survey publications, sells Survey maps
and books over the counter, and is a depository for
selected open-file reports.

Publications. "Publications of the Geological
Survey, 1879–1961," includes a listing of books,
maps and charts issued by the Survey and may
be obtained free on application to the U.S. Geological Survey, Washington, D.C., 20242, and Denver
Federal Center, Denver, Colo., 80225. Yearly supplements are issued to keep the material up to date.
They may also be obtained from the Public Inquiries Offices of the Survey. Details concerning
postage, quantity discounts, ordering instructions
and prices are contained in this publication.

Published quadrangle maps are shown on index
circulars available for each State, Puerto Rico,
and the Virgin Islands; these circulars are supplied free on request. The base map in each circular shows the outlines of all mapped quadrangles
and gives their names, survey dates, and the publishing agency (if not the Geological Survey).
The circulars also contain lists of special maps
and sheets with their prices, addresses of map reference libraries, commercial map dealers, and Federal map-distribution centers. Detailed directions
for ordering maps are included.

OFFICE OF MINERALS EXPLORATION, GEOLOGICAL SURVEY

FINANCIAL ASSISTANCE TO EXPLORE FOR CERTAIN MINERALS

The Office of Minerals Exploration, Geological
Survey, offers financial assistance to firms and individuals who desire to explore their properties or
claims for certain mineral commodities. This
help is offered to applicants who ordinarily would
not undertake the exploration under present conditions or circumstances at their sole expense and
who are unable to obtain funds from commercial
sources on reasonable terms.

The Government will contract with an eligible
applicant to pay up to 75 percent of the cost of

[1] The Public Inquiries Office in Los Angeles, Calif., will move
their offices about May 24, 1965. After the move their address
will be: Room 7638, Federal Building, 300 North Los Angeles
Street, Los Angeles, Calif.

exploring for silver and 50 percent of the cost of exploring for the other eligible mineral commodities. The Government's share may not exceed $250,000 per contract. The operator (applicant) does the work, pays the bills, and submits a monthly report of the work done and costs incurred.

An Office of Minerals Exploration field officer inspects and approves acceptable work, after which the Government reimburses the operator for one-half of the acceptable costs. The operator's time spent on the work and charges for the use of equipment which he owns may be applied toward his share of the cost.

Funds contributed by the Government are repaid by a 5-percent royalty on production from the property. If nothing is produced, there is no obligation to repay. The royalty is paid on any production during the period the contract is in effect; and if the Government certifies that production may be possible from the property, the royalty obligation continues until the Government's contribution is repaid with interest, or for the 10-year period usually specified in the contract. The royalty payment applies to both principal and interest, but it never exceeds 5 percent.

REGIONAL OFFICES

Information and application forms may be obtained from the Office of Minerals Exploration, Geological Survey, Department of the Interior, Washington 25, D.C., or from the following Regional Offices:

Office of Minerals Exploration, Geological Survey
Region I
South 157 Howard Street
Spokane, Wash. 99604

Office of Minerals Exploration, Geological Survey
Region II
Room 9007
450 Golden Gate Avenue
San Francisco, Calif. 94102

Office of Minerals Exploration, Geological Survey
Region III
Building 20
Federal Center
Denver, Colo. 80225

Office of Minerals Exploration, Geological Survey
Region IV
Room 11, Post Office Building
Knoxville, Tenn. 37902

PUBLICATIONS

"Minerals Exploration Program" free, available from any of the offices listed above. "Semiannual Report, Office of Minerals Exploration," Geological Survey, free, available from Washington office only.

BUREAU OF MINES

ADVICE AND GUIDANCE TO THE MINERAL INDUSTRIES, INCLUDING FUELS

Advice and guidance are given by the Bureau on technical problems pertinent to health and safety in the mineral industry as well as suitable processes for production, extraction, and utilization of minerals, metals, and fuels. The Bureau provides information on the location and character of known mineral deposits, and furnishes statistics on production, consumption, mining methods, and health and safety with respect to minerals. Requests should be made to the Director, Bureau of Mines, Department of the Interior, Washington, D.C., 20240, or one of the following offices:

Chief, Eastern Administrative Office
Bureau of Mines
Department of the Interior
4800 Forbes Avenue
Pittsburgh, Pa. 15213

Chief, Western Administrative Office
Bureau of Mines
Department of the Interior
Room 200, New Customhouse
Denver, Colo. 80202

General Manager, Helium Operations
Bureau of Mines
Department of the Interior
Post Office Box 10085
Amarillo, Tex. 79106

PUBLICATIONS

Bulletins. Report results of important Bureau programs and investigations of scientific, historical, or economic significance. Sold by the Superintendent of Documents, Government Printing Office, Washington, D.C., 20402.

Reports of Investigations and Information Circulars. The former series presents results of various phases of laboratory research. The latter consists of reports, reviews, and digests, whose primary purpose is to facilitate exchange of information between Government and industry. They include surveys of mineral resources and bibliographies. Most are obtainable from the Bureau of Mines, Publication Distribution Section, 4800 Forbes Avenue, Pittsburgh, Pa., 15213. A few are sold by the Superintendent of Documents, Government Printing Office, Washington, D.C., 20402.

Mineral Facts and Problems. Bulletin 630, 1965 Edition. An encyclopedic summary of the various minerals, metals, and fuels, giving information on resources, technology, uses, research, and outlook. Cloth bound, $6.75.

List of Publications. Published monthly, annually, and quinquennially by the Bureau of Mines. Obtainable free upon request. List of Publications of the Bureau of Mines issued from July 1, 1910, to January 1, 1960, with subject and author index, $4.25; List of Journal Articles by Bureau of Mines Authors published July 1, 1910, to January 1, 1960, with subject index, $1.75.

Mineral Statistics. These are published weekly, monthly, and quarterly or on other periodic bases for nearly all mineral commodities and also on accidents and fatalities in mining and quarrying. Obtainable from Bureau of Mines. Requests should indicate commodities or subjects of particular interest.

Minerals Yearbooks. Issued annually in 4 volumes. Volume I. Metals and Minerals (Except Fuels); Volume II, Fuels; Volume III, Area Reports: Domestic; and Volume IV, Area Reports: International. Available from Superintendent of Documents. Prices vary.

OFFICE OF COAL RESEARCH

DEVELOPMENT OF NEW AND EXPANDED COAL MARKETS

The Office of Coal Research (OCR) conducts a contract research program directed toward creating new and expanded markets for all types of coal. Contracts are awarded for work leading toward improved methods of mining, preparing, transporting, and utilizing coal, as well as for economic and marketing studies directed toward improved coal merchandising. The Office invites contract proposals from commercial organizations, educational institutions, trade associations, and agencies of States for consideration and evaluation.

PUBLICATIONS

A booklet, "Annual Report of the Office of Coal Research," describes work underway and completed in each calendar year and discusses the results obtained from the research undertaken. It is available without charge from OCR. In addition, a detailed report on work performed and results secured is made available at cost following the completion or termination of each contract. Information for ordering individual contract reports may be secured by writing OCR. The address is: Office of Coal Research, Department of the Interior, Washington, D.C., 20240.

OFFICE OF SALINE WATER

LOW COST PROCESSES FOR SALT WATER CONVERSION

The Office of Saline Water is responsible for developing low-cost processes for the conversion of saline water to fresh. The research program is carried on by means of contracts or grants with universities, private research organizations and industrial firms. The Office of Saline Water stands ready to evaluate research proposals to determine their technical merit or economic potential. Worthy proposals may be supported by a research and development contract.

SMALL BUSINESS COMPETENCE

Many small businesses may have competence in this area. The Office of Saline Water encourages their interest and participation in this program. Some businesses may face problems of water quantity or quality that may be solved by installing saline water conversion equipment. Information on the availability of such equipment can be obtained without charge from the Office of Saline Water. Technical information concerning the development status of saline water conversion processes is also available from the Office of Saline Water, Department of the Interior, Washington, D.C., 20240.

PUBLICATIONS

The Office of Saline Water publishes an annual report which gives a general description of research and development activities supported during the calendar year. This report is available to educational institutions, public libraries and agencies of National, State, and Municipal governments, without charge, from the Office of Saline Water. Others interested may obtain the report by sending $2.00 to the Superintendent of Documents, U.S. Government Printing Office, Washington, D.C., 20402.

Many technical reports covering research activities sponsored by the Office of Saline Water have been published. Some are for sale by the Clearing House for Federal and Scientific Information, 5285 Port Royal Road, Springfield, Va., 22151. Others are for sale by the Superintendent of Documents, U.S. Government Printing Office, Washington, D.C., 20402.

OFFICE OF OIL AND GAS

ADVICE AND ASSISTANCE ON OIL AND GAS MATTERS

The Office of Oil and Gas is a staff agency that provides advice and assistance on oil and gas policies, and on technical and economic aspects of the business. It serves as the principal channel of communication between the Federal Government and the Interstate Oil Compact Commission, State oil and gas regulatory bodies, and the petroleum and gas industries, and develops petroleum and gas mobilization and civil defense plans.

The advice and consultative services of the Office of Oil and Gas are available to both Federal and State agencies, the petroleum, gas, and allied industries, and the public on matters concerning worldwide petroleum and gas operations, including the short-term and long-range peacetime and wartime outlook for petroleum, gas, and products. Information and advice are also furnished regarding emergency plans, survival, and the continuity of oil and gas industries' operations in case of attack on the Continental United States.

REQUESTS FOR INFORMATION

Requests for advice or assistance on oil or gas matters may be directed to the Director, Office of Oil and Gas, Department of the Interior, Washington, D.C., 20240.

BUREAU OF RECLAMATION

ENGINEERING AND TECHNOLOGICAL DATA

The Bureau of Reclamation has a staff of skilled and experienced engineers, scientists, and other professional employees who are engaged in planning, designing, constructing and operating water resource development projects throughout the Western United States. In conducting this program, numerous engineering and other books and monographs are developed which would be useful to engineering, construction, architectural and other businesses engaged in water resource development and conservation activities.

PUBLICATIONS

A complete list of Reclamation publications available for free distribution and available for sale may be obtained by writing to the Bureau of Reclamation, Denver, Colo., 80225. A partial, representative, listing of Reclamation publications is shown below:

Reclamation Era. A quarterly magazine presenting various phases of land reclamation, including irrigation, crops, pasturing, and land recovery. Also lists major construction and materials for which future bids will be requested
. as well as recent major contract awards. Available from Superintendent of Documents, Washington, D.C., 20402. 50¢ a year.

Design of Small Dams. Illustrated book, mainly technical discussion of investigation, design, and construction of small dams. Available from Superintendent of Documents, Washington, D.C., 20402. $6.50.

Reclamation Project Data. Comprehensive, authoritative reference on Reclamation developments and works as they stood on June 30, 1958. Available from Superintendent of Documents, Washington, D.C., 20402. $6.75.

The Contribution of Irrigation and the Central Valley Project to the Economy of the Area and the Nation. Assesses the impact of irrigation and related developments on the local and national economy in a detailed study of the physical features of the projects in the Valley. Available free from Bureau of Reclamation, Denver, Colo., 80225.

Stress Analysis of Concrete Pipe. Engineering Monograph. Available from Bureau of Reclamation, Denver, Colo., 80225. 35¢.

A Rapid Method of Construction Control for Embankments of Cohesive Soil. Engineering Monograph. Available from Bureau of Reclamation, Denver, Colo., 80225. 60¢.

BUSINESS OPPORTUNITIES IN RECLAMATION CONSTRUCTION CAMPS AND TOWNS

The development of water resource projects in certain isolated areas of the western United States at times requires that the Bureau of Reclamation establish community facilities to be utilized by both Bureau and contractor employees. The communities of Page, Arizona, and Dutch John, Utah, are examples of Reclamation towns that have been recently established. When such conditions exist there are opportunities for private enterpreneurs to establish small businesses.

Requests for information concerning business opportunities in Reclamation construction camps should be sent to the Bureau of Reclamation, Department of the Interior, Washington, D.C., 20240.

BONNEVILLE POWER ADMINISTRATION

SET-ASIDES OF PROCUREMENT CONTRACTS FOR SUPPLIES AND MATERIALS

In accordance with General Services Administration and Departmental regulations, Bonneville Power Administration in its procurement contracts for supplies and materials, and construction, sets aside a portion of the requirements to be procured only from qualified small business firms. The Bonneville Power Administration Branch of Supply is located at 830 Northeast Holladay, Portland, Oreg., 97208.

LOW POWER RATES FOR INDUSTRY

Bonneville Power Administration's industrial rates—are the lowest in the Nation and have inspired a considerable growth of power-using industry, both large and small, within the Bonneville Power Administration area. The Administration's Branch of Power Marketing will gladly assist small industries wishing to locate near the Western market by putting them in touch with community development agencies who can provide information on resources, labor force, tax structure, and plant location.

NATIONAL PARK SERVICE

OPPORTUNITIES IN NATIONAL PARK AREAS

In carrying out the dual responsibility of preserving the areas of the National Park System for the enjoyment of this and future generations and at the same time making them available for public use, it is the policy to authorize only those public facilities and services reasonably necessary for the full enjoyment of the area. Where adequate accommodations exist or can be provided by private enterprise outside such areas, they are not authorized within them. In the older parks and monuments which have been established for some years, most necessary facilities and services are authorized to be provided by concessioners who have been operating in them for some time. Therefore, the majority of business opportunities exist, or will develop in the more recently established parks and monuments, and in the recreational areas. The types of facilities authorized will vary from area to area, depending on location, size, and need. In general, however, business opportunities will be for accommodations such as motels, restaurants, service stations, shops and stores of various kinds, saddle horse service, and marinas. A circular, described below, contains information concerning the procedures to be followed in the granting of these concessions.

PUBLICATIONS

Circular, "General Information Concerning the Granting of Concessions in the Areas Administered by the National Park Service."

For the circular and an application form to be completed by those wishing to receive prospectuses inviting offers for the installation and/or operation of concessions address: Director, National Park Service, Department of the Interior, Washington, D.C., 20240.

BUREAU OF LAND MANAGEMENT

TIMBER SET-ASIDES AND LAND USE

The Bureau of Land Management has a program of timber set-asides for small forest industries and stands ready to discuss with small business its land and resource needs and to expedite as far as possible under the Public Land Laws the sale, lease or issuance of permit for use of public lands. Any valid proposal for utilization of the public domain and its ground or surface resources will be given adequate review in the light of national policy and public law.

CONTACTS

Small Business should discuss its needs with the appropriate State directors of the Bureau of Land Management:

State Director
Bureau of Land Management
U.S. Department of the Interior
Federal Building and U.S. Court House, Room 4017
650 Capitol Mall, Room 4032
Sacramento, Calif. 95814

State Director
Bureau of Land Management
U.S. Department of the Interior
Post Office Box 11505
8217 Federal Building
Salt Lake City, Utah 84111

State Director
Bureau of Land Management
U.S. Department of the Interior
U.S. Post Office and Courthouse Building
2120 Capitol Avenue
Post Office Box 1828
Cheyenne, Wyo. 82001

State Director
Bureau of Land Management
U.S. Department of the Interior
U.S. Courthouse
300 Booth Street
Post Office Box 1551
Reno, Nev. 89505

State Director
Bureau of Land Management
U.S. Department of the Interior
323 Federal Building
Post Office Box 2237
Boise, Idaho 83701

State Director
Bureau of Land Management
U.S. Department of the Interior

Room 14023, Federal Building
1961 Stout Street
Denver, Colo. 80202

State Director
Bureau of Land Management
U.S. Department of the Interior
Room 3022, Federal Building
Phoenix, Ariz. 85025

State Director
Bureau of Land Management
U.S. Department of the Interior
316 North 26th Street
Billings, Mont. 59101

State Director
Bureau of Land Management
U.S. Department of the Interior
U.S. Post Office & Federal Building
South Place
Post Office Box 1449
Santa Fe, N. Mex. 87501

State Director
Bureau of Land Management
U.S. Department of the Interior
710 Northeast Holladay
Portland, Oreg. 97232

State Director
Bureau of Land Management
U.S. Department of the Interior
555 Cordova Street
Anchorage, Alaska 99501

State Director
Eastern States Office
Bureau of Land Management
U.S. Department of the Interior
1728 L Street NW.
Washington, D.C. 20240

PUBLIC LAND LAWS

A comprehensive discussion of the Public Land Laws which might be of interest to Small Business is contained in Title 43 of the Code of Federal Regulations.

BUREAU OF INDIAN AFFAIRS

INDIAN INDUSTRIAL DEVELOPMENT PROGRAM

The Bureau of Indian Affairs is the agency of the Federal Government concerned with the welfare of American Indians. In cooperation with communities, States, and other Federal Agencies, the Bureau is actively encouraging Indian tribes to explore industrial development opportunities and is helping them establish contact with industrial firms interested in new or branch plant loca-

tions. The Bureau also provides financial assistance for on-the-job training programs.

TECHNICAL ASSISTANCE

Assistance is available to tribal and reservation communities in the organization of local industrial development foundations and corporations, committees, and programs, and in the preparation of industrial fact sheets for determining which types of industries are most suited to the area. Field Industrial Development specialists located in metropolitan areas contact industrialists who are interested in plant expansion to acquaint them with the resources and opportunities available in reservation areas.

The Branch of Industrial Development of the Bureau of Indian Affairs functions as a connecting link between tribal or local community groups in Indian labor areas and industrial management. In this capacity, the Branch is in a position to furnish management with general information on local labor supply, occupational skills and productivity, resources and facilities available at the various proposed plant sites, available financial assistance, tax structure, transportation, and many other related items. Detailed information on specific locations is assembled on request.

Examples of industries located on Indian reservations include: Electronic components manufacture and assembly, plastic pipe, costume jewelry, precision gears, soft goods and quilts, women's apparel, tufted carpets, and fishing tackle assembly.

FINANCIAL ASSISTANCE

Financial assistance is available to employers for on-the-job training of Indian employees. Such help can be furnished by the Bureau of Indian Affairs under contracts with established corporations and associations that have recognized training programs in operation for their employees.

Financial assistance is also available from the Bureau's Revolving Loan Fund to assist eligible Indian tribes or groups and individual Indians in the development of business enterprises in reservation areas. Funds from this source are also available to eligible Indian tribes or groups to aid them in their efforts to attract industry to reservation areas.

CONTACTS

For further information, contact Commissioner of Indian Affairs, Department of the Interior, Washington, D.C., 20242 and Area Directors, Bureau of Indian Affairs, at the following locations: Juneau, Alaska; Phoenix, Ariz.; Sacramento, Calif.; Minneapolis, Minn.; Billings, Mont.; Gallup, N. Mex.; Anadarko, Okla.; Muskogee, Okla.; Portland, Oreg.; and Aberdeen, S. Dak.

PRINTED MATERIALS

The Indian Industrial Development Program— A New Industrial Opportunity (brochure); State and U.S. maps showing reservation locations; industrial fact sheets and brochures; and special reports on specific reservation areas. These are obtainable from the Bureau of Indian Affairs at no cost.

BUREAU OF COMMERCIAL FISHERIES

FISHERY LOANS

Loans are available to owners of fishing vessels and fishing gear to finance and refinance the purchase, construction, operation, maintenance, and repair of fishing vessels and gear, and for research into the basic problems of fisheries when conducted as an integral part of vessel or gear operation. The interest rate is 5 percent yearly and maturity of loans must not exceed 10 years. Security is required. Request for information should be addressed to the nearest field office listed below.

Bureau of Commercial Fisheries
408 Atlantic Avenue
Boston, Mass. 02210

Bureau of Commercial Fisheries
Post Office Box 6245
St. Petersburg Beach, Fla. 33706

Bureau of Commercial Fisheries
101 Seaside Avenue
Terminal Island, Calif. 90731

Bureau of Commercial Fisheries
Post Office Box 2481
Juneau, Alaska 99801

Bureau of Commercial Fisheries
2570 Dole Street
Honolulu, Hawaii 96812

Bureau of Commercial Fisheries
6116 Arcade Building
Seattle, Wash. 98101

Fishery Leaflet 542—*Fisheries Loans for Vessels, Gear, and Research* describes the program.

MORTGAGE INSURANCE

This program provides for insurance of loans and mortgages to lending institutions providing funds for construction, reconstruction, or reconditioning of fishing vessels. The interest rate is 5 percent except in cases where the Secretary finds that the money market requires a higher rate of not more than 6 percent. Requests for information should be made to the nearest field office listed above.

Fishery Leaflet 499—*Federal Fishing Vessel Mortgage and Loan Insurance* describes this program.

FISHING VESSEL CONSTRUCTION SUBSIDIES

This program is to provide financial assistance to correct inequities between foreign and domestic costs of constructing fishing vessels. The Secretary of the Interior is authorized to pay up to 50 percent of the cost of construction of a new fishing vessel provided the owner of the vessel, and the fishery in which the vessel will operate meet certain requirements. The amount that can be paid is limited to the difference between the cost of construction in domestic and foreign shipyards or 50 percent of the domestic cost, whichever is smaller. The determination of the foreign cost will be made by the Maritime Administrator. Requests for information should be made to the nearest field office listed above.

Fishery Leaflet 574—*Fishing Vessel Construction Differential Subsidy* describes this program.

TECHNICAL RESEARCH

A Branch of Technology is concerned with scientific studies designed to improve and develop methods of handling, processing, preserving, and distributing fish and shellfish. This Branch also develops information on sanitation measures and requirements for voluntary U.S. standards of grade and condition of fishery products. It also conducts USDI voluntary inspection and certification services for fishery products.

Contacts. Services can be obtained by contacting: Chief, Branch of Technology, Bureau of Commercial Fisheries, Washington, D.C., 20240 or Regional Offices as follows:

Region *Address*
1 Bureau of Commercial Fisheries, 6116 Arcade Building, Seattle, Wash., 98101.
2 Bureau of Commercial Fisheries, Don Ce-Sar Federal Center, Post Office Box 6245, St. Petersburg Beach, Fla., 33706.
3 Bureau of Commercial Fisheries, Post Office Building, Gloucester, Mass., 01930.
4 Bureau of Commercial Fisheries, 5 Research Drive, Ann Arbor, Mich., 48103.
5 Bureau of Commercial Fisheries, Post Office Box 2481, Juneau, Alaska, 99801.
6 Bureau of Commercial Fisheries, 101 Seaside Avenue, Terminal Island, Calif., 90731.

EXPLORATORY FISHING

A Branch of Exploratory Fishing especially plans and conducts programs to locate and determine the extent of new fishing grounds, and the size and character of the resource using specially equipped vessels. This Branch also designs, tests, and develops new types of fishing gear and equipment. Services can be obtained by contacting: Chief, Branch of Exploratory Fishing, Bureau of Commercial Fisheries, Department of the Interior, Washington, D.C., 20240, or Regional Offices listed herein.

ECONOMIC STUDIES

A Division of Economics performs studies concerning the economic position of the fishing industry in the national economy, and conducts basic and applied economic research studies on production efficiency, distribution problems, and consumption of fishery products. This Division furnishes consulting services on fishery economic problems including transportation problems and provides technical services for fishery cooperatives.

Economic reports are prepared on foreign and domestic fishery situation, the production and flow of fishery products from foreign producers which might affect domestic fisheries, and competitive position of domestic and foreign produced fishery products. This Division also conducts studies and provides services on foreign trade and tariff problems.

List of publications and reprints are available upon request. Services can be obtained by contacting: Assistant Director for Economics, Bureau of Commercial Fisheries, Department of the Interior, Washington, D.C., 20240.

FOREIGN FISHERIES

The Branch of Foreign Fisheries collects, coordinates, analyzes, and evaluates basic information and prepares reports on the technological, biological, and other aspects of the fisheries of foreign countries, and the effect of foreign developments on the U.S. fishery industry; conducts and coordinates Bureau participation in international organizations. The Branch also conducts studies and makes recommendations designed to aid the domestic industry by solving problems created by foreign fishery activities and developments and meet foreign competition. It also coordinates Bureau participation in the Public Law 480 research program, designed to develop fishery programs in foreign countries of mutual benefit to the U.S. fishing industry, and collaborates with the Agency for International Development (AID) in providing technical assistance in fisheries for the developing countries.

Services can be obtained by contacting: Chief, Branch of Foreign Fisheries, Bureau of Commercial Fisheries, Department of the Interior, Washington, D.C., 20240.

MARKETING

A Branch of Marketing develops markets for domestic fishery products. This is accomplished through (1) increasing the use of fishery products in school lunch and institutional menus, (2) special programs of market promotion, (3) forecasting future marketing conditions, (4) developing and expanding foreign markets, and (5) finding new uses for underutilized species. This Branch also conducts an educational service to promote fishery products by developing visual and other educational materials including test kitchen activities, fish cookery demonstrations, recipe development, and distribution of fishery motion pictures in cooperation with industry. It also issues Test Kitchen Series of fishery recipes. Motion pictures are distributed through: Bureau of Commercial Fisheries, University and Commercial Film Libraries.

Services can be obtained by contacting: Chief, Branch of Marketing, Bureau of Commercial Fisheries, Department of the Interior, Washington, D.C., 20240, or Regional Offices listed above.

STATISTICS

The Bureau of Commercial Fisheries assembles, tabulates, analyzes, and publishes fishery statistics on the volume and value of the catch by gear of capture and geographical areas; monthly landings of fish and shellfish in individual States; employment of fisherman, fishing craft, and gear in the fisheries, the volume and value of manufactured fishery products; stocks of frozen products; foreign trade in fishery commodities; and related information; and conducts staff activities relating to statistical matters. It also exercises staff supervision over Civil Defense activities of the Bureau and conducts a consulting service on fishery statistics.

Principal Field Offices

Gloucester, Mass., 01931, 14 Elm Street: Phone 283–3420.
Salisbury, Md., 21801, Post Office Building: Phone 749–6109.
Beaufort, N.C., U.S. Fisheries Laboratory, Post Office Box 500: Phone 728–4968.
Miami, Fla., 33149, 75 Virginia Beach Drive: Phone 350–5798.
New Orleans, La., 70130, Room 609, Federal Building: Phone 527–6151.
Galveston, Tex., 77550, 322 Custom House Building, 17th and Strand: Phone 762–7642.
San Pedro, Calif., 90733, Room 205, Post Office Building: Phone 831–9271.
Seattle, Wash., 98004, 706 Federal Office Building: Phone 583–5230.
Juneau, Alaska, 99801, Post Office Box 2481: Phone 586–3341.
Ann Arbor, Mich., 48105, 1451 Green Road: Phone 663–8453.

Publications

Fishery Statistics of the United States, Annual, Statistical Digest Series. Superintendent of Documents, Government Printing Office, Washington, D.C., 20401. $2.25
Fisheries of the United States, Current Fishery Statistics 3800, Annual. Office of Information, Publications Section, Fish and Wildlife Service, Department of the Interior, Washington, D.C., 20240. Free.
Fishery Statistical Publications of the Bureau of Commercial Fisheries, Fishery Leaflet 432. Office of Information, Publications Section, Fish and Wildlife Service, Department of the Interior, Washington, D.C., 20240. Free.

MARKET NEWS

The Branch of Market News collects, compiles, and analyzes information daily on landings, receipts, imports, rail and truck movements, cold-storage holdings, market conditions, and prices of fishery products and byproducts, and evaluates fisheries developments in the United States and foreign countries. The Bureau also collects, assembles, abstracts, tabulates, compiles, and prepares for release data giving the current status of the United States fisheries and distributes this information by telephone, telegraph, teletype, radio and daily mimeographed reports, monthly and annual summaries, and periodic summaries. A consulting service for market news problems is also conducted.

Publications

Commercial Fisheries Review, a monthly periodical containing current information on domestic and foreign fisheries, and related news is published by the Bureau and may be purchased at 60¢ per copy or $6.50 per year; $2 additional for foreign mailing, from the Superintendent of Documents, Government Printing Office, Washington, D.C., 20402.
"Separates"—Reprints of articles with names of authors in the fore section of the periodical and articles of special interest appearing in the trends and developments and foreign sections of *Commercial Fisheries Review* are published in the Separate series.
"Market News Leaflets"—Extensive reports on trends and developments in foreign fisheries, transmitted by the Department of State from foreign reporting posts, are published in the Market News Leaflet series.
Daily "Fishery Products Reports" issued from each of the field offices except Baltimore.
Monthly and annual summaries issued from same offices as daily reports including Baltimore.
Lists of Brokers and Importers issued for Boston, Mass.; New York City; Chicago, Ill.; Seattle, Wash.; San Francisco, San Diego, and Los Angeles Area; New Orleans, La., Houston, Tex.; and Miami, Fla.
Weekly Alaska Canned Salmon Pack Reports issued from Seattle.
Monthly Northwest Region Cold Storage Report of freezings and holdings of fishery products issued annually from Seattle.
Halibut and Troll Salmon Landings and Ex-Vessel Prices, for Seattle, Alaska Ports and British Columbia, issued annually from Seattle.
Explanatory Statement Reports issued by Boston, New York, San Pedro and Chicago field offices outlining contents of and procedures for collection of data for daily reports and summaries.

BUREAU OF SPORT FISHERIES AND WILDLIFE

[For regulations codified under this heading, see Code of Federal Regulations, Title 50, Chapter I]

OBJECTIVES

The objectives of the Bureau of Sport Fisheries and Wildlife are to insure the conservation of the

Nation's wild birds, mammals, and sport fish, both for their recreational and economic values, and to prevent their destruction or depletion while still encouraging the maximum possible present use of the Nation's fish and wildlife resources.

ORGANIZATION

The Bureau of Sport Fisheries and Wildlife consists of a headquarters office at Washington, D.C., five regional offices, and wildlife refuges, fish hatcheries, research laboratories, and other offices located throughout the United States.

ACTIVITIES

Migratory Birds.—The Bureau is responsible for the conservation of migratory bird resources pursuant to the Migratory Bird Treaty Act, other Federal acts, and treaties with the Governments of Canada and Mexico. Research is conducted on the histories, habits, distribution, and diseases of the species, and serves as a basis for management. Annual studies are made of breeding ground conditions, hunter kills, and the relative abundance of birds in cooperation wtih the States and the Governments of Canada and Mexico. The studies serve as the basis for promulgating Federal hunting regulations which are administered by the Bureau in cooperation with the States. Coordinated flyway management plans are developed in cooperation with State flyway councils, and take into account all factors affecting the resource, including the need for nesting, resting, and wintering sanctuaries.

Sport Fisheries.—A system of over 100 fish hatcheries is operated for the propagation and distribution of various species of sport fishes, including trout, salmon, bass, and catfish. The stocking of public waters and farm fish ponds is carried out in cooperation with State fish and game departments.

Research is conducted on the nutritional and disease factors that affect hatchery-raised fish and the factors that affect their survival and growth after they are planted in various waters.

The objective of the fishery management services is to increase the value to the public of hatchery-raised fish by coordinating the stocking program with State, Federal, and private agencies and by rendering an extension service to furnish these agencies modern techniques for the management of fishing waters for the maximum public enjoyment.

National Wildlife Refuges.—Approximately 300 national wildlife refuge areas, encompassing about 28,500,000 acres, are managed throughout the United States and Puerto Rico. These refuges variously provide nesting, resting, and wintering sanctuaries for migratory birds; range for big game, such as the bison, elk, and mountain sheep; and nesting grounds for upland birds and scarce exotic species, such as the whooping crane and the trumpeter swan. Portions of some of the areas are open to public hunting and fishing as biological conditions permit. When not incompatible with their wildlife management functions, the areas provide recreation for large segments of the public and economic benefits from agricultural crops, furs, timber, mineral royalties, and public concession fees.

Wildlife Services.—The basic objective of this program is the scientific management of wild animals to achieve the maximum desirable populations at times, places, and circumstances, in serving man's increasing interest in natural beauty and recreation. The Division's program has four basic functions: (1) Wildlife enhancement to improve conditions for wildlife; (2) pesticide surveillance and monitoring to prevent adverse effects of pesticides on wildlife resources; (3) animal control, as a management tool, to control those species which, under certain circumstances, adversely affect man's interests; and (4) education to improve public understanding of the management and enjoyment of wildlife resources and their environment.

Federal Aid to States and Possessions.—The Bureau administers the Federal aid in Fish and Wildlife Restoration Acts which authorize grants-in-aid to the States and Puerto Rico, Guam, and the Virgin Islands. Under this program grants-in-aid are authorized up to 75 percent of the cost of projects for investigation, acquisition of land, and development and maintenance of fish and wildlife habitat.

River Basin Studies.—This program examines the effects on fish and wildlife resources of water use projects of Federal agencies and public and private agencies under Federal license. It is authorized by the Fish and Wildlife Coordination Act, the Federal Power Act, and the Watershed Protection and Flood Prevention Act. Studies have as their objective the recommending of measures for the protection and improvement of fish and wildlife resources and are conducted in cooperation with State fish and game departments and conservation agencies.

REGIONAL OFFICES—BUREAU OF SPORT FISHERIES AND WILDLIFE

Region:	Headquarters
1. Pacific	Federal Building, Portland, Oreg., 97208.
2. Southwest	Federal Building, Albuquerque, N. Mex., 87103.
3. North Central	1006 West Lake Street, Minneapolis, Minn., 55408.
4. Southeast	809 Peachtree-Seventh Building NE., Atlanta, Ga., 30323.
5. Northeast	U.S. Post Office and Courthouse, Boston, Mass., 02109.

OFFICE OF TERRITORIES

LOANS TO SMALL BUSINESS

The Guam Economic and Development Authority is authorized to make loans to private enterprises. Inquiries should be directed to the Guam Economic Development Authority, Agana, Guam, 96910.

The Government of the Trust Territory of the Pacific Islands has a development loan fund from which loans are made to locally-owned private enterprises. Inquiries should be directed to the High Commissioner, Trust Territory of the Pacific Islands, Saipan, Mariana Islands, 96950.

TAX INCENTIVES

The three U.S. territories, American Samoa, Guam, and the U.S. Virgin Islands, have tax incentive programs to encourage the development and expansion of private enterprise. Inquiries regarding these programs should be addressed to the following officials:

Governor of American Samoa
Pago Pago, Tutuila
American Samoa, 96920

Director, Department of Commerce
Government of Guam
Agana, Guam, 96910.

Commissioner, Department of Commerce
Government of the Virgin Islands
St. Thomas, U.S. Virgin Islands, 00802

Department of Agriculture

INTRODUCTION

The U.S. Department of Agriculture (USDA) provides information on its procurement procedures in a publication "Selling to USDA." This publication indicates who does the buying, the types of items bought for the various programs, where the buying is done, and other general information. It includes a directory of purchasing offices and their locations. Copies are available at no cost from:

Contract and Procurement Management Division.
Office of Plant and Operations
U.S. Department of Agriculture
Washington, D.C. 20250

RURAL AREAS DEVELOPMENT

Rural areas development helps local people use Federal and State programs to promote economic growth, build community facilities, and develop job skills and abilities.

The Department of Agriculture began encouraging local people to organize rural areas development (RAD) committees in 1961. It backs up these local committees with on-the-spot technical advice from USDA and other Government employees in the area. The Government employees form Technical Action Panels to work with the local people.

By the start of 1965, more than 109,000 private citizens were serving on local RAD committees in 2,100 rural counties. They had carried out, or were working on, 13,500 community improvement projects.

Projects ranged from development of new industry to on-farm recreation for pay; from improved housing to installation of central water and sewer systems; from job training to better schools; and from special activities to help the poor to strengthening rural cooperatives.

In line with President Johnson's directive to the Department of Agriculture to see that "no service of the Federal Government stops at the city line," a new agency—the Rural Community Development Service—was created within USDA. Its job is to help make the services of *all* Federal agencies completely available in rural areas.

The Rural Community Development Service coordinates all USDA agency activities that contribute to rural development.

In the field the Technical Action Panels help RAD committees plan projects, find outside capital, and act, as requested, as coordinators between local people, who seek aid, and the Government agencies that may have the facilities to help.

CONTACT

Local RAD Chairman or write to Office of Information, U.S. Department of Agriculture, Washington, D.C., 20250.

GENERAL INFORMATION

Rural Areas Development At Work—PA-625.
Revitalizing America Today—PA-497.
Upswing in Rural America (Unnumbered).

SOIL CONSERVATION SERVICE

The Soil Conservation Service administers the national program of resource conservation on private land. Most of its work is done through nearly 3,000 locally organized and operated conservation districts.

Assistance to individual cooperators of soil conservation districts includes: (1) Giving the cooperator a soil and land-capability map of his land; (2) giving him information about practical alternatives for treating and using the land within its capabilities as indicated on the map; (3) helping him develop an orderly plan for installing the treatment measures and making the land use changes needed; and (4) helping him apply parts of the plan that require special skills or knowledge.

Part of the cost of conservation improvements may be shared under the Agricultural Conservation Program of Agricultural Stabilization and Conservation Service.

During the 30 years the program has been in operation, a new industry has emerged—land improvement contracting. More than 20,000 of these contractors, most of them in the small-business category, now are earning a living by helping landowners install conservation practices.

The SCS administers the watershed protection and flood prevention program; the Great Plains Conservation Program; the national inventory of soil and water conservation needs; and the Federal part of the National Cooperative Soil Survey.

The SCS has USDA leadership in recreation-for-pay developments on private land and in watershed projects: helps local sponsors in Re-

115

source Conservation and Development Projects; makes snow surveys for water forecasting in the West; and gives technical help in rural areas development, and related activities.

For more information, write: Soil Conservation Service, U.S. Department of Agriculture, Washington, D.C., 20250.

LOCATION AND ADDRESSES OF STATE OFFICES AND REGIONAL TECHNICAL SERVICE CENTERS

STATE OFFICES

William B. Lingle
Soil Conservation Building
Post Office Box 311
Auburn, Ala.　36830

Harold W. Cooper
Severns Building
Post Office Box F
Palmer, Alaska　99645

M. D. Burdick
230 North 1st Avenue
Federal Building
Room 6029
Phoenix, Ariz.　85025

William B. Davey
Federal Office Building
Room 5401
Little Rock, Ark.　72201

T. P. Helseth
Tioga Building, 2d Floor
2020 Milvia Street
Berkeley, Calif.　94704

Frederick A. Mark
12417 Federal Building
Denver, Colo.　80202

N. Paul Tedrow
Old Bookstore Building
Route 195
Storrs, Conn.　06268

William R. Ratledge
501 Academy Street
Post Office Box 418
Newark, Del.　19711

James W. Hammett
Federal Building
Post Office Box 1208
Gainesville, Fla.　32601

Cecil W. Chapman
Old Post Office Building
Post Office Box 832
Athens, Ga.　30601

Robert L. Brown
Post Office Box 1840
Honolulu, Hawaii　96805

Lee T. Morgan
5263 Emerald Street
Post Office Box 38
Boise, Idaho　83701

Lester H. Binnie
Nogle Building
605 South Neil Street
Champaign, Ill.　61823

Kenneth E. Grant
Room 212
311 West Washington Street
Indianapolis, Ind.　46204

Frank H. Mendell
Iowa Building, 4th Floor
505—6th Avenue
Des Moines, Iowa　50309

Morrie A. Bolline
760 South Broadway
Post Office Box 600
Salina, Kans.　67402

Homer A. Taff
1409 Forbes Road
Lexington, Ky.　40505

Joe B. Earle
3737 Government Street
Post Office Box 1630
Alexandria, La.　71301

Floyd W. Campbell
USDA Building
University of Maine
Orono, Maine　04473

Edward R. Keil
Hartwick Building
Room 522
4321 Hartwick Road
College Park, Md.　20742

Benjamin Isgur
27-29 Cottage Street
Amherst, Mass.　01002

V. M. Bathurst
Room 101, 1405 South Harrison Road
East Lansing, Mich.　48823

Herbert A. Flueck
517 Federal Courts Building
St. Paul, Minn.　55102

William L. Heard
Milner Building, Room 490
Lamar and Pearl Streets
Post Office Box 610
Jackson, Miss.　39205

Howard C. Jackson
Highway 40 and Illinois Avenue
Post Office Box 180
Columbia, Mo.　65202

A. B. Linford
33 East Mendenhall
Post Office Box 855
Bozeman, Mont.　59715

C. Dale Jaedicke
Room 604
134 South 12th Street
Lincoln, Nebr.　68508

Charles W. Cleary, Jr.
1479 Wells Avenue, Room 3
Reno, Nev.　89502

Albert C. Addison
Federal Building
Durham, N.H.　03824

Selden L. Tinsley
Feher Building
108 Bayard Street
Post Office Box 670
New Brunswick, N.J.　08903

Einar L. Roget
517 Gold Avenue SW.
Post Office Box 1348
Albuquerque, N. Mex.　87103

Wallace L. Anderson
400 Midtown Plaza
700 East Water Street
Syracuse, N.Y.　13210

Joseph P. Kuykendall
1330 St. Mary's Street
Post Office Box 12045
Raleigh, N.C.　27605

Lyness G. Lloyd
Federal Building
Post Office Box 1458
Bismarck, N. Dak.　58502

Raymond S. Brown
311 Old Federal Building
3d and State Streets
Columbus, Ohio　43215

Courtney A. Tidwell
Agricultural Center Building
Farm and Admiral Road
Stillwater, Okla.　74074

Albert J. Webber
1218 Southwest Washington Street
Portland, Oreg.　97206

Ivan McKeever
Central Industrial Building
100 North Cameron Street
Harrisburg, Pa.　17101

N. Paul Tedrow
(Rhode Island combined with Connecticut)

Albin T. Chalk
Federal Building, 6th Floor
901 Sumter Street
Columbia, S.C.　29201

Keith F. Myers
239 Wisconsin Avenue SW.
Post Office Box 1357
Huron, S. Dak.　57350

J. Ralph Sasser
561 U.S. Court House
Nashville, Tenn.　37203

Henry N. Smith
First National Bank Building 16-20 South Main Street
Post Office Box 648
Temple, Tex.　76502

J. A. Libby
125 South State Street
Federal Building, Room 4012
Salt Lake City, Utah　84111

Lemuel J. Peet
19 Church Street
Burlington, Vt.　05401

Tom F. McGourin
400 North 8th Street
Federal Building
Post Office Box 10026
Richmond, Va.　23240

Orlo W. Krauter
Bon Marche Building Room 840
Spokane, Wash.　99201

Thomas B. Evans
209 Prairie Avenue
Post Office Box 865
Morgantown, W. Va.　26505

William W. Russell
4601 Hammersley Road
Post Office Box 4248
Madison, Wis.　53701

Bernard H. Hopkins
Tip Top Building
345 East 2d Street
Post Office Box 340
Casper, Wyo.　82602

Harry M. Chambers
1409 Ponce de Leon Avenue
Post Office Box 9581
Santurce, P.R.　00908

REGIONAL TECHNICAL SERVICE CENTERS

H. G. Bobst
134 South 12th Street
Room 503
Lincoln, Nebr.　68508

S.J. Kortan
507 Federal Building
701 Northwest Glisan Street
Portland, Oreg.　97209

H. E. Tower
7600 West Chester Pike
Upper Darby, Pa.　19082

H. B. Martin
3600 McCart Street
Post Office Box 11222
Ft. Worth, Tex.　76110

Prepared by Administrative Services Division, Records and Communications Management Branch.

FARMERS HOME ADMINISTRATION

GENERAL

The Farmers Home Administration, a Department of Agriculture agency, provides supervised credit and management advice to farm and other rural people unable to get credit from any source at reasonable rates and terms. Programs administered by the agency strengthen family farms and rural communities.

LOANS

Operating Loans. Operating loans are made to help family farmers and ranchers make improved use of their land and labor. Loans may be used for equipment, livestock, feed, fertilizer and other farm and home operating needs; refinance chattel debts; improve the management of farm woodlands; and develop and operate income-producing recreation facilities.

Farm Ownership Loans. These loans are made to eligible farmers to enlarge, develop, and buy family farms, refinance debts, and install farmbased, income-earning recreation facilities.

Rural Housing Loans. This supervised credit is available to rural families to build, buy, and repair homes and farm buildings with special provisions for persons over 62. Loans are also available to build rental housing for elderly rural residents. There are also farm labor housing loans and grants to public agencies and nonprofit associations to construct or repair housing for farm workers.

Rural Community Water and Sewer System Loans. Loans and grants are extended to farmers and rural residents in towns of less than 5,500 for community water and sewer systems.

Recreation Area Loans. Funds are available to groups of farmers and rural residents in towns of less than 2,500 for development of nonprofit recreational areas.

Rural Renewal Loans. Such credit is made to public agencies in designated rural renewal areas, where family incomes are abnormally low, to help rebuild the area's economy. Some grant funds also may be made available for planning, surveys, feasibility and engineering studies, or similar planning essential to preparing the entire plan or for individual projects.

Emergency Loans. These loans are made to farmers or ranchers in designated areas where natural disasters, such as floods and drought have brought about the temporary need for credit not available from other sources. Loans may be made for purchase of feed, seed, fertilizer, replacement equipment, livestock, and for other items needed to maintain normal operations.

Watershed Loans. These loans are made to local organizations to help finance projects that protect and develop land and water in small watersheds. Loans are made only under watershed plans approved by the USDA's Soil Conservation Service.

Loans to Cooperatives. The agency—under the Economic Opportunity Act of 1964—makes loans to cooperatives which furnish essential processing, purchasing, and marketing services, supplies, or facilities to low-income rural families. A borrowing cooperative association must be operated for the mutual benefit of its members and under their control. At least two-thirds of the members must be low-income rural families. The loan funds can be used to develop facilities that are not otherwise available and which will serve to raise the income and living standards of member families.

Opportunity Loans. These Economic Opportunity Act loans are made to low-income rural families who need small amounts of capital to improve their earnings but are unable to obtain credit from other sources. Loans to nonfarm rural residents can finance a small business, trade, or service that supplements the family income. Such loans to farmers are made to finance farm operating expenses, improvements and development, including purchase of land, or to pay for the equipment, machinery, buildings or other items needed in a small family business, trade or service that will add to income from farming.

GENERAL INFORMATION BIBLIOGRAPHY

Farmers Home Administration in Brief—PA-547.

Farm Ownership Loans—PA-62.

Operating Loans for Better Farming, Better Living.—PA-182.

Loans to Rural Groups—PA-560.

Loans to Cooperatives—FHA Bulletin.

Opportunity Loans—FHA Bulletin.

Loans for Water Development and Soil Conservation—PA-554.

Watershed Loans—PA-406.

Rural Housing Loans—PA-476.

Housing for Senior Citizens—PA-640.

Loans for Farm Labor Housing—PA-521.

Emergency Loans—PA-490.

Loans to Family Farmers for Recreation Enterprises—PA-563.

Loans for Forestry Purposes—PA-624.

Most counties have a local Farmers Home Administration Office, often located in the courthouse or agricultural center; check the telephone directory under U.S. Government; or write: Farmers Home Administration, U.S. Department of Agriculture, Washington, D.C., 20250.

RURAL ELECTRIFICATION ADMINISTRATION

GENERAL

The REA, an agency in the Department of Agriculture, makes self-liquidating loans to rural electric cooperatives, public utility or power districts, municipalities, and power companies to bring initial and continued adequate electric service to persons in rural areas. REA loan funds may be used to finance facilities serving farms and nonfarm rural people, rural industries, and other enterprises. The REA also makes loans for extending or improving rural telephone service, and for financing house wiring, plumbing, and electrical appliances and equipment for rural consumers.

LOANS

Loans for Rural Electric Systems. The law provides that in making electrification loans, preference be given to public bodies, cooperatives, and nonprofit limited dividend associations. Loans are available for construction of electric generation and transmission facilities. Funds may be made available also to increase the capacity of existing lines (system improvements) to meet the increasing use by rural residents.

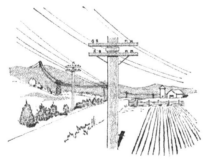

REA will assist also with problems of the borrower's plant design, construction, and operations. The Agency advises borrowers on accounting, engineering, and other management matters.

Loans for Wiring, and the Acquisition and Installation of Electrical and Plumbing Appliances and Equipment. Loans are authorized to finance the wiring of premises and acquisition and installation of electrical and plumbing appliances and

equipment, including machinery, for persons in rural areas receiving or about to receive electric service from REA electric borrowers. Such loans will generally be made for a period of 10 years, but may be made for a longer period in case of demonstrated need, not to exceed two-thirds of the estimated life of the equipment. No loans are made directly to the consumer. The funds are loaned to REA borrowers operating electric systems to finance these appliances of their members.

Rural Telephone Loan Program. Loans are made to independent telephone companies and cooperatives for extending or improving rural service. A specific requirement of rural telephone legislation is that the program be conducted so as to make telephone service available to the widest practical number of rural users.

Loan Terms. An amendment to the Rural Electrification Act established the rate of all REA loans at 2 percent and fixed the permissible loan period at a maximum of 35 years.

CONTACT

Applications must be made to Rural Electrification Administration, Department of Agriculture, Washington, D.C., 20250. Interested parties should secure copies of the recommended printed references which specify in detail the procedures to be used in making application.

CURRENT INFORMATION BULLETINS

"Electric Loan Policy for Section 4 Loans," REA Bulletin 20–2.
"Electric Loan Policy for Section 5 Loans," REA Bulletin 24–1.
"Preloan Procedures for Rural Telephone Cooperatives," REA Bulletin 320–1.
"Preloan Procedures for Telephone Loan Applicants," REA Bulletin 320–4.

THE FOREST SERVICE

The Forest Service works actively with the economic and business life of communities throughout the country, including small business. This is done through management of 154 National Forests, cooperative work with States, and forestry research.

Each year more than $125 million worth of National-Forest timber is sold to private sawmill operators. The Forest Service cooperates with the Small Business Administration to make sure that small businesses (those with fewer than 500 employees) get a fair share of timber sale offers. Of some 30,000 timber sales annually, about 90 percent are made to small businesses.

Many businesses operate on National Forests through special use permits issued to individuals or firms. These are recreational developments such as resorts, boat launching sites, campgrounds, stores, gas stations, and other facilities to serve the public.

Forest Service research develops new wood products, improves processing methods, and opens up new markets for forest products. For example, the manufacture of plywood from southern pine is a new industry that grew out of Forest Service research. Results of this broad research program are available to the public and the entire forest products industry. This is especially helpful to small wood-using industries who do not do research on their own.

The Forest Service provides advice and technical assistance to State, county, and community committees in the development of new business and industry from woodland management, processing of forest products, and outdoor recreation enterprises on private lands.

For more information, write: Forest Service, U.S. Department of Agriculture, Washington, D.C., 20250.

AGRICULTURAL STABILIZATION AND CONSERVATION SERVICE

RELATIONSHIPS WITH BUSINESS

The Agricultural Stabilization and Conservation Service requires the services of many businesses in supporting prices of farm commodities and in disposing of farm surpluses.

ASCS enters into contracts with business to buy, sell, process, package, store, and transport various price-supported and other farm commodities.

Certain processed products, particularly dairy, are purchased from processors to support farm prices of milk and butterfat. Under other surplus removal operations, processed products are purchased to stabilize farm prices and are distributed through school lunch programs and welfare organizations, both at home and abroad.

Commodities acquired in supporting farm prices are offered for sale to the trade to provide supplies needed for export and in some instances to augment supplies for domestic consumption.

In disposing of price-supported commodities to needy persons at home and abroad, services of the food processing and packaging industry are needed to transform the raw bulk product as acquired under the support program into a food product or in other instances to put a bulk product into consumer-sized packages.

Services of the warehouse industry are required to store the Commodity Credit Corporation inventory of price-supported commodities.

In managing the inventory in a businesslike manner, it is often necessary to move commodities to more advantageous storage points. Railroads, trucks, and barges are called upon to do this job and also to move commodities to ports for export.

To maintain exports of U.S.-produced farm commodities, export payments are made to exporters to enable them to offset the margin by

which domestic prices for farm commodities are above world prices.

Services of private lending agencies, mostly banks, are used for making price-support loans to farmers.

EXTENT OF SERVICES AND RELATIONSHIPS

CCC is directed by its charter to carry out its commodity operations—buying, selling, transporting, warehousing, milling, crushing or such other handling as may be needed—to the fullest extent practicable by utilizing "the usual and customary channels, facilities, and arrangements of trade and commerce."

Accordingly, ASCS uses storage facilities in thousands of warehouses, and uses the service of thousands of domestic and ocean carriers, processors, handlers, cooperative associations and exporters in carrying out its programs.

Lending agencies help in the price support program by making loans directly to cotton producers. Settlement of cotton loans is made in certificates of interest. Funds are advanced direct to grain farmers on certificates of interest. Lending agencies, including local banks, gins and warehouses, may hold these certificates of interest as an interest-bearing item, transfer them to another bank or cash them through the banking system.

CCC adapts its operations wherever feasible to adopted trade customs and practices. It carries on its day-to-day dealings with trade elements much as would a commercial corporation conducting a commercial-type business.

Information on CCC-owned commodities available for sale is contained in a Monthly Sales List issued by CCC on the last day of each month and effective for the following month. This list aids in moving CCC-owned commodities into domestic or export use through regular commercial channels. It specifies the kinds of commodites available, the terms and conditions under which the commodities are offered, and the numbers of the different sales announcements.

The job of carrying out these varied activities and of guarding the investment of post-farm operations for CCC lies primarily in the four ASCS Commodity field offices at Evanston, Ill., Kansas City, Mo., New Orleans, La., and Minneapolis, Minn.

The Evanston and Kansas City offices are grain and bean offices.

The New Orleans office handles the cotton price support program. Catalogs for upland and extra long staple cotton, showing quantities, qualities and locations, are issued every two weeks. They may be purchased for a nominal fee.

The Minneapolis office is responsible for all processed products, such as butter, cheese, nonfat dry milk, flour, cornmeal, linseed oil, honey and vegetable oil products. In addition, this office handles a variety of other products which are donated to the national school lunch program and other eligible groups.

Each of these field offices provides warehouse handbooks to assist businessmen in filing invoices with CCC for storage.

CONSERVATION

More than $400 million have been invested in conservation each year as result of the Agricultural Conservation Program.

Through this program the Government each year shares with more than a million land owners the cost of increasing soil, water, woodland, and wildlife conservation practices on farms and ranches.

Cost-shares may be in the form of either cash or a purchase order for a conservation service or material.

Under the cash plan, farmers and ranchers pay the total cost of establishing the approved practice and later are reimbursed for the Government's share of the cost.

Under the purchase order plan, the Government's cost-share is advanced through the purchase for farmers and ranchers of a conservation material, such as seed, trees, or essential minerals, or for a service, such as earth moving or tree planting.

Vendors who furnish the material or service bill the Government and receive payment for the Government's share of the cost. Ranchers and farmers pay the difference.

Conservation practices under ACP vary, bringing divergent activity to the local scene. These many activities stimulate need for fuel, tires, machinery, and the many other materials and services farmers require. They also provide jobs.

The ACP is administered locally by ASCS officials in more than 3,000 agricultural counties, usually located in county seat towns or cities.

STORAGE

Also stimulating the local economy is the storage program under which farmers borrow money from CCC to build new on-the-farm storage space to house commodities they put under price support. From July 1949 through November 1963, CCC had made about 182,000 loans. These loans are repaid in four installments over a period of 5 years, at 4 percent interest.

To keep commodities in on-the-farm storage in sound condition, 10,200 loans were made from December 1949 to November 1963 for drying equipment. Drying equipment loans are payable in three installments over a period of 3 years, also at 4 percent interest.

WHERE AND HOW SERVICES MAY BE OBTAINED BY BUSINESSMEN

Interested businessmen are invited to write to the Agricultural Stabilization and Conservation Service, U.S. Department of Agriculture, Washington, D.C., 20250, with respect to all commodities, or for specified commodities to the designated ASCS commodity office.

To be placed on the mailing list to receive CCC Monthly Sales List, address: Director, Procurement and Sales Division, ASCS, U.S. Department of Agriculture, Washington, D.C., 20250.

To receive offers based on announcements for purchasing or processing dairy products, other than those owned by CCC, milled rice, rolled wheat, bulgur, rolled oats and fats and oils, address: Director, Procurement and Sales Division, ASCS, U.S. Department of Agriculture, Washington, D.C., 20250.

To receive offers based on announcements for packaging or processing dairy products owned by CCC, address: Director, Minneapolis ASCS Commodity Office, 6400 France Avenue, South Minneapolis, Minn., 55410.

Programs on peanuts, tobacco, and rosin are handled in production areas by associations of producer cooperatives working under contractual agreements with CCC. For their names and locations, address: Director, Producer Associations Division, ASCS, U.S. Department of Agriculture. Washington, D.C., 20250.

GRAIN OFFICES

Evanston ASCS Commodity Office, 2201 Howard St., Evanston, Ill., 60202. Tel: Long Distance—University 9–0600 (Evanston exchange) local—Rogers Park 1–5000 (Chicago, Ill.). (Connecticut, Delaware, Florida, Georgia, Illinois, Indiana, Iowa, Kentucky, Maine, Maryland, Massachusetts, Michigan, New Hampshire, New Jersey, New York, North Carolina, Ohio, Pennsylvania, Rhode Island, South Carolina, Tennessee, Virginia, Vermont, and West Virginia.)

Branch Office—Minneapolis ASCS Branch Office, 310 Grain Exchange Building, Minneapolis, Minn., 55415, Tel: 334–2051. (Minnesota, Montana, North Dakota, South Dakota, and Wisconsin.)

Kansas City ASCS Commodity Office, 8930 Ward Parkway (P.O. Box 205), Kansas City, Mo., 64141. Tel: Emerson 1–0860. (Alabama, Arkansas, Colorado, Kansas, Louisiana, Mississippi, Missouri, Nebraska, New Mexico, Oklahoma, Texas, and Wyoming.)

Branch Office—Portland ASCS Branch Office, 1218 Southwest Washington Street, Portland, Oreg., 97205. Tel: Capitol 6–3361. (Alaska, Hawaii, Idaho, Nevada, Oregon, Utah, and Washington, and Arizona and California (export sales only).)

Branch Office—Berkeley ASCS Branch Office, 2020 Milvia Street, Berkeley, Calif., 94704. Tel: Thornwall 1–5121. (Arizona and California (domestic sales only).)

PROCESSED COMMODITIES OFFICE—(All States)

Minneapolis ASCS Commodity Office, 6400 France Avenue, South Minneapolis, Minn., 55410. Tel: 334-3200

COTTON OFFICES—(All States)

New Orleans ASCS Commodity Office, Wirth Building, 120 Marais Street, New Orleans, La., 70112. Tel: 529-2411.

Cotton Products and Export Operations Office, 80 Lafayette Street, New York, N.Y., 10013. Tel: Rector 2-8000.

Representative of General Sales Manager, New York area: Joseph Reidinger, 80 Lafayette Street, New York, N.Y., 10013. Tel: Rector 2-8000.

Representative of General Sales Manager, West Coast Area: Callan B. Duffy, Balboa Building, 593 Market Street, San Francisco 5, Calif. Tel: Sutter 1-3179.

CONSUMER AND MARKETING SERVICE

GENERAL

Small businessmen can benefit particularly from many of the programs of the Consumer and Marketing Service (established in February 1965).

These fall into broad groupings of Marketing Services, Regulatory Programs, Consumer Protection, and Consumer Food Programs.

MARKETING SERVICES

"*Market News*" reports on supply, demand, prices, and movement of all major farm commodities, issued daily (or seasonally for some commodities), provide small businesses with market information that narrows their handicap in competing with larger organizations.

Standards, grades and grading, acceptance services, and cotton classing offer small businesses a universal language of trade, and a variety of services that let them buy agricultural products, even in distant markets, without a personal representative to examine them; or sell agricultural products to distant customers—with assurance the quality will be as agreed upon. Although used by large companies as well, these services are especially helpful to smaller companies that cannot afford extensive brand promotion or sales representatives.

REGULATORY PROGRAMS

The Packers and Stockyards Act makes it unlawful for any packer or any live poultry dealer or handler to do anything that has the effect of creating a monopoly, manipulating prices, or restraining commerce. It is representative of many laws administered by the C&MS to maintain fair play and competition in marketing—with the effect

of helping many small businesses escape being squeezed out.

The United States Warehouse Act established a program both voluntary and regulatory. Businessmen who choose to apply for Federal warehouse licenses, furnishing the bonds and permitting the inspections that go along with it, gain several advantages—chiefly the confidence of their customers, and the ability of the owners of stored products to use warehouse receipts as security for loans.

CONSUMER PROTECTION

Inspection of farm products (compulsory for meat and poultry sold across State lines and voluntary for many other products) helps make U.S. food the safest, most wholesome in the world. Related requirements of plant sanitation and proper labeling of products build customer confidence in businesses, large and small—so much so that many companies advertise the fact their products have been inspected or graded by the USDA.

CONSUMER FOOD PROGRAMS

Commodity Distribution Programs are a meeting point for programs to make sure that all Americans (and many people in other lands) are adequately fed, and programs to make sure that farmers get decent incomes. Sometimes this means Federal purchase of processed or perishable foods specifically for distribution to low-income families, to institutions, or to schools. In general, small businesses are assured of an opportunity to share fairly in supplying such commodities.

The National School Lunch Program, requiring that Federal funds be matched at least three to one from State and local resources, creates local markets for foods worth $700 million to $800 million.

The Special Milk Program, through cash payments to schools and child care institutions, enlarges this local market for foods still more. Small businesses would do well to study their potential for sharing in these local markets.

The Food Stamp Program, made permanent in 1964 after a 3-year tryout, is expanding steadily to more areas and more people. Wherever it goes, local grocers and the many businesses that supply or service them are benefiting from the added food-buying power of low-income customers.

The Plentiful Foods Program helps all parts of the food industry, in many ways, to merchandise more of the foods that are particularly abundant at any given time.

CONTACT

Further information can be obtained from the Consumer and Marketing Service, U.S. Department of Agriculture, Washington, D.C., 20250; or from any of the following area offices of the Information Division, Consumer and Marketing Service, U.S. Department of Agriculture:

50 Seventh Street NE., Atlanta, Ga. 30823	346 Broadway New York, N.Y. 10013
536 South Clark Street Chicago, Ill. 60605	630 Sansome Street, San Francisco, Calif. 94111
500 South Ervay Street, Dallas, Tex. 75201	

COMMODITY EXCHANGE AUTHORITY

The Commodity Exchange Authority provides regulation of futures trading on licensed commodity exchanges. The agency maintains regional offices in Chicago, Minneapolis, Kansas City, New York and New Orleans. Major purposes of regulation by the agency are to maintain fair trading practices and competitive prices on the exchanges and to prevent price manipulation and other violations of the Commodity Exchange Act. Quotations from the exchanges are used for price basing of such leading commodities as wheat, corn, cotton, wool, soybeans, and vegetable oils, and their products and byproducts. The proper functioning of futures trading and pricing thus has a significant bearing on prices to producers and consumers. Regulatory services of the Commodity Exchange Authority include daily surveillance of large traders' operations, registration and auditing of brokerage firms to protect commodity customers funds, and investigations to provide evidence in prosecutions of persons and firms charged with violation of the Commodity Exchange Act.

CEA REGIONAL OFFICES

Commodity Exchange Authority, U.S. Department of Agriculture, 141 West Jackson Boulevard, Room 1200, Chicago, Ill., 60604.

Commodity Exchange Authority, U.S. Department of Agriculture, 854 Board of Trade Building, Kansas City, Mo., 64105.

Commodity Exchange Authority, U.S. Department of Agriculture, 44 Beaver Street, Room 1202, New York, N.Y., 10004.

Commodity Exchange Authority, U.S. Department of Agriculture, 510 Grain Exchange Building, Minneapolis, Minn., 55415.

Commodity Exchange Authority, U.S. Department of Agriculture, 508 Cotton Exchange Building, New Orleans, La., 70130.

FEDERAL CROP INSURANCE CORPORATION

Federal Crop Insurance has a double value to its farmer-policyholders and to the community and businessmen affected when crop failure occurs. It provides indemnity checks to replace money lost in the effort to produce a crop, and collateral for credit to continue farming.

Collateral assignments accepted on Federal Crop Insurance policies amount to several millions of dollars annually. Assignments against individual policies sometimes exceed $100,000.

Benefits of Crop Insurance extend far beyond the farmer. When crop disaster strikes, the stabilizing influence of Crop Insurance is of real value not only to the insured farmer, but those with whom he trades or from whom he borrows money. It has become almost automatic, when the impact of crop disaster is felt, for the farm and business community to request help from the Federal Government. They seek it for the very reason that Federal Crop Insurance was initiated and operates—to cushion the shock of the financial impact when there is little or no crop to sell or feed.

Bankers and others who extend credit on the basis of a crop mortgage realize that such collateral has value only if a crop is produced. However, this fact does not keep them from getting caught along with the farmer when crop disaster strikes.

Federal Crop Insurance is available in over 1,200 counties. Congress allows an addition of 150 counties yearly if funds are available. It insures against crop loss from drought, insect infestation, plant disease, flood, hail, wind, frost, freeze, excessive rain, hurricane, tornado, and over 100 other unavoidable causes.

To put up his Crop Insurance policy as collateral for a loan or credit, an insured farmer need only file an assignment form at the county Crop Insurance office. The Corporation will then pay an indemnity due by a joint check to the insured and the person or firm in whose favor the assignment was executed.

For more information, write: Federal Crop Insurance Corporation, U.S. Department of Agriculture, Washington, D.C., 20250.

ECONOMIC RESEARCH SERVICE

The Economic Research Service conducts research in agricultural economics and marketing, both domestic and foreign commerce.

Economic and Statistical Analysis.—Includes broad economic research and analysis on factors affecting agricultural prices and income, commodity outlook and situation, food demand and consumption, and relationships between agriculture and the national economy.

Marketing Economics.—Marketing research is concerned with market costs, structure, and development, market potentials, and the distribution and merchandising of agricultural products. Studies are conducted to determine the potentials for market expansion of agricultural products. Cost analysis research is conducted on the marketing of crops and animal products to determine ways of increasing efficiency and reducing costs, increasing returns to growers and providing consumers with the choices they desire. The research results are widely disseminated.

Farm Production Economics.—Research is conducted on the economics of farm organization and management, financial requirements and returns, adjustments in production to prospective market demands and changing technology, development of measures of output and productivity, and appraisal of alternative agricultural production policies and programs.

Natural Resource Economics.—Studied are the economics of use, conservation, development, management, and control of natural resources and their relationship to general economic activity. Included are economic analyses of land and water resources, and the economic and social conditions affecting their use.

Economic Development Research.—A broad research program is conducted on economic advancement of rural areas, the opportunities and employment available to the people in these regions, and the factors affecting them, such as local governments and other organizations. Special attention is given to problems of poverty among rural people.

Foreign Regional Analysis.—Effort is on economic analyses and interpretations of conditions and development affecting supply, demand, and trade in farm products in foreign countries and their impact on U.S. agricultural exports. Studies are conducted on the long-range outlook for U.S. agricultural exports, based in part on research contracts with foreign institutions to project the demand and supply of farm products in foreign countries for several years.

Foreign Development and Trade.—Economic development processes in foreign countries are analyzed to ascertain the contribution of agricultural development to general economic growth, the priority of various aspects of agricultural development, trends in national income, and economic effects of present and proposed Food for Peace programs.

STATISTICAL REPORTING SERVICE

The Statistical Reporting Service prepares estimates and reports of production, supply, price, and other aspects of the agricultural economy. These include prices received by farmers for products sold and prices paid by farmers for commodities and services; preparation of indexes of prices received and paid; and computation of parity prices, farm employment, and wage rates.

The reports include statistics on field crops, fruits and vegetables, and numbers of milk cows, livestock, livestock products, and poultry.

Other activities involve statistical standards, methodological research, automatic data processing, and special consumer surveys for the Department of Agriculture.

For lists of publications and research reports, including annual and monthly summaries, write to Division of Information, OMS, U.S. Department of Agriculture, Washington, D.C., 20250.

NATIONAL AGRICULTURAL LIBRARY

The National Agricultural Library cooperates jointly with the other national libraries, to collect, on a worldwide basis, publications in the sciences and organize them for best use. Its services are made available not only to the Department of Agriculture but throughout the world to research and educational institutions, scientists, industry, and the general public.

With resources of about 1,248,000 volumes, it is the largest agricultural library in the United States, covering the field of agriculture in its broadest sense—botany, zoology, chemistry, veterinary medicine, forestry, plant pathology, livestock, poultry, entomology, and general agriculture. Publications are received regularly from more than 200 countries, printed in approximately 50 different languages.

Information contained in the Library's collection is made available through loans of publications, reference services, photocopies of materials and bibliographies.

For more information, write: Program Coordination Services, National Agricultural Library, U.S. Department of Agriculture, Washington, D.C., 20250.

AGRICULTURAL RESEARCH SERVICE

Managers of small businesses involved in the production, processing, or marketing of goods—particularly those related to agriculture—can benefit in many ways from Agricultural Research Service programs. At the end of the fiscal year 1965, for example, there were 1,327 unexpired public service patents available for licensing. Many of these patents, all stemming from agricultural research, cover processes now being used by small businessmen.

In agricultural engineering, for example, research on farm equipment benefits not only the small business farmer who uses the equipment but also the small businessman who manufactures it. * * * In the area of marketing, numerous managers of egg crating and packaging plants have been able to mechanize their plants because of automatic candling equipment—an outcome of agricultural research. * * * Many businesses—both large and small—are licensed to use patents that have come out of utilization research. Examples are businesses that produced dehydrated potato products and concentrated fruit juices.

Information concerning patents may be obtained by writing to the Agricultural Research Service, U.S. Department of Agriculture, Washington, D.C., 20250.

Small businessmen are in regular contact with USDA's four Utilization Research and Development Divisions, where they obtain information on new or improved methods of utilizing agricultural materials, wastes, and byproducts.

Broiler plant operators faced a problem, for example, of getting rid of feathers—until utilization research found that they could be used in feed. Not only did the broiler operators benefit, but feed processors did, too.

USDA's four Utilization Research and Development Divisions, and their areas of work, are listed here and may be contacted with specific requests for information.

The Northern Division, 1815 North University Street, Peoria, Ill., conducts research on corn, wheat, and other cereal grains, soybeans, flaxseed, and other oilseeds of the region, and new crops to serve as profitable alternates to those in surplus.

The Eastern Division, 600 East Mermaid Lane, Philadelphia 18, Pa., conducts research primarily on livestock and dairy products and byproducts, eastern fruits and vegetables, and tobacco.

The Southern Division, Post Office Box 19687, New Orleans 19, La., conducts research on cotton and cottonseed, rice, citrus and other fruits of the region, sweetpotatoes and other southern vegetables, peanuts, and pine-gum products.

The Western Division, 800 Buchanan Street, Albany 10, Calif., conducts research on western fruits and vegetables, wheat, barley, rice, poultry, and eggs, sugarbeets, wool, alfalfa and other forage crops.

Results of agricultural research of interest and use to small businessmen are published regularly in trade papers, magazines, and newspapers. Trade groups keep in touch with this work through research advisory committees. At each of the four ARS utilization research division laboratories, a technically trained official is designated as liaison between the utilization division and industry. And USDA representatives attend meetings of industrial associations and discuss research results that pertain to many fields of interest to small businessmen.

Publications aimed specifically at helping a given trade are made available by the USDA. And frequently, when a research project has been completed and tested in a pilot plant, representatives of industrial groups are invited to see the operation and to discuss the possibilities of commercial adaptation.

FOREIGN AGRICULTURAL SERVICE

The Foreign Agricultural Service administers several programs which are of both immediate and long-range benefit to small business. Chief of these are a foreign market development program carried out in cooperation with agricultural trade organizations, sales of agricultural commodities on special terms under the Food for Peace program, a worldwide agricultural intelligence system through agricultural attaches abroad, and a continuing program of activities designed to improve access to foreign markets for U.S. farmers and agricultural trading firms.

The market development program is designed to develop increased markets for U.S. farm products in countries that buy for hard currencies. While promotional work is done chiefly by trade organizations, it is U.S. business firms which make the actual sales.

Approximately 50 trade organizations participate in this program. They carry on foreign promotion in behalf of producers, processors, handlers and exporters of farm commodities. Among the products represented are cotton, dairy products, poultry, dairy cattle, soybeans and soybean products, dried fruits, citrus fruits, cranberries, canned fruits, deciduous fruits, wheat and flour, feed grains, rice, dry beans and peas, seeds, lard, tallow, leather, beef, beef cattle, tobacco, and processed foods. Firms handling these or other exportable agricultural products may obtain additional information about the export market by communicating with their national association or writing to Foreign Agricultural Service, U.S. Department of Agriculture, Washington, D.C., 20250.

The Foreign Agricultural Service also makes available to U.S. farmers, processors, exporters, and other small business groups a wide range of information to aid foreign marketing. This information is published in the weekly magazine, "Foreign Agriculture," and in foreign agriculture circulars issued at irregular intervals. These publications cover such topics as world agricultural production, foreign competition, market prospects, trade promotion, and many other topics of concern to U.S. business in making necessary adjustments to meet changing market situations abroad. "Foreign Agriculture" is available on a subscription basis to business firms at $7 a year. Subscription orders should be placed with Superintendent of Documents, Government Printing Office, Washington, D.C., 20402. Write to Foreign Market Information Division, Foreign Agricultural Service, U.S. Department of Agriculture, Washington, D.C., 20250, for a sample copy of "Foreign Agriculture" or to be placed on the free list for foreign agriculture circulars.

The Food for Peace program makes farm commodities available on special terms to foreign countries that cannot pay cash. This provides immediate market outlets for U.S. agricultural business firms. It also stimulates the economic development of the recipient countries and speeds the time when they will be cash customers of U.S. business.

In this program, the Foreign Agricultural Service issues authorizations for purchase of commodities for shipment under Title I (sales for foreign currencies) and Title IV (long-term dollar credits). The actual exports in both cases are made by private U.S. business firms which deal with authorized purchasing agents of the recipient countries.

For further information, write Program Operations Division, Foreign Agricultural Service, U.S. Department of Agriculture, Washington, D.C., 20250.

HOW THE DEPARTMENT OF AGRICULTURE SERVES YOU

Every day your life and the lives of your family and friends are benefited by the services of the U.S. Department of Agriculture. It is involved directly or indirectly with—
The food on your table,
The cotton or wool in your clothes,
The wood in your house and its furnishings.

HOW IT STARTED

In 1862 President Lincoln approved an Act of Congress creating the Department of Agriculture "the general design and duties of which shall be to acquire and diffuse among the people of the United States useful information on subjects connected with agriculture in the most general and comprehensive sense of that word * * *."

In 1889 the Department, again by Act of Congress, became the eighth Executive Department in the Federal Government with Cabinet rank.

HOW IT WORKS

In Washington, D.C., the Secretary of Agriculture and his staff direct the programs and activities assigned to the Department by Congress. In every part of the United States, and in many foreign countries, employees administer programs and carry out responsibilities authorized by Congress.

As new laws have been added to its functions, the Department has grown. It currently is organized into various service and administrative agencies, which are divided into major groups. (See p. 128.) An Assistant Secretary or other designated official heads each group and interprets and executes its policies.

RELATIONSHIP TO LAND-GRANT COLLEGES

In 1862 Congress passed and President Lincoln signed the Land-Grant College Act. This Act donated 11 million acres of public lands to the States and Territories to provide colleges for the benefit of agriculture and the mechanical arts.

This Act was followed by others to strengthen the experimental and extension activities of the States in their relations with the Department.

In 1887 Congress authorized an agricultural experiment station in each State and Territory.

In 1914 it established the Cooperative Extension Service to extend agricultural and home economics research information of the Department and land-grant colleges to farmers and other people.

ACTIVITIES OF USDA

RESEARCH

Five USDA agencies conduct and administer research. The Director of Science and Education coordinates the work.

The Department works closely on research programs with State experiment stations, State departments of agriculture, schools of forestry, and cooperative and other public and private agencies. It administers Federal-grant funds voted for the States by Congress.

Agricultural Research Service. Carries out research on crops, soil and water conservation, agricultural engineering, livestock, human nutrition and home economics. Also develops new and expanded uses for farm commodities.

Conducts and administers a research program, using the physical and biological sciences to solve problems of market quality, transportation, and facilities.

Conducts control and regulatory programs, including plant and animal quarantines, meat inspection, and others.

Cooperative State Research Service. Administers Federal-grant payments to States under Hatch Act of 1955 and McIntire-Stennis Cooperative Forestry Research Act of 1962, for research at the agricultural experiment stations and eligible schools of forestry. Assists State experiment stations and USDA agencies in planning and coordinating scientific research programs.

Economic Research Service. Does research in general economic and statistical analysis, marketing economics, farm and resource economics, and foreign economic analysis.

Farmer Cooperative Service. Carries on research to help farmers market their products, purchase supplies, and obtain other business services through cooperatives.

Forest Service. Conducts research on growing and harvesting timber; improving water and range resources; protecting forests from fire, insects, and disease; the use of wood products and developing new ones; and improving methods of marketing forest products.

EDUCATION

Cooperative Extension Service is the field educational arm of the Department and land-grant colleges. Its work is jointly sponsored and financed by Federal, State, and local governments. The Federal Extension Service represents USDA in this activity.

In every rural county, extension workers conduct an educational program designed to help farm families and others use research findings and other Government aids. Through this program extension workers provide assistance toward more efficient production and marketing of agricultural products, improved family living, and the advancement of community affairs.

Farmer Cooperative Service carries on educational work to help farmers improve the effectiveness of their cooperatives. In these activities it cooperates with land-grant colleges, State extension offices and county agents, and with cooperatives, and the State and national organizations representing these farmer businesses.

The National Agricultural Library, largest agricultural library in the world, extends services to researchers, other libraries, institutions, and the general public; provides, at cost, microfilm and photocopy service of material in the collection; and issues monthly *Bibliography of Agriculture,* a comprehensive index to current agricultural literature.

INFORMATION

Each USDA agency provides information on its work for farmers, homemakers, and others. The Office of Information coordinates:

Publications, technical and popular, which present research results, program, regulatory, and other information on the work of USDA.

Current information, which includes press, radio and television materials, and special reports.

Visuals, which include exhibits, photos, graphics, and motion pictures.

MARKETING

The **Consumer and Marketing Service** carries out marketing and distribution programs and works with States on marketing problems.

Administers several regulatory acts relating to the marketing of farm products, and the national school lunch, food stamp, and other food distribution and surplus removal programs.

Administers marketing agreements and orders for milk, fruits and vegetables, and issues voluntary acreage marketing guides for vegetables.

Develops standards; grades and inspects a wide range of farm products.

Collects and disseminates market news on farm products in major producing and marketing areas.

The **Commodity Exchange Authority** keeps watch on and investigates traders' and brokers' operations on commodity exchanges, to prevent price manipulation and fraud, and to safeguard producer and consumer interests in pricing and marketing services of exchanges.

CONSUMER SERVICES

Consumers benefit from the work of all USDA agencies. Research is constantly serving the public interest through better plants and animals, food and nutrition, pest controls, and a host of other ways.

Consumers also gain through inspection and grading, school lunches, rural housing, electrification, conservation, and outdoor recreation programs. Send your name, address, and ZIP Code on a postcard to Office of Information for a copy of "Consumer's Guide to USDA Services." Ask for MP 959.

INTERNATIONAL AFFAIRS

The **Foreign Agricultural Service** administers USDA foreign programs in the interest of U.S. agriculture, with special emphasis on market promotion abroad. Attachés at 61 foreign posts maintain a constant flow of world agricultural intelligence.

The **International Agricultural Development Service** coordinates the Department's participation in overseas technical assistance programs. Its work includes sending agricultural technicians abroad, and training foreign specialists in the United States.

ECONOMICS

The **Economic Research Service** analyzes factors affecting farm production, prices and income, and the outlook for various commodities. It studies production efficiency, marketing costs and potentials, rural development, and agricultural finance problems. It also analyzes foreign agricultural trade, production, and Government policies.

The **Statistical Reporting Service** reports on crop and livestock production and prices paid and received by farmers; conducts surveys of consumer purchases and attitudes, and seeks to improve statistical methods in the Department.

CONSERVATION

The **Agricultural Stabilization and Conservation Service** administers the national Agricultural Conservation program that yearly shares with more than one million farmers and ranchers costs of approved soil and water conserving practices.

The **Soil Conservation Service** develops and carries out a national soil and water conservation program through 2,900 soil conservation districts.

Has USDA leadership for: Watershed protection projects, Great Plains Conservation Program, resource conservation and development projects, income-producing recreation enterprises, river basin investigations, and flood damage reduction in 11 major watersheds.

Administers the Federal part of the National Cooperative Soil Survey.

Makes and coordinates snow surveys for water forecasting in the Western States.

The **Forest Service** administers the National Forest System—186 million acres of forests and grasslands—for the best use and conservation of their resources, including water, timber, outdoor recreation, wildlife, and range. It manages publicly owned watersheds to regulate streamflow, control floods, protect water sources for industrial power, irrigation, and home use. It carries on cooperative work with States to aid private forest landowners.

STABILIZATION

The Agricultural Stabilization and Conservation Service is responsible for—

• Acreage allotments and marketing quotas, to help keep supplies in line with demand.

• Feed grain program, to divert corn, barley, and grain sorghum acreage to conservation use.

• Voluntary wheat program providing to cooperators domestic and export certificates, price-support loans, and payments for diversion of wheat acreage to conservation use.

• Cotton choice program providing domestic and export acreage allotments and price-support payments and loans to cooperators.

• Equalization payment for cotton designed to remove price inequity between domestic and foreign users of U.S. cotton.

• Cropland conversion program, on a pilot basis in 1963, to shift unneeded cropland to other uses such as grassland, trees, wildlife habitat, and recreational facilities. Continued administration of Conservation Reserve under which cropland has been shifted to conservation use.

• Price support for numerous commodities and management of commodity inventory.

• Reduction of surpluses through sales, transfers and other means. Assist Foreign Agricultural Service in foreign sales, donations, and barter of surpluses under Public Law 480 and the Agricultural Marketing Service in donating surplus commodities through domestic channels.

• Helping obtain adequate farm and commercial storage for farm products.

• Administering the Sugar Act, the National Wool Act, and the International Wheat Agreement.

• Assisting farmers in designated areas to meet conditions caused by natural disasters and other emergencies.

The **Commodity Credit Corporation** with its $14,-500,000,000 borrowing authority, finances such programs as price support, domestic and export surplus commodity disposal, foreign assistance, storage activities, and other varied operations of the U.S. Department of Agriculture.

The **Federal Crop Insurance Corporation** provides farmers "all risk" insurance protection of production expenses against unavoidable causes beyond their control such as weather, insects, and diseases. FCIC protection is available in more than one-third of the Nation's farm counties.

RURAL AREAS DEVELOPMENT

Through **Rural Areas Development (RAD)**, rural people work together in an organized fashion to improve their communities, to create new economic opportunities, and to upgrade their skills and human resources. The Department of Agriculture helps local people organize and survey their resources. Local people on the RAD committee decide what will be done, when, and how. USDA field personnel form a Technical Action Panel to work with the local organization in an advisory capacity and to help bring to the community the services of other Federal and State agencies.

The **Rural Community Development Service** has general responsibility to coordinate and expedite rural areas development programs at the Federal level, and to arrange full utilization of the Department's resources in advancing rural development objectives.

The **Farmers Home Administration** strengthens family farm and rural communities through credit accompanied by technical farm and financial management assistance.

Funds are advanced for farm operating expenses, the purchase, enlargement, and improvement of family farms, construction of rural homes and farm buildings, development of rural community water systems and recreational facilities; rural renewal projects, watershed development, soil and water conservation, shifts in land use, housing for senior citizens, farm labor housing, and the emergency credit needs of farmers.

Loans supplement and in no case compete with credit provided by other lenders. There is an FHA office serving every rural county of the United States.

The **Rural Electrification Administration** makes long-term loans to provide initial and continuing electric service in unserved rural areas. Most borrowers are nonprofit, consumer-owned cooperatives.

REA also makes loans to extend and improve telephone service in rural areas. Loans are made to telephone companies and to nonprofit associations.

Other USDA agencies that aid in rural areas development include Agricultural Stabilization and Conservation Service, Agricultural Research Service, Federal Extension Service, Forest Service, Soil Conservation Service, Farmer Cooperative Service, Consumer and Marketing Service, Cooperative State Research Service, Federal Crop Insurance Corporation, and Statistical Reporting Service.

EMERGENCY PROGRAMS

An emergency organization has been set up within USDA at national, State, and county levels to handle both natural disasters and defense programs. A special assistant to the Secretary coordinates and directs this work.

Those administering programs to feed people and to help farmers affected by floods, drought and other natural disasters would use this experience to meet USDA responsibilities in case of nuclear war. In the national defense program, USDA is responsible for food from farmer to retailer, for emergency food stockpiling, for radiological defense and fire control in rural areas, and biological and chemical warfare defense for animals and crops.

HOW USDA IS ORGANIZED

SECRETARY

UNDER SECRETARY

Deputy Under Secretary   Staff Assistants
General Counsel   Inspector General

DEPARTMENTAL ADMINISTRATION
    Administrative Assistant Secretary
        Budget and Finance, Office of
        Hearing Examiners, Office of
        Information, Office of
        Management Appraisal and Systems Development, Office of
        Management Services, Office of
        Personnel, Office of
        Plant and Operations, Office of
AGRICULTURAL ECONOMICS
    Director
        Economic Research Service
        Statistical Reporting Service
RURAL DEVELOPMENT AND CONSERVATION
    Assistant Secretary
        Farmer Cooperative Service
        Farmers Home Administration

RURAL DEVELOPMENT AND CONSERVATION—Continued
    Assistant Secretary—Continued
        Forest Service
        Rural Community Development Service
        Rural Electrification Administration
        Soil Conservation Service
AGRICULTURAL STABILIZATION
    Under Secretary
        Agricultural Stabilization and Conservation Service
        Commodity Credit Corporation
        Federal Crop Insurance Corporation
INTERNATIONAL AFFAIRS
    Assistant Secretary
        Foreign Agricultural Service
        International Agricultural Development Service
MARKETING AND CONSUMER SERVICES
    Assistant Secretary
        Commodity Exchange Authority
        Consumer and Marketing Service
SCIENCE AND EDUCATION
    Director
        Agricultural Research Service
        Cooperative State Research Service
        Federal Extension Service
        National Agricultural Library

Washington, D.C.   Revised December, 1965

INF-71

U. S. DEPARTMENT OF AGRICULTURE   OFFICE OF INFORMATION   WASHINGTON 25, D. C.

How To Get Information
FROM THE U. S. DEPARTMENT OF AGRICULTURE

Revised March 1965

This list gives sources of information in the USDA Office of Information and the various agencies of the Department. The chart on the last page shows the relationship of one agency to another.

Questions may be mailed to the Office of Information, U. S. Department of Agriculture, Washington, D. C. 20250, or telephone by using the "thru" dialing exchange, DUdley 8 plus the extension desired. (Example: The telephone number for the Director of Information is Dudley 8-5247.) If you are calling long distance, our "direct dialing" area code is 202.

For more detailed information, write or telephone the person in charge of information on the subject matter in which you are interested. When writing, address the person by name and title, the name of the agency, U. S. Department of Agriculture, Washington D. C. 20250. The room numbers are listed for the convenience of those who call in person.

OFFICE OF INFORMATION

This Office, a staff agency of the Secretary's Office, directs and coordinates information work with the various agencies and has final review of all informational materials involving departmental policy. It provides assistance and facilities in the production of motion pictures, still photography (including a Central Photo Library), exhibits, and art and graphics.

Title	Name	Room	Extension
DIRECTOR OF INFORMATION	Harold R. Lewis	402-A	5247-6311
DEPUTY DIRECTOR	Gordon Webb	406-A	7903
ASSISTANT DIRECTOR	James H. McCormick	409-A	4613
International Development Programs	Jon F. Greeneisen	105-A	6965
Chief, Press Service	Harry P. Clark	404-A	4026
Chief, Publications Division	Harry P. Mileham	500-A	6623
Chief, Radio & Television Service	Layne R. Beaty	406-A	5163
Chief, Special Reports Division	Daniel Alfieri	409-A	4335
Editor, USDA Farm Paper Letter	Edward D. Curran	460-A	5480
Editor, Food and Home Notes	Mrs. Jeanne S. Park 1/	461-A	5437
Consumer Information	Daniel Alfieri	409-A	4335
Great Plains Cons. Program News	Gordon Webb	406-A	7903
Rural Areas Development Program	Joseph T. McDavid	457-A	2505
Chief, Art & Graphics Division	Elmo J. White	516-A	6641
Chief, Exhibits Service	David M. Granahan	0338-S	4337
Chief, Motion Picture Service	Calle A. Carrollo	1081-S	6072-6073
Chief, Photography Division	Albert A. Matthews	412-A	6633
(Includes the Central Photo Library, filmstrips, and slide sets)

1/ Contact Mrs. Park for information of general interest in women's field. For detailed information in home economics and human nutrition, contact the Current Information Branch, Agricultural Research Service, Rm. 5141-S, extension 4435.

AGRICULTURAL STABILIZATION AND CONSERVATION SERVICE -- (Includes information service for CCC
and Agricultural Stabilization and Conservation Committees). Responsible for production
and adjustment activities including acreage allotments and farm marketing quotas; the Agricultural Conservation Program; the cropland conversion program, the stabilization of sugar
production and marketing; price support; foreign supply and purchase, commodity disposal,
storage facilities, and other assigned programs of CCC; and related services on assigned
purchase and export programs, drought emergency feed program; and for certain defense food
activities.

Director of Information Division	M. L. DuMars	24-W	5237
Dep. Dir. (Price Support & Commodity Operations)	James E. McMahon	24-W	5239
Dep. Dir. (Production Programs)	Willard Lamphere	30-W	4094

FEDERAL CROP INSURANCE CORPORATION -- Insures farmers against loss of crop investments due
to risk beyond their control.

Director, Sales Management	R. A. Dimock	4621-S	4364
Asst. Dir., Sales Management	M. G. Reed	4621-S	4364

SCIENCE AND EDUCATION

AGRICULTURAL RESEARCH SERVICE -- Conducts basic and applied research on the production and
utilization of plants and animals, and does research pertaining to human nutrition to do
with plant and animal quarantines, and control of diseases and insect pests of animals and
plants. Also conducts studies on methods of managing soil, water, machinery, and buildings
for more efficient farming.

Director, Information Division	Ernest G. Moore	5133-S	4433
Assistant Director	R. B. Rathbone	5133-S	5787
Chief, Audio-Visual Branch	H. G. Bass	5149-S	5082
Chief, Current Inf. Branch	James E. Reynolds	5141-S	4435
Chief, Program Services Branch	Val Weyl	5130-S	5533
Chief, Publications Branch	David G. Hall	5145-S	5923
Chief, Reports Branch	J. S. Silbaugh	5130-S	4048

COOPERATIVE STATE RESEARCH SERVICE -- Administers federal-grant funds for research at State
Agricultural Experiment Stations and coordinates agricultural research among States and
between States and the U. S. Department of Agriculture.

Asst. to Admin. (Res. Comm.)	Werner P. Meyer	316-A	3079
(See also, the listing under Office of Management Services below.)			

FEDERAL EXTENSION SERVICE -- Has primary responsibility for and leadership in USDA educational programs and coordination of all educational activities of the Department.

Director, Division of Information	Walter W. John	5503-S	6283
Assistant Director	Ralph M. Fulghum	5503-S	2805

NATIONAL AGRICULTURAL LIBRARY -- Provides reference, bibliographic, loan, and photocopy
services of technical agricultural literature and its related biological and chemical
science, and coordinates scientific information and documentation activities of the Department.

Asst. Dir. for Public Services	Angelina J. Carabelli	1059-S	7660
Asst. Dir. for Program Coord. Serv.	Blanche L. Oliveri	1420-S	3961

INTERNATIONAL AFFAIRS

FOREIGN AGRICULTURAL SERVICE -- Promotes export of U. S. farm products, protects domestic
agricultural markets from unfair foreign competition; serves as a basic source of information to American agriculture on world crops, policies, and markets.

Director, Foreign Mkt. Inf. Div.	K. W. Olson	5554-S	3448
Assistant Director	Robert H. Ingram	5554-S	7115
Assistant Director	Harry W. Henderson	5554-S	3448

INTERNATIONAL AGRICULTURAL DEVELOPMENT SERVICE -- Coordinates USDA programs in international
agricultural development in foreign countries and training in U. S. of foreign officials,
leaders and scientists in fields of agriculture and home economics.

(For information contacts, see listing under Office of Information, page 1)

MARKETING AND CONSUMER SERVICE

CONSUMER AND MARKETING SERVICE -- Responsible for consumer protection, consumer food programs,
marketing regulatory programs, and marketing services.

Director, Inf. Div.	Franklin Thackrey	1744-S	6766
Deputy Director	Philip V. Fleming	1744-S	6766

COMMODITY EXCHANGE AUTHORITY — Supervises futures trading on commodity exchanges to maintain fair trading practices and competitive pricing, and to prevent price manipulation and other violations of the Commodity Exchange Act.

Trading Division

Assistant Director	R. Corbin Dorsey	42-W	3030
Administrative Assistant	Ruth D. Grant	44-W	4987

FARMER COOPERATIVE SERVICE — Does research, educational, and service work for farmers who belong to agricultural marketing, purchasing, and service cooperatives, and provides statistics on trends in agricultural cooperatives.

(For information contacts, see listing under Office of Management Services, page 3)

FARMERS HOME ADMINISTRATION — Makes loans, accompanied to the extent necessary by technical assistance in farm and money management, for farm operating expenses, farm enlargement, improvement and purchase, rural housing, soil and water conservation, emergency credit needs, rural renewal, rural water systems, shifts in land use to recreation facilities and grazing purposes, watershed development, housing for senior citizens, and farm labor housing. Under Economic Opportunity Act of 1964, provides supervised credit to low-income families and cooperatives composed of low-income families to finance agricultural and non-agricultural enterprises which will increase their income and raise their standards of living.

Director, Information Division	Philip S. Brown	5340-S	4031

FOREST SERVICE — Responsible for applying sound conservation and utilization practices to the natural resources of the National Forests and National Grasslands, for promoting these practices on all forest lands through cooperation with States and private landowners, and carries out extensive forest and range research.

Director, Div. Inf. & Educ.	Clint Davis	3223-S	3760-5920
Assistant Director	Noland O'Neal	3219-S	3709
General Information	Barbara Spahn	3207-S	3957
Publications	C. J. Morquest	3205-S	3957

RURAL COMMUNITY DEVELOPMENT SERVICE — Provides leadership and coordination within the Department of Agriculture in the formulation of plans and programs for advancing and developing natural and human resources in rural communities; and maintains liaison with local organizations and leaders in helping them to locate and utilize the facilities and resources of private, State and Federal agencies for the improvement of economic conditions in rural areas.

(For information contact, see Rural Areas Development listing under Office of Information)

RURAL ELECTRIFICATION ADMINISTRATION — Makes loans to local cooperatives and other organizations to bring electric power and modern telephone service to rural areas and works with them to stimulate economic development in their service areas.

Director, Inf. Ser. Div.	William E. Spivey	4038-S	5606

SOIL CONSERVATION SERVICE — Carries on a national soil and water conservation program with the cooperation of landowners and operators and other Government agencies; administers the Department's Great Plains Conservation Program and Small Watershed Protection and Flood Prevention Program; carries on the National Cooperative Soil Survey; has departmental leadership in assisting landowners and local groups in Resource Conservation and Development projects and in establishment of income-producing recreation enterprises.

Director, Information Division	D. Harper Simms	5112-S	4543
Assistant Director	F. Glennon Loyd	5112-S	4544

ECONOMIC RESEARCH SERVICE — Conducts research in agricultural economics and marketing, domestic and foreign; analyzes factors affecting agricultural production, supplies, prices and income; reports outlook for major commodities; evaluates market potentials and development marketing costs; analyzes farm productivity costs, financing, use of resources, potentials of low income areas; studies U. S. trade in agricultural products, role of agriculture in economic development of other nations.

(For information contacts, see listing under Office of Management Services below.)

STATISTICAL REPORTING SERVICE — Prepares monthly, quarterly, or annual estimates of production, supply, prices of agricultural commodities, farm labor, livestock numbers, etc., nationally and by States.

(For information contacts, see listing under Office of Management Services below.)

OFFICE OF MANAGEMENT SERVICES

Services Economic Research Service, Farmer Cooperative Service, Statistical Research Service, and Cooperative State Research Service.

Director, Div. of Information	Wayne V. Dexter	1447-S	7133
Chief, Research & Stat. Inf. Br.	Joel W. Wheeler	1447-S	5455
Chief, Program Services Br.	Beryle E. Stanten	1474-S	6486
Chief, Publications Branch	James Madison	1467-S	6557

UNITED STATES DEPARTMENT OF AGRICULTURE

March 25, 1965

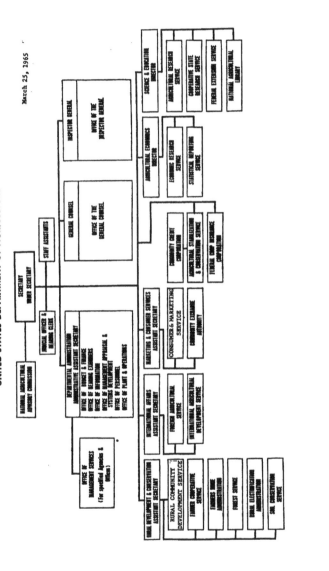

Department of the Treasury
Internal Revenue Service

GENERAL

The Internal Revenue Service of the Department of the Treasury has several programs designed to assist the businessman with his tax responsibilities.

MR. BUSINESSMAN'S KIT

A Mr. Businessman's Kit has been developed for presentation to operators of new businesses, as they are formed. Its purpose primarily is to encourage more effective voluntary compliance by helping new businessmen to become fully aware of their responsibilities for filing all the Federal tax returns for which they may be liable, and for paying the taxes due.

The kit is a four-pocket folder designed to hold forms and instructions for preparing most business tax returns.

On each pocket is a list of the various forms and documents applicable to the particular business. It also contains a check list of tax returns, a calendar of due dates for filing returns and paying taxes, a convenient place to keep employment tax information for employers, and a pocket for keeping retained copies of tax returns and related materials.

The principal feature of this program, however, is the *personal* presentation of the kit to the taxpayer. Internal Revenue Officers will present the kits and explain the various forms and documents applicable to the particular business. Thus each kit is tailored to the needs of the taxpayer.

The Revenue Officer will make every effort to assist and advise the businessman of his tax filing requirements. A place has been provided on the kit for the Revenue Officer's name, address and telephone number. The businessman will be encouraged to contact the Revenue Officer at any time to obtain further assistance or information.

TAX GUIDE FOR SMALL BUSINESS

The Internal Revenue Service publishes annually a *Tax Guide for Small Business* which explains Federal tax problems for sole proprietors, partners, partnerships and corporations.

Income, excise and employment taxes are explained in nontechnical language and many examples are used to illustrate the application of the tax laws.

A Check List, of particular interest to the new businessman, shows, at a glance, the taxes for which different kinds of business organizations and business activities may be liable and what the businessman should do about them.

A Tax Calendar is included, which explains, on a day-by-day basis, what the businessman should do in regard to his Federal taxes and when he should do it. The two pages may be removed from the booklet and posted in a prominent place as a reminder of the various due dates for the taxes discussed.

Establishing a new business, purchasing a going concern, operating a business, organizing a partnership and corporation, the sale of a business as a unit, the dissolution of a partnership, and the liquidation of a corporation are among the subjects covered in detail in the booklet.

The publication is revised annually to include new rules and changes in tax laws, regulations and rulings. Plain language is used in the text, supplemented by many examples explaining such things as: the need for adequate records and how long they should be retained; income averaging; declaration of estimated tax; business insurance; entertainment expenses; bad debts; rental expenses and leases; depreciation; educational expenses; how to compute net profit, the cost of goods sold and inventories.

The booklet is available at local Internal Revenue Service offices. It may also be ordered from the Superintendent of Documents, U.S. Government Printing Office, Washington, D.C., 20402, for 50¢ a copy. Quantities of 100 or more may be purchased at a 25 percent discount from the Superintendent of Documents.

PARTICIPATION IN TAX CLINICS

The Internal Revenue Service participates in tax clinics for small businessmen conducted jointly with the Small Business Administration, in cooperation with universities, chambers of commerce, and local civic groups.

The clinics have the general theme, "Tax Aspects of Small Business Management Decisions."

Internal Revenue technicians head discussions of such matters as the form of a business enterprise; the type of accounting methods that they may use; the different methods of taking depreciation and the advantages of each, and the tax problems that face a small, family-owned business.

These sessions are scheduled in accordance with the needs of each particular community. Information about the clinics is available from the Small Business Administration and the Internal Revenue Service.

133

Department of Justice

ANTITRUST ACTIVITIES

The Department of Justice is not a "service" agency furnishing direct aid to small businesses. As a law enforcement arm of the Federal Government, its principal duty is prosecuting violations of Federal laws entrusted to it by the Congress for enforcement.

However, small firms receive a great measure of indirect assistance from the Department's enforcement of the Federal antitrust laws. Small business is generally the primary victim of the illegal practices which those enforcement activities seek to eliminate.

The antitrust laws, most notably the Sherman Act and the Clayton Act, were designed to break up or prevent undue concentration of economic power in any business or industry. They prohibit conspiracies to restrain trade or commerce, monopolization or attempts to monopolize a field, and a variety of practices which may have the effect of substantially lessening competition or tending to create a monopoly. Thus, vigorous prosecution of the antitrust laws maintains free competition in the American economy, and permits the development and growth of a sound body of small business concerns.

Examples could be cited of many antitrust cases which have resulted in substantial benefits in many fields traditionally associated with small business firms. These include gas station operators, building contractors, grocery stores, funeral homes, fuel oil dealers, film processing, tabulating machines, motion picture exhibitors, and many others.

The Department's Antitrust Division has always been eager to assist small business firms in problems involving violation of the Federal antitrust laws. The Division welcomes, and is in great measure dependent upon, complaints from the small concerns about such violations. Its independent investigations of phases of the business economy are necessarily restricted by limitations in available manpower and financial resources. Therefore, the great majority of antitrust investigations and cases are initiated as a result of complaints from the public.

VIOLATIONS OF ANTITRUST LAWS

It is often difficult to determine what constitutes violations of the antitrust laws. Nevertheless, for the assistance of small business owners and managers, it may be possible to set forth some of the business practices in which, among others, the Antitrust Division is particularly interested:

134

(1) Any agreement to fix prices or to regulate prices.

(2) Any boycotting activities, involving, for example, members of a trade association agreeing to exclude competitors or a businessman inducing suppliers to withhold supplies from a competitor.

(3) Tie-in sales in which a businessman will sell a product, either patented or unpatented, to a customer only if the latter will purchase another product as well.

(4) Full-line forcing of products, whereby the purchaser must take all of his suppliers' line of products or get none at all.

(5) Agreements by competitors to assign each other separate sales territories, and to refrain from competing in each other's territories.

(6) Discriminatory pricing to some customers at the expense of others by means of rebates, discounts, service charges, and other excuses for price differentials.

(7) The obtaining by a business or group of businesses in an industry of a percentage of the market sufficient to have the power to control prices and exclude competition.

(8) The merger of two corporations by a transfer of stock of of assets which may have the effect of substantially lessening competition or tending to create a monopoly.

(9) Various general predatory practices, such as business espionage or the policing of competitors to ensure that they conform to the industry's traditions and customs.

Small businessmen who have observed any of these practices in their business experience or have had their business suffer as a result of such practices by competitors or suppliers, are invited to bring the facts of these cases to the attention of the Antitrust Division.

Letters may be addressed to the Antitrust Division, Department of Justice, Washington 25, D.C., or interviews may be arranged with officials of the Division at the Washington office, or at one of the field offices in New York, Philadelphia, Cleveland, Chicago, Los Angeles, San Francisco, or Honolulu. If these cities are too distant, the nearest local office of the Federal Bureau of Investigation may be contacted; the complaint will then be forwarded to the Washington office of the Antitrust Division.

FORM OF COMPLAINT

It must be understood that only a few of the foregoing list of business practices are illegal in and of themselves under the antitrust laws. Others may or may not be violations, depending upon the total factual picture. Therefore, to enable the Antitrust Division to make an accurate analysis of the problem, it is desirable that all the facts of the problem be stated in as much detail as possible.

A description must be included of the business or industry involved, all relevant dates, all names and addresses of the parties, and an indication of the size, importance, and percentage of the market held by each business involved, if such information is available. In addition, it would be helpful if copies of any relevant documents—such as price lists, agreements, minutes of meetings, or letters—were submitted.

The Antitrust Division has jurisdiction to take action only if these illegal activities affect the movement of goods or services in interstate commerce. Therefore, it is essential that statements show that the goods or services affected are in the stream of interstate commerce. If part of such goods or services are sold in interstate commerce and the rest wholly within the State, the relative percentage sold in interstate commerce should be indicated.

PROCESSING OF COMPLAINTS

When a complaint is submitted to the Antitrust Division, immediate institution of a suit cannot be expected. After a complaint is acknowledged, it is assigned to a member of the staff for analysis to determine whether it presents substantial questions under the Federal antitrust laws. It may be correlated with other complaints of a similar nature involving the same industry or business.

A preliminary investigation may be ordered and, if the facts warrant, a full-scale investigation of the problem will be undertaken. Therefore, unless the person submitting the complaint is contacted for further information, a considerable period may elapse between the time a complaint is received and the time when an interview is scheduled by a representative of the Antitrust Division or an agent of the Federal Bureau of Investigation.

Federal Trade Commission

ANTITRUST AND TRADE REGULATION LAWS

The Federal Trade Commission was established by Congress in 1914 to protect business and the public against unfair methods of competition and to prevent practices which would lessen competition or tend to create monopoly. The Commission is, in short, charged with the basic duty of protecting our competitive free-enterprise economy.

The Commission acts:

(a) To prevent the use of unfair methods of competition and unfair or deceptive acts or practices in interstate commerce, such as acts or practices which are unfair or oppressive or tend to monopoly; combinations which unreasonably restrain competition, and representations, express or implied, which have the capacity of misleading or deceiving members of the public with respect to commodities being offered for sale, all as prohibited by section 5 of the Federal Trade Commission Act.

(b) To prevent the dissemination of false advertisements of foods, drugs, cosmetics, and devices, as provided in sections 12 through 15 of the Federal Trade Commission Act.

(c) To prevent discriminations in price, services, or facilities, including quantity discounts which are unjustly discriminatory or promotive of monopoly, by the establishment, when necessary, of quantity limits; payment or receipt of brokerage, commissions, or discounts in lieu thereof; the use of tying or exclusive dealing leases, sales, or contracts; the acquisition by one corporation of stock or assets of another, and continuance of interlocking directorates among corporations, all under the circumstances of which these things are prohibited respectively by sections 2, 3, 7, and 8 of the Clayton Act as amended.

(d) To prevent the misbranding of wool or wool products through failure to comply with the provisions of the Wool Products Labeling Act of 1939.

(e) To prevent misbranding, false advertising, or false invoicing of furs or fur products through failure to comply with the Fur Products Labeling Act.

(f) To prevent the introduction or movement in interstate commerce of articles of wearing apparel and fabrics which are so highly flammable as to be dangerous when worn by individuals, in violation of the Flammable Fabrics Act.

(g) To prevent misbranding or false advertising of textile fiber products through failure to comply with the Textile Fiber Products Identification Act.

(h) To prevent unfair methods of competition and unfair or deceptive acts or practices in the business of insurance to the extent that such business is not regulated by State law, under the Federal Trade Commission Act and Public Law 15, of 1945 relating to the regulation of the business of insurance.

(i) To administer the provisions of the Export Trade Act, providing for the registration and operation of associations of American exporters engaging solely in export trade.

(j) To bring about the cancellation of registration of trade marks which have been illegally registered or which have been used for purposes contrary to the intent of the Trade Mark Act of 1946.

(k) To investigate the organization, business, conduct, practices, or management of corporations and to make public reports thereon as the Commission deems expedient in the public interest; to investigate, at the direction of the President or the Congress, and report upon alleged violations of the antitrust laws by corporations; to make various other investigations and reports, including recommendation to Congress for legislation, and reports to the Attorney General, to the extent and in the manner provided in section 6 of the Federal Trade Commission Act.

REQUESTS FOR COMMISSION ACTION

Any individual, partnership, corporation, association or organization may request the Commission to institute a proceeding in respect to any violation of law over which the Commission has jurisdiction. Such requests should be in the form of a signed statement setting forth the alleged violation of law and the name and address of the party or parties complained about. No formal procedure or forms are required. Requests should be mailed to Federal Trade Commission, Washington, D.C., 20580. The person making the request is not regarded as a party, for the Commission acts only in the public interest and its proceedings are for the purpose of vindicating public, not private, rights. It is Commission policy not to publish or divulge the name of an applicant or complaining party, except as required by law.

ADVISORY OPINIONS

It is the policy of the Commission to afford businessmen assistance in determining, in advance, whether a proposed course of action, if pursued, may violate any of the laws administered by the Commission, and, where practicable, to give them the benefit of the Commission's views.

Any person, partnership or corporation may request advice from the Commission as to whether a proposed course of action, if pursued, would probably violate any of the laws administered by the Commission. A request for advice should be addressed to the Secretary and should include complete information. Conferences with members of the Commission's staff may be held before or after the request is submitted. Submission of additional information may be required.

On the basis of the facts submitted, as well as other information available to the Commission, the Commission, when practicable, will advise the requesting party whether or not the proposed course of action, if pursued, would be likely to result in further action by the Commission. Any advice given is without prejudice to the right of the Commission to reconsider the questions involved and, where the public interest requires, to rescind or revoke the advice. However, information submitted will not be used as the basis for a proceeding until an opportunity is afforded for the party to discontinue the course of action pursued in good faith in reliance upon the Commission's advice.

EXPORT OPPORTUNITIES FOR SMALL BUSINESS

On April 9, 1963, the Federal Trade Commission created the Division of Export Trade in the Office of the General Counsel for the purpose of administering the Webb-Pomerene [Export Trade] Act of 1918.

This Division was successor to the Export Trade Division which was originally created in the Commission in 1918 to administer this Act which was entitled "An Act to promote export trade and for other purposes." The Webb-Pomerene Act provides exemptions from the Sherman Act of 1890 and the Federal Trade Commission and Clayton Acts of 1914 for cooperatively organized American exporters engaged solely in export trade.

Under the provisions of this Act members of associations are permitted to fix prices, allocate quotas for export and agree on terms and conditions for export. Export savings to association members may be realized through joint office management, allocation of expenses on export sales and the pooling of products for foreign shipment. Associations may also collect and disseminate trade information on market conditions abroad,

foreign exchange situations, tariff requirements, shipping rules and regulations and foreign laws affecting foreign trade.

At the present time there are 34 registered associations and many of the active members are small business concerns which have combined for the purpose of competing with foreign combines and cartels.

Legal formalities for setting up a Webb-Pomerene association are simple. The Act requires only that the association file with the Federal Trade Commission within 30 days after its organization a verified written statement setting forth the location of its offices or places of business; the names and addresses of all its officers, stockholders, and members; and if incorporated, a copy of the certificate or articles of incorporation and by-laws; or if unincorporated, a copy of the articles or contract of association.

Inquiries regarding the operations of the Webb-Pomerene Export Trade Act or information relating to the formation of a new export association can be addressed to the Assistant General Counsel for Export Trade, Federal Trade Commission, Washington, D.C., 20580.

FTC FIELD OFFICES

Field offices are maintained at Atlanta, Boston, Chicago, Cleveland, Kansas City, Los Angeles, New Orleans, Houston, New York, San Francisco, Seattle and Washington, D.C. (Falls Church, Va.) Their addresses are:

Federal Trade Commission
915 Forsyth Building
86 Forsyth Street NW.
Atlanta, Ga. 30303

Federal Trade Commission
Room 1001
131 State Street
Boston, Mass. 02109

Federal Trade Commission
Room 486
U.S. Courthouse and Federal Office Building
219 South Dearborn Street
Chicago, Ill. 60604

Federal Trade Commission
1128 Standard Building
Cleveland, Ohio 44113

Federal Trade Commission
2806 Federal Office Building
Kansas City, Mo. 64106

Federal Trade Commission
215 West Seventh Street
Room 1212
Los Angeles, Calif. 90014

Federal Trade Commission
1000 Masonic Temple Building
333 St. Charles Street
New Orleans, La. 70130

Federal Trade Commission
U.S. Courthouse Building
Room 10511
Post Office Box 61165
Houston, Tex. 77061

Federal Trade Commission
30 Church Street
New York, N.Y. 10007

Federal Trade Commission
450 Golden Gate Avenue
Box 36005
San Francisco, Calif. 94102

Federal Trade Commission
511 U.S. Court House
Seattle, Wash. 98104

Federal Trade Commission
450 West Broad Street
Falls Church, Va. 22046

For the limited purpose of administering the Wool, Fur, Textile Products, and Flammable Fabrics Acts, additional offices are located at Dallas, Charlotte, Denver, Los Angeles, Miami, Philadelphia, St. Louis, and Portland, Oreg.

The addresses of these Inspection and Industry Counseling Units are:

Federal Trade Commission
915 Forsyth Building
86 Forsyth Street
Atlanta, Ga. 30303

Federal Trade Commission
131 State Street, Room 1001
Boston, Mass. 02109

Federal Trade Commission
Cutter Building, Room 204
327 North Tryon Street
Charlotte, N.C. 28202

Federal Trade Commission
U.S. Courthouse and Federal Office Building, Room 486
219 South Dearborn Street
Chicago, Ill. 60604

Federal Trade Commission
1128 Standard Building
1370 Ontario Street
Cleveland, Ohio 44113

Federal Trade Commission
405 Thomas Building
1314 Wood Street
Dallas, Tex. 75202

Federal Trade Commission
18013 Federal Office Building
1961 Stout Street
Denver, Colo. 80202

Federal Trade Commission
U.S. Courthouse Building, Room 10511
Post Office Box 61165
Houston, Tex. 77061

Federal Trade Commission
2806 Federal Office Building
911 Walnut Street
Kansas City, Mo. 64106

Federal Trade Commission
215 West Seventh Street, Room 1212
Los Angeles, Calif. 90014

Federal Trade Commission
1631 New Federal Building
51 Southwest First Avenue
Miami, Fla. 33130

Federal Trade Commission
1000 Masonic Temple Building
333 St. Charles Street
New Orleans, La. 70130

Federal Trade Commission
30 Church Street
New York, N.Y. 10007

Federal Trade Commission
53 Long Lane
Upper Darby, Pa. 19082

Federal Trade Commission
231 U.S. Courthouse
Portland, Oreg. 97205

Federal Trade Commission
450 Golden Gate Avenue
Box 36005
San Francisco, Calif. 94102

Federal Trade Commission
511 U.S. Court House
Seattle, Wash. 98104

Federal Trade Commission
400 U.S. Court and Custom House
1114 Market Street
St. Louis, Mo. 63101

Federal Trade Commission
450 West Broad Street
Anderson Building
Falls Church, Va. 22046

Veterans Administration

GENERAL

The Veterans Administration, in carrying out its mission of administering veterans' laws, (1) provides a medical program equivalent to the finest in civilian practice, (2) operates the third largest ordinary life insurance program in the world, and (3) administers a wide variety of benefits, such as compensation and pensions for disabled veterans and dependants of deceased veterans, vocational rehabilitation and education, and guaranteed or insured loans.

While the major portion of our approximately $5 billion budget is expended in direct benefits to veterans, various aspects of our operations have considerable meaning to industry and business—both large and small. A prodigious amount of supplies, equipment and services are needed to support an operation employing approximately 172,000 persons and including a field network of 165 hospitals (8 percent of the Nation's hospital beds), 80 outpatient clinics, 6 domiciliaries, 57 regional offices, and 2 insurance offices.

CONTRACTS

The major categories of purchases are as follows:

1. Medical, surgical, dental, laboratory, X-ray, pharmaceutical and hospital equipment, supplies and services.

2. Foodstuffs, kitchen, laundry and plant maintenance equipment supplies and services.

3. Clothing, linens.

NOTE: The Veterans Administration contracts for the drugs and medicines, and nonperishable food items required by all civil agencies of Government.

For items centrally procured for all stations, Marketing Divisions in specific commodity areas have been established. Applications for inclusion on bidders lists should be addressed to the Marketing Division, Chief—

M1—Dental and Surgical Supplies and Equipment, VA Supply Depot, Hines, Ill.

M3—Hospital Furnishings, VA Supply Depot, Hines, Ill.

M4—Subsistence, VA Supply Depot, Hines, Ill.

M5—Drugs and Chemicals, VA Supply Depot, Somerville, N.J.

M6—Technical Medical, VA Supply Depot, Somerville, N.J.

M7—Laboratory and Physical Medical and Rehabilitation Supplies and Equipment, VA Supply Depot, Hines, Ill.

Books and Periodicals, VA Supply Depot, Somerville, N.J.

Motion Picture, VA Supply Depot, Somerville, N.J.

In addition, all VA hospitals procure in their local areas many off-the-shelf items such as perishable subsistence, maintenance supplies, etc. and services. Requests for bidders information should be addressed to the Chief, Supply Division, of the appropriate VA office. See List A.

ARCHITECTURAL AND PROFESSIONAL ENGINEERING DESIGN SERVICES

The Veterans Administration construction program involves the design and construction of complete new hospital facilities including auxiliary buildings and utilities as well as additions, conversions and alterations to existing hospital structures. The Veterans Administration uses private Architects, Architect-Engineers, and Professional Engineers to accomplish a major portion of its design mission.

Architectural, Architectural-Engineering and Professional Engineering firms interested in providing design and other professional services for the Veterans Administration should forward a completed Form 251, U.S. Government Architect-Engineer Questionnaire to the Chairman, Architect-Engineer Selection Board, Office of Assistant Administrator for Construction, Veterans Administration, Washington, D.C., 20420. These forms are available from the Chairman, Architect-Engineer Selection Board, as well as from other Government agencies using this form. It is important that firms submit complete, accurate and responsive information concerning their qualifications in executing this Form 251. The forms, and any additional brochure material which the firms may elect to submit, are filed in the Veterans Administration Architect-Engineer Library for use by the Architect-Engineer Selection Board.

There is no competitive bidding on design and other professional services contracts. The fee for such services is negotiated on a strictly professional basis.

CONSTRUCTION SERVICES

The Assistant Administrator for Construction Service, Veterans Administration, Washington, D.C., 20420, maintains a list of general contractors and electrical, plumbing, air conditioning, heating, and certain other categories, of subcontractors. Firms in these categories who are interested in bidding for VA construction should write to the Assistant Administrator for Construction. In reply, they will receive a questionnaire concerning their Small Business status and the categories of work which they desire to perform. When a project is ready for the market, the firms located within the state of the project and neighboring states, will be mailed copies of the Invitation for Bids.

VETERANS' LOANS

The VA guarantees or insures various types of loans made by private lenders (banks, savings and loan associations, and the like) to eligible World War II and Korean Conflict veterans. Under certain conditions, it also makes direct home loans to them.

Purpose: To assist in the purchase, construction, alteration, improvement and repair of home, farm, or business real estate, and the acquisition of supplies, equipment, and working capital.

Terms: The loan may be short-term (5 years and under), or long-term (amortized). If the maturity is 5 years or less, no payments on principal are required until maturity. With a long-term loan, regular amortization is required which will pay off the principal plus interest over the period of the loan.

The loan may be either guaranteed or insured by the VA. Generally, long-term loans are guaranteed and short-term non-real estate business and farm loans tend to be insured. If guaranteed, or if for real estate purposes, the interest rate on the loan may not exceed 5¼ percent per annum under present law. If insured, 15 percent of each loan is credited by the VA to an insurance account of the lender, limited by the entitlement available to the veteran borrower, from which the lender is paid for losses on such insured loans up to the amount of the insurance account. The interest rate on a non-real estate insured loan may not exceed 5.7 percent per annum, or 3 percent discount.

REAL ESTATE LOANS

A home or business real estate loan may be repaid up to 30 years and a farm real estate loan up to 40 years. The VA guaranty may not exceed $7,500, or 60 percent of a loan for the purchase, construction, alteration, improvement, or repair of residential property which the veteran will, or does, occupy as his some. Nonresidential real estate (farm or business) loans may be guaranteed up to a maximum of $4,000 or 50 percent of the loan. The purchase price of property (real or personal) being acquired with the proceeds of a guaranteed or insured loan may not exceed the reasonable value as determined by the Administrator.

NON-REAL ESTATE LOANS

These are for the purchase of property other than real estate, such as machinery, tools, equipment, livestock, and working capital required in the operation of a farm or business. This type of loan may be repaid in up to 10 years and may be guaranteed by VA up to a maximum of $2,000 or 50 percent of the loan.

DIRECT LOANS

Under certain conditions the VA makes direct loans to veterans for the purchase, construction, alteration, improvement, and repair of residential property (including a farm residence) which the veteran will, or does, occupy as his home. Direct loans are not authorized for business purposes. Such loans may not exceed $15,000 and may only be made in specified direct loan areas. The interest rate on a direct loan is 5¼ percent per annum, the same as a guaranteed home loan, and may be repaid in up to 30 years. The security is the property being acquired with the proceeds of the loan.

CONTACTS

All active lenders are aware of the VA's loan program. For additional information VA Pamphlet 26–4, "Questions and Answers on Guaranteed and Direct Loans for Veterans," and VA Fact Sheet 1S–1, "Federal Benefits for Veterans and Dependents," may be obtained at the nearest Veterans Administration Regional Office as indicated on List B.

NOTE: Veterans have eligibility for loan benefits for 10 years from the date of discharge or release from the last period of active duty, any part of which occurred during World War II or the Korean Conflict, plus one year of eligibility for each 3 months (90 days) of active wartime duty. Eligibility of World War II veterans will not extend beyond July 25, 1967. Eligibility of Korean Conflict veterans will not extend beyond January 31, 1975.

VETERANS ADMINISTRATION HOSPITALS BY STATES

ALABAMA

VAH Birmingham 3
VAH Montgomery 10, Perry Hill Rd.
VAH Tuscaloosa
VAH Tuskegee

ARIZONA

VAH Phoenix, 7th St. and Indian School Rd.
VAH Tucson
VAC Whipple

ARKANSAS

VAH Fayetteville
VAH Little Rock, 300 E. Roosevelt Rd.

CALIFORNIA

VAH Fresno, 2615 Clinton Ave.
VAH Livermore
VAH Long Beach, 5901 Seventh St.
VAC Los Angeles 25, Sawtelle and Wilshire Blvds.
VAH Martinez, 150 Muir Road
VAH Oakland 12, 13th and Harrison Sts.
VAH Palo Alto
VAH San Fernando
VAH San Francisco 21, 42d Ave. and Clement St.
VAH Sepulveda
VASD Wilmington, 2401 E. Pacific Coast Highway

COLORADO

VAH Denver 20, 1055 Clermont St.
VAH Fort Lyon
VAH Grand Junction

CONNECTICUT

VAH Newington 11
VAH West Haven 16, W. Spring St.

DELAWARE

VAH Wilmington

DISTRICT OF COLUMBIA

VAH Washington, 50 Irving St., NW. 20422

FLORIDA

VAC Bay Pines
VAH Coral Gables
VAH Lake City

GEORGIA

VAH Atlanta 19, 4158 Peachtree Rd., NE.
VAH Augusta
VAC Dublin

IDAHO

VAC Boise, 5th and Fort Sts.

ILLINOIS

VAH Chicago 11, 333 E. Huron St.
VAH Chicago 12, 820 S. Damen Ave.
VAH Danville
VAH Downey
VAH Hines
VAH Marion
VASD Hines, P.O. Box 27

INDIANA

VAH Fort Wayne 3, 1600 Randalia Dr.
VAH Indianapolis 7, 1481 W. 10th St.
VAH Marion

IOWA

VAC Des Moines 8
VAH Iowa City
VAH Knoxville

KANSAS

VAC Wichita 18, 5500 E. Kellogg
VAH Topeka, 2200 Gage Blvd.
VAC Wadsworth

KENTUCKY

VAH Lexington
VAH Louisville 2, Mellwood and Zorn Ave.

LOUISIANA

VAH Shreveport 12, 510 E. Stoner Ave.
VAH Alexandria
VAH New Orleans 12, 1601 Perdido St.

MAINE

VAC Togus

MARYLAND

VAH Baltimore 18, 3900 Loch Raven Blvd.
VAH Fort Howard
VAH Perry Point

MASSACHUSETTS

VAH Bedford
VAH Boston 30, 150 S. Huntington Ave.
VAH Brockton
VAH Northampton
VAH West Roxbury 32, Veterans of Foreign Wars Parkway

MICHIGAN

VAH Ann Arbor, 2215 Fuller Rd.
VAH Battle Creek
VAH Dearborn
VAH Iron Mountain
VAH Saginaw, 1500 Weiss St.

MINNESOTA

VAH Minneapolis 17, 54th St. and 48th Ave., S.
VAH St. Cloud
VAC St. Paul 11, Fort Snelling

MISSISSIPPI

VAC Biloxi
VAC Jackson

MISSOURI

VAH Jefferson Barracks St. Louis 25
VAH Kansas City 28, 4801 Linwood Blvd.
VAH Poplar Bluff
VAH St. Louis 6, 915 N. Grand Blvd.

MONTANA

VAC Fort Harrison
VAH Miles City

NEBRASKA

VAH Grand Island
VAH Lincoln 1
VAH Omaha 5, 4101 Woolworth Ave.

NEVADA

VAC Reno

NEW HAMPSHIRE

VAH Manchester, Smyth Rd.

NEW JERSEY

VAH East Orange
VAH Lyons
VASD Somerville

NEW MEXICO

VAH Albuquerque

NEW YORK

VAH Albany
VAH Batavia
VAC Bath
VAH Bronx 68, 130 W. Kingsbridge Rd.
VAH Brooklyn 9, 800 Poly Pl.
VAH Buffalo 15, 3495 Bailey Ave.
VAH Canandaigua
VAH Castle Point
VAH Montrose
VAH New York 10, First Ave. at E. 24th St.
VAH Northport, Long Island
VAH Syracuse 10, Irving Ave. and University Pl.

NORTH CAROLINA

VAH Durham, Fulton St. and Erwin Rd.
VAH Fayetteville
VAH Oteen
VAH Salisbury

NORTH DAKOTA

VAC Fargo

OHIO

VAH Brecksville
VAH Chillicothe
VAH Cincinnati 20, 3200 Vine St.
VAH Cleveland 30, 7300 York Rd.
VAC Dayton

OKLAHOMA

VAH Muskogee, Memorial Station, Honor Heights Dr.
VAH Oklahoma City 4, 921 N.E. 13th St.

OREGON

VAD White City
VAH Portland 7, Sam Jackson Park
VAH Roseburg

PENNSYLVANIA

VAH Altoona
VAH Butler
VAH Coatesville
VAH Erie 5, 135 E. 38th Street Blvd.
VAH Lebanon
VAH Philadelphia 4, University and Woodland Ave.

141

PENNSYLVANIA—Con.
VAH Pittsburgh 6, Leach Farm Rd.
VAH Pittsburgh 40, University Dr.
VAH Wilkes-Barre, East End Blvd.

PUERTO RICO
VAC San Juan, 521 Ponce de Leon Ave.

RHODE ISLAND
VAH Providence 8, Davis Park

SOUTH CAROLINA
VAH Columbia

SOUTH DAKOTA
VAC Sioux Falls
VAH Fort Meade
VAC Hot Springs

TENNESSEE
VAH Memphis 15, Park Ave. and Getwell St.
VAH Murfreesboro
VAC Mountain Home
VAH Nashville 5, 90 White Bridge Rd.

TEXAS
VAH Amarillo
VAH Big Spring
VAC Bonham
VAH Dallas 2
VAH Houston 31, 2002 Holcombe Blvd.
VAH Kerrville
VAH Marlin
VAC Temple
VAH Waco, Memorial Dr.

UTAH
VAH Salt Lake City 1

VERMONT
VAC White River Junction

VIRGINIA
VAC Kecoughtan
VAH Richmond 19, Broad Rock Rd., and Belt Blvd.
Salem VA Hospital (Roanoke)

WASHINGTON
VAH American Lake
VAH Seattle 8, 4435 Beacon Ave.
VAH Spokane 15, N. 4815 Assembly St.
VAH Vancouver

Abbreviations used:
VAC—Veterans Administration Center
VAD—Veterans Administration Domiciliary
VAH—Veterans Administration Hospital
VASD—Veterans Administration Supply Depot

WASHINGTON—Con.
VAH Walla Walla

WEST VIRGINIA
VAH Beckley
VAH Clarksburg
VAH Huntington 1, 1540 Spring Valley Dr.
VAC Martinsburg

WISCONSIN
VAH Madison
VAH Tomah
VAC Wood

WYOMING
VAC Cheyenne, 2360 E. Pershing Blvd.
VAH Sheridan

List B
VETERANS ADMINISTRATION REGIONAL OFFICES

ALABAMA Montgomery
ALASKA Juneau
ARIZONA Phoenix
ARKANSAS Little Rock
CALIFORNIA Los Angeles, San Francisco
COLORADO Denver
CONNECTICUT Hartford
DELAWARE Wilmington
DISTRICT OF COLUMBIA Washington
FLORIDA St. Petersburg
GEORGIA Atlanta
HAWAII Honolulu
IDAHO Boise

ILLINOIS Chicago
INDIANA Indianapolis
IOWA Des Moines
KANSAS Wichita
KENTUCKY Louisville
LOUISIANA New Orleans
MAINE Togus
MARYLAND Baltimore
MASSACHUSETTS Boston
MICHIGAN Detroit
MINNESOTA St. Paul
MISSISSIPPI Jackson
MISSOURI St. Louis
MONTANA Fort Harrison

NEBRASKA Lincoln
NEVADA Reno
NEW HAMPSHIRE Manchester
NEW JERSEY Newark
NEW MEXICO Albuquerque
NEW YORK Brooklyn, Buffalo, New York City
NORTH CAROLINA Winston-Salem
NORTH DAKOTA Fargo
OHIO Cleveland
OKLAHOMA Muskogee
OREGON Portland
PENNSYLVANIA Philadelphia, Pittsburgh
PHILIPPINES Manila

PUERTO RICO (and VIRGIN ISLANDS) San Juan
RHODE ISLAND Providence
SOUTH CAROLINA Columbia
SOUTH DAKOTA Sioux Falls
TENNESSEE Nashville
TEXAS Houston, Waco
UTAH Salt Lake City
VERMONT White River Junction
VIRGINIA Roanoke
WASHINGTON Seattle
WEST VIRGINIA Huntington
WISCONSIN Milwaukee
WYOMING Cheyenne

Atomic Energy Commission

The bulk of the procurement of supplies and services in connection with AEC programs is done by the contractors which operate AEC plants and laboratories. The AEC's small business program centers around these operating contractors, and a large number of the opportunities for small business participation arises with them. However, emphasis is also placed on small business participation with prime contractors other than those operating AEC plants.

It is the policy of AEC to provide the broadest opportunity for business concerns to participate in meeting the procurement needs of the atomic energy programs and to give special attention to assisting small business concerns, and concerns, located in labor surplus areas. A booklet "Selling to AEC" has been prepared to provide general information helpful to those who want to do business with AEC or its contractors. This booklet (which may be purchased at nominal cost from the Superintendent of Documents, Government Printing Office, Washington, D.C., 20402) indicates generally what is bought, how much is bought, who does the buying, and where procurement offices are located. Other items include information which should assist concerns interested in the atomic energy industry, and provides guidance as to the sources of technical information, availability of royalty-free patents, and industrial uses of radioisotopes. The booklet, as an aid to manufacturers of reactor components, also lists the companies that have built, are building, or propose to build reactors.

LOCATION OF PRINCIPAL OFFICES

(a) The agency Headquarters is located at Germantown, Md. Headquarters office facilities are also maintained in the District of Columbia at 1717 H Street NW. The mail address of the Headquarters is Washington, D.C., 20545.

(b) The major operating field offices are located as follows:

Albuquerque Operations Office Post Office Box 5400 Albuquerque, N. Mex. 87115	Grand Junction Office Grand Junction, Colo. 81502
Brookhaven Office Upton, N.Y. 11973	Idaho Operations Office Post Office Box 2108 Idaho Falls, Idaho 83401
Chicago Operations Office 9800 South Cass Avenue Argonne, Ill. 60439	Nevada Operations Office Post Office Box 1676 Las Vegas, Nev. 80101

New York Operations Office
376 Hudson Street
New York, N.Y. 10014

Oak Ridge Operations Office
Post Office Box E
Oak Ridge, Tenn. 37831

Pittsburgh Naval Reactors Office
Post Office Box 109
West Mifflin, Pa. 15122

Richland Operations Office
Post Office Box 550
Richland, Wash. 90352

San Francisco Operations Office
2111 Bancroft Way
Berkeley, Calif. 94704

Savannah River Operations Office
Post Office Box A
Aiken, S.C. 29802

Schenectady Naval Reactors Office
Post Office Box 1069
Schenectady, N.Y. 12301

OPERATION OF AEC PLANTS AND LABORATORIES

Most AEC work is accomplished by contractors. There are more than 135,000 persons working directly in the program, of which approximately 7,000 are AEC employees. The rest work for AEC contractors. At present, the AEC investment in plant, equipment, and real estate is approximately $8 billion, and operating costs are at an annual level of approximately $2.7 billion. These Government-owned facilities are managed and operated for the AEC by contractors. AEC operating contractors comprise a variety of industrial, academic and not-for-profit organizations.

The addresses of AEC principal operating contractors, names of individuals who may be contacted, and lists of supplies, materials, equipment and services purchased for the AEC are contained in the booklet "Selling to AEC."

RESEARCH

(a) *Basic Research.*—In addition to the research conducted at its national laboratories and other major research centers, the AEC makes arrangements for the conduct of basic research in fields related to nuclear energy with institutions of higher education and other nonprofit research organizations. Such research contracts are granted on the basis of solicited or unsolicited proposals submitted to and approved by AEC in Washington.

Those interested in obtaining contracts for basic research may obtain a copy of a "Guide for the Submission of Research Proposals" from the U.S. Atomic Energy Commission, Washington, D.C., 20545 or from any AEC field office.

(b) *Applied Research and Development.*—Some AEC program requirements for applied research and development are performed by private con-

143

cerns in their own facilities pursuant to contracts and subcontracts administered by AEC field offices and cost-type contractors. Interested parties should contract the appropriate AEC field offices for information concerning these contracts.

SECURITY REQUIREMENTS

Vendors of material, equipment, supplies, and services who solicit business from the AEC, its contractors, subcontractors, or access permit holders may be affected by the security provisions of the Atomic Energy Act of 1954, as amended, and other Federal laws governing the handling of classified defense information. The Atomic Energy Act defines certain information relating to the design, manufacture, production, or use of special nuclear material as "Restricted Data" and prescribes conditions under which access to Restricted Data may be granted. One of the important provisions pertains to AEC authorization for access to Restricted Data.

In any case where access to Restricted Data is required in order for a vendor to furnish—or negotiate in connection with furnishing—material, equipment, supplies, or services to the AEC or its contractors, subcontractors, or access permit holders, the vendor must obtain access authorization from the AEC for all personnel who will require access to the Restricted Data involved. The AEC field offices and their contractors have full information concerning this and other applicable AEC security requirements.

In most cases discussions with vendors can be handled without Restricted Data becoming involved and in these instances AEC access authorization is not required. When access to Restricted Data is required, the AEC, its contractors or subcontractors will initiate action to obtain the necessary access authorization.

PATENTS

Commission-owned patents constitute a source of opportunity for manufacturers who are interested in entering the atomic energy field. More than 3,000 U.S. patents are available for licensing at this time. Abstracts of issued patents are published in Nuclear Science Abstracts, a Commission publication, and in the publications of the Small Business Administration and the Department of Commerce.

Patents held by the Commission cover all phases of the atomic energy field including nuclear reactors and components, processes for producing source and special nuclear materials, processes for producing other materials required in atomic energy work, special fabrication techniques, instrumentation, and a wide variety of mechanical equipment and apparatus.

Patents have not been issued on some significant inventions because of the classified nature of the subject matter. Many of the inventions covered by Commission-held patents have actual or potential use outside the atomic energy field.

On request, the Atomic Energy Commission grants nonexclusive, royalty-free, revocable licenses on the patents for which it has the right to grant licenses. Policies and rules governing licenses were published on page 606 of the Federal Register, January 27, 1956, and also appear in Part 81, Title 10, Code of Federal Regulations.

Applications for licenses should contain the number of the patent, the name and address of the applicant, and the state of incorporation, if the applicant is a corporation.

Requests for further information and applications for licenses should be directed to the Assistant General Counsel for Patents, Office of the General Counsel, Atomic Energy Commission, Washington, D.C., 20545.

RADIOISOTOPES

Radioisotopes are unstable isotopes of an element that decay or disintegrate spontaneously, emitting radiation. They are potentially applicable to a wide range of industrial activities. The Oak Ridge National Laboratory is still the primary source of supply; however, several other AEC laboratories are also distributing radioisotopes. Several dozen firms now act as retailers and secondary distributors of the more than 100 different radioisotopes which are produced by the various AEC laboratories and distributed by the Atomic Energy Commission. In addition, radioisotopes are now being produced to a limited extent in privately-owned reactors.

Individuals and concerns wishing to obtain additional information regarding radioisotopes, radioactive materials, or information regarding general industrial applications of atomic energy should direct their inquiries to either the Division of Isotopes Development or the AEC's Division of Reactor Development, Washington, D.C., 20545.

LICENSING REQUIREMENTS

The Atomic Energy Act of 1954, as amended, established a system of licensing requirements applicable to virtually all private activities involving the use of by products, source, special nuclear materials, or production and utilization facilities, all of which are defined in the Act. Under this system, which is administered by the Director of Regulation, anyone who wants to possess or use these materials must get a license from the AEC's Division of Materials Licensing, Atomic Energy Commission, Washington, D.C., 20545, except in States which have entered into agreements with the Commission pursuant to Section 274 of the Atomic Energy Act. This provides that the Commission is authorized to enter into agreements with the Governor of any State providing for discontinuance of the regulatory authority of the Commission with respect to any one or more of the following materials within the State:

(a) byproduct materials;
(b) source materials; and
(c) special nuclear materials in quantities not sufficient to form a critical mass.

Under such an agreement, the State has authority to regulate the materials covered by the agreement for the protection of the public health and safety from radiation hazards.

As of April 1965, nine States—Arkansas, California, Florida, Kansas, Kentucky, Mississippi, New York, North Carolina, and Texas—have entered into such agreements with AEC.

REGULATIONS

The Atomic Energy Commission's Rules and Regulations are published in Title 10, Chapter 1, of the Code of Federal Regulations.

The Atomic Energy Commission's Procurement Regulations, which implement and supplement the Federal Procurement Regulations, are published in Title 41, Chapter 9, of the Code of Federal Regulations.

Copies of either of these regulations may be purchased at nominal cost from the Superintendent of Documents; Government Printing Office, Washington, D.C., 20402.

NUCLEAR REACTORS BUILT, BEING BUILT, OR PLANNED

Many of the commercial business opportunities that grow out of the development of nuclear reactors undoubtedly will occur at the level of the first and second tier of subcontracts. The opportunities probably will involve the components, materials, and services which are required for the construction and operation of nuclear reactors. A number of industrial concerns have built, are building, or plan to build nuclear reactors. List of contractors, designers, shipbuilders, and facility operators are compiled in the booklet "Nuclear Reactors Built, Being Built, or Planned in the United States" (latest revision) and is available from the Clearinghouse for Federal Scientific and Technical Information, National Bureau of Standards, U.S. Department of Commerce, Springfield, Va., at nominal cost.

Tennessee Valley Authority

MANAGEMENT SERVICES AND COUNSEL

Fertilizer Production Technology developed by TVA is freely available to small business. Results of research and the development of new or improved processes for the manufacture of fertilizers are made available to prospective users through technical reports, articles published in trade and technical journals, various meetings, correspondence and visits. Those cooperating directly in TVA's fertilizer development programs are given technical assistance with problems and opportunities in the use of TVA produced materials. Representatives of companies may visit the TVA laboratories and plants at Muscle Shoals, Ala., to observe tests, pilot-plant demonstrations of new fertilizer processes, and large-scale manufacturing operations, and to consult with TVA scientists and engineers. Patents covering new processes and equipment are obtained by TVA, and licenses for use of the developments are granted without royalty. By April 1965, TVA had granted 409 licenses to 254 companies for the use of patented developments in 390 plants.

In the distributor demonstration program, an educational program designed to encourage scientific use of fertilizer, limited quantities of TVA fertilizers are made available to interested manufacturers and distributors for improving products and processes, and systems of fertilizer distribution. A field staff gives technical educational and engineering advisory service in connection with use of the experimental TVA materials. During fiscal year 1964, TVA fertilizers were used by 204 firms in 40 States in projects to encourage improved fertilization practices on farms, and to reduce plant nutrient costs in fertilizers through improved products and manufacturing processes. The participation of small businesses is encouraged. Currently, three-fourths of the firms having contracts to handle TVA fertilizers for the educational programs are small businesses.

Forest Resources of the Tennessee Valley are inventoried by TVA, making timber quantity and quality data available in a form that can be used by local industry. Studies of sawmill and logging operations provide information which is passed on to the industry through literature and sawmill conferences.

TVA Fisheries Investigations include inventories of fish populations in reservoirs, testing of new types of commercial fishing gear, and development of new markets for rough fish—nongame species for which markets are now inadequate or nonexist-

ent. Studies aimed at maintaining and developing the mussel population and shell harvest are also underway.

TVA Assistance on Navagiation Matters relative to the Tennessee waterway is available to barge lines and industries. State agencies and waterfront communities are also assisted in providing developmental services. These services include identification of sites suitable for river terminals and for waterfront industries requiring water transportation and processing water supply; engineering data in respect to channel depths and reservoir levels; and information on barge line and other transportation services.

Assistance Is Available on Regional and Local Economic Analyses and in obtaining related information on resources of importance to business activity through business and industry work groups of Tributary Area Development Associations.

TVA Sells Power to 156 municipal and cooperative distributors who retail the power to their industrial and other customers. TVA also sells power directly, at retail, to a few industries with large or unusual power requirements. The distributors have their own engineering and sales staffs and, in most areas, engage the services of professional industrial developers. TVA offers, in addition, advisory engineering services to assist the distributors with special customer problems.

Engineering Information resulting from many years of experiment and study is available to small business. TVA's Engineering Laboratory in Norris, Tenn., has developed useful know-how in hydromechanics, in the field of air and gas handling equipment, and in the uses of instrumentation to record and analyze data collected in the Laboratory and in the field.

The Laboratory's *Water Quality Management Studies*, for example, are developing the means to predict water temperatures, dissolved oxygen content and general water quality in Tennessee Valley streams and reservoirs. These continuing studies will provide information concerning plant location and the proper uses of water intake structures for those facilities requiring water in processing.

TVA maintains and operates streamflow, rainfall, and evaporation stations for operational and water management purposes, and collects information on the quality of water within the Tennessee River basin in connection with water management and pollution studies.

TVA has published local flood reports for most of the communities in the region that experience

146

periodic flooding. These reports contain data on historic floods as well as those which may occur in the future. This information is useful in evaluating the risk associated with developments in the flood plain.

Topographic Maps of standard 1 : 24,000 scale are available for the entire Tennessee Valley area, and may be purchased from TVA. Also, prints of aerial photographs and copies of compilation manuscripts used in the preparation of these maps may be had at reproduction cost.

GOVERNMENT CONTRACTS

In its contracting for materials, equipment, and supplies, small business is given the following preferences:

(1) Bidders' mailing lists on certain selected items are limited to small business concerns.

(2) Where a small business and a large one are equal low bidders and have equal labor surplus area classification, the small business is given the award.

(3) In evaluating foreign bids a factor of 12 percent is added to them when the low domestic bidder is a small business concern.

In addition, some of TVA's purchasing policies directly benefit small concerns. For example, the practice of buying part of its coal requirements in small quantities over short terms permits small producers to share in supplying coal to TVA. In fiscal year 1964, about 46 percent of TVA's coal purchases were from small business concerns. TVA makes wide use of motor carriers and contract barge lines for shipments to, from, and within TVA; these carriers are principally small business concerns. For fiscal year 1964, about $146 million or 43 percent of the total amount of TVA contracts went to small business.

NEW BUSINESS OPPORTUNITIES

RESEARCH AND DEVELOPMENT

TVA advances in fertilizer technology are being adopted by members of the industry and by new producers at an increasing rate. The expanding need for production of liquid and suspension fertilizers, high-analysis granular fertilizers of various types, and intermediate materials of high concentration offer new business opportunities in which TVA can be of considerable assistance. TVA developments in these and other fertilizer fields are becoming increasingly important in improving and lowering the costs of fertilizers. Availability of improved fertilizer materials under the TVA distributor demonstration program, open to any firm willing to carry on designated developmental activities, has enabled many companies to try out applications of new technology or new types of operation.

TVA has done research and development work

on laminated hardwood flooring, wood molasses, and wood preservation with oil-soluble preservatives. Analysis reports on additional hardwood and pine pulpmill sites were published recently. Integrated wood utilization centers are being encouraged through publications that analyze resources, markets, and economic opportunities for specific areas. Research is underway with the U.S. Forest Products Laboratory on continuous wood laminating processes, treatment of wood with polyphosphates to make it fire resistant, and increased chemical utilization of hardwoods. Other investigations are aimed at cutting the cost of harvesting and delivering wood to processing plants and developing new methods for reducing roundwood to fibers.

GENERAL INFORMATION BIBLIOGRAPHY

OFFICE OF AGRICULTURAL AND CHEMICAL DEVELOPMENT PUBLICATIONS

Fertilizer Science and the American Farmer.
General Outline of Chemical Engineering Activities.
Fertilizer Trends and the Scope of TVA's Fertilizer Activities.
TVA Fertilizers in the Distributor Demonstration Program.

Abstracts of TVA reports on such subjects and publications on research and development projects of possible interest to small concerns, are sent periodically to the Small Business Administration.

DIVISION OF FORESTRY DEVELOPMENT PUBLICATIONS

Skidding [Logs] with Rubber-Tired Wheel Tractors.
A Guide for Evaluating Black Walnut Sawlog Quality.
Quality Control in Circular Sawmill Operation.
Utilizing Pine Sawmill Residue for Pulp Chips.
Harvesting Pine Pulpwood.
Pulpwood Marketing Trends in the Tennessee Valley.
A Forest Restored—An Industry Expanded.
An Industrial Opportunity for Southwest Virginia—Hardwood Furniture Dimension.
Furniture Industry Expansion in the Tennessee Valley.
Hardwood Utilization Centers.
Hickory—Wood with a Future.
Forest Industry Prospects for Upper French Broad Watershed.
A Forest Industry Prospectus for East Tennessee.

OFFICE OF POWER PUBLICATIONS

Power Annual Report (TVA).
Annual Summary of New and Expanded Industrial Plant Announcements.

Export-Import Bank

The basic purpose of the Export-Import Bank (EXIMBANK) is to facilitate the foreign trade of the United States. Eximbank has three major programs which benefit U.S. exporters:

1. Export Credit insurance issued to U.S. suppliers in cooperation with the Foreign Credit Insurance Association (FCIA) covering political and commercial risks on both short- and medium-term export sales transactions.

2. Guarantees offered to commercial banks furnishing nonrecourse financing to U.S. exporters on their medium-term sales.

3. Direct loans to foreign borrowers to assist them in financing the purchase of U.S. goods and services.

EXIMBANK's operations are guided by the following principles:

Loans, guarantees, and insurance are extended for the primary purpose of promoting the export of U.S. materials, equipment and services.

Loans, and guaranteed or insured credits, are in dollars and payable in dollars.

Each transaction must offer reasonable assurance of repayment.

Eximbank cooperates with and assists private capital and does not compete with it.

EXPORT CREDIT INSURANCE

A small businessman desiring to increase sales abroad but uncertain about extending credit overseas, or who may be forced to meet credit terms offered by his foreign competitors, may find it helpful to make use of the credit insurance program now available through the Foreign Credit Insurance Association (FCIA).

The Foreign Credit Insurance Association—an unincorporated group of more than 70 major American marine, casualty, and property insurance companies—was formed in 1961 with the support of Eximbank to provide U.S. exporters with insurance of their short- and medium-term accounts receivable arising out of export sales. By the end of calendar year 1964 cumulative insurance authorizations had totaled about $2 billion. Coverage is provided for either comprehensive risks (both political and credit risks) or for political risks only. Also, the proceeds of the FCIA insurance policy may be assigned to a commercial bank, thus making it easier for the exporter to obtain financing if needed.

Payment of principal (and interest up to 6 percent) is insured from the time of shipment of the goods—or, if the insured desires, from the date the order is received—until final payment date.

Short-term policies provide coverage during a 1-year period on all credit sales transactions to all or selected countries where the term extended by the exporter does not exceed 180 days. The comprehensive policy covers 90 percent of losses due to credit risks and 95 percent for political risks. FCIA will negotiate policies excluding particular markets if the remaining markets provide a reasonable spread of risk.

Medium-term policies (payment from 181 days up to 5 years) permit the exporter to insure a single sale, or repetitive sales to one buyer during 1 year; the policy covers 90 percent of losses due to either credit or political risks.

For further information, U.S. exporters may apply either through their insurance broker or directly to the Foreign Credit Insurance Association, 250 Broadway, New York, N.Y., 10007.

COMMERCIAL BANK GUARANTEE PROGRAM

The small businessman may more easily obtain financing from his commercial bank on his medium-term sales abroad because of the guarantees offered to the banks by the Export-Import Bank. By the end of 1964 nearly $1 billion of guarantees had been authorized under this program. If a commercial bank desires to obtain a guarantee from Export-Import Bank it must be willing to provide credit to the exporter on a nonrecourse basis. The commercial bank prepares and submits to Eximbank an application for a guarantee which covers the commercial bank against the risk of nonpayment by the foreign buyer for either political or commercial reasons. To be eligible for a guarantee the underlying sales transaction must provide for an initial cash payment by the foreign buyer (usually 20 percent of the contract price), the exporter must retain for his own account 10 percent of the balance or financed portion, and financing for the remaining 90 percent of the financed portion of the sale is to be provided without recourse on the exporter. Guarantee fees vary according to the term of the credit and the degree of risk in the particular market.

For further information, exporters should contact their commercial banks or through them a correspondent bank in a major city.

LONG-TERM CAPITAL LOANS

Also, small businessmen may benefit directly or indirectly when Eximbank finances exports through long-term capital loans extended directly to private and public borrowers abroad. The amount of these loans varies from a few thousand to many millions of dollars. They may be used to finance the dollar cost of such varied projects as the purchase of equipment for plant expansion, the erection of a bridge, the equipping of a huge electric power station, or the construction of a complex chemical plant. These loans currently carry a standard interest rate of 5½ percent per annum regardless of where the project is located, and maturities of from 5 to around 20 years as may be appropriate. Such credits enable the U.S. suppliers of equipment, materials, and services to receive prompt and full payment in cash from the foreign buyer. Since Eximbank's establishment in 1934, such direct loans have totalled nearly $15 billion and have benefited not only the principal suppliers but thousands of subcontractors and small manufacturers throughout the United States.

OTHER PROGRAMS

In addition to the three major export financing programs described above, some of the Bank's other activities which may be of special interest to the small businessman are: The issuance of guarantees on U.S. goods shipped abroad for display at trade fairs and exhibits or on lease or consignment, or on the sale abroad of U.S. technical services such as engineering studies and reports, economic surveys, and design and architectural services, and direct commodity credits to oversea purchasers of agricultural commodities.

O

89th Congress } COMMITTEE PRINT
1st Session }

ACT

LIST OF PUBLICATIONS

ISSUED BY THE

SELECT COMMITTEE ON SMALL BUSINESS

UNITED STATES SENATE

81ST CONGRESS, 2D SESSION (1950)

THROUGH

88TH CONGRESS, 2D SESSION (1964)

Ɜ

REVISED MARCH 31, 1965

Printed for the use of the Select Committee on Small Business

---

U.S. GOVERNMENT PRINTING OFFICE

WASHINGTON : 1965

47-481

LIST OF PUBLICATIONS

ISSUED BY THE

SELECT COMMITTEE ON SMALL BUSINESS

UNITED STATES SENATE

81st Congress, 2d Session (1950), through the 88th Congress, 2d Session (1964)

81st Congress, 2d Session, 1950

HEARINGS

Small Business and Credit, Reconstruction Finance Corporation: The degree of availability of Reconstruction Finance Corporation funds to small business, June 14, 1950.[1]

Small Business and Procurement, Department of Commerce: Dissemination of procurement information; technical and management aids to small business, June 15, 1950.[1]

Small Business and Procurement, Department of Defense: Participation of small business in Government procurement, June 19, 1950.[1]

Small Business and Procurement, General Services Administration and Veterans Administration: Participation of small business in Government procurement, June 20, 1950.[1]

Small Business and Procurement, Economic Cooperation Administration: Participation of small business in Government procurement, June 21, 1950.[1]

Fuel Situation in Chicago, Chicago, Ill., December 14, 1950.[1]

REPORT

Senate Report No. 2633: The New England Fuel Situation and Prospects. Report of the Select Committee on Small Business, United States Senate, pursuant to S. Res. 344. December 14, 1950.[1]

COMMITTEE PRINTS

No. 1. The New England Fuel Situation and Prospects. Report of the Subcommittee on Fuel of the Select Committee on Small Business, United States Senate, October 21, 1950.[1]

Small-Business Clinic—Proceedings of small-business clinic held at Tucson, Ariz., December 15, 1950, including excerpts from the Oklahoma City clinic, December 16, 1950.[1]

Selling to Your Government: Data prepared by the Select Committee on Small Business, United States Senate, relative to participation of small business in the Federal Procurement Program in National Defense, 1950.[1]

82d Congress, 1st Session, 1951

HEARINGS

Material Shortages:
Part I. Impact on Small Business, January 18, 1951.[1]
Part II. Steel: Impact on Small Business, January 19, 20, 1951.[1]
Part III. Plastics: Impact on Small Business, January 23, 1951.[1]
Part IV. Aluminum: Impact on Small Business, January 26, 1951.[1]

Industrial Manpower: Subcommittee on Manpower, March 6, 7, 22, 1951.[1]

Rubber Survey: Subcommittee on Rubber. March 26, 27, 28, 29, 30, April 2, 3, 4, 5, 9, 10, 1951.[1]

[1] Supply exhausted.

Role of Irregular Airlines in United States Air Transportation Industry: Sub-
    committee on Irregular Airlines, April 23, 24, 25, 27, 30, May 1 and 5, 1951.[1]
Small Business Participation in the Military Procurement Program, May 21, 23,
    24, 28, 29, 1951.[1]
Price Discrimination and the Basing-Point System: Subcommittee on Price Dis-,
    crimination and the Basing-Point System, July 13, 16, 17, 18, 19, 23, 24, 25,
    26, and 27, 1951.[1]
Small-Business Problems in the Mobilization Program: Subcommittee on Military
    Procurement, Detroit, Mich., July 14 and 16, 1951.[1]
Nickel Gray Market: Subcommittee to Study the Gray Market in Nickel, August
    21, 22, and 28, 1951.[1]
Small-Business Programs of the National Production Authority, October 4, 1951.
Steel Gray Market: Subcommittee on Mobilization and Procurement, Pittsburgh,
    Pa., October 25, 1951; Chicago, Ill., November 20, 1951; Detroit, Mich., No-
    vember 29 and 30, 1951; Cleveland, Ohio, December 19, 1951.[1]
Steel Outlook for 1952: Subcommittee on Mobilization and Procurement, Decem-
    ber 3, 1951.

JOINT HEARINGS

Small-Business Participation in Military Procurement: Joint hearings before the
    Senate and House Select Committees on Small Business, May 7, 8, 14, 15, and
    16, 1951.[1]
Production and Allocations: Joint hearing before the Senate and House Com-
    mittees on Banking and Currency and the Senate and House Select Committees
    on Small Business, October 12, 1951.[1]

REPORTS

Senate Report No. 2: Annual Report of the Select Committee on Small Business.
    January 15, 1951.
Senate Report No. 77: Report on Material Shortages, February 5, 1951.
Senate Report No. 438: Report on Small-Business Manpower Problems—Indus-
    trial Manpower, June 18, 1951.
Senate Report No. 469: Report on Participation of Small Business in Military
    Procurement, June 21, 1951.
Senate Report No. 540: Report on Role of Irregular Airlines in United States Air
    Transportation Industry, July 10, 1951.
Senate Report No. 551: Concentration of Defense Contracts, July 19, 1951.
Senate Report No. 586: Report on Price Discrimination and the Basing-Point
    System, July 30, 1951.
Senate Report No. 785: The Gray Market in Nickel, September 18, 1951.

COMMITTEE PRINTS

Supplies for a Free Press: A preliminary report on newsprint by the Subcommittee
    on Newsprint of the Select Committee on Small Business, United States Senate,
    1951.
Prevalence of Price Cutting of Merchandise Marketed Under Price Maintenance
    Agreements: Study prepared for the Joint Committee on the Economic Report
    and the Select Committee on Small Business, United States Senate, May 28
    through June 25, 1951.[1]
Second Report of the Attorney General of the United States, prepared pursuant
    to section 708(e) of the Defense Production Act of 1950, April 30, 1951.[1]
Small Defense Plants Administration: Section 714 of the Defense Production Act
    of 1950, October 15, 1951.
New England Fuel Supplies: Staff report to the Subcommittee on Fuel of the
    Select Committee on Small Business, December 5, 1951.
Aluminum Inventories of West Coast Aircraft Industry: Staff Report, December
    26, 1951.

82d Congress, 2d Session, 1952

HEARINGS

Small Business Participation in Military Procurement, No. 3: Plant expansion,
    part 1, Air Force program on landing gear struts.   January 30 and 31, 1952.
Machine-Tool Shortages: The impact of machine-tool shortages on small manu-
    facturers.   February 27, 28, and 29, March 10, 11, 12, 14, 17, 18, and 19, and
    April 1 and 2, 1952.

---

[1] Supply exhausted.

Small Business Participation in Military Procurement, No. 4: Administration of
Public Law 921, 81st Congress, an act whereby the Department of Defense
received authority to grant relief to contractors suffering hardships under fixed-
price contracts. February 13 and 14, 1952.[1]
Aluminum Supply: Outlook for small aluminum fabricators. March 7, 1952.
Defense Manpower Policy No. 4: The implementation of defense manpower policy
No. 4, issued February 7, 1952, by the Director of Defense Mobilization, and
its impact on small business. March 20, 1952.
Tax Problems of Small Business, Part I: Impact of Federal tax programs on small
business concerns: [1]
    March 13, 1952, Bridgeport, Conn.
    March 14, 1952, Newark, N.J.
    March 28, 1952, Los Angeles, Calif.
    April 4, 1952, Minneapolis, Minn.
    April 10, 1952, Birmingham, Ala.
    May 15, 1952, Chicago, Ill.
Tax Problems of Small Business, Part II: Impact of Federal tax program on small
business concerns: July 15, 1952—Cleveland, Ohio.
Rubber Program: The conduct of the rubber program. March 27 and 28, 1952.
Use of Unauthorized Aluminum in the Storm-Window Industry. April 21 and 22,
1952.
Military Procurement, No. 5: Participation of small business in military procure-
ment. April 28 and 29, May 2, 5, 6, and 8, 1952.
Monopoly and Cartels, Part I: The impact of monopoly and cartel practices on
small business. April 23 and 29, May 23, July 16 and 17, 1952.

REPORTS

Senate Report No. 1068: Annual Report of the Select Committee on Small
Business, United States Senate. January 21, 1952.[1]
Senate Report No. 1141: The Gray Market in Steel: Impact of gray market in
steel on small manufacturers and fabricators. January 31, 1952.
Senate Report No. 1404: Newsprint for Tomorrow: Report and conclusions of
the Select Committee on Small Business, including individual views of Senator
Thye and statement of Senator Schoeppel. April 7, 1952.[1]
Senate Report No. 1459: The Administration of Public Law 921, 81st Congress
April 16, 1952.
Senate Report No. 1597: Defense Production Pools. May 26, 1952.
Senate Report No. 1860: The Unauthorized Use of Aluminum in the Storm-
Window Industry. June 27, 1952.
Senate Report No. 1988: Machine-Tool Shortages: Impact of machine-tool
shortages on small manufacturers. June 30, 1952.
Senate Report No. 2070: Military Procurement: Participation of small business
in military procurement. July 2, 1952.[1]

COMMITTEE PRINTS

No. 1. Monopolistic Practices and Small Business: Staff report to the Federal
    Trade Commission for the Subcommittee on Monopoly of the Select
    Committee on Small Business, United States Senate. March 31, 1952.
No. 2. The Distribution of Steel Consumption, 1949–50: Report of the Federal
    Trade Commission to the Subcommittee on Monopoly of the Select
    Committee on Small Business, United States Senate. March 31, 1952.
No. 3. A Study of the Development of the Antitrust Laws and Current Problems
    of Antitrust Enforcement: Report of the Department of Justice to the
    Subcommittee on Monopoly of the Select Committee on Small Business,
    United States Senate. May 23, 1952.
No. 4. The Public Utility Holding Company Act of 1935: Report of the Securities
    and Exchange Commission to the Subcommittee on Monopoly of the
    Select Committee on Small Business, United States Senate. June 3,
    1952.
No. 5. Foreign Legislation Concerning Monopoly and Cartel Practices: Report
    of the Department of State to the Subcommittee on Monopoly of the
    Select Committee on Small Business, United States Senate. July 9,
    1952.
No. 6. The International Petroleum Cartel: Staff report to the Federal Trade
    Commission submitted to the Subcommittee on Monopoly of the Select
    Committee on Small Business, United States Senate. August 22, 1952.[1]

[1] Supply exhausted.

No. 7. Concentration of Banking in the United States: Staff report to the Board of Governors of the Federal Reserve System, submitted to the Subcommittee on Monopoly of the Select Committee on Small Business, United States Senate.   September 10, 1952.
No. 8. The Cost and Availability of Credit and Capital to Small Business: Staff report to the Board of Governors of the Federal Reserve System, submitted to the Subcommittee on Monopoly of the Select Committee on Small Business, United States Senate.   October 30, 1952.
No. 9. The Role of Competition in Commercial Air Transportation: A report by the Civil Aeronautics Board, submitted to the Subcommittee on Monopoly of the Select Committee on Small Business, United States Senate.   November 24, 1952.

JOINT COMMITTEE PRINT

The Third World Petroleum Congress: A report to the Select Committee on Small Business, United States Senate, and the Select Committee on Small Business, House of Representatives.[1]

83d Congress, 1st Session, 1953

HEARINGS

Military procurement, participation of small business in; March 5, May 4, 8, 9, 11, 13, 14, and 15, 1953.[1]
Future of irregular airlines in the United States air transportation industry; March 31, May 1, 4, 5, 6, 7, and 8, 1953.[1]
Motion-picture distribution trade practice—Problems of independent motion-picture exhibitors relating to distribution trade practices; Los Angeles, Calif., March 31, April 1 and 2, 1953; Washington, D.C., April 15, 16, 17, 27, 28, 29, 30, May 28, and July 10, 1953.[1]
Battery AD–X2: Investigation of battery additive AD–X2; March 31, June 22, 23, 24, 25, and 26, 1953.[1]
Aluminum sweating operations, the extent of Government competition with private enterprise; September 28, 1953.
Petroleum marketing and distribution problems of independent west coast marketers; Seattle, Wash., November 16 and 17, 1953.

REPORTS

Senate Report 49: Annual Report of the Select Committee on Small Business, United States Senate; March 2, 1953.
Senate Report 206: Small Business and Defense Subcontracts; April 28, 1953.
Senate Report 442: Tax Problems of Small Business; June 18, 1953.
Senate Report 882: Future of Irregular Airlines; July 31, 1953.
Senate Report 835: Problems of Independent Motion-Picture Exhibitors; August 3, 1953.

COMMITTEE PRINTS

Effect of battery additive AD–X2 on lead acid batteries; report of the Massachusetts Institute of Technology submitted to the Select Committee on Small Business, United States Senate, April 6, 1953.[1]
Problems of independent tire dealers, staff report to the Select Committee on Small Business, United States Senate, July 27, 1953.
Small Business Administration: Title II of Small Business Act of 1953 (Public Law 163, approved July 30, 1953), August 10, 1953.

83d Congress, 2d Session, 1954

HEARINGS

Military Procurement Program, 1954: Participation of Small Business in Military Procurement; March 17, 19, 24, 25, 31, April 2, 7, 8, 13, and 14, 1954.[1]
Small Business Administration Loan Policy; May 13, 1954.[1]
Navy Procurement of Tugboats: Participation of Small Business in Military Procurement; May 19 and 20, 1954.

---

[1] Supply exhausted.

REPORTS

Senate Report 1092: Annual Report of the Select Committee on Small Business;
   March 25, 1954.[1]
Senate Report 2487: Military Procurement, 1954: Participation of Small Busi-
   ness in Military Procurement; August 14, 1954.[1]
Senate Report 2506: Navy Procurement of Tugboats; August 24, 1954.[1]

84th Congress, 1st Session, 1955

HEARINGS

Small Business Administration Progress Report, March 21, 1955.
Government Competition With Private Business, April 6, 1955.
Military Procurement, 1955—Participation of Small Business in Military Pro-
   curement, April 20, 21, 22, 25, May 4 and 5, 1955.
Report of the Attorney General's National Committee to Study the Antitrust
   Laws—To consider the report of the Attorney General's National Committee,
   April 27, 28, and 29, 1955.
Maintenance of the Mobilization Base—Policies of the Office of Defense Mobili-
   zation and the Department of Defense, as they affect small business (DMO
   VII-7; DOD 3005.3), July 20, 1955.
Gasoline Price War in New Jersey—A Study of Petroleum Marketing Practices
   in New Jersey; July 22, 1955, part 1.
Gasoline Price War in New Jersey—A Study of Petroleum Marketing Practices
   in New Jersey, October 19 and 20, 1955 (Newark, N.J.), part 2.
Administration of the Motor Carrier Act by the Interstate Commerce Commission,
   as it affects small truckers and shippers; November 30, December 1 and 2, 1955.[1]

REPORTS

Senate Report No. 129: Annual Report of the Select Committee on Small Busi-
   ness, United States Senate, March 30, 1955.
Senate Report No. 1272: Maintenance of the Mobilization Base: Directives and
   Orders Relating to the Maintenance of the Mobilization Base, July 30, 1955.
Senate Report No. 1273: Military Sea Transportation Service Bidding Pro-
   cedures, July 30, 1955.
Senate Report No. 1274: Military Procurement, 1955: Participation of Small
   Business in Military Procurement, July 30, 1955.

COMMITTEE PRINT

Small Business Act of 1955—Text of Small Business Act of 1953 (Public Law
   163, 83d Cong., 1st sess.), as amended by Public Law 268 of the 84th Congress,
   1st session; August 20, 1955.[1]

84th Congress, 2d Session, 1956

HEARINGS

Military Procurement, 1956: Small Business Problems in Military Procurement,
   January 9 and 10, 1956.
Machine-Tool Programs: Mobilization Planning, Reserve and Replacement
   Programs, February 7 and 8, 1956.
Gasoline Price War in New Jersey: A Study of Petroleum Marketing Practices in
   New Jersey, December 15 and 16, 1955, and February 18, 1956, part 3.[1]
Motion-Picture Distribution Trade Practices, 1956: Problems of Independent
   Motion-Picture Exhibitors, March 21, 22; May 21 and 22, 1956.[1]
Small Business Administration, 1956: Progress Report of the Small Business
   Administration, April 18 and 19, 1956.
Supply and Distribution of Nickel: The Impact of the Nickel Shortage on Small
   Electroplaters, May 30 and 31, 1956.
Government Procurement, 1956: Small Business Policies and Programs of
   Government Agencies, March 28, 29; May 22, 23, 24; June 26 and 27, 1956.

[1] Supply exhausted.

Senate Report No. 1368: Sixth Annual Report of the Select Committee on Small Business, United States Senate, January 12, 1956.
Senate Report No. 1693: Competition, Regulation, and the Public Interests in the Motor Carrier Industry—Administration of the Motor Carrier Act by the Interstate Commerce Commission, together with minority views, March 19, 1956.
Senate Report No. 1723: Military Procurement, 1956—Military Procurement Practices—Case Studies—April 3, 1956.
Senate Report No. 2229: Machine-Tool Program—Mobilization Planning, Reserve and Replacement Programs, June 14, 1956.
Senate Report No. 2810: Gasoline Price War in New Jersey—A Study of Petroleum Marketing Practices, July 26, 1956.[1]
Senate Report No. 2818: Motion-Picture Distribution Trade Practices, 1956: Problems of Independent Motion-Picture Exhibitors, July 27, 1956.
Senate Report No. 2819: Fair Trade—A study on Fair Trade, Based on a Survey of Manufacturers and Retailers, July 27, 1956.
Senate Report No. 2826: Supply and Distribution of Nickel and the Impact of the Nickel Shortage on Small Electroplaters, August 1, 1956.
Senate Report No. 2827: Government Procurement, 1956—Small Business Participation in Government Procurement, August 1, 1956.

Material Relative to Competition in the Regulated Civil-Aviation Industry, 1956, transmitted by the Civil Aeronautics Board to the Select Committee on Small Business, United States Senate, April 18, 1956.
Tax Guide for Small Business—Transmitted by the Internal Revenue Service of the Department of the Treasury to the Select Committee on Small Business, United States Senate, December 1956.[1]

85th Congress, 1st Session, 1957

Government Procurement, 1957: Case Studies in Government Procurement, March 11, 12, and 13, 1957.
Small Business Administration, 1957: Annual review of the activities of the Small Business Administration, March 14 and 15, 1957.
Government Competition with Private Business, 1957: Progress report on discontinuance of commercial-type operations by the Federal Government, April 16 and May 22, 1957.[1]
Daytime Radio Broadcasting, 1957: Problems arising out of the petition filed by the Daytime Broadcasting Association, Inc., with the Federal Communications Commission for extended hours of operation, April 29 and 30, 1957.[1]
Trucking Mergers and Concentration: Mergers and possible growth of concentration in the trucking industry (and an appendix entitled, "Trucking Mergers, Concentration, and Small Business: An Analysis of Interstate Commerce Commission Policy, 1950–56," prepared by Dr. Walter Adams and Dr. James B. Hendry, for the Senate Small Business Committee), July 1, 2, 11, and 12, 1957.
Small-Business Participation in Government Procurement, 1957: Small-business policies and programs of Government agencies, June 25, 26, 28, July 11, 12, and 30, 1957.[1]
Tax Problems of Small Business: The impact of Federal taxation on small business, part 1:[1]
    September 16, 1957, Phoenix, Ariz.
    September 18, 1957, Los Angeles, Calif.
    September 20, 1957, San Francisco, Calif.
    September 30, 1957, Boston, Mass.
    October 2, 1957, New York, N.Y.
Tax Problems of Small Business: The impact of Federal taxation on small business, part 2:[1]
    November 5, 1957, Miami, Fla.
    November 12, 1957, Chicago, Ill.
    November 13, 1957, Minneapolis, Minn.
    November 15, 1957, Portland, Oreg.

[1] Supply exhausted.

Tax Problems of Small Business: The impact of Federal taxation on small business, part 3: [1]
  November 20, 1957, Denver, Colo.
  November 22, 1957, Wichita, Kans.
  December 2, 1957, Birmingham, Ala.
  December 4, 1957, Dallas, Tex.
  December 10, 1957, Milwaukee, Wis.
Small-Business Problems in the Pacific Northwest, 1957, Portland, Oreg., November 14, 1957.

REPORTS

Senate Report No. 46: Seventh Annual Report of the Select Committee on Small Business, United States Senate, February 1, 1957.[1]
Senate Report No. 1015: Government Competition With Private Business: Discontinuance of commercial-type operations by the Federal Government, August 19, 1957.
Senate Report No. 1111: Government Procurement, 1957: Case studies in Government procurement, August 23, 1957.[1]
Senate Report No. 1168: Daytime Radio Stations: Extended hours of operation for daytime radio stations, September 11, 1957.
Senate Report No. 1170: Government Procurement Policies: Small-Business participation in Government procurement, 1957, December 30, 1957.

DOCUMENTS

Senate Document No. 32: The Right To Buy—And Its Denial to Small Business: A report prepared by Dr. Vernon A. Mund for the Select Committee on Small Business, United States Senate, March 1957.

85th Congress, 2d Session, 1958

HEARINGS

The Role of Private Antitrust Enforcement in Protecting Small Business, 1958: The extent to which private enforcement of the antitrust laws offers a practical form of protection to small business, victims of predatory pricing practices and other antitrust wrongdoing, March 3 and 4, 1958.[1]
Small Business Administration, 1958: Annual review of the activities of the Small Business Administration, March 25, 1958.
The Role of Small Business in Defense Missile Procurement, 1958: The participation of small business in the missile, rocket, and outer space exploration programs of the Department of Defense, April 29, 30, and May 1, 1958.
Discount-House Operations: Competitive impact of discount-house operations on small business, June 23, 24, and 25, 1958.[1]
Small-Business Participation in Government Procurement, 1958: Small-business programs, policies, and procedures of Government agencies, July 23 and 24, 1958.[1]
Competitive Problems of Independent Flat-Glass Dealers: Dual distribution methods of flat-glass producers and competitive problems of independent flat-glass dealers and distributors, July 30 and 31, 1958; October 9 and 10, 1958.
Independent Logging and Sawmill Industry, 1958: Problems of the independent logging and sawmill industry, November 13, 1958, Superior, Wis., part 1.[1]

REPORTS

Senate Report No. 1237: Tax Problems of Small Business, January 30, 1958.
Senate Report No. 1282: Eighth Annual Report of the Select Committee on Small Business, United States Senate, February 10, 1958.
Senate Report No. 1441: Mergers and Concentration in the Trucking Industry, together with minority views of Mr. Schoeppel and Mr. Goldwater, April 21, 1958.
Senate Report No. 1855: The Role of Private Antitrust Enforcement in Protecting Small Business, July 18, 1958.
Senate Report No. 2499: The Role of Small Business in Defense Missile Procurement, September 30, 1958.

[1] Supply exhausted.

Senate Report No. 2504: Discount-House Operations: Summarizing Testimony on Competitive Impact of Discount-House Operations on Small Business, November 28, 1958.

Senate Report No. 2505: Small-Business Participation in Government Procurement, December 30, 1958.

COMMITTEE PRINTS

The General Accounting Office and Small Business: Staff report to the Select Committee on Small Business, United States Senate, January 21, 1958.

Financing Small Business: Report to the Committees on Banking and Currency and the Select Committees on Small Business, United States Congress, by the Federal Reserve System (pts. 1 and 2), April 11, 1958.[1]

Small Business Act of 1958: Text of Small Business Act of 1958, Public Law 536, 85th Congress, 2d session, July 23, 1958.[2]

Small Business Investment Act: Text and explanation, Public Law 699, 85th Congress, 2d session, September 5, 1958.[2]

Small Business Tax Adjustments (contained in the Technical Amendments Act of 1958, Public Law 85-866), September 15, 1958.[1]

Briefing on the Investment Act: Briefing session on the Small Business Investment Act of 1958, sponsored by the American Management Association in New York, December 1 and 2, 1958.

MIMEOGRAPH

Statistical Data on Small Business, prepared by the Select Committee on Small Business, United States Senate, 1958.[1]

86th Congress, 1st Session, 1959

HEARINGS

ndependent Logging and Sawmill Industry, 1959: The problems of the independent logging and sawmill industry (pt. 2, continued from 85th Cong.), January 31, 1959.

Case Problems in Government Procurement: Government procurement problems of Aerosonic Corp., Clearwater, Fla.; and Hastings-Raydist, Inc., Hampton, Va., March 19 and 20, 1959.

State Taxation on Interstate Commerce, 1959 (pt. 1), April 8, 1959.

State Taxation on Interstate Commerce, 1959 (pt. 2), May 1, 1959.

State Taxation on Interstate Commerce, 1959 (pt. 3): Written statements submitted for the record, New York, N.Y., and Newark, N.J., June 19, 1959.

Small-Business Participation in Defense Subcontracting, April 22, 23, and 24, 1959.

Shopping Centers, 1959: Alleged discriminatory practices against small-business concerns in suburban shopping centers, April 28 and 29, 1959.

Small Business Administration, 1959: Review of current programs and activities of Small Business Administration, June 3, 1959.

Dual Distribution in the Automotive Tire Industry, 1959 (pt. 1), June 17, 18, and 19, 1959.

Dual Distribution in the Automotive Tire Industry, 1959 (pt. 2) (Supplemental material to hearings), June 17, 18, and 19, 1959.

Problems of the Scrap-Steel Industry, 1959: Technological and competitive problems of independent scrap-steel dealers, June 24, 1959.

Mergers and Unfair Competition in Food Marketing: The interim report of the Federal Trade Commission on its economic inquiry into food marketing, July 2, 1959.

Tax Depreciation Allowances on Capital Equipment: The effect of current Federal tax depreciation policies on small business, July 24, 1959.

Patent Policies of Departments and Agencies of the Federal Government: The effect of Federal patent policies on competition, monopoly, economic growth, and small business, December 8, 9, and 10, 1959.

REPORTS

Senate Report No. 6: Ninth Annual Report of the Select Committee on Small Business, United States Senate, January 23, 1959.

[1] Supply exhausted.
[2] Revised in 1965.

Senate Report No. 240: The Small Independent Firm's Role in the Forest Products Industry: Problems of the independent logging and sawmill industry, together with a staff report, May 5, 1959.
Senate Report No. 453: State Taxation on Interstate Commerce: Problems faced by small business in complying with multistate taxation of income derived from interstate commerce, June 30, 1959.
Senate Report No. 716: Small Business Participation in Defense Subcontracting, August 13, 1959.
Senate Report No. 1013: Monopoly and Technological Problems in the Scrap Steel Industry, together with individual views, October 16, 1959.
Senate Report No. 1015: Studies of Dual Distribution: The Flat-Glass Industry—Dual-distribution methods of flat-glass producers and competitive problems of independent flat-glass dealers and distributors, together with individual views and staff report, December 31, 1959.

COMMITTEE PRINTS

The Right To Buy, 1959: Staff report prepared by the Select Committee on Small Business (updated through February 1959), July 9, 1959.
Set-Asides in Sale of Government Timber: Small Business Administration hearing on set-asides in sale of Government timber, together with SBA's summary, Portland, Oreg., August 26–27, 1959.
Appendix to a Staff Report entitled "Dual Distribution Methods and Competitive Problems of Independent Flat-Glass Dealers and Distributors," prepared by the Select Committee on Small Business, United State Senate, December 31, 1959.

CONGRESSIONAL RECORD REPRINT

Significant Small-Business Legislation Passed by the 86th Congress, 1st Session: Remarks by Hon. John Sparkman, chairman, Select Committee on Small Business, United States Senate, appearing in Congressional Record, September 14, 1959, p. 19983.

86th Congress, 2d Session, 1960

HEARINGS

Small Business Investment Act, 1960: Review of the operations of the Small Business Investment Act, February 23, 24, and 25, 1960.
Small Business Administration, 1960: Annual review of programs and activities of the Small Business Administration, March 22, 1960 (pt. 1).
Small Business Administration, 1960: Review of lending policies of the Small Business Administration, July 1, 1960 (pt. 2).
Government Procurement, 1960: Lack of competition in military procurement and its impact on small business, April 5, 6, 7, and 8, 1960.
Case Study in Subcontracting by Weapon-System Contractor: Excessive costs of the ground-support air-conditioning equipment for the B-58 bomber program, April 28, 1960.
Government Competition With Business—Liquid Oxygen Production: Air Force plan to build liquid oxygen plants in competition with private enterprise, May 12 and 13, 1960.
Government Competition With Business—Refrigerated Warehousing: Use of Government-owned facilities in competition with private commercial refrigerated warehouses, June 15, 1960.
Impact of Imports on American Small Business. June 16, 1960.
Food-Marketing—Report of the Federal Trade Commission: Federal Trade Commission inquiry into concentration and integration in food marketing, June 22, 1960.
Small Business Exports and the World Market, 1960: New York City, November 17, 1960; New Orleans, La., December 9, 1960; San Francisco, Calif., December 14, 1960.

REPORTS

Senate Report No. 1044; Tenth Annual Report of the Select Committee on Small Business, U.S. Senate, January 28, 1960.
Senate Report No. 1016: The Impact of Suburban Shopping Centers on Independent Retailers: Alleged discriminatory practices against small-business concerns in suburban shopping centers, together with individual views, January 5, 1960.

Senate Report No. 1017: Tax Depreciation Allowances on Capital Equipment: The effect of current Federal tax depreciation policies on small business, together with supplemental views, January 7, 1960.[1]

Senate Report No. 1031: Case Problems in Government Procurement: Government procurement problems of Aerosonic Corp., Clearwater, Fla.; and Hastings-Raydist, Inc., Hampton, Va., January 20, 1960.

Senate Report No. 1293: Small Business Investment Act, 1960: Review of the operations of the Small Business Investment Act, April 27, 1960.

Senate Report No. 1588: Government Competition With Business—Liquid Oxygen Production: Air Force plan to build liquid oxygen plants in competition with private enterprise, June 15, 1960.

Senate Report No. 1908: Impact of Imports on Small Business, August 23, 1960.

Senate Report No. 1947: Case Study in Subcontracting by Weapon-System Contractor: Excessive costs of the ground-support air-conditioning equipment for the B-58 bomber program, September 16, 1960.

Senate Report No. 1948: Government Competition with Business—Refrigerated Warehousing: Use of Government-owned facilities in competition with private commercial refrigerated warehousing, December 30, 1960 (pt. 1). Supplemental views of Senator Andrew F. Schoeppel, December 31, 1960 (pt. 2).

COMMITTEE PRINTS

Ten-Year Record of the Select Committee on Small Business, U.S. Senate, 1950–60: Statement by Senator John Sparkman, chairman, and list of committee publications for the 81st Congress, 2d session, through 86th Congress, 1st session, February 20, 1960.

Patent Policies of Government Departments and Agencies, 1960: Conference on Federal patent policies—Senator Russell B. Long, chairman, Subcommittee on Monopoly of the Select Committee on Small Business, U.S. Senate, and Vice Adm. H. G. Rickover, U.S. Navy, April 8, 1960.

Small Business Act (approved July 18, 1958): Text of Small Business Act, (Public Law 536, 85th Congress, 2d session, as amended by Public Law 85–699 and Public Law 86–367, October 5, 1960).[2]

Small Business Investment Act, Public Law 699, 85th Congress, 2d session, as amended: Text, explanation and related tax provisions, October 5, 1960.[2]

87th Congress, 1st Session, 1961

HEARINGS

The Role of Small Business in Government Procurement, 1961: Small business procurement program of the administration, April 25 and 26, 1961.

Small Business Administration, 1961: Annual review of the operations of the Small Business Administration, June 21 and 22, 1961.

Space Satellite Communications: Public policy questions on the ownership and control of a space satellite communications system, August 2, 3, 4, 9, 10, and 11, 1961 (pt. 1).[1]

Space Satellite Communications: Review of the Report of the Ad Hoc Carrier Committee, November 8 and 9, 1961 (pt. 2).

Lease Guarantees, 1961: Feasibility of a Program of Federal Guarantees for Small Business Leases, December 18 and 19, 1961.

REPORTS

Senate Report No. 51: Eleventh Annual Report of the Select Committee on Small Business, U.S. Senate, together with supplemental views, February 16, 1961.

Senate Report No. 4: Government Procurement, 1960: Lack of competition in military procurement and its impact on small business, together with supplemental views, January 17, 1961.

Senate Report No. 30: Review of the Small Business Administration Activities, 1959–60: Report of the Select Committee on Small Business, U.S. Senate, on the Small Business Administration, February 3, 1961.

---

[1] Supply exhausted.
[2] Revised in 1965.

Senate Report No. 89: Small Business Exports and the World Market: Report of the Select Committee on Small Business, U.S. Senate, on encouragement and expansion of exports by small business, March 27, 1961.
Senate Report No. 355: The Role of Small Business in Government Procurement, 1961: Report of the Select Committee on Small Business, U.S. Senate, on small business procurement program of the administration, June 7, 1961.

COMMITTEE PRINTS

American Management Association Seminar: Going abroad; the profit opportunities of international business for the smaller company. Briefing session on the profit opportunities of international business for the smaller company, Sponsored by the International Management Division of the American Management Association, Inc., held in New York City June 26, 27, and 28, 1961, published July 31, 1961.[1]
Small Business Investment Act: 1961 Text, Explanation, and related Tax Provisions, published October 31, 1961.[2]
Small Business Act: Text of Small Business Act (Public Law 536, 85th Cong., 2d sess.) as amended by Public Law 85–699, Public Law 86–367, Public Law 87–70, Public Law 87–198, Public Law 87–305, Public Law 87–341, and Public Law 87–367, published November 27, 1961.[2]
A Primer on Government Contract Claims, published December 20, 1961.

87th Congress, 2d Session, 1962

HEARINGS

Operations of Small Business Investment Companies: A review of the operations of small business investment companies: Portland, Oreg., February 24, 1962; Chicago, Ill., February 26, 1962; New York, N.Y., March 16, 1962; Atlanta, Ga., March 30, 1962; Washington, D.C., April 17–18, 1962.
Government Patent Policies in Meteorology and Weather Modification, 1962: The effect of Federal patent policies on competition, monopoly, economic growth and small business, March 26, 27, and 28, 1962.
World Trade—The Small Business Potential, 1962: Opportunities for small business in world trade discussed by recipients of the President's E award for export expansion, May 23, 1962.
Small Business Failures—Management Defects Held Largely Responsible: An inquiry into the availability and the adequacy of management counseling services for very small businesses, June 25, 26, and 27, 1962.
Impact of Defense Spending on Labor Surplus Areas, 1962: Effect of defense spending on small business in labor surplus areas, August 29, 1962.
The Role of Small Business in Government Procurement, 1962–63: Small business procurement programs of the Administration, September 12, 1962.

REPORTS

Senate Report No. 1491: Twelfth Annual Report of the Select Committee on Small Business, U.S. Senate, May 15, 1962.
Senate Report No. 1532: Small Business Lease Guarantees: Feasibility of a program of Federal guarantees for small business leases, May 24, 1962.
Senate Report No. 2270: Small Business Failures: Report of the Select Committee on Small Business, U.S. Senate, on factors influencing small business failures and the availability of management counseling to small firms, October 3, 1962.
Senate Report No. 1117: Small Business Administration, 1961: Report of the Select Committee on Small Business, U.S. Senate, on annual review of the operations of the Small Business Administration together with individual views, January 15, 1962.

COMMITTEE PRINTS

Recent Developments in the Structure of Banking—A Supplemental to Concentration of Banking in the United States: Special staff report of the Board of Governors of the Federal Reserve System, submitted to the Select Committee on Small Business, U.S. Senate, January 15, 1962.

[1] Supply exhausted.
[2] Revised in 1055.

Federal Handbook for Small Business: A survey of small business programs in the Federal Government agencies, sponsored by the Select Committee on Small Business, U.S. Senate; Select Committee on Small Business, U.S. House of Representatives; White House Committee on Small Business, and the Small Business Administration, 1962.

88th Congress, 1st Session, 1963

HEARINGS

Economic Aspects of Government Patent Policies: Impact of Government patent policies on economic growth, scientific and technological progress, competition, monopoly, and opportunities for small business, March 7, 8, 13, and 14, 1963.

Impact of Current Tax Proposals on Small Business: Impact upon small business of the 1963 tax proposals of the administration, April 29 and 30, 1963.

The Role and Effect of Technology in the Nation's Economy: A review of the effect of Government research and development on economic growth, May 20, 1963 (pt. 1).

The Role and Effect of Technology in the Nation's Economy: A review of the effect of Government research and development on economic growth, June 5 and 6, 1963 (pt. 2).

The Role and Effect of Technology in the Nation's Economy: A review of the effect of Government research and development on economic growth, June 20, December 17 and 18, 1963 (pt. 3).

Advertising Allowances: Competitive antitrust aspects of joint advertising programs by retailers, and the nature and purpose of advertising allowances given to retailers by manufacturers and wholesalers, September 11, 1963.

Small Business Administration—1963: Annual review of the operations of the Small Business Administration, December 2, 1963.

REPORTS

Senate Report No. 104: Thirteenth Annual Report of the Select Committee on Small Business, U.S. Senate, April 2, 1963.

Senate Report No. 161: Operations of small business investment companies: Report of the Select Committee on Small Business, U.S. Senate, on the operations of small business investment companies, April 25, 1963.

Senate Report No. 397: Impact of current tax proposals on small business: Report of the Select Committee on Small Business, U.S. Senate, on the impact upon small business of the 1963 tax proposals of the administration, August 15, 1963.

COMMITTEE PRINTS

Addenda to committee print of the Small Business Investment Act, Public Law 699, 85th Congress, 2d session, as amended October 31, 1961, issued by the Select Committee on Small Business, U.S. Senate, March 25, 1963.[3]

Small Business Act: Text of the Small Business Act, Public Law 536, 85th Congress, 2d session, as amended by Public Law 85–699, Public Law 86–367, Public Law 87–70, Public Law 87–198, Public Law 87–305, Public Law 87–341, Public Law 87–367, and Public Law 87–550; issued by the Select Committee on Small Business, U.S. Senate, March 25, 1963.[4]

Conference Relating to Subcontractors' Claims, by staff members of the Select Committee on Small Business, U.S. Senate, with representatives of the Department of Defense, Small Business Administration, National Aeronautics and Space Administration, General Accounting Office, and General Services Administration, May 28, 1963.

Economic and Legal Problems of Government Patent Policies: Report prepared for the Subcommittee on Monopoly of the Select Committee on Small Business, U.S. Senate, June 15, 1963.

Impact of Defense Spending on Labor-Surplus Areas: Report of the Subcommittee on Retailing, Distribution, and Marketing Practices to the Select Committee on Small Business, on Government programs and policies as they relate to the use of procurement in redeveloping distressed areas and a compilation of policy directives, statutes, and regulations relating to procurement in distressed areas, August 19, 1963.

---

[3] Small Business Investment Act revised in 1965.
[4] Revised in 1965.

Conference Relating to Small Business Participation in Government Procurement—1963, by staff members of the Select Committee on Small Business, U.S. Senate, with representatives of the Departments of the Army, Navy, and Air Force, Defense Supply Agency, National Aeronautics and Space Administration, and the Small Business Administration, September 24, 1963.

Small Lumber Companies in Western Oregon, October 1, 1963.

The Federal Disaster Relief Program: A concise and practical guide to all disaster relief programs, prepared for the Select Committee on Small Business, U.S. Senate, December 15, 1963.

88th Congress, 2d Session, 1964

HEARING

Ford Tractor Distributors: The circumstances and effects of termination by the Ford Motor Co. of the franchises of its independent distributors of tractors and implements in the United States, February 10, 1964.

Tax treatment of U.S. Concerns With Puerto Rican Affiliates: The economic development program, April 16 and 17, 1964.

The Role of Small Business in Government Procurement—1964: A review of the progress made in small business participation in Government procurement programs, June 2, 3, and 4, 1964.

Small Business Conversion Problems—1964: The impact of defense spending shifts and curtailments on small business; conversion problems of smaller firms, June 23 and July 7, 1964.

Oil Import Allocations: The impact of the system of allocations of crude oil under the mandatory oil import program on small business refiners, August 10 and 11, 1964.

Advertising Allowances—1964: Competitive and antitrust aspects of joint advertising programs by retailers, and the nature and purpose of advertising allowances given to retailers by manufacturers and wholesalers, August 12, 1964.

Impact of Defense Spending on Labor Surplus Areas—1964: The positions of various Government agencies with regard to implementation of Defense Manpower Policy No. 4 and other policies and programs for the placing of defense contracts and facilities in labor surplus areas, August 13, 1964.

REPORT

Senate Report No. 1180: Fourteenth Annual Report of the Select Committee on Small Business, U.S. Senate, July 9, 1964.

COMMITTEE PRINTS

Studies of Dual Distribution—The Automotive Tire Industry: Report of the Subcommittee on Retailing, Distribution, and Marketing Practices to the Select Committee on Small Business, U.S. Senate, January 15, 1964.

American Management Association Briefing Session—Planning to Meet Major Shifts in Defense Programs: Briefing session on the problems of defense-oriented companies in converting to commercial products, sponsored by the American Management Association, Inc., New York, N.Y., July 9 and 10, 1964.

O

4. Sm 1/2: P96/2/1950 —66

Y4 ... 1 ... .. / 16

| 89th Congress | } COMMITTEE PRINT |
| 2d Session | |

ACT

LIST OF PUBLICATIONS

ISSUED BY THE

SELECT COMMITTEE ON SMALL BUSINESS

UNITED STATES SENATE

81ST CONGRESS, 2D SESSION (1950)

THROUGH

89TH CONGRESS, 2D SESSION (1966)

ᒣ

ber 1, 1966
n)

Printed for the use of the Select Committee on Small Business

U.S. GOVERNMENT PRINTING OFFICE
71-726   WASHINGTON : 1966

IRARY
' 1955
CALIFORNIA
EY

SELECT COMMITTEE ON SMALL BUSINESS

[Created pursuant to S. Res. 58, 81st Cong.]

JOHN SPARKMAN, Alabama, *Chairman*

RUSSELL B. LONG, Louisiana
GEORGE A. SMATHERS, Florida
WAYNE MORSE, Oregon
ALAN BIBLE, Nevada
JENNINGS RANDOLPH, West Virginia
E. L. BARTLETT, Alaska
HARRISON A. WILLIAMS, Jr., New Jersey
GAYLORD NELSON, Wisconsin
JOSEPH M. MONTOYA, New Mexico
FRED R. HARRIS, Oklahoma

LEVERETT SALTONSTALL, Massachusetts
JACOB K. JAVITS, New York
JOHN SHERMAN COOPER, Kentucky
HUGH SCOTT, Pennsylvania
WINSTON L. PROUTY, Vermont
NORRIS COTTON, New Hampshire

LEWIS G. ODOM, Jr., *Staff Director*
BLAKE O'CONNOR, *Assistant Staff Director*
ROBERT R. LOCKLIN, *General Counsel*
ELIZABETH A. BYRNE, *Chief Clerk*

II

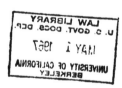

LIST OF PUBLICATIONS

ISSUED BY THE

SELECT COMMITTEE ON SMALL BUSINESS

UNITED STATES SENATE

81st Congress, 2d Session (1950), through the 89th Congress, 2d Session (1966)

81st Congress, 2d Session, 1950

HEARINGS

Small Business and Credit, Reconstruction Finance Corporation: The degree of availability of Reconstruction Finance Corporation funds to small business, June 14, 1950.[1]

Small Business and Procurement, Department of Commerce: Dissemination of procurement information; technical and management aids to small business, June 15, 1950.[1]

Small Business and Procurement, Department of Defense: Participation of small business in Government procurement, June 19, 1950.[1]

Small Business and Procurement, General Services Administration and Veterans Administration: Participation of small business in Government procurement, June 20, 1950.[1]

Small Business and Procurement, Economic Cooperation Administration: Participation of small business in Government procurement, June 21, 1950.[1]

Fuel Situation in Chicago, Chicago, Ill., December 14, 1950.[1]

REPORT

Senate Report No. 2633: The New England Fuel Situation and Prospects. Report of the Select Committee on Small Business, U.S. Senate, pursuant to S. Res. 344. December 14, 1950.[1]

COMMITTEE PRINTS

No. 1. The New England Fuel Situation and Prospects. Report of the Subcommittee on Fuel of the Select Committee on Small Business, U.S. Senate, October 21, 1950.[1]

Small Business Clinic—Proceedings of small business clinic held at Tucson, Ariz., December 15, 1950, including excerpts from the Oklahoma City clinic, December 16, 1950.[1]

Selling to Your Government: Data prepared by the Select Committee on Small Business, U.S. Senate, relative to participation of small business in the Federal Procurement Program in National Defense, 1950.[1]

82d Congress, 1st Session, 1951

HEARINGS

Material Shortages:
Part I. Impact on Small Business, January 18, 1951.[1]
Part II. Steel: Impact on Small Business, January 19 and 20, 1951.[1]
Part III. Plastics: Impact on Small Business, January 23, 1951.[1]
Part IV. Aluminum: Impact on Small Business, January 26, 1951.[1]
Industrial Manpower: Subcommittee on Manpower, March 6, 7, 22, 1951.[1]

---

[1] Supply exhausted.

6. The maximum authorized term for all SBA disaster loans was increased from 20 years to 30 years, and SBA specifically authorized to suspend temporarily repayments by disaster loan borrowers in certain hardship cases. During such suspensions, SBA could make the payments on or purchase the privately financed share of any such loan.

7. The authorization for appropriations to SBA's revolving fund was increased from $1,666 million to $1,721 million; the amount authorized to be outstanding for business- and disaster-loan purposes was increased from $1,325 million to $1,375 million; the amount authorized to be outstanding for functions under the Small Business Investment Act of 1958 was increased from $341 million to $461 million; and $5 million was authorized for transfer to the new lease guarantee fund established by Public Law 89–117.

A related provision of law, title IV of Public Law 88–452 (the Economic Opportunity Act of 1964), is also included at the end of the committee print. This new program of small business loans is particularly directed at reducing long-term unemployment. It is administered by SBA under a delegation from the Office of Economic Opportunity.

Another related provision of law which is included at the end of the committee print is the new lease guarantee provision contained in Public Law 89–117. Under this new authority, SBA may guarantee the payment of rentals on leases of commercial or industrial property by small concerns displaced by Federal or federally aided construction or on leases by small concerns eligible for antipoverty loans under title IV of the Economic Opportunity Act of 1964, to enable such concerns to obtain such leases.

These new provisions represent significant steps forward in assisting and preserving the small business segment of the American economy.

JOHN SPARKMAN,
Chairman, Select Committee on Small Business,
U.S. Senate.

AUGUST 30, 1965.

CONTENTS

ACT

SMALL BUSINESS ACT

(as amended)

SEC. 1. This Act may be cited as the "Small Business Act." — *Citation.*

SEC. 2. (a) The essence of the American economic system of private enterprise is free competition. Only through full and free competition can free markets, free entry into business, and opportunities for the expression and growth of personal initiative and individual judgment be assured. The preservation and expansion of such competition is basic not only to the economic well-being but to the security of this Nation. Such security and well-being cannot be realized unless the actual and potential capacity of small business is encouraged and developed. It is the declared policy of the Congress that the Government should aid, counsel, assist, and protect, insofar as is possible, the interests of small-business concerns in order to preserve free competitive enterprise, to insure that a fair proportion of the total purchases and contracts or subcontracts for property and services for the Government (including but not limited to contracts or subcontracts for maintenance, repair, and construction) be placed with small-business enterprises, to insure that a fair proportion of the total sales of Government property be made to such enterprises, and to maintain and strengthen the overall economy of the Nation.[1] — *Policy of Congress. 15 U.S.C. 631.*

(b) Further, it is the declared policy of the Congress that the Government should aid and assist victims of floods and other catastrophes, and small-business concerns which are displaced as a result of federally aided construction programs.[2]

SEC. 3. For the purposes of this Act, a small-business concern shall be deemed to be one which is independently owned and operated and which is not dominant in its field of operation. In addition to the foregoing criteria the Administrator, in making a detailed definition may use these criteria, among others: Number of employees and dollar volume of business. Where the number of employees is used as one of the criteria in making such definition for any of the purposes of this Act, the maximum number of employees which a small-business concern may have under the definition shall vary from industry to industry to the extent necessary to reflect differing characteristics of such industries and to take proper account of other relevant factors. — *Small business defined. 15 U.S.C. 632.*

[1] The subcontracts of contractors performing work or rendering services under Government procurement contracts were included within the policy statements of this section by section 6 of PL 87-305.
[2] The last 15 words of this subsection added by section 305(b) of PL 87-70.

Small Business
Administration.
15 U.S.C. 633.

Under President.

Independent agency.

Administrator.

Deputy Administrators.

15 U.S.C. 636,
637, 661 note.

SEC. 4. (a) In order to carry out the policies of this Act there is hereby created an agency under the name "Small Business Administration" (herein referred to as the Administration), which Administration shall be under the general direction and supervision of the President and shall not be affiliated with or be within any other agency or department of the Federal Government. The principal office of the Administration shall be located in the District of Columbia. The Administration may establish such branch and regional offices in other places in the United States as may be determined by the Administrator of the Administration. As used in this Act, the term "United States" includes the several States, the Territories and possessions of the United States, the Commonwealth of Puerto Rico, and the District of Columbia.

(b) The management of the Administration shall be vested in an Administrator who shall be appointed from civilian life by the President, by and with the advice and consent of the Senate, and who shall be a person of outstanding qualifications known to be familiar and sympathetic with small-business needs and problems. The Administrator shall not engage in any other business, vocation, or employment than that of serving as Administrator. The Administrator is authorized to appoint three Deputy Administrators to assist in the execution of the functions vested in the Administration.[3]

(c) There is hereby established in the Treasury a revolving fund, referred to in this section as "the fund", for the Administration's use in financing the functions performed under sections 7(a), 7(b), 7(c)(2), and 8(a) and under the Small Business Investment Act of 1958, including the payment of administrative expenses[4] in connection with such functions. All repayments of loans and debentures, payments of interest, and other receipts arising out of transactions financed from the fund shall be paid into the fund. As capital thereof, appropria-

---

[3] Section 201 of the Small Business Investment Act provides for a fourth Deputy Administrator, as follows:

"SEC. 201. There is hereby established in the Small Business Administration a division to be known as the Small Business Investment Division. The Division shall be headed by a Deputy Administrator who shall be appointed by the Administrator, and shall receive compensation at the rate provided by law for other deputy administrators of the Small Business Administration. The powers conferred by this Act upon the Administration and upon the Administrator, with the exception of those conferred by titles IV and V hereof, shall be exercised through the Small Business Investment Division and through the Deputy Administrator appointed hereunder. The powers conferred by this Act upon the Administration and upon the Administrator by titles IV and V hereof shall be exercised through such division, section, or other personnel as the Administrator in his discretion shall determine. In the performance of, and with respect to the functions, powers, and duties vested by this Act, the Administrator and the Administration shall (in addition to any authority otherwise vested by this Act) have the functions, powers, and duties set forth in the Small Business Act, and the provisions of sections 15 and 16 of that Act insofar as applicable, are extended to apply to the functions of the Administrator and the Administration under this Act." Public Law 89-117 excepted titles IV (lease guarantees) and V (development company loans) from the requirement that all authority contained in the Small Business Investment Act be administered through the Investment Division and the Deputy Administrator for Investment.

[4] That portion of former section 4(c) specifying the purposes for which the revolving fund might be used was rewritten, and specific authority to charge the revolving fund with administrative expenses applicable to operations under the Small Business Investment Act was included by sections 11(h)(3) and 11(h)(4) of PL 87-341. The inclusion of such authority was believed necessary in view of section 202(b) of the SBIA, which was repealed by section 11(h)(1) of PL 87-341. PL 89-59 added authority to use the fund for section 7(c)(2).

tions not to exceed $1,721,000,000 [6] are hereby authorized to be made to the fund, which appropriations shall remain available until expended. Not to exceed an aggregate of $1,375,000,000 [6] shall be outstanding at any one time for the purposes enumerated in the following sections of this Act: 7(a) (relating to regular business loans), 7(b) and 7(c)(2) (relating to disaster loans), and 8(a) (relating to prime contract authority): *Provided*, That the Administration shall report promptly to the Committees on Appropriations and the Committees on Banking and Currency of the Senate and House of Representatives whenever (1) the aggregate amount outstanding for the purposes enumerated in sections 7(a) and 8(a) exceeds $1,222,-000,000, or (2) the aggregate amount outstanding for the purpose enumerated in sections 7(b) and 7(c)(2) exceeds $103,000,000.[7] Not to exceed an aggregate of $461,-000,000 [6] shall be outstanding from the fund at any one time for the exercise of the functions of the Administration under the Small Business Investment Act of 1958: *Provided*, That such limitation shall not apply to functions under title IV thereof. The Administration shall pay into miscellaneous receipts of the Treasury, following the close of each fiscal year, interest on the outstanding cash disbursements from the fund, at rates determined by the Secretary of the Treasury, taking into consideration the current average yields on outstanding interest-bearing marketable public debt obligations of the United States of comparable maturities as calculated for the month of June preceding such fiscal year.[9]

> Business loans and prime contracts:
> $1,375,000,000.
> 15 U.S.C. 636.
> 15 U.S.C. 637.

> Disaster loans:
> $103,000,000.

> Small Business Investment Act:
> $461,000,000.

(d) There is hereby created the Loan Policy Board of the Small Business Administration, which shall consist of the following members, all ex officio: The Administrator, as Chairman, the Secretary of the Treasury, and the Secretary of Commerce. Either of the said Secretaries may designate an officer of his Department, who has been appointed by the President by and with the advice and consent of the Senate, to act in his stead as a member of the Loan Policy Board with respect to any

> Loan Policy Board.

[6] Increased from $650,000,000 to $900,000,000 by section 202(a)(1) of PL 85-699 and from $900,000,000 to $975,000,000 by PL 86-367, from $975,000,000 to $1,000,000,000 by PL 87-70, from $1,000,000,000 to $1,020,000,000 by PL 87-198, from $1,020,000,000 to $1,125,000,000 by section 3 of PL 87-305 and from $1,125,000,000 to $1,200,000,000 by section 12(1) of PL 87-341. Further increased to $1,566,000,000 by PL 87-550, to $1,716,000,000 by PL 88-56, and to $1,721,000,000 by PL 89-117. PL 89-117 also authorized transfer of $5,000,000 to a lease guarantee fund.

[6] The amount of authorized aggregate advances for section 7(a) was increased from $300,000,000 to $575,000,000 by PL 86-367 and from $575,000,000 to $595,000,000 by PL 87-198. This authorization was raised to $700,000,000 and combined with the existing $25,000,000 authorization for section 8(a), by section 3 of PL 87-305. Further increased to $1,225,000,000 by PL 87-550, and to $1,375,000,000 by PL 89-59.

[7] Increased from $125,000,000 by section 305(c)(2) of PL 87-70. PL 87-550 reduced this amount from $150,000,000 to $103,000,000.

[6] Increased from $250,000,000 by section 12(2) of PL 87-341; further raised to $341,000,000 by PL 87-550, and to $461,000,000 by PL 89-78. The statement that the limitation does not apply to lease guarantee functions under title IV of the Small Business Investment Act was added by PL 89-117.

[9] Those portions of this section authorizing expenditure of funds from the revolving fund in the exercise of the functions of the Administration under the Small Business Investment Act of 1968, and setting a limit upon the aggregate advances for such purposes, originated from section 202(a)(2) and section 202(a)(3) of PL 85-699. The entire section 4(c) was generally revised by section 3 of PL 87-305 and further revised by PL 87-550. References in the section to section 7(c)(2) were added by PL 89-59.

matter or matters. The Loan Policy Board shall establish general policies (particularly with reference to the public interest involved in the granting and denial of applications for financial assistance by the Administration and with reference to the coordination of the functions of the Administration with other activities and policies of the Government), which shall govern the granting and denial of applications for financial assistance by the Administration.[9a]

Administrative
powers.
15 U.S.C. 634.

SEC. 5. (a) The Administration shall have power to adopt, alter, and use a seal, which shall be judicially noticed. The Administrator is authorized, subject to the civil-service and classification laws, to select, employ, appoint, and fix the compensation of such officers, employees, attorneys, and agents as shall be necessary to carry out the provisions of this Act; to define their authority and duties; to provide bonds for them in such amounts as the Administrator shall determine; and to pay the costs of qualification of certain of them as notaries public. The Administration, with the consent of any board, commission, independent establishment, or executive department of the Government, may avail itself on a reimbursable or nonreimbursable basis of the use of information, services, facilities (including any field service thereof), officers, and employees thereof, in carrying out the provisions of this Act.[10]

Administrator
may:

(b) In the performance of, and with respect to, the functions, powers, and duties vested in him by this Act the Administrator may—

Sue and be sued.

(1) sue and be sued in any court of record of a State having general jurisdiction, or in any United States district court, and jurisdiction is conferred upon such district court to determine such controversies without regard to the amount in controversy; but no attachment, injunction, garnishment, or other similar process, mesne or final, shall be issued against the Administrator or his property;

Dispose of
property.

(2) under regulations prescribed by him, assign or sell at public or private sale, or otherwise dispose of for cash or credit, in his discretion and upon such terms and conditions and for such consideration as the Administrator shall determine to be reasonable, any evidence of debt, contract, claim, personal property, or security assigned to or held by him in connection with the payment of loans granted under this Act, and to collect or compromise all obligations assigned to or held by him and all legal or equitable rights accruing to him in connection with the payment of such loans until such time as such obli-

⁹ᵃ The SBA Loan Policy Board was abolished by Reorganization Plan No. 4 of 1965 (effective July 27, 1965; 30 F.R. 9353) and its functions transferred to the SBA Administrator.

¹⁰ The last sentence of former section 5(a), authorizing 15 positions within SBA to be placed in grades 16, 17, and 18 of the General Schedule established by the Classification Act of 1949, was deleted by section 103(3) of PL 87-367.

gations may be referred to the Attorney General for suit or collection;

(3) deal with, complete, renovate, improve, modernize, insure, or rent, or sell for cash or credit upon such terms and conditions and for such consideration as the Administrator shall determine to be reasonable, any real property conveyed to or otherwise acquired by him in connection with the payment of loans granted under this Act; *Utilise property.*

(4) pursue to final collection, by way of compromise or otherwise, all claims against third parties assigned to the Administrator in connection with loans made by him. This shall include authority to obtain deficiency judgments or otherwise in the case of mortgages assigned to the Administrator. Section 3709 of the Revised Statutes, as amended (41 U.S.C., sec. 5), shall not be construed to apply to any contract of hazard insurance or to any purchase or contract for services or supplies on account of property obtained by the Administrator as a result of loans made under this Act if the premium therefor or the amount thereof does not exceed $1,000. The power to convey and to execute in the name of the Administrator deeds of conveyance, deeds of release, assignments and satisfactions of mortgages, and any other written instrument relating to real property or any interest therein acquired by the Administrator pursuant to the provisions of this Act may be exercised by the Administrator or by any officer or agent appointed by him without the execution of any express delegation of power or power of attorney. Nothing in this section shall be construed to prevent the Administrator from delegating such power by order or by power of attorney, in his discretion, to any officer or agent he may appoint; *Collect claims.*

(5). acquire, in any lawful manner, any property (real, personal, or mixed, tangible or intangible), whenever deemed necessary or appropriate to the conduct of the activities authorized in sections 7(a) and 7(b); *Acquire property.*

(6) make such rules and regulations as he deems necessary to carry out the authority vested in him by or pursuant to this Act; *Issue regulations.*

(7) in addition to any powers, functions, privileges, and immunities otherwise vested in him, take any and all actions, including the procurement of the services of attorneys by contract, determined by him to be necessary or desirable in making, servicing, compromising, modifying, liquidating, or otherwise dealing with or realizing on loans made under the provisions of this Act; but no attorneys' services shall be procured by contract in any office *Services of attorneys.*

where an attorney or attorneys are or can be economically employed full time to render such services;

Employ and
reimburse
temporary
employees.

(8) pay the transportation expenses and per diem in lieu of subsistence expenses, in accordance with the Travel Expense Act of 1949, for travel of any person employed by the Administration to render temporary services not in excess of six months in connection with any disaster referred to in section 7(b) from place of appointment to, and while at, the disaster area and any other temporary posts of duty and return upon completion of the assignment; and

Accept free
services.

(9) accept the services and facilities of Federal, State, and local agencies and groups, both public and private, and utilize such gratuitous services and facilities as may, from time to time, be necessary, to further the objectives of section 7(b).

Employ
consultants.

(c) To such extent as he finds necessary to carry out the provisions of this Act, the Administrator is authorized to procure the temporary (not in excess of one year) or intermittent services of experts or consultants or organizations thereof, including stenographic reporting services, by contract or appointment, and in such cases such services shall be without regard to the civil-service and classification laws and, except in the case of stenographic reporting services by organizations, without regard to section 3709 of the Revised Statutes, as amended (41 U.S.C., sec. 5). Any individual so employed may be compensated at a rate not in excess of $50 per diem, and, while such individual is away from his home or regular place of business, he may be allowed transportation and not to exceed $15 per diem in lieu of subsistence and other expenses.

(d) Section 3648 of the Revised Statutes (31 U.S.C. 529) shall not apply to prepayments of rentals made by the Administration on safety deposit boxes used by the Administration for the safeguarding of instruments held as security for loans or for the safeguarding of other documents.[11]

Depositaries
of funds.
15 U.S.C. 635.

SEC. 6. (a) All moneys of the Administration not otherwise employed may be deposited with the Treasury of the United States subject to check by authority of the Administration. The Federal Reserve banks are authorized and directed to act as depositaries, custodians, and fiscal agents for the Administration in the general performance of its powers conferred by this Act. Any banks insured by the Federal Deposit Insurance Corporation, when designated by the Secretary of the Treasury, shall act as custodians and financial agents for the Administration. Each Federal Reserve bank, when designated by the Administrator as fiscal agent for the

---

[11] Subsection 5(d) added by section 4 of PL 87-305.

Administration, shall be entitled to be reimbursed for all expenses incurred as such fiscal agent.

(b) The Administrator shall contribute to the employees' compensation fund, on the basis of annual billings as determined by the Secretary of Labor, for the benefit payments made from such fund on account of employees engaged in carrying out functions financed by the revolving fund established by section 4(c) of this Act. The annual billings shall also include a statement of the fair portion of the cost of the administration of such fund, which shall be paid by the Administrator into the Treasury as miscellaneous receipts. *Retirement contributions.*

SEC. 7. (a) The Administration is empowered to make loans to enable small-business concerns to finance plant construction, conversion, or expansion, including the acquisition of land; or to finance the acquisition of equipment, facilities, machinery, supplies, or materials; or to supply such concerns with working capital to be used in the manufacture of articles, equipment, supplies, or materials for war, defense, or civilian production or as may be necessary to insure a well-balanced national economy; and such loans may be made or effected either directly or in cooperation with banks or other lending institutions through agreements to participate on an immediate or deferred basis. The foregoing powers shall be subject, however, to the following restrictions and limitations: *Business loans. 15 U.S.C. 636.* *Restrictions on loans.*

(1) No financial assistance shall be extended pursuant to this subsection unless the financial assistance applied for is not otherwise available on reasonable terms. *Not elsewhere available.*

(2) No immediate participation may be purchased unless it is shown that a deferred participation is not available; and no loan may be made unless it is shown that a participation is not available. *Priority on types of loans.*

(3) In agreements to participate in loans on a deferred basis under this subsection, such participation by the Administration shall not be in excess of 90 per centum of the balance of the loan outstanding at the time of disbursement. *90 percent maximum SBA participation.*

(4) Except as provided in paragraph (5)(A), no loan under this subsection shall be made if the total amount outstanding and committed (by participation or otherwise) to the borrower from the revolving fund established by this Act would exceed $350,000; (B) the rate of interest for the Administration's share of any such loan shall be no more than 5½ per centum per annum; and (C) no such loan, including renewals or extensions thereof, may *$350,000 maximum SBA share.* *5½ percent maximum SBA interest.*

10-year
maximum
term.

be made for a period or periods exceeding ten years except that a loan made for the purpose of constructing facilities may have a maturity of ten years plus such additional period as is estimated may be required to complete such construction.

(5) In the case of any loan made under this subsection to a corporation formed and capitalized by a group of small-business concerns with resources provided by them for the purpose of obtaining for the use of such concerns raw materials, equipment, inventories, supplies or the benefits of research and development, or for establishing facilities for such purpose, (A) the limitation of $350,000 prescribed in paragraph (4) shall not apply, but the limit of such loan shall be $250,000 multiplied by the number of separate small businesses which formed and capitalized such corporation; (B) the rate of interest for the Administration's share of such loan shall be no less than 3 nor more than 5 per centum per annum; and (C) such loan, including renewals and extensions thereof, may not be made for a period or periods exceeding ten years except that if such loan is made for the purpose of constructing facilities it may have a maturity of twenty years plus such additional time as is required to complete such construction.

Pool loans:
Maximum
limit.

Interest
between 3 and
5 percent.

Maximum
period.

(6) The Administrator is authorized to consult with representatives of small-business concerns with a view to encouraging the formation by such concerns of the corporation referred to in paragraph (5). No act or omission to act, if requested by the Administrator pursuant to this paragraph, and if found and approved by the Administration as contributing to the needs of small business, shall be construed to be within the prohibitions of the antitrust laws or the Federal Trade Commission Act of the United States. A copy of the statement of any such finding and approval intended to be within the coverage of this section, and any modification or withdrawal thereof, shall be furnished to the Attorney General and the Chairman of the Federal Trade Commission when made, and it shall be published in the Federal Register. The authority granted in this paragraph shall be exercised only (A) by the Administrator, (B) upon the condition that the Administrator consult with the Attorney General and with the Chairman of the Federal Trade Commission, and (C) upon the condition that the Administrator obtain the approval of the Attorney General before exercising such authority. Upon withdrawal of any request or finding hereunder or upon withdrawal by the Attorney General of his approval

SBA may
encourage
formation of
pools.

Antitrust
exemption.

granted under the preceding sentence, the provisions of this paragraph shall not apply to any subsequent act or omission to act by reason of such finding or request.

(7) All loans made under this subsection shall be of such sound value or so secured as reasonably to assure repayment. *Reasonable assurance of repayment.*

(b) The Administration also is empowered [13]—

(1) to make such loans (either directly or in cooperation with banks or other lending institutions through agreements to participate on an immediate or deferred basis) as the Administration may determine to be necessary or appropriate because of floods or other catastrophes; *Disaster loans.*

(2) to make such loans (either directly or in cooperation with banks or other lending institutions through agreements to participate on an immediate or deferred basis) as the Administration may determine to be necessary or appropriate to any small business concern located in an area affected by a disaster, if the Administration determines that the concern has suffered a substantial economic injury as a result of such disaster and if such disaster constitutes— *Economic injury disaster loans.*

(A) a major disaster, as determined by the President under the Act entitled "An Act to authorize Federal assistance to States and local governments in major disasters, and for other purposes", approved September 30, 1950, as amended (42 U.S.C. 1855–1855g), or

(B) a natural disaster, as determined by the Secretary of Agriculture pursuant to the Consolidated Farmers Home Administration Act of 1961 (7 U.S.C. 1961);

(3) to make such loans (either directly or in cooperation with banks or other lending institutions through agreements to participate on an immediate or deferred basis) as the Administration may determine to be necessary or appropriate to assist any small business concern in reestablishing its business, if the Administration determines that such concern has suffered substantial economic injury as a result of its displacement by a federally aided urban renewal or highway construction program or by any other construction conducted by or with funds provided by the Federal Government; and the purposes of a loan made pursuant to this paragraph may, in *Displaced business disaster loans.*

[13] A number of recent amendments have been made to subsection 7(b):
PL 87–70 added paragraph (3);
PL 88–264 added paragraph (4) and extended paragraph (2) beyond its former scope relating solely to drought and excessive rainfall disasters; and
PL 88–560 added the phrase after the word "Government" in paragraph (3).
PL 88–69 extended the maximum term of disaster loans to thirty years, and provided for suspension of repayments in certain hardship cases.

the discretion of the Administrator, include the purchase or construction of other premises whether or not the borrower owned the premises from which it was displaced;

(4) to make such loans (either directly or in cooperation with banks or other lending institutions through agreements to participate on an immediate or deferred basis) as the Administration may determine to be necessary or appropriate to assist any small business concern in reestablishing its business if the Administration determines that such concern has suffered substantial economic injury as a result of the inability of such concern to process or market a product for human consumption because of disease or toxicity occurring in such product through natural or undetermined causes.

Product disaster loans.

No loan under this subsection, including renewals and extensions thereof, may be made for a period or periods exceeding thirty years: *Provided,* That the Administrator may consent to a suspension in the payment of principal and interest charges on, and to an extension in the maturity of, the Federal share of any loan under this subsection for a period of not to exceed five years, if (A) the borrower under such loan is a homeowner or a small-business concern, (B) the loan was made to enable (i) such homeowner to repair or replace his home, or (ii) such concern to repair or replace plant or equipment which was damaged or destroyed as the result of a disaster meeting the requirements of clause (A) or (B) of paragraph (2) of this subsection, and (C) the Administrator determines such action is necessary to avoid severe financial hardship: *Provided further,* That the provisions of paragraph (1) of subsection (c) of this section shall not be applicable to any such loan having a maturity in excess of twenty years. The interest rate on the Administration's share of any loan made under this subsection shall not exceed 3 per centum per annum, except that in the case of a loan made pursuant to paragraph (3), the rate of interest on the Administration's share of such loan shall not be more than the higher of (A) 2¾ per centum per annum; or (B) the average annual interest rate on all interest-bearing obligations of the United States then forming a part of the public debt as computed at the end of the fiscal year next preceding the date of the loan and adjusted to the nearest one-eighth of 1 per centum, plus one-quarter of 1 per centum per annum.[13] In agreements to participate in loans on a deferred basis under this subsection, such participation by the Ad-

Maximum term 30 years. Interest rate 3 percent.

Maximum participation 90 percent.

[13] The interest rate applicable to loans made pursuant to subsection 7(b)(3) was specified by section 305(4) of PL 87-70.

ministration shall not be in excess of 90 per centum of the balance of the loan outstanding at the time of disbursement.

(c)(1) The Administration may further extend the maturity of or renew any loan made pursuant to this section, or any loan transferred to the Administration pursuant to Reorganization Plan Numbered 2 of 1954, or Reorganization Plan Numbered 1 of 1957, for additional periods not to exceed ten years beyond the period stated therein, if such extension or renewal will aid in the orderly liquidation of such loan.

Terms may be extended.

(2) During any period in which principal and interest charges are suspended on the Federal share of any loan, as provided in subsection (b), the Administrator shall, upon the request of any person, firm, or corporation having a participation in such loan, purchase such participation, or assume the obligation of the borrower, for the balance of such period, to make principal and interest payments on the non-Federal share of such loan: *Provided,* That no such payments shall be made by the Administrator in behalf of any borrower unless (i) the Administrator determines that such action is necessary in order to avoid a default, and (ii) the borrower agrees to make payments to the Administration in an aggregate amount equal to the amount paid in its behalf by the Administrator, in such manner and at such times (during or after the term of the loan) as the Administrator shall determine having due regard to the purposes sought to be achieved by this paragraph.[14]

(d) The Administration also is empowered to make grants to any State government or any agency thereof, any State-chartered development credit or finance corporation, any land-grant college or university, any college or school of business, engineering, commerce, or agriculture, or to any corporation formed by two or more of the entities hereinabove described which are eligible to receive such grants, for studies, research, and counseling concerning the managing, financing, and operation of small business enterprises and technical and statistical information necessary thereto in order to carry out the purposes of section 8(b)(1) by coordinating such information with existing information facilities within the State and by making such information available to State and local agencies. The Administrator may recommend to grant applicants particular studies or research which are to be financed by such grants. The total of all grants (including amendments and modifications thereof) made under this subsection within any one State in any one year shall not exceed $40,000. The Administration may require, as a condition to any grant (or amendment or modification thereof) made under this subsection, that

[14] Paragraph 7(c)(2) added by PL 89-59.

an additional amount not exceeding the amount of such grant be provided from sources other than the Administration to assist in carrying out the purposes for which such grant is made: *Provided*, That if such grant or any part thereof is to be utilized for the purpose of providing counseling services to individual small business enterprises the Administration shall require that such additional amount be provided and in an amount which is equal to the amount of such grant. What constitutes such additional amount may be defined by the Administration.[14]

SEC. 8. (a) It shall be the duty of the Administration and it is hereby empowered, whenever it determines such action is necessary—

(1) to enter into contracts with the United States Government and any department, agency, or officer thereof having procurement powers obligating the Administration to furnish articles, equipment, supplies, or materials to the Government. In any case in which the Administration certifies to any officer of the Government having procurement powers that the Administration is competent to perform any specific Government procurement contract to be let by any such officer, such officer shall be authorized in his discretion to let such procurement contract to the Administration upon such terms and conditions as may be agreed upon between the Administration and the procurement officer; and

(2) to arrange for the performance of such contracts by negotiating or otherwise letting subcontracts to small-business concerns or others for the manufacture, supply, or assembly of such articles, equipment, supplies, or materials, or parts thereof, or servicing or processing in connection therewith, or such management services as may be necessary to enable the Administration to perform such contracts.

(b) It shall also be the duty of the Administration and it is hereby empowered, whenever it determines such action is necessary—

(1) to provide technical and managerial aids to small-business concerns, by advising and counseling on matters in connection with Government procurement and property disposal and on policies, principles, and practices of good management, including but not limited to cost accounting, methods of financing, business insurance, accident control, wage incentives, and methods engineering, by cooperating and advising with voluntary business, professional, educational, and other nonprofit organizations, associations, and institutions and with other Federal and State agencies, by maintaining a clearinghouse for information concerning the managing, financing,

---

[14] Former subsection 7(d) was rewritten by section 9 of PL 87-305.

and operation of small-business enterprises, by disseminating such information, and by such other activities as are deemed appropriate by the Administration;

(2) to make a complete inventory of all productive facilities of small-business concerns or to arrange for such inventory to be made by any other governmental agency which has the facilities. In making any such inventory, the appropriate agencies in the several States may be requested to furnish an inventory of the productive facilities of small-business concerns in each respective State if such an inventory is available or in prospect; *Make inventory of small business facilities.*

(3) to coordinate and to ascertain the means by which the productive capacity of small-business concerns can be most effectively utilized; *Coordinate utilization of small business.*

(4) to consult and cooperate with officers of the Government having procurement or property disposal powers, in order to utilize the potential productive capacity of plants operated by small-business concerns; *Consult with Government procurement and disposal officers.*

(5) to obtain information as to methods and practices which Government prime contractors utilize in letting subcontracts and to take action to encourage the letting of subcontracts by prime contractors to small-business concerns at prices and on conditions and terms which are fair and equitable; *Obtain information on subcontracting.*

(6) to determine within any industry the concerns, firms, persons, corporations, partnerships, co-operatives, or other business enterprises which are to be designated "small-business concerns" for the purpose of effectuating the provisions of this Act. To carry out this purpose the Administrator, when requested to do so, shall issue in response to each such request an appropriate certificate certifying an individual concern as a "small-business concern" in accordance with the criteria expressed in this Act. Any such certificate shall be subject to revocation when the concern covered thereby ceases to be a "small-business concern". Offices of the Government having procurement or lending powers, or engaging in the disposal of Federal property or allocating materials or supplies, or promulgating regulations affecting the distribution of materials or supplies, shall accept as conclusive the Administration's determination as to which enterprises are to be designated "small-business concerns", as authorized and directed under this paragraph; *Define what is small within industries.* *Certify concerns as "small."*

(7) to certify to Government procurement officers, and officers engaged in the sale and disposal of Federal property, with respect to the competency, as to capacity and credit, of any small-business concern or group of such concerns to perform a specific Government contract. In any case in which a small- *Issue certificates of competency.*

business concern or group of such concerns has been certified by or under the authority of the Administration to be a competent Government contractor with respect to capacity and credit as to a specific Government contract, the officers of the Government having procurement or property disposal powers are directed to accept such certification as conclusive, and are authorized to let such Government contract to such concern or group of concerns without requiring it to meet any other requirement with respect to capacity and credit;

Obtain reports from Government procurement agencies.

(8) to obtain from any Federal department, establishment, or agency engaged in procurement or in the financing of procurement or production, such reports concerning the letting of contracts and subcontracts and the making of loans to business concerns as it may deem pertinent in carrying out its functions under this Act;

Obtain reports from Government disposal agencies.

(9) to obtain from any Federal department, establishment, or agency engaged in the disposal of Federal property such reports concerning the solicitation of bids, time of sale, or otherwise as it may deem pertinent in carrying out its functions under this Act;

Obtain information on allocation of materials.

(10) to obtain from suppliers of materials information pertaining to the method of filling orders and the bases for allocating their supply, whenever it appears that any small business is unable to obtain materials from its normal sources;

Study procurement and disposal programs.

(11) To make studies and recommendations to the appropriate Federal agencies to insure that a fair proportion of the total purchases and contracts for property and services for the Government be placed with small-business enterprises, to insure that a fair proportion of Government contracts for research and development be placed with small-business concerns, to insure that a fair proportion of the total sales of Government property be made to small-business concerns, and to insure a fair and equitable share of materials, supplies, and equipment to small-business concerns;

Insure fair treatment for small business.

(12) to consult and cooperate with all Government agencies for the purpose of insuring that small-business concerns shall receive fair and reasonable treatment from such agencies;

Establish advisory groups.

(13) to establish such small business advisory boards and committees truly representative of small business as may be necessary to achieve the purposes of this Act; and

Assistance to businesses to be displaced by urban renewal.

(14) to provide at the earliest practicable time such information and assistance as may be appropriate, including information concerning eligibility for loans under section 7(b)(3), to local public agencies (as defined in section 110(h) of the Housing

Act of 1949) and to small-business concerns to be displaced by federally aided urban renewal projects in order to assist such small-business concerns in reestablishing their operations.[16]

(c) The Administration shall from time to time make studies of matters materially affecting the competitive strength of small business, and of the effect on small business of Federal laws, programs, and regulations, and shall make recommendations to the appropriate Federal agency or agencies for the adjustment of such programs and regulations to the needs of small business. *(margin: Study competitive position of small business.)*

(d)(1) Within ninety days after the effective date of this subsection, the Administrator, the Secretary of Defense, and the Administrator of General Services shall cooperatively develop a small business subcontracting program which shall contain such provisions as may be appropriate to (A) enable small business concerns to be considered fairly as subcontractors and suppliers to contractors performing work or rendering services as prime contractors or subcontractors under Government procurement contracts, (B) insure that such prime contractors and subcontractors will consult through the appropriate procuring agency with the Administration when requested by the Administration, and (C) enable the Administration to obtain from any Government procurement agency such available or reasonably obtainable information and records concerning subcontracting by its prime contractors and their subcontractors as the Administration may deem necessary: *Provided*, That such program shall not authorize the Administration to (i) prescribe the extent to which any contractor or subcontractor shall subcontract, (ii) specify the business concerns to which subcontracts shall be granted, or (iii) vest in the Administration authority respecting the administration of individual prime contracts or subcontracts: *Provided further*, That such program shall provide that in evaluating bids or in selecting contractors for negotiated contracts, the extensive use of subcontractors by a proposed contractor shall be considered a favorable factor. The Secretary of Defense and the Administrator of General Services each shall promulgate regulations implementing the program as developed: *Provided*, That prior to the promulgation of such regulations, or any changes therein, the concurrence of the Administration shall be obtained, and if such concurrence cannot be obtained the matter in disagreement shall be submitted to the President who shall make the final determination. In addition, the Administrator of General Services and the Secretary of Defense may issue such other regulations concerning subcontracting not inconsistent with the small business subcontracting program as they each deem necessary or appropriate to effectuate their functions and responsibilities. *(margin: Small business subcontracting program.)*

[16] Paragraph 14 of section 8(b) was added by PL 88–660.

Contracts
included.

(2) Every contract for property or services (including but not limited to contracts for research and development, maintenance, repair and construction, but excluding contracts to be performed entirely outside of the United States or its territories) in excess of $1,000,000 made by a Government department or agency, which in the opinion of the procuring agency offers substantial subcontracting possibilities, shall require the contractor to conform to the small business subcontracting program promulgated under this subsection, and to insert in all subcontracts and purchase orders in excess of $500,000 which offer substantial possibilities for further subcontracting a provision requiring the subcontractor or supplier to conform to such small business subcontracting program.

SBA report
and recom-
mendations.

(3) The Administration shall include in any report filed under section 10(b) of this Act, information and such recommendations as it may deem appropriate, with respect to the administration of the small business subcontracting program established under this subsection.

Proprietary
rights protected.

(4) Nothing in this subsection shall be construed to authorize the Administrator, the Secretary of Defense, or the Administrator of General Services to secure and disseminate technical data or processes developed by any business concern at its own expense. [17]

Proposed
procurements
publicised daily
by Secretary of
Commerce.

(e) It shall be the duty of the Secretary of Commerce, and he is hereby empowered, to obtain notice of all proposed defense procurement actions of $10,000 and above, and all civilian procurement actions of $5,000 and above, from any Federal department, establishment, or agency engaged in procurement of supplies and services in the United States; and to publicize such notices in the daily publication "United States Department of Commerce Synopsis of the United States Government Proposed Procurements, Sales, and Contract Awards", immediately after the necessity for the procurement is established; except that nothing herein shall require publication of such notices with respect to those procurements (1) which for security reasons are of a classified nature, or (2) which involve perishable subsistence supplies, or (3) which are for utility services and the procuring agency in accordance with applicable law has predetermined the utility concern to whom the award will be made, or (4) which are of such unusual and compelling emergency that the Government would be seriously injured if bids or offers were permitted to be made more than 15 days after the issuance of the invitation for bids or solicitation for proposals, or (5) which are made by an order placed under an existing contract, or (6) which are made from another Government department or agency, or a mandatory source of supply, or (7) which are for personal or professional services, or (8) which are for services from educational institutions, or (9) in which only

---

[17] Entire section 8(d) was added by section 7 of PL 87-305.

foreign sources are to be solicited, or (10) for which it is determined in writing by the procuring agency, with the concurrence of the Administrator, that advance publicity is not appropriate or reasonable.[18]

SEC. 9. (a) Research and development are major factors in the growth and progress of industry and the national economy. The expense of carrying on research and development programs is beyond the means of many small-business concerns, and such concerns are handicapped in obtaining the benefits of research and development programs conducted at Government expense. These small-business concerns are thereby placed at a competitive disadvantage. This weakens the competitive free enterprise system and prevents the orderly development of the national economy. It is the policy of the Congress that assistance be given to small-business concerns to enable them to undertake and to obtain the benefits of research and development in order to maintain and strengthen the competitive free enterprise system and the national economy. *[Research and development. 15 U.S.C. 638.]* *[Policy of Congress.]*

(b) It shall be the duty of the Administration, and it is hereby empowered— *[SBA shall:]*

(1) to assist small-business concerns to obtain Government contracts for research and development; *[Assist in obtaining research contracts.]*

(2) to assist small-business concerns to obtain the benefits of research and development performed under Government contracts or at Government expense; and *[Assist in obtaining benefits of research.]*

(3) to provide technical assistance to small-business concerns to accomplish the purposes of this section. *[Provide technical assistance.]*

(c) The Administration is authorized to consult and cooperate with all Government agencies and to make studies and recommendations to such agencies, and such agencies are authorized and directed to cooperate with the Administration in order to carry out and to accomplish the purposes of this section., *[Other agencies to cooperate with SBA.]*

(d) (1) The Administrator is authorized to consult with representatives of small-business concerns with a view to assisting and encouraging such firms to undertake joint programs for research and development carried out through such corporate or other mechanism as may be most appropriate for the purpose. Such joint programs may, among other things, include the following purposes: *[Joint research and development programs.]*

(A) to construct, acquire, or establish laboratories and other facilities for the conduct of research; *[Acquisition of facilities.]*

(B) to undertake and utilize applied research; *[Utilization of applied research.]*

(C) to collect research information related to a particulate industry and disseminate it to participating members; *[Collection of research information.]*

---

[18] Section 8(e) was added by section 8 of PL 87-305.

Applied research
programs.

(D) to conduct applied research on a protected, proprietary, and contractual basis with member or nonmember firms, Government agencies, and others;

Apply for
patents.

(E) to prosecute applications for patents and render patent services for participating members; and

Grant licenses.

(F) to negotiate and grant licenses under patents held under the joint program, and to establish corporations designed to exploit particular patents obtained by it.

Antitrust
exemption.

(2) The Administrator may, after consultation with the Attorney General and the Chairman of the Federal Trade Commission, and with the prior written approval of the Attorney General, approve any agreement between small-business firms providing for a joint program of research and development, if the Administrator finds that the joint program proposed will maintain and strengthen the free enterprise system and the economy of the Nation. The Administrator or the Attorney General may at any time withdraw his approval of the agreement and the joint program of research and development covered thereby, if he finds that the agreement or the joint program carried on under it is no longer in the best interests of the competitive free enterprise system and the economy of the Nation. A copy of the statement of any such finding and approval intended to be within the coverage of this subsection, and a copy of any modification or withdrawal of approval, shall be published in the Federal Register. The authority conferred by this subsection on the Administrator shall not be delegated by him.

(3) No act or omission to act pursuant to and within the scope of any joint program for research and development, under an agreement approved by the Administrator under this subsection, shall be construed to be within the prohibitions of the antitrust laws of the Federal Trade Commission Act. Upon publication in the Federal Register of the notice of withdrawal of his approval of the agreement granted under this subsection, either by the Administrator or by the Attorney General, the provisions of this subsection shall not apply to any subsequent act or omission to act by reason of such agreement or approval.

Reports:
Operations
under Act.
15 U.S.C. 639.

SEC. 10. (a) The Administration shall make a report on December 31 of each year of operations under this Act to the President, the President of the Senate, and the Speaker of the House of Representatives. Such report shall include the names of the business concerns to whom contracts are let and for whom financing is arranged by the Administration, together with the amounts involved, and such report shall include information on the progress of the Administration in liquidating the assets and winding up the affairs of the Reconstruction Finance Corporation, and such other information and such comments and recommendations as the Administration may deem appropriate. The requirement contained in this subsection with respect to the inclusion of information respecting the progress of the Administration in liquidating the assets and winding up the affairs of the Reconstruction Finance Corporation in such report shall be in lieu of any requirement, pursuant to section 106(b) of the Reconstruction Finance Corporation Liquidation Act, and Reorganization Plan Numbered 1 of 1957, that progress reports with respect to such liquidation or winding up of affairs by the Administration be made to the Congress on a quarterly basis.[19]

(b) The Administration shall make a report to the President, the President of the Senate, and the Speaker of the House of Representatives, to the Senate Select Committee on Small Business, and to the House Select Committee To Conduct a Study and Investigation of the Problems of Small Business, on December 31 of each year, showing as accurately as possible for each such period the amount of funds appropriated to it that it has expended in the conduct of each of its principal activites such as lending, procurement, contracting, and providing technical and managerial aids.[20] *{Expenditure of funds.}*

(c) (1) The Attorney General is directed to make, or direct the Federal Trade Commission to make for him, surveys of any activity of the Government which may affect small business, for the purpose of determining any factors which may tend to eliminate competition, create or strengthen monopolies, promote undue concentration of economic power, or otherwise injure small business. *{Antitrust reports.}*

(2) The Attorney General shall submit to the Congress and the President, at such times as he deems desirable, but not less than once every year, reports setting forth the results of such surveys and including such recommendations as he may deem desirable.[21]

(d) For the purpose of aiding in carrying out the national policy to insure that a fair proportion of the total purchases and contracts for property and services for the Government be placed with small-business enterprises, and to maintain and strengthen the overall economy of the Nation, the Department of Defense shall make a monthly report to the President, the President of the Senate, and the Speaker of the House of Representatives not less than forty-five days after the close of the month, showing the amount of funds appropriated to the Department of Defense, which have been expended, obligated, or contracted to be spent with small-business concerns and the amount of such funds expended, obligated, or contracted to be spent with firms other than *{Defense procurement reports.}*

[19] Former subsection 10(a) was rewritten and the reporting requirement changed from semiannual to annual by section 5(a)(1) of PL 87-305.
[20] The reporting requirement of subsection 10(b) was changed from semiannual to annual by section 5(a)(2) of PL 87-305.
[21] Former subsection 10(c) was rewritten and annual reports by the Attorney General made mandatory by section 5(a)(3) of PL 87-305.

small business in the same fields of operation; and such monthly reports shall show separately the funds expended, obligated, or contracted to be spent for basic and applied scientific research and development.

Maintenance of records.

(e) The Administration shall retain all correspondence, records of inquiries, memoranda, reports, books, and records, including memoranda as to all investigations conducted by or for the Administration, for a period of at least one year from the date of each thereof, and shall at all times keep the same available for inspection and examination by the Senate Select Committee on Small Business and the House Select Committee To Conduct a Study and Investigation of the Problems of Small Business, or their duly authorized representatives.

Consultation with other Government agencies.

(f) To the extent deemed necessary by the Administrator to protect and preserve small-business interests, the Administration shall consult and cooperate with other departments and agencies of the Federal Government in the formulation by the Administration of policies affecting small-business concerns. When requested by the Administrator, each department and agency of the Federal Government shall consult and cooperate with the Administration in the formulation by such department or agency of policies affecting small-business concerns, in order to insure that small-business interests will be recognized, protected, and preserved. This subsection shall not require any department or agency to consult or cooperate with the Administration in any case where the head of such department or agency determines that such consultation or cooperation would unduly delay action which must be taken by such department or agency to protect the national interest in an emergency.

15 U.S.C. 640.

SEC. 11 (a) The President is authorized to consult with representatives of small-business concerns with a view to encouraging the making by such persons with the approval of the President of voluntary agreements and programs to further the objectives of this Act.

Defense production pools.

(b) No act or omission to act pursuant to this Act which occurs while this Act is in effect, if requested by the President pursuant to a voluntary agreement or program approved under subsection (a) of this section and found by the President to be in the public interest as contributing to the national defense, shall be construed to be within the prohibitions of the antitrust laws or the Federal Trade Commission Act of the United States. A copy of each such request intended to be within the coverage of this section, and any modification or withdrawal thereof, shall be furnished to the Attorney General and the Chairman of the Federal Trade Commission when made, and it shall be published in the Federal Register unless publication thereof would, in the opinion of the President, endanger the national security.

(c) The authority granted in subsection (b) of this section shall be delegated only (1) to an official who shall for the purpose of such delegation be required to be appointed by the President by and with the advice and consent of the Senate, (2) upon the condition that such official consult with the Attorney General and the Chairman of the Federal Trade Commission not less than ten days before making any request or finding thereunder, and (3) upon the condition that such official obtain the approval of the Attorney General to any request thereunder before making the request.

(d) Upon withdrawal of any request or finding hereunder, or upon withdrawal by the Attorney General of his approval of the voluntary agreement or program on which the request or finding is based, the provisions of this section shall not apply to any subsequent act, or omission to act, by reason of such finding or request.

SEC. 12. The President may transfer to the Administration any functions, powers, and duties of any department or agency which relate primarily to small-business problems. In connection with any such transfer, the President may provide for appropriate transfers of records, property, necessary personnel, and unexpended balances of appropriations and other funds available to the department or agency from which the transfer is made. Transfer of small-business functions. 15 U.S.C. 641.

SEC. 13. No loan shall be made or equipment, facilities, or services furnished by the Administration under this Act to any business enterprise unless the owners, partners, or officers of such business enterprise (1) certify to the Administration the names of any attorneys, agents, or other persons engaged by or on behalf of such business enterprise for the purpose of expediting applications made to the Administration for assistance of any sort, and the fees paid or to be paid to any such persons; (2) execute an agreement binding any such business enterprise for a period of two years after any assistance is rendered by the Administration to such business enterprise, to refrain from employing, tendering any office or employment to, or retaining for professional services, any person who, on the date such assistance or any part thereof was rendered, or within one year prior thereto, shall have served as an officer, attorney, agent, or employee of the Administration occupying a position or engaging in activities which the Administration shall have determined involve discretion with respect to the granting of assistance under this Act; and (3) furnish the names of lending institutions to which such business enterprise has applied for loans together with dates, amounts, terms, and proof of refusal. Listing of agents and attorneys. 15 U.S.C. 642. Employment agreement.

SEC. 14. To the fullest extent the Administration deems practicable, it shall make a fair charge for the use of Government-owned property and make and let contracts on a basis that will result in a recovery of the direct costs incurred by the Administration. Charges for Government-owned property. 15 U.S.C. 643.

Joint-determination program for awarding contracts or selling property.
15 U.S.C. 644.

SEC. 15. To effectuate the purposes of this Act, small business concerns within the meaning of this Act shall receive any award or contract or any part thereof, and be awarded any contract for the sale of Government property, as to which it is determined by the Administration and the contracting procurement or disposal agency (1) to be in the interest of maintaining or mobilizing the Nation's full productive capacity, (2) to be in the interest of war or national defense programs, (3) to be in the interest of assuring that a fair proportion of the total purchases and contracts for property and services for the Government are placed with small-business concerns, or (4) to be in the interest of assuring that a fair proportion of the total sales of Government property be made to small-business concerns; but nothing contained in this Act shall be construed to change any preferences or priorities established by law with respect to the sale of electrical power or other property by the Government or any agency thereof. These determinations may be made for individual awards or contracts or for classes of awards or contracts. Whenever the Administration and the contracting procurement agency fail to agree, the matter shall be submitted for determination to the Secretary or the head of the appropriate department or agency by the Administrator.

Penalty for false statements.
15 U.S.C. 645.

SEC. 16. (a) Whoever makes any statement knowing it to be false, or whoever willfully overvalues any security, for the purpose of obtaining for himself or for any applicant any loan, or extension thereof by renewal, deferment of action, or otherwise, or the acceptance, release, or substitution of security therefor, or for the purpose of influencing in any way the action of the Administration, or for the purpose of obtaining money, property, or anything of value, under this Act, shall be punished by a fine of not more than $5,000 or by imprisonment for not more than two years, or both.

Penalty for wrongful conduct.

(b) Whoever, being connected in any capacity with the Administration, (1) embezzles, abstracts, purloins, or willfully misapplies any moneys, funds, securities, or other things of value, whether belonging to it or pledged or otherwise entrusted to it, or (2) with intent to defraud the Administration or any other body politic or corporate, or any individual, or to deceive any officer, auditor, or examiner of the Administration, makes any false entry in any book, report, or statement of or to the Administration, or, without being duly authorized, draws any order or issues, puts forth, or assigns any note, debenture, bond, or other obligation, or draft, bill of exchange, mortgage, judgment, or decree thereof, or (3) with intent to defraud participates or shares in or receives directly or indirectly any money, profit, property, or benefit through any transaction, loan, commission, contract, or any other act of the Administration, or (4) gives any unauthorized information concerning any future action or plan of the Administration which might affect the value of securities, or, having such knowledge, invests or speculates, directly or indirectly, in the securities or property of any company or corporation receiving loans or other assistance from the Administration, shall be punished by a fine of not more than $10,000 or by imprisonment for not more than five years, or both.

(c) Whoever, with intent to defraud, knowingly conceals, removes, disposes of, or converts to his own use or to that of another, any property mortgaged or pledged to, or held by, the Administration, shall be fined not more than $5,000 or imprisoned not more than five years, or both; but if the value of such property does not exceed $100, he shall be fined not more than $1,000 or imprisoned not more than one year, or both.[22]

SEC. 17. Any interest held by the Administration in property, as security for a loan, shall be subordinate to any lien on such property for taxes due on the propery to a State, or political subdivision thereof, in any case where such lien would, under applicable State law, be superior to such interest if such interest were held by any party other than the United States. *(Subordination of SBA collateral. 15 U.S.C. 646.)*

SEC. 18. The Administration shall not duplicate the work or activity of any other department or agency of the Federal Government and nothing contained in this Act shall be construed to authorize any such duplication unless such work or activity is expressly provided for in this Act. *(Avoidance of duplication. 15 U.S.C. 647.)*

SEC. 19. If any provision of this Act, or the application thereof to any person or circumstances, is held invalid, the remainder of this Act, and the application of such provision to other persons or circumstances, shall not be affected thereby. *(Separability. 15 U.S.C. 648.)*

SEC. 20. There are hereby authorized to be appropriated such sums as may be necessary and appropriate for the carrying out of the provisions and purposes of this Act other than those for which appropriations to the revolving fund are authorized by section 4(c).[23] *(Authorization for appropriations. 15 U.S.C. 649.)*

SEC. 21. All laws and parts of laws inconsistent with this Act are hereby repealed to the extent of such inconsistency. *(Repeal of inconsistent laws. 15 U.S.C. 650.)*

---

[22] Subsection (c) of section 16 was added by PL 88-264.
[23] The clause excluding the appropriation authority covered by section 4(c) was added by section 11(h)(2) of PL 87-341.

RELATED PROVISIONS OF LAW

PUBLIC LAW 536—85TH CONGRESS
APPROVED JULY 18, 1958

Amendment
of Federal
Reserve Act.

SEC. 3. The fourth paragraph of section 24 of the Federal Reserve Act is amended (1) by striking out "or the Small Business Administration" and "or of the Small Business Act of 1953,", and (2) by adding at the end thereof the following new sentence: "Loans in which the Small Business Administration cooperates through agreements to participate on an immediate or deferred basis under the Small Business Act shall not be subject to the restrictions or limitations of this section imposed upon loans secured by real estate."

Extension
of certain
RFC loans.

SEC. 4. The Secretary of the Treasury is hereby authorized to further extend the maturity of or renew any loan transferred to the Secretary of the Treasury pursuant to Reorganization Plan Numbered 1 of 1957, for additional periods not to exceed ten years, if such extension or renewal will aid in the orderly liquidation of such loan.

PUBLIC LAW 550—87TH CONGRESS
APPROVED JULY 25, 1962

15 U.S.C. 639a.

Review by
Congress.

1(b) It is the sense of the Congress that the regular business loan program of the Small Business Administration should be reviewed by the Congress at least once every two years. It is further the sense of the Congress that the Small Business Administration should submit its estimated needs for additional authorization for such program to the Congress at least one year in advance of the date on which such authorization is to be provided, in order to assure an orderly and recurring review of such program and to avoid emergency appeals for additional authorization. Compliance by the Small Business Administration with the foregoing policy will enable the Congress hereafter to provide additional authorization for such program on a two-year basis.

Trade
Adjustment
Assistance.
15 U.S.C. 637a.

2(a) The Small Business Administration is empowered to make loans (either directly or in cooperation with banks or other lenders through agreements to participate on an immediate or deferred basis) to assist any firm to adjust to changed economic conditions resulting from increased competition from imported articles,[24] but only if (1) an adjustment proposal of such firm has been certified by the Secretary of Commerce pursuant to the Trade Expansion Act of 1962, (2) the Secretary has referred such proposal to the Administration under that Act and the loan would provide part or all of the financial assistance necessary to carry out such proposal, and (3) the Secretary's certification is in force at the time the Administration makes the loan.

[24] This section was added by PL 87-550 in connection with the Trade Expansion Act of 1962, PL 87-794, approved October 11, 1962.

(b) The Small Business Administration's authority to make loans under this section shall be in addition to and separate from its authority to make loans under the Small Business Act. With respect to loans made under this section the Administration shall apply the provisions of sections 314, 315, 316, 318, 319, and 320 of the Trade Expansion Act of 1962 as though such loans had been made under section 314 of that Act. *15 U.S.C. 631 note.*

(c) There are hereby authorized to be appropriated, without fiscal year limitation, such sums as may be necessary to carry out this section.

(d) This section shall take effect on such date (on or after the enactment of the Trade Expansion Act of 1962) as the President may specify in a proclamation duly published in the Federal Register but in no case later than 60 days after the date of the enactment of such Act.

PUBLIC LAW 846—87TH CONGRESS APPROVED OCTOBER 22, 1962

SEC. 213. (a) The Secretary of the Treasury shall pay out of the War Claims Fund on account of awards certified by the Commission pursuant to this title as follows and in the following order of priority: *War Claims Act of 1948. 76 Stat. 1111*

(1) Payment in full of awards made pursuant to section 202(d) (1) and (2), and thereafter of any award made pursuant to section 202(a) to any claimant certified to the Commission by the Small Business Administration as having been, on the date of loss, damage, or destruction, a small business concern within the meaning now set forth in the Small Business Act, as amended. *15 U.S.C. 631 note.*

ECONOMIC OPPORTUNITY ACT OF 1964

PUBLIC LAW 88–452—APPROVED AUGUST 20, 1964

TITLE IV—EMPLOYMENT AND INVESTMENT INCENTIVES [26]

STATEMENT OF PURPOSE

SEC. 401. It is the purpose of this title to assist in the establishment, preservation, and strengthening of small business concerns and improve the managerial skills employed in such enterprises; and to mobilize for these objectives private as well as public managerial skills and resources. *Small business concerns, assistance.*

[26] 78 Stat. 526–7; 42 U.S.C. 2901–7 (codification to be published summer of 1965.)

LOANS, PARTICIPATIONS, AND GUARANTIES

72 Stat. 384.

SEC. 402. The Director is authorized to make, participate (on an immediate basis) in, or guarantee loans, repayable in not more than fifteen years, to any small business concern (as defined in section 3 of the Small Business Act (15 U.S.C. 632) and regulations issued thereunder), or to any qualified person seeking to establish such a concern, when he determines that such loans will assist in carrying out the purposes of this title, with particular emphasis on employment of the long-term unemployed: *Provided, however*, That no such loans shall be made, participated in, or guaranteed if the total of such Federal assistance to a single borrower outstanding at any one time would exceed $25,000. The Director may defer payments on the principal of such loans for a grace period and use such other methods as he deems necessary and appropriate to assure the successful establishment and operation of such concern. The Director may, in his discretion, as a condition of such financial assistance, require that the borrower take steps to improve his management skills by participating in a management training program approved by the Director. The Director shall encourage, as far as possible, the participation of the private business community in the program of assistance to such concerns.

COORDINATION WITH COMMUNITY ACTION PROGRAMS

SEC. 403. No financial assistance shall be provided under section 402 in any community for which the Director has approved a community action program pursuant to title II of this Act unless such financial assistance is determined by him to be consistent with such program.

FINANCING UNDER SMALL BUSINESS ACT

76 Stat. 220.
72 Stat. 387;
75 Stat. 167;
Ante, p. 7.

SEC. 404. Such lending and guaranty functions under this title as may be delegated to the Small Business Administration may be financed with funds appropriated to the revolving fund established by section 4(c) of the Small Business Act (15 U.S.C. 633(c)) for the purposes of sections 7(a), 7(b), and 8(a) of that Act (15 U.S.C. 636(a), 636(b), 637(a)).[38]

LOAN TERMS AND CONDITIONS

Sec. 405. Loans made pursuant to section 402 (including immediate participation in and guaranties of such loans) shall have such terms and conditions as the Director shall determine, subject to the following limitations—

---

[38] Authority to carry out title IV of PL 88-452 has been delegated to the Small Business Administration by the Director of the Office of Economic Opportunity (29 Federal Register 14764, October 29, 1964).

(a) there is reasonable assurance of repayment of the loan;

(b) the financial assistance is not otherwise available on reasonable terms from private sources or other Federal, State, or local programs;

(c) the amount of the loan, together with other funds available, is adequate to assure completion of the project or achievement of the purposes for which the loan is made;

(d) the loan bears interest at a rate not less than (1) a rate determined by the Secretary of the Treasury, taking into consideration the average market yield on outstanding Treasury obligations of comparable maturity, plus (2) such additional charge, if any, toward covering other costs of the program as the Director may determine to be consistent with its purposes: *Provided, however,* That the rate of interest charged on loans made in redevelopment areas designated under the Area Redevelopment Act (42 U.S.C. 2501 et seq.) shall not exceed the rate currently applicable to new loans made under section 6 of that Act (42 U.S.C. 2505); and 75 Stat. 47.

(e) fees not in excess of amounts necessary to cover administrative expenses and probable losses may be required on loan guaranties.

LIMITATION ON FINANCIAL ASSISTANCE

SEC. 406. No financial assistance shall be extended pursuant to this title where the Director determines that the assistance will be used in relocating establishments from one area to another or in financing subcontractors to enable them to undertake work theretofore performed in another area by other subcontractors or contractors.

DURATION OF PROGRAM

SEC. 407. The Director shall carry out the programs provided for in this title during the fiscal year ending June 30, 1965, and the two succeeding fiscal years.

Public Law 89–117 added the following new title IV to the Small Business Investment Act of 1958 (see also footnotes 3 (p. 2) and 5 (p. 3)):

TITLE IV—LEASE GUARANTEES

AUTHORITY OF THE ADMINISTRATION

SEC. 401. (a) The Administration may, whenever it determines such action to be necessary or desirable, and upon such terms and conditions as it may prescribe, guarantee the payment of rentals under leases of commercial and industrial property entered into by small business concerns that are (1) eligible for loans under section 7(b)(3) of the Small Business Act, or (2) eligible for loans under title IV of the Economic Opportunity Act of 1964, to enable such concerns to obtain such leases. Any such guarantee may be made or effected either directly or in cooperation with any qualified surety company or other qualified company through a participation agreement with such company. The foregoing powers shall be subject, however, to the following restrictions and limitations:

(1) No guarantee shall be issued by the Administration (A) if a guarantee meeting the requirements of the applicant is otherwise available on reasonable terms, and (B) unless the Administration determines that there exists a reasonable expectation that the small business concern in behalf of which the guarantee is issued will perform the covenants and conditions of the lease.

(2) The Administration shall, to the greatest extent practicable, exercise the powers conferred by this section in cooperation with qualified surety or other companies on a participation basis.

(b) The Administration shall fix a uniform annual fee for its share of any guarantee under this section which shall be payable in advance at such time as may be prescribed by the Administrator. The amount of any such fee shall be determined in accordance with sound actuarial practices and procedures, to the extent practicable, but in no case shall such amount exceed, on the Administration's share of any guarantee made under this title, 2½ per centum per annum of the minimum annual guaranteed rental payable under any guaranteed lease: *Provided*, That the Administration shall fix the lowest fee that experience under the program established hereby has shown to be justified. The Administration may also fix such uniform fees for the processing of applications for guarantees under this section as the Administrator determines are reasonable and necessary to pay the administrative expenses that are incurred in connection therewith.

(c) In connection with the guarantee of rentals under any lease pursuant to authority conferred by this section, the Administrator may require, in order to minimize the financial risk assumed under such guarantee—

(1) that the lessee pay an amount, not to exceed one-fourth of the minimum guaranteed annual rental required under the lease, which shall be held in escrow and shall be available (A) to meet rental charges accruing in any month for which the lessee is in default, or (B) if no default occurs during the term of the lease, for application (with accrued interest) toward final payments of rental charges under the lease;

(2) that upon occurrence of a default under the lease, the lessor shall, as a condition precedent to enforcing any claim under the lease guarantee, utilize the entire period, for which there are funds available in escrow for payment of rentals, in reasonably diligent efforts to eliminate or minimize losses, by releasing the commercial or industrial property covered by the lease to another qualified tenant, and no claim shall be made or paid under the guarantee until such effort has been made and such escrow funds have been exhausted;

(3) that any guarantor of the lease will become a successor of the lessor for the purpose of collecting from a lessee in default rentals which are in arrears and with respect to which the lessor has received payment under a guarantee made pursuant to this section; and

(4) such other provisions, not inconsistent with the purposes of this title, as the Administrator may in his discretion require.

POWERS

Sec. 402. Without limiting the authority conferred upon the Administrator and the Administration by section 201 of this Act, the Administrator and the Administration shall have, in the performance of and with respect to the functions, powers, and duties conferred by this title, all the authority and be subject to the same conditions prescribed in section 5(b) of the Small Business Act with respect to loans, including the authority to execute subleases, assignments of lease and new leases with any person, firm, organization, or other entity, in order to aid in the liquidation of obligations of the Administration hereunder.

FUND

Sec. 403. There is hereby established a revolving fund for use by the Administration in carrying out the provisions of this title. Initial capital for such fund shall consist of not to exceed $5,000,000 transferred from the fund established under section 4(c) of the Small Business Act: *Provided*, That the last sentence of such section 4(c) shall not apply to any amounts so transferred. Into the fund established by this section there shall be deposited all receipts from the guarantee program authorized by this title. Moneys in such fund not needed for the payment of current operating expenses or for the payment of claims arising under such program may be invested in bonds or other obligations of, or bonds or other obligations guaranteed as to principal and interest by, the United States; except that moneys provided as initial capital for such fund shall be returned to the fund

established by section 4(c) of the Small Business Act, in
such amounts and at such times as the Administrator
determines to be appropriate, whenever the level of the
fund herein established is sufficiently high to permit the
return of such moneys without danger to the solvency
of the program under this title.

○

SMALL BUSINESS INVESTMENT ACT

1965 TEXT, EXPLANATION, AND RELATED TAX PROVISIONS

SELECT COMMITTEE ON SMALL BUSINESS
UNITED STATES SENATE

APRIL 1, 1965

Printed for the use of the Select Committee on Small Business

---

U.S. GOVERNMENT PRINTING OFFICE

45–500 O

WASHINGTON : 1965

For sale by the Superintendent of Documents, U.S. Government Printing Office
Washington, D.C., 20402 - Price 15 cents

FOREWORD

The Small Business Investment Act of 1958 (Public Law 85–699) was signed into law on August 21, 1958, less than 7 years ago.

Since that date, the Act has undergone three major revisions—one in each of the three succeeding Congresses. Public Law 86–502, approved June 11, 1960, authorized SBIC's to acquire a wide range of equity securities from small business concerns financed by them and doubled the amounts that banks might invest in the stock of SBIC's. Public Law 87–341,.approved October 3, 1961, increased from $150,000 to $400,000 the amount of funds that the Small Business Administration might contribute to the capital of an SBIC. Public Law 88–273, approved February 28, 1964, further increased the matching Government funds provision to $700,000 and eliminated a previous restriction relating to the maximum amount an SBIC might invest in any one small business concern. Public Law 88–273 also added to the statute a direction to the Small Business Administration that it adopt effective regulations dealing with the matter of conflicts of interest.

These and all other changes made in the Act are detailed in the following pages, where the Select Committee on Small Business of the United States Senate sets out the full text of the Small Business Investment Act of 1958 as it stands today, together with the related provisions of our tax laws and regulations.

These changes in the law afford concrete evidence of the continuing interest of the Congress in the SBIC program and its determination to provide those statutory tools necessary to the realization of the program's mission "to stimulate and supplement the flow of private equity capital and long-term loan funds which small business concerns need for the sound financing of their business operations and for their growth, expansion and modernization."

JOHN SPARKMAN,
Chairman, Select Committee on Small Business,
United States Senate.

APRIL 1, 1965.

CONTENTS

TEXT OF ACT

SMALL BUSINESS INVESTMENT ACT OF 1958

(Public Law 699, 85th Cong., 2d sess., as amended)

AN ACT To make equity capital and long-term credit more readily available for small-business concerns, and for other purposes

Be it enacted by the Senate and House of Representatives of the United States of America in Congress assembled,

TITLE I—SHORT TITLE, STATEMENT OF POLICY, AND DEFINITIONS

SHORT TITLE

SEC. 101. This Act, divided into titles and sections according to the following table of contents, may be cited as the "Small Business Investment Act of 1958."

TABLE OF CONTENTS

---

[1] Previous sec. 309 repealed by sec. 11(e) of Public Law 87-341 and new sec. 309 is added by sec. 9 of Public Law 87-341.
[2] This new section added by sec. 9 of Public Law 87-341.
[3] This new section added by sec. 9 of Public Law 87-341.
[4] Added by Public Law 88-273.

STATEMENT OF POLICY

15 U.S.C. 661.

SEC. 102. It is declared to be the policy of the Congress and the purpose of this Act to improve and stimulate the national economy in general and the small-business segment thereof in particular by establishing a program to stimulate and supplement the flow of private equity capital and long-term loan funds which small-business concerns need for the sound financing of their business operations and for their growth, expansion, and modernization, and which are not available in adequate supply: *Provided, however,* That this policy shall be carried out in such manner as to insure the maximum participation of private financing sources.

It is the intention of the Congress that the provisions of this Act shall be so administered that any financial assistance provided hereunder shall not result in a substantial increase of unemployment in any area of the country.

DEFINITIONS

15 U.S.C. 662.

SEC. 103. As used in this Act—

(1) the term "Administration" means the Small Business Administration;

(2) the term "Administrator" means the Administrator of the Small Business Administration;

(3) the terms "small business investment company", "company", and "licensee" mean a company approved by the Administration to operate under the provisions of this Act and issued a license as provided in section 301(c);[5]

(4) the term "State" includes the several States, the Territories and possessions of the United States, the Commonwealth of Puerto Rico, and the District of Columbia;[6]

(5) the term "small-business concern" shall have the same meaning as in the Small Business Act;

(6) the term "development companies" means enterprises incorporated under State law with the authority to promote and assist the growth and development of small-business concerns in the areas covered by their operations; and

(7) the term "license" means a license issued by the Administration as provided in section 301(c).[7]

TITLE II—SMALL BUSINESS INVESTMENT DIVISION OF THE SMALL BUSINESS ADMINISTRATION

ESTABLISHMENT OF SMALL BUSINESS INVESTMENT DIVISION

15 U.S.C. 671.

SEC. 201. There is hereby established in the Small Business Administration a division to be known as the Small Business Investment Division. The Division shall be headed by a Deputy Administrator who shall be appointed by the Administrator, and shall receive compensation at the rate provided by law for other deputy administrators of the Small Business Administration The powers conferred by this Act upon the Administration shall be exercised by the Administration through the Small Business Investment Division, and the powers herein conferred upon the Administrator shall be exercised by him through the Deputy Administrator appointed hereunder. In the performance

---

[5] This new language substituted by sec. 2(1) of Public Law 87-341.
[6] Amended by sec. 3 of Public Law 86-502 to reflect admission of Alaska and Hawaii to the Union.
[7] This new language inserted by sec. 2(2) of Public Law 87-341.

of, and with respect to the functions, powers, and duties vested by this Act, the Administrator and the Administration shall (in addition to any authority otherwise vested by this Act) have the functions, powers, and duties set forth in the Small Business Act, and the provisions of sections 13 and 16 of that Act, insofar as applicable, are extended to apply to the functions of the Administrator and the Administration under this Act.

[Funds for exercise of functions under this Act authorized in sec. 4(c) of Small Business Act (15 U.S.C. 633(c)). Present authorization for appropriations for these functions is $341,000,000.]

TITLE III—SMALL BUSINESS INVESTMENT COMPANIES

ORGANIZATION OF SMALL BUSINESS INVESTMENT COMPANIES

SEC. 301. (a) A small business investment company shall be an incorporated body, organized and chartered under State law solely for the purpose of performing the functions and conducting the activities contemplated under this title, which has succession for a period of not less than thirty years unless sooner dissolved by its shareholders and possesses the powers reasonably necessary to perform such functions and conduct such activities. The area in which the company is to conduct its operations, and the establishment of branch offices or agencies (if authorized by the articles of incorporation), shall be subject to the approval of the Administration.[8]   15 U.S.C. 681.

(b) The articles of incorporation of any small business investment company shall specify in general terms the objects for which the company is formed, the name assumed by such company, the area or areas in which its operations are to be carried on, the place where its principal office is to be located, and the amount and classes of its shares of capital stock. Such articles may contain any other provisions not inconsistent with this Act that the company may see fit to adopt for the regulation of its business and the conduct of its affairs. Such articles and any amendments thereto adopted from time to time shall be subject to the approval of the Administration.

(c) The articles of incorporation and amendments thereto shall be forwarded to the Administration for consideration and approval or disapproval. In determining whether to approve such a company's articles of incorporation and permit it to operate under the provisions of this Act, the Administration shall give due regard, among other things, to the need for the financing of small-business concerns in the area in which the proposed company is to commence business, the general character of the proposed management of the company, the number of such companies previously organized in the United States, and the volume of their operations. After consideration of all relevant factors, if it approves the company's articles of incorporation, the Administration may in its discretion approve the company to operate under the provisions of this Act and issue the company a license for such operation.[9]

CAPITAL STOCK AND SUBORDINATED DEBENTURES

SEC. 302. (a) Each company authorized to operate under this Act shall have a paid-in capital and surplus equal to at least $300,000. In order to facilitate the formation and growth of small business investment companies, the Administration is hereby authorized notwithstanding any other provisions of law (but only to the extent that the necessary funds are not available to the   15 U.S.C. 682.

---

[8] New language, contained in sec. 11(a) of Public Law 87-341.
[9] New language in second and third sentences substituted by sec. 11(b) (1) and (2) of Public Law 87-341. Previous subsecs. (d) and (e) struck out by sec. 11(b)(3) of Public Law 87-341.

company involved from private sources on reasonable terms), to purchase the debentures of any such company in an amount not to exceed the lesser of $700,000 or the amount of the paid-in capital and surplus of the company from other sources; but debentures of a small business investment company may be purchased by the Administration under this subsection only during such period (in no case ending more than five years after the date of the issuance of its license under sec. 301(c) or the date of the enactment of the Small Business Investment Act Amendments of 1963,[10] whichever is later) as may be fixed by the Administration.[11]   Any debentures purchased by the Administration under this subsection shall be subordinate to any other debenture bonds, promissory notes, or other obligations which may be issued by such companies, and shall be deemed a part of the capital and surplus of such companies for purposes of this section and sections 303(b) and 306 of this Act.

(b) Notwithstanding the provisions of section 6(a)(1) of the Bank Holding Company Act of 1956,[12] shares of stock in small business investment companies shall be eligible for purchase by national banks, and shall be eligible for purchase by other member banks of the Federal Reserve System and nonmember insured banks to the extent permitted under applicable State law; except that in no event shall any such bank hold shares in small business investment companies in an amount aggregating more than 2 percent of its capital and surplus.[13]

(c) The aggregate amount of shares in any such company or companies which may be owned or controlled by any stockholder, or by any group or class of stockholders, may be limited by the Administration.

BORROWING POWER

15 U.S.C. 683.   SEC. 303. (a) Each small business investment company shall have authority to borrow money and to issue its debenture bonds, promissory notes, or other obligations under such general conditions and subject to such limitations and regulations as the Administration may prescribe.

(b) To encourage the formation and growth of small business investment companies, the Administration is authorized (but only to the extent that the necessary funds are not available to the company involved from private sources on reasonable terms) to lend funds to such companies either directly or by loans made or effected in cooperation with banks or other lending institutions through agreements to participate on an immediate or deferred (standby) basis.   Such loans shall bear interest at such rate (in no case lower than the average investment yield, as determined by the Secretary of the Treasury, on marketable obligations of the United States outstanding at the time of the loan involved) and contain such other terms as the Administration may fix, and shall be subject to the following restrictions and limitations:

(1) The total amount of obligations of any one company which may be purchased and outstanding at any one time by the Administration under this subsection (including commitments to purchase such obligations) shall not exceed 50 per centum of the paid-in capital and surplus of such company or $4,000,000, whichever is less.

(2) All loans made under this subsection (b) shall be of such sound value as reasonably to assure repayment.[14]

---

[10] "Small Business Investment Act Amendments of 1963" was enacted on Feb. 28, 1964.
[11] This second sentence contains new language substituted by sec. 3(a) of Public Law 87-341, and amended by Public Law 88-273.
[12] Added by Public Law 86-502.
[13] This amount raised from 1 to 2 percent by Public Law 87-341.
[14] This subsection contains much new language inserted by Public Law 87-341 and by Public Law 88-273.

PROVISION OF EQUITY CAPITAL FOR SMALL-BUSINESS CONCERNS [15]   15 U.S.C. 684.

SEC. 304. (a) It shall be a function of each small business investment company to provide a source of equity capital for incorporated small-business concerns, in such manner and under such terms as the small business investment company may fix in accordance with the regulations of the Administration.

(b) Before any capital is provided to a small-business concern under this section—

(1) the company may require such concern to refinance any or all of its outstanding indebtedness so that the company is the only holder of any evidence of indebtedness of such concern; and

(2) except as provided in regulations issued by the Administration, such concern shall agree that it will not thereafter incur any indebtedness without first securing the approval of the company and giving the company the first opportunity to finance such indebtedness.

(c) Whenever a company provides capital to a small-business concern under this section, such concern shall have the right, exercisable in whole or in such part as such concern may elect, to become a stockholder-proprietor by investing in the capital stock of the company 5 per centum of the amount of the capital so provided, in accordance with regulations prescribed by the Administrator.

(d) Equity capital provided to incorporated small-business concerns under this section may be provided directly or in cooperation with other investors, incorporated or unincorporated, through agreements to participate on an immediate basis.[16]

LONG-TERM LOANS TO SMALL-BUSINESS CONCERNS

SEC. 305. (a) Each company is authorized to make loans, in the manner   15 U.S.C. 685.
and subject to the conditions described in this section, to incorporated and unincorporated small-business concerns in order to provide such concerns with funds needed for sound financing, growth, modernization, and expansion.

(b) Loans made under this section may be made directly or in cooperation with other lenders, incorporated or unincorporated, through agreements to participate on an immediate or deferred basis.[17] In agreements to participate in loans on a deferred basis under this subsection, the participation by the company shall not be in excess of 90 per centum of the balance of the loan outstanding at the time of disbursement.

(c) The maximum rate of interest for the company's share of any loan made under this section shall be determined by the Administration.

(d) Any loan made under this section shall have a maturity not exceeding twenty years.

(e) Any loan made under this section shall be of such sound value, or so secured, as reasonably to assure repayment.

(f) Any company which has made a loan to a small-business concern under this section is authorized to extend the maturity of or renew such loan for additional periods, not exceeding ten years, if the company finds that such extension or renewal will aid in the orderly liquidation of such loan.

[15] Prior to its amendment by sec. 6 of Public Law 86-502, sec. 304 authorized SBIC's to furnish equity capital only through the purchase of convertible debentures and required, rather than permitted, borrowing small-business concerns to purchase stock in the lending SBIC. Subsec. (c) was also rewritten by sec. 6 of Public Law 86-502.
[16] This new subsection added by sec. 5 of Public Law 87-341.
[17] This sentence rewritten by sec. 6 of Public Law 87-341.

AGGREGATE LIMITATIONS

15 U.S.C. 686.   SEC. 306. Without the approval of the Administration, the aggregate amount of obligations and securities acquired and for which commitments may be issued by any small business investment company under the provisions of this Act for any single enterprise shall not exceed 20 per centum of the combined capital and surplus of such small business investment company authorized by this Act.[18]

EXEMPTIONS

SEC. 307. (a) Section 3 of the Securities Act of 1933, as amended (15 U.S.C. 77c), is hereby amended by inserting at the end thereof the following new subsection (c):

"(c) The Commission may from time to time by its rules and regulations and subject to such terms and conditions as may be prescribed therein, add to the securities exempted as provided in this section any class of securities issued by a small business investment company under the Small Business Investment Act of 1958 if it finds, having regard to the purposes of that Act, that the enforcement of this Act with respect to such securities is not necessary in the public interest and for the protection of investors."

(b) Section 304 of the Trust Indenture Act of 1939 (15 U.S.C. 77ddd) is hereby amended by adding the following subsection (e):

"(e) The Commission may from time to time by its rules and regulations, and subject to such terms and conditions as may be prescribed herein, add to the securities exempted as provided in this section any class of securities issued by a small business investment company under the Small Business Investment Act of 1958 if it finds, having regard to the purposes of that Act, that the enforcement of this Act with respect to such securities is not necessary in the public interest and for the protection of investors."

(c) Section 18 of the Investment Company Act of 1940 (15 U.S.C. 80a–18) is amended by adding at the end thereof the following:

"(k) The provisions of subparagraphs (A) and (B) of paragraph (1) of subsection (a) of this section shall not apply to investment companies operating under the Small Business Investment Act of 1958."

MISCELLANEOUS

15 U.S.C. 687.   SEC. 308. (a) Wherever practicable the operations of a small business investment company, including the generation of business, may be undertaken in cooperation with banks or other investors or lenders, incorporated or unincorporated, and any servicing or initial investigation required for loans or acquisitions of securities by the company under the provisions of this Act may be handled through such banks or other investors or lenders on a fee basis. Any small business investment company may receive fees for services rendered to such banks and other investors and lenders.[19]

(b) Each small business investment company may make use, wherever practicable, of the advisory services of the Federal Reserve System and of the Department of Commerce which are available for and useful to industrial and commercial businesses, and may provide consulting and advisory services on a fee basis and have on its staff persons competent to provide such services. Any Federal Reserve bank is authorized to act as a depository or fiscal agent for any company operating under the provisions of this Act.[20] Such companies

---

[18] This section rewritten by Public Law 87-341 and by Public Law 88-273.
[19] This subsection rewritten by sec. 8 of Public Law 87-341.
[20] The last seven words of this sentence added by sec. 11(c) of Public Law 87-341.

may invest funds not reasonably needed for their current operations in direct obligations of, or obligations guaranteed as to principal and interest by, the United States, or in insured savings accounts (up to the amount of the insurance) in any institution the accounts of which are insured by the Federal Savings and Loan Insurance Corporation.[21]

(c) The Administration is authorized to prescribe regulations governing the operations of small business investment companies, and to carry out the provisions of this Act, in accordance with the purposes of this Act. Each small business investment company shall be subject to examinations made by direction of the Administration by examiners selected or approved by the Administration, and the cost of such examinations, including the compensation of the examiners, may in the discretion of the Administration be assessed against the company examined and when so assessed shall be paid by such company. Every such company shall make such reports to the Administration at such times and in such form as the Administration may require; except that the Administration is authorized to exempt from making such reports any such company which is registered under the Investment Company Act of 1940 to the extent necessary to avoid duplication in reporting requirements.

(d) Should any small business investment company violate or fail to comply with any of the provisions of this Act or of regulations prescribed hereunder, all of its rights, privileges, and franchises derived therefrom may thereby be forfeited. Before any such company shall be declared dissolved, or its rights, privileges, and franchises forfeited, any noncompliance with or violation of this Act shall be determined and adjudged by a court of the United States of competent jurisdiction in a suit brought for that purpose in the district, territory, or other place subject to the jurisdiction of the United States, in which the principal office of such company is located. Any such suit shall be brought by the United States at the instance of the Administration or the Attorney General.

(e) Nothing in this Act or in any other provision of law shall be deemed to impose any liability on the United States with respect to any obligations entered into, or stocks issued, or commitments made, by any company operating under the provisions of this Act.[22]

SUSPENSION OF LICENSES; CEASE AND DESIST ORDERS

SEC. 309.[23] (a) A license may be suspended by the Administration— 15 U.S.C. 687a

> (1) for false statements knowingly made in any written statement required under this title, or under any regulation issued under this title by the Administration, for the purpose of obtaining the license;
>
> (2) if any written statement required under this title, or under any regulation issued under this title by the Administrator, for the purpose of obtaining the license, fails to state a material fact necessary in order to make the statement not misleading in the light of the circumstances under which the statement was made;
>
> (3) for willful or repeated violation of, or willful or repeated failure to observe, any provision of this Act;

[21] Last sentence revised by Public Law 88–273 to permit deposits of idle SBIC funds in insured savings accounts.
[22] The last seven words added by sec. 11(d) of Public Law 87–341. The same subsection also struck out the previous subsecs. (e) and (f); and redesignated this subsection (formerly (g)) as (e). The former subsecs. (e) and (f) were rewritten and expanded by Public Law 87–341 and are now designated as secs. 309, 310, and 311.
[23] Secs. 309, 310, and 311 are all new sections added by sec. 9 of Public Law 87–341. The previous sec. 309 was repealed by sec. 11(e) of Public Law 87–341.

(4) for willful or repeated violation of, or willful or repeated failure to observe, any rule or regulation of the Administration authorized by this Act; or

(5) for violation of, or failure to observe, any cease and desist order issued by the Administration under this section.

(b) Where a licensee has not complied with any provision of this Act, or of any regulation issued under this Act by the Administration, the Administration may order such licensee to cease and desist from such action or failure to act; and the Administration may further order such licensee to take such action or to refrain from such action as the Administration deems necessary to ensure compliance with the Act and the regulations. The Administration may also suspend the license of such licensee until the licensee has complied with such order.

(c) Before suspending a license pursuant to subsection (a), or issuing a cease and desist order pursuant to subsection (b), the Administration shall serve upon the licensee involved an order to show cause why an order suspending the license or a cease and desist order should not be issued. Any such order to show cause shall contain a statement of the matters of fact and law asserted by the Administration and the legal authority and jurisdiction under which a hearing is to be held, and shall inform the licensee that a hearing will be held before the Administration at a time and place stated in the order. If after hearing, or a waiver thereof, the Administration determines on the record that an order suspending the license or a cease and desist order should issue, it shall promptly issue such order, which shall include a statement of the findings of the Administration and the grounds and reasons therefor and specify the effective date of the order, and shall cause the order to be served on the licensee.

(d) The Administration may require by subpena the attendance and testimony of witnesses and the production of all books, papers, and documents relating to the hearing from any place in the United States. Witnesses summoned before the Administration shall be paid by the party at whose instance they were called the same fees and mileage that are paid witnesses in the courts of the United States. In case of disobedience to a subpena, the Administration, or any party to a proceeding before the Administration, may invoke the aid of any court of the United States in requiring the attendance and testimony of witnesses and the production of books, papers, and documents.

(e) An order issued by the Administration under this section shall be final and conclusive unless within thirty days after the service thereof the licensee appeals to the United States court of appeals for the circuit in which such licensee has its principal place of business by filing with the clerk of such court a petition praying that the Administration's order be set aside or modified in the manner stated in the petition. After the expiration of such thirty days, a petition may be filed only by leave of court on a showing of reasonable grounds for failure to file the petition theretofore. The clerk of the court shall immediately cause a copy of the petition to be delivered to the Administration, and the Administration shall thereupon certify and file in the court a transcript of the record upon which the order complained of was entered. If before such record is filed the Administration amends or sets aside its order, in whole or in part, the petitioner may amend the petition within such time as the court may determine, on notice to the Administration. The filing of a petition for review shall not of itself stay or suspend the operation of the order of the Administration, but the court of appeals in its discretion may restrain or suspend, in whole or in part, the operation of the order pending the final hearing and determination of the petition. The proceedings in such cases in the court of appeals shall be made a preferred cause and shall be expedited in every way. The court may affirm, modify, or set aside the order of the Administration. If the court determines that the just and proper disposition of the case requires the taking of additional evidence, the court shall order the Administration to reopen the hearing for the taking of such evidence, in such manner and upon such terms and conditions as the court may deem proper. The Administration may modify its findings as to the facts, or make new findings, by reason of the additional evidence so taken, and it shall file its modified or new findings and the amendments, if any, of its order, with the record of such additional evidence. No objection to an order of the Administration shall be considered by the court unless such objection was urged before the Administration or, if it was not so urged, unless there were reasonable grounds for failure to do so. The judgment and decree of the court affirming, modifying, or setting aside any such order of the Administration shall be subject only to review by the Supreme Court of the United States upon certification or certiorari as provided in section 1254 of title 28, United States Code.

(f) If any licensee against which an order is issued under this section fails to obey the order, the Administration may apply to the United States court of appeals, within the circuit where the licensee has its principal place of business, for the enforcement of the order, and shall file a transcript of the record upon which the order complained of was entered. Upon the filing of the application the court shall cause notice thereof to be served on the licensee. The evidence to be considered, the procedure to be followed, and the jurisdiction of the court shall be the same as is provided in subsection (e) for applications to set aside or modify orders. The proceedings in such cases shall be made a preferred cause and shall be expedited in every way.

INVESTIGATIONS

SEC. 310.[23] The Administration may make such investigations as it deems necessary to determine whether a licensee or any other person has engaged or is about to engage in any acts or practices which constitute or will constitute a violation of any provision of this Act, or of any rule or regulation under this Act, or of any order issued under this Act. The Administration shall permit any person to file with it a statement in writing, under oath or otherwise as the Administration shall determine, as to all the facts and circumstances concerning the matter to be investigated. For the purpose of any investigation, the Administration is empowered to administer oaths and affirmations, subpena witnesses, compel their attendance, take evidence, and require the production of any books, papers, and documents which are relevant to the inquiry. Such attendance of witnesses and the production of any such records may be required from any place in the United States. In case of contumacy by, or refusal to obey a subpena issued to, any person, including a licensee, the Administration may invoke the aid of any court of the United States within the jurisdiction of which such investigation or proceeding is carried on, or where such person resides or carries on business, in requiring the attendance and testimony of witnesses and the production of books, papers, and documents; and such court may issue an order requiring such person to appear before the Administration, there to produce records, if so ordered, or to give testimony touching the matter under investigation. Any failure to obey such order of the court may be punished by such court as a contempt thereof. All process in any such case may be served in the judicial district whereof such person is an inhabitant or wherever he may be found.

15 U.S.C. 687b.

---

[23] Secs. 309, 310, and 311 are all new sections added by sec. 9 of Public Law 87-341. The previous sec. 309 was repealed by sec. 11(e) of Public Law 87-341.

INJUNCTIONS AND OTHER ORDERS

15 U.S.C. 687c.

SEC. 311.[23] (a) Whenever, in the judgment of the Administration, a licensee or any other person has engaged or is about to engage in any acts or practices which constitute or will constitute a violation of any provision of this Act, or of any rule or regulation under this Act, or of any order issued under this Act, the Administration may make application to the proper district court of the United States or a United States court of any place subject to the jurisdiction of the United States for an order enjoining such acts or practices, or for an order enforcing compliance with such provision, rule, regulation, or order, and such courts shall have jurisdiction of such actions and, upon a showing by the Administration that such licensee or other person has engaged or is about to engage in any such acts or practices, a permanent or temporary injunction, restraining order, or other order, shall be granted without bond. The proceedings in such a case shall be made a preferred cause and shall be expedited in every way.

(b) In any such proceeding the court as a court of equity may, to such extent as it deems necessary, take exclusive jurisdiction of the licensee or licensees and the assets thereof, wherever located; and the court shall have jurisdiction in any such proceeding to appoint a trustee or receiver to hold or administer under the direction of the court the assets so possessed.

CONFLICTS OF INTEREST

15 U.S.C. 687d.

SEC. 312. For the purpose of controlling conflicts of interest which may be detrimental to small business concerns, to small business investment companies, to the shareholders of either, or to the purposes of this Act, the Administration shall adopt regulations to govern transactions with any officer, director, or shareholder of any small business investment company, or with any person or concern, in which any interest, direct or indirect, financial or otherwise, is held by any officer, director, or shareholder of (1) any small business investment company, or (2) any person or concern with an interest, direct or indirect, financial or otherwise, in any small business investment company. Such regulations shall include appropriate requirements for public disclosure (including disclosure in the locality most directly affected by the transaction) necessary to the purposes of this section.[24]

[All of title IV of Public Law 85-699 was repealed by sec. 11(f) of Public Law 87-341.]

TITLE V—LOANS TO STATE AND LOCAL DEVELOPMENT COMPANIES

15 U.S.C. 695.

SEC. 501. (a) The Administration is authorized to make loans to State development companies to assist in carrying out the purposes of this Act. Any funds advanced under this subsection shall be in exchange for obligations of the development company which bear interest at such rate, and contain such other terms, as the Administration may fix, and funds may be so advanced without regard to the use and investment by the development company of funds secured by it from other sources.

(b) The total amount of obligations purchased and outstanding at any one time by the Administration under this section from any one State development company shall not exceed the total amount borrowed by it from all other

---

[23] Secs. 309, 310, and 311 are all new sections added by sec. 9 of Public Law 87-341. The previous sec. 309 was repealed by sec. 11(e) of Public Law 87-341.
[24] Added by Public Law 85-273.

sources. Funds advanced to a State development company under this section shall be treated on an equal basis with those funds borrowed by such company after the date of the enactment of this Act, regardless of source, which have the highest priority, except when this requirement is waived by the Administrator.

SEC. 502. The Administration may, in addition to its authority under 15 U.S.C. 696. section 501, make loans for plant construction, conversion or expansion, including the acquisition of land, to State and local development companies, and such loans may be made or effected either directly or in cooperation with banks or other lending institutions through agreements to participate on an immediate or deferred basis: *Provided, however,* That the foregoing powers shall be subject to the following restrictions and limitations:

(1) All loans made shall be so secured as reasonably to assure repayment. In agreements to participate in loans on a deferred basis under this subsection, such participation by the Administration shall not be in excess of 90 per centum of the balance of the loan outstanding at the time of disbursement.

(2) The proceeds of any such loan shall be used solely by such borrower to assist an identifiable small-business concern and for a sound business purpose approved by the Administration.

(3) Loans made by the Administration under this section shall be limited to $350,000 [25] for each such identifiable small-business concern.

(4) Any development company assisted under this section must meet criteria established by the Administration, including the extent of participation to be required or amount of paid-in capital to be used in each instance as is determined to be reasonable by the Administration.

(5) No loans, including extensions or renewals thereof, shall be made by the Administration for a period or periods exceeding twenty-five years [26] plus such additional period as is estimated may be required to complete construction, conversion, or expansion, but the Administration may extend the maturity of or renew any loan made pursuant to this section beyond the period stated for additional periods, not to exceed ten years, if such extension or renewal will aid in the orderly liquidation of such loan. Any such loan shall bear interest at a rate fixed by the Administration.[27]

TITLE VI—CHANGES IN FEDERAL RESERVE AUTHORITY

[Omitted as no longer current.]

TITLE VII—CRIMINAL PENALTIES

[This title amends the U.S. Code to include certain actions by persons affiliated with or dealing with SBIC's as Federal crimes. See 18 U.S.C. 212, 213, 216, 657, 1006, and 1014.]

[25] This limitation was raised from $250,000 to $350,000 by sec. 10(1) of Public Law 87-341.
[26] This limitation was raised from 10 years to 25 years by sec. 10(2) of Public Law 87-341.
[27] Previous limitation on the life of sec. 502 (June 30, 1961) was repealed by sec. 26 of Public Law 87-27 (the Area Redevelopment Act).

TEXT OF TAX PROVISIONS

SECTION 57 OF TECHNICAL AMENDMENTS ACT OF 1958

*　　　*　　　*　　　*　　　*　　　*　　　*

SEC. 57. SMALL BUSINESS INVESTMENT COMPANIES.

(a) Losses on Small Business Investment Company Stock and Losses of Small Business Investment Companies.—Part IV of subchapter P of chapter 1 (relating to special rules for determining capital gains and losses) is amended by adding at the end thereof the following new sections:

26 U.S.C. 1242.
"**SEC. 1242. LOSSES ON SMALL BUSINESS INVESTMENT COMPANY STOCK.**

"If—

"(1) a loss is on stock in a small business investment company operating under the Small Business Investment Act of 1958, and

"(2) such loss would (but for this section) be a loss from the sale or exchange of a capital asset,

then such loss shall be treated as a loss from the sale or exchange of property which is not a capital asset. For purposes of section 172 (relating to the net operating loss deduction) any amount of loss treated by reason of this section as a loss from the sale or exchange of property which is not a capital asset shall be treated as attributable to a trade or business of the taxpayer.[28]

26 U.S.C. 1243.
"**SEC. 1243. LOSS OF SMALL BUSINESS INVESTMENT COMPANY.**

"In the case of a small business investment company operating under the Small Business Investment Act of 1958, if—

"(1) a loss is on convertible debentures (including stock received pursuant to the conversion privilege) acquired pursuant to section 304 of the Small Business Investment Act of 1958, and

"(2) such loss would (but for this section) be a loss from the sale or exchange of a capital asset,

then such loss shall be treated as a loss from the sale or exchange of property which is not a capital asset."[29]

(b) Dividends Received by Small Business Investment Companies.— Section 243 (relating to dividends received by corporations) is amended—

(1) by striking out in subsection (a) "In the case of a corporation" and inserting in lieu thereof "In the case of a corporation (other than a small business investment company operating under the Small Business Investment Act of 1958)";

(2) by redesignating subsection (b) as (c), and by inserting after subsection (a) the following new subsection:

26 U.S.C. 243(b).
"(b) Small Business Investment Companies.—In the case of a small business investment company operating under the Small Business Investment Act of 1958, there shall be allowed as a deduction an amount equal to 100 percent of the amount received as dividends (other than dividends described in paragraph (1) of section 244, relating to dividends on preferred stock of a

---

[28] Under Internal Revenue Service Income Tax Regulation § 1.1242–1(a) sec. 1242 ordinary loss deductions are made clearly available to subsequent purchasers as well as to original investors in SBIC stock.

[29] Sec. 304 of the Small Business Investment Act of 1958 was amended in 1960 to permit SBIC's, under SBA regulations, to accept securities other than convertible debentures in exchange for equity capital supplied to small concerns. However, only convertible debentures and stock acquired by exercise of the conversion privilege are specifically covered by sec. 1243 of the Internal Revenue Code.

public utility) from a domestic corporation which is subject to taxation under this chapter.''; and

(3) by striking out in subsection (c) (as redesignated by paragraph (2)) "subsection (a)" and inserting in lieu thereof "subsections (a) and (b)".

(c) TECHNICAL AMENDMENTS.—

(1) Section 165(h) (relating to deduction for losses) is amended by adding at the end thereof the following new paragraphs:

"(3) For special rule for losses on stock in a small business investment company, see section 1242.

"(4) For special rule for losses of a small business investment company, see section 1243.''

(2) Section 246(b)(1) (relating to limitation on aggregate amount of deductions for dividends received by corporations) is amended by striking out "243" each place it appears therein and insert in lieu thereof "243(a)".

(3) The table of sections for part IV of subchapter P of chapter 1 is amended by adding at the end thereof

"Sec. 1242. Losses on small business investment company stock.
"Sec. 1243. Loss of small business investment company."

(d) EFFECTIVE DATE.—The amendments made by this section shall a ply with respect to taxable years beginning after the date of the enactment of this Act.

SECTION 3 OF PUBLIC LAW 86-376

SEC. 3. (a) Section 542(c) of the Internal Revenue Code of 1954 (relating to exceptions from definition of a personal holding company) is amended— 26 U.S.C. 542(c).

(a) by inserting ";" in lieu of "." at the end thereof and

(b) by adding at the end thereof the following new paragraph (11)[30]:

"(11)[30] A small business investment company which is licensed by the Small Business Administration and operating under the Small Business Investment Act of 1958 and which is actively engaged in the business of providing funds to small business concerns under that Act. This paragraph shall not apply if any shareholder of the small business investment company owns at any time during the taxable year directly or indirectly (including, in the case of an individual, ownership by the members of his family as defined in section 544(a)(2) a 5 per centum or more proprietary interest in a small business concern to which funds are provided by the investment company or 5 per centum or more in value of the outstanding stock of such concern."

(b) The amendment made by this section shall apply to taxable years beginning after December 31, 1958.

[30] Renumbered as par. (8) by Revenue Act of 1964.

ACCUMULATED EARNINGS SURTAX EXEMPTION

Treasury Decision 6652, published May 13, 1963, added the following language to Income Tax Regulation § 1.533–1:

"(d) *Small business investment companies.* A corporation which is licensed to operate as a small business investment company under the Small Business Investment Act of 1958 (15 U.S.C. ch. 14B) and the regulations thereunder (13 CFR Part 107) will generally be considered to be a "mere holding or investment company" within the meaning of section 533(b). However, the presumption of the existence of the purpose to avoid income tax with respect to shareholders which results from the fact that such a company is a "mere holding or investment company" will be considered overcome so long as such company:

"(1) Complies with all the provisions of the Small Business Investment Act of 1958 and the regulations thereunder; and

"(2) Actively engages in the business of providing funds to small business concerns through investment in the equity capital of, or through the disbursement of long-term loans to, such concerns in such manner and under such terms as the company may fix in accordance with regulations promulgated by the Small Business Administration (see secs. 304 and 305 of the Small Business Investment Act of 1958, as amended (15 U.S.C. 684, 685)). On the other hand, if such a company violates or fails to comply with any of the provisions of the Small Business Investment Act of 1958, as amended, or the regulations thereunder, or ceases to be actively engaged in the business of providing funds to small business concerns in the manner provided in subparagraph (2) of this paragraph, it will not be considered to have overcome the presumption by reason of any rules provided in this paragraph."

RESERVE FOR BAD DEBTS

Following is the text of Revenue Ruling 64–48, published February 10, 1964:

"*Reserve for bad debts: Small business investment companies: Bad debt reserve ceilings.*—For a period of 10 years beginning with 1959, small business investment companies are allowed bad debt reserve ceilings equal to ten percent of their outstanding loans as reasonable reserves under Code Sec. 166(c). When the ten-year period expires, a small business investment corporation's own loss experience will be used to determine the reasonableness of further additions to its reserve.

"Small business investment companies (SBIC) are allowed to establish bad debt reserve ceilings equal to ten percent of their outstanding loans as reasonable reserves under section 166(c) of the Internal Revenue Code of 1954. The ten-percent ceiling applies for a period of ten years beginning with 1959. When the ten-year period expires an SBIC's own loss experience will be used to determine the reasonableness of further additions to its reserve. After 1968 a new SBIC, or one that has not been in existence a sufficient number of years to provide adequate loss experience data for establishing reasonable bad debt reserves, will be permitted to use an average loss experience factor computed on an industry-wide basis until it has sufficient loss experience of its own.

"In allowing a flat percentage as a reasonable reserve ceiling, consideration has been given to the fact that the SBIC industry has been in existence only since 1959 and has no available bad debt loss experience of its own which would afford an adequate basis for determining reasonable bad debt reserves. There is no similar industry which could provide the SBIC industry with comparable bad-debt experience data.

"The ten-percent ceiling was arrived at after a thorough study of the nature of the SBIC industry and the inherent risks involved in the type of loans made. The increasing amount of charge-offs under current business trends and a comparison of the principal features of the SBIC industry with those of other types of lending institutions were other factors considered.

"The determination of the period of ten years as an appropriate length of time for the application of the ten-percent ceiling factor resulted from an analysis of the loan portfolio turnover of the SBIC industry."

EXPLANATION OF THE ACT

ESTABLISHMENT OF SMALL BUSINESS INVESTMENT DIVISION IN THE SBA

The Act establishes a division of the Small Business Administration known as the Small Business Investment Division. This Division is headed by a Deputy Administrator appointed by the Administrator of the Small Business Administration. Through such Division, the Administrator of SBA (a) licenses, regulates, and examines small business investment companies, (b) lends funds to such investment companies, and (c) lends funds to State and local development companies. The Small Business Administration can suspend licenses of investment companies or issue cease and desist orders.

The Act provides that the functions to be performed by the Small Business Administration shall be carried out in such manner as to insure the maximum participation of private financing sources and shall be administered so that any financial assistance shall not result in a substantial increase of unemployment in any area of the country.

PROVISION OF FUNDS

The Act provides funds for the program by authorizing $341 million of appropriations to the existing revolving fund of the Small Business Administration which was established by the Small Business Act of 1953. These funds are to be used, however, only to carry out the purposes of the Small Business Investment Act, i.e., to make loans to small business investment companies, and to make loans to State and local development companies.

SMALL BUSINESS INVESTMENT COMPANIES

Formation.—Small business investment companies formed to operate under this Act must be incorporated under State law solely for the purpose of conducting the activities contemplated by the Act. The SBA, in determining whether to permit a company to operate under this Act, shall consider the need for small-business financing in the area where the proposed company is to operate, the character of the proposed management of the company, and the number of such companies already formed in the United States and the volume of their business.

The primary function of these small business investment companies is to provide equity capital and long-term loans to small business concerns.

Capital stock requirements.—A small business investment company is required to have a minimum paid-in capital and surplus of $300,000 before it may commence business. Stock in such companies may, subject to State law, be purchased by individuals, partnerships, corporations, insurance companies, and financial institutions, including Federal Reserve member banks and nonmember insured banks. No Federal Reserve member bank nor any nonmember insured bank, however, may hold shares in such companies in an amount aggregating more than 2 percent of its capital and surplus.

In order to encourage the formation and growth of small business investment companies, the SBA is authorized to match, during such period as may be fixed by SBA, private funds on a dollar-for-dollar basis up to $700,000 for each company formed, through the purchase of subordinated debentures, to the extent necessary funds are not available from private sources on reasonable terms. These debentures are subordinate to any other obligations issued by a company, and are considered as part of such company's paid-in capital and surplus for purposes of the minimum capital required under the Act for formation of an investment company and for other specified purposes.

Borrowing power.—Small business investment companies are authorized to borrow money from private sources under such conditions and subject to such limitations and regulations as are prescribed by the SBA.

To encourage the formation and growth of these companies, the SBA is authorized to lend them money on terms and at a rate of interest set by the SBA, through the purchase of their obligations and to the extent necessary funds are not available from private sources on reasonable terms. Such SBA assistance may be provided either directly or through participations with banks or other lending institutions on an immediate, deferred or guaranty basis. The amount the SBA may so lend (or commit to purchase such obligations) and have outstanding to any company may not exceed $4 million or 50 percent of the paid-in capital and surplus of such company, whichever is the lesser. The subordinated debentures of a company which are purchased by the SBA are, for purposes of the 50-percent limitation, treated as part of the capital and surplus. This limitation on the amount the SBA may lend to an investment company is to prevent such companies from serving merely as intermediates in the disbursement of Government funds to small business concerns. The SBA funds advanced to the small business investment companies are to encourage and facilitate the formation and growth of such companies. Ultimately, the major portion of their funds are expected to come from private sources.

Equity capital for small businesses.—Small business investment companies are authorized, in cooperation with other investors, to provide equity capital to small business concerns under such terms as the companies fix under SBA regulations.

Before an investment company provides equity capital, it may require the small business concern to refinance its outstanding indebtedness so that the investment company is the only holder of indebtedness of such concern. Furthermore, to protect the investment company, such small business concern may be required to agree not to incur further indebtedness without approval of the investment company.

Whenever an investment company provides capital to a small business concern, such concern may purchase stock in the investment company in an amount up to 5 percent of the amount of the capital provided, as established by SBA regulation.

Loans to small-business concerns.—Small business investment companies are authorized to make loans "of such sound value, or so secured, as reasonably to assure repayment" to small-business concerns. These loans may be made directly or in participation with other lenders, incorporated or unincorporated. The maximum interest rate on such loans is to be set by the SBA. The maximum maturity of such loans is set at 20 years, but an investment company may extend the maturity of a loan for an additional 10 years if such extension will aid in the orderly liquidation of a loan.

Without approval of the SBA, the total amount which a small business investment company may lend to or invest in a single small-business concern may not exceed 20 percent of the combined capital and surplus of such investment company. Subordinated debentures purchased by the SBA are treated as part of capital and surplus for purposes of the 20-percent limitation.

Exemptions from securities acts.—The Securities and Exchange Commission is granted the authority to exempt securities which are issued by small business investment companies from the regulatory provisions contained in the Securities Act of 1933 and the Trust Indenture Act of 1939, if it finds that such exemption will not jeopardize the protection of investors or the public interest.

The Act also provides a specific exception from the Investment Company Act of 1940 for small business investment companies, releasing them from the three-to-one asset coverage in connection with borrowings. The SBA may prescribe limitations on borrowing by small business investment companies. No definite debt-to-capital ratio is prescribed in the Act because of the experimental nature of the program. By regulation, SBA has authorized a 4-to-1 debt-to-equity ratio for SBIC's.

SBA can suspend licenses and issue cease and desist orders. Further, after court action, SBA can terminate a license.

SBA LOANS TO STATE AND LOCAL DEVELOPMENT COMPANIES

The Act recognizes that State and local development companies can play an important role in meeting the needs of small businesses for long-term credit.

Section 501 authorizes interest-bearing loans by the Administration to State development companies to assist in carrying out the purposes of the Act. The amount of such a loan shall not exceed the total amount borrowed by the company from all other sources. Unless waived by the Administration, such loans must rank equally with those loans from other sources having the highest priority and made to the company subsequent to the enactment of the Act.

Section 502 provides for interest-bearing secured loans by the Administration to both State and local development companies for site acquisition and plant construction, conversion, or expansion. Such loans may not exceed $350,000 and the proceeds must be used solely to assist an indentifiable small business concern, and for a sound business purpose approved by the Administration. They may be made directly or in cooperation with banks or other lending institutions. Participation may be on an immediate or deferred basis and SBA's share may not exceed 90 percent of the balance outstanding at the time of disbursement. The term of such loans may not exceed 25 years, except that the Administration may extend or renew for periods not exceeding 10 additional years where such extension or renewal will aid in the orderly liquidation of the loan.

TAX PROVISIONS

Taxpayers investing in the stock of small business investment companies will be allowed an ordinary-loss deduction rather than a capital-loss deduction on losses arising from worthlessness or sale of such stock. Small business investment companies will also be allowed an ordinary-loss deduction, rather than a capital-loss deduction, on losses sustained on convertible debentures, including stock received pursuant to the conversion privilege.[31] The loss

---

[31] Sec. 304 of the Small Business Investment Act of 1958 was amended in 1960 to permit SBIC's, under SBA regulations, to accept securities other than convertible debentures in exchange for equity capital supplied to small concerns. However, only convertible debentures and stock acquired by exercise of the conversion privilege are specifically covered by sec. 1243 of the Internal Revenue Code.

deduction will include losses due to worthlessness as well as those arising from sale or exchange of the security.

Such companies will also be allowed a deduction of 100 percent of dividends received from a taxable domestic corporation rather than the 85-percent deduction allowed corporate taxpayers generally.

Section 542(c)(8) of the Internal Revenue Code of 1954 qualifiedly exempts small business investment companies from the personal holding company surtax.

Acting under its administrative authority, the Internal Revenue Service has given SBIC's a qualified exemption from the surtax on accumulated earnings and has authorized a bad-debt reserve equal to 10 percent of outstanding loans.[12]

---

[12] See p. 14, supra.

SMALL BUSINESS PROCUREMENT CONFERENCES

By Staff Members of

SELECT COMMITTEE ON SMALL BUSINESS UNITED STATES SENATE

with

REPRESENTATIVES OF SMALL BUSINESS

NOVEMBER 15, 1965—SHREVEPORT, LA.
NOVEMBER 16, 1965—BIRMINGHAM, ALA.
NOVEMBER 18, 1965—JACKSONVILLE, FLA.

Printed for the use of the Select Committee on Small Business

U.S. GOVERNMENT PRINTING OFFICE
58-119   WASHINGTON : 1966

1:

d

sa

re
d

sn

h
a
—

FOREWORD

It continues to be the policy of your committee to maintain a constant, close relationship with individual small businessmen as an essential to a full appreciation of the needs and problems confronting small entrepreneurs generally. To this end, your committee directed its staff members to conduct a series of conferences with representative groups of small businessmen in Shreveport, La., Birmingham, Ala., and Jacksonville, Fla. Conferees were selected with the assistance of the chambers of commerce in the three cities, and, in Birmingham and Jacksonville, of the district offices of the small Business Administration.

In an informal setting, participants were encouraged to bring to light and discuss problems arising in the course of doing business under Government contracts either as a prime contractor or subcontractor and to express their views on any serious problems presented to the small businessman as a result of requirements placed on him and his business by the Federal Government.

The following is a transcript of these proceedings.

JOHN SPARKMAN,
Chairman, Select Committee on Small Business, U.S. Senate.
FEBRUARY 21, 1966.

1
de
sa

re
de

sn

ha
ar

CONTENTS

CONFERENCE DATES

SMALL BUSINESS PROCUREMENT CONFERENCES

MONDAY, NOVEMBER 15, 1965

U.S. SENATE,
SELECT COMMITTEE ON SMALL BUSINESS,
Shreveport, La.

The staff conference met, pursuant to notice, in the offices of the chamber of commerce, at 1 p.m.

Present: William T. McInarnay, counsel, and E. Wayne Thevenot, professional staff member, Senate Small Business Committee (presiding).

Also present: Richard Thevenot, public and governmental affairs director, chamber of commerce, Shreveport, La.; and representatives of small businesses in the area.

Mr. DICK THEVENOT. Gentlemen, I called you on the telephone the other day about the Select Committee on Small Business, and these two gentlemen are here from Washington, representing the committee. They do not propose to bring any specific solutions to your problems but they do wish to let you voice your opinions as to what can be done for the small businessman. They are looking into how some of your problems may be eliminated and what some of your problems are.

Mr. McInarnay is the committee counsel.

My brother, Wayne Thevenot, is a professional staff member of the committee.

These gentlemen will discuss the purpose of the meeting.

Mr. WAYNE THEVENOT. Mr. McInarnay and I represent the U.S. Senate Select Committee on Small Business, which is chartered by the Congress to deal with the problems that face small business and to oversee the Federal Government's role in matters affecting the small business community.

We are not a legislative committee. Bills pertaining to small business are not referred to us for committee action. We do have a great deal of influence in connection with the Federal Government's actions which affect small business.

This conference, which is to be one of a series of meetings, results from the belief on the part of members of the committee, specifically Senator Long and Senator John Sparkman, who is chairman of the Senate Small Business Committee, that it would be of great benefit to planning future committee action if the staff could sound out the thinking of small businessmen themselves—the people who have to deal with the day-to-day problems in the business world.

They thought it would be helpful if the staff members could get as close to these people as possible, listen to their problems, and hear their suggestions. This is the first stop in a three-stop trip through the South. From here we are going to Birmingham, Ala., and Jacksonville, Fla., for similar conferences in these cities.

We hope to have a fruitful meeting with you gentlemen. You were carefully selected as representative of small business in Shreveport and the surrounding area. We hope you will be able to give us some new insights which we can follow as guidelines for future investigations, and give some direction to our continuing efforts on your behalf.

Mr. McInarnay, you may want to add something.

Mr. McINARNAY. I will say this: this type of approach to the American small businessman is somewhat new to the committee.

Senator Sparkman has been chairman most of the 15 years of the committee's existence, and Senator Long is the ranking majority member, and they are intensely interested in the problems small businessmen face.

We have made various visits to many places in the United States, often to Army bases and military bases where they do a heavy load of Government contracting. The idea of going out into the cities of the country and sitting down with businessmen and getting from them, firsthand, the problems they experience in doing business is somewhat unique in the history of small business.

The committee, as a whole, is intensely interested in this effort and anxious to find out what can be developed in the way of expanding our thinking on the problems you face.

The Small Business Committee is a different animal from the Small Business Administration. The Small Business Administration is an agency of the executive branch of the Government. It is the agency that counsels small business. It renders management assistance. It helps with Government contracting as it pertains to small business. It is heavily involved in small-business financing in a number of ways.

Our committee is not a part of the executive branch of the Government. It is part of the Congress. It was chartered to investigate the problems of American small business. Those are the exact words in the resolution. We have broad authority and responsibility in this area.

One of the principal functions of the committee is contained in the Small Business Act itself, which says our committee is to survey and look over the accomplishments of the Small Business Administration and be sure their activities are best geared to small businessmen.

I think it should be stressed, with importance, that you understand what your goal is to be. In a sense, you represent all the small businessmen in Louisiana and the entire country. Obviously, we cannot get around the entire country but we hope to get enough of a cross section by listening to the small businessmen discuss various problems and make various recommendations so that we will be able to come up with a good overall view.

What you have to say is extremely important to us. I wouldn't be concerned if you find one person talks about something you want to talk about because the very duplication of the particular idea would have some weight and merit in our consideration.

Would you like to go on with the format?

Mr. WAYNE THEVENOT. We have reserved the area to be covered by this discussion to two broad categories. One, Government procurement. This is doing business with the Government under Government contracts. If any of you are doing business with the Federal buying agencies, you know of the myriad problems inherent in this.

The other area we would like you to cover is what problems face small businesses as a result of the requirements placed on them by the Federal Government. By this we mean difficulties in meeting reporting requirements under the wage and hour law, the requirements of the Census Bureau, the Internal Revenue Service—any of these forms or reports that are required of you by the Federal Government.

It would be a great help to the orderly presentation of the record if you would first give us your name, the business you represent, who you do business with, and give us some idea of the size of your business. After everyone has been introduced, we will go back and let each of you make whatever statements you would like in connection with your various problems and present any recommendations you might have.

Mr. A. I am president of the AA Co.[1]

Mr. WAYNE THEVENOT. What type business is this?

Mr. A. Mainly oilfield supply business.

Mr. WAYNE THEVENOT. Mr. B?

Mr. B. I am in the laundry and uniform service and we supply both laundry service and some uniform service to some Federal Government agencies.

Mr. WAYNE THEVENOT. Not the uniforms themselves?

Mr. B. These are workmen's uniforms, not the Army or Air Force or Navy uniforms.

Mr. WAYNE THEVENOT. Mr. C?

Mr. C. I am treasurer of the CC Hardware Co., a wholesale hardware concern.

Mr. WAYNE THEVENOT. Mr. D?

Mr. D. I am with the DD Co. We do sell the Government sometimes.

Mr. WAYNE THEVENOT. Mr. E?

Mr. E. I am vice president of the EE Co., primarily electrical contractors and retail supplies.

Mr. WAYNE THEVENOT. Mr. F?

Mr. F. I am in the commercial job printing business, representing the FF Printing Co. I am also a member of the Legislature of the State of Louisiana.

Mr. WAYNE THEVENOT. Mr. G?

Mr. G. I am manager of the GG Electrical Association.

Mr. WAYNE THEVENOT. Mrs. H?

Mrs. H. I am president of the HH Electric Motors. We are rebuilders of automotive parts and sell to automotive supply houses.

Mr. WAYNE THEVENOT. Mr. I?

Mr. I. I am president of the II Corp., department stores.

Mr. WAYNE THEVENOT. Mr. J?

Mr. J. I am president of the JJ Co., a Chevrolet dealership.

Mr. WAYNE THEVENOT. In keeping with our orderly procedure, Mr. A, do you have any statements you would like to make or do you have any views you would like to bring out?

Mr. A. Nothing at this time.

Mr. WAYNE THEVENOT. Mr. B?

Mr. B. I would like to wait and give my time to Mr. C.

[1] Identities of participating businessmen at Shreveport conference concealed, at their request.

Mr. C. I don't have all that much to say. Are we speaking only about our business relations with the Federal Government and the agencies thereof?

Mr. WAYNE THEVENOT. Your business with everybody. We would welcome any problems you may have in doing business with the Government.

Mr. C. Is this a gripe session?

Mr. WAYNE THEVENOT. Certainly, gripes may be a part of it.

Mr. McINARNAY. We will welcome your gripes and also welcome any particular recommendations you might have.

Mr. C. Some of these problems I have here are probably common with everybody in here.

The first is we now have become tax collectors for too many different taxing agencies. It has become very onerous and we are having trouble keeping our customers happy because they blame us for collecting taxes. It is not only Federal taxes but State taxes too.

The Louisiana Legislature imposed a sales tax on wholesalers making sales to retailers and that has been a tremendous headache. That, together with these other taxes for the State of Louisiana and the Federal Government, we are now collecting social security taxes, State income taxes, and also Federal income taxes—collecting State income taxes for Louisiana and Arkansas, and we are paying unemployment taxes on our payroll for Louisiana, Texas, and Arkansas and the Federal Government. We are also collecting the State sales tax, as I said. Those are the main taxes we are collecting.

The sum of all these taxes represents a real substantial bookkeeping problem and also a public relations problem with our employees and customers. For a small concern that is not heavily computerized, we think it has become a substantial problem in our operation, and any assistance that can be given to us, either at the State or Federal level, would be a help for us as small business people.

Mr. McINARNAY. Do you have any estimate of the amount of man-hours and money it costs you to collect these various taxes?

Mr. C. I daresay, in the aggregate, it probably takes one full-time person doing nothing but that, although we don't have anybody in that category. We have a number of people that work at it from different angles.

In our company, which employs between 45 and 50 people and with traveling outside salesmen in a 3-State area, that would be 2 or 2½ percent of our personnel engaged full time in this business of paying taxes and making up reports and writing checks.

Mr. McINARNAY. You might be interested to know there has been an awful lot of pressure from the Congress to the executive agencies, particularly to the Revenue Service, to decrease the requirements of reporting, particularly on small businessmen.

From the survey that Mr. Thevenot and I read on the way down here from Washington, it seems that the biggest problem is the form 941, the social security form which is required quarterly, and a lot of businessmen believe this should be put on an annual basis. Others have said: "Why don't you let us give you a declaration of how much we paid and let the employee himself be responsible for the tax?"

There is a Federal Reports Act which was passed in 1942, which many people would say hasn't been tremendously effective, but lately it has because they have cut down on a number of reports.

I want you to know there is pressure building up in Congress principally through the work of a subcommittee of the House of Representatives to decrease this requirement.

Mr. WAYNE THEVENOT. This is part of a broad study being done by the Post Office and Civil Service Committee of the House.

Mr. C. One of the most onerous reports has been from the Bureau of the Census. It is almost impossible for us to make out an accurate report.

Mr. DICK THEVENOT. There is a bill to be considered during the next Congress to have a census every 5 years instead of every 10 years.

Mr. WAYNE THEVENOT. This is a problem which has been given a great deal of attention.

As soon as President Johnson came into office he issued a directive to the Bureau of the Budget—which is the coordinating arm of the Federal executive branch—to completely review all of reporting requirements made on the business community. This directive has resulted in a tremendous number of forms being eliminated. The Bureau of the Budget now oversees every new form that requires more than 10 respondents.

If a branch of one of the executive departments comes out with a form that touches more than 10 respondents this has to go before the Department Review Board and goes before the Board of the Bureau of the Budget. Any new form has to stand a test of a great deal of justification.

There is considerable emphasis being put on this. Not only does it cost the Federal Government an awful lot of money but, as you say, it puts a burden on the small businessman who is not equipped with manpower and finances to make out all these reports.

Mr. C. Speaking of burdens, I understand there is legislation which did not get through this session but may get through next time to increase the minimum wage from $1.25 to $1.75.

I have written both our Senators and Congressmen about this legislation. This is about a 40-percent increase in payroll. It will probably be 40-percent increase across the board over a period of 3 years and that amounts to about three times what we have left after taxes—that increase in payroll would amount to what our little company has after taxes.

We think that would just about be the coup de grace if that legislation is passed for people in our line.

Let us pass on to somebody else.

Mr. D. One of my problems is the system of communications from the higher level to the lower.

Publications come out, particularly referring to the wage and hour board. They have men that come to our place spasmodically and check and every time they will come up with, "Didn't you know?" And say, "Read this." They will hand you a big thick publication and I am not fixing to read it. We have many more things we have to do.

We need some sort of simplified communication, which is necessary in every organization, as far as getting work done.

They will make a check on us and they will find a difference of a minute nature—talking about the wage and hour board—and the small businessman will pay it because he doesn't have the time to check on it.

We definitely need a system to keep us informed as to what we have to do.

Talking about this census report, I have thrown the thing in the trash and they keep writing. So far I have gotten away with it. There is a limit to what we can do. I am president of the DD Co., Inc.

Mr. McINARNAY. Do you have any ideas as to how communications might be improved?

Mr. D. Yes. They seem to be able to write about every report. At least, they can keep it to simplified English so we can understand what we are reading and know what we are doing. If we can keep it in a simplified form it will keep us abreast. Until we can get some sort of simplified form, we have to wait until it is brought to our attention by somebody else.

Mr. McINARNAY. In other words, you feel the agency bringing about the change should be responsible to get the information to you in the simplest possible way?

Mr. D. Yes. They don't mind writing us about flowers, or something like that, but when it comes down to the basic thing, they will say, "Didn't you know?"

Mr. McINARNAY. Other than the forms that they give you, which are very thick and complicated, don't you now receive any communications from the various agencies?

Mr. D. None whatever. The next time I look at the man, he will make a demand and I will sit down with him.

The last time the gentleman said I had to do it at that very moment and I was about to go to lunch and I told him that I wasn't about to read this booklet at that very moment and that he didn't have that prerogative, and from then on I have had a complex for these people.

I know the job must be accomplished. The agency must be there and there is a reason for its creation. But, on the other hand, we have little enough privileges left in our organization and I believe if we could be informed in some simplified way we could be abreast and cognizant of what is expected of us and not some upstart coming in and saying, "Didn't you know?"

Mr. McINARNAY. To what extent do you have difficulties with the individuals involved who have this responsibility to come to you?

Mr. D. We are at the mercy of the individual who walks in the door. The interpretation he gives to us, in many cases, would not be correct.

As a small businessman, you do not have time to go back and make a complete check. If it amounts to a few dollars, you pay it and get it out of the way, but it always sticks in your craw.

Mr. McINARNAY. The Department of Commerce puts out a publication—I know it lists all the contracts the Government puts out. It is called the Commerce Business Daily. It seems to me something like that would be directed to businessmen all over the country and would be an informative document.

Mr. D. That's right. It would keep us abreast of what is going on.

Like the other gentleman just mentioned, the minimum wage is going to eliminate the small businessman to some extent. This is one of my major problems—let me know before they walk in the door instead of waiting for you to come in. This has not happened on only one occasion. There have been several occasions similar to this.

Mr. McINARNAY. I wonder if any of these problems have affected any of you gentlemen? If they have, please feel free to join in.

Do you have any other particular areas?

Mr. E. Mr. C. mentioned some of mine.

Are we at liberty to discuss Government contracts?

Mr. WAYNE THEVENOT. Very much so, sir.

Mr. E. In fact, the job is in progress now. It was a competitive job. It is under the Navy at Barksdale Field. A typical example written in the job is that the maximum you would be allowed is 10 percent on your labor, 6 percent on your overhead, and 5 percent for profit. In any electrical contractor's business in this area, and probably anywhere in the United States, the labor is over 10 percent. There is no way you can break even at 10 percent. I would say a minimum of 13 percent, which means you automatically lose 3 percent in changes.

Things like that written in specifications—I don't know whose responsibility it is, but there is no way that a man who bids on a highly competitive job and is awarded the job and there are change orders, he is going to lose. On small amounts, the contractor just forgets about it. He will lose money by the time he gets into the paperwork.

Mr. WAYNE THEVENOT. You are talking about excessively restrictive specifications?

Mr. E. I don't know where they obtained 10 percent on the labor charge.

Mr. WAYNE THEVENOT. Are you talking about negotiated contracts?

Mr. E. This is a contract which is existing and if you have a change order, like you have on all jobs, you would be allowed 10 percent on your labor. There is no way you can break even.

Mr. McINARNAY. You won the contract originally by sealed bid?

Mr. E. Yes.

Mr. WAYNE THEVENOT. This is written in the specifications?

Mr. E. Yes. This is in progress at this time.

Mr. WAYNE THEVENOT. This precludes you from actually doing much negotiation.

Mr. E. If it was me, I would go ahead and do it and forget about the charge because you would be better off dollarwise not mentioning it. There was a change for $3.85 and the man had to leave the office and go to Barksdale Field and we would be allowed 6 percent and it wouldn't cover the paperwork on a change order like that.

Lately, I have not been bidding these highly competitive Government jobs. One of the main reasons is that they have a person in charge of construction who knows as much about construction as I know about small business in Washington. It is usually a career man in the Navy or Air Force and he is not qualified to be a person in charge of construction, whether it be electrical, plumbing, or what have you.

Mr. WAYNE THEVENOT. This is the man who is inspecting your work?

Mr. E. Yes. In the majority of cases they have civilian inspectors and you don't have problems with them. It is usually a career man where you have your problems.

Mr. McINARNAY. Are they military or civilian people?

Mr. E. A lot of them are military. They are totally unqualified. They wouldn't know an I-beam from a T-beam. This is true with general contractors or subcontractors.

Mr. WAYNE THEVENOT. Where is the big difficulty with his changing things?

Mr. E. Usually, his inability to comprehend construction, as such. That is primarily all I have to mention other than what Mr. C hit on, and he hit pretty close to what I was going to say.

Mr. McINARNAY. The limitations placed on the overhead, profits, and labor in change orders, is that a standard clause?

Mr. E. Not always in this percentage; no, sir.

In all fairness, the Corps of Engineers—in past years I have negotiated with them on a time and material basis, which is cost plus, and we have been having very satisfactory arrangements on both sides.

Mr. WAYNE THEVENOT. This is a fixed-fee situation?

Mr. E. Yes. With the Corps of Engineers in Little Rock, we have had very little difficulty. When they write things of this character in the specifications, the person who is low bidder better be very cautious because the change orders will eat it up, and the change orders are bound to be there.

When they write in 10 percent for labor, 6 percent for overhead, and 5 percent for profit, there is no way to make it.

Mr. WAYNE THEVENOT. Is this an unusual situation?

Mr. E. I would not bid such a job as this. I am not involved in it.

Mr. WAYNE THEVENOT. You are talking about an experience you are familiar with?

Mr. E. Yes, sir.

Mr. WAYNE THEVENOT. This is the reason you didn't bid?

Mr. E. Yes.

Mr. WAYNE THEVENOT. Not only are there problems after you get the contract, but very often the Government is hurt by contractors not willing to get involved in this type of thing. This cuts down on competition.

Mr. E. There is one other thing that crossed my mind and it is a very delicate subject and I don't have a solution to it and it has to do with qualified people to do certain types of work.

For example, an Air Force official called me about bidding on an underground electrical system. I told him that there were some people that were qualified to do it. He asked who it was, and he said it was a new setup from Fort Worth and there would be three or four bidders who did this type of work. But when you ask a person who knows nothing about it and some local man bids low, he usually goes broke.

Mr. WAYNE THEVENOT. Was this a request for a proposal on bidding?

Mr. E. It was a request to see if we were interested in bidding this specific job.

The point I am getting at is to see if the firm is qualified to bid this particular type of work.

Mr. WAYNE THEVENOT. Of course, the responsibility is with the contracting officer to establish the competency of their bidders. I am sure that is what they attempt to do.

Mr. E. It is a delicate thing.

Mr. McINARNAY. Manufacturing, for example, in some products they have what is called a qualified products list and your product has to be on that list before you are eligible to bid.

Mr. E. I have heard something about it.

As Mr. Thevenot said, the responsibility lies with the contracting officer to decide whether an individual is the lowest qualified bidder and not just a low bidder.

I have no solution for it. It is a problem.

Mr. WAYNE THEVENOT. The Small Business Administration itself enters this field too by a certificate of competency program whereby a company bids on a job and if the company is determined by the contracting officer not to be capable of performing this contract, the bidder may appeal to the Small Business Administration. The Small Business Administration comes into his plant and makes a determination as to his capabilities with regard to facilities and financing. If he is found to be thus capable of performing the contract, he is issued a certificate of competency which is binding on the contracting officer. The contracting officer must award the contract to the low bidder.

Mr. B. They do this locally, and they investigate the plant and I think they use several agencies aside from the Small Business Administration. The Small Business Administration can come in and perhaps loan him the money to buy the equipment to perform the contract, but they do investigate it.

Mr. WAYNE THEVENOT. This is very often a thorn in the side of the Defense Department. They may determine a company, for whatever reason, not competent to fulfill a contract and the Small Business Administration says they are. It is binding on the contracting officer, and the Department of Defense, or whatever agency involved, has to award the contract.

Mr. McINARNAY. The Small Business Administration is proud of its record for having salvaged contracts where they may have been turned down.

Mr. WAYNE THEVENOT. They attempt, within limits, to help the business measure up. It has saved a great many small businessmen by being able to get Government contracts.

Mr. E. I wish there was some setup where they couldn't do that on the subcontracting end of the business.

Mr. B. I think maybe it is wrong in this respect for the Small Business Administration to come in. You might get a fly-by-night outfit to come in and bid a contract and the outfit goes to the Small Business Administration and gets enough money to compete against this fellow with Government money, which I am not sure is a good policy.

Mr. McINARNAY. There the man has to prove himself in more than one way. For example, in order to get that money he has got to have sufficient collateral and reasonable assurance of ability to repay. He has to prove technical competence. So that in those cases I would assume that the Small Business Administration thinks the man is well qualified except for the money problem.

Mr. F. I believe I could make a speech. It may take up so much time that I would rather hear from others and then come in later.

I do have some things which affect the morale of the business people. Being in politics myself, I can hear these things from the people. Actually, I can certainly sympathize with them and agree with them. The gripes I have heard are in my mind, and I have listed them here, but I would rather let someone else talk.

Mr. WAYNE THEVENOT. Mr. G?

Mr. G. I have nothing at this time.

Mr. WAYNE THEVENOT. Mrs. H?

Mrs. H. I agree with Mr. C about the reports. I have that pretty well whipped. I had to buy office equipment which would eliminate one employee. Of course, that was bad, but it helped me out.

Mr. WAYNE THEVENOT. This is what type equipment?

Mrs. H. Posting machines that would do the work. I took it over and did the work. We carry about 20 to 30 employees, but my main concern is the taxes heaped on me. I can't raise my prices and I am in competition even with General Motors and with these larger rebuilders, and you know how that is. They get their merchandise cheaper than I can get mine because I am small. That is one of the main things.

In January I have got to go up on my prices because of the social security going up so much as it has. I have held it down for 3 years now. We use a lot of copper and it has gone up about 7 percent and I have got to make a profit and have to compete with large companies.

Mr. WAYNE THEVENOT. Do you have the problem of competing with companies—for instance, General Motors—with companies affiliated with General Motors?

Mrs. H. Yes. They put out rebuilt generators and I don't think they have gotten into starters yet.

Mr. WAYNE THEVENOT. This dual distribution is a problem Senator Long has been deeply involved in for a number of years.

We have one of our staff members working practically full time on the problem of the small man in competition with the large manufacturer that has retail outlets all over the country.

Mrs. H. Volume buying is hurting a lot of small businesses.

I have also run into the same problem that Mr. D has in connection with getting a reply from the proper person in the Revenue Department in connection with excise taxes that we have to pay and I have written several letters to the Revenue Department and I still don't know what the outcome is.

Mr. McINARNAY. What effect did the tax cuts last year have? Did they help to any extent?

Mrs. H. My employees ended up paying more and they have quite a gripe because I didn't take out quite enough withholding.

Mr. WAYNE THEVENOT. This is a one-time problem because of when the tax cut came about.

Mrs. H. I hope it is.

Mr. WAYNE THEVENOT. What effect has the excise tax had on your business?

Mrs. H. I don't know. I am still paying 8 percent for the new parts going in the rebuilt units.

I tried to get that situation straightened out with the Internal Revenue Department two or three times and I haven't heard from them.

Mr. McINARNAY. I suspect if you wrote a letter to Senator Long's office you would get an answer right quick.

Mrs. H. This minimum wage has affected us quite a bit.

Mr. McINARNAY. Mr. I.

Mr. I. I want to mention something about this minimum wage. We are operators of small stores and all except one or two come under the minimum wage. There are a lot of people in Louisiana and in other areas who operate four or five small general stores such as we operate and if they have to pay $1.75 they will have to close their stores because we can't afford to pay $1.75, because most of our people are inexperienced people and we can't pay it out of profit. You have to pay it out of capital and we are not about to do that and we will close.

I have had many people talk to me about it and they have asked me what I was going to do with my business.

It is like a man who operates a filling station. They claim because there are a lot of Texaco filling stations that they should be under the minimum wage. About 80 or 85 percent of the people are small businessmen or just working people and if I were a politician I would think about them because they are in the majority.

I have had people contact me about whether or not I would be interested in a certain location, but I am not going to do it as long as we are faced with $1.75 an hour. This is a serious thing for small retailers. We have telephone calls every week about a location in a small town. I don't even look at them because I couldn't afford to take it. In the past, I could afford to look at a store that would gross $200,000 or $250,000.

Another thing, just as fast as we can we are changing our stores to semiself-service and cutting down on our employees. With the prospect of a $1.75 minimum, it will put a lot of people out of work. In stores where we have four cash registers, we will change it to one and put it at the door and instead of employing six women, we will employ two.

Even S.R. Co. will not hire any more help than they have to at $1.75 minimum. They just don't need any more.

We will depend on the people that come in our stores to pick up their own merchandise. We can't afford to pay $1.75.

Another thing is the proposed increase in social security and unemployment compensation. I am not real familiar with this. I have a certified public accountant and I don't spend too much time worrying with it.

I ask myself who is going to pay that? It is going to be us. The taxpayer will have to pay it. This is an incentive for what we call the deadbeats to just work for a little while and get laid off and go for a year without having to do anything if this unemployment compensation is raised to 52 weeks. You wouldn't believe it if you knew how much of that is being done.

We work anywhere from 250 to 600 people, depending on the time of year. Those people say that they only want to work a few weeks and then start getting unemployment. They say that it doesn't cost us anything anyway. It is a moral thing. The people just don't care.

Mrs. H. A lot of housewives do that. They take a vacation on the money they get from their unemployment. I know this to be a fact because it happens in my place.

Mr. I. There isn't any housewife without experience that is worth $14 a day wrapping merchandise, and the same thing goes for the porters. When you have a porter working in your store, you have to point out everything he does just about every day. Is he worth $1.75? Is a housewife worth $14 a day that doesn't have any experience? This increase has to come out of profit, and whenever you buck a big competitor, who is not supposed to be represented here in this group, I can tell you now it is a real big problem and there is no incentive for a small businessman to try to expand his business knowing these things are against him. With these increases and these various tax structures it takes just about all the profit away.

If I were a politician, I would look a long time before I would increase the minimum wage from $1.25 to $1.75.

If they would come out to some of these small towns where small business is involved and find out what is going to take place, then I think they would be against it. The big stores are already paying the minimum because they can do it, and in that way it makes it easier to get help and they pay a little more than we do and get the cream of the crop.

I have had more than one small businessman say that he was going to close his business and go to work for one of the big ones. When he does something like that, he becomes a competitor for the other people looking for jobs. It means the small towns are getting smaller and the big towns are getting bigger.

We have many girls working for us in small towns that earn $250 a month. We also have the deadbeat type that work a while and draw unemployment and come back and work a while and go back on unemployment.

On this poverty thing—there are people looking for something like that and they don't want to work hard as long as the Government is taking care of them. These are plain facts.

You can't go to the big city and talk to the big politicans and find out these things and you can't find it out in Washington. All you have to do is go to Jonesboro, Arcadia, Minden, and De Ridder and walk up and down the streets and see what is going on and you will find out that what I am talking about is true.

In a little town of Hugo, Okla., a supermarket man told me that he surveyed the town with the idea of putting in a supermarket. He did some checking and found out that 65 percent of the people were drawing some sort of Government compensation—old age, unemployment, and various other things—65 percent of the people were living off the Government. It is not hard for me to understand why he didn't consider that for a supermarket. That town has already been through the wringer. There is no industry there and there won't be any. Those people are not in the habit of working.

I am not against the poverty program, but I am telling you what the small businessman is up against. We have 23 stores and we have investors looking for a return on their investment and when we talk about little towns they say: "Don't go there. You got to go where you can do enough volume to pay the minimum wage."

These are real problems that we, as small business people, have to face.

Mrs. H. We have employees who make $1.65 an hour. Every time the social security goes up or the witholding goes up it makes it hard on them and they want to make a living. They don't want to get on relief.

Mr. I. This is in the form of a gripe: I write to Washington quite a bit to Russell Long and Senator Ellender and Joe Waggonner and also Wright Patman. I know him. They will say: "They will take it under advisement."

That means "No" in my book.

Once in a while you will get one that will tell you he is already for it but not very many. Most of the time they will tell you how happy they are to take it under advisement, but to me that just means "No."

Mr McINARNAY. There are times, regrettably, where you are unable to help.

Mr. I. I understand that, but there is an answer to section 14(b) and he can say "Yes" or "No" and there is an answer to the minimum wage and he can answer "Yes" or "No." Joe Waggonner will tell you he is against it and some of the others will, too.

Mr. McINARNAY. You mentioned you were going into self-service anyhow?

Mr. I. I am buying that particular kind of fixture. However, there is nothing better than a woman waiting on somebody to make a sale.

Mr. WAYNE THEVENOT. Is this your reason for going into self-service?

Mr. I. There is nothing that takes the place of a saleslady who knows what she is doing.

Mr. WAYNE THEVENOT. The prospects of an increase in the minimum wage would cut you back?

Mr. I. I know I am going to do less volume. I know I am, but I also know I am going to have the payroll, too.

Mr. J. When I first sat down I wrote out a few notes and almost everything I have written down has been covered in some shape or form.

I am a Chevrolet dealer, and in this area probably a large Chevrolet dealer, but I am in a small pond compared to dealerships in Dallas, Memphis, New Orleans, and so on.

Mention has been made about General Motors in this meeting and I have no General Motors stock nor does the general confide in me when he goes up, down, or sideways in his price.

As a matter of fact, I sell General Motors products and I am still a small businessman because the general doesn't pay any of my expenses, nor does he subsidize me in any way. When I buy something from him it is cash as it leaves the factory gate and not on consignment or pay next month.

I am in as much a competitive small business situation as anyone in the room.

The No. 1 thing I wrote down when I first started making notes had to do with taxes. I have been in the car business 12 years, and in years gone by we used to figure our mechanics' wages on Saturday morning and pay them Saturday noon. This was 12 years ago.

Right now we have a National Cash Register machine and two ladies to run it so that we can do the accounting we used to do by hand with one lady. Granted our business has increased, but we have to cut off Thursday night at midnight in order to pay Saturday noon and work like the devil to get the things out on Saturday noon. We have to figure all the deductions and the taxes for the State and the Federal Government and all that has to be done so that we can pay our people by Saturday noon.

I have talked to other dealers in the Southwest part of the United States and they cut off around Wednesday noon or Wednesday night so that they can pay on Saturday, and in some cases they cut off Saturday so they can pay the following Saturday.

Let me give you another example of the problems we face: We will get an application for a Federal job from some bureau. It might be in Washington or some place else. It will be on a former employee of ours and it takes my personnel at least 30 minutes to fill out the application on somebody who might have worked a short time 4 or 5 years ago. We put their name and social security number down and send it back to them with one or two other things we can remember, but it certainly is an involved form for what we are going to get out of it.

Twelve years ago we paid our starting workers in every department $35 a week. They worked 55 hours.

In the car business you have to stay open early and stay open late so you can service the customer when he has time to see you.

Arbitrarily, I went to the minimum wage myself because I figured I could command a higher quality of personnel by paying whatever the minimum wage was, although according to the law the car dealers are exempted.

Another reason, to be perfectly honest, why I went to the minimum wage because I was sure I would be under it sooner or later and I might have the advantage in hiring a better class of employee when it was an employer's market, so to speak, than to wait until I am forced into it and get the dregs or not get credit for having done anything the Government didn't force me to do.

If and when the time comes that $1.75 is the minimum wage—just this morning I was reading an automotive news report, which is the journal of the industry and it says the average dealer so far this year has averaged slightly more than 2 percent profit of the dealers reported on this national survey, whereas last year it was slightly less than 2 percent. As long as I can recall, dealerships have never made 2 percent profit on sales. When you talk about 2 percent profit on sales and you talk about 40 percent minimum wage increase, naturally, it means in a very short time everybody will go up 40 percent or some pretty good percent. Two percent and 40 percent of the largest expense that you have in your business or I assume anybody has in their business, does not jibe and there will be an awful lot of car dealers who will go out of business. Maybe the bigger car dealers in the bigger towns will survive. I think we will survive because we are in a bigger town where industry is growing.

But you take a little place where a car dealer is located and they are not getting any new industry and not getting any bigger and their population can't afford to pay the higher rates for servicing and parts, and so on, those are the ones that will fold, I believe.

If we are going to continue to increase the amounts we spend on individual employee benefits in the dealership—for example, Christmas bonuses or paid vacations or sick leave or major medical or the other fringe benefits which have come along in the little time I have been in the business and at the same time have big brother watching over you who says that you got to do this besides what you are already doing, you will very soon reach the point of no return. You have got to raise your prices. The public is either going to pay or the business is going to fold.

We talked about General Motors, and I would like to throw this in as a side shot. Maybe there are only a few giants in the aluminum and steel business, and maybe there are only a few giants in the car business. But when you are in a competitive business, and my business is competitive—Mr. Ford may not outsell me today but he might put me out of business via the Studebaker people.

Whatever happens in big business, whether we like it or not, affects us in a little business. I know my cost of doing business has increased and I don't see how big business costs have not increased.

The right-to-work law seems to me the wrong thing to have happen. in other words, I don't see that it is fair to legislate an organization into existence which should have to compete—a union—which should have to compete on its own merits.

If a union is good for employees in my business and I am not man enough or human enough or whatever it is to convince my people that I am a good man and I have to have somebody from out of town tell me how to run our organization, then it is my own fault. A union can come in and compete and be there. But for the Federal Government to tell my employees that all a union has to do is get in there one time and there is nothing they can do, then I don't think it is fair.

A new employee cannot go to work for me unless he joins the union and pays dues no matter how much they do good or how much they do bad for that man. That, to me, is absolutely wrong.

In my opinion, small business or large business or in between business—right is right and wrong is wrong and that isn't one of the right things.

I don't do business with Government agencies on a contract basis except once in a while we have supplied Chevrolet parts to Barksdale or the ordnance plant on a bid. Recently the procurement people at Barksdale put out a new set of rules. For instance, they might have a hundred trucks that are Chevrolet trucks and I feel that my genuine Chevrolet parts are as good as, and perhaps as competitive as anybody's. In order for me to bid on them, I must bid on running a store at Barksdale. In other words, physically have a man in a store at Barksdale to supply all the parts for all the brands that they have out there whether it be Ford, Chevrolet, Chrysler, or whatever it is. There is no way a Chevrolet dealer can be a Ford dealer at the same time. What happens is that I immediately back out of the bid based on the specifications being such that I cannot bid. I could, I guess, but if I am going to be a genuine Chevrolet dealer and back up my product I can't go into the off brand, or whatever you want to call it, and handle other merchandise.

Along comes a jobber who handles some other brand than Chevrolet parts and it might be as good as Chevrolet parts but it is never any better—the quality I mean—and he bids for this opportunity and the people who are capitalized and have the manpower and equipment to handle Chevrolet and Ford and Chrysler best are out of the picture.

There is no way that I can, in my opinion, bid on the stuff and, therefore, there are no Chevrolet dealers supplying Chevrolet parts to Barksdale.

Mr. WAYNE THEVENOT. What would you suggest as a remedy for that situation?

Mr. J. I would suggest we bid it for a percentage above or below the book value on specific brands or parts. In other words, if we can supply all the Chevrolet parts, let me bid on them. If you can supply the Ford parts, bid on them.

Mr. WAYNE THEVENOT: The Air Force wants to put in an office which keeps in stock parts to service all their vehicles?

Mr. J. That's right. They have done that for the last year and a half or two years, as I recall.

Mr. WAYNE THEVENOT: They have done it the other way?

Mr. J. Yes, and all of a sudden they came along with the store proposition on the base where you are stocking the material. As I understand it, you are not specifically bidding on any brand of parts. You are bidding on whatever you want to provide. It looks like it is not good business from the Government or taxpayer's standpoint or the public's standpoint.

Mr. WAYNE THEVENOT. Mrs. H, are you in the parts business?

Mrs. H. We are rebuilders. We sell to jobbers and they, in turn, retail them, but we do not go direct to Barksdale Field. They asked us to bid on a certain amount.

Mr. WAYNE THEVENOT. You could conceivably subcontract to the jobber?

Mrs. H. We would retail to them.

Mr. J. So could we. Since we are talking about Government and small business, there is nothing I know of which says this man has to buy genuine Chevrolet parts, or anything else, and I don't know that the quality is good. From the Government's standpoint, it is possible they could get rooked.

Mr. I. Do you represent Senator Long?

Mr. WAYNE THEVENOT. I am on the Senate Small Business Committee and I do a good deal of Senator Long's small business work.

Mr. I. You should be able to explain the advantage of 14(b).

Mr. WAYNE THEVENOT. No, sir; that is not within my purview at all.

Mr. McINARNAY. This comes under an entirely different committee.

Mr. WAYNE THEVENOT. Do you have any more comments?

Mr. J. It seems to me that certainly you don't want to get down to one General Motors or one United States Steel or anything like that. As long as there are three or four competitors who are at each other tooth and nail and if you can make the product better by doing it yourself on a small basis, which I think in a lot of cases you can, then we, the small businessmen, should survive.

But if we are doing something in an inefficient manner compared to large business, personally, I don't see anything wrong with large business as such. I don't think because large business can do it better and cheaper that it makes it wrong.

Mrs. H. I have to compete with them and the Government makes my taxes higher.

Mr. I. If they will leave me alone I will make it.

All I am asking is that they leave me alone. Don't legislate me out of business. I can't do it if they legislate me out of business.

I don't know how I am going to hire a tailor to measure men's clothes when I don't know whether it is going to be a woman or a man. In other words, a woman can sue me for not giving her a chance to measure men's clothing. I am endeavoring to create an application blank that will be acceptable to Uncle Sam and at the same time keep me out of jail. I don't think we will have a problem with this if they leave us alone. The fellow who wrote that doesn't know what he is doing.

Mr. B. I know how Senator Long feels about the minimum wage. We have about 200 employees and we employ semiskilled people. They are women that supplement the family income in most cases. We feel actually that the minimum wage law would deprive the small wage earner of the right to make a living. We won't be able to employ unskilled people at $1.75 an hour. We figure that with the gross income of our business, we would have to lay off about 40 people. We are paying over a dollar an hour voluntarily because we have a union and the lowest scale in the union is 65 cents. What we will be doing is raising the deadbeats by raising the pay because there wouldn't be any incentive. We do have girls working in our plant that earn $2 and $2.25 an hour.

My thoughts to Senator Long would be that this proposed minimum wage increase would be actually depriving low-wage earners of a living.

I would like to add one thing about the Government contracts. We have had pleasant working conditions with the Government in our contract work, and on occasion when we have run into problems with someone who doesn't know anything about the laundry business—it is always a career man in the service who gets his information from a manual—there is always a recourse to a little bit higher echelon where we find we have been given fair treatment.

Mr. WAYNE THEVENOT. Most of your business is under the small business set aside program?

Mr. B. That's right.

Mr. WAYNE THEVENOT. Mr. F.

Mr. F. The only thing I was going to say was in summation, but I believe you can perhaps get all of the unsatisfactory and unacceptable measures from the Federal or the State Government from the office accountants or the bookkeepers in small businesses because they are the ones who are fighting this problem constantly and daily. Naturally, they are calling it to the attention of management.

In the last several years, and you can hear it practically from anybody, and particularly small business people, that there is no more incentive in business—there is no more initiative by business people.

Just as was mentioned here a while ago, all of these broad regulations are destroying initiative and incentive, and I have heard small business people say it would be wiser for them to get a job somewhere and be relieved of all these regulations and requirements by both the Federal and State Governments than it would be to remain in business. Naturally, that isn't only demoralizing but it is destructive to business when you run small businessmen out of business and you are creating vacancies in all your buildings. That is taking money from the assessment rolls and the tax rolls. The fact that small businessmen are going out of business affects the Government, because it takes money for the Government to operate.

Because of the vast amount of paperwork, and I particularly know this as a printer, that is required of business today is so enormous that it requires additional employees and then it throws the management into almost an utter state of confusion. He doesn't know where he is. He has lost control over his business. There is no more personal authority on the part of management or the owner of a business as there used to be.

Just like Mr. I explained a while ago, he doesn't know how to go about getting an employee because of the fear of innocently violating some regulation of the Government.

Small business people, as well as anybody in business, want to cooperate with Government. I have seen it in my experience. They want to be sure they are doing it right but they have the constant fear of innocently violating some part of the form as required by the business people to be filled out.

Of course, with reference to taxes we had the withholding tax to come up in the State legislature. The State was suffering from lack of finances. The Governor appealed and everyone else appealed to the legislature to please put this into effect, that it would produce such revenue as the State needed for its services. I voted against it and I thought it was wrong and I never heard so much hollering from the people in Caddo Parish as I did from my own bookkeeper.

In addition to the Federal requirements of tax collections, it makes the burden considerably heavier when you have to collect State taxes also.

I have always heard about the specifications in Government bidding. The Government is my biggest competitor, but when it comes to receiving any specifications from the Federal Government, before I would attempt to read the specifications, much less attempting to comply with them and bidding on the job, I wouldn't make any money on the job after I got it by the fact that I would have to offset the time required in reading and attempting to follow the requirements of the specifications.

There is one thing that I think ought to be looked into and studied very, very strongly and that is a form of taxation that may simplify the burden of paying taxes by our State or Federal Government that is now being assessed upon the people. They have so many different taxes that are being paid, such as your unemployment tax and your workmen's compensation tax and social security tax and income tax and all the other forms of taxes we have. If there was some way somebody could come up with a good solution of paying one tax it would certainly simplify the burden. We are going to come up with more and more taxes and more different kinds of taxes. Who thinks of them, I don't know.

The Government is becoming so great and complex that it is working a hardship on the people who have to support the Government. There are experts in these fields and they have to come up with solutions, but I believe firmly that if we were represented—we who are in management—were represented by our accounting offices, you could get the story in a mighty complete form.

Mr. McINARNAY. Mr. F, you might have seen Senator Long on television yesterday where he explained his program for simplifying income tax forms. As chairman of the Finance Committee and with his ability to get various legislative programs, I would say it stands a very good chance, and it will greatly simplify an individual's difficulty in filling out income tax forms.

Mr. I. It seems to me that if we had 10 or 15 businessmen—not career Government men--they might be able to come up with a lot of simplified ideas which would save the Government a lot of money in having to handle all these forms that have to be sent in.

Mr. McINARNAY. There is an advisory board on Federal reports made up of businessmen all over the country—12 or 15 of them—which meet periodically with the Bureau of the Budget people. I assume they will be playing a more and more prominent role.

Mr. I. I haven't any gripe as far as the Government is concerned. I don't think the Government is doing anything dishonest. It just gets bigger and bigger and they don't know what else to do but send out more reports.

Mr. WAYNE THEVENOT. As of quite recently there is a great deal of work going on, not only in Congress, but in the executive branch to eliminate this. It is recognized as a tremendous problem.

Mr. McINARNAY. I haven't heard from Mr. A. Do you have anything to add?

Mr. A. I am in an ambiguous position. We hire less than 500 people. We are large in the amount of business we do. As far as profits go, we are a charitable organization. We are beset by all the ills outlined here today and probably some I don't know of.

We have legal counsel in 13 States and in Washington, D.C. When most of these things come up we refer it to accountants or legal counsel and go from there. What it costs us, I don't know. I think our comptroller figures 40 percent of our accounting procedure is keeping records for some Government agency, not only Federal, but State and city in making out reports as these gentlemen have outlined.

Mr. WAYNE THEVENOT: Mr. G.

Mr. G. Are you people making this swing through the South and then there will be other people coming here later?

Mr. WAYNE THEVENOT: This is more or less a pilot program to determine whether it will benefit the committee. It will possibly be expanded to cover representative communities throughout the country. It is an attempt to get the staff very close to the businessmen and listen to them personally to ascertain what problems they have.

It is difficult sitting at a desk in Washington to get a feel for what problems the businessmen are having. We handle case after case. These are the unusual problems and we are familiar with those because we handle them from day to day. But the feel of the business community is what we are trying to assay.

We certainly appreciate you gentlemen taking the time to come here and give us a very candid view of your business situation and problems.

Thank you very much.

(Whereupon the meeting was adjourned at 3:30 p.m.)

1

de
sa

re
de

sn

ha
ar

SMALL BUSINESS PROCUREMENT CONFERENCES

TUESDAY, NOVEMBER 16, 1965

U.S. SENATE,
SELECT COMMITTEE ON SMALL BUSINESS,
Birmingham, Ala.

The staff conference met, pursuant to notice in the offices of the Chamber of Commerce Building, at 1:30 p.m.

Present: William T. McInarnay, counsel, and E. Wayne Thevenot, professional staff member, Senate Small Business Committee (presiding); and R. H. Bartlett, Chief, Financial Assistance Division, and J. C. Barksdale, loan specialist, of the Birmingham regional office, Small Business Administration; and E. Cary Nall, department manager, Birmingham Chamber of Commerce.

Also present: J. L. Corley, Mrs. Gayle Roadruck, Dean Jemison, Alvin Klein, V. C. McNamee, Frank L. Salzmann, Jr., Carl Taylor, F. R. Hall, Oden Proctor, Hugh W. Mitchell, Frank P. Self, Forest M. Self, James B. Sykes.

Mr. McINARNAY. Wayne, do you want to start off by explaining our procedures and purposes to Mr. Corley and Mrs. Roadruck?

Mr. THEVENOT. As you know, we represent the Senate Small Business Committee, which is charged with the responsibility of looking after the interest of small business in this country and to oversee those functions in the Federal Government that are set up to assist the small businessman. Senator John Sparkman of Alabama, as you know, is chairman of the Small Business Committee. He has instructed the staff, rather than spend most of our time holding hearings in Washington, to get out and talk to small business people themselves in order to get as closely as possible a feeling for their problems and to solicit recommendations from them. The areas we are primarily interested in are Government procurement, both prime contracting and subcontracting, and the small businessman's problems arising out of requirements that the Federal Government places on them, such as the reports required from the Bureau of the Census, wage and hour laws, and the Internal Revenue Service, this type of thing.

We are taking a tour through the South right now and have been to Shreveport, La. Birmingham is our second stop. We are going on to Jacksonville for a meeting with representatives of small business. Our object is to listen to your problems and try to elicit suggestions from you as the basis for our future efforts on the committee.

Mr. McINARNAY. I think it might be worthy to note that the type of things that you bring up we will consider as representative of small businessmen's problems all over the country. This is in the nature of a pilot project.

We think what you have to say is terribly important, and even though you might both bring up the same thing, that would be important to us because it would indicate some breadth to the problems you

21

raise. We also solicit your recommendations on any particula₁ subject you bring up, because these, too, would be important for us to consider.

I think perhaps first we might ask Mr. Corley to just tell us what kind of business you are in.

STATEMENT OF J. L. CORLEY, SOUTHERN PRECISION, INC., BIRMINGHAM, ALA.

Mr. CORLEY. We are in a jobbing pattern business which was established 20 years ago this month. We started out as a three-man partnership and grew reasonably. I would say inside of 6 months we had a 12-man operation. That type of pattern work that we started doing was primarily metal patterns. There were jobbing pattern jobs in this locality that we are doing woodwork, but practically all, I would say more than 90 percent of all of the metal patterns that are being used in this area were being made in other localities, around the Cleveland or St. Louis area or Cincinnati or somewhere in that area, so it left the field pretty well open for us.

We encountered, of course, growing pains throughout the years. We now have an operation employing 73. I understand that the small business is considered 500 or under.

Mr. THEVENOT. It is different for different types of businesses.

Mr. CORLEY. Yes, sir. Well, we currently are probably about the fourth largest jobbing pattern shop in the United States. We do business in about 23 States.

We do about 10 percent of our business in the State of Alabama, about 20 percent in Texas, about 20 percent in Tennessee, and we do about close to 10 percent out in California.

It is primarily where there are large foundry areas that we do our principal business.

In recent years, we have been doing probably half of the business that we do in the State of Alabama with Hayes Aircraft, which comprises roughly 3 to 6 percent of our total business with Hayes Aircraft, and this year I anticipate it might run as high as 10 percent.

Mr. McINARNAY. This would put you in the category of defense subcontractor, then, with the Government work?

Mr. CORLEY. Yes, sir. We have supplied castings to Hayes-Huntsville branch. We supply some pattern equipment and castings to the Chrysler Corp., and others who are doing subwork up in the arsenal.

We have done some work from time to time for the arsenal.

The comment I had in mind was differentiating between Hayes-Birmingham and Hayes-Huntsville. It is Hayes International. We have no associations or dealings with other branches other than the Huntsville branch and the local modification center here in Birmingham.

Mr. McINARNAY. Now, that more or less summarizes the business you are in?

Mr. CORLEY. Yes, sir; we are primarily producing patterns, castings and machining operations, and sometimes submachining for Hayes International.

Mr. McINARNAY. Do you do any work directly for the Government?

Mr. CORLEY. We seldom have any opportunity to quote on them directly.

Mr. McINARNAY. Can you think of anything in any area that you would want to comment on?

If not, Mrs. Roadruck, would you give us a brief summary of the type of business that you are in and who you do business with.

STATEMENT OF MRS. GAYLE ROADRUCK, ROADRUCK TOOL CO., GUNTERSVILLE, ALA.

Mrs. ROADRUCK. We are in the machine shop business manufacturing custom-made metal parts and automated machinery, mostly prototype work,

We have been in business here in Alabama for 7½ years.

Mr. McINARNAY. How many employees do you have?

Mrs. ROADRUCK. We have 10 right now, and this hinges on part of our trouble. It goes up and down so. It fluctuates so.

Mr. THEVENOT. Most of it is prototype work?

Mrs. ROADRUCK. Yes, sir, and 4 months out of the year we may have 20 people work and then, boom, in 2 months we are without work and they leave our area and go elsewhere and it is hard to get them back.

Mr. THEVENOT. These are skilled employees?

Mrs. ROADRUCK. Skilled help. We use all skilled help and assembly help. Assembly help is very easy to get and very easy to train in our area. We do business with prime contractors in approximately six States. Ten percent of our business is out of the missile and rocket industry. About 90 percent of it is Government, subcontract work.

Mr. McINARNAY. Now, Mr. Corley, if you would begin just to tell us in your own words any particular things that you would like to touch upon. We welcome hearing from you.

Mr. CORLEY. Having very limited experience with any of the Government agencies other than through Hayes International and the others I have mentioned, I really don't know just what would be feasible.

We, once in a while, have inquiries from, say, TVA, or some other Government agency, and when you speak of problems, one of the biggest problems there is that we have encountered when we have these inquiries, there is a multitude of paperwork to fill out and it just looks like a lot more stipulations than would be worth the while to try to get into to get Government contracts direct.

Now, we have excellent associations with Hayes International. They need something and they call us in and we quote on it and we are able to work with a local organization and in the procurement division and also the engineering division, and, of course, being here locally and doing most of our work for the Birmingham center, it means that probably at least 90 percent of all of the work that we do that goes into the defense effort is through Hayes International.

Mr. McINARNAY. So that you find that for your business at least it is better to deal at the subcontract level, remain at the subcontract level rather than to——

Mr. CORLEY. I would feel definitely that way. At the present, just about 2 or 3 weeks ago, we had an inquiry from TVA asking for a quote on a pattern. They gave us no indication as to how much usage was going to be expected, who would make the castings, or what type of pattern equipment was needed, whether it would be for 1 casting or 50, or anything of that sort.

Mr. THEVENOT. There were just inadequate specifications to enable you to make a responsive proposal?

Mr. CORLEY. Yes, sir; and about four or five different pages to be filled out in triplicate along with this inquiry just for one pattern.

Mr. MCINARNAY. I would be interested to know whether, as a result of your extensive experience as a contractor, and your somewhat limited, and I take it, unhappy experience in dealing directly with Government agencies, if you have any recommendations as to how the Federal Government, the executive agencies that procure, for example, TVA, and the Army, etc., anything they might learn from the subcontractor that could be applied in dealing directly with these smaller businessmen.

Mr. THEVENOT. Perhaps, in the working relationship that you have with prime contractors as opposed to dealing directly with the Government.

Mr. CORLEY. Well, just use this TVA inquiry for an example. They were specifying a nihard casting. That is a trade name for a type of casting that is very brazen resistant, and I know of one foundry in this locality that makes that kind of metal. It is Thomas Foundry.

I called them to find out if they had had any inquiry for the casting, because it is quite important many times when you are quoting on pattern equipment to know who is going to run the casting.

Different foundries will have their preferences about types of pattern equipment, and I called them and they said that they had not had an inquiry, that in recent years they had found so much redtape to making the quotes that it didn't really concern them whether they got the inquiry or not, but if they did get it, they would be glad to cooperate with me and tell me what type of pattern equipment they would prefer if they got the casting.

I wound up calling two or three others I thought might be prospects, and I didn't find anyone that was particularly interested in getting the inquiry for that reason, the same type of reason.

Mr. MCINARNAY. Are there any other areas of concern that you would like to mention?

Mr. CORLEY. I don't think of any in particular right now. I would be glad to answer any questions you might have. Our time is getting close on the half hour. Perhaps Mrs. Roadruck should——

Mr. MCINARNAY. Mrs. Roadruck, how about you? Could you give us the benefit of your views on this?

Mrs. ROADRUCK. On subcontracting?

Mr. MCINARNAY. On that or any other aspect of doing business as a small business.

Mrs. ROADRUCK. Well, we have done them on about three prime contracts, and the paperwork was thick, but we had a lot of help from the ordnance on the packaging and the DD-250's, etc., and we got through it just fine, but then we got nothing else to bid on, and when we went to Atlanta to a—it was some kind of a meeting where they had a lot of forms to fill out to do contracting, and we were encouraged to do this by Mr. Turbeville in Atlanta, head of Decast, and everything that we got to bid on after all of these extensive forms we filled out were too large for our shop.

There are page after page of things that you are supposed to cross that your shop can do. We never got anything to bid on in our capacity. It was always over our capacity, or——

Mr. THEVENOT. Over your capacity?

Mrs. ROADRUCK. In size of machinery.

Mr. THEVENOT. You could have handled a smaller portion of the same?

Mrs. ROADRUCK. Oh, yes, and then there was a fact I was going to mention just now, and I forgot what it was.

Mr. THEVENOT. The paperwork you are talking about is required in order to be put on the bidder's list?

Mrs. ROADRUCK. Yes, sir; in order to get on the bidder's list, you have hours and hours of work on every procuring office, and, as I said, when you do get something to bid on, the paperwork is so thick to bid on it and most of it that we have gotten, all of it has been too large for us, but almost all of it someone else already owns the tooling and, therefore, your bid would be out of line completely, so why fill out the bid when it is obvious that expensive tooling is held by someone else, so we find that subcontracting for Hayes International, as for Thiokol, is simplified for us because they know and they have our machinery list just like we presented it to all of the ordnances, but they send us prints to quote on within our limit of machinery.

Mr. THEVENOT. You have to make out separate reports for each ordnance?

Mrs. ROADRUCK. Yes, sir, for every Air Force base.

Mr. THEVENOT. This could be coordinated, you think?

Mrs. ROADRUCK. Yes, sir. I have had not less than one dozen applications.

Mr. THEVENOT. Is this your suggestion?

Mrs. ROADRUCK. Yes, that it be combined into one, and whatever is marked on those pages should be adhered to.

Mr. THEVENOT. You are, of course, talking about one Federal Government?

Mrs. ROADRUCK. Yes, sir; that is true, but it is not combined into one and then if they would observe after they are filled out what you mark on there and send you what you could quote on, it would save a lot of time for the procurements, too.

Mr. MCINARNAY. Do you have any indication that there is work to be done in the area that you are qualified to perform that you are not getting an opportunity to bid on?

Mrs. ROADRUCK. Yes, sir.

Mr. THEVENOT. With the people to whom you have given information about your company?

Mrs. ROADRUCK. Yes, sir.

Mr. THEVENOT. You are not being invited to bid on projects?

Mrs. ROADRUCK. Yes, sir.

Mr. THEVENOT. You are a known subcontractor and a known producer in this field?

Mrs. ROADRUCK. Yes, sir, that is right. We have had visitors, you know, like Mr. Turbeville from the Air Force. We have had several surveys from various sources and we have been encouraged to find these things. We weren't really interested, but they insisted that we turn in our information.

Mr. THEVENOT. Very often when you are asked to do it you would be asked to bid on contracts beyond your capacity?

Mrs. ROADRUCK. Beyond the size of our machinery, yes, that is true. We get between 25 and 50 percent of all our business from Hayes-Birmingham and Hayes-Huntsville, and the balance of it comes from other places.

The only customer that we have in the commercial line is Goodyear for automating machinery, and, as I said, our help goes from around 25 down to 10 and sometimes it goes down to 5 when we do not get enough to bid on, and we are competitive, qualified, and passed all of the surveys.

Mr. McINARNAY. Is there any other area in Government contracting that either you or Mr. Corley want to touch upon?

Mrs. ROADRUCK. We do not get enough of it to know. We had two or three small prime contracts and filled them, and this was several years ago and never have gotten any more, and this came out of the Birmingham procurement before it was dissolved.

Mr. THEVENOT. And most of your competitors in this field are in the small-business category?

Mrs. ROADRUCK. Yes, sir.

Mr. McINARNAY. What procurement offices are letting contracts for your type of work?

Mrs. ROADRUCK. We have made application to Detroit—let's see, what is the name of it? They use this—it is not Detroit Ordnance. It is in Detroit, Mich. It is in the Army.

Mr. THEVENOT. Army Ordnance?

Mrs. ROADRUCK. It is an ordnance and then Middletown Air Force Base, and Warner Robbins and then in Atlanta with Mr. Turbeville.

Mr. McINARNAY. What is the name of that office; do you know?

Mrs. ROADRUCK. Yes, sir. It is the Air Force. It was changed last February. They have seven States under them now.

Mr. McINARNAY. Defense Contract Administration Service?

Mrs. ROADRUCK. Yes, sir. I cannot remember the exact name of the office, that they come out of.

Mr. McINARNAY. We will be glad to take up this point with the various offices you mentioned, the military services, and see why you have not been receiving bids.

Mrs. ROADRUCK. Bids within our range.

Mr. McINARNAY. Right. Now, is there any other area that concerns you generally as a small business that you would like to bring up?

Mr. THEVENOT. Are there problems in the way of requirements put on you by the Federal Government for reporting, for instance, with the Census Bureau or Internal Revenue Service or wage and hour laws?

Mrs. ROADRUCK. Do you mean by this census that——

Mr. THEVENOT. Part of their survey of business.

Mrs. ROADRUCK. It is once a year, isn't it?

Mr. THEVENOT. In some cases. In some cases, they ask for a little more information, depending on what the size and what the type of business you run.

Mrs. ROADRUCK. I just wonder if that is the form I am thinking of, but I don't like it.

Mr. THEVENOT. In previous conferences, we have had a good deal of discussion of what was considered by small-business people to be excessive paperwork and excessive reports required by the Government. I just wondered if you had a comment on that?

Mrs. ROADRUCK. I don't have any complaint about anything except the paperwork that is just less, and like quoting on things that you know you are not going to get.

Mr. THEVENOT. But this is on bids and specifications and this type of thing?

Mrs. ROADRUCK. Yes, sir.

Mr. THEVENOT. Mr. Corley, do you have any comments on this?

Mr. CORLEY. Well, we have grown up sort of getting used to this sort of thing. They have come on gradually over a period of 20 years; and when something new comes along, we have an office manager who is a pretty well qualified auditor. We send him to New Orleans once a year down to the seminar they have regarding the new regulations, and things of that sort.

He handles most of that sort of thing, and I have not heard any new complaints in that field. It is just one of those things that I guess it is necessary to a large extent in helping to make sure that everybody pays their fair share to help finance the tremendous load that is being carried with the Federal Government nowadays.

Mr. McINARNAY. Do you speak of the seminar in New Orleans, the Internal Revenue Service?

Mr. CORLEY. Yes, sir.

Mr. McINARNAY. Well, we want to thank you both very much for coming and expressing your views and helping us to establish a record here to be taken back to Washington.

Mr. THEVENOT. You have been very helpful in giving us an idea of where the thrust of our effort in the committee should be in the coming months.

Mr. CORLEY. I am just wondering, if it is not too personal, has your company ever applied for a small business loan?

Mrs. ROADRUCK. No.

Mr. CORLEY. We have not, either. We considered it one time, and we felt like that the amount of information required and perhaps some of the possible restrictions didn't warrant it.

We have been able to establish satisfactory credit with a local banking agency to be able to meet all our working capital needs, and I just wondered, you were asking about problems in particular. The biggest complaint that I ever heard about in the Small Business Administration is the loans when you got this to them, it seems like unduly restrictive and we considered it one time and we decided that unless it became necessary, that we just felt like that would not be the proper way to try to finance the expansion we had in mind.

Mr. THEVENOT. Are you referring to the amount of justification or collateral you had to provide in order to get a loan?

Mr. CORLEY. I think we have done that already. It seemed that the amount of information of the follow-up would have been considerably more for the Administration than it would have been for local banking facilities. We have had them ranging up as high as $92,000 with local banking at times, and I am sure that some small businesses would not be able to satisfy banking a lot of times where a Small Business Administration can feel justified when they go to the extreme limits of getting this information, but that has not been a real personal problem with us. That is just by way of comment.

Mr. McINARNAY. Do you have any particular thing that you would like to discuss about that? Mr. Bartlett is in charge of the

Financial Assistance Division of the local Small Business Administration Office and is here with us today.

Mr. THEVENOT. I am sure they would be very glad to help you in the future, should you have any problems.

Mr. CORLEY. We hope so. Our business is all locally owned and all six stockholders are active in the business, and we have tried to be conservative in keeping within our range, you know, to where it has not been necessary to get bailed out by the Small Business Administration.

There are some businesses who have tried to expand too fast.

Mr. THEVENOT. Mrs. Roadruck, have you gone to the Small Business Administration in an effort to be put on the bidding list?

Mrs. ROADRUCK. No.

Mr. THEVENOT. You know they have a very active program in this line. They will——

Mrs. ROADRUCK. I didn't know that.

Mr. THEVENOT. They can provide a great deal of assistance when you are seeking out new markets for your business, and I am sure they could be of great benefit to you.

Mrs. ROADRUCK. Where would you contact them?

Mr. THEVENOT. I am sure Mr. Bartlett could give you an idea.

Mr. McINARNAY. Where is your office located, Mr. Bartlett?

Mr. BARTLETT. 2030 First Avenue North, in Birmingham.

Mr. THEVENOT. I am sure they could have been of assistance to you. You might want to comment on that.

Mr. BARTLETT. Mr. Jim Allen is our procurement manager and assistant representative. He is the one you would get in touch with. Any problem you have in this area, he would be of assistance to you.

We will work with you in the Financial Assistance Division on any of your financial problems to see if we can be of assistance to you in that way.

Now, I would suggest that you drop us a line to tell us what your problems are, whether you are interested in a loan, either visit with us or write to us and tell us whether you are interested in a loan or in contract assistance or both, and we will be glad to furnish you with the information on both of them.

Mrs. ROADRUCK. Fine.

Mr. BARTLETT. I will say this: That our loan program has been considerably streamlined. In fact, it has been streamlined to the extent now that we are out of money.

The only way we can consider a loan at the present time is on our loan guarantee program. If a bank will participate with us on our loan guarantee program, then we can accept an application, but in the meanwhile, we would be glad to discuss your financial situation with you and to see if we can be of service to you in locating funds through private enterprise, through small business investment companies, or other sources.

Mr. McINARNAY. I think our time is about up. I want to thank you again for coming.

(Whereupon, Mr. Corley and Mrs. Roadruck were excused.)

Mr. McINARNAY. Gentlemen, I see that they have scheduled us so tightly, and to keep the schedule, we may not be able to cover as much as we would like. We are going to be here, I suppose, at least until 4:30, or so, and you can stay as long as you like. We will be in town until 10:30 tonight, so if you have anything that you would like to discuss further after this little brief session here, we will be glad to talk with you.

Let me just say very briefly that Senator Sparkman, as you know, is chairman of the Small Business Committee. We are both staff members—Mr. Thevenot and myself. Senator Sparkman asked us to come down. We have been to Shreveport, La., we are in Birmingham today, and on Thursday, we will be in Jacksonville, Fla., meeting with small businessmen. The conference in each instance is being set up by the chamber of commerce in each community.

Our purpose is to get down and talk to the businessmen in their own town and to learn directly from them anything that they may have on their mind in the problems that arise as a result of doing business directly with the Government or as a subcontractor, or in any particular problem that might arise in your business as a result of requirements imposed upon you by the Federal Government, so with that I think I will start with Mr. Jemison.

Will you briefly tell us the nature of your business, who you do business with, the number of employees you have, and then perhaps we might hear from you as to any points you particularly want to comment on.

STATEMENT OF DEAN JEMISON, LYNN MACHINE & MANUFAC-TURING CO., BIRMINGHAM, ALA.

Mr. JEMISON. Primarily, we are a small business, of course, and 95 percent of our work is Government subcontract work. We subcontract from Hayes here in Birmingham.

We contract from the Engel Shipbuilding Corp. in Pascagoula, Miss., and also from Defoe Shipbuilding, Avondale Shipyards, primarily as Government subcontractors.

We employ about 25 people, including out staff, overhead, etc.

At the present time, I have no questions until we get further into this thing about finances, etc. We find that our biggest problem is the technical end, meeting the Government specifications for requirements such as material, etc.

This is our biggest problem. Sometimes this problem creates a financial problem, but if you stay at it long enough everything irons itself out.

Mr. McINARNAY. Is this where you attempt to do business directly with the Government or in your subcontracts?

Mr. JEMISON. Just in subcontracts, primarily with Engel's.

Mr. McINARNAY. But these requirements are placed upon you not by the prime contractor but by the Government; is that correct?

Mr. JEMISON. Yes, sir. In order to sell it to the Government, and I speak of a nuclear-powered submarine, for instance, which is naturally for the Government, and the requirements on this thing is extremely strict.

Lots of times material is rejected just for being, say, 1 percent, the chemical analysis being 1 percent off, such as too high in one particular content, zinc, and what have you.

This is our biggest problem, and, of course, this creates financial problems sometimes.

Mr. THEVENOT. Your feeling is that these specifications are overdrawn for their intended use.

Mr. JEMISON. I wouldn't say that they are overdrawn. I would say that they have multiplied 10 percent, or I would say 10 times since the *Thresher* went down. I think this has created a problem.

Of course, it may be a justified problem. I am sure it is, but, nevertheless, we are stuck with it. We are not stuck with it. We quote on the work and we expect to do the work according to the specifications.

Mr. THEVENOT. Do you find the specifications clearly enough drawn so that they are sufficiently easy to understand?

Mr. JEMISON. If you can acquire the specifications they are there. Sometimes they are not as easy to get as you might like them to be. For instance, we had an ordnance group down here in town.

Mr. THEVENOT. This was prior to your bid?

Mr. JEMISON. At any time. You could call down there and you could call ordnance down here in town and ask for a certain military specification on any particular item, anything, welding, material, packing, shipping, anything that you wanted to know.

Now, they have cut that out. You have to go directly to the Naval Depot in Philadelphia, Pa., to get it.

Mr. THEVENOT. Are these security items?

Mr. JEMISON. No, not security items. This is anyone, any contractor can get it, provided he has a contract number, Government contract number.

Mr. THEVENOT. They are slow in coming, or don't come at all?

Mr. JEMISON. Well, they are not, you might—I wouldn't say they were slow. You have to go to Philadelphia for it, but it was right here on hand, you see, downtown where we could get it the next day through the mail or we could go down and pick it up immediately.

Mr. THEVENOT. But the Engel organization moved it to Philadelphia?

Mr. JEMISON. Now you have to go to Philadelphia to get the specifications.

Mr. McINARNAY. I think for the time being perhaps we will move on to Mr. Klein and then come back.

STATEMENT OF ALVIN KLEIN, STEEL COT CORP., BIRMINGHAM, ALA.

Mr. KLEIN. All right. Steel Cot Corp. is a metal fabricating and assembly organization. We press metal, stamp metal parts, and assemble, weld, et cetera, making either subassemblies or complete assemblies.

We are a small business ranging in the neighborhood of 10 to 25 people, depending on the volume of work.

We have some products of our own that I would say are subcontract work, probably consists of 75 percent of our business.

We have not been able to obtain any prime contract work for a number of reasons. The removal of the Birmingham Ordnance District is a hardship on us locally, but generally we don't get a chance to bid on too much.

We probably don't have our application forms into enough agencies, which we will try to take care of by sending them to the local office. I didn't realize that they had that phase of their work to help us along that line.

We have no particular problem in our subcontract work at all. I think everything is going along smoothly there.

Mr. McInarnay. I might mention that in addition to working with the local Small Business Administration office which we would encourage you to do, you can also write directly to Senator Sparkman and he will contact the offices and see that you are placed on all of the bidder's lists.

Mr. Thevenot. We on the committee have very close contact with all branches of the armed services, and with all civilian branches. We can find out through them very quickly who is buying your type item.

Mr. McInarnay. And have them contact you directly and see that you are put on the bidding list for these items.

Mr. Klein. We would write to the Senator directly?

Mr. Thevenot. Write to Senator Sparkman, chairman of the Small Business Committee.

Mr. Klein. Most of our subcontract work has been with Hayes locally and we find that their engineering department and all phases of their operation very easy to work with. In other words, we shortcut all of these difficulties we would have on a prime contract by working through them.

Mr. McInarnay. They are the ones that have the burden of dealing directly with the Government, which is the heavy responsibility off your shoulders.

Mr. Klein. Yes, sir; very true.

Mr. McInarnay. Mr. McNamee.

STATEMENT OF V. C. McNAMEE, SCHWACHA MACHINE CO., BRIGHTON, ALA.

Mr. McNamee. Well, Schwacha Machine Co. is primarily a tool and die shop and we do a certain amount of subcontract work. As Mr. Klein says, we prefer to work with people like Hayes. We are so small—we only have seven employees, so we don't have a staff to go through these specifications, packing specifications, material specifications, et cetera. Fifty percent of our business is subcontract work for various prime contractors with governmental agencies, and 50 percent would be civilian work.

As I say, you know it, we couldn't, when we find out the requirements, and all that, and then consequently we do business through Hayes and they assume all of that burden, and that is about it. Of course, there is one thing. I don't know whether Senator Sparkman is on to it or not, but I remember the National Association of Independent Businesses. They worked very closely with the Senator and I have got one thing there that would be extremely beneficial to small businesses, such as myself, and that is stopping some of the paperwork that we have to do in connection with the payrolls.

I think that one annual report—well, the W-2 instead of the quarterly returns. I mean, you are paying money every month on withholding taxes, and every 3 months, and in my case it is me making the return for the quarter, and then you have to balance it out at the end of the year anyway, so why not do it just once.

Mr. McInarnay. This is form 941, social security?

Mr. McNamee. Social security and withholding taxes and quarterly returns, and then the W-2 forms and the final recapitulation at the end of the year. That would cut out 75 percent of our paperwork.

Mr. Thevenot. Once a year, is this the major——

Mr. McNamee. It is something that has been brought up and it is in my mind.

I don't believe that the census comes once a year. It took an accountant to help me fill that out. As I say, you balance your taxes and you pay the Government your money every month.

I don't see the need or necessity for a quarterly return.

Mr. McInarnay. I think the National Federation of Independent Businessmen did a survey. You might have gotten a copy of that and the other people recommended that this form——

Mr. McNamee. Actually, I didn't think it up myself. That is where it came from, and I know Mr. Burger in Washington and Mr. Harder in California are very closely working with the Senator on that.

Mr. McInarnay. Mr. George Burger I know very well.

Mr. Thevenot. There is a great deal of effort going on in the Congress and in the executive department now to do whatever can be done about eliminating some of these problems and shortcutting this paperwork requirement. A great deal of progress has been made and I hope there will be a great deal more.

Mr. McNamee. That is one thing I was thinking about. As I say, it is something I have to do myself, so I am in favor of stopping it if I can.

Mr. McInarnay. Is there any other particular area that may not concern you so much as a Government subcontractor, but just as a small businessman that you would like to bring up?

Mr. McNamee. Well, another thing that irks me—to put it that way, and I am sure it does everybody else—this is not at the national level, but this is at the State and municipal level.

All of these various and sundry sales taxes and where you are doing business in one State and according to your terms of delivery, while you are doing business in, say, an adjacent State here and you wind up later on and find out that you are responsible for a sales tax in a different State because the product was delivered f.o.b. delivery rather than f.o.b. point of manufacture.

Mr. Thevenot. Mr. Jemison, you mentioned something about financing that you would like to discuss.

Do you have any comment on that?

Mr. Jemison. Well, not really. We have found Engel's to be extremely helpful in cases of financing a large contract.

Mr. Thevenot. Engel's?

Mr. Jemison. Engel's Shipbuilding in Pascagoula. For instance, when we have a job, say, $100,000 job, the material alone runs $25,000 or $30,000.

We have found Engel's to be more than helpful in purchasing the castings. In other words, we place the order with the company and Engel's will send a check payable to us, and this company for these castings which relieves us considerably on the financial end of buying and purchasing all of this material.

Most of it is a nonferrous and very expensive material, but like I say, they have been very helpful and, of course, Hayes Aircraft furnishes their own material.

Mr. THEVENOT. Helpful with advance payments on your contract?

Mr. JEMISON. It is possible, but we never have delved into that. Advanced payment is possible. Hayes, for instance, they will furnish their own material.

Therefore, you do not have to worry about chemical and physical analysis, material, and specifications, and so forth. About the only thing they require is that you send them a certificate of compliance saying the material they sent you is the exact material that you used to accomplish a certain job.

Mr. THEVENOT. This relieves you?

Mr. JEMISON. Yes, sir, any material, like I say, is usually a special material. When you are dealing with the Government, it is—95 percent of it is a special material.

Mr. THEVENOT. Do you have difficulty in securing this type of material?

Mr. JEMISON. Sometimes you do, especially in small quantities. Sometimes it is almost impossible to buy a certain material in a small quantity. Sometimes you might—sometimes you need 5 pounds of a certain material and they want a 500-pound mill run to produce this material. In other words, the mill is set up to make this particular material to a certain specification for 500 pounds, but we really don't have any problems as long as we are dealing with Hayes on this, because they furnish their own material, and Engel's, like I say, will help you out financially if you need to purchase a large quantity, a large amount of material.

Of course, progress payment is possible if it becomes necessary, but we have never tried it.

Mr. THEVENOT. Have you ever had occasion to go to the Small Business Administration for a loan?

Mr. JEMISON. No, sir, I don't think so.

Mr. McINARNAY. Is there any other area that any of you gentlemen would like to touch upon?

Mr. KLEIN. I would like to ask one question. This is something that is a personal business problem.

We have been trying to get some space in the Childersburg Ordnance Works which is under the Corps of Engineers out of Mobile, and we had a negotiation going on on a building which we wanted and need very badly and all of a sudden we find out that whole thing was tied up under some sort of a verbal option or something or somebody was apparently trying to put a chemical plant together and sell it down there.

We were wondering, my company was wondering whether the Senator would have any influence in finding out whether or not a building can be pulled out of that thing for the use of a small business company, such as our own, or would this be out of his realm?

Mr. McINARNAY. I think very definitely he could find out that information for you. I will recommend if it isn't too much trouble for you if you would drop him a letter. Would you do this?

Mr. KLEIN. I would.

Mr. McINARNAY. Write him directly and explain precisely what it is you want to know and he will find out for you.

Mr. KLEIN. Thank you. I hate to bother him.

I think a meeting like this is really a help to small businesses, for example, not knowing that the local office had the facilities to help us in obtaining work to bid on. This is something we should have known.

Mr. THEVENOT. The Small Business Administration offers a very wide variety of services to the small businessman, and I think their services are probably not widely enough known. For instance, there is the loan program, the loan guarantee program, and other financial assistance programs. There is help available to small businesses in getting on bidding lists and finding markets for their products. There is also technical and managerial assistance.

This can be very helpful to the small businessman. The Small Business Administration has experts in just about every field, who will come into your shop and give you an analysis of what they consider to be your problem and suggest possible solutions.

I would suggest that you take any problems you have to the Small Business local office and if they don't have the answer there, they can find it for you. They can be a great deal of assistance to you.

Mr. McINARNAY. Do you have that address?

Mr. KLEIN. Yes, sir; I have it.

Mr. McINARNAY. Well, we want to thank each of you for coming and giving us the benefit of your views, and if at any time you have any problems that arise in connection with your relations with either the Government contractor or any other aspect of the Federal Government and which the Federal Government is involved in, don't hesitate to write to the Senator. I don't want you to feel that you don't want to bother him, because that is what he feels he is there for and if we can help you, we certainly will.

Thank you so much.

(Whereupon, Mr. Jemison, Mr. Klein, and Mr. NcNamee were excused.)

Mr. McINARNAY. I have a report just handed me from Mr. Oden Proctor, director of procurement for Hayes International Corp. of Birmingham—a report on the period from January to September of 1965—which indicates that the total number of purchase orders made during that period was 46,620, for a total value of $14,774,239.

The number of purchase orders, out of the total, that went to small businesses was 37,803, or 83.2 percent.

As to dollar value, the amount that went to small businesses was $8,910,487, or 60.3 percent of total dollar value of their subcontracts, which by the way, is a very fine record in anyone's book for small business programs.

I think the record might indicate that Mr. Oden Proctor, the director of procurement for Hayes International, is in the conference.

Mr. Salzmann, would you begin by giving us an indication of the type of business you are in, how many people you employ, and who you do business with, and then go right into, if you will, any particular area you would like to cover.

STATEMENT OF FRANK L. SALZMANN, JR., MANAGER, UTILITY TOOL CO., BIRMINGHAM, ALA.

Mr. SALZMANN. Well, I have a machine shop, fabricating shop, and I employ approximately 20 people. I have been doing business with Hayes International, Fontaine, Parker, Aircraft, Gulf States Paper, and miscellaneous companies around town.

Mr. THEVENOT. How many people do you employ, Mr. Salzmann?

Mr. SALZMANN. Twenty; it is actually between 20 and 22. It varies in that area. It has just been built up. I started in June and I have been building up since then.

Mr. MCINARNAY. You started the business in June?

Mr. SALZMANN. Yes, sir. I have been doing a lot of Hayes International bidding and getting some and not getting some, but that is normal.

Mr. MCINARNAY. Is there any particular thing you would like to cover, any particular area?

Mr. SALZMANN. No. The only point I have tried to get in with, I would say, is the small business end of Redstone, and I have put in about—I would say about 12 or 15 bids and I have not heard whether I have got any or didn't get any, or anything, so it is a little disheartening when you do not hear, so that is about all I could say. My business has been very good.

Mr. THEVENOT. Are you being offered an opportunity to bid on the Redstone Arsenal projects as often as you think you should.

Mr. SALZMANN. I think about—well, I was trying to get in up there, trying to get forms and all for that and get them out right and think that is as big a problem as any. When they were down here at the fair, I had about 14 items I bid on.

Mr. THEVENOT. This is on prime contracts?

Mr. SALZMANN. I have not heard whether I got them or didn't get them, or kiss my foot or what. Maybe they don't answer back.

Mr. MCINARNAY. Do you know Jeff Darwin up there?

Mr. SALZMANN. No.

Mr. MCINARNAY. Jeff Darwin is in charge of small business in the Redstone Arsenal and can be very helpful to you.

Mr. SALZMANN. I went out here at the Small Business Office and they gave me some forms and I found out through Redstone that they are not the right forms, that I have to get another set. What was his name?

Mr. MCINARNAY. You should contact Jeff Darwin. He is an employee of the U.S. Army. He is a small business specialist in the Department of the Army at Redstone Arsenal.

Mr. SALZMANN. OK.

Mr. MCINARNAY. He has been active a long time and knows an awful lot about it, and I think he could help you.

Mr. SALZMANN. Other than that, I have had a very satisfactory business. I have been busy.

Mr. MCINARNAY. Well, that is good. That is the acid test.

Mr. SALZMANN. Yes, sir.

Mr. MCINARNAY. Mr. Taylor?

STATEMENT OF CARL TAYLOR, VICE PRESIDENT, FOSTER MACHINE & MANUFACTURING CO., INC., BIRMINGHAM, ALA.

Mr. TAYLOR. Are you ready for my résumé?

Mr. MCINARNAY. Yes, sir.

Mr. TAYLOR. Well, we have a machine shop. We do a lot of precision machine parts. We do fabrication, assemblies, quite a diversified coverage of different types of machine work.

We have certified welders. We are very familiar with all of the military specifications on material and the chemical and physical analyses of materials and we have done work with just about every type of material that there is. Well, not all. I am just saying what is usually used in the Government work.

We do work for Hayes, Chrysler Corp., Brown Engineering, Spaco, Inc., Thiokol Chemical Co., Chemstrand, Sperry Rand, IBM, Northrop, and I think that is about enough to cover it.

Mr. MCINARNAY. Did you cover how many employees you have?

Mr. TAYLOR. We have approximately 45, and that ranges up to around 80, depending on the workload. Actually, we utilize a lot of part-time help that work at other companies and we use them either during the day or at night.

Generally, we try to stay away from that for the simple reason that it does present a certain amount of problems, a man coming in on the job that a full-time man has been working on and he doesn't know where to pick up, and so on, so we try to stay away from using part time if we possibly can, but we do use them occasionally.

Other than that, I mean, you will have to ask me questions. I don't actually have any problems. We are enjoying a very good business as of right now, and we have been for the last 90 days, and we also have some customers at the present time where I would say about 35 percent of the work we have in our shop is on a price-advise basis; and, of course, I would like to have 100 percent if I could, but——

Mr. MCINARNAY. What is the meaning of that term?

Mr. TAYLOR. Well, you do the job for them and you advise them of the price after the completion of the job after the hours you have worked on it and the cost of the material, and so forth.

Mr. THEVENOT. And you give them a fixed fee?

Mr. TAYLOR. No. We have an hourly rate and so many hours involved in the job, plus material, and then whatever the total figure comes up to is what the job will amount to.

Mr. PROCTOR. I would like to make one thought. I would like to have Carl tell you he doesn't get that kind of work out of Hayes if these other fellows expect to get the same kind.

Mr. THEVENOT. Or with the Government.

Mr. TAYLOR. No. This is strictly private enterprise, and we get this kind of work from——

Mr. MCINARNAY. What percentage of your work is commercial rather than Government?

Mr. TAYLOR. Well, actually, I would say that 95 percent of our work is Government work and the other 5 percent usually is just ordinary commercial work for people that are not in Government type of work.

Mr. THEVENOT. What part of this is subcontracting and what is prime?

Mr. TAYLOR. Well, I would say that roughly we do possibly 10 percent prime contracts with the Government and the balance is all strictly subcontracting.

Mr. MCINARNAY. What offices do you do prime contracting work with?

Mr. TAYLOR. Well, we have done them with the arsenal, the Army in Huntsville, and we have also done prime contracting work through the prime procurement district, and we do occasionally when jobs come up.

Now, like Mr. Salzmann said, we have bid on quite a few jobs and we don't get all that we bid on. We get our share, so we are not complaining.

Mr. McINARNAY. How do you find the relative problems that arise as a prime contractor versus a subcontractor?

Mr. TAYLOR. Well, the only problems that come up occasionally would be on prime contract if the Government issues a certain set of specifications that you must follow, and you possibly might run into some problems on certain military specifications on material or welding or cleaning or painting that occasionally it might be an obsolete specification, and you just have to get with the right people and find out what the proper specification is that covers the one that had been deleted or omitted.

But other than that, we don't have any problems other than what I have just covered.

Mr. THEVENOT. Is there any great difference in promptness of payment?

Mr. TAYLOR. You are talking about payment on prime contracts with the Government?

Mr. THEVENOT. As opposed to subcontracts.

Mr. TAYLOR. No. I would say that mostly on the average the Government may take a few days longer to pay than a private individual or a private corporation, but we have not noticed anything that was just out of this world, I mean, as far as late in payment.

Mr. McINARNAY. Mr. Hall?

STATEMENT OF F. R. HALL, SUPERIOR ENGRAVING CO., BIRMINGHAM, ALA.

Mr. HALL. We are in the recess engraving business. We do engraving in the aircraft and missile end of it for panels and ID plates and placards and such as that. We do a majority of our business that is different from his in the fact that the majority of ours comes from other sources other than that particular item.

We also make plastic or laminated signs for offices and desk plates and badges, and such as that, and we sell trophies and awards and items of that nature.

Of the type of work in that end, the majority of our business is for, I would say, Hayes in Birmingham. Of course, we do it also for the Air Force, and in the past we have done some for the Air Force and some for the Social Security and the Treasury Department, and we have done—we do quite a bit of work for a number of machine shops around in the Huntsville and Birmingham area.

So far as problems, I don't know of any that we have.

Of course, like Frank, we have been on the bidders' list up at Huntsville now for a couple of years and I have not gotten a bid yet. Maybe they don't have anything in my line.

Mr. THEVENOT. You have not gotten an invitation to bid?

Mr. HALL. Right.

Mr. THEVENOT. Do you know if you are currently on their bidding list?

Mr. HALL. I was up a couple of months ago and checked and I was still on it at that time. Of course, the problem could be there that the type of work I do primarily would be of a subcontract nature for

Hayes or some of the machine shops around. So far as prime contracts in my line, there would be very few, except in signs.

We did a hospital up in Shell Air Force Base not too long ago. Other than that, I wouldn't think there would be too many prime contracts that come out for me.

Mr. THEVENOT. Have you done any business with the General Service Administration? They, as you know, purchase a great deal of these laminated signs and that type of thing.

Mr. HALL. No.

Mr. THEVENOT. Maybe you could see whether it is to your advantage to get on their list.

Mr. McINARNAY. They have a catalog. It is almost like Sears, Roebuck. It is where they have national buying schedules and terms.

Mr. HALL. Right, and I have that information, but——

Mr. THEVENOT. You may want to check into that and see if your products are put on their catalog list. There may be a source of business there.

Mr. McINARNAY. I think they have a regional office in Atlanta, if I am not mistaken, but if you would like to pursue that, I suggest that you write to Senator Sparkman and send him a brochure if you have one of the type of work that you do and an indication of what you would like to do and he in turn would get in touch with the General Service Administration and have them contact you or see that you get the proper information, because that may be a very good source.

Mr. HALL. Yes, sir.

Mr. THEVENOT. And another source would be the Defense Supply Agency, which is the common purchaser for all three military services of this type item, but as Mr. McInarnay says, if you will contact our office, Senator Sparkman's office, we will seek these out for you and see that the information is gotten to you on that.

Mr. HALL. Okay. I will do this. We have seven people employed and we work for contractors, building contractors, such as that quite a bit.

Mr. McINARNAY. Mr. Reporter, in each instance do we have the address of the businessmen who have been here today, the street address?

The REPORTER. Yes, sir.

Mr. McINARNAY. Do you make the directories that appear inside of the building?

Mr. HALL. Yes, sir.

Mr. McINARNAY. I wonder if either of you gentlemen have anything in particular you would like to comment on as a small businessman that may not necessarily be in the area of Government contracts, but would just be perhaps something that might arise as a result of various requirements that the Federal Government imposes upon your business.

Mr. THEVENOT. This is in the way of reports?

Mr. TAYLOR. Not unless you can eliminate income taxes.

Mr. HALL. And tax forms.

Mr. McINARNAY. I don't think we can eliminate them, but perhaps we will see them reduced again. I hope so.

Mr. HALL. I cannot think of anything in that area.

Mr. TAYLOR. The only thing I can say is just let business stay as it is for another year and I will be all right.

Mr. McINARNAY. We are in a prosperous area.

Mr. TAYLOR. It seems to be generally everywhere, and, of course, in some areas it may be slow, but there it depends on the individual whether they are progressive enough to get up and get out and beat the bushes and find out where the work lies.

You do have to keep on your toes, there is no question about that. Occasionally, somebody might come to your place and ask for a bid, but that is not too often. Usually, you have to get out and make yourself known and let the people know what your capabilities are and go from there.

Mr. McINARNAY. And you have to call on them not just once, but——

Mr. TAYLOR. You have to follow it up. You can call one time, and that is fine. They remember you then, but a month from now if you don't follow it up, they will forget about you unless you had something that is pretty unique that they have to have and they cannot get it from anybody else, which doesn't exist.

It is just a matter of keeping with it. I even have to call Mr. Proctor every now and then.

Mr. SALZMANN. When you once get a job in a spot, then your contact is pretty well made inside and it starts moving in that direction.

Mr. THEVENOT. This is your particular problem in regards to Huntsville?

Mr. SALZMANN. Yes, sir, and knowing who to hit.

Mr. THEVENOT. I would suggest that you might get in touch with Jeff Darwin personally about that.

Mr. SALZMANN. I have tried other rounds and it doesn't seem to come out.

Mr. McINARNAY. Well, if you don't have anything else, I want to thank you on behalf of Senator Sparkman and the committee, and Mr. Thevenot for coming to share your views and helping us to help you in any field we can.

Thank you.

(Whereupon, Mr. Salzmann, Mr. Taylor, and Mr. Hall were excused.)

Mr. McINARNAY. Mr. Mitchell, briefly, Senator Sparkman, as you know, is the chairman of the Senate Small Business Committee.

Mr. MITCHELL. Yes, sir.

Mr. McINARNAY. He asked Mr. Thevenot and me to come to the southeastern States. We have been to Louisiana and now Alabama today, and on Thursday we will be in Florida to meet with the small businessmen to learn first-hand of them any particular problems that they might have, either as a result of doing business with the Federal Government, either on the prime or subcontract level, or as a result of requirements imposed by the Federal Government on businessmen, so we are very anxious to hear your comments. Anything you might say is very important to us because it makes up the composite of what the small businessman's views are today.

I would like for you to start, if you would, by identifying the type of business you are in and who you do business with and the number of employees you have, etc.

STATEMENT OF HUGH W. MITCHELL, EXECUTIVE VICE PRESIDENT, SOUTHERN PRODUCTS CO., INC., BIRMINGHAM, ALA.

Mr. MITCHELL. We are a very small precision machine shop, and we do business with Hayes and Hardie-Tynes Manufacturing Co. The principal part of our Government business comes from Hardie-Tynes Manufacturing Co., with quite a bit coming from Hayes.

We do very little bidding direct. As small as we are, we would much rather have the subcontracting from firms who have the better engineering and quality control and all of those things and go ahead as a subcontractor. We do bid direct occasionally.

Mr. McINARNAY. How many employees did you say you had?

Mr. MITCHELL. Twenty.

Mr. PROCTOR. Mr. Mitchell, I don't know of a stick of work that we have out there that isn't Government work.

Mr. MITCHELL. All we get from you would be Government work.

Mr. McINARNAY. Do you do any commercial?

Mr. MITCHELL. It is a little hard to get. Probably 50 percent is commercial. That comes from people like Central Foundry Co., Stewart Machine Co. here in town, and Pulman Standard—in fact, anybody we can get it from. We are simply a contract shop. We are very limited due to the small equipment that we have.

Mr. McINARNAY. Are there any particular areas of the Government contract field that you would like to bring to the committee's attention and comment on?

Mr. MITCHELL. I wouldn't have any criticism of any area of the Government contracting, for instance, all of the small businesses have problems, don't you fellows misunderstand me, but we do not have problems of such a nature that you could solve.

Mr. THEVENOT. The reasons you do not bid on prime contracts are what?

Mr. MITCHELL. My thinking is we are simply too small. We do not have the engineering, the quality control, and various other things to justify direct bidding with the Government.

Now, frankly, I would rather give Mr. Proctor the headaches and just go ahead and enjoy myself, you see, subcontracting with him. Really, that is the way it is.

Mr. THEVENOT. The prime contractor you feel——

STATEMENT OF ODEN PROCTOR, DIRECTOR OF PROCUREMENT, HAYES INTERNATIONAL CORP., BIRMINGHAM, ALA.

Mr. PROCTOR. For the record, we have a full ground quality assurance department, and I think a good one. We have liaison engineers and the type of people that will support Mr. Mitchell and his endeavor.

We provide source inspection where required, and anything that can help him cross the hurdles. Our purchase orders reflect certain certifications that must be made, and among them which was mentioned earlier, and a very important one, any material that we furnish is certified material and we ask them to certify such material as material we are sending back forms in some manner, so there is not a subcontractor in the area that we don't know about, and it isn't necessarily related to the Birmingham facility.

We hand work to small businesses throughout the entire United States, the west coast, Detroit area, New England States, the Middle Atlantic States, and if we were dependent upon small business in many cases to do the type of things that we insist be done, we just couldn't patronize them.

We couldn't give them the business, because as Mr. Mitchell indicates, they don't have a full quality assurance division to support some of the things that we ask for.

I would like to make one other statement. I had people say to us, and it has been quoted by some of my people, that this is a Government contract, I don't want it because it isn't worth the effort.

I personally say don't worry about it. We are the prime contractor on this. We will take care of your paperwork and help you through it, because of redtape, and I think it is something we must recognize.

I know the Small Business Committee is attempting to help the small businessmen, and we too are. We think it is real important, but some of the imposition on small business is such that a particularly small business just cannot cope with it.

Mr. McINARNAY. The small business program principally within the Defense Establishment because that is where the big money is.

Mr. PROCTOR. That is right.

Mr. McINARNAY. This is a two-pronged effort, and small businessmen receive about as much by way of subcontracts as they do by the prime contract route.

Mr. MITCHELL. Right.

Mr. McINARNAY. And perhaps you would find that the small businessmen who get the bulk of prime contract work are rather large, but small businessmen by Mr. Mitchell's standards.

Mr. MITCHELL. That is right. Hardie-Tynes Manufacturing Co. is a small business. Forty percent of my business comes from them. They have the facilities, engineering, financial, accounting, attorneys—there are a lot of things I think Mr. Proctor's statement was very good in, things they can do.

They can hire the men to do these things and we, naturally, can't do it because we don't have the production capacities to produce anything to pay for such people.

It makes a much better relationship for—frankly, I think for any firm our size to deal as a subcontractor rather than a direct bidder, it is better.

Mr. McINARNAY. Well, there is another point, too, isn't there, that by not having these people on your payroll, your overhead is substantially reduced and you can be far more competitive?

Mr. MITCHELL. That is it exactly. We would not be competitive in any way without additional equipment if we had to hire the additional personnel to do the things that must be done, and I understand it must be done in any Government contract. There are things that have to be done that a small firm just cannot do.

Mr. PROCTOR. We feel, and I think it may be one of them, that the smaller subcontractors with whom we deal we consider a real valuable adjunct to our operation. They are, if you please, an extension of our own shop and we attempt to support these people as we support our own shop.

Mr. MITCHELL. They do. This is true. They cooperate in every way in the world with us.

Mr. McINARNAY. By the same token, Mr. Proctor, if the small businessmen had the means to hire quality control people and various experts and specialists, they would charge you more and you would have to charge the Government more and you would be less competitive; isn't that correct?

Mr. PROCTOR. Very true. They would price themselves completely out of the business.

Mr. McINARNAY. Very likely you would be doing work in-house?

Mr. PROCTOR. That is right, if we could. I will tell you, it is simple where a man has a relatively small organization up to 100 people, the support personnel for that 100 people where his overhead may now be 50 percent could conceivably go to 100 or 125, so the small business, in order to maintain all of the pertinences necessary to 'do prime contracting, and I am sympathetic with them. They simply couldn't compete. They couldn't compete with us. Their overhead would be completely higher than ours.

Mr. McINARNAY. Your company has such an outstanding record in subcontracting with small business. I wonder if you have ever been commended by the military?

Mr. PROCTOR. Yes, sir.

Mr. McINARNAY. I wonder if they have been——

Mr. PROCTOR. We have a man by the name of Turbeville assigned to the Atlanta office. I have not seen him in months. He comes over frequently. He never leaves our operation without he says we are doing an outstanding job in supporting small business.

We had a letter written by his colonel commending us for small business. We are not big. We have 5,300 people. We are a little bit too big to be little, but we are not big enough to be big.

Mr. McINARNAY. You are one of those medium-size businesses?

Mr. PROCTOR. Yes; we are constantly fighting the battle on these.

Mr. MITCHELL. There is another angle of this, too, that we have not discussed, that is very important.

Just using Hayes as an example, they bid on large contracts, contracts that I would assume have to be let by the Air Force or whoever may be doing the job. These contracts have to be let to one firm, and if they did not bid on that job, certainly I could not bid on it, don't you see.

All right, there are many items on this job that we can actually produce more economically than he can, but I couldn't go to the Air Force and bid directly on them because it is an overall job that has to be let in one contract, and an overflow of many items that these small businesses such as I can do more economically than he can gives us a place in the program without being required to have the high-priced personnel that a large firm necessarily has to have.

Mr. PROCTOR. Well, not necessarily, Mr. Mitchell, more economical. We have schedules to maintain and that is saying that it isn't necessary, but it does not necessarily follow that it is.

We have schedules to maintain; and, of course, we are out bidding on business and sometimes we superimpose business on top of business and we find an overload in our own area.

This, of course, we altogether subcontract due to overload conditions not necessarily because it is more economical and in many cases it could be.

For example, we will bid by virtue of our overhead we will bid, and the fact that we have much Government-owned equipment within our plant, which may be a composite machine rate of say $6.20 an hour.

There have been some times that we have subcontracted heavy work and paid $20 an hour on it on fixed-priced contracts in order to maintain the schedule, but we also go to Small Business in order to get it accomplished, so it isn't necessarily—it doesn't necessarily mean it is more economical, and these boys bid it competitively, too, every one of them.

There is no favoritism shown, and I think Mr. Mitchell will bear this out, and anyone you talk with.

Mr. MITCHELL. Yes.

Mr. PROCTOR. We get at least three bids and send out the drawings and place it on a competitive basis, which we must do.

Mr. THEVENOT. If your subcontractors are bidding and making mistakes in their bids, do you have any program of assisting them to comply or be responsive in their bids, or do you give them other counseling?

Mr. PROCTOR. Only to this extent. If someone comes in with a ridiculously low bid we like to say are you sure you understand the task.

Now, we know that in any given group of three or four subcontractors we are not completely aware of their shop load. Now, they have to maintain their machinists and their capacity or their management capabilities and one time they may bid inordinately high. We don't rule them off on this basis.

The next time we go out and even Mr. Mitchell, we may find that he is real competitive. I can only ask this question to myself, and it is obvious that he needs the work in the shop, and he needs something to keep these people together.

If you let it go down and not have people, then he loses his work force.

Mr. THEVENOT. It is to your advantage to keep as many people going as possible.

Mr. PROCTOR. That is right.

Mr. THEVENOT. To gain competition?

Mr. PROCTOR. Exactly. When someone comes in with a ridiculously low bid, we will say you are sure you understand this clause and if he says he does, we will take it, but we have never forced anyone into bankruptcy by forcing it on them, nor do we intend to.

Mr. THEVENOT. There is a great deal of emphasis being put on encouraging prime contractors, more specifically in the Department of Defense, to institute the type of program that you are saying that Hayes has in operation now, a broad-scale subcontracting or small business program to assist as many as possible of the small business people to participate in your business. It is an extremely important part of the small business program.

Mr. PROCTOR. We recognize it as being so. We solicit. I have a couple of fellows that will go out and if someone comes and solicits us in business in machinists, subcontracting, a couple of things happen. They give us an equipment list.

Now, we can pretty well judge from this type of equipment what they are capable of doing and try to tailor it to their capabilities in the type of work we allow them to go on. We will send out a quality assurance man to check out their inspection facilities and whether or not they are qualified to do the work that we give them.

We always get a Dun & Bradstreet report. We don't want to be in a position, and we don't want to be caught in a position of having work out and someone is eminently bankrupt, because this can hurt our programs, so we get financial backing, a financial report, and it would be pretty obvious that if someone had a shaky financial condition we wouldn't give them as large a job as we would someone who had a sound financial standing.

We would rather work with them and build them up so their financial standing would be better and we consider them simply, as I said before, an extension of our own capabilities.

Without them we would be in a heck of a mess.

Mr. McINARNAY. Do you receive any consideration in your bidding on Government prime contracts as a result of your outstanding small business subcontracting program?

Mr. PROCTOR. Mr. McInarnay, I cannot say this has—I would not like to say inasmuch as I am not in the contract section. I am sure that we talk about it and we probably will do anything in our power to point out that we are supporting small business. Whether or not this influences the decision as the prime, I cannot say.

Mr. THEVENOT. Are you familiar with the weighted guidelines program in the Department of Defense?

Mr. PROCTOR. Yes, sir.

Mr. THEVENOT. I was sure that your company was very aware of this, because of its superior small business program.

Mr. PROCTOR. We think we have. We have no reason to believe that we have not. Certainly, if you weight just that one factor, I think we are somewhat eminent in supporting small business. I honestly think that. We think of it as an extension of our own capabilities.

Now, as far as bidding the job is concerned, we have estimators in the house and at the time we estimate a job where there is a considerable amount of machinery, we don't ask people to give us their estimate of cost. We estimate an in-house cost factor. Time doesn't permit us to go out and do this.

Now, if we get the job, much of it, and certainly I will be real honest to say that that is within our capabilities of meeting the schedule, we are going to do, but unfortunately, or fortunately, for small business, there is a whole lot of that we cannot do and we must rely on small business to support us.

We don't have a program that is a definite set aside. We don't feel that we need to bid the statistics that we have generated. We are well over the majority, I would say, but we do not bid with the thought of subcontracting. We cannot bid with the thought of subcontracting, nor can these people bid with the thought of subcontracting. They bid on what they think the job is worth.

Mr. McINARNAY. Mr. Mitchell, do you have any further comment you would like to make?

Mr. MITCHELL. I don't think so. I think this pretty well covers it. I have found the cooperation all around from both governmental agencies and the prime contractors, and we have problems from time to time, but back to the question Mr. Proctor discussed about our doing things that they could not do, I used Hayes as a specific example.

Maybe I should have used Hardie-Tynes Manufacturing Co. as a specific example. They bid, for instance, on air compressors and there are many parts on those—this is for the U.S. Navy. There are many parts that are very, very small and intricate and highly precisioned parts and we can actually manufacture them more economically than Hardie-Tynes can, and for that reason we get a lot of business from them such as that, and to me that is much better than having a contract direct with the Government for a firm the size and the facilities that we have.

Mr. McInarnay. Mr. Mitchell, on behalf of Senator Sparkman and the Small Business Committee and Mr. Thevenot, I want to thank you for coming here today and sharing your views with us. We really appreciate it.

Thank you, sir.

(Whereupon, Mr. Mitchell was excused.)

Mr. McInarnay. Gentlemen, as you no doubt know, Senator Sparkman is chairman of the Senate Small Business Committee, and he asked Mr. Thevenot and me to come into the Southeast. We were in Louisiana yesterday. We are here in Birmingham today, and on Thursday we will be in Florida meeting with small businessmen in conferences set up by the chamber of commerce, and in some instances, in cooperation with the Small Business Administration Office.

Senator Sparkman wanted us—Mr. Thevenot and me, who are staff members of the Senate Small Business Committee—to undertake somewhat of a pilot project in coming into local communities and sitting down with small businessmen across the table and learning directly from them any particular problems that they have.

(1) As arising out of doing business directly with the Government, either as a prime contractor of a subcontractor; and

(2) Problems that may arise as a result of requirements that are placed on businessmen by the Federal Government: rules and regulations.

So that is why we are here. We solicit your comments. We are very anxious to know what you have to say. We feel that what you have to say would be very important in our study which may be extended into other States and other communities around the country, so we look forward to having your comments today.

I think that we will start off with Mr. Self. If you would tell us a little bit about your company, the type of business you are in, whom you do business with, and the number of employees you have and how long you have been in business, this sort of thing, and then go into any particular area you might want to cover.

STATEMENT OF FRANK P. SELF AND FOREST M. SELF, EXCELLO MACHINE CO., BIRMINGHAM, ALA.

Mr. Frank Self. Well, I have been in business about 25 years. Well, I started in 1942. It would be 23 years I have been in business.

I have found that subcontracting from the prime contractor is better for me because it is so much easier for me to do my bookkeeping, and everything that way. I don't really have the backing and everything to take prime contracts. My company is not big enough for that.

Mr. McINARNAY. How many employees do you have?

Mr. FRANK SELF. It varies. I have had as many as 25, and it varies from 5 or 6 up to 25. It is according, you know, to what amount of work we have to do.

Mr. THEVENOT. What kind of products do you have?

Mr. FRANK SELF. We machine products, metal machine products, component parts, you might say, and I have done work with Thiokol.

Now, I made the Falcon nozzle, the exit cone, you might call it, for the Falcon. I made 5,000 of those for Thiokol, and what was that other company's name up there in Pittsburgh?

Mr. FOREST SELF. Scaife Co.

Mr. FRANK SELF. Scaife Co., and I have subcontracted work for Hardie-Tynes on air compressor valves, and I guess, well, now, you might say that the work that I subcontracted from Thiokol and Scaife Co. on the missiles, amounted to around—I would say $900,000.

Mr. McINARNAY. Over what period?

Mr. FRANK SELF. Over a period of about 8 years, and from Hardie-Tynes, I guess I have done around $750,000 worth for them on subcontracts. That was on air compressor valves and other parts, too.

I have found that I can do better business with them than I could trying to go direct to the Government, and I have one complaint about the Small Business Administration.

Now, I went to Huntsville up there and I figured a job one time when I had—it was about 250 shafts to make, and I went up there for the opening bid and I found that they had 42 bidders on that one job, and the one that bid the lowest price, if he was in an area where there was, you know, where they needed help, why, he would get it anyway, and anytime that there were as many as 42 bidders, especially where there is a small business, somebody is going to make a mistake and bid too low, that wouldn't help the small business. It would put them out of business, because they would bid too low, and they would lose money, and they would have to finance that part as a loss, and I think it is wrong for them to have that many bidders on one job.

Mr. THEVENOT. But it is not the Small Business Administration, this is one of the procurement offices. Was it a subcontract or prime contract?

Mr. FRANK SELF. It was a prime contract from the Small Business Administration in Huntsville, there were 42 bidders on one job.

Mr. McINARNAY. I suspect this might have been a contract set aside for the small business.

Mr. FRANK SELF. It was several years ago. Anyway, the fellow was very nice, and he told me, he said, "I am sure sorry you missed this job," but he said, "You just keep on bidding and maybe you will get one."

I said that I didn't want to keep on bidding because if I was to get one it would scare me to death. I knew I was going to lose money on it if 42 bidders turned in a price on it, and that is one objection I have to the Small Business Administration, but I know that——

Mr. McINARNAY. Let me say this. There is often a confusion about the difference between the Small Business Committee, which we represent, and which is a part of the Congress. It is a committee set up by the U.S. Senate to look into the problems of business.

One of our responsibilities, specific responsibilities is to oversee the activities of the Small Business Administration.

The Small Business Administration is a part of the executive branch of the Government. It is one of the agencies of the executive branch of the Government, and it is an entirely different thing from the committee.

The committee is what Senator Sparkman is chairman of. The Small Business Administration does buy some things, but only housekeeping items, and mostly around Washington where its headquarters are, but it probably wasn't a purchase directly by the Small Business Administration.

Now, what it might well have been was a contract that had been set aside so that only small businessmen could bid on it.

Mr. FRANK SELF. Now, I understand that. I am sure it was.

Mr. McINARNAY. If it was Redstone it probably in those days was the Army. I can readily understand that when you have 42 bidders how it might be that a man might come in with a bid that is entirely unreasonable and perhaps he might end up losing money on it and certainly he would if he took the job at that price.

Mr. FRANK SELF. That is right.

Mr. McINARNAY. This is a very difficult problem for the procuring agencies, the Army, Navy, and Air Force, whoever it might be, because if you put a bid out on formalized competitive sealed bid processes, then the principal thing that a businessman does is fill in a figure, the price at which he is willing to do that work for.

Now, if the XYZ company comes in with $2 and the next lowest bidder is $10, there may be a presumption that the XYZ company doesn't understand the bid, but the burden is upon that particular agency to look into this small business, or whatever size business, and to determine whether he is qualified and whether he is responsive to the bid, whether he is a responsible contractor, and if he meets all of those tests, it is up to them to give him the bid anyhow.

So it is rather complicated and difficult for the agencies in the case like that.

Mr. FRANK SELF. We will go back to those prices, and I might say that those prices ranged from $39 a piece down to $3.25 a piece, and I was in between, and the material would have cost more than $3.25 a piece.

Mr. THEVENOT. Then the presumption is that that bidder was desperately trying to buy into a market or else he misunderstood very badly the specifications.

Mr. FRANK SELF. Anyway, he got the bid. That was one small businessman gone out of business.

Mr. THEVENOT. This is not to the advantage of the U.S. Government.

Mr. FRANK SELF. It is not any help to the Small Business to put out that many bids for him to bid against. Limit the number of bids that go out.

Mr. THEVENOT. Or break the procurement down to several parts and allow several bidders on each of the parts.

Mr. FRANK SELF. I think so. I don't think it is a fair bid when there is that many people bidding on one job. Somebody is bound to be wrong. When there are two or three bids on it, you can still bid low, but you are not as apt to bid that low.

Mr. THEVENOT. But it goes back to what Mr. McInarnay said, it is the responsibility of the contractor also to ascertain whether this bidder was a responsible and responsive bidder.

Mr. FRANK SELF. Well, now, the one that got that contract, he had been checked and he was responsible, but somewhere there was a misunderstanding. There had to be one because the material cost more than what he was actually charging for the job.

Mr. McINARNAY. Have there been any recent problems of this nature?

Mr. FRANK SELF. No, I have not made any more bids on them.

Mr. McINARNAY. Your business is exclusively that of subcontractor?

Mr. FRANK SELF. Yes, sir.

Mr. McINARNAY. And that is what you prefer?

Mr. FRANK SELF. Well, I believe I would. I think I would prefer to do subcontracting, unless they cut those bids down.

Mr. THEVENOT. This is your principal complaint about bidding?

Mr. FRANK SELF. Yes, sir. There are too many bidders.

Mr. THEVENOT. Are there other problems that you run into in bidding?

Mr. FRANK SELF. No, nothing except that—I think there are too many bids that go out on a job. If there were 5 or 6 or 7, I would still think that would be fair, but when we get up to 40 and 45 bids, why, I think I am putting in too much time in estimating a job, then if I get one, I am afraid I am going to lose money when I get it because there are too many bidding there.

Mr. McINARNAY. You don't have all of these complications at the subcontract level?

Mr. FRANK SELF. No, I don't. Usually, there will hardly ever be more than six or seven bidders on a job where you are subcontracting, because they just don't send out that many bids, and where the prime contractor can naturally get more for it than a subcontractor can, they take the complete job, where I couldn't take the complete job.

I couldn't build a battleship, but I could build a hydrant or something to go on it.

Mr. McINARNAY. Are there any other problem areas that you are aware of that you would like to mention?

Mr. FRANK SELF. No.

Mr. McINARNAY. Are there any problems that you are finding in just doing business as a small businessman as a result of any particular requirements that the Federal Government imposes?

Mr. FRANK SELF. Well, it might be a lot of paperwork that I wouldn't like to go through. I wouldn't have an office staff big enough to take care of a prime contract on most of the work that they have.

Mr. McINARNAY. I wonder if Mr. Forest Self has anything.

Mr. FOREST SELF. No, I don't have anything to say. I think he has said about all of it.

Mr. McINARNAY. Mr. Sykes, would you tell us a little bit about your company and whom you do business with and the number of employees, and that sort of thing, and discuss anything you would like to discuss?

JAMES B. SYKES, SOUTHEASTERN PRODUCTS CORP., PELHAM, ALA.

Mr. SYKES. We manufacture mechanical packing. Primarily, that is our line of manufacturing. Now, we also are in the fabricating business and related line of gaskets, and we handle molded extruded rubber items, and principally, our business is with the large industry, and OEM.

Mr. McINARNAY. Who is that?

Mr. SYKES. Original Equipment Manufacturers, such as—well, people who manufacture valves. We supply one component part of the valve. That would be the ceiling or the valve seat, probably, for one instance.

Our dealings with the different Government agencies are primarily limited to relatively small requirements. We may get through the mail a list of the requirements, and we would just take the list and pick out the items that we feel we can furnish and will bid a price that we feel that we can handle profitably, and pretty much that is our dealing with the Government agencies.

They are thinking primarily now about an installation such as Brookley or the different airbases in the area.

We do a lot of business with TVA. We have just received a contract for next year's soft packing requirements, and the Authority has their packing requirements broken into five schedules.

We are approved to all five of TVA's packing requirement schedules, and this is something that we are proud of. We had to work for it, and you have to qualify.

You have to submit samples of your products for approval, and once you are approved, then your name is on the bid list, and we bid and along with the other major packing manufacturers within our industry, and we were just successful this year. We had not had it before.

Mr. THEVENOT. Are your competitors primarily other small businesses?

Mr. SYKES. No. In fact, our principal competitors in this area and in the TVA area would be large business. In fact, I would imagine of the competitors that we have we are the only one that would qualify as a small business. It would be Garlock, Johns Manville, and Raybestos, Manhattan, John Crane, and I mention these because I know they are some who are approved to the various schedules, but I think I am correct that we are the only sole-source for all five schedules.

I don't think any of the others have been approved and they may not have submitted samples for approval in all areas, but we have and are approved and we enjoy a good business with TVA.

Mr. THEVENOT. Are these procurements very often set aside for small business? Do you know?

Mr. SYKES. No, I don't think so.

Mr. McINARNAY. How many employees do you have? Did you cover that?

Mr. SYKES. We have about 60. Now, this is pretty stable. We do not fluctuate very much. Sixty would be including our sales force and our manufacturing and management and clerical level; 60 total.

Mr. McINARNAY. Are there any particular problem areas that you would like to bring up?

Mr. SYKES. I don't know of any particular problem that we are having involving Government agencies or the Small Business Administration.

Mr. THEVENOT. Are there a good many other small businesses engaged in this type of work aside from yourself?

Mr. SYKES. There are no manufacturers that I know of. There are some fabricators; yes, sir.

Mr. THEVENOT. This explains perhaps the reason that there have been no set-asides, because probably there was not enough competition among the small businesses.

Mr. SYKES. Right. Now, in the Arsenal area, there are several fabricators that I am familiar with, and—I think I am correct—there is a 30-mile range. I am not sure. I don't even know what type of contract would be involved, but I understand there is some geographical range that you have to be within in order to participate in some of the smaller contracts that are awarded through Redstone Arsenal.

We cannot participate in this because we are not within the geographical location. I cannot give you any more information, and I get this information through one fabricator that we furnished some raw materials to in the area, and he qualifies us of his locations to participate in some of the business, and we are not given an opportunity to do this.

This is no particular problem to us, but it is a small thing really, but we do participate secondhand, so to speak, through this fabricator in furnishing his raw material requirements.

Mr. McINARNAY. Is there anything that you might like to bring up in any particular problem area as a result of the requirements placed upon your business by the Federal Government that do not necessarily relate to Government contracting.

Mr. SYKES. No, I don't know of any at all. Now, there may be some that I am not aware of. Now, I am sales manager and I am here because the president of the company had to be out of town this week, and he may have something or some comment that I would not cover or wouldn't really be aware of, but I don't know of any.

We have not had any problems, particularly in the sales end of it, or in manufacturing, to my knowledge, or any other area.

Mr. McINARNAY. Mr. Self, do you have any further comments?

Mr. FRANK SELF. No; I think John Sparkman will be mad at me, though, because that was his pet project when he had that Small Business Administration up there.

Mr. McINARNAY. Do you mean John Horne?

Mr. FRANK SELF. I said "Sparkman will probably be mad at me because that was his pet project," that Small Business Administration, and I criticized that the way they were doing it up there, putting out so many bids, it was really hurting the small businessmen.

Mr. McINARNAY. I am sure Senator Sparkman will not be mad at you. He wants to know what small businessmen are thinking. As chairman of the committee, he wants to do anything he can to help you, and if there is any area or any problem that you have, he is interested in it.

Mr. THEVENOT. If you face this problem, chances are others face the same problem, and it gives us an idea in which areas future effort ought to be placed.

Mr. FRANK SELF. Well, that was the only complaint I had, was just so many bids being put out on one shop to the small business, and I think that was hurting them instead of helping them.

Mr. BARTLETT. I would like to get a little something in the record. This is the first time I have had the pleasure of meeting Mr. Sykes. We are familiar with the president of his company. The regional office here in Birmingham has participated with the Exchange Security Bank and made a couple of loans to this company, so it made us feel good that this is about the only small business of its type in a competitive structure, and, of course, we can take some pride in what little contribution we have made, because this new building that they are in in Pelham, with the Exchange Security Bank as a participant, we about a year ago, I think, approved a $250,000 loan to this company so it could expand its operations and get in the present position it is in.

Mr. McINARNAY. I think when we find in small businesses the only one in its field or at least the only one that is, like you say, qualified in such a broad area, it is really a great honor and it indicates that that is a business really on its toes.

Mr. SYKES. Maybe I should say to qualify this a little further that we are not the only one in the business. We are the only one in our area. We are the only one qualified to all five TVA schedules, to my knowledge, but we are not the only manufacturer of mechanical packings that would qualify as small business.

Now, of the ones that we were talking about we are the only small business, but there are some others in the Mechanical Packing Association which is an industry association in the Middle West and in the Northeast that are old companies.

They are as small, some of them, as we, and some may be even smaller. Their range is considerably smaller, their capabilities are considerably smaller, and they are pretty well specialized in a much, much narrower field than we, but in this area, I don't know of any other manufacturer of branded mechanical packings.

Mr. PROCTOR. I could add one thing here, perhaps. Southeastern Products and I had never met Mr. Sykes before this afternoon, although I know we have some business through them, and they have been real fine in supporting requirements for certain types of extruded material and gasket material, and that sort of thing, and they have supported this real well.

Now, we asked them to come today, because they were another small business somewhat disassociated from the normal—the majority of the people that we had—in that they are manufacturers in the small business.

I don't know what the dollar volume is that we do with Southeastern Products, except that I hear some nice things about them.

Mr. McINARNAY. Well, gentlemen, Mr. Self, and Mr. Self, and Mr. Sykes, on behalf of Senator Sparkman and the Small Business Committee and Mr. Thevenot, I want to thank you very much for coming here and taking the time away from your business, which I know is a sacrifice, in making yourself available to the committee and giving us the benefit of your views, which I can assure you will be helpful to us.

(Whereupon, at 4:05 p.m. the conference in the above-entitled matter was concluded.)

1

de
sa

re
de

sn

ha
ar

SMALL BUSINESS PROCUREMENT CONFERENCES

U.S. SENATE,
SELECT COMMITTEE ON SMALL BUSINESS,
Jacksonville, Fla.

The staff conference met, pursuant to notice, at 1 p.m., in board room, Chamber of Commerce Building, Jacksonville, Fla., William T. McInarnay, counsel; E. Wayne Thevenot, professional staff member, Senate Small Business Committee (presiding); Kennon Turner, regional manager, Small Business Administration, Jacksonville, Fla.; and Joseph D. Kelly, director, trade development, Jacksonville Area Chamber of Commerce, Jacksonville, Fla.

Also present: Wilbur H. Mason; Henderson Boree, Charles P. Greeg, Roger M. Painter, Edward A. Koester, Jr., Walter Hohenhausen, Jr., George M. Goodloe, Dan Hufnagel, and Eldon Dickson, all of Jacksonville.

Mr. McINARNAY. Gentlemen, I think we should begin. I want to thank each of you for coming here today and I want to thank also Mr. Kelly and the Jacksonville Chamber of Commerce, as well as Mr. Turner, regional manager of the Small Business Administration, who together sponsored this meeting and gave us this opportunity to come down and listen to the small businessmen of Jacksonville.

I am Bill McInarnay, counsel for the Senate Small Business Committee. I have been with them since 1958.

This is Mr. Wayne Thevenot, who is a professional staff member of the same committee.

I would like to have Mr. Thevenot, if he would, explain a little bit to you about the Senate Small Business Committee's function.

Mr. THEVENOT. Well, by the committee's charter, we are to look into the problems facing small business and do whatever is necessary to give small businesses a fair break in getting their share of the economy of this country. In doing so, a part of our job is to hold hearings in Washington and throughout the country. This particular session is sort of a pilot program, as far as the committee is concerned. Generally, the hearings are held in Washington, and, while some of them are held out of Washington, they are formal hearings where businessmen are brought in to present their formal statements and officials from the Federal Government are present.

This meeting is intended to be quite informal as you see and Senator John Sparkman, who is chairman of the committee, and Senator Smathers were interested in seeing that the staff gets as closely as possible into the small business community to hear about the problems that face you day to day and to get us more acquainted with them, to give us some basis for further action by the committee in the months to come.

And, this is why Mr. McInarnay and I are now going through the South—we have been in Shreveport, La., Birmingham, Ala., and now to Jacksonville. We hope that from these meetings we will get a better view of what problems the business community is encountering and hopefully to give us some direction to be of whatever assistance we can be to the small business community.

Mr. McInarnay. There are two areas on which we would like to hear from you.

One is any problem that might arise as a result of doing business with the Government, either as a prime contractor or a subcontractor.

The other is more general—one that affects every small business—and that is the various problems, any problem, that might arise as the result of requirements imposed upon you as a small businessman by the Federal Government.

As Mr. Thevenot said, this is somewhat of a pilot project. We have been in three States. While we don't have any further conferences scheduled, it may be that we will in the future go into other areas of the country. You represent to us a cross section of the small business community, not only in Jacksonville, but the Nation, because of the problems that you face. They are the problems that men face all over the country.

So, what you have to say is very important to us and we would like for you to be very frank in discussing your views about various things that affect you as a small businessman, because whatever you say will be most helpful to the committee in discharging its responsibility to investigate the problems of American small business and make recommendations to the Senate for legislative changes or to the various executive agencies for administrative changes that will help you.

I might differentiate here for a moment—a point that is rather confusing to a lot of people, not only outside of Washington, but inside Washington also. We represent a committee of the U.S. Senate. We are charged by the Senate with looking into the problems of small business. Under the Small Business Act of 1958, one of the duties of this committee is to act as a surveillance group over the activities of the Small Business Administration, which Mr. Turner represents. He is the regional manager here in Jacksonville.

The Small Business Administration is an agency of the executive branch of Government. We, however, are in the legislative branch. It is the SBA, the Small Business Administration, which has the various loan programs, financial assistance, management assistance, and assistance in Government contracts and subcontracts.

Now, as the format today, what we would like to do is start with Mr. Painter, and, first, I will ask you, going around the room, to identify yourselves, if you would. Please tell us what type of business you are in and a little bit about your business—the number of employees, size of the business, and the nature of the business, and so forth. So, I wonder if we could do that, and then we will come back and begin and give each of you an opportunity to express your views about small business today.

Mr. Painter?

ROGER M. PAINTER, PAINTER'S POULTRY CO., INC., JACKSON-VILLE, FLA.

Mr. PAINTER. Well, I am Roger M. Painter and I represent Painter's Poultry Co., Inc., and its affiliated companies. We have been in the poultry business—my brother has, primarily, some close to 60 years in the same community.

We have grown during that period of time today to where we really don't qualify as small business as such, but we put ourselves up against some rather big businesses and we still consider ourselves small business. But we do have now about 225 employees and we have sales up close to $10 million a year.

We are a fully integrated poultry operation, all the way from having our own breeders in the field to supply our hatching eggs, to supply our hatchery, to supply our broiler farms with baby chicks. We have our own feed mill where we mix our feed to supply these same farms and bring those finished birds in into our processing plant, which we process and we sell strictly wholesale. We also have branches throughout the State, and so we go into the distribution end as an additional step toward integration.

That is about the story, as far as our company is concerned.

Mr. McINARNAY. Thank you, Mr. Painter.

Mr. Koester?

EDWARD A. KOESTER, JR., DOUGLAS PRINTING CO., INC., JACK-SONVILLE, FLA.

Mr. KOESTER. My name is Ed Koester, Jr., and I represent Douglas Printing Co.

Our firm is one of the older printing companies in the area, being established in 1898. Our family has had the business since 1926, and in the early thirties we were the first printing house in town—in fact, in this area, we were the pioneer in the photo-offset process. We employ, at present, between 40 and 50 people in our plant. We were the first company in town—printing company—to install commercial two-color equipment. Our volume, at present, is scraping close to $750,000 a year, which for us seems phenomenal. We never thought we would get this far.

At the present time, we have plans under way for expansion of our facilities, due to the fact that we have been able to enter several new markets, and in order to meet this demand, we are going to have to expand one way or another, so we are taking things in hand and somehow or another we are going to expand.

Our market is primarily in this region; however, we sell in many States, and we have had substantial inquiries from the North, and at least in our business, the future looks fairly good.

Mr. McINARNAY. Did you say how many employees you had, Mr. Koester?

Mr. KOESTER. Yes, sir; between 40 and 50. It fluctuates according to the demand of work in process.

Mr. McINARNAY. Do you do any business with the Federal Government?

I suppose we want to get into that a little later?

Mr. KOESTER. Yes.

Mr. McINARNAY. And I think the record should reflect that Mr. Kennon Turner, regional manager of the Small Business Administration, is present, and Mr. Joe Kelly, the assistant general manager of the Jacksonville Area Chamber of Commerce. Is that correct?

Mr. KELLY. Yes; among a few other things.

Mr. McINARNAY. By the way, Mr. Turner and Mr. Kelly, I skipped you. Is there anything you would like to say at this time?

Mr. TURNER. No, sir.

Mr. KELLY. No, thank you.

Mr. McINARNAY. If, at any time, you do have anything to say, either now or during the discussion period, I wish you would feel free to speak up.

Mr. TURNER. All right. Thank you.

Mr. KELLY. Yes, sir.

Mr. McINARNAY. Mr. Mason?

WILBUR H. MASON, OPERATIONS MANAGER, FLORIDA TRACTOR EQUIPMENT CO., JACKSONVILLE, FLA.

Mr. MASON. Yes. I am Will Mason, operations manager and secretary of the Florida Tractor Equipment Co., in Jacksonville.

I am here today in the absence of Gert Schmidt, our president, who could not be here. We are the only distributors of tractors and implements—farm equipment—in the State of Florida. We were formerly the Florida Ford Tractor Co., which was in business since 1947, and, of course, Ford elected to distribute under their own distribution pattern last year, and we elected to stay in the business and we are continuing on.

However, we dropped from having 78 employees to 7 last March and we are back up to 36 now, so we are growing rapidly. We at Florida Ford did set a pace of around $10 million a year. We are at a pace now of $3 million—$3 million-plus, this year—our first full year.

We don't do any business with the Federal Government, or we haven't done any business directly with the Federal Government agencies. We have had some bids in and we do some with the State government, but we are not too successful right now with that.

As far as Florida Tractor Equipment Co., we cover an area of Florida and southeast Georgia, and we have another company in Decatur, Ga., the Southeast Tractor Corp., which handles the same David Brown tractor and the lines that we have, out of that area, covering towns in Georgia, Alabama, 14 counties in Tennessee and 5 counties in South Carolina.

Mr. THEVENOT. What is your major line of farm equipment?

Mr. MASON. Our major line is David Brown tractors, along with farm equipment to go with it—not David Brown equipment, but lines from suppliers throughout the country, parts and service, and related items.

We also distribute, along with farm equipment, Bolens power equipment; the lawnmowers, riding mowers, and compact tractors in Florida, Georgia, and Alabama. Another line we distribute is the Lawn Boy Mowers in two-thirds of the State of Florida. Bolens, all of Florida; Bolens, all of Georgia and Alabama.

Bolens is a subsidiary of Food Machines Corp.

Mr. McINARNAY. Thank you, Mr. Mason.

Mr. Hohenhausen?

WALTER HOHENHAUSEN, JR., GENERAL MANAGER, PENINSULA PEST CONTROL SERVICE, INC., JACKSONVILLE, FLA.

Mr. HOHENHAUSEN. My name is Walter Hohenhausen, Jr., and I am representing Earl Dixon, who is out of town, and he is the president of Peninsular Pest Control Service, Inc.

We are a fairly new concern with respect to pest control in this area, having been in business about 10 years. However, we are enjoying very rapid growth, and at the present time, we probably are second in the industry in the area to the national concern, which is Orkin.

We employ, according to the seasons, between 20 to 30 people, and our main business is pest control in the homes, in industry, and we also have a division devoted to lawn pest control, as well as termite work, and tent fumigation.

Most of our work with respect to the Federal Government is concerned with subcontracting to general contractors on Federal projects, requiring soil poisoning for new construction.

Mr. McINARNAY. Thank you, sir.

Mr. Goodloe?

GEORGE M. GOODLOE, SECRETARY, PARKHILL-GOODLOE CO., INC., JACKSONVILLE, FLA.

Mr. GOODLOE. I am George Goodloe, with Parkhill-Goodloe Co. I am pinchhitting for my brother who is out of town. He is more familiar with the problems we have.

We are in the dredging business and the parent company was formed approximately 75 years ago. The bulk of our work—perhaps 90 percent of it—is with the Government through the Corps of Engineers.

We operate 3 dredges and have from 50 to 100 employees, depending on our workload. We now do in excess of a million dollars worth of business a year.

Mr. McINARNAY. Thank you, sir.

Mr. Hufnagel?

DAN HUFNAGEL, OF THE JACK R. WINTERBURN CERTIFIED PUBLIC ACCOUNTANTS FIRM, JACKSONVILLE, FLA.

Mr. HUFNAGEL. Well, I represent the CPA firm, Jack R. Winterburn. I am a senior accountant associated with Mr. Winterburn, and I am more or less substituting for him here today. We didn't know exactly what we were invited for, but we are here and pleased to be here, so as to have a better picture of what some of our local business people have to do. We have at times furnished financial information used in connection with some formalities of the SBA, and Jack and I have both been in public accounting for 20 years or more, and we wanted to listen to the proceedings and participate if we can.

Mr. McINARNAY. We are very glad to have you, Mr. Hufnagel.

It just so happens that in the meeting in Shreveport, one of the gentlemen spoke up and said that, "What you fellows really need to do is have our accountants in, because they run into these problems daily, and they could really discuss them."

So we are particularly happy to have you here.

Mr. HUFNAGEL. Thank you.

Mr. McINARNAY. Mr. Boree, we are glad to have you here.

We have been discussing a little bit about our mission here. We are here to listen to the small businessmen about any particular problem that affects them, that the Federal Government has anything to do with, and we have been around the room identifying ourselves and our companies, the types of business we are in, numbers of employees and with whom we do business, and that sort of thing.

I wonder if you would do that for us?

HENDERSON BOREE, BOREE CONCRETE BLOCK CO., INC., JACK-SONVILLE, FLA.

Mr. BOREE. Well, I am Henderson Boree of the Boree Concrete Block Manufacturing Co.

The number of men, I don't know exactly right now. I would say around 24 employees, and you want to know who we sell?

Mr. McINARNAY. Yes.

Mr. BOREE. We sell anybody—one, or as many as they want, of concrete blocks.

Mr. McINARNAY. Are you still located around Stockton and Edison—out in there?

Mr. BOREE. Dennis Street—2036 Dennis.

What else did you want to know?

Mr. McINARNAY. Who you do business with—you said everybody. Do you do any business with the Federal Government?

Mr. BOREE. Directly with the Federal Government?

Mr. McINARNAY. As a subcontractor?

Mr. BOREE. As a subcontractor, yes, commercial jobs—large—well, we have a lot of commercial work right at present that is going on at Cecil Field and Mayport, and school jobs, and individuals also—homebuilders or anybody. It doesn't matter who it is.

Mr. McINARNAY. Well, we are very glad to have you here today.

Mr. BOREE. We also have the only autoclave block in Jacksonville. That is a high-pressure cure, so the Government accepts that as—on their jobs—a 3-day hold period on their jobs is all that is required, but on air dried block, it is a 28-day holding period on the job, so therefore, it is an advantage for an autoclave, and that is an advantage for the contractor.

Mr. McINARNAY. What do you sell, other than concrete blocks? Did you say you had other products?

Mr. BOREE. Well, we don't specialize in any. We sell mortar and steel rods.

Those are about the leading ones that we have. I don't know of anything else to add, unless somebody wants to buy some blocks.

Mr. McINARNAY. Now, what we have been doing—we went around the room and identified ourselves, and then we are going to go back around and ask for various viewpoints. I hope that we will try to expedite this as much as possible and I hope that most of you will be able to stay and contribute to the dialog as we go along.

I know that some of you are under particular pressure, on time. Mr. Mason mentioned that he had something to get to.

Now, I wonder if there is anyone else who is fighting the clock? I know you are all doing that, but——

Mr. BOREE. I am pushed for time.

Mr. McINARNAY. Thank you. If you don't mind, then, we will call on Mr. Mason first and solicit his views on any particular thing he would like to bring up at this time.

We will then go from there.

Mr. Mason?

Mr. MASON. Well, fine. Thank you.

I would like to say that in previous remarks I should have included our active participation with some of the Federal agencies, 4–H Clubs, FFA organizations, Soil Conservation—we do work actively with those people and their projects throughout the State, the projects we can participate in.

Mr. McINARNAY. Mr. Mason, would you mind speaking up a little bit?

Mr. MASON. All right.

I don't have any particular thing, I guess, that I could bring before this group. My own personal views on where help could be given to to the small businessman—there have been clinics and so on in management for the small businessman. These programs are going on— still going on. The biggest need, having worked closely with dealers of farm equipment for the last 15 years—and is the major problem— is management, and assistance in training them. There is a real, real big need. The associations are into this quite actively and by having their schools—management schools, the major manufacturers are more getting into this management training, but outside of those major lines, there are a number of small farm equipment dealers whose real problem is the lack of management knowledge.

Mr. THEVENOT. Are they getting assistance from the Department of Agriculture on this?

Mr. MASON. Not that I know of, from the Department of Agriculture. The Small Business Administration had clinics for the small business, for management, but not specifically in the field of farm equipment.

Mr. THEVENOT. Have your people participated in these?

Mr. MASON. Our people have participated.

Mr. McINARNAY. Do you have any recommendations as to the way that these management assistance programs might be improved?

Mr. MASON. It is real hard to get people to attend these types of clinics.

Your mention here of assistance from the Department of Agriculture—here to me, is a place where this could very well be worked in for these people, and I am speaking primarily of those who are not handling a major line of tractors—there are quite a number that are not.

As a personal experience, not too long ago, we got hold of a young fellow down in Dade City who was in this type of business and didn't have a tractor business, but he had a tractor repair business—some small implements, but didn't know much about running the business, so we took him under our wing and developed him into a David Brown tractor dealer and set up his accounting for him and trained his girls— his wife, in fact, on accounting and we follow through with him every month or two. And he has come along real well.

Now, some kind of training such as this on these small independent farm equipment dealers certainly would be real helpful because this is their biggest problem.

They might be able to sell merchandise but they can't make money.

Mr. THEVENOT. This is primarily the dealers of small equipment manufacturers? The larger ones have their programs, of course?

Mr. MASON. Yes; the larger ones have incoming programs that cover this area of training, yes.

Mr. THEVENOT. What are some of these companies that handle— that produce this type of equipment, besides the one you represent?

Mr. MASON. You mean the smaller companies?

Mr. THEVENOT. Smaller farm equipment manufacturers.

Mr. MASON. I don't quite follow you.

You have a number of major lines of tractors—Massey-Ferguson, Case, John Deere, Oliver, Ford, Minneapolis-Moline, John Deere— there are so many of them. All of these have a training program for their dealers—some sort of management training, and this has developed in the last few years—the last 4 or 5 years that they have gone into this.

The need, I think, is for those dealers who do not have a tractor line where they do not have this backup training. This is the part that I can't spell out—who they are individually, or where they are, but there are quite a number of them in the State of Florida, and Georgia.

Mr. THEVENOT. The other major lines is what I was getting at— the other types of tractors.

Mr. MASON. Most of those have—I think all of them have some management training programs.

Mr. McINARNAY. I think your company testified before our committee a year or two ago when the decision was made by the large companies to change their way of distribution, did you not?

Mr. MASON. You are right.

Mr. Gert Schmidt, our president, testified. We have not been involved in this very much. We did file—I guess it goes to the Atlanta regional office—a form to get put up on the bid list for all the products we handle. We get very little information, very few bids sent to us. We did get one just recently, which I have here in front of me, from the Housing and Home Finance Agency, Public Housing Administration of Atlanta, which is an open-end kind of contract. I ran into a little difficulty with this because of the fact that they don't—in the bid itself, they don't refer to the specifications—and, this is on lawnmowers, incidentally—and in the bid, there are no specific specs, but it does refer to interim Federal specifications, 00M00681B, and different numbers throughout the bid.

Then, in another place, it says the specs can be gotten from the regional office, and of course, we wrote for those, and we haven't received them yet, although we submitted a bid we hope is within the specs. We think we are, and we hope we are.

Mr. THEVENOT. How long ago have you written for these?

Mr. MASON. Well, we received this—let's see if I have the date.

It has been 3 or 4 weeks ago. This was issued on October 28. We received it a few days thereafter and November 9 was the deadline for getting it in, and from the date we received this we wrote for the specifications and we haven't received them yet. We had to get it in

November 9, so we sent it in without receipt of the specifications. We are just hoping we are all right.

This is probably an oversight somewhere along the line, but my point on this is, if there are specifications on the bid, then they ought to be with the bid. This is my point—not to say, just send for the specifications, particularly when they give you just 10 days to get your bid in.

Mr. THEVENOT. This was inadequate information for a responsive proposal on your part, sir?

Mr. MASON. You are so right.

So, there is not enough time involved—not enough time within the bid time and the let time, or the opening time, to really get what you need to bid the job.

Mr. McINARNAY. This does not appear to be an emergency procurement, by any means?

Mr. MASON. It is not.

Mr. McINARNAY. I believe, under the regulations generally, they are supposed to give you at least 30 days, and it seems to me that this is something that should be called to the agency's attention—well, this was issued October 28, ending November 9, 2 p.m., eastern standard time.

Mr. THEVENOT. Ten days for your bid?

Mr. MASON. Yes.

Mr. McINARNAY. Often, it is much less than that, and also without any good reason.

Mr. MASON. It is not an emergency for the period of January 1, 1966, through December 31, 1966—so, it is not a real emergency.

Mr. McINARNAY. Have you ever done any business with the General Services Administration?

Mr. MASON. No.

Mr. McINARNAY. Have you ever made any effort to do so?

Mr. MASON. No, we haven't tried to. We have just in the last year gotten into this lawnmower part of the business, and we want to get in—get all the information we can where we can get into submitting bids—get on the list to be able to submit bids.

Mr. McINARNAY. You drop Senator Smathers a line and we will see that you get on the bidders list—whatever bidders lists are available for your type of product in the General Services Administration, and possibly in the Defense Supply Agency, which purchases thousands of miscellaneous type items for the three military services.

Mr. MASON. Fine.

Mr. McINARNAY. Are there any other major problem areas you would like to cover?

Mr. MASON. No, I don't think I have anything that I could be of any help on.

Mr. THEVENOT. Mr. Mason, had the specifications been included in this bid, would the 10 days then have been an excessively short period for you to be responsive?

Mr. MASON. There would have been sufficient time.

Mr. THEVENOT. So, you are not manufacturing. This is a line that you could just supply immediately?

Mr. MASON. That is right.

Mr. McINARNAY. Have you done business with any agencies other than the public housing? I think this was public housing; was it, Mr. Mason?

Mr. MASON. Yes; Housing and Home Finance.

Mr. McINARNAY. Housing and Home Finance.

Mr. MASON. No, not since we have been the Florida Tractor Equipment Co.

Mr. THEVENOT. Do you have any comments on the requirements that the Federal Government places on you as a small business firm?

I am referring generally to the reporting requirements.

Mr. MASON. Well, just like everyone else, the more reports there are the higher the cost of operation is, and of course, the Federal Government reporting—they have so many different agencies—Social Security, your withholding tax—all these increase costs, but I am sure they are all necessary.

Mr. McINARNAY. Do you have any specific recommendations on the manner in which the Federal Government asks you for various reports? Any ideas you might have for simplifying these?

Mr. THEVENOT. Are they sufficiently clear in their requests?

Mr. MASON. All those that I have been in contact with, I would say are sufficiently clear for our purposes.

If I run into any problem, I can call my CPA.

Mr. McINARNAY. Well, thank you very much, Mr. Mason, for giving us the benefit of your views.

We would like for you to stay as long as you can; but, any time you have to leave, just feel free to do so.

Mr. MASON. Thank you, sir.

Mr. McINARNAY. Before we go back to Mr. Boree, Mr. Gregg has joined us.

The first thing that we did was to go around the room and identify ourselves, our business, the type of business it is, whom we do business with, the size of the business and that sort of thing. I wonder if you will do that for us, Mr. Gregg?

CHARLES P. GREGG, LIBERTY IRON WORKS, JACKSONVILLE, FLA.

Mr. GREGG. My name is Charles P. Gregg, with Liberty Iron Works, and ours is primarily with central and southern Florida flood control, which of course is Government, but second-hand Government, because we don't go straight through the Government. Ours goes through a prime, and sometimes we are the second or third down the line.

Mr. McINARNAY. What kind of products?

Mr. GREGG. Flood control downstate, gates and so on.

Mr. McINARNAY. I am familiar with the central and southern Florida flood control district.

What type of products do you manufacture for them?

Mr. GREGG. Miscellaneous metals and the gates that go in there — you know, there is a scad of anchor bolts and all kinds of sleeves and guardrails and handrails, side seals, bottom seals, top seals.

Mr. THEVENOT. Valves and so on?

Mr. GREGG. Valves, stilling wells.

Mr. McINARNAY. How many employees do you have?

Mr. GREGG. Fifteen in the plant and about six helpers.

Mr. McINARNAY. How long have you been in business?

Mr. GREGG. Since 1959— January 1, 1959.

Mr. McINARNAY. Do you sell to any other Government agencies, either as a prime contractor or a subcontractor?

Mr. GREGG. No; no other Government agencies. Ours have all been through the U.S. Engineers, other than one set of gates that we shipped to Pittsburgh.

We bid it out of a Government agency pamphlet, the Commerce Daily, and we bought the steel in Pittsburgh. It was shipped down here. We put it in the gates and shipped it back.

Mr. MCINARNAY. I see.

Mr. GREGG. That was in the paper, and I might add we lost $4,000 on it.

Mr. MCINARNAY. You were low bidder?

Mr. GREGG. Only by $300.

Mr. MCINARNAY. Is that right?

Mr. GREGG. But what caused that—we bid it, taking it by barge, and the particular barge company in town that gave us the estimate flubbed the dub. We found out we couldn't even take it by barge. I made a trip to Tampa and tried to find out about it, but the barge cost would have been absolutely prohibitive. The only way possible that that thing could have been taken by barge and we could have come out on it, would have been that the man was going to make the trip absolutely—if he had a little spot in back that he could put it at no cost to him—practically no cost. That was the only way, so we had to ship it by rail.

That means we had to break it down and go to Pittsburgh and put it back together again.

Mr. MCINARNAY. Thank you, Mr. Gregg. We will come back to you and solicit your general views on small business.

Mr. Dickson has joined us.

The first order of business we had, Mr. Dickson, was to go around asking each person to identify himself as to his type of business, with whom he does business, the number of employees and that sort of thing. We will then go around again and solicit general views from each one of you.

I wonder if you would be good enough now to identify yourself and tell us a little bit about your company?

ELDON DICKSON, DICKSON TIRE CO., JACKSONVILLE, FLA.

Mr. DICKSON. Well, my name is Eldon Dickson, and my business is Dickson Tire Co., and we are located at Edison and College Streets here in Jacksonville.

I have been in business 35 years totally, in business for myself 21 years. Would you like for me to give you a little bit about our operations?

Mr. MCINARNAY. Yes, sir.

Mr. DICKSON. Well, we are distributors for two of the major rubber companies, B. F. Goodrich and Mohawk Rubber Co., and we also have our own recapping plant. We do tire recapping for both truck and passenger cars—the small compacts and all, and we do repairing, such as vulcanizing, section repairing to truck tires, tractor tires, grader tires, and then we have a front-end department—wheel alinement and balancing, brake service, shock service.

We employ 11—we have 11 in our employ.

Anything further you would like to discuss at this time—I mean, going into detail?

Mr. THEVENOT. Do you do any business with the Government directly?

Mr. DICKSON. Yes; we do recapping for the Government, the U.S. Post Office Department, Cecil Field, Mainside, Naval Air Station, and some at Mayport—recapping and vulcanizing.

Mr. McINARNAY. This is all with local Government offices?

Mr. DICKSON. Right.

Mr. McINARNAY. All right, sir.

We are glad to have you here today, Mr. Dickson, and we will come back to you in just a few minutes.

Mr. Boree, I wonder if you would give us the benefit of your views about the small businessman as you see him, and anything in particular that relates to doing business with the Federal Government, either as a prime contractor or a subcontractor—any particular problem that may arise as a result of requirements imposed upon your business by the Federal Government.

Mr. BOREE. Well, I haven't had any problem in that respect. My problem is mostly collecting from contractors and individuals.

So, I mean, as far as the Government, with my loan with them, I have no complaint.

Mr. McINARNAY. You say you have a loan. Is that with the Small Business Administration?

Mr. BOREE. Yes; nobody bothers me and I pay my bills when they are made, and I have never been late yet. I might have been a little pushed sometimes, but I have got by; so, as far as any problem with the Government, I haven't any.

Mr. THEVENOT. Your big problem, though, is receiving prompt payment from the prime contractors you do business with. Is that right?

Mr. BOREE. Right; individuals, too.

Most of your larger contractors pay you. You have no problem there, but you take so many individuals, you know, the time runs out and they don't have it, but I don't know of any problems that I have.

Mr. McINARNAY. What was your experience with the SBA loan?

Mr. BOREE. Well, I have enjoyed doing business with them. There is only one problem. They want it back with interest, though, you see.

Mr. THEVENOT. Maybe there ought to be an SBA grant program?

Mr. BOREE. Yes. I have paid back what I borrowed, but then that interest—I would like to get it cut in half instead of carrying these boys that go bankrupt.

Mr. McINARNAY. Your loan was on what term?

Mr. BOREE. Ten years.

Mr. McINARNAY. Ten years?

Mr. BOREE. Yes.

Mr. McINARNAY. I think that is the maximum on these 7(a) loans. I think for working capital you usually restrict that to 6 years, don't you, Mr. Turner?

Mr. TURNER. Yes.

Mr. McINARNAY. It makes a lot of difference in that term of loan, I guess for a businessman—between 3-year money and 10-year money.

Mr. TURNER. When a man is growing fast, it is—it isn't how much money he is making. He plows it all back into his business. Even though he could pay it back, he could continue to use it.

Mr. McINARNAY. I suppose some of you gentlemen may know that the Small Business Administration is having some—I would suppose you would call it growing pains of its own. It is out of money, and they didn't ask Congress for enough last time. I suppose they wanted it, but the Bureau of the Budget wouldn't let them ask for it, and of course the Bureau of the Budget sort of runs things in Washington and the agency has to go through them, no matter what they want, to get a clearance. They are a very powerful group.

But, as of now, the 7(a)—7(a) is the section in the Small Business Act that covers ordinary business loans and as of now they are not accepting any applications. I think Mr. Turner could tell you that the loan guarantee program, where the banks make the loans—SBA guarantees 90 percent of it—as well as a few of the other programs; the local development company and small business investment companies programs are active at the present time, and I think by December 1, Mr. Turner, they are hoping to lift that flat restriction. It may be that they won't be able to loan $350,000, but they are hoping at least to accept some business loans by that time.

That is what they told us just before we came down here.

Mr. TURNER. That is good.

Mr. McINARNAY. Well, Mr. Boree?

Mr. BOREE. Why do they have different interest in different places? You can get a lower rate out of some areas than you can another. Why do we have to be penalized and pay a much higher rate than some other area, or is that just a law? I guess that is the law.

Mr. McINARNAY. It is the law, Mr. Boree—the so-called ARA areas—the area redevelopment areas—I am not sure of all the figures. I think they are all——

Mr. TURNER. They have just done away with all of that.

Mr. McINARNAY. It is now the EDA, isn't it?

Mr. TURNER. Well, the ones who get the benefit of the loans are the EDA.

Here until just recently, up until 2 weeks ago, any business located in an ARA county did have the benefit of the 4-percent interest rate, but now that no longer is available. They have done away with it. They pay the usual rate of 5½ percent now.

That is recently—just 2 weeks ago.

Mr. McINARNAY. Now, disaster loans are, of course, 3 percent; right? That is by special act of Congress.

Mr. MASON. Any time you need money it is a disaster.

Mr. BOREE. That is what mine was.

Mr. HOHENHOUSEN. It still is.

Mr. McINARNAY. The SBA has to get this money from the Treasury, and I don't know exactly what they have to pay for it, but it is more than 3 percent.

Mr. TURNER. It is the average rate that the Government pays each year. It is adjusted.

Mr. McINARNAY. So, on 3-percent loans, the SBA, interestwise, is losing.

Mr. TURNER. We pay about 3¼ percent, and let it out at 3.

Mr. BOREE. But, I think they should lower the rate if a man needs the money and is going to pay—they should give him a different rate.

Mr. McINARNAY. Well, at the very least, I would hope that SBA in the future has adequate money, and I'm sure that Mr. Kennon·

Turner will echo this, so that he can accept and approve good applications, and not be in the predicament he is in right now, where he has no money to loan out. That is even worse.

Mr. BOREE. Well, if they would save that money they are sending overseas and bring it back where they need it at home they would get along better with the family, you know.

Mr. TURNER. Well, Mr. Boree, we can't compete with the banks, you know. We can't lend money to folks when you can go to the bank and get it at five—and it wouldn't be fair. We would put the banks out of business.

Mr. MCINARNAY. Do you have any other comments, Mr. Boree?

Mr. BOREE. No. No more gripes.

Mr. MCINARNAY. Well, we welcome them.

Mr. THEVENOT. That is what we are here for.

Mr. MCINARNAY. We like to hear your sentiments completely on anything.

Mr. BOREE. That is all.

Mr. MCINARNAY. Thank you so much, and we hope you can stay as long as possible.

Mr. BOREE. To hear some other complaints?

Mr. MCINARNAY. Yes, sir; and feel free to chime in with anything you have to say as the discussion moves along.

Mr. BOREE. Thank you.

Mr. MCINARNAY. Mr. Gregg, I wonder if you would give us the benefit of your views on small business—any particular point you would like to cover, any problem areas that you see, either as a result of doing business with the Government or any particular requirements that the Federal Government places upon you that are unduly harsh.

We would like to hear from you.

Mr. GREGG. Well, you can immediately eliminate the SBA, because if all the dealings we have had to have with people were as pleasant as they have been with the SBA on three loans, we wouldn't have a problem. We would be in paradise. So that takes them out of the picture.

Now, we do strike another thing, though, in invitations for bids that come out that say this is a small business set-aside—in other words, there are certain stipulations that constitute a small business—so many employees, so much money, so much business done within a period of time. We have lost several because of that, and not because of the fact that a small business didn't get it, even though it was marked a small business set-aside. A larger company doesn't do a thing in the world except form an outside corporation—and, it is no longer small.

Now, I understand that that is not supposed to be, but it is done, because we are doing a contract now that, all told, the company must have 5,000 employees on the payroll and maybe do $20 or $30 million a year—maybe more.

Mr. MCINARNAY. The Small Business Act provides that a company, to be small, must be independently owned and operated and not dominant in its field.

Mr. GREGG. That is right.

Mr. MCINARNAY. And there are very strict rules that apply there.

Of course, the Administrator of the Small Business Administration has the authority to classify businesses in more specific categories, as to whether they are large or small. However, anytime you encounter a thing of this sort, where you feel that a business is large, and yet, is competing on a small business set-aside, you have the right to protest that to the Small Business Administration, and they will make a determination. They have the authority to make a determination as to whether one of the competitors is in fact small business.

I don't know whether you were aware of your authority to do that.

Mr. GREGG. I was aware of that. I didn't think it was worth it, really, from the standpoint of the time it would take to do it and all that, and then, if we were successful, we would be so far behind that we would come out at the little end of the horn anyway.

Mr. McINARNAY. Well, I don't know what the particular circumstances are in that case.

Mr. GREGG. Well, I have reference to a particular flood control project on which we are just about 60 percent through now. We bid this, and when we bid it we knew that the man was a little branch off a big one. We knew that, but he got the job, and so did we.

But, that is not true every time, because sometimes the big contractor—you know, he takes it where he wants it to go.

Mr. McINARNAY. I am sure there are a lot of factors that enter into a decision as to whether you would want to protest, but I would suggest that if all other things are equal, and that comes up again——

Mr. GREGG. Well, when that came up, the company out of Alabama—they bid it out of Alabama and they were low on it—no, I am wrong. They set up an office in Tampa immediately beforehand with the home office in Alabama, and this is a branch, but they got the small business set-aside and have had several of them. But, our correspondence goes back to Alabama, not Tampa. Our checks come out of Alabama, so that should be proof within itself that it is not a small business; if it were entirely separate, we certainly wouldn't be getting our checks out of Alabama. We should be getting them from Tampa.

Mr. McINARNAY. Sometimes—I don't know what this company is in size, but sometimes a company can have some affiliates and still in sum total be classified as a small business.

Mr. GREGG. Well, I guess you are right.

However, you cannot do the canal work that is necessary on this, when they are $8 or $10 million jobs, and build superhighways and dams in other States and all that, and be classified as small business. You can't do it.

Mr. McINARNAY. I would recommend that if this comes up again it would be very simple to get in touch with Mr. Turner here, who is in charge of the local SBA office, and I am sure that he could be of some rapid assistance to you in coming to the bottom of it.

You mentioned the Commerce Business Daily a few moments ago. Have you found that to be a useful publication?

Mr. GREGG. We take it.

Mr. McINARNAY. Do you subscribe to it?

Mr. GREGG. Yes. We read it religiously.

Mr. McINARNAY. Does it help you? I see you obtained a contract, but lost money.

Mr. GREGG. Well, we have had two or three out of it.

Mr. McINARNAY. Have you?

Mr. GREGG. Yes.

Mr. McINARNAY. Do you find that the bid notices in there give you sufficient time to get in your bid?

Mr. GREGG. Hardly, and it takes a Philadelphia attorney to understand it. It would take you 6 weeks to begin to know what you are reading, but one time you do learn what you are looking for and where to find it, there is some good information in it.

But, at the beginning, no.

Mr. McINARNAY. Do you have any specific ideas on how that publication might be improved?

Mr. GREGG. Yes, but don't ask me right now. If you would give me a little bit of time to think it over, I could tell you. Something that might help, and I don't know whether it would or not, because we are only interested in one thing. That is the only thing we are looking for, and there is too much in it.

We have to look two or three places to find what we are hunting.

Mr. McINARNAY. If you think of some other factors you would like to bring up later on, we would be glad to receive a letter from you, and include it in the record of this proceeding.

Mr. GREGG. OK.

Mr. McINARNAY. You also mentioned earlier the impossibility of barging your product to Pittsburgh.

Now, I wonder if that was in the specifications, or did you just assume you could barge it up there?

Mr. GREGG. No, the delivery was Pittsburgh. They didn't care if we took it by helicopter. Our estimator received a barging quotation which we used in our estimate. The estimate of the cost of moving this to Pittsburgh by barge. Actually, the cost seemed to be in line. It was comparable to what we had figured, but when he went out of business—or died—and we tried it from other sources, the figures that he had submitted were just a small fraction of the actual cost.

I went to the port authority in Tampa to try to find out about the barge charges from there, assuming that if we could get it to Tampa we could put it on a barge there, but that was prohibitive.

We had planned to build it in one piece, which would have been the two leaves, but we had to build it in three pieces each—due to the size, which of course, was an additional cost. We had to set it up for Government inspection, then take it down, transport it to the rail yard, into a car, and the height of it caused a commotion with the railroad. We thought at one time that we wouldn't get it there at all, as there was 1 inch clearance on a bridge in Pittsburgh.

Mr. McINARNAY. I wonder, Mr. Gregg, if there is any particular——

Mr. GREGG. Oh, another thing I might add to that—they wouldn't take it in hot weather, and that delayed it. We had $1,400 in liquidated damages waiting for the cold weather, for the steel to shrink so they could take it through that 1 inch. If it had been hot, it wouldn't have gone through.

Mr. BOREE. What do these gates weigh?

Mr. GREGG. Well, from 15 to 38 to 40 tons.

Mr. McINARNAY. I wonder if there is any particular legislation that you would like to see Congress enact, or not enact, that would affect your business?

Mr. GREGG. Yes; take this darned Census report that is about so thick—if any of you gentlemen have ever had one——

Mr. KOESTER. I had that down on my list.

Mr. GREGG. That is enough to drive anyone out of his mind, and I never have been able to understand what they get out of it, because they call for things—the last one I got out there, they wanted to know how much aluminum we had bought, where we bought it, how we used it, so many tons, and so forth—how it was bought, what we use it for, what grade it as, what classification aluminum.

They wanted the same thing out of carbon steel. They wanted it out of stainless steel.

On top of that, they wanted to know how many man-hours was applied to this particular part, and to the other part—how many man-hours were lost due to accidents, I think, in this one particular category, how many man-hours we had in an entire year, how much we had lost—oh, I could go on and on. I never did even send it in, because I figured if I sent it in I would make a bigger fool out of myself than if I didn't.

Mr. BOREE. Well, what would they do to you if you don't send it in?

Mr. GREGG. Well, they threatened a lawsuit, but they haven't been down yet.

Mr. KOESTER. Ours came marked with all sorts of beautiful penalties. We had 10 days to do it in.

Mr. McINARNAY. How often do you get this?

Mr. GREGG. Once a year.

Mr. BOREE. I thought it was once every 5 years—or, is it the same one I am thinking about?

Mr. GREGG. I don't know. It is on big, yellow paper.

Mr. PAINTER. It is annual.

Mr. McINARNAY. That is the one that won't fit in a typewriter?

Mr. GREGG. It won't fit in anything. It won't fit in anyone's head.

Mr. PAINTER. It takes a rail car to send it back.

Mr. THEVENOT. Is that the kind of information you could fill out in-house, or would you have to get some outside help to get it?

Mr. GREGG. It would take a bevy of CPA's I don't know how long to go through our books to fill that thing out, and fill it out correctly. It would take a complete audit.

Mr. BOREE. Well, you couldn't fill mine in correctly, and my CPA—I give it to him. He kept it a week, sent it back and said, "You are going to have to help me with it or we will have to throw it away." I said, "Well, throw it away." I was too busy, and so he laid it on the desk and it stayed there. I got three or four threats, and I finally sent in what he filled out and let it go.

I couldn't answer it correctly—and he couldn't either.

Mr. GREGG. If Mr. Turner had to fill out one of those he would quit.

Mr. McINARNAY. Are there any other reports that the Government requires of you that fall in this category?

Mr. GREGG. No.

No, sir; they are all right. That is the only one. The rest of them all make sense.

Mr. BOREE. Who cooked this up, anyway?

Mr. McINARNAY. I would assume the Census Bureau.

Mr. KOESTER. Wasn't it the Commerce Department?

Mr. THEVENOT. Which is a part of—the Census Bureau, of course, is a part of the Commerce Department.

Mr. PAINTER. Well, we got one on a water survey there. I looked at that, and I figured in the first place if I had kept that kind of record in our place on the use of water, I would have been a world wonder, because they asked so many different questions—how much water, how many gallons you bought for the year from outside sources, how many gallons came out of the artesian wells, and what percentage of your water was treated, where it went out, and what percentage went some other place.

I mean, the average company, I don't think, keeps records like that. So, I got busy and did a little mental arithmetic and I wrote some figures down and sent it in. Now, as far as them wanting accurate information—of course, they do say to make it as approximate as you can, but I just gave them a brief outline there on the questions they asked. Even going into the kilowatt-hours of power. They come up with a lot of stuff like that.

Now, just merely estimating pointblank how many kilowatts per year do you use—that is fairly simple. I mean, you could look it up but they diverge so much from that and try to break it down into all different kinds of uses and things, and this leaves you just completely bewildered.

The rest of our forms that we get—as I say, I have just reached the point where I turn them over to our CPA's and let them bother with them. We have a lot of forms from the Labor Department, and things like that—statistical, and we can fill those out. I let the CPA's do it, because I couldn't take—it would take too much of our time in the office to do that.

Mr. GREGG. Well, we had to do this to each figure that they asked for in the census—and, incidentally, the census we are talking about contains water information, too—it has got that in there. It would take four full-time employees, and I don't know how many pounds of paper to have it available where you could turn to it and say at this date it was so-and-so.

And, it would take the same amount of man-hours at the end of the year if you didn't have it like that.

Mr. McINARNAY. I wonder if the Census Bureau makes any effort to explain the importance to them of this information when they send you a questionnaire of this sort? Do they explain why they want the information and why it is important to them, and so forth?

Mr. GREGG. I don't recall seeing that. The only thing I recall seeing is that they tell you what to do, what they want, and what they will do if you don't.

That is about the gist of it. They don't say that the first time—that is the second or third time they ask you for it. Then they begin to get nasty.

Mr. McINARNAY. Are there any other areas, other than the report—we have heard a lot of this in these various cities. It seems to be the general consensus of the small businessman that this is an undue burden placed upon them, and particularly the census report you mentioned.

Mr. GREGG. I am glad.

Mr. BOREE. This must just have been opening up a job for people.

Mr. GREGG. Didn't they have one man in Washington who got lost down in the bottom somewhere? He had been there clipping paper for a long time, ever since World War I, and they had forgotten about him. Well, it must have been someone like that who dug this up.

Mr. THEVENOT. You might say there has been a great effort going on in the Congress and in the executive department of the Government to do a complete survey of all of the reporting requirements on any report that requires more than 10 respondents to it, and they have been successful, in the brief period that they have been doing this, in eliminating a good many forms and simplifying a good many others.

There is a committee of the House of Representatives, a subcommittee of the Committee on Government Operations, that has gone into extensive study and continued to study this, and hopefully, out of this will come some kind of shortening and cutting back on the reporting requirements on businessmen.

Mr. GREGG. To simplify it?

Mr. THEVENOT. To simplify it.

I know that any new form that is—that a Government agency wishes to put out now must go through a lengthy and rather arduous course and set of reviewing boards. One of the boards is made up of representatives from private industry. It must go through this gantlet before it is ever put out for information, and there is hopefully going to be a great deal of progress made in this.

Mr. GREGG. That would be fine, if they just don't get the industry too high, to where the man that is sitting on it will look at it and say, well, my CPA will take care of that, and so forth. When it gets down small, that will be good.

Mr. McINARNAY. They have had legislation on the books since 1942—the so-called Federal Reports Act, which attempts to limit and restrict the inquiries made of citizens and businessmen, and so forth, but only since 1960 has there been a concerted effort, and I think that the time was coincident with the time when Congress began its comprehensive inquiry into just what the executive agencies were asking businessmen and citizens, that they began putting some extra effort into this, and they have cut down a considerable number of these reports.

Unfortunately, it has not eliminated all of the onerous ones yet.

By the way, the report put out by the subcommittee—its title gives you some indication of the feeling of Congress on what the executive agencies ask for—it is called the Federal paperwork jungle, and it is available to anyone who wants to have a copy of it.

Mr. Gregg, did you have any further comments on any area you would like to cover?

Mr. GREGG. No.

I've got lots of areas, but I don't think this will cover them.

Mr. McINARNAY. Well, it may be that if you would bring up some of these, some of the others participating here would have ideas to add, and it would build a good record of recommendations, and critiques for the committee to consider.

Mr. GREGG. OK. When the U.S. Engineers give a contract for digging a canal, putting structures in—which pertains to gates and so forth—that job is 100 percent bonded. The prime contractor that takes that contract must produce, or the bonding company, one or the other. The Government is not going to lose any money.

Now, the prime contractor again may require a bond from a sub. In this instance, we had to produce a $200,000 bond. The job was $5 million. Our part of it, building these two gates, was $202,000. The contractor went broke. I'm not sure he actually went broke.

Anyway, the bonding company had to take it over. We sweated it out for 19 months—for a little over $20,000. Of course, now, this is no problem of the Government, but as Mr. Turner well knows, it nearly put us under. There is no way under God's earth to get money, except by the bonding company. Our material is incorporated into the job—accepted by the Government, and the Government paid the contractor. The Government didn't owe anything on it. They had paid the contractor for it. He had used the funds otherwise.

And, his bonding company had to take the job over and complete it, but nevertheless, our materials were installed and operable, but we waited 19 months for the money, and only collected it last month.

Mr. McINARNAY. Now, you say this was the fault of the bonding company not making more prompt payment?

Mr. GREGG. Well, it is no fault of the Government. The Government had paid it, but a little businessman—that could ruin him.

Mr. THEVENOT. Did you have to go to the courts?

Mr. GREGG. No. Oh, it was suggested we take it to court and try to collect it, but I couldn't see it, I knew eventually we would get our money.

The only question was when we would get it. There was no reason why we shouldn't, because there it was—physical evidence.

Mr. McINARNAY. Is there any action that the Federal Government could take—any requirements that it could place on bonding companies that would assure some expeditious treatment on payment of claims in cases like this?

Mr. GREGG. You boys work it out. I wish you could. That would be good, if you could just do that. That would be well worth while.

Mr. McINARNAY. Do you have any ideas about that?

Mr. GREGG. Well, it would seem—the prime contractor sent in his estimate to the Government, stating—it is on his forms—our material is on the jobsite, inspected before it left our plant, inspected again when it reached the jobsite, installed in the lock, and operable. The Government paid the man.

All right. Their skirts are clear. They can't go any further. They could have required from this man, I think, evidence that he had paid what he asked for, what he had on his estimate sheet when he made it up, which included moneys due Liberty Iron Works.

Mr. BOREE. An affidavit?

Mr. GREGG. Now, had that been done, then—I don't know how it could be worked out, but it looks to me like there ought to be some way to work it out where we wouldn't have to wait like that, and I think we've got another contract that might be the same way.

Mr. McINARNAY. This is not an unreasonable request, is it, in the sense that in an ordinary commercial business if you pay a prime contractor and don't have the assurances of subcontractor payment, then the subcontractor can file a lien against your building for his payment.

Mr. GREGG. No, you can't. That would be——

Mr. MCINARNAY. But, you can't do that with the Federal Government.

Mr. GREGG. No; you can't do it.

Mr. MCINARNAY. You are suggesting that some system like this be set up for the protection of small subcontractors?

Mr. GREGG. That is right, because had that been an individual, we could do that, but not with the Government.

If we tried to institute a suit against the Government for payment of that, they would say, heck, we paid for it. If he didn't pay you, that is your problem—which is true.

Mr. BOREE. You know, I think they should get an affidavit just like other people require when they have something built.

Mr. GREGG. I have primary reference to one estimate on which this company listed Liberty Iron Works, $35,906. He asked the Government for that and by so doing he made a statement that he owed Liberty Iron Works $35,906, he didn't say so, but you would be led to believe since he was asking the Government for that amount of money that he in turn was going to turn around and pay it out to Liberty Iron Works—less 10 percent, of course, for retainage.

But, we didn't get it. We didn't get any of it, and by constant pounding, and driving back and forth every week or so. If you called, it wouldn't do any good because he was always out—so I left several times at 2 o'clock in the morning and would be hidden on the highway near his office, and when I would see him go in I would follow him in quick before he could get out.

Mr. MCINARNAY. I think it is very unfortunate that the small subcontractor is placed in the position of mercy, really.

Mr. GREGG. It is mercy, begging.

Mr. MCINARNAY. And, it shouldn't be. There should be some system worked out so that the small sub is protected if he does the work and the work is accepted, and as you say, installed. He shouldn't be placed at the mercy, in the case like this, as you were. It is something that we will look into a little further.

Mr. GREGG. And remember, on top of that, you can't talk about material shortages or discrepancies, because it is inspected and approved before it leaves our plant.

Mr. MCINARNAY. And also inspected at the site?

Mr. GREGG. Yes, again.

Mr. GOODLOE. Did you go to the Government after you found out that he had been paid?

Did you go to the contracting office?

Mr. GREGG. I sure did.

Mr. MCINARNAY. Were they of any help to you at all?

Mr. GREGG. They can't. I went straight over to head of construction, U.S. Engineers.

Mr. MCINARNAY. In Jacksonville?

Mr. GREGG. Yes; they advised me that it had been paid.

Mr. MCINARNAY. Well, the subcontractor has for a long time been in a bad position because of the so-called privity-of-contract rule. The Government's position—that of the General Accounting Office, which audits many Government contracts—is that the Federal Government has no privity of contract with anyone other than the prime contractor.

Mr. GREGG. That is right.

Mr. McINARNAY. So therefore, the subcontractor is left out in the weather. It is unfortunate.

Mr. GREGG. Yes, it is true to the extent that it is hilarious.

We have a job building a gate—St. Johns lock, Florida Cross Barge Canal. The prime contractors are at 360 Lexington Avenue in New York City. We have to make up drawings. Now, at our expense, we ship those drawings all the way to New York City. They put another label on it—sometimes they don't even open it; ship it back to the Corps of Engineers here at Jacksonville. The Jacksonville Engineers go over it and send it back to New York City. They slap another label on it—it is true in many instances they haven't even opened it; and it comes back to us.

We would be happy to carry it over to the Corps of Engineers, because it would save 2 weeks.

Mr. McINARNAY. Also, you would be in a position to deal directly with those responsible for overseeing it?

Mr. GREGG. That is right, since the Engineers are the ones who have the say-so as to whether they want this angle changed or they want something else changed. The Engineers are the ones who do it, but we are the ones who are going to do the actual changing, not the prime contractor.

Mr. THEVENOT. The Engineers are doing all the inspection?

Mr. GREGG. All of it.

You see, the prime contractor doesn't care anything about the drawings; not a thing. The only thing he requires is when it get to the jobsite it must fit.

It is not so much the money involved, but the time.

Mr. McINARNAY. Do you have any further comments that you would like to make, Mr. Gregg, any other areas?

Mr. GREGG. Well, I could expound on that a little bit, because it puts us behind the eight ball. To make drawings to cover this contract may require 50 or 60 sheets. We are afraid to order the materials and supplies necessary for fabrication until after final drawing approval.

We do not carry an inventory of steel. It is too varied, so we order steel for each job. Now, if we go ahead and assume nothing can be wrong, which we have done in the past, and assumed they can't or won't change this, and we go ahead and order the material, darned if they won't come in and change it. That is the one drawing they will change every time.

We buy it when it is approved, and some drawings take three trips, which consumes valuable time. That is their prerogative. Example: Let's say we have four items equally spaced on the drawing and they decide they don't want them equally spaced. They want this one here, this one here, this one a little bit closer, and this one a little bit closer. That changes no material, but the time involved going to New York City, back again, back to New York, back again.

So, we don't buy material before prior approval.

In the meantime, though, we do need to start work on it, and at the final end of it then, they are hollering, and if we don't get it out on time—liquidated damages of so much a day.

But, that is not as important as the money part of it.

Mr. McINARNAY. Well, thank you so much, Mr. Gregg.

Mr. Painter, I wonder if you would give us your views?

Mr. PAINTER. Well, I really have very little to talk about, as it relates to your main purpose here, doing business with the Government. We as such do very little business with the Federal Government. We sell a few small isolated agencies here and there, like the veterans' hospital down at Clearwater or something like that. We find no problem in that type of business. It isn't big business, of course, but in our case, if we want to bid on Army requirements—they asked us to, out of Columbia, S.C.—and have called us long distance several times, and they have put us on their list. I mean, they have approached us, rather than we trying to go through a lot of redtape on getting on such a list, but we are not in a position to consider that type of business, primarily due to lack of sufficient supplies.

We stay, basically, with the ice-packed chicken or the fresh-cut-up chicken which we sell on the Florida market. We do no business with the Federal Government which would upset us or come up with a lot of petty problems. I could take the liberty—I don't like to bring up somebody else's problems, as I don't understand enough of them, but when Mr. Kelly called me and I got Mr. Turner's letter, I did make inquiry among a couple of my business associates that I know do come probably within the scope of your inquiries—they should be up here, and I tried to get them to come up, but it was so late in the week and they had other plans. They are in the fabrication business, you know and bid on various jobs, or what have you.

As I say, I know nothing about their businesses sufficiently to sit here and be a qualified expert talking about it, but they did mention a couple of things about—is it permissible to bring this up, or would you rather I not?

Mr. McINARNAY. By all means.

Mr. PAINTER. One of them, and I can mention this again, because they asked me to—David Hess of Hescom Roofing Co.—they not only build roofs, they do a lot of work pertinent in that respect—metalwork and stuff like that. He had wanted to get more into Government business, but he has found that most of the jobs are too big, that they are really geared to big business—the lot, quantity lot—and if they could be broken down in any way, where the smaller manufacturer could get a share of them, why, he would be in a position, but since that door is closed he just has to forget it now. That is one thing he brought up.

Mr. McINARNAY. I wonder if he has made any effort to act as a subcontractor on the jobs that his company is qualified for?

Mr. PAINTER. Well, as I said, I am not that well acquainted with his business to answer the problems.

Mr. McINARNAY. I would make two recommendations to him. I don't know whether this particular problem can be solved. It is always a question of the economy and so-called efficiency of the agency, the procuring agency, to buy in large lots, rather than breaking purchases down in the quantities that a small businessman can bid on. It is a constant battle, but it may be that if he would write directly to Senator Smathers, we could look into this with the agency and see if something couldn't be done.

Also, he might contact Mr. Turner here in the local SBA office, and maybe there is something that his procurement specialist could look into for him, and it might just possibly be of some help to him.

Mr. PAINTER. I have one more. Time is running on here and I don't want to take too much of it.

I talked to Mr. Willie Mick, of Parker & Mick Co., which is another rapidly expanding Florida organization. I believe they now have three plants in Florida and they have come along real fast, and I had hoped that Mr. Mick could be here today.

He said they would like to feel they could get a little share of Government business. Maybe they didn't have it—they said one problem they had, and again I can't go into detail on it—was that they had made some inquiry on bidding on certain equipment they manufacture—machinery and stuff like that. They have a big tool works and things of that sort to manufacture machinery. You know, kind of heavy work.

But, they had asked to bid on certain materials, and they found that in order to be eligible to bid, their plant had to have the fabrication equipment in the plant to bid on this particular job, and he said he knew there wasn't any banker who was going to lend him money to put in special types of equipment to bid on a job on business that he didn't even know whether he was going to get or not.

And, he said he would be a foolish businessman to even do it even if the banker would give it to him. I don't know whether there is any area there, but I will pass those two on.

With that, I do, in closing, though, want to corroborate Mr. Gregg's feelings about the Small Business Administration, Mr. Turner in particular.

We have had a very wonderful relationship with them, now going on to about 7 years, and we are reaching a point where, in another 2 or 3 years, we hope we will liquidate it, but during all that time they have been most helpful to us, meeting our situations as they have come up, and relieving us of certain restrictions under our mortgage. We have reached that point where it is as it should be, and not before. I don't think they have given us anything they felt they should not have given us, but I will say that they have been fine people to do business with, and I just hope that that is one agency of the Government that will be here a long, long time.

Mr. MCINARNAY. Well, thank you so much, Mr. Painter. We like to hear that.

I deal with Mr. Turner quite a bit, as well as with Tom Butler who is in charge of the Miami office of SBA, and Mr. Turner and Mr. Butler have always been most cooperative. When a company doesn't meet SBA's minimum requirements for financial assistance, and other types of assistance, their hands are tied.

But, they have always been most cooperative in bending over to help a company many times, so I am really very glad to hear you echo those sentiments of Mr. Gregg.

Mr. Koester?

Mr. KOESTER. Thank you very much.

You know, I was amazed that so many people would bring up this Commerce Department census form. Washington must be a truly wonderful place, because it seems like they have a battery of people plus IBM computers, waiting until just the point when we are the busiest, and then here comes the form to be filled out in 10 days. This means that our bookkeeper has to drop everything he is doing. The payroll goes to smash, all records go to smash. It is a crash program getting this stuff out. We don't really know whether we have the information precisely the way they want it or not. We always hope for the best.

I have a suggestion on getting away from this mess. I am sure all of us belong to various trade associations—associated in our fields. For instance, in the printing field, there is the Printing Industry of America—the PIA, which has offices in Washington. Most of your printing plants belong to this association. Our books are set up in the manner that the PIA has their books set up. Every year we fill this information out and send it off to PIA, and then back comes the ratio to us, some study that shows exactly where we place among all the printers in the country in our particular category, all broken down in fractional percentages.

The Government could go to these trade associations without having to bother the individual. That is only a suggestion. There is the Graphic Arts Technical Foundation in Pittsburgh; there is the Printing Industry of Florida in Miami. It is a wonderful thing, because it allows us to see exactly where our cost structure is in relation to printing plants all over the Nation in our size areas.

All this information goes into Washington, but we don't see anything come back except more forms. I think that if the Government needs this information, that would be a more logical place to go instead of bothering all of us poor little taxpayers.

Mr. MCINARNAY. I think that recommendation is particularly appropriate for one reason, and, that is—I don't know how it could be implemented, but the Department of Commerce, under which the Census Bureau rises, also has an Office of Trade Associations, so that they know pretty well all of the trade associations in the country, and it may just possibly be that some effort could be worked out with them, rather than contacting the individual businessman.

And, if they could standardize what the Government wants with what the trade associations need, and work something out——

Mr. KOESTER. There could be an interchange.

Mr. MCINARNAY. Right.

Mr. KOESTER. But we found it better to set our books up according to the way PIA has theirs set up, because then we can get the information to them quicker. We can interpret the information that comes back to us quicker. It works out better all the way around, and I am sure there are adequate trade associations for every field of endeavor in the country.

Mr. GREGG. Might I add, Ed, though, that there is no industry comparable—I mean, another industry that has the setup that PIA has.

Mr. KOESTER. Well, it is a beautiful setup. It is very thorough.

Mr. GREGG. I know there is none in our line. In fabrication, there is nothing—I have never seen a setup of a trade association that would equal PIA.

Mr. KOESTER. Maybe it could be taken off of the printers' backs—maybe that could be a good starting point.

Mr. GREGG. Yes.

Mr. KOESTER. But, it works a hardship on us. We have one book-keeper—we have one girl that works a bookkeeping machine to run the figures for the company, and when you have got to pull them off of everything and work on these fool studies, it throws us into a book-keeping tailspin. It just isn't fair, I don't believe.

So, if they can't do it that way, then they ought to put it on a basis where it is not compulsory. Then those industries that have the work force to put on it can do so and those that don't, they can get it out when they jolly well please, if they want to at all.

But, we take a sort of bad outlook on it, because we don't see anything come back. It looks like a gigantic hopper where you put all this information in. It comes from all over the country and nothing comes out, so what worth is it? But, if it is needed to be gotten up, I suggest they try the PIA for printers.

I am really not too well versed on the Small Business Administration's role. We have never taken out an SBA loan, or applied for one. I know some of our competition has, but in line—in the light of our prospective enlargement, I do take heart in the fact that the local newspaper says our factory is located in a poverty pocket. Maybe we can qualify for some poverty aid; I don't know.

One other thing that I was thinking of—in doing business with the Government back in World War II, we did a few things for the air station, mainside, out here, and then they put in their own printing plant, and for years and years and years we couldn't ever get to first base in doing any work for the Government. The closest thing we ever did was a whole bunch of these class books from the training schools, that they put out during the war, and then about 1960 or 1961, somewhere around there, in came a whole bunch of people from General Electric, Daytona, and they were on an inspection tour. General Electric was going to put in a facility in Daytona and they had to get somebody who could turn out their printing requirements, and they wanted to inspect all of the places in town, in the Jacksonville area, so they could line up a source of supply.

Well, they finally decided we had an adequate plant and they said, "Well, now, we will have to have your place cleared for security."

So, we said, "Well, be our guest and go ahead."

What we were in for.

Comes all sorts of forms, all sorts of paperwork, very accommodating people in security from Atlanta. We were working on the thing for years. We spent hundreds and hundreds of dollars getting the thing up. We published a standard practice and procedural manual. I make a chance remark that I have got an opportunity to go to Europe. Whoops, wait a minute, you've got to have permission to go, so I finally get permission from the Government so I can go to Europe, and I come back and I have to give them a report of where I have been, what I was doing, all this, that, and the other.

So finally they said, "Now, you are clear. You are classified as secret," which is next to top secret. That is the ultimate; the next I guess is "Burn before reading."

But, we were secret classification, so I told them, "Fine. How about notifying General Electric? We are ready to go. We are ready to do business."

So, they said, "Well, we have already notified General Electric. That is part of it. They requested this security. They have got the answer. You are cleared. Go out and get the business."

So, I go down to General Electric: "Well, we don't need you. We have got our own plant now."

So, I told the security officer the next time I saw him, "Well, General Electric is out. Where do I go from here?"

"Well, you might try the air stations, naval installations in Jacksonville."

So, I try all of them.

"We don't need you. We have our own printing plant."

Why should I bust my brains against a brick wall going through all of this security garbage when I can't do anything with it? It is silly. Here I am out hundreds of dollars in cash put out. I am out countless man-hours assembling all this mess. I have got a security cabinet I bought. I have got security garbage cans I bought. I have got security incinerators I bought. I have got a ridiculous situation plus a sheaf of records I am told I've got to keep for the next 10 years.

I don't really know why, we haven't had a sniff of our first classified work yet. My point is this: We are willing to go through all this rigmarole if there is something to be gained, but if everybody is going to put in their own printing plant, what is the point?

So, we have about adopted the point that we are going to send the security stuff back to them, tell them they can take their clearance back, that we have no need of it, and just concentrate on work that we can get, because we find far less trouble in dealing with commercial enterprises than what could ever be gained in going through all this Government redtape.

Mr. McINARNAY. Is it your contention, from your own experience, that the Government is competing with private enterprise?

Mr. KOESTER. Definitely.

Mr. McINARNAY. Unreasonably, in this area?

Mr. KOESTER. Definitely.

There is a need for the Bureau of Printing in Washington. They've got to print up the money, print up the bonds, the postage stamps and things like that, but, for instance, in the shore installations in the Navy, if there is any possibility of having the work done on the outside, on a secure level, at fair rates, I see no reason for the Government to be in competition.

Mr. McINARNAY. The fact that the Federal Government is in competition with you is something that is not just in this area? Have you heard of it in other parts of the country?

Mr. KOESTER. No; not just in this area.

Though I don't know it to be a conclusive fact, and I am not a gambling man, I would be willing to bet you a steak that you show me the Government installation and I will show you a printing plant in it.

Mr. THEVENOT. Is this one of the problems that your association is contending with? Are they making an effort to do something about this?

Mr. KOESTER. I don't know just how you could get at the problem. It is deep seated. I am glad that Eldon Dickson here can recap tires for the Navy. They haven't put in a recapping plant yet. I am glad that Mr. Painter can sell the Navy chickens. They haven't got a hatchery out at the air station yet.

I just think it is unfair competition.

Mr. McINARNAY. This is one of the areas in which our committee has been interested for a long time. I don't know that we have ever looked into specifically this area. I know we have in laundry operations.

At Orlando Air Force Base, for example, they put in a million-dollar laundry and fought to take away its work with the private contractors in that part of Florida, and we were successful in getting them to reconsider.

Refrigerated warehouses was another activity where the Federal Government in areas of the east coast were competing with private enterprise.

Mr. THEVENOT. Liquid oxygen.

Mr. McINARNAY. Liquid oxygen manufacture was another one, so we would be happy to look into this to just see what could be done.

Mr. KOESTER. There is a need, I concede, for instantaneous printing, such as letter forms.

Mr. THEVENOT. Orders and this type of thing?

Mr. KOESTER. Yes. Which is usually produced on Multilith equipment, but that also proves to be a steppingstone. Some officer in procurement says, "Well, that is great. Your Multilith is working fine."

Then, here comes another one.

"Now, if we just had this other model, you could turn out this size, and then if you had this press, you could turn out this size. If you had this press, you could turn out this size."

The next thing you know, they have got a whole battery of equipment there which is in direct competition.

Now, for instance, our two-color press back in 1950—I believe it was—we paid almost $50,000 less trade-in for the thing. The press that we are contemplating now will cost us $90,000. Now, Mister, it takes a lot of impressions to pay for that. It takes a lot of letterheads. It takes a lot of business forms. It takes a lot of brochures to make expenditures like that worth while to little fellows like us, but we are willing to do it if we have a market.

Now, I don't say take the printing department out of the U.S. Navy establishment in Jacksonville and give it to Douglas Printing.

Of course not—give it to printers of the area. They can leave Douglas Printing out of it entirely, but give it to the printers of the area, if they can do it, and if they are qualified to do it.

Mr. THEVENOT. Is this equipment that the Government owns rather sophisticated printing equipment—color?

Mr. KOESTER. I have not been able to see the department. I talked with the procurement officer out at Mainside—or, the printing supervisor at Mainside, and I was questioning him about the various articles that we could turn out, such as maps.

He said, "No, we have our own equipment for that." Well, now, that takes the sort of size equipment that we have, that Miller Press has, that Paramount Press has, that Ambrose has.

Mr. McINARNAY. Now, you are a printer by profession.

In this business, would you say that the Government could purchase their printing needs on the outside more economically than than can support their own printing establishments?

Mr. KOESTER. That is not only my contention, that has been the contention of the trade associations in our field for years.

There has been many an instance such as—I believe RCA decided they were in the electronics business and not the printing business, and they sold their printing plant. There have been other companies, such as Sears, Roebuck & Co. I can get the information and I can get the names of companies who have sold their printing plants because they have suddenly awakened to the fact that it costs them a lot more than just the cost of the equipment to run it.[1]

Mr. McINARNAY. Let me suggest, if you will, that you document a case pretty thoroughly to support your contention and send it to Senator George Smathers, Senate Office Building, Washington, D.C. He is a member of the Senate Small Business Committee—as a matter of fact, he is chairman of the Subcommittee on Government Procurement, and it is an area that we would like to look into very thoroughly.

We can never promise the kind of response that perhaps you would like to see, but you never can tell unless you make the effort; if you are willing to put the case together, we are willing to take it to the appropriate people in Washington to just see if something can't be done.

Mr. KOESTER. I wish something could be done about simplifying the security data. It is such a complicated bunch of stuff, even the security officer from Atlanta was in the office one time trying his best to figure out what the regulation said, and he couldn't do it. It is terribly topheavy.

Mr. McINARNAY. We will be glad to look into that, too. As I recall—and it has been a long time since I was cleared—when you are working for the Government, what they require is not so comprehensive; so I just don't know why they require so much of you.

Mr. KOESTER. I don't know either, but there are five copies of four-page forms, the history form, and so on.

Mr. THEVENOT. This is on everyone in your plant?

Mr. KOESTER. Yes. You have two fingerprint cards, you've got one more form there somewhere—several copies of that.

And that all goes up—now, it goes to DISCO in Columbus, Ohio, and it takes weeks or longer to process anything, and it is wild. They send me these security booklets with a whole bunch of information in there, exhorting you to use the security posters they send you.

I haven't seen the first one yet. I would be willing to put them up, but they have never sent them to us.

There is a whole list of friendly foreign countries. If you want to go outside the United States, you don't decide right now, I've got to go on a business trip to West Germany or to England or to France. No—each country has its own number of waiting days as to how much leadtime you've got to advise the security office before you can be given permission to go. And, to me, this kind of rankles me.

Mr. McINARNAY. Well, obviously, there are some requirements that they need to impose. It appears from what you have said that very possibly they go overboard in what they require of the ordinary businessman in fulfilling their various regulations.

So, this is something we would be very glad to take up with——

Mr. KOESTER. Especially with nothing to be gained at the end.

We are still a secure plant, but we have never had the first bit of work to do.

---

[1] The information referred to was not received at time of going to press.

Mr. GREGG. Ed, wouldn't you think that the business itself is one thing that would call for tighter security regulations, so to speak, rather than ours, where we are putting together nothing except steel?

I mean, the printing industry itself—I don't know why it should be, but I just would——

Mr. KOESTER. Well, in our industry you have a collection of intelligence, I guess you could put it, whereas in your industry you have a hunk of iron.

Unless you know the application, it wouldn't mean a lot.

Mr. THEVENOT. How expensive is it to maintain this security, once you have established the security at your plant and for its personnel? There is a continuing security program that must be maintained; is that right?

Mr. KOESTER. Perhaps I led you to the wrong idea. It doesn't cost me anything to maintain it, because there is nothing for me to do, except for the fact that every new employee I get in I am supposed to have him cleared.

The way our security is set up, if I should get a secured job in, all those employees who have not been cleared would be banned from the plant until that job was out and delivered, and the necessary steps taken all along the route. So, rather than go through all that monumental effort again, I just haven't bothered applying for any further security clearance on employees.

Mr. McINARNAY. Are there any other areas you would like to bring up?

Mr. KOESTER. Well, our social security and income tax will be with us until the millenium. There is nothing that can be done about that anyway.

So, I doubt if the paperwork will be reduced materially in that line. It looks like it is a necessary evil. Taxes in the excise region have been reduced. I don't know what is going to happen when the full impact of the civil rights business hits us.

I attended a seminar on what the equal opportunity section is going to mean when it finally filters down to our particular level of employment, and it does sound bizarre, but there again, that is on the books, and I don't think that is liable to be changed. So, like the income tax, we will have to live with that.

So, I am afraid I have no other comments.

Mr. McINARNAY. Thank you very much, Mr. Koester.

Mr. HOHENHAUSEN. As I mentioned earlier, we really don't do much direct business with the Federal agencies—mostly in the capacity of a subcontractor, and usually of a very minor nature, and probably the only remark that would be fitting here is the fact that as a subcontractor on these Government projects, even though we are a minor subcontractor in most cases where the project being built involves millions of dollars, our contract is usually only for several hundreds of dollars.

Yet, we apparently are burdened with the same amount of paperwork that the general contractor has to put up with, and in many cases, even though as I say our contract might only be for several hundred dollars over a period of several months, and we continually have to fill out these elongated forms for the Government—affidavits, and so forth. In many instances, where we have only spent 1 or 2 man-hours in a whole month on a project, whereas another subcontractor or the general contractor might be compiling thousands or hundreds of thousands of man-hours in a period of time—we have to fill out the exact same forms for maybe 1 or 2 man-hours, and it takes up an awful lot of office worktime doing it.

Mr. McInarnay. You are referring to which forms?

Mr. Hohenhausen. Oh, I can't remember them all now, but every month they come in. We are doing a couple of projects out at Cecil Field now—soil poisoning for some new hangars, and so forth, and it is forms reporting the number of man-hours, and affidavits attesting that we are complying with the wage and hour laws, and so forth and so on.

It would seem to me that a simplified form for a small subcontractor on a large project could be considered that could cover the length of the project in reflection to the amount of money involved, as far as the contractor is concerned. As I say, we have to make these forms out week after week, and in most cases on these projects we would spend at the maximum 5 or 6 man-hours a month on them, but at the same time, we still have all these different papers which we have to fill out for the Government, and, in turn, resubmit them to the general contractor who, I suppose, turns them in to the Government agencies at the end of each month.

I think that there should be some set of short forms for a small subcontractor to fill out either at the termination of his subcontract or at intermediate periods of his contract, rather than fill out these voluminous reports every week.

There isn't that much money involved in this thing for potential violations of the law.

Mr. McInarnay. And, these are principally in wage and hour areas?

Mr. Hohenhausen. That is right. Contractors weekly payroll statement, form No. 879, plus copies of payroll.

Mr. McInarnay. Now, these are forms you do not have to fill out if you are not performing a contract?

Mr. Hohenhausen. No, even if we have a month where we don't perform any man-hours, we still have to fill out the forms and say we didn't perform any man-hours that month, and so forth.

Mr. McInarnay. On a Government contract?

Mr. Hohenhausen. On Government contracts—and, I say, ours is probably the smallest subcontract in most cases of any subcontract on the job, but we are still burdened with the same amount of paperwork as a large subcontractor, and it takes a lot of our man-hours—office man-hours, which we normally don't even compute when we are pricing the job.

Mr. McInarnay. Are there other areas you would like to cover?

Mr. Hohenhausen. No, sir. That is—as far as I say, we don't do much business with the Federal Government.

As far as pest control is concerned, the naval air stations seem to have some of their own pest control operators trained by the Navy, evidently doing some of this work.

Mr. Koester. You, too?

Mr. Hohenhausen. Yes. It has bothered us, particularly as far as potential pest control work and termite treating is concerned.

Recently, I think, was the first time—a housekeeping contract they let for the Capehart housing project out at Mayport—they included pest control work in with the housekeeping contract, which the successful contractor for that, of course, sublet the pest control to some other company. We worked with a janitorial service company which was not the successful bidder. The State of Florida now is enforcing some very strict regulations with respect to pest control operators, but it normally doesn't affect the Federal property.

So, there is some competition from the Government of a small nature. We actually go on the Government premises in some cases, as in this Capehart housing project, officers, families want some professional insect control job done on these houses, and they will pay for it out of their own pockets, even though there are some facilities available at the station for that.

Mr. McINARNAY. Thank you so much, Mr. Hohenhausen.

Mr. Goodloe?

Mr. GOODLOE. We are very much interested in this small business set-aside program. It has affected our business, helped us out immeasurably, and we have gotten contracts that we would not have gotten had it not been for the set-aside program, so we are very much interested in the problems and some of the loopholes that are in the setup itself.

Mainly, in regard to the way big business is getting around the intent of the set-aside program—jobs that are set up for small business organizations are being performed by big business and their equipment. All of our work is in the dredging business, dredging work, and most of it—or the bulk of it—is for the Government through the Corps of Engineers.

Mr. McINARNAY. Mr. Goodloe, how do the large business firms manage to make themselves qualified to compete on a small business set-aside?

Mr. GOODLOE. They do it either through the method of leasing equipment to a small company and the big business equipment performs the work, or by having a small business concern bid the work; on most of the bids you are required to list the equipment that the job will be performed with. Dredges are described as to the size, the name of the dredge, and so forth, and then we have numerous listings in records where small businesses have put in bids and listed equipment belonging to big business.

And, they are getting around that all the time.

Mr. McINARNAY. Do they take the job as a prime contractor and then subcontract most of it out to the large businesses?

Mr. GOODLOE. No; a big contractor can locate a small firm that is willing to bid the work for—say, a certain fee. They will put in the bid and then actually all the work is performed by the big business.

Mr. THEVENOT. Performed by the big business machinery, not their employees?

Mr. GOODLOE. Machinery, employees, and everything.

Now, a lot of these Government contracts with the Corps of Engineers, for instance, a certain percentage is set up for the prime contractor—percentage of work is set up for him that he has to perform—20 percent of the work in some cases. That is what it is now.

In some districts—in the Savannah district, the contracts we performed the first of this year, completed the first of this year, were set up as 50 percent. The prime contractor had to perform 50 percent of the work. Now, that is good. That cuts out some of the contracting to big business, but not unless there is some control over the lease, the lease type of performance.

Mr. THEVENOT. Is this a small business set-aside or a labor surplus area set-aside?

Mr. GOODLOE. No; it is a small business set-aside contract.

We belong to an association, the Southeastern Dredge Owners Association, and we were requested to attend the hearing by the Select Committee on Small Business of the House of Representatives last—I believe it was in August of this year. My brother attended that, and in that session they did bring out some of these problems that we are having directly, and the other members of this association. There are approximately 10 or 12 firms belonging to the association, all businesses on the southeast coast, and they are all well-established firms—have been in business for quite a few years. Primarily, most of their business is with the Government.

I don't know whether this would be in place, but we have a letter that was written by Representative Multer, who is chairman of the Subcommittee on Small Business. He was at this hearing, and it is addressed to Ross D. Davis, the Executive Administrator of the Small Business Administration, which brought out some of the things that were brought up there. I don't know whether you would want that written into the record here or not.

Mr. McINARNAY. I think it would be a good idea to include that in the record at this point, if you could, Mr. Reporter.

Mr. GOODLOE. But, we are trying to get something done along these lines.

One thing is to increase the percentage of the work required of the prime contractor, and in this type of work, it is not unreasonable to require——

Mr. McINARNAY. Would you be good enough to make that copy available to the reporter, so that he can include that in the record, or is that your only copy?

Mr. GOODLOE. This is our only copy.

Mr. HOHENHAUSEN. Can you make a copy of that, Joe?

Mr. KELLY. Is it an original or a copy? We can make copies of originals, but we will know in a few minutes.

(The letter referred to follows:)

SELECT COMMITTEE ON SMALL BUSINESS,
HOUSE OF REPRESENTATIVES OF THE UNITED STATES,
Washington, D.C., October 8, 1965.

Hon. ROSS D. DAVIS,
Executive Administrator,
Small Business Administration,
Washington, D.C.

DEAR MR. DAVIS: This is in reference to the protest of Southeastern Dredge Owners Association against procurement regulations and practices of the military departments in awarding construction-dredging contracts set aside for small business.

This matter is being studied by our Subcommittee on Small Business and Government procurement in connection with our review of small business subcontracting and set-aside programs. Witnesses testified in our recent hearings that Defense Department's regulations permit the subcontracting of 80 percent and, in certain instances, 100 percent, of the set-aside contract to large business. They state that existing regulations encourage collusive bidding by brokers and small firms who are not equipped to perform themselves but who act for the benefit of large concerns. This practice tends to defeat the purpose of the set-aside program.

The witnesses also complain that current Defense Department practices and regulations allow a contracting officer to make an award while a size determination appeal to Small Business Administration is pending. It is pointed out that this deprives the small business of its remedy against collusive bidders in set-aside procurements and renders SBA appeal procedures meaningless. Industry recommends remedial action through administrative changes in procurement regulations and procedures.

We enclose copies of the witnesses' statements for your attention. Your comments will be helpful to our subcommittee in its study of this problem and in reaching appropriate conclusions and recommendations.[3]

We will appreciate your response in six copies for our hearing record by October 18.

Sincerely yours,

ABRAHAM J. MULTER,
Chairman, Subcommittee No. 2 on
Small Business and Government Procurement.

Mr. GOODLOE. Another thing—another point I would like to bring out is that the contracting officer can award a job to a big business firm—I mean, to a firm, I shouldn't say big business firm—even though this is up for protest to the Small Business Administration, the Size Appeal Board.

Recently a contract was awarded to a firm while a determination was underway by the Size Appeal Board. If it is emergency work, of course, they should be allowed to waive that. I mean the contracting officer should, of course, have the right to go ahead and award that contract, but we have protested the award of the contract to a firm which was low bidder on a job. We were second low, and we had reason to believe that they were big business under the rules, and we protested and it was successful. We were awarded the contract, but in some cases it doesn't work that way.

In some cases, the award is already made before the determination is made.

Mr. GREGG. Wouldn't an affidavit of some kind, when it was a small business set-aside, if it was a requirement by the contracting officer that it be submitted at the same time as his bid came in—wouldn't that put an end to this?

Mr. GOODLOE. One of the difficulties now is that there is no penalty for violations of this.

Mr. GREGG. Yes, I know that.

Mr. GOODLOE. A bidder can submit a bid whether he is big business or small business, and even knowing that he is big business, and there is no penalty for that. If no one protests the award of that work to that firm, the award is made. There is no—there are no teeth in the setup now to prevent this sort of thing.

Mr. GREGG. But, if he had to declare his status right along with his bid, then he could be—that would be perjury there.

Mr. MCINARNAY. Well, they do—they do have to certify themselves as being small business, and that stands unless one of the other bidders protests.

Mr. THEVENOT. Unless the contracting officer makes a determination that he is large business.

Mr. GREGG. In other words, then, a big business—he does certify to that and he perjures himself whenever he does it, and there is no penalty involved? In other words, it doesn't matter how big

---

[3] Enclosures referred to not included in the exhibit submitted by the witness.

he is, if he wants to do so, then he can sign this affidavit and send it right along saying, "Yes, I am small."

Mr. McINARNAY. Well, I was assuming that any of these cases— that is an honest mistake on their part. They might not know what the particular rules are in their industry. I don't know.

Because certainly, the other companies in that industry in that area know, and they would be awake to their ability to make a protest.

Mr. GOODLOE. Well, we have records pertaining to bid openings we have attended, and members of our organization, too, have attended, and have obtained the information as far as the bidder and the equipment that he proposes to use in performing the work, and we would be glad to make available to you some of that information, if you would like specific information.

Mr. McINARNAY. We would like to have it, and you could include that in a letter to Senator Smathers, and we would look further into it for you to see what assurances can be given a truly small businessman on a small business set-aside, that they are in fact, competing only with small business firms.

Mr. GOODLOE. All right.

If some pressure could be put on the Government agency, such as the Corps of Engineers, to increase this percentage of required work by the prime contractor, that would help the situation, too. It varies in different districts.

Mr. McINARNAY. How has it been in the Jacksonville district?

Mr. GOODLOE. Twenty percent now, some up to—it depends on the size of the contract.

Twenty percent on the ones we bid.

Mr. McINARNAY. In Savannah it is 50 percent?

Mr. GOODLOE. The last contract we bid on and performed in Savannah was 50 percent.

Mr. McINARNAY. Do you have any other areas you would like to cover?

Mr. GOODLOE. Well, we do have some competition from the Government in the dredging field, which we contend that we can perform or work at less expense than it is being performed, and they are in direct competition with the dredging business.

Mr. McINARNAY. Is this the Corps of Engineers?

Mr. GOODLOE. Yes.

Mr. McINARNAY. Jacksonville district?

Mr. GOODLOE. No, not primarily Jacksonville district. The Savannah district and in the Mississippi area, it is quite prevalent there.

Private industry equipment is available to do the work and there are many dredges idle at this time, but the Government dredges are working.

Mr. McINARNAY. Do you have anything further, Mr. Goodloe?

Mr. GOODLOE. I believe that about covers it.

Mr. McINARNAY. All right, sir.

Well, thank you very much.

Mr. McINARNAY. Mr. Hufnagel?

Mr. HUFNAGEL. Well, our function, of course, is strictly a service, and I think the accounting profession in recent years is gradually becoming more and more of a peacemaking organization—I mean, between the taxpayer or the businessman and the Federal Government.

Of course, most of our work is with the Internal Revenue Service, and we along with those people in that department are constantly fighting their ADP machine up there in Chamblee, Ga., which seems to send out more mail than any other agency that I know of. I would like to comment on this matter of the census and I say more or less being in between our client and the Federal Government, 9 times out of 10, if a client receives something from some Government agency, State included, they don't bother to look at it any more. They just put it in an envelope and send it to us, you know, and we make a decision one way or the other.

And, being independent, a lot of times our judgment is a little bit more reserved, but we go ahead and handle it and get rid of it the best way we can. So, in my opinion, the accounting profession is performing a real function in these days of automation that we are getting into here now. We are trying to keep everybody happy. We know that the people in the Internal Revenue Service over here are fighting their machine just as much as the accountants are.

As to the Small Business Administration, our relationship there has always been very pleasant. We haven't had too much of it, but sitting here and listening to the various problems of operations as these gentlemen face them from day to day, it appears that it is an agency that is doing something good, and I would naturally like to see it continued and expanded, and checked out, such as you are doing right at this moment.

I think if something like that was done, a lot of other agencies—for example, the Census Bureau—we might find out where all this stuff finally winds up, you know.

Mr. GREGG. That is a bad word.

Mr. HUFNAGEL. It is to you, Mr. Gregg, but we have made out lots of them, and it seems that sometimes they do get carried away. We have one client, a very small business, and, since this thing started 8 or 10 years ago, I know that she gets this regular attack once a year, just as regular as the years go around, and that, to me, seems unfair, as this is a very small business, and what good could her little figures contribute to the entire community, unless they just pick out one.

Mr. MCINARNAY. Are you now referring to the census report?

Mr. HUFNAGEL. Yes; but I mean we have never discouraged anyone to not fill them out. We fill them out as best we can, based on the information that comes off the client's books or, if we have the books in our office, we give it to them as straight as we can, and we haven't had too much trouble, but it does seem that certain individuals get a pretty steady dose of it, you know. They might try the guy next door the next time.

Mr. GREGG. You know, come to think of it, I don't remember getting one of those last year or the year before either.

Prior to that, though, for 5 years they were regular and the last one was an improved one, and it was much thicker than the others. That was the one they called for all this breakdown of aluminum, steel, ingots, on castings, and so forth, and I was crazy by the time I read through it. I think I wrote across it in red that it was impossible to supply it, but if they wanted to go across the books and bear the expense, I would be happy to open the doors to them—something like that—and sent it back.

Mr. HUFNAGEL. Well, we have handled quite a number of them for many of our clients, and in some cases, their accounting department or their comptroller, or someone, makes it out and we will review it before it goes in.

We have even had them down to the 11th hour where some people have gotten a telegram—you know, it has got to be filed today.

Mr. GREGG. Yes; that is right.

Mr. HUFNAGEL. That sort of thing, you know.

Mr. GREGG. I got it.

Mr. HUFNAGEL. Well, maybe we didn't know about it until that day.

Mr. McINARNAY. Do you have any particular recommendations on how these Government forms might be improved, these reports that are required?

Mr. HUFNAGEL. Well, I find it more and more difficult to read taxbooks every day. We had a problem come up yesterday, and when you get through reading all the information that is given by the tax services, you are generally hesitant about whether you are right or wrong about the matter.

It seems they try to put too many words in them. In many situations, a lot of words could be left out, could be condensed in some manner to make it simple for people to understand.

Mr. THEVENOT. And, you say that as an accountant, an expert in the field?

Mr. HUFNAGEL. I would say that.

Mr. THEVENOT. To the layman, it would be much more difficult, of course?

Mr. HUFNAGEL. Yes, of course, it is just difficult to read some of these things.

The new code in 1954 did make some good changes. But, I think there is an awful lot of paperwork that most businesses have to face, not only from the Federal Government, but from the State as well, and we naturally in our business try to keep everybody out of trouble if we can.

Mr. McINARNAY. Do you have any ideas on the way the various Small Business Administration programs of assistance to small business might be improved?

Mr. HUFNAGEL. No, I am not familiar enough with it. I mean, we haven't had enough contact in our clientele for me to pass judgment in that matter.

But, I can see that with the gentlemen present, that they must have had their accountants work it out or help them work out their problems at the time they were going through an application for loan or something of that nature, whatever the circumstance was.

I think that is about all I have to add here. I enjoyed being here, and listening to the proceedings.

Mr. McINARNAY. Thank you, Mr. Hufnagel.

Mr. KOESTER. If I may interject a thought here, Mr. McInarnay?

Mr. McINARNAY. Yes, sir.

Mr. KOESTER. I have just been sitting here and thinking this is just absolutely wonderful. It is nothing ususual for Congressman Bennett to come here during his off times in Congress, you know, and see you and shake hands and say, "How are you doing?" Or, "What can I do for you in Washington?"

But this is the first time I have ever seen something such as this, where Senators Smathers and Long have taken the trouble to send you and Mr. Thevenot down here, to bring this thing here and say, "What can we do to help you?"

It is wonderful. I think it is very nice of you gentlemen to do this, and I certainly deeply appreciate it.

Mr. THEVENOT. It has been a great deal of help to us. As staff members, we are responsible for carrying out the intent of the Congress and our committee in getting very close to you people and hearing first-hand what is actually bothering you it gives us a good indication as to where the thrust of our efforts should be.

Mr. KOESTER. This is something that can't possibly do anything but improve Government, as I see it.

Mr. McINARNAY. Well, we hope so, and we thank you very much for those comments, Mr. Koester.

As Mr. Thevenot has said, we just hope that some of the things we have been apprised of as a result of these meetings throughout the Southeast will assist us to assist you, and that is our purpose in being here.

Now we want to hear from Mr. Dickson.

Mr. DICKSON. I would like to concur with what Ed Koester just said. That was one of the things that I wanted to mention, because certainly this is the first time in the many years I have been in business that I have been given an opportunity to sit down and just discuss things in our small business. We are one of the smallest of the small.

First of all, I would like to say this, that in our business with the various governmental agencies or divisions, such as the U.S. Post Office Department and Naval Air Station, Cecil Field and all, in recapping and repairing tires, our relations have been very satisfactory. We have not done a great deal of this; however, I think we have had our fair share, and that is about all anybody in business could ask.

We have not secured any loans through the Small Business Administration, but probably will have to one of these days. I have been up and talked to Mr. Turner, and have had very pleasant relations and all, and so it may be that we will need to seek help there in the not too distant future.

Aside from some of the things that we have discussed, here is, I think, the main problem of the independent tire distributor, not only in Jacksonville, but across the country. Our biggest problem is this. The manufacturers are our greatest competitors.

I have been in the tire business 35 years. I worked for another concern 14, and I have been in business for myself 21, and the independents across the country have been fighting this thing through their National Independent Tire Dealers Association for 7 years. So far, we have not been able to come up with any help.

Actually, it has grown worse. For example, the tire manufacturer will go out to these large concerns, such as the trucklines—now, the railroads have the piggyback operations and big fleets, in other words—and give them the same price that they sell us for. In other words, we are the distributors. Where we used to be able to sell those people and make a very small profit, today if we sell them we will have to sell them at the same price the manufacturer sells to us.

I think it is a very unfair practice, and certainly the small independent cannot exist if this thing continues to prevail.

Now, in the retail market, it is the same way, of course; "the manufacturer" is opening more and more company-owned stores every day. Now, we have to be competitive, of course, and we are competitive, and I think any independent—I know this is true in Jacksonville— if you called any independent tire company for a price on the same quality product, the same type tire, you would receive within pennies the same price, because we have to keep abreast of what they are doing. When I say "they," I mean the manufacturer, the store, the company-owned store.

And, we have to be and we are competitive, and we can fairly well live with that. It is a very, very low percent profit, but by volume, we could live with it, but the large user, as I mentioned earlier, we cannot sell at the same price we buy at, and still stay in business. It can't be done.

Mr. THEVENOT. This, I might say, sir, is a problem that Senator Russell Long, of Louisiana, who is the ranking majority member of the committee, and with whom I work very closely—this is a problem that he has been very much interested in, and has proposed several bills in the Senate to curb this whole dual distribution problem. We have on the Small Business Committee a very competent lawyer, Mr. Ray Watts, who is working almost exclusively on this problem, and it not only covers the tire industry, but also a great many other industries where the company-owned outlet is in competition with the independent businessman, and hopefully some of the legislation that has been gleaned from all of this research will get on the books and will be of a great deal of benefit to you and other small businesses.

Mr. DICKSON. I might add this in closing.

A few years ago, Franklin D. Roosevelt, Jr., was in Jacksonville, and at that time had a hearing with some small businessmen, with reference to the thing that I just mentioned, company-owned operations, manufacturers selling direct, and I know that he was trying to bring this to light and trying to help the small businessman.

However, we haven't gotten any relief from it as far as the tire industry, and I understand that neither have many other lines, as you have mentioned.

Mr. McINARNAY. Are there any other areas that you would like to cover, Mr. Dickson?

Mr. DICKSON. Well, I could expand on this considerably, but I think that in light of the time and all, I think that I have covered the main points.

I would like to say in closing again that I appreciate the opportunity of being here, and expressing my views, because certainly what I have said with regard to our business, the independent tire distributors— something is going to have to happen in the not too distant future, or you are going to have a lot of small independent businesses, not only tires, but others, that can't survive.

Mr. McINARNAY. Well, thank you so much for coming and sharing with us your views.

I just want to say on behalf of Senator Smathers, with whom I work directly, and certainly, I am sure, Senator Long, for whom Mr.

Thevenot works, and for both of us, and on behalf of Senator Sparkman, and the Small Business Committee of which he is chairman, I want to thank the Jacksonville Area Chamber of Commerce and Mr. Joe Kelly, in particular, and the Small Business Administration office here in Jacksonville, Mr. Kennon Turner, regional manager, for setting up this meeting and making it possible for us to come here and meet with you.

And, we certainly want to thank each and every one of you for coming here and sharing your views, and taking time out of your work, which I am certain has been a sacrifice on the part of each of you—to come here, and I just want to say again that what you have had to say has been extremely important to us, and I hope that as a result of what we have heard today we will be able to do a better job for you.

So, thank you very much for coming.

(Whereupon, at 4:15 p.m., Thursday, November 18, 1965, the conference adjourned.)

O

CPSIA information can be obtained
at www.ICGtesting.com
Printed in the USA
BVHW08*1223021018
529052BV00008B/613/P

9 780484 621076